THE
CRUISING GUIDE
TO THE
LEEWARD ISLANDS

11th Edition

ANGUILLA
ST. MARTIN & ST. MAARTEN
SABA
SINT EUSTATIUS (STATIA)
ST. CHRISTOPHER (ST. KITTS)
NEVIS
REDONDA
MONTSERRAT
ANTIGUA
BARBUDA
GUADELOUPE
MARIE GALANTE
ILES DES SAINTES (THE SAINTES)
DOMINICA

Chris Doyle

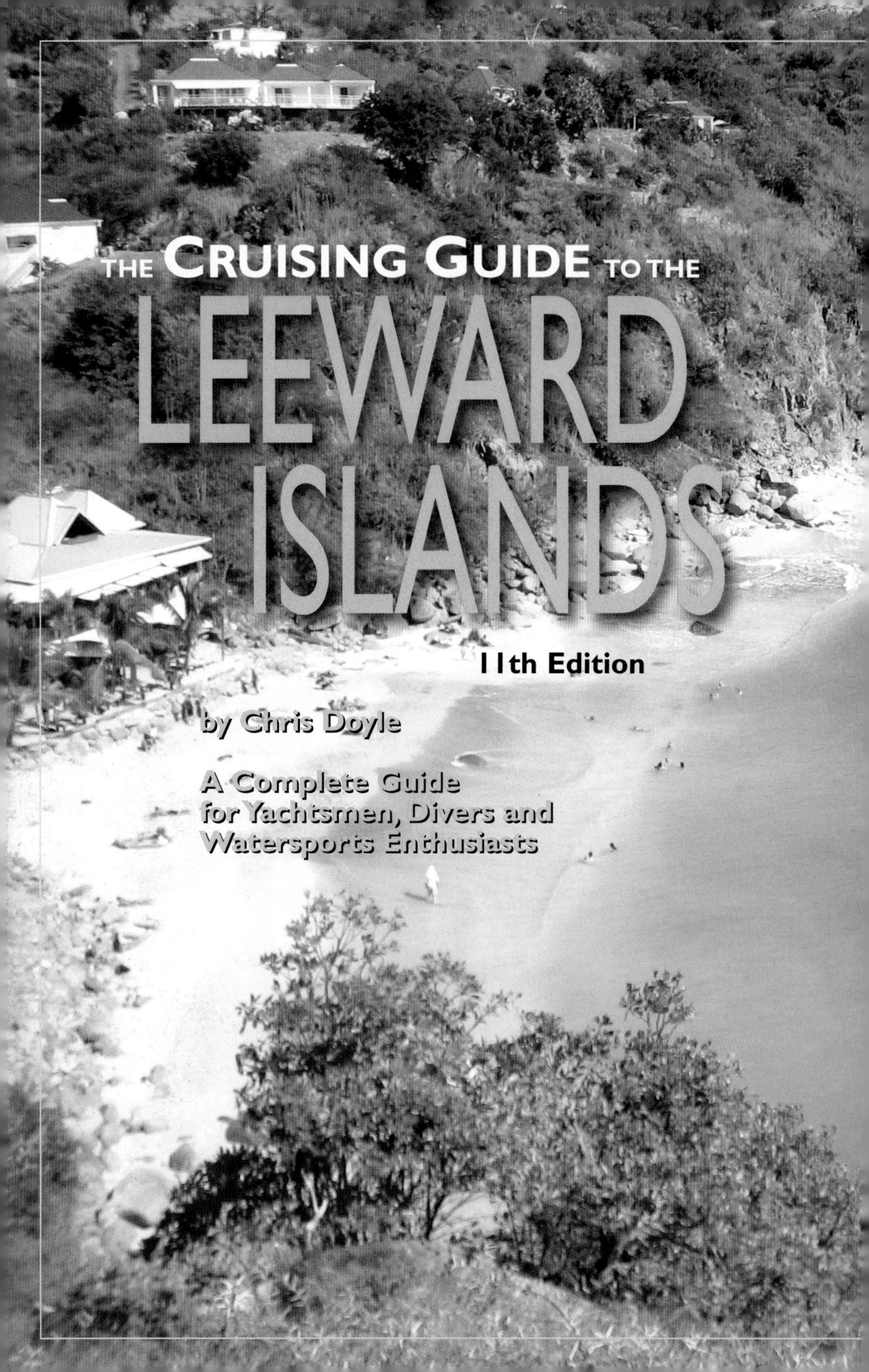

THE **CRUISING GUIDE** TO THE
LEEWARD ISLANDS

11th Edition

by Chris Doyle

A Complete Guide
for Yachtsmen, Divers and
Watersports Enthusiasts

Published by
Cruising Guide Publications, Inc.
P. O. Box 1017, Dunedin, FL 34697-1017
(727) 733-5322   Fax (727) 734-8179
(800) 330-9542
info@cruisingguides.com
Website: **www.cruisingguides.com**

Author: Chris Doyle
Editor: Nancy Scott, Ashley Scott
Book Design/Layout: Carol Dioca-Bevis - Carol Design Inc.
Cover Design/Layout: Carol Dioca-Bevis - Carol Design Inc.
Photography: Chris Doyle
Color Charts: Chris Doyle
Marketing and Advertising Sales: Maureen Larroux
Advertising Coordinator: Ashley Scott

This guide is intended for use with official navigational charts. Every effort has been made to describe conditions accurately, however, the publisher makes no warranty, expressed or implied, for any errors or for any omissions in this publication. The skipper must use this guide only in conjunction with charts and other navigational aids and not place undue credence in the accuracy of this guide. This guide is not to be used for navigational purposes.

Eleventh Edition (2010 - 2011)
Printed in China
ISBN 0-944428-87-8

TABLE OF CONTENTS

continued on page viii

TABLE OF CONTENTS (con't)

Chris Doyle

LIST OF SKETCH CHARTS

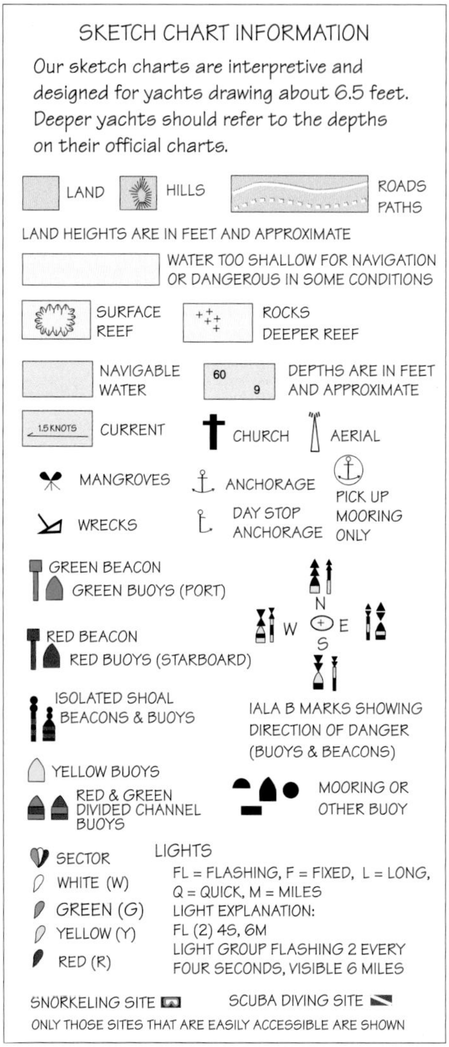

SKETCH CHART INFORMATION
Our sketch charts are interpretive and designed for yachts drawing about 6.5 feet. Deeper yachts should refer to the depths on their official charts.
LAND
HILLS
ROADS
PATHS
LAND HEIGHTS ARE IN FEET AND APPROXIMATE
WATER TOO SHALLOW FOR NAVIGATION OR DANGEROUS IN SOME CONDITIONS
SURFACE REEF
ROCKS
DEEPER REEF
NAVIGABLE WATER
60
9
DEPTHS ARE IN FEET AND APPROXIMATE
1.5 KNOTS
CURRENT
CHURCH
AERIAL
MANGROVES
ANCHORAGE
PICK UP MOORING ONLY
WRECKS
DAY STOP ANCHORAGE
GREEN BEACON
GREEN BUOYS (PORT)
N
W
E
S
RED BEACON
RED BUOYS (STARBOARD)
ISOLATED SHOAL BEACONS & BUOYS
IALA B MARKS SHOWING DIRECTION OF DANGER (BUOYS & BEACONS)
YELLOW BUOYS
RED & GREEN DIVIDED CHANNEL BUOYS
MOORING OR OTHER BUOY
SECTOR
WHITE (W)
GREEN (G)
YELLOW (Y)
RED (R)
LIGHTS
FL = FLASHING, F = FIXED, L = LONG, Q = QUICK, M = MILES
LIGHT EXPLANATION:
FL (2) 4S, 6M
LIGHT GROUP FLASHING 2 EVERY FOUR SECONDS, VISIBLE 6 MILES
SNORKELING SITE
SCUBA DIVING SITE
ONLY THOSE SITES THAT ARE EASILY ACCESSIBLE ARE SHOWN

NOTICE

No warranty, expressed or implied, is made by the publisher with respect to accuracy. This guide and these charts are the work of one individual. There may be errors and omissions – so undue credence should not be placed in this guide. This guide should be used with navigational charts and other navigational aids. This guide should not be used for navigation.

PLANNING
YOUR CRUISE

Anse de Columbier, St. Barts

Chris Doyle

Introduction

*T*HE LEEWARD ISLANDS span some 200 miles and include 10 major islands operating as different nations. Some are French, some Dutch, and some independent with an English tradition. You can find sophisticated nightspots with entertainment and gambling, as well as deserted and under-populated areas where you feel at the outer edge of the world. Some areas make for easy cruising with short sails, others include romping across longer open ocean passages. Still others make demands on your reef navigating skills. The variety is unparalleled.

It takes several months to explore the Leewards in depth, and only a lucky few will have that kind of time to spend. Most will have to make choices about what they want to see and, partly as an aid to this, we have divided this book into three areas to make it more manageable. These are functional rather than official groupings, so we named them ourselves.

The Renaissance Islands include St. Martin, St. Barts, and Anguilla. Their stable governments, sunny climate, and spectacular beaches have led them into a startling economic and social rebirth. They are now major destinations for discriminating visitors who want fun and amenities, but enjoy them tinged with a certain degree of character and without too many high-rises. St. Martin is the Caribbean's major base for power superyachts, and many of the world's most majestic private craft gather here for the winter. St. Martin is also a popular bareboating and cruising base. Both groups appreciate the easy sailing conditions among islands that are close to one another and offer an exhilarating wide choice of anchorages.

The Islands that Brush the Clouds form the northern tail of a volcanic chain that begins in Grenada. They are strung between Saba and Montserrat and form a natural link between the Renaissance Islands and Guadeloupe. These islands are all small, steeply mountainous, and surrounded by deep water. Some lack natural secure harbors, which has meant that access has not

always been easy. As a result each has developed in a certain degree of isolation and they are individually distinctive. All are scenic and offer fascinating cruising for the adventurous who like to explore ashore and are not afraid of coping with sometimes difficult anchorages and occasionally uncomfortable nights.

The remaining islands follow the compass north from Dominica to Barbuda. We call them **The Islands of Mountains and Mangroves**. They include the largest of the Leewards, as well as some of the smallest. Guadeloupe, the largest, is in reality two islands divided by a narrow navigable mangrove channel. The western half is typically volcanic, with steep mountains covered in tropical rainforest the eastern half is low and flat. The Saintes are tiny, yet picture perfect. Dominica is the most mountainous and rugged island, offering hikers unequaled scenery of great dramatic beauty. Antigua and Barbuda lie on their own large shallow bank. They are outside the volcanic chain and while Antigua has hills of over a thousand feet, Barbuda is very flat. In these two islands, navigation can be tricky amid numerous reefs, some of which are poorly charted. In recompense, Antigua and Barbuda have an amazing variety of anchorages, a wealth of bird and sea life and some outstanding beaches.

The north-south alignment between Barbuda and Dominica gives some great reaching passages in open water for those who enjoy fairly long sails (20-35 miles). Conditions here are a little more challenging than in the Renaissance Islands, which is perhaps why Antigua has become the Caribbean's main base for the world's finest mega sailing yachts, providing a great spectacle during the winter season. Both Antigua and Guadeloupe have many bareboat charter companies and are home to many cruising yachts.

Whether you manage to see all the Leewards, or sample just a few, we wish you fair winds and fine cruising.

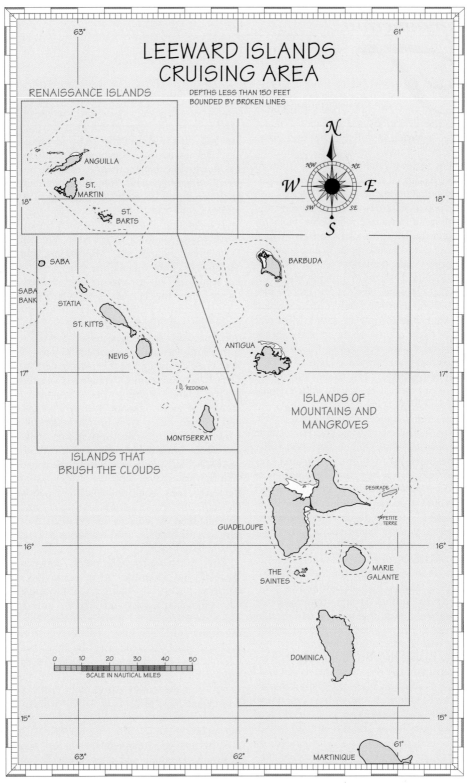

LEEWARD ISLANDS CRUISING AREA

RENAISSANCE ISLANDS

DEPTHS LESS THAN 150 FEET
BOUNDED BY BROKEN LINES

63°

61°

ANGUILLA

ST. MARTIN

ST. BARTS

18°

18°

N

NW NE

W E

SW SE

S

SABA

BARBUDA

SABA BANK

STATIA

ST. KITTS

NEVIS

ANTIGUA

17°

17°

REDONDA

ISLANDS OF MOUNTAINS AND MANGROVES

MONTSERRAT

ISLANDS THAT BRUSH THE CLOUDS

DESIRADE

PETITE TERRE

GUADELOUPE

16°

16°

THE SAINTES

MARIE GALANTE

0 10 20 30 40 50

SCALE IN NAUTICAL MILES

DOMINICA

15°

15°

63°

62°

61°

MARTINIQUE

Antigua Slipway, English Harbour. Chris Doyle

Planning Your Cruise

CURRENCY

Dominica, Montserrat, St. Kitts, Nevis, Anguilla, Antigua, and Barbuda share a British heritage and a common currency. They all use the Eastern Caribbean (EC) dollar. Banks give a fixed rate of around 2.67 EC to one dollar US. Shops, restaurants, and taxi drivers will take US and give about 2.60 EC. Taxi drivers frequently quote in US, as do restaurants in Antigua and Anguilla. Asking "what kind of dollars" avoids a lot of confusion. Spend all the EC you have, because if you take it back home to change, your bank will probably laugh at you.

In Guadeloupe, St. Barts, and French St. Martin the currency is the Euro, which can vary on either side of the US dollar. For those who need to know how it stands we give a link to a currency converter site on www.doyleguides.com. In these countries US dollars are also universally accepted except for Guadeloupe where they are slowly becoming more widely accepted.

In all the other islands US dollars are universally accepted and used. In the Dutch islands (Saba, Statia, and St. Maarten) prices are often quoted in guilders (rate varies).

TOURIST SEASON

People flock to the Caribbean to escape the chill, so the winter months (November to mid-April) are the fullest. Hotels and charter companies offer discounts for the rest of the year. The best sailing is between mid-April and early June. It is generally dry with easy breezes too late for northerly swells, too early for hurricanes, and one can get it at bargain rates. Restaurant and bar prices stay the same the year round. During the very slowest months (September and October), some small hotels close down and everyone goes on holiday.

WHAT TO BRING

One needs very little in the islands – some bathing things, a few shirts and pairs

3

of shorts, and a simple dress or light slacks and open necked shirts for the evening. These should be packed in a soft bag.

Remember to bring your camera, lots of sunblock, a long loose shirt and trousers, plus a hat and socks against sunburn. If you need prescription drugs, bring ample supplies and make sure they stay in your carry-on bag. Snorkelers and divers will want to bring their favorite masks and fins. Divers may also want to bring regulators and BCs, though it is probably easier to rent tanks and weight belts in the islands than to carry them with you.

LANGUAGE

English is spoken widely throughout the area with the exception of Guadeloupe, where you will find people who speak only French. In this case Cathy Parsons little book "French for Cruisers" is very helpful with everything from eating out to engine parts.

LOCAL CUSTOMS

People in the Leewards are often rather conservative at heart, and quite particular about dress. It will look weird to them if you wander into town or a supermarket in a bathing suit or bikini. Away from the beach, even in that tiny waterfront village, people generally wear at least a shirt and pair of shorts or skirt. In the major towns people dress much as you would if you were going to your local town.

Great store is set on greetings such as "good morning" or "good afternoon" (or in the French islands, "bon jour" or "bon nuit"). It is considered rude to approach people with a question or to transact business without beginning with the appropriate greeting.

Everyone likes to be tipped, but it is not always expected. In restaurants where no service charge is added, a 10% tip is normal. If service has already been included (as it is by law in the French territories), a little extra is appreciated, but not mandatory. I would tip taxi drivers if they give extra service, such as carrying your bags.

WATER SKIING

Local laws require that a water ski vessel have two persons on board and water skiing or speeding on a jet ski or aquatic scooter within 100 yards of the beach, or in harbors where yachts are anchored, is strictly forbidden.

GREEN FLASH

While you sip your sundowner, you can also try to spot the elusive "Green Flash." This happens as the sun disappears over the horizon. The last vestige of the sun turns bright green. It barely lasts a second and only happens on a clear horizon in the right atmospheric conditions. Binoculars make it easier to see.

HAZARDS

Biting insects are not usually a problem on board because of the breeze, but you may occasionally get bitten while ashore for the cocktail hour or a beach barbecue. The culprits could either be mosquitoes or the tiny sandflies whose diminutive size has earned them the name "no-see-ums." They can be kept at bay with any brand of bug repellent.

Scorpions and centipedes also live on the islands. They can give a bad sting, but are not generally deadly. You are unlikely to see one, but it is worth looking before you sit down in the scrub on the edge of the beach.

**Manchineel with flower
manchineel apple inset**

Chris Doyle

A much more real danger is the manchineel tree (Hippomane mancinella) which grows abundantly along some beaches. This pretty tree with its yellow-green apples is toxic and the leaves can produce a rash like poison ivy. It is all right to take shade under the tree, but avoid brushing through the leaves or standing under it in the rain. Putting a branch on a beach fire will quickly scatter your barbecue guests. Any sap in your eye is likely to cause blindness, which luckily often turns out to be temporary (about three days). The worst danger comes from eating the apples. They can cause blisters from stem to stern and could be deadly.

SEA SAFETY

Swimming and snorkeling are among the great pleasures of being in the Leewards and they are quite safe provided one uses reasonable common sense. The most serious threat to life and limb comes from speeding dinghies and fishing boats – you need to be on guard against these especially in harbor.

Accidental drowning deaths are rare and are usually caused when someone gets carried away by currents that can build up once you get away from the beach. Be cautious about swimming far from the beach and look over the side to check for current before you dive off the yacht.

You are likely to see plenty of sea urchins. They are black spiny creatures, best avoided because of their prickles that easily penetrate skin and break off on contact. This is quite painful, especially for the first few hours. If you do bump into one, do not try to remove imbedded spines. It is better to treat them with hot lime juice which will help dissolve them.

Caribbean sharks and barracudas have been much maligned in popular adventure stories. They have yet to attack anyone in these waters unless harassed, and so are not considered a danger here. Barracudas are very curious and have a habit of following you around. Some people advocate not wearing reflective jewelry as it resembles trolling spinners. On the other hand, diving tank stems are brightly reflective and none have yet been attacked. Moray eels also suffer from bad press, but they are in fact short sighted and timid and will not come out and bother you. It would be pushing your luck to stick your hand into holes among rocks or coral.

Some corals are poisonous and all are delicate, so look and do not touch them. Coral scratches can become infected, and if you get one, scrub it well with soap and fresh water. Stinging jellyfish do exist but are uncommon and occasionally the swimmer may feel a mild tingling from a small variety of jellyfish known as "sea ants".

Swimming at night is generally discouraged. If anything does happen, no one is going to be able to see you, and so few people swim at night that little is known about possible dangers.

If you want to scare yourself, look for horrors in any good book on dangerous marine animals. You are most unlikely to come to any harm, provided you watch where you put your hands and feet and keep an eye on sea conditions and passing craft.

DRUGS

Alcohol, tobacco, and coffee are acceptable. All other mind-altering substances are taboo. New antidrug attitudes through the islands have resulted in heavy penalties. Expect jail, enormous fines, and confiscation of the yacht you are on. People offering illegal substances may be in league with the police. If your mind needs bending, try a rum punch!

SUNTAN

Those who say "I never burn" will meet their match in the tropical sun, often deceptively masked by cool breezes. Over exposure is the major cause of sickness and discomfort among visitors. Use block out (preferably 30+) and keep covered most of the day. Loose, long sleeved cotton clothing, hats, and sunglasses are a must, as are light cotton socks to protect the tops of your feet. Heavy burning can occur even on cloudy days and in the shade.

PHOTOGRAPHY

The islands are so photogenic that it can be difficult to stop taking pictures. Luckily with modern digital photography, this is easy; just make sure your camera card has a few gigs of storage. If you are still back in the film age, bring plenty with you.

Polarizing filters will bring out the water colors. You get the effect you want by twisting the filter as you look through the viewfinder.

Some local people strongly object to being photographed. Always ask if you are taking a picture of an individual, and be prepared to stop if someone objects when taking groups or a crowd scene.

FISHING

Why not troll for dinner as you sail through the islands? It is often hard to buy fish ashore and those you catch yourself will be fresher. All you need is about 100 yards of 80 to 100 lb test line, a wire leader, swivel, hook, and lure. Rig the line with a clothespin so you can see if you have caught anything, or check it every few minutes.

Hand-lining at anchor is also often rewarded. Fish from your yacht, using a light line and a hook baited with a piece of fish or shrimp. Fish often start biting after dark. From late afternoon to dusk, trolling from your dinghy with a small spinner and light line may be the best strategy.

Ciguatera fish poisoning does exist in the Leewards, and it is supposed to be particularly bad around Redonda Rock. It can be serious. Common symptoms are a bad stomach upset followed later by various neurological ailments, such as tingling sensations and pains in the joints.

Unfortunately testing a fish before eating it is a complicated process that requires a special chemical kit. Local sailors consider tuna, dolphin, sailfish, wahoo, and marlin safe whatever their size. Many take a chance on small barracuda, Spanish mackerel and kingfish (4lbs or less), but the big ones are thrown back.

Spearfishing can be very damaging to the fragile reef ecology and, in addition, the presence of ciguatera (mentioned above) makes the eating of reef fish in this area an unpredictable enterprise. Many governments have banned spearfishing and the others are moving in that direction.

Chris Doyle

CARIBBEAN REGATTAS

Both racers and party-goers might be interested in knowing about some of the Caribbean's major sailing events. Both Antigua Race Week and Tobago Race Week have large charter classes using regular charter yachts. Since our publication is two-yearly I can only give a general idea of the dates for these events which change every year. For detailed dates consult the free newspapers: All at Sea and Caribbean Compass

Most of the events below are part of the Caribbean Sailing Association racing program.

January
Round the Island Race in Antigua
Grenada Sailing Festival

February
Valentines Regatta, Antigua (Jolly Harbour)
Schoelcher Sailing week (Martinique)

March
Heineken Regatta in St. Martin
North Sails Cup in Guadeloupe
Trophy Gardel - round Petit Terre race from St, Francois.

April
Antigua Classics Yacht Regatta
Antigua Mega Yacht Challenge
Antigua Sailing Week
Bequia Easter Regatta
BVI Spring Regatta
Rolex Cup Regatta in St. Thomas
Round Grenada Easter Regatta
(Easter events can be March)

May
Angostura Yachting World Tobago Race Week
Tour de la Guadeloupe

June
Mount Gay Regatta in Barbados (ends on the first Sunday in June - so can start late May)
Regattas de Juin in Martinique
Carib Cup Regatta in BVI
Guavaberry Offshore Regatta starting in St. Maarten
La Regate des Saintes (from Guadeloupe)

July
Green Island Weekend (Antigua)

August
Carriacou Regatta

October
Jolly Harbour Regatta (Antigua)
Caribbean Team Championships in Antigua
Triskell Cup in Guadeloupe

November
Queen's Cup/ Independence Day in Antigua
St. Maarten Day Regatta
Carriacou November Regatta with TTYA
St. Francois Sailing Week (Guadeloupe)

December
St. Barth Round the Island Race
La Grande Galette (to Marie Galante from Guadeloupe)

Chris Doyle

READING AND VIDEO

FREE MAGAZINES AND NEWSPAPERS:

All at Sea, available in most islands is a fine nautical newspaper, full of local and international stories of interest to yachtspeople. Useful information includes all the bridge opening times into Simpson Bay.

Caribbean Compass published in the Windward Islands is available in the Leewards. This free paper has excellent general interest stories and editorially is the Rolls Royce of the free press in this area. (As a regular contributor, I may be biased.)

Every island has its own glossy tourist magazines, with information on restaurants and nightlife. These are free and available at tourist offices and in most hotels.

by Chris Doyle. These are the only comprehensive dive guides to this area. Most dives and dive shops are covered, and dives that can be done from your yacht are described. ISBN, Vol 2: 0-944428-48-7, Vol 3: 0-944428-42-8. Complete Dive Guide Publications are available through Cruising Guide Publications. (1-800-330-9542) *Volume 1: Puerto Rico and the Virgin Islands* is also available.*

Scuba Diving from Your Yacht. Free booklet given out by the Scuba Shop in Oyster Pond, St. Martin. Call: 011-5995-70823. Describes easy to use scuba sites in St. Martin and St. Barts for those diving from their own boats.

Reef Creatures, Reef Fish, and Reef Coral, a series by Paul Humann. The best identification books for snorkelers and divers. Beautiful color photographs. The only identification source for many creatures. Widely available in dive shops. ISBNs: Creatures, 1-878348-31-0; Fish, 1-878348-30-2; Coral, 1-878348-32-9.*

Divers and Snorkelers Guide to the Fishes and Sea Life, Joseph Stokes. Comprehensive guide to the fish you meet on the reefs or are likely to catch on a line. Good color illustrations. Easy to use. Academy of Natural Sciences of Philadelphia Publishers. ISBN 0-910006-46-6.

Coral Reefs, a Peterson Field Guide. A detailed look at the ecology of reefs. Good for those who want to know why as well as what. Houghton Mifflin Co., ISBN 0-618-00211-1.

Marine Plants of the Caribbean, Diane Scullian Littler et al. Good for identifying underwater plants and algae. Smithsonian

BOOKS

Photo

Leeward Anchorages, Chris Doyle, Larger (8.5 by 11 inches) aerial photos of most anchorages in the Leewards with brief descriptions. Safe passages, markers, buoys and hazards included. Cruising Guide Publications. ISBN 0944428-57-6

Snorkeling and Diving

The Complete Diving Guide: The Caribbean, Volume 2 (out of print), Anguilla to Guadeloupe; and Volume 3: Dominica to Tobago. Colleen Ryan and Brian Savage, with shore sections

Institution Press, ISBN 0-87474-607-8

General Nature

The Nature of the Islands, Plants and Animals of the Eastern Caribbean, Chris Doyle Publishing. You may find the odd copy of this book around - if you can grab it. We are working on a new edition but it will be a while.
Southeastern and Caribbean Seashores, a Peterson Filed Guide, by Eugene Kaplan, Plants, shells, crustacea, and more. Both above and below the water. Houghton Mifflin Co., ISBN 0-395-46811-6

Plants

200 Tropical Plants, John M. Kingsbury. This is the best general purpose plant identification book for visitors we have seen. Good color photographs and a very wide coverage. Bullbrier Press, ISBN 0-9612610-2-1.

Birds

Birds of the Eastern Caribbean, Peter Evans, Good coverage of all the birds you are likely to see in the Leewards with many color photographs, Macmillan Caribbean, ISBN 0-333-52155-2

Birds of the West Indies, James Bond. Thorough treatment of all Caribbean birds and it includes many line drawings and color plates. Collins, ISBN 0-61-8002-1-03.

History

The Dominica Story, Lennox Honychurch. A great history of Dominica which reads as easily as a novel. If all history books were written like this, there would be more enthusiasm for the subject. Dominica Institute, Box 89, Roseau, Dominica. Also available in bookshops in Dominica.

*Available from Cruising Guide Publications 1-800-330-9542/ 1-727-733-5322
www.cruisingguides.com

Chartering in the Leeward Islands

*W*hether you dream of easy sails amid protected bays, long passages in open water, or gunkholing off the beaten track, you will find a holiday in The Leewards to fit the bill. You can stand at the wheel, captaining your boat to lands unknown, or you can lie back sipping an exotic drink being completely coddled by professional crew. All kinds of craft are available; the choice is entirely yours.

Unquestionably, the waters surrounding St. Martin, St. Barts, and Anguilla have become a popular bareboating area in the Leewards, and for good reason. Passages are satisfyingly crisp, yet short, and anchorages offer a variety of sandy coves and unspoiled beaches, yet there is plenty of action ashore for those who seek it.

This area is a little more challenging than the Virgin Islands, but still very easy, with the added advantage that those who crave a slightly longer passage can include Saba, Statia, or St. Kitts and Nevis, any one just a day's sail away.

St. Martin is also the Caribbean capital of large powered luxury mega yachts, many of which charter. Charters on such boats are usually arranged through brokers. A 10% tip to the crew of the charter price is normal.

Charter Companies in St. Martin
(see also overseas agents)

Anchorage Multicoques, 0590-51-90-37, F: 0590-51-11-12, sxm@anchorage-multicoques.com, catamaran charter, bare and skippered

Anyway Marine, 0590-87-91-41/29-35-93, F: 0590-29-34-76, anyway@wanadoo.fr

Horizon Yacht Charters, 0690-88-56-88, 599-544-3329, F:599-544-3330, info@horizonsxm.com, Davikd Duong

International Yacht Collection, 599-544-3780/2515, F: 599-544-3779, mel-liot@yachtcollection.net, maxi yacht agent.

No Limits Charters and the Maritime School of the West Indies, 599-523-7671, 0590-87-22-68, info@nolimitsyachts.com crewed charters and serious maritime school for yacht-master courses.

Reve Marine, 0690-40-10-05, revemarine@stmartin.com, power boats

Sunsail, 0590-29-50-50, F: 0590-87-31-58, VHF: 74, stmartinbase@sunsail.com, bareboat and skippered charters, one-way charters from Antigua

The Cruise Club, 599-542-9337, F: 599-542-9338, info@cruise-club.cc, sailing holidays by the berth.

The Moorings, 0590-87-32-55, F: 0590-87-32-54 customer@domaccess.com, Bareboats and crewed yachts, one way charters available

Trade Winds Club Cruises, 784-457-3407, reservations@tradewindscruiseclub.com,

VPM Best Sail, 0590 29-41-35, F: 0590 29 42 75, saintmartin@vpm-best-sail.com, All kinds of charter, monohulls and multihulls

Charter Companies in St. Barts

Nautica FWI, 0590-27-56-50, F: 0590-27-56-52, nfyachts@wanadoo.fr or nfyachts @compuserve.com. All kinds of charter from superyachts to bareboat.

Ocean Must, 0590-27-62-25, F: 0590-27-95-17, VHF: 10, oceanmust@wanadoo.fr. Small power bareboats, day trips, and skippered boats, deepsea fishing

Master ski Pilou, 0590-27-91-79, 0690-27-55-70, lepilou@wanadoo.fr, skippered power boats.40-65'.

Guadeloupe is another excellent charter destination. Anchorages abound in all directions and this area will appeal to those who

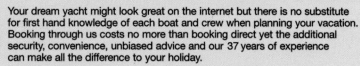
PLANNING YOUR CRUISE

like to spend some time studying the area and plotting out their own cruise.

The whole area is relatively uncrowded and very pleasant with spectacular beaches. Gunkholers will enjoy going through the Rivière Salée and circumnavigating Basse Terre, taking in the Saintes. Hikers will want to visit the Saintes and Dominica. Beach lovers might be content with a cruise around the Saintes, Marie Galante, and southeast Guadeloupe. Some will want to cruise to Antigua and Barbuda and back. Anyone with a mask and snorkel will want to visit to the Cousteau Underwater Park at Pigeon Island.

Where charter companies do not have a USA representative, it is easy to get their rates and charter conditions by sending them an email or fax. They all speak English.

Charter Companies in Guadeloupe

Ad Location, 0690-55-20-42, small power boat charter, day and term.

Antilles-Sail.com, 0590-90-16-81, F: 0590-90-16-82, c.a.loc@wanadoo.fr, bareboat and with skipper. Includes many interesting craft like aluminum center-board yachts.

Caraibes-Charter.com, 0590-90-81-61/90-29-12, F: 0590-90-80-13, info@caraibe-yachts.com, bareboat and skippered private yachts.

Sea & Sail, 0590-20-75-24, 0690-86-57-17, F: 0590-20-53-26, seaandsail@wanadoo.fr, bareboat and with skipper.

Sparkling Charter, 0590-90-85-75, F: 0590 90-88-19, Guadeloupe@sparkling-charter.com

Sun Evasion, 0690-35-03-18, F: 0590-84-72-54, saphir2@wanadoo.fr

Sunsail, 0590-90-92-02, F: 0590-90-97-99. sunsail.guadeloupe@wanadoo.fr bareboat and skippered charters, cats and monohulls, one-way charters.

Tip Top Croisieres, 0590-84-66-36/0690-35-17-92, F: 0590-84-46-15, tiptopcruise@wanadoo.fr, all kinds of charter.

Those that like out-of-the way places will love a cruise in Antigua and Barbuda. It has a wealth of beautiful anchorages, many of which you can have to yourself.

Navigation can be tricky and it is best for those that have experience in eyeball navigation. This is also a good place for starting one way charters to St. Martin, or taking a cruise to Guadeloupe, the Saintes and Dominica and back.

Antigua is the crewed sailing charter capital of the Leewards; many large luxury yachts are based here for the season. Even some really experienced sailors enjoy a fully-crewed charter. You get to sail the yacht when you wish, and at other times you can hand it over to the skipper. You have a cook to look after your every need and taking a fully-crewed yacht can expand your horizons. You can plot a course to the more difficult islands and leave the headaches to the skipper. You can usually pick up and drop off at different points at no extra charge. If you change your mind about where you want to go in the middle of the charter, there is a good chance the crew can arrange alternative flights for you. When you include the cost of provisioning, some crewed charters compare favorably with bareboating, even when you add the 10% you will be expected to tip the crew.

Charter Companies in Antigua
(see also overseas agents)

Antigua Yacht Charters, 268-463-7101/464-7662, charters@candw.ag, fully crewed yachts

Nicholson's Yacht Charters and Services, 268-460-1530, F: 268-460-1531, 305-433-5533, info@nicholson-charters.com Skippered charters

Horizon Yacht Charters, 268-562-4725, 268-562-4726, info@antiguahorizon.com, bareboat charters, skippers available.

Sunsail, 268-460 2615, F: 268-460 2616, VHF: 68, charterservices@candw.ag, bareboat with skippers, cooks and one way trips to St. Martin available

Trade Wind Cruise Club, 784-457-3407, reservations@tradewindscruiseclub.com, charter holidays on large cats.

For some, there is no thrill like that of a real voyage. Starting in one island and hopping down the chain to another. For this kind of holiday one often needs to

Dominica Hot Springs

Chris Doyle

make a schedule, and it suits people who like to spend most of their vacation out on the ocean rather than at anchor.

Many of the bareboat companies listed offer one way charters. Many Guadeloupe charter companies can arrange trips between Guadeloupe and St. Martin and even down to the Windwards.

Sunsail and Horizon offer one way charters between Antigua and St. Martin or the Virgins.

Keep in mind that the trip should be done in this direction, because the trip back from St. Martin to Antigua involves a really tough 55-mile beat to windward (Nevis to Antigua) which is almost impossible to complete during daylight hours.

USA and Overseas Charter Agents

Barefoot Yacht Charters, 784-456-9526, F: 784-456-9238, barebum@caribsurf.com

Catamaran Charter, 800-262-0308/ 305 462-6706, F: 305-462-6104

Ed Hamilton & Co, 800-622-7855/ 207-549-7855, F: 207-882-7851

Horizon Yacht Charters, 877-494-8787, 284-494-8787, F: 284-494-8989, info@horizoncharters.com,

Nicholson's Yachts Worldwide, 800-662- 6066/ 617-225-0555, F: 617-225-0190

Sailing Vacations www.ebare.com, an Internet company.

Sunsail (USA), 800-327-2276, 410-280-2553, F: 410-280-2406

Sunsail, (UK), (2392) 222-300, Fax: (2392) 222-333

Swift Yacht Charters and Villas, 800-866-8340, www.swiftyachts.com

Tradewind Yachts 800-825-7245, 804-694-0081, F: 804-693-7245

Wilder Adventures, 860-693-8523, F: 860-674-2693, shipslog@ibm.net

Check the website: www.doyleguides.com for links to charter websites.

15

CRUISING
INFORMATION

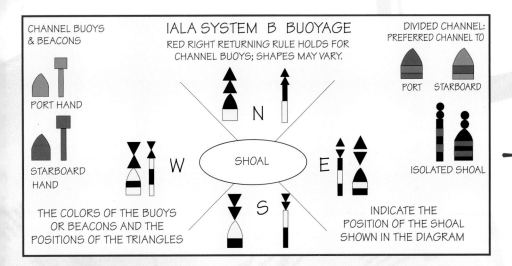

IALA SYSTEM B BUOYAGE
RED RIGHT RETURNING RULE HOLDS FOR CHANNEL BUOYS; SHAPES MAY VARY.

CHANNEL BUOYS & BEACONS

PORT HAND

STARBOARD HAND

THE COLORS OF THE BUOYS OR BEACONS AND THE POSITIONS OF THE TRIANGLES

DIVIDED CHANNEL: PREFERRED CHANNEL TO

PORT   STARBOARD

ISOLATED SHOAL

INDICATE THE POSITION OF THE SHOAL SHOWN IN THE DIAGRAM

SHOAL

N W E S

NAVIGATION

Most sailing in the Leewards is in sight of land. You will usually be able to see the island you are heading for before the last island disappears behind you.

The equatorial current flows in a north-westerly direction. Sometimes it may be imperceptible; at other times you may find a knot or more. It can intensify around the ends of the islands, and is offset for a few hours on the rising tide. When you are crossing channels, it is worth taking back bearings to assess the extent of the set. The tidal range is only about one and a half feet.

BUOYAGE SYSTEM

There are not many buoys in the Leewards. Those that exist are mainly for commercial traffic and mark channels into the larger harbors. The IALA "B" buoyage system is in use throughout the Leewards. This places red buoys on your right hand side and green buoys on your left hand as you go into harbor (the red-right-returning rule). Occasionally a shoal surrounded by deep water will be marked with a yellow and black buoy on which mounted triangles indicate the direction of the shoal. (See our diagram.)

WEATHER

Caribbean weather is famous for being sunny and breezy, with a smattering of showers and rainy days thrown in. The winds are nearly always northeast to southeast at 10 to 25 knots. In the winter months the winds get stronger and more northeasterly. In the summer they are more gentle and southeasterly. There are very occasional calms. Rain usually arrives in short intense squalls that can be seen coming from afar. Sometimes they lay you flat with gusts of over 40 knots; usually they do not. There is no way to tell before they arrive.

During the winter, high-pressure systems often build to the northeast of the Leewards. If they become strong they generate brisk easterly winds of 20-25 knots, sometimes 25-30 knots, and are known locally as "Christmas winds". You can occasionally get a year with weeks of strong Christmas winds. These winds scoop enough moisture off the sea to produce frequent showers, though for the most part conditions are sunny, if blustery.

These high-pressure systems are offset by cold fronts that sweep southeast from the USA. These usually stall, weaken, and dissipate before they reach the Leewards, but they do sometimes make it into the area. Before the cold front the weather is usually very pleasant and calm, with light variable winds, often from the south to west. If the cold front gets stalled, these conditions can last several days. The cold front arrives with a buildup of cloud, northwesterly swells, and a shift in the wind. In the northwest part of the Leewards, the wind may switch to northwest and blow at about 16 knots for some hours. It then switches to north or northeast and often blows at 20-25 knots (with stronger gusts in rain showers) for a day or two. From Barbuda to Dominica a northwesterly wind is rare, but you do get northeasterly winds and northwesterly swells.

A combination of factors can give rise to unusual winds and weather. It is rare, but I have seen the wind blow from both the north and the northwest for some days, and also I have seen squalls produce quite strong westerly winds for some hours.

Cruising is good year round, but winter swells and the hurricane season can affect your planning. Northerly swells roll down from time to time in the winter months. They usually come as a result of cold fronts and storms north of the Leewards. Out at sea they are of no consequence, but along the coast normally tranquil anchorages may

become uncomfortable or dangerous. Northerly swells are most frequent from November to January, though they have been known as late as April. In the exposed islands of Saba and Statia you may have to put to sea, even at night, if bad swells arrive. In other places you have to be selective about where you anchor overnight.

The hurricane season is from June until October. The months of June, July and October only average one hurricane every three years for the whole western Atlantic, including the Caribbean Sea and the Gulf of Mexico. Both August and September, average around five a year. Hurricanes frequently start far south, but head northwest to pass through the Leewards. Luckily, forecasts are fair and one usually gets several days advance notice. Hurricane winds can come from any direction, turning normal anchorages into deadly lee shores. They can also produce swells far from their centers. Only three of the Leewards have good hurricane holes, and this has to be borne in mind when planning a cruise, especially in August and September. In Guadeloupe you can find protection in Pointe à Pitre, or in the Rivière Salée, which can be approached from north or south. In Saint Martin,

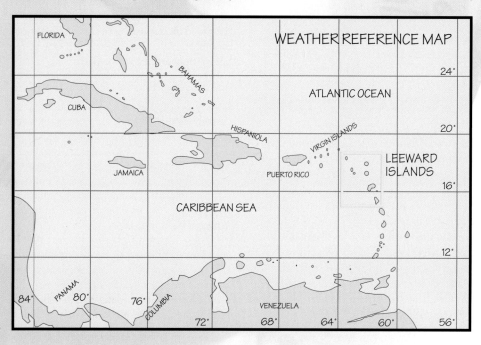

Simpson Bay Lagoon, Anse Marcel and the Oyster Pond are used for refuge. Antigua has many good harbors, but the most used are English Harbour in the south and Parham in the north. In a category 4 or 5 hurricane, no harbor can be considered really safe, though English Harbour has the best track record.

In the hurricane season it is essential to listen to the forecasts. Check out times and frequencies on our radio page. For northerly swells and lesser weather systems ZBVI is the best, and can often be reached throughout the Leewards, except in St. Kitts and Nevis where it clashes with a powerful religious station. This may help those who prefer to pray about the weather than to trust forecasts. You can also go online. Both cruisingguides.com and doyleguides.com give links to weather.

Listen closely when you hear about a Tropical Disturbance, Tropical Wave, or Upper Level Trough. These are poorly organized weather systems associated with rainsqualls of varying intensity, but they can develop. Get to shelter for a Tropical Depression (an organized weather system with rain and sustained winds of up to 35 knots), a Tropical Storm, (lots of rain and sustained winds of 35 to 63 knots), or a Hurricane (sustained winds of more than 64 knots).

Seasons are not well differentiated, but the wettest time of the year is from August to November and the driest is from February to June. Temperatures are 70 to 85 degrees Fahrenheit year round.

Visibility is often more than 30 miles. Strong winds can put enough water in the atmosphere to cut visibility to 15 miles, but occasional hazier days are caused by dust from Africa. Sometimes reddish traces may be found on the cabin and decks. Even in hazy conditions visibility is 5 to 15 miles.

CUSTOMS AND IMMIGRATION

The Leeward Islands include many different nations, each with its own customs and immigration formalities to be dealt with on arrival and departure. These are not generally difficult.

Typically you are asked to fill in forms supplied by the officer.

Always carry your boat papers, passports and a blue or black pen (red and green are unacceptable) when you visit customs and immigration, as well as some blank paper in case they ask you to make your own crew list.

Details are given under island and harbor headings.

The customs officers have to wear uniforms and sit in offices all day. They, like you, would probably prefer to be having fun, so if you arrive looking too relaxed they will refuse to deal with you. At minimum wear flip-flops, a presentable t-shirt and shorts.

In some countries customs can be very late on arrival, so if you need to get going in the morning, clear the day before. Those with pets on board will be able to walk them ashore in the Dutch islands. The French islands will allow them ashore, provided they have a rabies certificate. Anguilla, St. Kitts and Nevis, Montserrat, Antigua, and Dominica are free of rabies and will not allow pets off the boat.

Eseaclear.com is a new system of form filling which can be done online. It works for St. Kitts and Nevis, and will probably be introduced soon for Dominica and Antigua.

COMMUNICATIONS

There have been rapid changes in yacht communications over the last few years. These days the only good reason not have a phone on board is if you went sailing to leave all that behind. For the rest of us, this new era is a big improvement. I, for one, am happy to no longer have to wait in line at a public phone and then try to balance a notebook on my knee using one hand to hold the phone and the other to try and write some important incoming information down; information that I can barely hear, because a car has just pulled into the parking lot with its stereo going at full blast. Modern communications are a big improvement, and not only can we phone

from our boats, but in most cases we can also send and receive emails.

GSM phones are now widely available in the Leewards and work well on yachts. With a GRSM enabled phone or PCMIA slot aerial card, you can use this system for both phone calls and internet connection. While some companies may now cover most islands, roaming charges can be prohibitive, so often it pays to buy a new sim (about $10 US) when you get to a new area. It is easiest for the cruiser to buy the sims that use the prepaid cards that you can top up when you want.

Digicel has very wide coverage and uses standard top-up cards wherever you are. Cable & Wireless Bfree also works for many islands, but the cards do not – instead you take your phone into one of the many Bfree agents and they top it up for you.

Card Orange works in Martinique, Dominica, Guadeloupe, St. Barts and St. Martin. But while the cards from the French islands are interchangeable, those from Dominica are not. In St. Martin you can get by on both sides with a Card Orange, but if you need a phone to work in Saba and Statia, you will need to get a local sim for these islands. If you are buying a phone, get a four-band phone for the greatest flexibility.

You can store numbers in your GSM phone either in the phone itself or on the sim card. Selection is normally through the contacts setup menu. If you are going to be changing sims, store valuable numbers in the phone, not on the sim.

Satellite phones connect well throughout the Caribbean. Because you are tuning to a satellite and not a fixed tower, you may lose your connection more often than with GSM, especially on long calls. Satellite phones are also more complex than GSM phones, so they may not be quite as reliable. They will often not be suitable for local Caribbean calls, as these can incur high roaming charges. In the directory in the back of this book we list both the area code and the phone number for each country. You will also need the information in

RADIO
For local News, Views & Weather Forecasts

AM Band

ANTIGUA BROADCASTING SERVICE AM 620: Weather 0750

ZBVI (VIRGIN ISLANDS) AM 780.
Good weather forecast 0730 and 0805 daily except Sunday when it is at 0945.
Updates on most hours and half-hours

FM Band

ANGUILLA RADIO 1000

ANTIGUA BROADCASTING SERVICE 90.5: Weather 0750

RADIO ST. BARTH 98.7: Weather at 0730, 1230 and 1730

GEM RADIO IN ST. MARTIN 88.9. In the other islands look for Gem between 92 and 95. Weather usually on the hour and half hour

ISLAND 92 (91.9) ST. MARTIN: weather and bridge times 0900, Monday to Friday, upgrades given where necessary at 1000 and on weekends. Frequent updates for hurricanes. Marine Trades Calender weekdays at 0945, All at Sea marine program weekdays at 0845.

VOICE OF ST. MARTIN (PJD3) 102.7 MHz: Sundays at 0900–hour long nautical program for St. Martin, St. Barts and Anguilla, designed with cruisers in mind. If you have a TV try channel 09 for news and weather

VHF

CHANNEL 14 IN ST. MARTIN has daily cruisers net at 0730.
This is also used as the cruisers calling channel.

CHANNEL 06 IN ANTIGUA at 0900 (announced on Channel 68 just prior to broadcast), English Harbour Radio presents the "Not the nine o'clock news", and excellent weather forecast and general information from Jol Byerley.

In Guadeloupe MRCC- MARTINIQUE gives forecasts in French at 0800, 0810, 0820 and 0830. Listen to VHF: 16 and they will direct you to the appropriate channel. You can also contact them on VHF: 16 any time for weather news in English.

SSB & Ham

Caribbean weather net on 8104 USB at 0830 (Safety and Security net 0815)
Caribbean emergency net weather on 7162 kHz LSB at 0635
Caribbean emergency net weather on 3815 kHz LSB at 1835
Eric, weather on 3855.0 LSB at 0630 & 1830
NMN Offshore forecast 4426, 6501 & 8764 USB at 0530 & 2330
NMN Offshore forecast 6501 & 8764 & 13089 USB at 1200 & 1800
Southbound 11 12359 USB at 1600
Cocktail and Weather net 7086 LSB at 1630 (not normally Sunday)
Weather Fax for radio information check website:
http://205.156.54.206/om/marine/radiofax.htm

Internet

Both www.cruisingguides.com and www.doyleguides.com give links to weather.

Chris Doyle

the box on page 22.

Wifi internet coverage is new and a huge boon to cruisers as it brings broad-band high-speed internet access right into your boat, and makes surfing the web on board really practical. Various companies are supplying this service, and it is generally only available where yachts congregate, which means in or somewhere near a marina. So, to be able to get onboard email over the

whole area we cover, you would need to combine wifi with either satellite or GRSM. The company with the most stations at this point is Hot Hot Hot Spot.

It is easy enough for a wifi company to set up a shore station powerful enough to cover an area like English Harbour, but internet is a two way process so this is not a big help if you are using a weak system like a laptop with a regular wifi card. To take full

Overseas CALLS

From local private, public and GSM phones, this is what you dial from the following islands:

French Islands: 00 + country & area code + number

Netherlands Antilles: 00 + country & area code + number

NANP countries: country & area code + number for Zone A

NANP countries: 011 + country & area code + number for Zone B

Calling all countries from overseas: if the first digit of an area code is 0, omit it.

Notes

French St. Martin, St. Barts and Guadeloupe work like one country with one area code. When calling from overseas, the number is + 590 590 + 6 digits (regular phones) or +590 690 + 6 digits (mobile phones). When calling internally all number are: 0590 + 6 digits or (mobile) 0690 + 6 digits

Calling within French territories is not considered overseas. Just dial the area code and number

Calling within the Netherlands Antilles is not considered overseas, just dial 0 and the last 7 digits. If you are calling within one island, just dial the last 7 digits.

Within NANP countries, if your area code is the same as the one you are calling (for example if you calling Antigua and using an Antigua phone) you omit the area code and just dial the last 7-digits.

SIM phones are often smart enough to recognize where you are. When this happens you need only dial as you would if your phone was from the country you are in, even though your phone's area code is different. (For example in NANP countries just dial the last 7 digits). The converse side of this is if you are dialing the same area code as your phone, but you are in a different island, you may well have to dial 1 + the area code + the number.

SATELLITE PHONES

For each phone we give the same example for calling Antigua 460-1156

GLOBALSTAR

If you use a Globalstar phone set up for the Americas, it works just like a USA phone: For NANP countries dial 1 + the country & area code, + 7 digits. To call overseas dial 011 + country & area code, + numberExample, dial: 1-268-460-1156

IRIDIUM

Dial 00 + the country & area code - e.g. for NANP countries dial 001 then the area code + 7 digitsExample, dial: 00-1-268-460-1156

INMARSAT

Dial 00 + the country & area code - e.g. for NANP countries dial 001 then area code + 7 digits + #. The # key is used after all numbers are entered to initiate the call. Example, dial: 00-1-268-460-1156-#

Country Codes

Zone A NANP

(North American Numbering Plan)

USA . . . . .1-(area code)
Anguilla . . . . .1-(264)
Antigua . . . . .1-(268)
Barbados . . . . .1-(246)
Dominica . . . . .1-(767)
Grenada . . . . .1-(473)
Montserrat . . . . .1-(664)
St. Lucia . . . . .1-(758)
St. Vincent . . . . .1-(784)
St. Kitts . . . . .1-(869)
Trinidad . . . . .1-(868)

Zone B

Guadeloupe 590
Martinique 596
Netherlands Antilles . . .599
UK 44
Australia 61
Austria 43
Germany 49
Denmark 45
France 33
Italy 39
Sweden 46
Switzerland 41

advantage of Caribbean wifi you will need some sort of booster aerial. Whatever you buy needs to operate on the IEEE 802.11 b and/or g standard, and have an output power of at least 100mw.

This is not to say a laptop with a regular wifi system is useless, but being close to the supplier's transmitter (hot spot) becomes very important. Some suppliers have multiple hot spots to extend the range, in which case you may get fair reception when you are in or very close to a marina. The position of your computer is important and you can often significantly improve a weak signal by moving from down below to up into the cockpit or on deck. The regular wifi laptop is also excellent for taking ashore to a wifi internet cafe.

Using wifi is simple. Normally you just click on the wireless connection icon on your laptop and follow the directions. Occasionally you may need to go ashore to pay. Receiving emails and surfing the web is easy, and outgoing mail through webmail outfits like hotmail is no problem. If you are using Outlook Express with an STMP address for your outgoing mail, this will be seamless with some operators, but with others you may have to add a new address into your system.

VHF radio is still widely used in the Leeward Islands, both by vessels and shore-side stations such as charter companies, dive shops, and restaurants. It is still a good form of local communication, though completely open to the listening public, and you cannot beat the price.

Channel 16 is for emergency and raising other stations only. As soon as you have made contact, switch to another channel. In Antigua, shore stations stand by on channel 68 and in St. Martin they use 14. So in these islands use these channels only for contact, and then switch.

SECURITY ABOARD

Most islanders and yachtspeople are very honest, but one finds the occasional bad apple, so it is worth taking reasonable precautions, much as you would at home.

Lock your outboard onto your dinghy and lock the dinghy onto the dock when you go ashore. At night, hoist the dinghy or lock it to the boat. Remove the outboard and lock it onto the stern rail. Close up and lock your yacht when you leave it alone. Do not leave valuables unattended on the beach or in the dinghy.

One night we were eating out on a balcony about 8 feet above the beach when a thief attempted to grab the pocketbook of a nearby guest, cutting one of the straps with a knife. The thief had built himself a platform on the beach out of an old table and chair. So when you eat out, think about where you are putting your possessions.

While you are unlikely to suffer a theft, it is best to plan your trip so that such an event would not be a disaster. Avoid bringing large amounts of cash to the islands. Use credit cards and travelers checks, which are replaceable. Valuable jewelry is best left at home and it is advisable to take holiday insurance on expensive cameras and binoculars. Be a little cautious about walking at night down small side streets or away from town.

GARBAGE

There are garbage facilities in just about every community in the Leewards. In those anchorages without, you can bag garbage and lash it to the stern deck till the next stop. Barbuda is as far as you will get from garbage disposal facilities, so take plenty of bags. It is quite okay to throw food scraps overboard in deep water, but everything else should be kept. Under no circumstance should you throw plastic bags over the side. Some turtles which feed on jelly fish eat plastic bags by mistake and die. Better they live and eat those jelly fish!

ENVIRONMENTAL NOTES

Please help preserve the water we all enjoy. Care should be taken while anchoring. Anchors can do great harm to coral, which is very slow growing. Never anchor in living coral. If you are not sure of the nature of the bottom, snorkel before you anchor and take a look.

When anchoring let out anchor line equivalent to at least five times the depth of water. Dragging across the seabed and ploughing the sea-grass is also harmful.

Be selective about the handicrafts you buy. When you buy straw work, woven mats, cloth, clothing, woodcraft, coconut-craft, jewelry made from seeds and conch shells, and other renewable resources, you are supporting the local economy without damaging the environment. Please do not buy anything made from coral or turtle shell. Reefs are badly damaged by coral collectors, and all the local turtles are endangered species.

Coral reefs require clean nutrient-poor water to thrive. An excess of nutrients allows the rapid growth of algae which smothers the coral. Most detergents, soaps, and shampoos are now phosphate free, but even the new ones can be somewhat harmful. Bleach on the other hand will kill everything, including fish, so be very parsimonious in the use of these products, especially when anchored near rocks or reefs.

Avoid wearing gloves when diving or snorkeling, and be careful not to touch or stand on coral, you may well damage it.

There are anchorages in the Leewards where you may be very close to nesting seabirds. If so, be careful not to disturb them. Loud music and shouting may scare them away.

Little Bay, Anguilla   Chris Doyle

25

LEEWARD VIEW OF

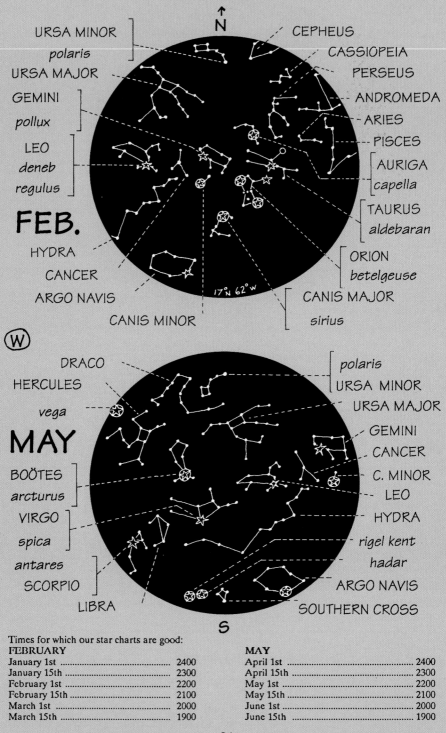

URSA MINOR
polaris
URSA MAJOR
GEMINI
pollux
LEO
deneb
regulus

FEB.

HYDRA
CANCER
ARGO NAVIS

CANIS MINOR

CEPHEUS
CASSIOPEIA
PERSEUS
ANDROMEDA
ARIES
PISCES
AURIGA
capella
TAURUS
aldebaran
ORION
betelgeuse
CANIS MAJOR
sirius

17° N 62° W

Ⓦ

DRACO
HERCULES
vega

MAY

BOÖTES
arcturus
VIRGO
spica
antares
SCORPIO
LIBRA

polaris
URSA MINOR
URSA MAJOR
GEMINI
CANCER
C. MINOR
LEO
HYDRA
rigel kent
hadar
ARGO NAVIS
SOUTHERN CROSS

S

Times for which our star charts are good:

FEBRUARY		MAY	
January 1st	2400	April 1st	2400
January 15th	2300	April 15th	2300
February 1st	2200	May 1st	2200
February 15th	2100	May 15th	2100
March 1st	2000	June 1st	2000
March 15th	1900	June 15th	1900

26

THE CONSTELLATIONS

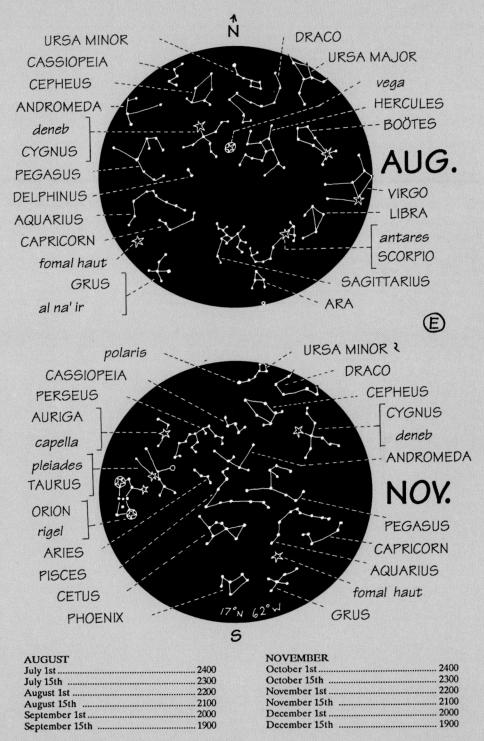

N

URSA MINOR
CASSIOPEIA
CEPHEUS
ANDROMEDA
deneb
CYGNUS
PEGASUS
DELPHINUS
AQUARIUS
CAPRICORN
fomal haut
GRUS
al na' ir

DRACO
URSA MAJOR
vega
HERCULES
BOÖTES

AUG.

VIRGO
LIBRA
antares
SCORPIO
SAGITTARIUS
ARA

Ⓔ

polaris
CASSIOPEIA
PERSEUS
AURIGA
capella
pleiades
TAURUS
ORION
rigel
ARIES
PISCES
CETUS
PHOENIX

URSA MINOR ♌
DRACO
CEPHEUS
CYGNUS
deneb
ANDROMEDA

NOV.

PEGASUS
CAPRICORN
AQUARIUS
fomal haut
GRUS

17°N 62°W

S

AUGUST	
July 1st	2400
July 15th	2300
August 1st	2200
August 15th	2100
September 1st	2000
September 15th	1900

NOVEMBER	
October 1st	2400
October 15th	2300
November 1st	2200
November 15th	2100
December 1st	2000
December 15th	1900

DISTANCE TABLE FOR THE LEEWARDS

The distance you sail will depend very much on the wind and current. This distance table is approximate and for planning only.

The routes given are via the leeward coast of Guadeloupe. If you go through Rivière Salée you can save 41 miles from Pointe à Pitre to Antigua or Barbuda, and 39 miles from Point à Pitre to Montserrat and all the islands to its northwest.

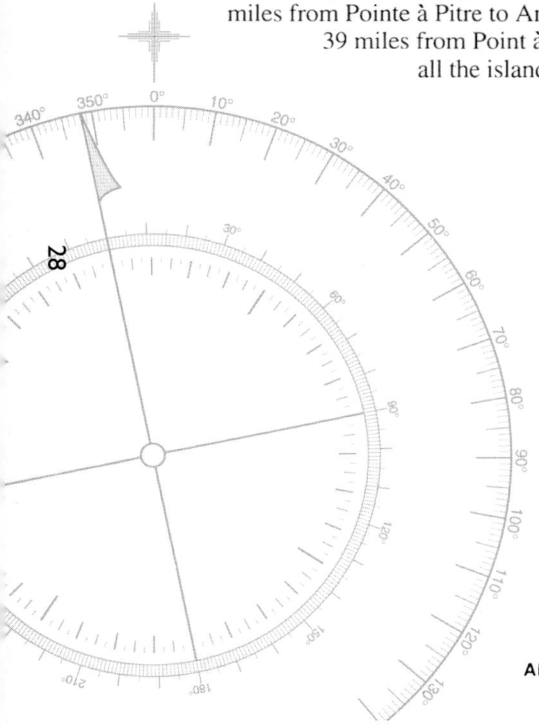

	ST. PIERRE	ROSEAU	PRINCE RUPERT BAY	THE SAINTS	POINTE À PITRE	BASSE TERRE	DESHAIES	MONTSERRAT	NEVIS	ST. KITTS	ST. EUSTATIUS	SABA	ST. BARTS	ST. MARTIN (PHILIPSBURG)	ANGUILLA (ROAD BAY)	ANTIGUA (ENGLISH HARBOUR)
BARBUDA (SPANISH POINT)	181	145	126	108	123	96	79	58	57	61	70	86	68	80	95	39
ANTIGUA (ENGLISH HARBOUR)	144	108	91	73	88	61	42	36	52	62	77	93	85	97	112	
ANGUILLA (ROAD BAY)	250	214	195	175	182	155	145	110	77	68	46	39	32	20		
ST. MARTIN (PHILIPSBURG)	230	194	175	158	172	145	130	92	60	51	32	28	14			
ST. BARTS	216	180	165	150	160	133	117	81	52	43	27	28				
SABA	212	176	160	144	158	131	116	80	46	37	17					
ST. EUSTATIUS	196	160	145	131	143	115	98	65	30	22						
ST. KITTS (BASSETERRE)	172	144	127	107	126	96	80	46	11							
NEVIS (CHARLESTOWN)	167	133	117	98	115	87	70	35								
MONTSERRAT (PLYMOUTH)	135	100	83	64	80	53	36									
DESHAIS	100	66	50	32	47	20										
BASSE TERRE	83	47	30	12	27											
POINTE À PITRE	94	60	40	23												
THE SAINTES	72	38	20													
PRINCE RUPERT BAY	54	19														
ROSEAU	36															

GPS

SATELLITE NAVIGATION
in the Leeward Islands

The GPS positions
given here have ID numbers
that are shown on our sketch charts.
You can download all these
waypoints directly to your GPS
by visiting www.doyleguides.com,
where I have posted
the waypoints and a
link to the appropriate software.

ID	LATITUDE	LONGITUDE	COMMENT
LANG01	N18°13.30'	W063°04.50'	Crocus Bay
LANG02	N18°12.00'	W063°05.90'	Road Bay
LANG03	N18°09.40'	W063°10.70'	Anguillita
LANG04	N18°15.70'	W063°10.70'	Prickly Pear Cays
LANG05	N18°16.00'	W063°15.00'	Dog Island
LANG06	N18°16.00'	W062°57.00'	Scrub I passage S approach
LSTM01	N18°00.40'	W063°03.30'	Philipsburg
LSTM02	N18°01.30'	W063°06.80'	Simpson Bay
LSTM03	N18°04.90'	W063°06.10'	Marigot near unlit buoys
LSTM04	N18°03.50'	W063°09.30'	Point Basse Terre
LSTM05	N18°06.80'	W063°03.80'	Grande Case
LSTM06	N18°06.20'	W062°59.90'	Orient Bay entrance
LSTM07	N18°03.00'	W063°00.40'	Oyster Pond entrance
LSTM08	N18°07.40'	W063°02.50'	Anse Marcel approach
LSTM09	N18° 06.00'	W063° 04.70'	Friar's Bay
LSTB01	N17°55.50'	W062°52.80'	Anse de Colombier
LSTB02	N17°54.30'	W062°52.00'	Gustavia (N.entrance)
LSTB03	N17°51.00'	W062°50.00'	South approach to St Barts
LSTB04	N17°57.30'	W062°54.70'	Ile Forchue
LSTB05	N17°55.00'	W062°56.00'	West approach St. Barts
LSTB06	N17°52.40'	W062°49.10'	approach to Saline Bay
LSTB07	N17° 54.7'	W062° 50.00'	approach b. St. Jean
LSAB01	N17°36.80'	W063°15.40'	Fort Bay
LSAB02	N17°39.00'	W063°15.50'	Saba NW approach
LSAB03	N17°37.00'	W063°13.00'	Saba SE approach
LSTA01	N17°29.00'	W062°59.50'	Orangestad
LSTA02	N17°32.00'	W063°00.00'	Statia N approach
LSTA03	N17°27.40'	W062°58.00'	Statia S approach
LSKT01	N17°24.60'	W062°52.60'	Off northwest coast St Kitts
LSKT02	N17°17.00'	W062°43.00'	Basseterre
LSKT03	N17°15.80'	W062°37.50'	North approach to the Narrows
LSKT04	N17°21.40'	W062°51.60.'	Sandy Point Town
LSKT05	N17°15.00'	W062°40.00.'	Approach to White House Bay
LSKT06	N17°20.30'	W062°50.10.'	St. Kitts Marine Works
LNVS01	N17°08.60'	W062°38.00'	Charlestown
LNVS02	N17°05.00'	W062°39.00'	Nevis SW Approach
LNVS03	N17°12.00'	W062°37.30'	Nevis approaches Oualie,Tamarind
LMTS01	N16°48.40'	W062°12.80'	Little Bay
LMTS02	N16°44.3'	W062°14.50'	Old Road Bay
LMTS03	N16°50.00'	W062°10.00'	NE Montserrat
LMTS04	N16°41'00'	W062°15.00'	SE Montserrat
LMTS05	N16°47'00'	W062°07.50'	East Montserrat
LMTS06	N16°38.50'	W062°09.00'	South Montserrat
LBAU01	N17°34.00'	W061°51.50'	0.9 NM south Palmetto Point
LBAU02	N17°32.10'	W061°43.50'	Entrance to Spanish Pt
LBAU03	N17°33.00'	W061°46.90'	Approach to Cocoa Pt. anchorage
LBAU04	N17°40.50'	W061°54.50'	Approach to Cedar Tree Point
LBAU05	N17° 35.08'	W061° 49.50	Barbuda Boat Harbour
LBAU06	N17°38.80'	W061°52.30'	Approach to Low Bay
LBAU07	N17°36.00'	W061°53.00'	Outside 9-foot Bank
LANT01	N17°00.00'	W061°45.80'	English Harbour approach
LANT02	N17°00.00'	W061°47.00'	Falmouth Harbour approach
LANT03	N16°59.80'	W061°44.30'	Indian Creek approach
LANT04	N17°00.20'	W061°43.80'	Mamora Bay approach
LANT05	N17°03.70'	W061°39.20'	Just south of Green I

These should not be used for navigation without first checking the data out against current DMA or BA ch

ID	LATITUDE	LONGITUDE	COMMENT
LANT06	N17°04.10'	W061°39.10'	Just East of Green I
LANT07	N17°12.00'	W061°53.50'	Just west of Diamond Bank
LANT08	N17°11.20'	W061°52.20'	Diamond Channel south
LANT09	N17°12.40'	W061°52.20'	Diamond Channel north
LANT10	N17°09.20'	W061°46.30'	Maiden Island approach
LANT11	N17°09.60'	W061°51.40'	Dickenson Bay
LANT12	N17°07.90'	W061°52.30'	St. John's entrance
LANT13	N17°07.50'	W061°54.00'	Deep Bay approach
LANT14	N17°04.50'	W061°54.70'	Jolly Harbour approach
LANT15	N16°59.00'	W061°53.00'	One NM south of Cades Reef
LANT16	N17°10.04'	W061°43.50'	Outside Bird I. Channel
LGUA0A	N16°21.69'	W061°34.35'	Cul de Sac Marin channel Passe Colas
LGUA0B	N16°21.10'	W061°34.11'	Cul de Sac Marin channel one
LGUA0C	N16°20.61'	W061°34.50'	Cul de Sac Marin channel two
LGUA0D	N16°19.53'	W061°34.14'	Cul de Sac Marin channel three
LGUA0E	N16°18.93'	W061°34.23'	Cul de Sac Marin channel four
LGUA0F	N16°17.52'	W061°33.47'	Cul de Sac Marin channel five
LGUA0G	N16°18.49'	W061°35.00'	C-de-S Marin mahault approach 1
LGUA0H	N16°17.24'	W061°35.14'	C-de-S Mahault approach 2
LGUA0I	N16°18.14'	W061°35.93'	C-de-s Grand Rivière approach
LGUA0J	N16°19.00'	W061°35.40'	C-de-s turn for west fajou
LGUA0K	N16°20.90'	W061°35.90'	Ilet à Fajou west anchorage
LGUA0L	N16°20.82'	W061°36.88'	Park marker
LGUA01	N16°18.30'	W061°48.50'	Deshais
LGUA02	N16°10.00'	W061°47.00'	Pigeon Island area
LGUA03	N16°05.30'	W061°46.30'	Anse a la Barque
LGUA04	N15°58.90'	W061°43.40'	Marina Riviere Sens approach
LGUA05	N16°25.00'	W061°32.50'	Port Louis
LGUA06	N16°12.50'	W061°31.90'	Pointe a Pitre entrance
LGUA07	N16°12.00'	W061°30.00'	Ilet à Gosier
LGUA7A	N16°11.70'	W061°26.10'	Petit Havre approach
LGUA08	N16°13.00'	W061°22.90'	St.Anne
LGUA8A	N16°12.90'	W061°23.90'	St.Anne (Club Med)
LGUA09	N16°14.85'	W061°15.30'	St. Francois Approach
LGUA10	N16°17.80'	W061°04.30'	La Desirade approach
LGUA1D	N16°10.70'	W061°07.20'	Iles de la Petite Terre
LGUA1A	N16°10.61'	W061°07.15'	Petite Terre bar crossing
LGUA1B	N16°10.52'	W061°07.05'	Petite Terre bar crossing
LGUA1C	N16°10.50'	W061°06.93'	Petite Terre bar crossing
LMGT01	N15°57.60'	W061°19.70'	St. Louis
LMGT02	N15°52.80'	W061°19.40'	Grand Bourg approach
LSNT01	N15°53.00'	W061°37.50'	Northwest approach
LSNT02	N15°53.00'	W061°35.50'	Cabrit/Baleine approach
LSNT03	N15°49.60'	W061°36.20'	South of La Coche & Grande Ile
LSNT04	N15°52.00'	W061°36.00'	Just north of Pain de Sucre
LSNT05	N15°53.10'	W061°34.70'	Approach Baie de Marigot
LDOM01	N15°35.00'	W061°29.00'	0.3 nm west Cabrits–Prince Rupert Bay
LDOM02	N15°33.00'	W061°29.00'	Prince Rupert Bay (approaching from the south)
LDOM03	N15°27.00'	W061°27.50'	Batali Beach
LDOM04	N15°24.70'	W061°25.90'	Castaways
LDOM05	N15°20.00'	W061°24.00'	Canefield (Donkey Beach)
LDOM06	N15°18.00'	W061°23.60'	Roseau (0.25 NM east of Queens River)
LDOM07	N15°17.55'	W061°23.20'	Approach to Fort Young Hotel anchorage
LDOM08	N15°16.90'	W061°22.80'	Approach to Hotels anchorage
LDOM09	N15°13.00'	W061°23.20'	0.5 NM west of the Pinnacle (Scotts Head)

Professional Yachts

*D*URING THE WINTER season, the Leewards have become a major cruising area for a fleet of some of the largest and most magnificent yachts in the world. These yachts are either for charter or for the use of the owner and his friends. Either way, time and efficiency are more important than cost for their captains. In this volume you will find excellent coverage of marinas, services and restaurants, and we often mention when these are particularly suitable for larger yachts.

Below is just a brief overview of what to expect in Leewards, along with a few useful contacts – people you can count on to help out when you have a lot that needs doing in a short time and don't have the time to look for individual services.

St. Martin

St. Martin is one of the two main mega-yacht bases and the largest for power yachts. You will find everything you need to support your yacht here. Most marinas have a full organization for helping superyachts and these include:

Marina Fort St. Louis,
0590 51 11 11, F: 0590 51 11 12, VHF: 16, marinafortlouis@domaccess.fr

Palapa Marina,
599-545-2735, F: 599-545-2510, VHF: 68, office@palapamarina.com

Yacht Club Port de Plaisance
599-544-4565, Fax: 599-544-4566, VHF: 16/78, info@yachtclubportdeplaisance.com

Simpson Bay Marina,
599-544-2309, F: 599-544-3378, VHF: 16/79A, sbm@igymarinas.com

Yacht Club Isle de Sol,
599-544-2408, F: 599 544-2906, IDS@igymarinas.com.You can also find superyacht agents who will arrange everything for you:

Dockside Management
599-542-4096, F: 599-544-4097, office@docksidemanagement.net

International Yacht Collection,
(Simpson B.), 599-544-3780, F: 599-544-3779, mark@yachtcollection.net

Mega Yacht Services
599-544-4440, Cell: 599-520-1530, F: 599 544-2526, harrison@megayachtservice.com

Super Yacht Services
599-544-2436/522-9746 simon@superyachtservices.net

Yacht Services,
590-52-92-38, 0690-88-88-47 F: 599-553-7526. VHF: 68, yachtservices@caribserve.net

St. Barts

The Port of Gustavia has a fair amount of dock space for yachts less than 60 meters, and the anchorage is large. The fuel dock is often out of commission. One agency specializes in arranging everything for supery-achts: Nautica FWI, 0590-27-56-50, F:590-27-56-52. nfyachts@wanadoo.fr

Statia

Fuel can be taken on in Statia. Contact The Port Authority, 599-318-2888, VHF:16, 14

St. Kitts/Nevis

Serviciz is a superyacht agency run by Rickie Browne. He will make all the arrangements you need. 869-762-8130/663-8130, Fax: 464-4188 . rickie@serviciz.com.

As far as facilities are concerned, large yachts (up to 200 feet and 15 foot draft) can find space outside the marina wall in an area protected by the outer breakwater. Fuel can be arranged in this berth.

Port Zante

869-466-5021, F: 869-466-5020, VHF:68, udcorp@caribsurf.com

If there is space they can also use the cruise ship dock by arrangement with the port authority.

In Nevis use ship's agent:

A&M Enterprises,

869-469-5966, F: 869-469-5966, caribsurfqueen@hotmail.com

Antigua

Antigua is one of the two main mega-yacht bases in the Leewards and the largest for sailing yachts. You will find everything you need to support your yacht here. The superyacht marinas have organizations to support their customers:

Antigua Yacht Club Marina,

(FH), 268-460-1544, F: 268-460-1444, VHF: 68, falcones@candw.ag

Falmouth Harbour Marina,

268-460-6054, F: 268-460-6055, VHF:68

Jolly Harbour Marina,

268-462-6042, F: 268-462-7703, VHF: 68, jollymarina@candw.ag In addition there are agencies that can arrange everything for you:

Antigua Yacht Services,

268-460-1121, F: 268-460-1123, VHF: 68. ays@candw.ag

Caribbean Concierge Services,

268-726-2271, 462-2271, 401-662-3360, csantigua.com tina@ Jane's Yacht Services, 268-460-2711, F: 268-460-3740, VHF: 68, antyacht@candw.ag

Jane's Yacht Services,

268-460-2711, F: 268-460-3740, VHF: 68, antyacht@candw.ag

Guadeloupe

Guadeloupe has the infrastructure to support visiting superyachts with many repair facilities. Marina Bas du Fort recently dredged part of their marina for larger craft. Yachts with depths of up to 14.5 feet and 75 meters long are welcome.

Ariane Concierge Services, Marina Bas du Fort,

0590-93-66-20, F: 0590-90-81-53. Ariane will handle all superyacht needs in the area.

Gerard Petreluzzi is a customs clearance, ship and super-yacht agent and can handle all yacht needs. 0690-35-31-58, Petreluzzi.gerard@wanadoo.fr

Caribbean Luxury Cars also run a concierge service and they can come visit all ports in Guadeloupe, contact: Jimmy, 0690-93-03-56, caribbeanluxurycars@yahoo.fr

Dominica

Fuel can be arranged in Dominica, either in Portsmouth or Roseau. Contact:

National Petroleum, 767-448-7423 / 449-2415, F: 767-449-2477.

There are quite a few young men, trained as Indian River Guides, who have become adept at getting anything you need arranged while in Dominica. This includes customs clearance and taking on fuel.While these people are stationed in Portsmouth, they all own buses and can come to Roseau to tend to your needs.

Martin Carriere, Providence Boating, Portsmouth, 767-445-3008, F: 767-445-5181, VHF: 16, Carrierre@hotmail.com

Jeffrey, Sea Bird Tours, 767-245-0125, VHF:16

Cobra Tours and Yacht Services,

767-245-6332, VHF:16/10, info@cobratours.com

In Roseau Hubert Winston at **Dominica Marine Center** will take care of all your needs from fueling to provisioning. He also has a few moorings capable of taking some super-yachts, 767-448-2705/275-2851, info@dominicamarinecenter.com.

The best facility for shore access for guests is to use the dock at Fort Young Hotel. They will also be very supportive in arranging anything you may need.

Fort Young Hotel, Roseau, 767-448-5000, F:767-448-5006, fortyoung@cwdom.dm

Scuba Diving

EARLY EVERYONE WHO dives successfully is hooked. Few sports attract such dedicated adherents. Yet those who have not dived have little conception of what it is all about. This is not surprising because the world underwater is totally alien from life on land and language does a poor job of describing it. A major difference is in locomotion. One is weightless underwater and movement more closely resembles flying or drifting in outer space than walking or running.

We find ourselves gliding into a brand new environment with a fluidity and ease known only in our dreams. And as soon as we relax enough to look around, we realize that life under the sea is very strange indeed. The background color is in the restful blue-green spectrum, yet painted on top of this are some of the brightest colors imaginable: sponges that look like ancient urns glow a luminous blue, there are huge schools of fish

in brilliant reds, mauves, yellows and blues. It is a topsy-turvy world full of wonders. Tall soft waving plants that are really colonies of tiny animals, little squids moving by a kind of jet propulsion, and rays gliding with elegant ease. Best of all it has been barely touched by man so most of the fish are not frightened. Indeed the tiny damselfish, which can easily fit in the palm of a hand, regards a diver as another big fish and will charge headlong to protect its territory with such gallant determination that is hard not to laugh. If we put an upside down hand out among the cleaning shrimp, they will crawl aboard and clean our skin. We can swim close by schools of fish whose very numbers are astonishing

Diving is easy. Anyone who just wants to give diving a go can do so very quickly with a 'resort course.' It will take one whole morning or afternoon. First you get a one-hour talk that tells you in simple language what diving is all about. Then you try out the equipment in shallow water and, lastly, you go for your first dive. A resort course only qualifies you to dive under the close supervision of an instructor at the same dive shop.

34

The next step from the resort course is the new Scuba Diver course put out by PADI. This two-and-a-half day course certifies you to dive with any dive master at any shop to a depth of 40 feet. It is a good introduction and, being short, it is easy to do on holiday. You can complete your training on your next holiday, as this course counts as credit towards being an independent open water diver.   A full diving course in the islands takes about four or five days and includes a couple of hours of instruction each day, followed by a dive, during which you increase your practical skills.

The same tremendous variety that makes the Leewards so appealing as a cruising area extends underwater. The nature of the land is often reflected beneath the sea. Islands like Dominica and Saba that are rugged and dramatic onshore have breathtaking walls, pinnacles and rocks below. Islands with a more gentle form such as Antigua and St. Martin have huge forests of coral below and the diving is easy and relaxing. Cruising divers are especially lucky because they can try a dive in each island, sampling a smorgasbord of the area's very best dives.

In Saba, Statia, St. Kitts, Nevis and Dominica, diving is forbidden except with a local dive shop. Everywhere else you can dive from your yacht with your own or rented equipment.

We try to give adequate information for those dive sites that are suitable for diving straight from your boat or dinghy. We mark many of these on our sketch charts. For more information check the Complete Dive Guide series that describe all the dives in great detail including underwater plans.

Sometimes sea conditions make sites unsuitable; divers must judge for themselves. Those diving in St. Martin and St. Barts should contact the Scuba Shop in Oyster Pond, the owners put out a free booklet with maps describing sites suitable for yachts.

We also describe some sites that are out of reach of most yacht dinghies. In these cases it is best to go with a local dive shop. We strongly recommend that newly qualified divers and those who have not dived recently do their first dive with a dive shop.

Coral reefs are particularly fragile and it is essential that all of us sports divers take the greatest care to preserve this natural wonderland. Coral reefs are made up of colonies of small creatures called polyps that bond together to make up the huge structures we see. Many are sensitive to handling, and a small amount of damage can lead to the introduction of hostile sponges, which could slowly destroy a large clump of coral. Unlike plants, corals grow extremely slowly, so any damage is long lasting.

The diver can damage coral by kicking it with fins, grabbing it or bumping into it. Underwater photographers can also damage it by lying on it or supporting themselves on the coral while taking pictures. There are several things that can help. Never wear gloves when you dive, they decrease your sensitivity and you will be tempted to grab onto coral.

When you first go down, try to descend onto a sand patch beside the reef. This way you will be kicking sand rather than reef while you get your balance and buoyancy under control. Never take underwater souvenirs, be they live shells, hard coral or seafans. Not only is it illegal in every country, it will eventually destroy the reef. It is tempting to think that one little thing is not going to make much difference, but you are not the only one out there, and if you take something you can be sure there will be hundreds more who will do the same.

It is very beautiful down below and the fish and sea creatures are unafraid and, in many cases, downright curious. Enjoy it and help keep it wonderful.

A list of dive shops of the Leeward Islands is given in the *Directory* at the back of this book.

CRUISING INFORMATION

35

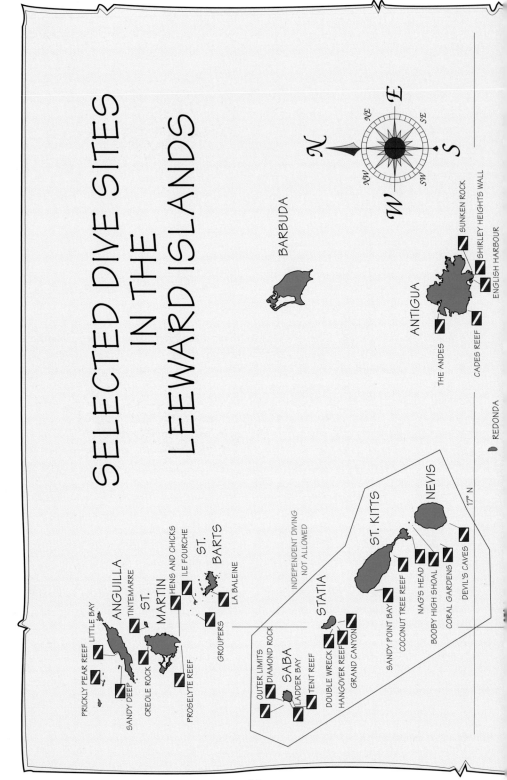

SELECTED DIVE SITES
IN THE
LEEWARD ISLANDS

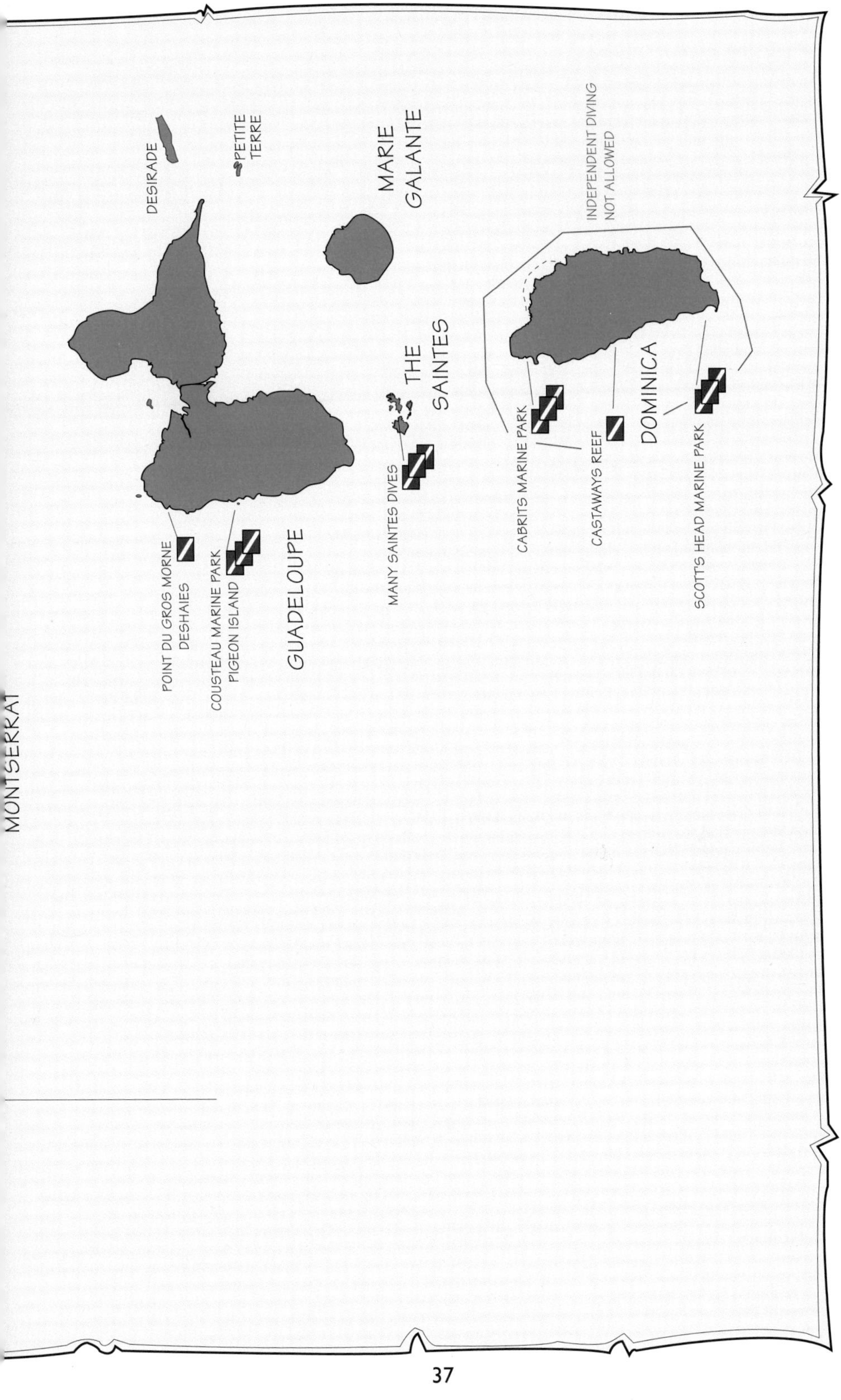

MONTSERRAT

DESIRADE

PETITE
TERRE

MARIE
GALANTE

INDEPENDENT DIVING
NOT ALLOWED

THE
SAINTES

POINT DU GROS MORNE
DESHAIES

COUSTEAU MARINE PARK
PIGEON ISLAND

GUADELOUPE

MANY SAINTES DIVES

CABRITS MARINE PARK

CASTAWAYS REEF

DOMINICA

SCOTT'S HEAD MARINE PARK

the anchorages of the
RENAISSANCE
ISLANDS

anguilla • st. martin • sint maarten • st. barthelemy (st. barts)

Anse de Columbier Chris Doyle

Oyster Pond   Chris Doyle

The Anchorages Of
The Renaissance Islands

IN THE LESSER ANTILLES there are two kinds of islands, both volcanic. The young ones, which are mountainous and steep, form a gentle arc from Grenada to Saba. The older islands were once like the youngsters, but have eroded to nearly flat and at some time sank below sea level where they acquired limestone cappings before being uplifted and resurfacing. St. Martin, St. Barts, and Anguilla are of the older type and they lie together on a large bank, 30 miles to the north of Statia and Saba. They are less mountainous than their volcanic cousins and consequently drier. The relatively shallow water has allowed for the growth of corals, shells and algae, which over millions of years have been transformed into long white sandy beaches.

The early success of plantations on these islands was short lived. Rainfall was inadequate for agricultural crops and the thin soil was quickly depleted. As a consequence, their economies and populations declined until quite recent times. With the coming of the leisure age, they have begun a renaissance that promises to far exceed any past splendor. A major contributing factor has been the pleasant dry climate that worked against these islands earlier. St. Martin led the way, with its duty free status, tolerant French/Dutch administration, and the easy access provided by a large airport. Hotels and condominiums have rapidly replaced the dry scrub behind the beaches and the population has more than tripled over the last 40 years. As St. Martin boomed, those wanting a quieter, more exclusive type of island have looked to St. Barts and Anguilla.

Politically, St. Martin is divided in two. The northern part is French (Saint Martin) and the southern part Dutch (Sint Maarten), but to make life easy we refer to the whole island as St. Martin. St. Barts is also French, and both St. Barts and French St. Martin have now separated from Guadeloupe and are like towns in France. Sint Maarten has a similar relationship with Holland. Anguilla is still British, though largely self-governing. From our perspective, all these islands are part of the Leewards, but some people get confused because in the old days the Dutch used to call them the Windwards – which they are compared to the other Dutch territories, Aruba and Bonaire.

Attractions for yachtspeople include short but invigorating passages between the islands and a wide variety of anchorages. One can suit one's mood with either peaceful hideaways or bustling ports with restaurants, shops, and nightlife. St. Martin in particular offers first rate duty free provisioning, some of the Caribbean's largest chandleries, and its most efficient yacht services.

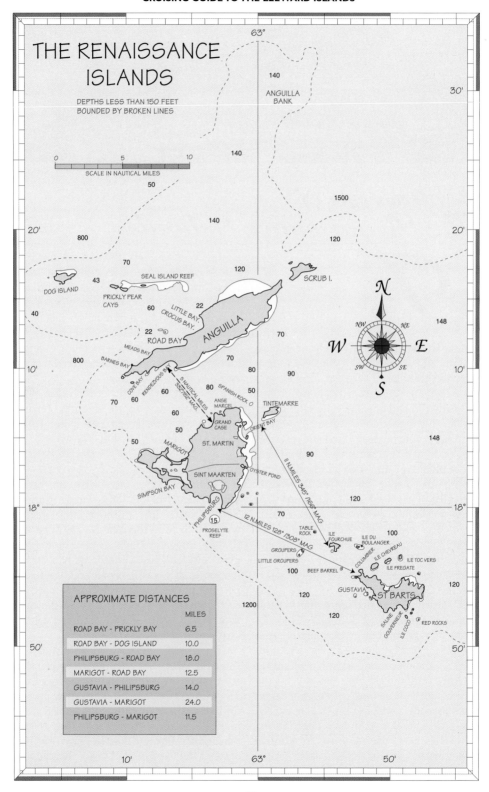

THE RENAISSANCE ISLANDS

DEPTHS LESS THAN 150 FEET
BOUNDED BY BROKEN LINES

0   5   10
SCALE IN NAUTICAL MILES

ANGUILLA BANK

Anguilla

DOG ISLAND

SEAL ISLAND REEF

PRICKLY PEAR CAYS

SCRUB I.

LITTLE BAY.
CROCUS BAY.

ROAD BAY

MEADS BAY

BARNES BAY

COVE BAY

RENDEZVOUS BAY

6 NAUTICAL MILES
205°/182° MAG.

SPANISH ROCK

ANSE MARCEL

GRAND CASE

ST. MARTIN

TINTEMARRE

ORIENT BAY

MARIGOT

SINT MAARTEN

OYSTER POND

11 N.MILES 345°/106° MAG.

SIMPSON BAY

PHILIPSBURG

15

PROSELYTE REEF

12 N.MILES 128° /308° MAG.

TABLE ROCK

ILE FOURCHUE

ILE DU BOULANGER

ILE CHEVREAU

ILE TOC VERS

ILE FREGATE

GROUPERS

LITTLE GROUPERS

BEEF BARREL

COLUMBIER

GUSTAVIA

ST BARTS

SALINE

GOUVERNEUR

ILE COCO

RED ROCKS

N NW NE W E SW SE S

APPROXIMATE DISTANCES	
	MILES
ROAD BAY - PRICKLY BAY	6.5
ROAD BAY - DOG ISLAND	10.0
PHILIPSBURG - ROAD BAY	18.0
MARIGOT - ROAD BAY	12.5
GUSTAVIA - PHILIPSBURG	14.0
GUSTAVIA - MARIGOT	24.0
PHILIPSBURG - MARIGOT	11.5

Anguilla

NGUILLA IS A LOW island surrounded by spectacular white sand beaches and banks of coral. For the most part it has a wonderful sense of peace and the people are outstandingly friendly and honest. However, development is continuing apace, lots of cars are being imported, so to find the peace you now have to get off the main roads. The population of 12,000 relies on tourism as the major industry. In 1967, Britain lumped Anguilla with St. Kitts and Nevis and made them an autonomous state. This awkward parceling conveniently filed them away for the British Colonial Office, but ignored both the social and geographical realities. Anguillans were dead set against this arrangement and wanted to remain with England. They rebelled against the rule of St. Kitts' Premiere Bradshaw who told them he "would show them who was boss" and threatened to "turn Anguilla into a desert." An amazing armed rebellion followed in which there were only minor casualties and no fatalities. The Anguillan rebels would open fire on the police station – manned from St. Kitts – at all hours of the night or day until the police were quite unnerved. A large armed crowd then gave the police an ultimatum to leave the island and they blocked the runway to stop reinforcements from arriving.

The Anguillans, fearing an armed invasion from St. Kitts, decided to take the offensive and invade St. Kitts themselves. A small boatload of men went there, aided by two American mercenaries. The invasion was a complete fiasco. A big hole got blown in the ground near the defense force headquarters and there was a shoot-out at a police station. There were no casualties. However, after that no one in St. Kitts

Pricky Pears Cays

Chris Doyle

RENAISSANCE ISLANDS

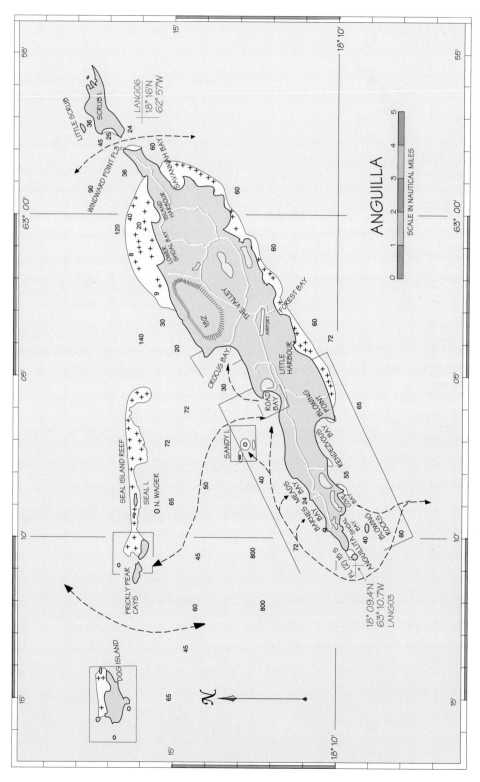

ANGUILLA

SCALE IN NAUTICAL MILES

0 1 2 3 4 5

LANG06
18° 16'N
62° 57'W

LITTLE SCRUB

SCRUB I.

WINDWARD POINT FL3

SAVANNAH BAY

ISLAND HARBOUR

LOWER SHOAL BAY

THE VALLEY

CROCUS BAY

SEAL ISLAND REEF

SEAL I.

O. N. WAGER

PRICKLY PEAR CAYS

DOG ISLAND

SANDY I.

ROAD BAY

BLOWING POINT

FOREST BAY

LITTLE HARBOUR

AIRPORT

RENDEZVOUS BAY

BARNES BAY

MEADS BAY

COVE BAY

BLOWING BAY

ANGUILLA SHOAL BAY

FL (2) 15 S

18° 09.4'N
63° 10.7'W
LANG03

Anguilla

Regulations

Yachts should proceed directly to Road Bay, the main port of entry. Blowing Point is also a permissible point of entry, but it is commercial and not recommended for yachts. The fisheries department does not allow anchoring in certain areas; we note these in our harbor descriptions. Yachts anchoring outside Road Bay need a cruising permit and many yachts will need to pay charges. We give full customs details under Road Bay. The waters all around Anguilla are protected by law. Nude bathing, spearfishing and the collecting of coral or live shells are strictly forbidden. You are not allowed to make fires on any beach. You must also be careful not to damage coral in any way (watch your anchor). In addition, in the marine park areas, waterskiing, fishing, pumping bilges or heads, and the taking of anything (except pictures) is banned. The marine park is open from 0600-1900; yachts may not overnight in the park.

Telephones

Public phones, coin or card, are next to customs, at Roy's and near Three C's Supermarket. For a collect or credit card call, dial 0, then the number. Telephone cards are available in town. The area code for Anguilla is 264. Cable and Wireless and Digicel cell phones work well here.

Shopping hours

Normal shopping hours are 0800-1200 and 1300-1600.

Transport

Anguilla's airport takes all inter-island airlines, but is not jumbo-jet sized. American Eagle has direct flights to Puerto Rico and other airlines have good linkage to neighboring islands. Easy connections can be made via St. Martin. There is also a ferry service that runs about every 45 minutes between Blowing Point and St. Martin. Airport departure tax is $20US.

The easiest way to get around in Anguilla is to use one of the taxis from the stand next to customs. Taxi rates are calculated by dividing Anguilla into zones. If you stay in the same zone, fares are usually $8US. The farthest fare is $32US.

Example rates in $US are:
Road Bay to The Valley	$12
Road Bay to the airport	$12
Tours, 1.5 hours	$50

Longer tours are $10 per extra half hour.
These rates are for one or two people. Extra people are charged $3 for regular runs, $5 for island tours.

Rental cars are easily available (You can rent one from Connor's Taxi Service VHF: 16). You will need to buy a local license for about $20 US. Drive on the left.

Holidays

- January 1
- Good Friday and Easter Monday (Easter Sunday is April 4, 2010; April 24, 2011)
- May 1 (Labor Day)
- Second Saturday in June (Queens Birthday)
- Whit Monday 50 days after Easter Sunday : (May 24, 2010, June 13, 2011)
- Last Friday in May (Anguilla Day)
- First Monday and Tuesday, Thursday and Friday in August (Carnival, August Thursday and Constitution Day)
- December (mid/variable) (Separation Day)
- December 25-26

Anguilla, Admiralty Leisure Folio 5641-1, 5641-5, 5641-6

really wanted to mess with the Anguillans. Several Americans thought up fancy schemes to help the Anguillans finance their island, and, in 1969, Britain, under the mistaken impression the island had been taken over by the Mafia, invaded. Armed men waded ashore onto the beaches to be met by goats and curious small boys. After the embarrassment died down, Anguillans got what they wanted and are again administered by the British.

Road Bay, the main anchorage in Anguilla, is a charming village set on a lovely beach. The sail to and from St. Martin is usually a pleasant haul over turquoise water. From Road Bay you can visit other anchorages along Anguilla's south and north coasts, as well as making day stops offshore at Sandy Island, Dog Island, and Prickly Pear Cays. There may be fees involved. (See under Road Bay.)

You must clear into Anguilla, and the proper place to do this is Road Bay. Customs can also be found at Blowing Point, but the anchorage is rolly and used only by commercial craft and ferries. From Road Bay you can get a cruising permit to explore other anchorages, some of which are in the marine park. The Anguilla Sailing Association runs the annual Anguilla regatta during the second weekend in May. It is fun, with Anguilla racing boats, visiting yachts, and the 12-meter fleet from St. Martin. They also organize the Anguilla Youth Sailing Club, which teaches local kids to sail. So far they have eight Optimists and a J-24. The sailing program is open to everyone, with scholarships for those that cannot afford it. In this endeavor they have had support from local businesses all over Anguilla, including those in Sandy Ground.

APPROACHING ROAD BAY FROM THE SOUTHWEST

From St. Martin, Anguilla appears low-lying and rather uniform. Toward the western end there are some very white ultra-modern buildings that almost glow in the sunlight behind Shoal Bay. Hideous or inspired, depending on your taste. Behind Maunday's Bay and at the headland linking

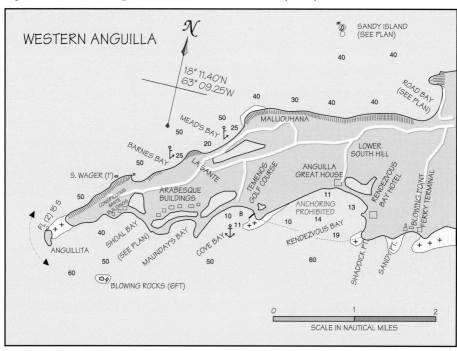

it to Cove Bay are some white buildings of distinctively Arabesque architecture. The next serious large group of houses is in the area of Blowing Point. However, new buildings are appearing all the time.

The shoreline from Rendezvous Bay around Anguillita to Road Harbor is fairly free of shoals, and you can sail just a couple of hundred yards off the coast. Offshore you will see the large, flat 6-foot-high Blowing Rocks. You can sail either side of these, but do not approach too closely.

When passing the western tip of Anguilla, always go outside Anguillita. The water between Anguillita and Anguilla contains underwater rocks. The sea has sculpted interesting cliff formations from Anguillita to Barnes Bay. Pass outside South Wager. This rock, which used to be 15 feet high and beautifully undercut into the shape of a head, was decapitated in a hurricane some years ago and is now barely awash. Between Sandy Island and Anguilla

there is a mile of clear water to sail in, but avoid the 5-foot patch that lies a few hundred yards to the south of Sandy Island. This is normally easy to see as light green water.

Between Anguillita and Road Bay, anchoring is sometimes possible in Meads Bay and Barnes Bay. You must clear into Road Bay before visiting these bays.

Barnes Bay and Meads Bay

Barnes Bay and Meads Bay are two long strips of beautiful white sand, separated by a cliffy headland. There are hotels at the eastern ends of both bays. On suitable days, these bays make a great temporary anchoring spot for lunch or a swim. You can anchor in 20 to 30 feet of water quite close to shore, good sand holding. There are no dinghy docks and trying to beach the dinghy could

RENAISSANCE ISLANDS

Road Bay

Chris Doyle

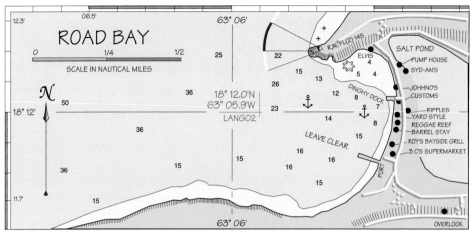

be hazardous in any kind of swell.

Meads Bay is somewhat more protected and has the advantage of the grand Mediterranean style Malliouhana Hotel. Put on your best beach shirt, land your dinghy, and wind your way along the path up the cliff. The restaurant has a panoramic view over the bay, and you can enjoy such delicacies as lobster crepes. Bring a credit card for the elegant La Romana boutique. At the end of Barnes Bay there is a place where you can swim with captive dolphins.

Road Bay

Road Bay is the main port of entry for yachts and one of the most pleasant anchorages in the northern Leewards. It is a long bay fringed by a perfect powdery beach. Along the beach is Sandy Ground Village and its collection of bars and restaurants, some of which are excellent. The atmosphere is quiet and peaceful. Behind the beach large salt ponds attract a wonderful array of egrets and wading birds, especially in the late afternoon.

Navigation

As you approach Road Bay, keep clear of the shoals along the southern shore. Otherwise, the bay is wide open. Avoid the northern tip of the bay, which is shoal. Anchor anywhere in the bay except in the main shipping passage. Road Bay is normally an excellent overnight anchorage, even in moderate northerly swells. In choosing your anchoring spot, keep in mind that late night live music is likely at Johnno's and Elvis from Wednesday to Saturday. If this will disturb you, anchor well away from the dinghy dock. The light on the northern headland often does not work.

Regulations

When you arrive in Road Bay, you must anchor. Do not pick up a mooring; they are all privately owned.

Personal watercraft of all types, including Jet Skis are strictly forbidden in Anguilla.

Do not be put off by tales of high entry fees in Anguilla. Many yachts are under 20 tons registered tonnage, in which case there is no charge to visit Road Bay, which is one of Anguilla's most attractive anchorages. The entry fee structure is shown below. Once there, you can look at the cruising fees and see if you want to venture farther.

Check in with customs and immigration behind the dinghy dock. Opening hours are daily 0830-1200 and 1300-1600. The customs staff is friendly and helpful. If you are not changing crew, you can clear in and out at the same time and pay all the fees. However, you do have to return within 24-hours before leaving to pick up the clearance. Entry charges into Road Bay in $EC are as follows:

Under 20 tons there is
currently no charge.
20-50 tons $50EC

50-100 tons	$90
100-250 tons	$180
250-500 tons	$240
500-1000 tons	$350
1000-2000 tons	$500
over 2000 tons	$800

(divide by 2.67 for $US)

There is a departure tax of $5US per person. If you are not sailing beyond Road Bay, these are the only fees you pay.

Anguilla has several other attractive anchorages that you can sail to. The regulations are more restrictive than anywhere else in the Eastern Caribbean – the only two anchorages where you may overnight are Road Bay and Crocus Bay. All other permissible anchorages are for day-use only. To visit any anchorage outside Road Bay you need a cruising permit, which you can get when you clear in.

The daily cruising permit, which applies to all yachts is as follows in $EC

	Up to 5 tons	5 -20 tons	over 20 tons
Day:	$25	$100	$150
Week:	$150	$600	$900

Monthly, quarterly, and yearly rates are available on request. Tonnage is checked against yacht papers. A bonus to these charges is that they deter people, so the anchorages outside Road Bay are generally quiet and uncrowded. Anchorages you may visit outside the marine park are Cove Bay, Maunday's Bay, and Crocus Bay.

The marine park areas include: Dog Island, Prickly Pear Cays and the whole of Seal Island Reef, Sandy Island, Little Bay, and, for shallow boats with local knowl-edge, Shoal Bay and Island Harbour. Anchoring in the Park areas is restricted to demarcated areas (see our harbor sections). The park is only open 0600-1900, and additional fees apply. These are:

Private yachts up 55 feet: $15 US per day. Yachts over 55 feet and all charter yachts: $23 per day. Yacht moorings have been placed in many marine park areas, which you are welcome to use.

Yacht moorings are white and designed for yachts up to 55 feet. Note that when you pick up a mooring, you must put your own dock line through the end of the pick up line to allow more scope. If you want a bridle, use two ropes, one on each side. A single line bridle will chafe through as the boat swings. Yachts of over 55 feet should ask for anchoring instructions.

Dive moorings are red and are for local dive boats only. Do not tie your yacht or tender to them.

Those wanting to dive in the marine park should discuss it with the park authorities. They would prefer that you dive with Carty (see water sports), but they may let you dive on some sites on your own. In the park, there is a $4US per dive fee. All the dive places we mention in this book come under the parks.

Communication, General Services

Roy has a good internet room with plenty of computers. If you bring your own computer in, Roy, Syd-An, Ripples, Elvis, and some of the others offer free wifi; you

RENAISSANCE ISLANDS

may be able to pick one of them up from your boat. Behind the dinghy dock are public toilets and free showers. Jerry jugging water is a possibility in an emergency. A couple of people have private water lines to the dock. You would have to find one of them and negotiate. Ripples, Johnno's, and Three C's Suprmarket sometime sell ice.

Any taxi driver should be able to help you get your cooking gas bottles filled.

For anything else and for all superyachts, Super Yacht Services has an agent here: Gabi Gumbs who also owns the Pump House. You can call her on her cell: 476-7972.

Chandlery, Technical Services

David Carty, at Rebel Marine, is a custom boat-builder of power boats. His yard is shared with Anguilla Techni Sales who fit out the boats. Techni Sales keeps a fair stock of chandlery: all the things they install on their boats. They are the agents for Bombardier (Evinrude/Johnson) outboards and they can fabricate both stainless and aluminum and do any installation work. They also sell industrial and medical gasses. You will find them at North Hill, not far from Sandy Bay. Ask to speak to Chris Carty.

A ham radio operator called Bobcat monitors 146.76 and can help out with electrical and refrigeration problems. (264-497-5974).

For tools and general hardware, visit the big Ace Hardware at the top of the hill as you leave Road Bay.

A number of yachts cruising the Caribbean are registered in Anguilla, which is currently under the British Registry system. Non-British applicants need to form an Anguillan company to do this. Stott Marine can provide any of these services and the local surveyor, Richard West, is very helpful. The process tends to be lengthy.

Transport

Several taxi drivers, including Stevens, base themselves at Sandy Ground.

Connor's Taxi Service is a good professional taxi and car rental company run by Wendell and Celsa Connor. You can call them on VHF: 16.

Provisioning

Three C's Supermarket, a few steps back from the main ship dock, is clean and modern and has enough to help keep your supplies topped up, including bags of ice. The owner comes and goes, so it hard to specify opening hours, but he is often open. Three C's is also an inn with six rental apartments upstairs. You can buy top-up cards for Digicel and C&W here.

If you need a big supermarket, then you will find three in the Valley. These are modern and complete, good enough for a full provisioning. From a yachting perspective, Proctor's is the newest and probably the best. It is open weekdays 0800-2000, Saturdays, 0800 to 2100. Albert's is also large and good and if you are planning to buy in bulk they have a wholesale department. It opens 0800-2030 weekdays, and 0800-2130 on Saturdays. IGA Food Center is in a shopping mall in The Valley and the only one to open on Sundays (0800-1200) weekday hours are 0800-2100.

An at Syd-An's has a tiny food store with essentials. However, if you need a few things from the bigger supermarkets,; some fresh fruts or vegetables or a special can of something, give her a call, and she will bring it in for you, saving you the taxi to town. Syd-An's also has an ATM cash machine outside.

Fun Shopping

An, at Syd-An's, has a small convenience store, but she also has a collection of rather fine art collected in Santa Domingo that she sells at very reasonable prices. An also has 16 rooms for rent at reasonable rates.

Caribbean Affairs Boutique, with lots of souvenirs, is on the road leading out of Sandy Ground, just as the hill starts.

Imzala Boutique and hair salon and Body and Soul fitness and massage are right on the beach.

ROAD BAY

Restaurants

Most of Road Bay's casual waterfront restaurants have ideal beach-front locations where you can eat fresh seafood to the sound of lapping waves. All are within easy walking distance, so you can stroll down the beach and take your pick. A variety of nationalities and cuisines are available and some of the restaurants are superb, providing a good reason to sail to Road Bay. You can walk in to most places, but best make reservations for dinner at Roy's and Barrel Stay; both are really popular.

Roy's Bayside Grill is just next to the port. It is open for lunch (1200-1500) and dinner (1800 to 2200 or later) every day. The dining area is perched on the beach, open to the sea and air, and has a romantic feel. This restaurant is perfection through simplicity. They use the very best ingredients that can be found. All the beef is certified prime Angus. The fish is local and fresh, or imported Scotch salmon, and the lobsters are fresh from Anguilla. They also do chops and chicken. The food is grilled just the way you ask for it, adding just enough marinade to bring out the flavors and the result is delicious. The lobster soup is wonderful. They have a happy hour from 1700-1900.

The Barrel Stay is light and breezy, with a high roof supported on mast-like poles and open walls. Graham Belcher and Jill Shepherd own this restaurant and bring top-end cuisine to Sandy Ground. Graham is a world-class modern chef who has worked in Michelin-class restaurants, London's best hotels, and as executive chef for prestigious companies. Graham cooks as an art form, creating sophisticated gourmet food, with everything, including the decorative pasta and the dessert ice cream, being made in his kitchen from the freshest ingredients. Graham and Jill do all this in an informal atmosphere where kids are welcome and especially catered to. The crème brûlée, which is served with a raspberry sorbet contained in a biscuit that rises like a half a moon and topped with decorative spun sugar, is positively celestial. They decided to carry on with the tradition of Barrel Stay's world famous fish soup, which has been featured in both Gourmet Magazine and Food and Wine and makes a fine, light lunch. If there is some dish you really love that is not on the menu, discuss it well advance, as Graham likes a challenge. The lunch menu is light, but if you want a big lunch, you can choose from the dinner menu. They open nightly for dinner except Wednesday and they open for lunch from Saturday to Monday.

Reggae Reef, is a pleasant, informal restaurant open to the beach and run by David from Atlanta and Rick from Florida, sailors both. They are very friendly and especially welcome those on yachts. They open every day for breakfast, lunch, and dinner, chalking up the next meal's offerings on a board. Lunch includes Black Angus burgers, salads, and local fish. They do an excellent fish soup. Dinner also features fresh fish and lobster whenever available from the local fishermen (all ingredients are local and fresh). The southern US influence also shows in their famous pulled pork. Their sunset special happy hour is 1600-1800, with half-price mixed drinks. They have background live music three nights a week.

Yard Style is owned and run by Carlett from Jamaica, who will look after you well. She offers local food and Jamaican specialties such as jerk meat, with all local vegetables, including yam and breadfruit: a good place to come for the local experience. For lunch you can get simple things like hamburgers. She puts out seats and sunshades by day so you can enjoy the beach. Yard Style is open every day from until 1000 until late at night.

Johnno's (closed Monday) is rough, ready, and right by the dinghy dock. Johnno makes great rum punches, tasty local seafood meals, and snacks, and he often has live music: Wednesday and Friday evenings (Mussinton brothers), Saturday (steel band), and Sunday (jazz starts around noon). Dinner at night, with tables out on the beach, makes you feel like you are in a top restaurant.

If you walk back to the road and turn left, you will come to a restaurant and lively nightspot called The Pump House. This atmospheric bar is built in the old salt workhouse. You can still see all the old machinery used for grinding up the salt prior to export. They open for dinner, and the bar often keeps going until the wee hours, with live music most nights of the week. Food is available with a varied menu – everything from a big steak meal to pizzas, salads, and burgers. Outside they post both a music menu and a food menu, so you can check it out. Owner Laurie Gumbs is from Anguilla and his wife, Gabi, is from Germany. The atmosphere is informal and friendly. They open from 1800 and close on Mondays.

Sammy's Bar is cheap, cheerful and local. Sit and drink beers with the locals and eat ribs and chicken off the grill at local prices. Sammy opens every day from 0900 to midnight.

At the north end of the beach, Elvis has

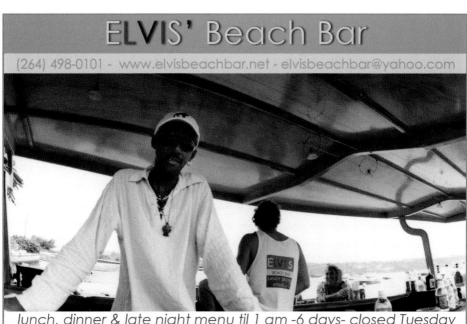
RENAISSANCE ISLANDS

51

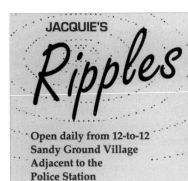
a great beach bar hang out, with a bar built out of an old Anguilla racing sloop. He opens every day except Tuesday, from noon untill way late at night. By day, a quiet hang-out; by night, the party place, with live music from Friday to Sunday, and a wild all-night party on the full moon. Elvis does a world-famous rum punch and special Mannawanna cocktail. Light food, like hamburgers, spicy wings, chicken and shrimp is available.

Ripples Bar and Restaurant is your friendly pub and eatery presided over by the owner, Jacquie, who is English. They serve fresh local seafood; fish, lobster, and conch; pub specials such as beef and Guiness or cottage pie, and also Indian and Thai curries. Glendon, the chef, got the Caribbean Chef of the Year award in 2007. Stella draft on tap and the prices are reasonable. Ripples opens daily from 1200 to 2400 or later, especially when customers get into the party mood, which is often. It is easy to find: just walk back to the main road from the dinghy dock and turn right. Don't miss Saturday's happy hour from 1700 to 1900, with a meat, fish, or a vegetarian special for $12 US. You can also buy takeout pizza.

The fanciest restaurant in Sandy Ground is Veya (open from Monday to Saturday for dinner only from 1800-2200). It is set back from the road leading to town, on the left before the hill gets steep. (A good appetite walk.) Veya is in a Caribbean style building with a big open room leading onto the eating verandah, and furnished with subtle elegance. Carrie Bogar, the chef, has had a passion for cooking since childhood. She studied at the Culinary Institute of America and owned a gourmet restaurant in Pennsylvania. Jerry, her husband, will welcome you. Everything from the bread to the ice cream is made on the premises and Carrie calls her food "cuisine of the sun" – worldwide flavors from warmer areas: African, Asia, Europe, and the Caribbean. This gives her the opportunity to create an interesting and varied menu. Carrie has the master's touch of combining just the right flavors with a touch of contrast that that will delight, and all is beautifully presented. This is a great choice for a special night out, when you want a change from the beach. It can be popular, so make a reservation.

Downstairs, is the café at Veya. This popular café is open Monday to Saturday from 0630-1700. They serve breakfast and lunch, including Panini sandwiches and 15 kinds of salad for lunch, and you can always get fresh croissants, muffins, and pastries. They do rotisserie chicken, which people often take out. Overlook is another fancy restaurant within walking distance of Road Bay. A path goes up the hill from the first small road on your right as head out of Sandy Ground. The road ends and becomes a path. They also offer a free shuttle service to and from the dock. Just call 264-497-4488 and ask. It has a fabulous view over the bay that is best enjoyed on a full moon night. Overlook only opens in the evening from 1900. Jamaican owner and chef, Deon Thomas, cooks a wide range of local fish and he won the 1995

Chef of the Year award. He does a good rack of lamb and if you want to try something different, order his braised goat shoulder with flambéed prunes. Deon is only here during the winter months. During the summer he has two restaurants on the east coast of the States.

On the way to Overlook, Dale Carty's Tasty's Restaurant, has an excellent reputation. If you are driving around and would like something local and inexpensive, visit Mala's Cottage Roti Hut on the road to the Valley. The traditional building is cute and they serve rotis (curry wrapped in a tortilla-like skin) of chicken, conch, shrimp, goat, or vegetables. Local meals with vegetables and fresh juices are available.

Ashore

How about going inland? Any taxi will take you on a tour or you can rent a car. Anguilla's many magnificent beaches and coves are its strong points and they are easily visited by land. Lower Shoal Bay is perhaps Anguilla's most picture-perfect beach,

with a mile of powdery sand that dissolves into luminous green and turquoise water. Plenty of places are open for lunch.

By complete contrast, Junk's Hole and Savannah Bays are wild and wonderful, especially when Christmas winds are at their strongest. Line after line of breakers smash as they approach this rugged coast, filling the air with misty spindrift. Great for surfers – others can swim in the protected water close to the beach. Palm Grove, a beach shack bar, is fine for lunch.

Just about any road leading to the coast will reveal a delightful view. Make sure you include the picturesque fishing port, Island Harbour Village, where meals are available on Scilly Cay, in the middle of the bay.

Serious bird watchers will want to explore Caul's Pond, a saltwater pond that is a bird sanctuary. The best approach is down a small road close to a concrete plant in Deep Waters, north of the pond. It ends at a unused power plant where you can park.

You may also want to visit the main

Chris Doyle

town, The Valley. It should be noted that The Valley is a long, but not unreasonable walk from Crocus Bay. In the Valley, the Anguillan Craft Shop, run by the National Council of Women, sells handicrafts that Anguillans make in their own homes. Stop by the Anguilla Drug Store, owned by Olive Hodge. As well as OTC drugs and health care products, she sells English language newspapers, beachwear, souvenirs, and t-shirts. Nico's is a great cheap and cheerful restaurant in town where you can get a tasty local lunch. A fancy and good restaurant is the Koal Keel in a lovely historic old building. While in The Valley, visit the tourist office and they will give you maps, visitor magazines, and helpful information.

Shopping in Anguilla is spread throughout the island, and as you drive around you will come upon little shops in the most unexpected places. Drive slowly and be prepared to stop and look.

Temenos has St. Regis, a professional, 18-hole, Greg Norman-designed golf course It was closed in early 2009, but may reopen.

Water Sports

Anguilla is surrounded by reefs and lies on white sand, so the diving is good. In addition, seven old ships have been sunk upright to make new dive sites. These attract huge schools of fish. A very old wreck was recently discovered. It had been carrying monks.

There are over 16 good dive sites. Diving from your yacht is a possibility. There is a charge of $4US per dive if you are diving in the park area. You need to talk to the park about diving before you go. However, diving is not easy as you cannot use the local dive boat moorings, and not too many good sites are right by the moorings. So you might have to use a manned dinghy.

Douglas Carty has a dive shop and will be happy to take you diving. You can take Padi courses from him, and do a resort course. Douglas works out of his home, but can often be found by Johnno's in Sandy Ground. You can call him on the phone (264-497-4567/ 235-8438). He has a good 30-foot dive boat with a bimini cover. Douglas is good at spotting and pointing out fish and sea creatures that others miss. If you are diving on your own, he can help you get your tanks filled.

If you moor at Sandy Island, there are several dives. Sandy Island (30 to 70 feet) has a delightful profusion of sea fans and soft corals and is home to many small reef fish. Sandy Deep (15 to 60 feet) is inside the shoal patch to the south of Sandy Island. Dive down a small wall covered in hard corals with abundant fish. When you reach the sand bottom below, there is a good chance of seeing stingrays.

Prickly Pear dive is about quarter of a mile north of Prickly Pear West and 30 to 70 feet deep. It is a beautiful underwater canyon amid a forest of elkhorn, where many ledges and caverns provide habitat for all kinds of fish. Nurse sharks are often seen resting on the sandy bottom.

The Little Bay dive is one of the easier ones to do from your yacht if you start off snorkeling along the cliff to the end where the water gets deeper. You have a chance of seeing eagle rays, manta rays, and turtles. It should be noted that most other dives, especially the wreck sites, are beyond the range of a dinghy and best visited with a dive shop. Frenchman's Reef (10 to 40 feet) lies a little farther southwest, down the coast from South Wager. Parts of the cliff have fallen into the sea, providing a beautiful garden of giant boulders. Here you will find soft corals and huge schools of brightly-colored reef fish. It makes an ideal first dive or refresher dive.

The wreck of the Ida Maria (60 feet) lies about one and a half miles northwest of Sandy Island. Deliberately sunk in 1985, this 110-foot freighter sits semi-intact on the bottom. Large groups of schooling fish make this an exciting dive. The Oosterdiep (75 to 80 feet) is a wrecked freighter which sits upright on the seabed about three quar-

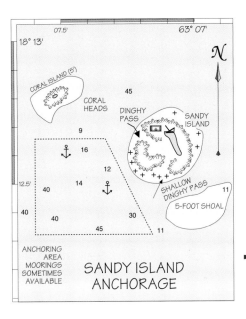

ters of a mile off Barnes Bay. It attracts large numbers of fish, including French angelfish. You can dive into the hold. There is a side trip to a reef about 100 yards away where you will find soft and hard corals and more angelfish. In the sand between the wreck and the reef are garden eels, rays, and conch. Paintcan Reef (80 feet) is about half a mile northwest of Oosterdiep. This reef covers several acres, with clear visibility and lush coral growth. As well as all the usual reef fish, large pelagic fish are sometimes seen.

Grouper Bowl (25 to 50 feet) lies about halfway down Seal Island Reef. This won-

RENAISSANCE ISLANDS

DINGHY IN

ANCHORING AREA

PRICKLY PEAR CAYS

derful elkhorn coral forest provides homes for a multitude of fish. Apart from the above, there are many more wreck sites, including the wrecks of the MV Sarah, MV Meppel, MV Lady Vie, and MV Commerce. These planned wrecks are excellent dive sites and have given Anguilla the reputation of being the wreck dive capital of the Leewards.

ANGUILLA'S OFFSHORE ANCHORAGES

Anguilla's offshore reefs are protected by the fisheries department. Below we mention places that yachts may visit. Please note that anchoring anywhere else on the offshore reefs, including the whole of Seal Island Reef, is strictly forbidden. In all sensitive areas mooring buoys are in place, so there is no danger of anchors tearing up seagrass or reef structures. Note the correct mooring procedure: pick up the buoy, attach your own docking line through the eye splice on top of the buoy and leave plenty of scope. Do not attach the pick up line directly to your yacht. Moorings are only for yachts less than 55 feet long. Customs will be able to give you the latest mooring information when you clear in.

Sandy Island

Sandy Island, one and half miles northwest of Road Bay, is a circle of sand with a

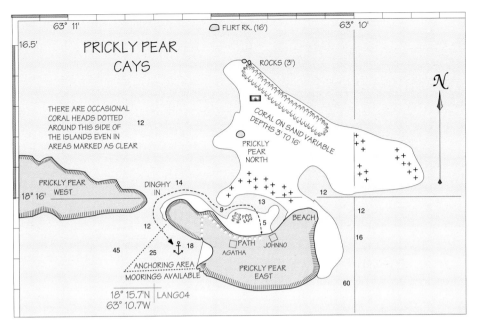

few baby palm trees. There are both shoals and reefs here, so only approach in good light conditions. It is part of the park, so open 0600-1900.

A coral island, about 5 feet high, is clearly visible northwest of Sandy Island. The water around this island has many coral heads, especially in the direction of Sandy Island. Give it wide clearance. There is a 5-foot shoal to the south of Sandy Island, which is clearly visible as turquoise water. Do not cross this, even in a shoal draft boat, as it generates large waves that sometimes break. There is a navigable passage some 30 feet deep between this shoal and Sandy Island. Sandy Island is surrounded by reef, which is quite visible; do not approach too closely.

Anchoring around Sandy Island is regulated because of possible damage to underwater reefs. The only permissible anchoring area suitable for yachts is shown on our sketch chart. Mooring buoys may be provided, but if not, you can anchor in the same area. Make sure you are anchored on an area of clear sand with no coral heads. There is a dinghy passage through the reef on the north side to get to the beach. You can beach your dinghy, or if it is too large for that, anchor in the clear sand directly to the west of Sandy Island. You can snorkel from the beach, but anchoring your dinghy on the reefs is forbidden.

Ashore

The island is all beach and if you search close to the water's edge you can find small pretty shells. The snorkeling is fair. Ashore is a shack, which, if open, will sell you a good-sized fresh lobster or a plate of fish or chicken. For details call Crusoe's (264-772-0787).

Prickly Pear Cays

These cays represent many a sailor's dream of paradise. Geologically, they are old reefs that have been uplifted to their present height of 60 feet. The sea has slowly eroded them to produce intricate rocky sculptures of fascinating design. There is a perfect creamy white beach that melts into the sea in translucent shades of pale green, turquoise, blue, and brown. The cliffs are picturesque, with many seabirds.

It is not worth venturing out here in unsettled conditions, in winds of more than 20 knots, or if there is a northerly swell. On the other hand, in settled light easterly or southeasterly winds, it makes a

heavenly lunch stop. Overnighting is not currently allowed and could be a nightmare if the weather were to change.

Navigation

People normally approach Prickly Pear Cays from Road Bay. You can see them in the distance. Pass to the east of Sandy Island and head out, approaching along the southern side of the islands. The only permissible anchorage is in the lee of Prickly Pear East, where a headland provides a little protection. If possible, use the moorings provided. If not, there is a shelf of 25 to 35 feet, with sand and rock bottom, and good holding in places. There are many underwater rock ledges and it is easy get your anchor stuck in one of these. The best way to avoid this is to tie a trip line to the bottom end of your anchor and buoy it. If it does get caught you can pull it out backwards with the trip line.

Ashore

Dinghy around to the relatively calm beach on the north side of the island. You can walk back across the island if you want to see your yacht from the rocks. The rocks ashore on the yacht anchorage side are sharp, but well worth exploring. There is a round rock pool fed by the sea. If you listen beside the pool, you can hear a rock sighing as the incoming water forces air down a tiny hole. There are more of these strange 'whistling' rocks and at low tide there are many tide pools. The underwater parts of these rocks are similarly strange and provide unusual snorkeling.

Day charter catamarans, laden with passengers from St. Martin, often visit the main beach in Prickly Pear. There are lounging seats and two lunchtime bar/restaurants. If you want a beach away from the herd, just keep walking – it goes on a long way.

For lunch, check out the restaurants. Prickly Pear Bar and Restaurant [VHF: 16] had a big overhaul a few years ago and is run by Alan who has taken over from his mother, Agatha, who did it for years before that. It has new a big deck and thatch shelters by the water. They open Tuesday through Saturday starting around 1000. You get a plate of great local food featuring local vegetables and their famous sautéed potatoes with your choice of chicken, ribs, or fish. Lobster is available by special request with advance notice. If you are low on cash they accept the Visa and Master card.

Johnno's will open for big groups and is most likely to be there on Wednesdays, Saturdays, and Sundays. It is easy to check with Johnno in Sandy Ground.

Water Sports

Hurricanes and swells have taken their toll on the snorkeling reefs, but if you have fair weather, and dinghy around to all the little reefs and rocks north of Prickly Pear East, you will find it worthwhile. Since anchoring your dinghy on the coral is not allowed, drift with it, or designate a boatman to follow the snorkelers. You can also dive here if you get permission from the park.

ANCHORING AREA

DOG ISLAND

Dog Island

Dog Island is for the adventurous who want somewhere perfect and private and are willing to make an extra effort to get it. The beach at Great Bay will satisfy the fussiest aficionado. A perfect stretch of brilliant white sand merges into bright turquoise water. The best part is that there are no bars or regular day charter boats, and the odds are you will get it to yourself. Ashore you can often find fine small shells high up on the beach.

Navigation

Dog Island is 10 miles from Road Bay and you may not stay overnight. It is worth

setting out early so you have plenty of time to explore, eat lunch, and beat back to Anguilla afterwards. The only permissible anchorage is Great Bay, which is usually rolly, but acceptable for lunch in moderate easterly and northeasterly winds (less than 20 knots). Don't bother going if heavy swells are running. If you are susceptible to a roll, prepare the picnic in advance.

You will usually be approaching from the east or southeast. It is easy to make out the conspicuous yellow-brown cliffs on the southeast coast. As you approach Great Bay, the 3-foot Bay Rock, which lies about 200 yards off the western end of the beach, stands out as a landmark. This is the only

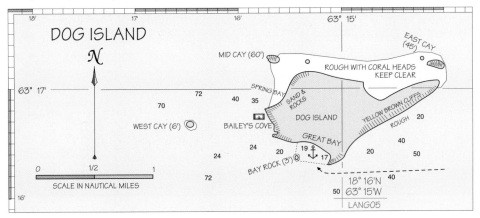

obstruction.

Anchor in the middle of the beach in about 18 feet of water. Make sure the anchor is well dug in and put out a second for added security. For the most part, the bottom is sand, but there are occasional slabs of white rock. Leave again by the south and keep well clear of Dog Island's rough and rocky northern coast.

Ashore

The surf is often heavy enough along the beach to make landing the dinghy risky. I would not try it with an outboard. If you do get the dinghy ashore, pull it up very high. Otherwise put your lunch and shore things in a watertight container, anchor the dinghy just beyond the surf line and swim in. Not easy, but that is why you get such a lovely beach to yourself.

The island was owned by the late Jeremiah Gumbs, who was once going to develop it and built an airstrip. There were rumors of drug traffickers using it, so it was closed again. The family keeps livestock here and no one is permitted beyond the beach. (All Anguillan beaches are open to the public.)

Conditions permitting, you will find good snorkeling around Bay Rock and Bailey's Cove.

ANGUILLA'S NORTH COAST EAST OF ROAD BAY

To the east of Road Bay there is an attractive sweeping bay some two miles long. Crocus Bay is the most protected part of this and is an excellent overnight anchorage.

Crocus Bay

Navigation

If you are approaching along the coast from Road Bay, stay a few hundred yards offshore until you pass Katouche Bay, as shoals extend 60 yards or more offshore. If you are approaching from out to sea, Crocus Bay has a paved road that runs up the hill, a big square apartment block sitting on top of the hill, and at the left hand end of the beach is a large tin building that houses a water desalinization plant. Anchor anywhere off Crocus Bay beach south of Pelican Point. Anchor a fair way out as the wind can drop and a swell could carry your yacht toward the shore. Use plenty of scope. The attractions are good snorkeling, the beach, easy access to Little Bay, and The Valley is within walking distance for shopping. (You can pull your

Crocus Bay. Note the conspicuous desalination plant on the right.   Chris Doyle

ANGUILLA

View of Crocus Bay from da'Vida

www.daVidaAnguilla.com

Celebrate Life.

Crocus Bay has long been one of
Anguilla's best kept secrets! Now you can
'discover' this tranquil and secluded getaway
in Anguilla, while you enjoy the inspiration and
atmosphere at da'Vida Restaurant & Spa. Indulge
in our exquisite lunch & fine dining menus,
unwind at the Bayside Bar & Grill or just be
caressed by the cool tropical breezes as you
lounge on the beach. Be Intentional, and
Celebrate Life with da'Vida!

da'Vida

Crocus Bay • Anguilla
www.**daVidaAnguilla**.com

OPENING HOURS & CALENDAR OF EVENTS:
Open: Tuesday to Sunday
Lunch: 11am - 3pm w Dinner: 6pm - 10pm
Live Entertainment, Friday - Sunday

INTERLINC COMMUNICATIONS EGK-20920-593

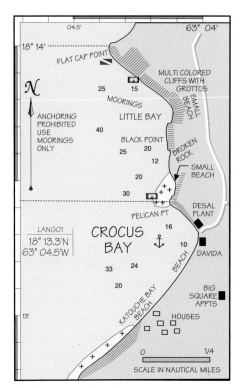

several years creating this delightful collection of paintings, and he will happily tell you all about the artists, most of whom he knows personally. His range includes some fine Haitian paintings as well as sheet metal art. Artists from Anguilla and many other islands are represented. Prints are for sale as well as originals, and occasionally you will find model traditional Anguillan sailing boats. A few steps beyond the art gallery is a lovely and also quite fancy restaurant; the Koal Keel, which is set in a lovely, historic old building. This is a great place to come for dinner.

Water Sports

When the visibility is good (the only time it is not is when northerly swells stir things up), the snorkeling off Pelican Point is excellent. You should visit Little Bay by dinghy or yacht.

Little Bay

For those addicted to undeveloped natural beauty, Little Bay is outstanding, even by Caribbean standards. Along the shore, 70-foot cliffs rise from turquoise water. They are multicolored, in reds, pinks, greys, and whites; textured by holes, caves, and grottos, which are home to tropicbirds, pelicans, and kingfishers. The pelicans spend much of the day dive-bombing schools of fish off the beach; the tropicbirds circle overhead and chatter; agile goats wander to the edge of the precipice. One can sit here for hours, just enjoying the view. You cannot anchor here, but you can pick up one of the moorings during the day. It is part of the park, so open only from 0600-1900. If all moorings are taken (rare), anchor in Crocus Bay and dinghy down.

Ashore, there are two small but delightfully secluded beaches. The only way to get to these by road is to climb up a cliff aided by a rope. Take a cooler and enjoy this fabulous place. If you spend the day at Little Bay, you can stay overnight next door at Crocus Bay.

Water Sports

The snorkeling is excellent (except in poor visibility, during and after northerly

dinghy up the beach near the road, but it could be dangerous in swells.) Apart from Road Bay this is the only anchorage where you may stay overnight.

Ashore

Da Vida is an super new up-market restaurant right on the beach, in the building that used to house Roy's. It is owed by Anguillan brother and sister team David and Vida who have created an ambiance of beach-side luxury, with decor that includes a wall waterfall. Dinner is excellent, gourmet, and artistically served. Visit also for a relaxed, lighter lunch; the coconut shrimp is highly recommended. Samplers will enjoy the tapas menu available from 1600-2100.

If you stroll up the hill and down the other side towards The Valley, you will come to Savannah, one of Anguilla's best art galleries. It is set in two lovely authentic old buildings. The outside is small, but as you enter, it opens up in an almost Alice-in-Wonderland kind of way into a house of many rooms. Owner Frank Costin has spent

LITTLE BAY

swells). Along the cliffs all the way to the point are little caves, overhangs, and small walls with a variety of hard and soft corals and many small fish. About 20 yards out, you find a rather flat bottom with sand, weeds, and occasional stands of coral. Out here, there is a good chance of seeing turtles, spotted eagle rays, and barracudas. You can also do this as a dive. (Talk to the park authorities.)

East of Little Bay

The coast is fairly clear for almost 2 miles to the east of Little Bay. Then a large expanse of reefs and rocks extends up to a mile offshore. Embedded in the reef system are two small harbors, suited only to shoal draft boats. They are called Lower Shoal Bay and Island Harbour. It is possible to thread through a passage between the reefs, but once you are past Shoal Bay it can be

rough and hazardous. To make it worse, you will be in the teeth of the wind heading east, or dead down wind going west. The best thing to do with this coast is give it wide clearance.

If you are going east, you can take a good long tack out to sea – but don't hit Seal Island Reef. When you get to Scrub Island, you will see a wild and tempting beach on it's western shore. Unfortunately, there is no good anchorage here. Reef extends a long way from the beach, and the bay is shoal toward its northern end. There is one sand strip that runs into the beach. Should you happen by on a very calm day, you could try to anchor about one or two hundred yards off the beach in about 36 feet of water, but landing the dinghy is likely to be hazardous. In 2001, an old landing strip on Scrub was rebuilt, and the island was used to make a soft drink commercial.

There is no problem in rounding the

COVE BAY

eastern tip of Anguilla between Windward Point and Scrub Island. Stay in the middle of the channel and do not go too close to the Anguillan shore.

ANGUILLA'S SOUTH COAST

There are lots of reefs along this coast all the way to Rendezvous Bay. While some bays are tucked in the reefs, none of them are well enough protected to be worth consideration for the passing cruiser. Give the coast a wide berth. Cove Bay is a fair anchorage and is described below.

Rendezvous Bay

This is a large bay with over a mile of perfect white sand beach. Yachts that have official yacht agents, can get special permission to anchor here. Otherwise, anchoring is forbidden. Do not enter too close to Shaddick Point, as it is shoal.

Cove Bay & Maunday's Bay

Cove Bay lies to the west of Rendezvous Bay. Although much smaller than Rendezvous Bay, it too has a perfect beach and makes a fair anchorage in settled conditions. You need to tuck up in the eastern corner to get protection from the reef off its eastern point. A fancy new dock, used mainly by the small fishing fleet that anchors here, makes a convenient place to leave your dinghy. Things are changing as the surrounding land has now been taken over by Temenos who own the big adjacent golf course.

Maunday's Bay also has good protection in most conditions. The development behind is private, but there is another splendid beach here and all beaches are public. The fisheries department does not allow overnight stays in either of these bays.

Altamar Marina

A new and very fancy marina is being planned just to the west of Maunday's Bay, at Altamar Resort. A salt pond is to be dredged, which will give a completely protected area and a breakwater cut through from the sea. This will be a high-end establishment with berths for all sizes of yacht, up to 200-feet. It will be many years before this is finished.

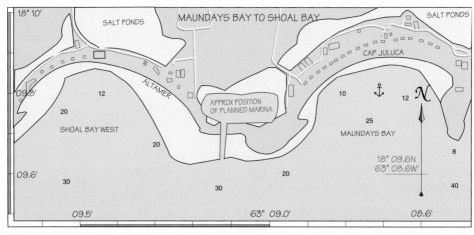

65

Simpson Bay, Marigot Chris Doyle

Sint Maarten & St. Martin

*A*LTHOUGH THIS island is barely 7 miles in each direction, it is perhaps the best-known holiday destination in the Leewards. It is blessed with a multitude of superb white sand beaches, backed by pleasantly scenic hills. Its fame has come from the way it has embraced tourism wholeheartedly, with casinos, condominiums, and scores of hotels. The whole island is one duty-free shopping plaza. Shopping is not restricted to cruise ship passengers. Two of the Caribbean's biggest chandleries are based here: Budget Marine and Island Water World. With the help of their customers, they have generated enough buying power to be able to offer excellent prices to yachts. Their catalog prices are a little higher than some US discount stores, but in duty-free St. Martin a further ten percent discount for cash is normal, and you can often negotiate more substantial discounts, depending on the items ordered and how much you are spending.

St. Martin is divided across the middle. The northern part is French; the southern part Dutch. There is a charming story, completely unsupported by historical fact, that the French and Dutch were so civilized that, rather than fight over the island, they had a Frenchman armed with a bottle of wine walk in one direction and a Dutchman equipped with a flask of gin take the other. Where they met became the boundary, and the French ended up with a bit more because the gin was stronger than the wine.

In the early days, the island was important to the Dutch because of the salt ponds in the southern part, which is why they settled that half. St. Martin was successful for a time as a producer of tobacco, and then of sugar. With the collapse of the sugar market, it started a long decline. In 1939 an attempt was made to halt this downward trend by making the island completely duty-free.

The strategy worked: St. Martin became the Caribbean's number one shopping mall.

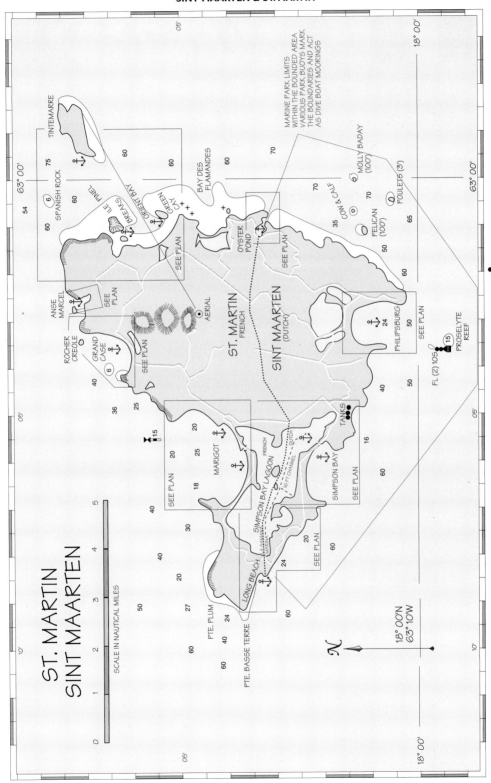

ST. MARTIN
SINT MAARTEN

RENAISSANCE ISLANDS

SCALE IN NAUTICAL MILES

MARINE PARK LIMITS
WITHIN THE BOUNDED AREA
VARIOUS PARK BUOYS MARK
THE BOUNDARIES AND ACT
AS DIVE BOAT MOORINGS

TINTEMARRE

SPANISH ROCK

ILE PINEL

BREAKS

ORIENT BAY

GREEN CAY

BAY DES FLAMANDES

OYSTER POND

SEE PLAN

MOLLY BADAY (100')

POULETS (3')

CON & CALF

PELICAN (100')

PROSELYTE REEF

FL (2) 10S

PHILIPSBURG

ANSE MARCEL

SEE PLAN

AERIAL

ST. MARTIN
FRENCH

SINT MAARTEN
(DUTCH)

ROCHER CREOLE

GRAND CASE

SEE PLAN

MARIGOT

SEE PLAN

SIMPSON BAY LAGOON

MARINA

16 FT CHANNEL

FRENCH

DUTCH

SIMPSON BAY

SEE PLAN

TANKS

LONG BEACH

SEE PLAN

PTE. PLUM

PTE. BASSE TERRE

18° 00'N
63° 10'W

St. Martin

Regulations

You need to check with the port authority and immigration on arrival and departure, even when sailing from one side to the other. There are clearing posts in Philipsburg and Simpson Bay, on the Dutch side, and in Marigot on the French side. On the Dutch side you pay $2 for boats up to 99 tons and $5 for boats between 100 and 499 tons, with $9 for boats over 500 tons when you clear out. In addition there is a fee for being in Simpson Bay either in the lagoon or outside. This charge does not apply in Philipsburg or Oyster Pond. For details see Simpson Bay page 86. Once you are in either side, you are absolutely free to visit the other by dinghy, car or on foot.

Telephones

The French side is treated as part of France; the Dutch side as part of the Netherlands. The two sides have different phone books and number systems.

All French St. Martin numbers now start 0590 (regular) or 0690 (cellular). If you are dialing into St. Martin from a non-French territory, you have to dial the country code first, which is also 590, then leave off the first 0 of the number. Thus if calling from the US, for regular numbers you will dial: 011-590-590, + 6 digits, for cell numbers 011-590-690 + 6 digits.

If calling the Dutch side from the French, dial 00, then the full number, and if you are calling the French from the Dutch, dial 00-590 590 (or 590 690 cell) + 6 digits. If you are calling within the Dutch side, just dial the last 7 digits; within the French side dial the 10-digit number.

It is easy to make phone calls from such business as Mailbox and Business Point.

Both sides have public telephones that take telephone cards, available from the post office and some shops. But the cards for each side are different. On the French side, lift the phone, put in the card, close the door (if applicable), wait until it shows your credit, and then dial. To get out of the country, dial 00, then the code of the country you are calling (US is 1, UK is 44). For ATT direct, dial (0800)-99-00-11. All French phone booths have numbers posted so you can get someone to call you back. The Dutch side also has blue phones that connect direct to the international operator and take credit cards. As with all credit card phones, you need to check carefully on how much you will be charged.

The GSM mobile phones are the most popular. You can buy a phone or a local sim and prepaid cards for UTS, Telcel (Dutch), or Carte Orange or Digicel (French)

Shopping Hours

Normal shopping hours are 0800-1200 and 1500-1800, but many shops are open over lunch.

Transport

Flying in and out is easy as St. Martin has a large international airport serviced by many major airlines. The airport is close to Simpson Bay Lagoon, just across the road from the Aqua Restaurant dinghy dock, so it is practical to pick up and drop off passengers by dinghy. When you leave, the current departure tax is $25 US.

Ferries run about once every 45 minutes between Marigot and Anguilla, and you catch them on the ferry dock, or less frequently, smaller ferries leave the immigration dock in Simpson Bay. Taxi stand numbers are: Philipsburg, 147; Marigot, 0590-87 56 54/77 13 42

For taxi rates, the island is divided into 21 zones. Rates are $6 inside one zone up to $30 between the most distant zones.

Typical taxi rates in $US are:

Philipsburg to Food Center	$8	Marigot to airport	$16
Simpson Bay to Philipsburg	$15	Philipsburg to airport	$16
Oyster Pond to airport	$22	Anse Marcel to Airport	$30

There are extra charges for the number of people over 2, for extra bags over 1, between 2200 and 0600 and, in some cases, if you call them to come by phone.

St. Martin also has an inexpensive regular bus system connecting the towns of Philipsburg, Marigot, and Grand Case.

Holidays

Holidays, both French and Dutch sides:
- Jan 1
- Good Friday and Easter Monday (Easter Sunday is April 4, 2010; April 24, 2011)
- May 1 (Labor Day)
- Ascension Day (May 13, 2010, June 2, 2011)
- Whit Monday, 50 days after Easter Sunday (May 24, 2010, June 13, 2011)
- All Saints (Nov 1)
- December 25

Holidays, French St. Martin only:
- Jan 6, Epiphany
- Carnival Monday & Tuesday (Monday - Tuesday, 46 days before Easter: Feb 15-16, 2010; March 7-8, 2011)
- May 8 (V.E. Day)
- July 14 (Bastille Day)
- July 21 (Victor Schoelcher Day)
- August 15 (Assumption of Virgin Mary)
- Nov 1 (All Saintes Day)

Holidays, Dutch Sint Maarten only:
- April 30 (Queen's Birthday)
- May 5 (Liberation Day)
- July 1 (Emancipation Day)
- Last Monday in July and the following Tuesday - Carnival
- Nov 11 (Sint Maarten Day)
- December 15, (Kingdom Day)
- December 26

St. Martin, Admiralty Leisure Folio 5641-1, 5641-6, 5641-7

Today it thrives, hosting about a million visitors annually. Hotels are everywhere, cruise ships call daily, and there are many hundreds of duty-free shops and restaurants, as well as over a dozen casinos. The current boom has created so much work that many cruising yachts-people have found temporary jobs here and there are excellent facilities for most kinds of yacht work.

Both the French and the Dutch sides have yacht clubs (Sint Maarten Yacht Club and Yacht Club International de Marigot). Between them they organize informal races, which can help the cruising sailor get to know the local yachting community. There is also the Heineken Regatta on the first full weekend in March, a world-famous international event that draws many famous yachts. But earlier, in January, St. Martin has its classics regatta, a great spectacle to view or join in. Smaller events include a race to Anguilla in November, and the St. Martin's Day Regatta on November 11, which is sponsored by Mount Gay rum. Perhaps the nicest race is the Course D'Alliance, a three day race from St. Martin to St. Barts, then Anguilla. You will also find a race to Statia in January. A big Laser regatta takes place on the first weekend in June. The Guavaberry Regatta to St. Kitts and Nevis offers the best cruising fun. It is held on the last full moon in May or the first full moon in June. Monohulls start at midnight; fast multihulls the next morning. The first stop is St. Kitts, followed by a race over to Nevis and a return race to St. Martin. There are plenty of social events with local people, plus you can try drinking Guavaberry Liquor. There are also several informal yacht races and many beach cat races out of Orient Bay. If interested, ask at the yacht club in Simpson Bay, or check their web site: www.smyc.com.

Marine parks exist on both sides. Yachts can anchor or pick up a mooring in all their usual haunts. Fishing, including spearfishing, is not allowed near any of the popular dive sites, including most of

RENAISSANCE ISLANDS

the offshore islands and rocks. Moorings for divers and snorkelers have been laid on many of the sites. These are not for yachts, though yacht moorings are planned. The French marine park goes from Oyster Pond to Anse Marcel, but excludes much of Orient Bay. Fishing, taking of anything, polluting, jet skiing, and water-skiing are all banned within this area.

St. Martin has good medical and dental facilities. A good clinic, easily accessible to the yachts, is in the complex by Simpson Bay Marina. Check with Dr. Datema or Dr. Ubbo Tjaden. You will also find a modern dental clinic with dentists, hygienists, and an orthodontist. Both the French and the Dutch have emergency lifeboats, from a large rigid inflatable to an ocean-going rescue vessel. Call VHF: 16 or dial 911.

SOUTH COAST OF SINT MAARTEN

Apart from Proselyte Reef, the south coast of St. Maarten is free of shallows and a quarter of a mile offshore clears all shoals. Proselyte Reef lies about 1.5 miles south of Philipsburg. It is 15 feet deep, so it is really only a problem for deep draft boats. Despite a buoy, cruise ships have managed to hit it.

With the creation of the marine park, various buoys have been placed to mark dive sites and more have been placed on the park limits. Most are unlit, so keep a good lookout. Some are in open water, where they may be a hazard to an unaware navigator, though happily most are soft plastic.

When you are sailing from St. Barts to Philipsburg, short steep seas can build up around Pte. Blanche. If you are towing a dinghy, keep an eye on it.

Philipsburg

Philipsburg is the capital of Sint Maarten and lies at the head of Great Bay. Over the last few years the focus of yachting has switched more towards Simpson Bay. At the same time, the whole town of Philipsburg has been vastly upgraded with a long, boardwalk behind the beach and the rebuilding of Front Street with cobblestones, fancy new lampposts and street décor, including fully-grown palms planted all the way along. While Front Street

PHILIPSBURG

allows cars, priority has been given to pedestrians, making it a pleasant place to walk. It is a major cruise ship stop and there are always plenty of people about. It is an excellent place to shop, sit in a bar or café, watch life go by, and eat out.

Navigation

The best way to approach is to pass by the new cruise shop docks and then head in. Depths reduce suddenly from 30 feet to about 15 feet, then become rather bumpy, mainly between 9 and 12 feet, all the way in. Both marinas have done some dredging and are deeper than the approaches: Bobby's is now mainly 12 feet deep and Great Bay Marina has about 12 feet at the deepest part, shoaling to about 5 feet in the southern corner.

Most of the passenger ferry traffic now passes from the cruise ships to Bobby's Marina. Quite a lot of boat traffic also comes and goes from the marinas, so it is best to leave a clear passage for this thoroughfare.

Anchor anywhere else in the bay. Philipsburg is a good anchorage in most conditions, though it gets very rolly when the wind switches to the southeast, and during the day cruise ship tender wakes make it rolly, which can be uncomfortable for monohulls. A couple of times a year a strong southerly is likely to make it untenable. At such times, proceed down the coast to Simpson Bay Lagoon or to Marigot. Under no circumstances should you be in Philipsburg in a hurricane or seriously disturbed weather.

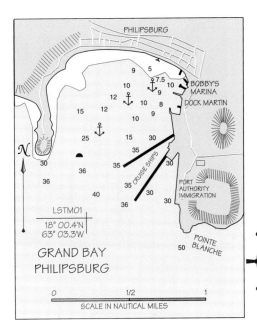

Regulations

In order to clear in or out of Dutch Sint Maarten, take your passports and ship's papers to the commercial port. Check with immigration and the port authority. You have to pay a small departure tax when you clear out. Office hours are Monday to Friday, 0800-1200 and 1300-1600; and Sundays, 0900-1500.

Communications

You will find phones by the Greenhouse. Cyber Surf on Front Street is one of several places that will get you online. Or take your computer to Chesterfields or Greenhouse, buy a coffee and use the com-

RENAISSANCE ISLANDS

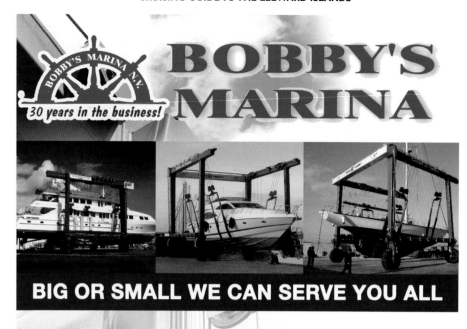

plimentary wifi. You can also try the bay-wide "Smart Wifi".

General Yacht Services

Dock Martin is a small marina, usually full of day charter yachts, with very occasional space for a transient. They plan an expansion of the outer wall, which will allow them to offer about 15 berths for superyachts. At the same time they will be building a large shopping and restaurant area. You are welcome to use their dinghy dock, which was being built in January 2009.

Bobby's Marina (VHF: 16) welcomes short-term visitors when there is space. The outside has expanded to include a big pay car park and gas station. They also have a fuel dock, are happy to have you use their dinghy dock, and they offer showers and toilets. Bobby's Marina group includes this marina and another facility in Simpson Bay Lagoon that has a large haul out area as well as some docks. A third facility is under construction in Simpson Bay to the north of New Wave Marine. This will be Bobby's largest haul out, with a travel lift that can take superyachts. Their current travel lift is 150-tons. Right now, some boats are hauled out in Philipsburg, but by the time this guide comes out, these will have been shifted to the Bobby's haul out in Simpson Bay and the yard replaced by a shopping, restaurant and services area. All Bobby's marinas are well managed by Jeff Howell who has an excellent record of keeping boats upright in hurricanes, even in killer Hurricane Luis, which battered the island for about 36 hours. He removes and stores masts on monohulls as a matter of course, and has his own system of wooden stands for storage. There is a plan to extend Bobby's outside breakwater to allow berthing for about eight mega-yachts on a short-term basis, allowing them to fuel and provision without going through the Simpson Bay Bridge. This dock will also be open to cruising yachts when space is available. This will probably not happen during the life of this guide. If you need laundry done, talk to one of Bobby's security guards; they can get a Chinese laundry to pick it up.

Chandlery

Island Water World in Bobby's Marina is an excellent general chandlery. They keep a stock of paints, anti-foulings, and all the resins and cloth you need to fix your boat before you paint it. You will also find much general gear, including ladders, dinghies, outboards, solar panels, ropes, and fittings. This store is part of the larger Island Water World in Simpson Bay; so if you don't see what you need, ask.

Caribbean Auto, the Napa agent, has an excellent stock of filters, engine parts, spares, and accessories. Their shop is on A.T. Illedge Road, behind the salt pond.

Radio Shack is in Philipsburg at Longwall Road. They are ideal for wire, switches, and fuses, when you have some boat project in mind, or TVs and electronics for after the work is done. Many yachts buy short-wave radios and mobile phones here.

Technical Yacht Services

Bobby's has a large and very professional fabrication department where you can get all kinds of machining and welding done, including aluminum and stainless steel. Making complex custom fittings is no problem. Bobby's also has a full mechanical shop for engine repairs, up to and including complete rebuilds.

Transport

Johan Romney (552-2213/553-2333) is a friendly and willing taxi driver who will take care of you. Avis car rental is outside Dock Martin. The main pier taxi stand number is 599-542-2359.

Provisioning

You should be able to pry some cash from your card at the ATM machine right near The Green House, otherwise try the Windward Islands Bank, near the police station, which is the place to get cash from a Visa or MasterCard. The American Express agent is Maduro Travel.

Provisioning is easy. Sang's Supermarket, across the road from Bobby's, is a big modern supermarket that will have most things you need, and it includes a wholesale department. For moderate orders, you can borrow carts from Sang's to wheel your groceries back to the docks; wholesale orders will be delivered. Sang's is also a great lunch place; they have deli section with lots of prepared foods.

Try also the fun of visiting a monster supermarket. Take a cab or catch a bus (from Back Street near the police station) to Le Grande Marché, a state-of-the-art supermarket that is new, flashy, and huge, with produce from all over the world. They open daily 0800-2000, except Sundays; 0900-1400. You will find everything you need, and they will deliver it back to any of the marinas for you. Almost opposite is St. Martin's first giant warehouse store; Cost-U-Less. This giant store has a full range of

supermarket items, as well as many other departments, including house wares, office supplies, appliances, electronics, and health and beauty products. They open daily 0900-2100, except Sundays, when they close at 1500.

Up the road from Le Grande Marché is Kooyman's hardware giant.

Fun Shopping

Shopping in St. Martin is all duty-free and boutique lovers will be in seventh heaven. Philipsburg has two main streets: Front Street and Back Street. Front Street has the flashier, more expensive stores. Back Street is great for the bargain hunter, especially those looking for clothes. On Front Street you will find endless shops, selling everything from fine porcelain and jewelry to videos, cameras, and TVs.

Shipwreck Shop, also on Front Street, is the best place for art, handicrafts, magazines, local books, nautical clothing, and nice spray jackets. Philipsburg has the widest selection of electronics in St. Martin. The fashion-conscious can check out such stores as Benetton and Beach Stuff for trendy, chic, casual wear. There will be plenty of places to buy "I was in St. Martin" t-shirts. The Central Drugstore, just across from the police station, fills prescriptions and has a wide range of vitamins, cosmetics, and healthcare products. You can get real bargains in the big new craft market behind the courthouse. Practical stuff is harder; you may have to get over to the bigger stores we mentioned above.

Front Street, Philipsburg

Chris Doyle

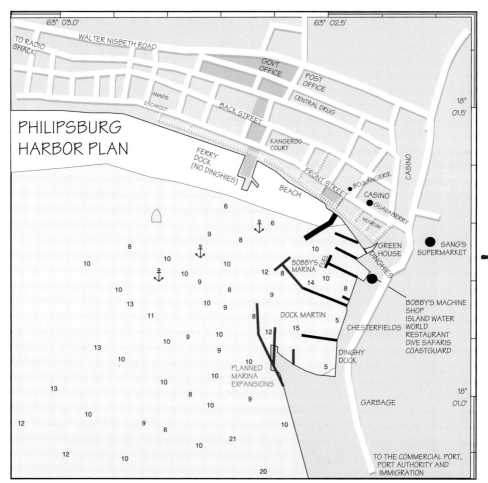

PHILIPSBURG
HARBOR PLAN

Philipsburg has a small museum down an alley that goes back from the waterfront. The museum shop sells maps, prints, and books, including a hiking book. Gamblers will find two casinos very close by.

Restaurants

Many good restaurants are within an easy stroll of the marinas, several with happy hours patronized by yachtspeople. The closest are on the waterfront among the marinas. Chesterfield's offers first rate dining right on the water and has a happy hour from 1700-1830, featuring lower priced drinks and snacks. It is popular with the quieter crowd out for a relaxing rendezvous. They have daily lunch specials, and a good dinner menu. From time to time, in season, they put on live back-ground music. They also have free wifi.

The young active crowd gathers at The Greenhouse from 1630-1830 daily for the liveliest happy hour in St. Martin. Expect lots of bustle, invigorating music, two-for-one drinks, and half-priced appetizers. Things quiet down about 1900 when the dinner crowd arrives, livening up again about 2100 when the DJ begins.

Bobby's plans a new restaurant to replace the old one that was on the waterfront.

Walk along the board-walk or front street and take your choice. La Baguette is a great little French boulangerie with espresso coffee, fresh baguettes, croissants, pain au chocolat for breakfast and snacks, and good lunchtime sandwiches and salads. Owner Catherine is on hand and helpful.

Oualiche and Passanggrahan both have a good reputation. L'Escargot on Front Street is set in a traditional old Antillian house. You will eat excellent seafood here, carefully prepared in the classical French style. They are open for both lunch and dinner. L'Escargot is on a corner. If you walk down the side street at this corner, appetizing smells will greet you from Anand's, an East Indian and Créole restaurant serving great food for the cheap and cheerful crowd. It is open from 1200-1500 for lunch and 1800-2200 for dinner. You can choose whether you want your dishes mild, spicy, hot, or hot as hell. The Kangaroo Court is in a pretty historic courtyard building on the side street by the courthouse. It has a delightful ambience if you visit on a non-cruise-ship day. They serve great salads, sandwiches, desserts, and coffee. It opens daily for lunch, coffee, and snacks

Water Sports

Dive Safaris is a dive shop at Bobby's that works closely with Scuba Shop in Oyster Pond. They can take 18 people out in their boats, they cater to the yachting trade as well as to cruise ships, and they fill tanks and rent equipment. Diving gear at good prices can be purchased. Courses for non-divers are available. Shark feeding sessions are a specialty.

Scuba Fun has a branch shop at Great Bay Marina. This is a small operation; they dive every day with small groups, and rent equipment to yachts.

Proselyte Reef is St. Martin's most popular dive. It lies south of Philipsburg, in depths of 20 to 70 feet. Plenty of soft and hard corals, lots of fish, and old cannons, anchors, and artifacts from the famous wreck of the HMS Proselyte, which went aground here in 1802. Another popular dive is the Amazing Maze, a series of rock formations that make you think you are in a fairyland. Abundant fish enhance the effect.

If the weather is calm, ask about the area's most dramatic dive, Moonhole. This open crater looks as though it was created

The beach in Philipsburg   Chris Doyle

by a meteor that punched a hole some 60 feet deep into the reef. The top almost breaks the surface, so the only approach is down a channel that leads into it. The walls are bare and moon-like; hence the name, but there are often sharks and rays, as well as many reef fish, inside. The reef outside is attractive.

Other dives within easy reach of Philipsburg include Hens and Chicks, which offers a forest of elkhorn coral from 20 to 70 feet with good visibility and lots of fish. Teigland is the wreck of a German freighter (60 feet deep) and the dive here has a reef with an old tugboat cable draped over it. The wreck is near a drop off. There is a good chance of seeing barracuda, turtles, and schools of pelagic fish.

You cannot help but notice a few sleek yachts having races just outside the bay. This is the brainchild of Colin, who assembled a fleet of five 12-meter America Cup thoroughbreds, including Stars and Stripes 55 and 56, Canada II, and True North 1 and 4. He thought it would be great to share the thrill and excitement of being part of a 12-meter crew with everyone who felt like it. These magnificent machines race several times a day with three trained crew on each boat and the rest of the muscle power supplied by the paying passengers. This participator sport is popular with cruise ship passengers. Enthusiasts of 12 meters can sign on at Bobby's Marina.

SIMPSON BAY AND SIMPSON BAY LAGOON

Simpson Bay is a large and pleasant bay surrounded by beaches. The eastern part makes a good sheltered anchorage. Simpson Bay Lagoon is about 12 square miles of completely protected, landlocked water. Access is by a channel and lifting bridge from Simpson Bay. Inside you are free from ocean swells. It is large enough for a good sail and open to exploration for those who like something a bit different. Simpson Bay Lagoon is the yachting center of St. Martin. Many marinas and marine businesses surround the lagoon on both the Dutch and French sides, and you can dinghy between the two. In recent years professional megayachts have become a large focus in the yachting scene, with several marinas built especially for them. However, the cruiser is also still highly thought of, as many people involved in the boating industry are cruisers themselves who washed ashore here. Even by Caribbean standards, they are a friendly and pleasant group. You will find many happy hours in bars around the waterfront. A stop in Simpson Bay is likely to be happy and convivial.

RENAISSANCE ISLANDS

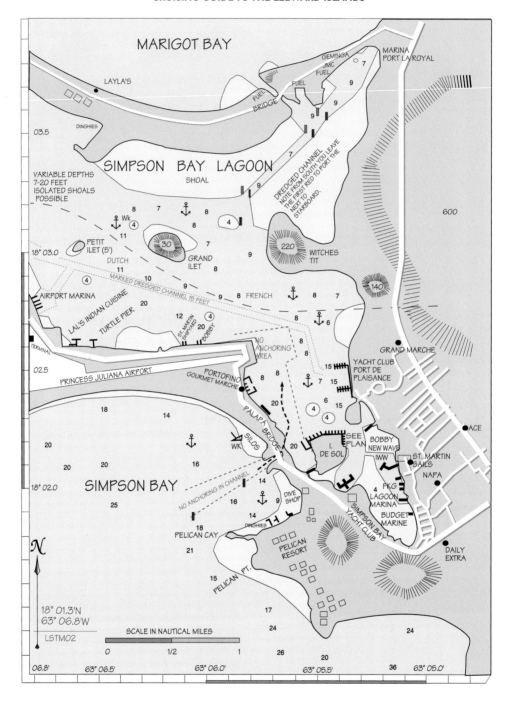

Navigation

When approaching Simpson Bay from the east, swing out in an arc well outside Pelican Point and Pelican Cay. When you are past the island, head into the anchorage between Pelican Resort and the bridge. Holding in the anchorage is good in sand, 9 to 14 feet deep. This is a good overnight anchorage that is not too bad even in southeasterly winds.

The swing bridge is a conspicuous structure, currently painted blue. The entrance is down a small channel and is clearly visible. The center of the entrance channel has been dredged to 19 feet, though either side of center there are spots as shallow as 15 feet, so if you need the 19 feet, get your marina to pilot you in. The bridge is 56 feet wide. The summer (May to November) bridge opening times are 0930, 1100, and 1730. Outgoing yachts leave before incoming ones. In the winter the traffic is so heavy they have to separate the ingoing from the outgoing yachts to give cars a chance to cross in between. So from December to April the times are as follows: 0900 outbound, 0930 inbound; 1100 outbound, 1130 inbound; 1630 outbound, 1730 inbound. The bridge does not operate in extremely strong winds. It may also have to close suddenly. For these reasons always keep your radio onto VHF 12 when transiting. You can call for information on 545-3183. Wait outside until the light turns green, as there is current in the channel.

Much dredging has taken place in Simpson Bay. Almost no room is deep enough for megayachts to swing at anchor, so they best go to one of the marinas. Contact a marina and be guided by their staff, who will send out a boat to bring you in through the bridge to the marina, according to your draft. Yachts going into Palapa (which is the deepest) need to stay really close the mooring buoys as in some places it shallows fast outside.

For other yachts, I have given the depths I found on the sketch chart. Judging by the size of anchored yachts, these may be pessimistic – it could be the echo sounder is picking up a foot or so of navigable suspended mud. Watch out for the unmarked shoals north of Snoopy Island. Leave a clear fairway into the channel and to the airport, with plenty of room for large yachts to maneuver into Palapa Marina. Anchor anywhere else except in the buoyed channels or off the end of the runway. (See our sketch chart, page 78.) It is

possible to get a dinghy under the bridge that goes to Snoopy Island, take either side, go slowly and stay in the middle.

Our sketch chart shows the dredged channels into the marinas. Cruising through the rest of the lagoon looks interesting. We show the obvious shoal areas. The rest of it is navigable, with depths of 7 to 12 feet, though there are several shoals within 100 yards of the shore and there may be uncharted shoals farther out. Unmarked wrecks occasionally get left over from hurricanes, so navigate with caution. There is a dredged channel (about 7 feet deep) over to the French side of the bay (see Marigot) and another bridge on that side. The channel is very clearly marked, but has the curiosity that heading north you leave the first red buoy to port and thereafter leave red buoys to starboard. Before you go, check that the buoys are still in place. A 16-foot deep channel has been dredged to the very inner part of the lagoon, where a fancy super-yacht marina at La Samanna hotel is about half-built. It is well buoyed as far as a side channel to the Airport Marina, thereafter not.

Regulations

When you arrive, visit the immigration and port authority station in the new building on the northwest side of the entrance channel. They have a big dinghy dock The immigration office is open from 0800-1800 weekdays, 0800-1500 on weekends. At the same time you have to check with the Simpson Bay Lagoon Authority, which is open 0800-1800 every day, including holidays. Take your ship's papers, passports, and your last clearance with you. The Simpson Bay Lagoon Authority will charge whether you go in the lagoon or stay outside. On entry, you should tell them on which day you plan to leave, and you then pay a fee. For a week (or portion thereof) it is as follows: (all US$), $20 for boats from 9 to 12 meters long; $30 for boats 12-15 meters long; $60 for boats 15-18 meters long; $120 for boats 18 to 22 meters long, $200 for boats 22-28 meters long, $300 for boats 28-36 meters long, and

SIMPSON BAY

$500 for those over 36 meters.

Everyone who passes inwards through the bridge during their normal opening pays fees as follows: (all US$). $10 for boats from 9 to 12 meters long; $30 for boats 12-15 meters long, $60 for boats 15-18 meters long, $120 for boats 18 to 22 meters long, $200 for boats 22-28 meters long, $300 for boats 28-36 meters long, and $500 for those over 36 meters. Special bridge openings are available by request between 0600 and 1800 for $1,000.

You also have to pay a clearance fee ($7-$29) when you clear out.

Communications

A cruiser's net is on the air Monday to Saturday at 0730 on (VHF: 14). This gives a morning weather forecast, followed by helpful information on getting gas tanks filled, local entertainment, and coming events. From time to time there have been water delivery services in the lagoon; ask on the net for the latest information. Cruisers use channel 14 as a calling frequency, switching after contact. Never use channel 12 for chat; it is strictly for commercial use. While in St. Martin, pick up the free Marine Trades Directory from most businesses.

Wifi at anchor is offered by Caribserve,

Network IDL, and Netstar, among others. During the season, big yachts provide so much electronic interference that you will need a really powerful aerial to make a connection. Be careful if you come in and sign up over New Year when everyone is out: you may lose your connection when the yachts come back in.

The Mailbox office is in an expanded location on the ground floor behind La Palapa Marina; the entrance is from the road. Many yachts use this efficient communications center with phone, message, fax, broadband internet access, and mail services. You can also send and receive Fedex here: they are an authorized dealer. Wifi hookup can be arranged, but may not be easy (see notes above). Mailbox phone rates to the US are excellent, and you can now rent prepaid cellular phones as well as buy prepaid phone cards. They have lots of good deals on email, including email happy hour (weekdays 1800-2000), and cut-rate block plans. They run an express mail service to the US and sell US stamps. They can also send packages worldwide. You can use their US address. They also provide secretarial and copy services and have a color copier. The Mailbox is open weekdays 0800-2000; Saturdays, 0900-1700, Sundays

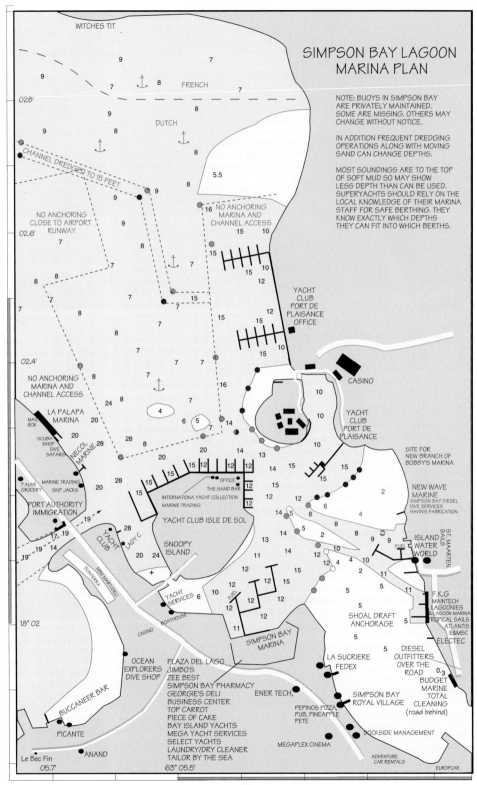

SIMPSON BAY LAGOON
MARINA PLAN

NOTE: BUOYS IN SIMPSON BAY
ARE PRIVATELY MAINTAINED.
SOME ARE MISSING. OTHERS MAY
CHANGE WITHOUT NOTICE.

IN ADDITION FREQUENT DREDGING
OPERATIONS ALONG WITH MOVING
SAND CAN CHANGE DEPTHS.

MOST SOUNDINGS ARE TO THE TOP
OF SOFT MUD SO MAY SHOW
LESS DEPTH THAN CAN BE USED.
SUPERYACHTS SHOULD RELY ON THE
LOCAL KNOWLEDGE OF THEIR MARINA
STAFF FOR SAFE BERTHING. THEY
KNOW EXACTLY WHICH DEPTHS
THEY CAN FIT INTO WHICH BERTHS.

1000-1400.

Over in the Simpson Bay Marina Plaza Del Lago, the Business Point (VHF: 14) offers phone and fax, mail and courier services, and a fast internet service. Use their computers or bring your own in for wifi in the office. They also rent cell phones and Hyacinth will arrange airline tickets and tours, including The Edge ferry to Saba. You can browse their book swap and look at yachting magazines. Their office opening hours are weekdays 0800-1800, Saturdays 0900-1600.

Ric's Café offers free wifi, with a small charge for electrical hookup, and Jimbo's offers free wifi – no electrical outlets. For those anchored out in the bay, Picante, may have free wifi (it was being rebuilt in 2009). For mobile phones, Telcel has an office on the left side of the road as you walk from Palapa Marina away from the bridge.

General Yacht Services

Simpson Bay Marina (VHF: 16 or 79A), is an Island Global Yachting (IGY) top quality marina, with generously wide, tile-decorated docks carrying electricity (110/220-volt, 60-cycle, 3-phase, and 100-volt single phase), water, telephone, and satellite TV. They also offer wifi, but it may not reach all slots. Facilities include full communications, showers, and toilets. The channel is dredged up to 16 feet and they can accommodate about 130 boats and up to 30 megayachts of 170 feet or more. This marina also caters to small yachts and they have many in the 40- to 50-foot range. Anyone unsure of the way in, and all megayachts, should call from outside the bridge and they will guide you into your slip. They have a fuel dock with ice, and arrange high-speed fuel bunkering for megayachts. Anything their megayachts customers need, they will get, including repairs, boat care, provisioning, laundry, and car rentals. It is usually necessary to book a place in advance.

Ashore is Plaza del Lago, a pleasant shopping and restaurant complex, which includes a bank with an ATM machine. Some of the restaurants, shops, and businesses are covered in different sections of this chapter. The plaza also contains a medical and dental clinic, a hair salon, and there are casinos and a cinema nearby.

You will also find Bay Island Yachts here. This is a big brokerage with world-

Simpson Bay   Chris Doyle

wide connections where Heather will help you sell your boat or find you a new one.

La Palapa Marina (VHF: 68) offers stern-to docking (any length) for about 25 boats. The water here is deep: if you can get through the bridge, you can get into La Palapa. This has made them very popular with megayachts, and it is not unusual to see a dozen or more yachts here between 100 and 200 feet long. Water and electricity (110, 220-volt, 3-phase, 60-cycle), phones, and cable TV are available on the dock; a wifi system keeps you online. They have full communications, washrooms, showers, and a convenient laundry, which is also open to the general public. Several large charter yachts use La Palapa Marina as a base. Their staff, headed by Valeska

Luckert, attends to all the needs of their customers and offers full provisioning.

Island Global Yachting, with marinas in several Caribbean islands, runs Yacht Club Isle de Sol (VHF: 78A/16), on Snoopy Island. It was built specifically for large yachts, with docks about 10 feet off the water. They have 220, 380 and 480-volt single or 3-phase electricity, with satellite TV, phone, and high-speed wifi or cable internet hookup at each slip, and full ISPS security. Water and fuel are delivered to all berths. Facilities include tennis courts, a swimming pool, a restaurant, provisioning, air conditioned gym and a chandlery. A lower dinghy dock can be found in the southeastern part of the marina. The staff will cater to all the needs of their cus-

tomers.

Yacht Club Port de Plaisance, by Princess Casino (VHF: 16/78), is built like a Mediterranean port, and is St. Martin's fanciest yachting facility, with full ISPS security. The service is geared to superyachts and they send tenders to meet every customer to make sure they navigate the bridge and channel with no problem. They can take about 100 yachts, including the largest superyachts in their new docks to the northwest. While Yacht Club Port de Plaisance is very much geared to megayachts, several berths in the prettier south harbor are suitable for cruising yachts.

The marina staff will take care of your fuel and water needs anywhere on their docks, and power (220, 380-volt single or 3-phase), cable TV, and wifi are provided. As you would expect from a marina of this caliber, they can supply just about anything. The swimming pools, health spa, gyms, lounging chairs, tennis courts, and other facilities reserved for resort guests are open to the crew and guests of boats on their dock. Customers can also rent hull cleaning rafts and electric baggage carts. The marina is next to a casino and several shops and restaurants (see our ashore section) that are open to the general public. The best place to leave your dinghy is close to the port office on the long wall in the new harbor.

International Yacht Collection, a superyacht charter brokerage, and crewfinder agency has offices both in the Yacht Club Port de Plaisance (Princess Marina) and in Yacht Club Isle de Sol. They open during the season (December through April) to look after their yachts in a princely fashion. They have both a private plane and helicopter to help move guests around or help provision your yacht down-island. They offer free internet access for crews from their yachts.

Portofino Marina is another IGY marina to the north of La Palapa, just after the big fuel dock and gas station. This is a facility for smaller yachts and powerboats. All the inside berths are designed to hoist power cruisers out of the water for storage between trips. They have a long dinghy dock at the northern end of the marina.

In this same complex is Weather Eye Yacht Sales, a brokerage run by Reg Bates. Island Water World (VHF: 74) is a full-service marina with room for about 55 boats. They cater specifically to regular cruising boats. They have a fuel dock with the availability of water and electricity alongside, also with cable TV for long-term guests. The entrance channel has been dredged to 9 feet. To get there, follow the main channel toward Simpson Bay Marina and turn to port into the Island Water World channel, shortly after Princess Yacht Club, and long before Simpson Bay Marina. It is not very well marked at this point, but is in line with the dinghy dock at Isle de Sol and the first dock in Island Water World.

FKG Rigging also has some berths. For details, look under Technical Yacht Services.

Lagoon Marina has been completely renovated, with a new dock that is more reasonably priced than many, and it has a big security gate. They have water, elec-

tricity (110/220-volt), internet hookup and cable TV on the dock. In the building are several technical services, Horizons Charter Company, and Lagoon Marina's laundromat, showers, and toilets. Most of the big services are very close by. Laggonies Bar and Restaurant is famous among cruisers (see ashore section). The easiest way in is to head into Island Water World. When you reach their first dock, follow it closely around into FKG. Go starboard into FKG, staying inside all the buoys, follow along the shore over to Lagoon Marina. The deep water is marked; outside that it is only about 4 feet.

Bobby's Marina has a haul out facility on the airport road close to the Red Cross (VHF: 14). This facility includes stern-to docking, with both 110 and 220-volt electricity, showers and toilets. Haul out is done with a 55-ton Travelift and they have room to store about 80 yachts. Bobby's Marina is also building a new marina and haul out yard between New Wave Marine and Princess Yacht Club. Access will be

directly in, past Princess Marina. The plans are for a large haul out yard, capable of taking both small yachts and super yachts. They currently have a 150-ton marine hoist up to 36-foot beam and a 75-ton hoist with a 25-foot beam. Jeff Howell tells me this will be operating before December 2009.

Next to Bobby's on the airport road is St. Martin Shipyard, behind Harry's Bar. They have a travel lift and can haul yachts, with long term plans for a superyacht hauling facility.

A new marina designed for larger yachts is very close to the airport, in an ideal position to collect or leave anyone travelling by plane. There is a channel, at least 16 feet deep to the marina from the deep water at Port de Plaisance (see our sketch chart). No Limits Charters is above McDonalds, a few steps toward the bridge from La Palapa. It is run by Jan Roosens in the Caribbean and Lou Hofman in the US. Apart from charter, they offer yacht management, large yacht brokerage, marine photography, and a marine school where you can get an IYT master's certificate up to 200 tons. Along with this is a crew placement service. Jan is also pivotal in organizing the St. Martin Classic Yacht Regatta in January.

Garbage bins can be found in, or just outside, all major marinas. The government empties these and this is part of where you monthly fee goes. If you need a vet, Dr. Gary Swanston has an excellent reputation and is just a short ride away (call 599-542-0111). The chandleries help out with the filling of cooking gas bottles. You take them before 0900 and collect them later in the day. The current schedule is Island Water World on Mondays and Budget Marine on Wednesdays.

General Yacht Services, Boat/Carpet Cleaning

David Clech of Yacht Assistance Caraibes does first rate carpet and upholstery cleaning, as well as glass, stainless, aluminum, and pvc surfaces. He works very closely with Superyacht Services.

Boat Cleaning and Services do exterior and interior detailing, look after boats, and will help with any kind of custom job that needs doing.

Total Cleaning are on Waterfront Road just behind Budget Marine. (Turn left out of Budget and you come to them.) They offer every kind of interior cleaning, from a carpet job to top-to-bottom cleaning by a willing and helpful team. However, do not expect any of them to remove the barnacles (see Lagoon Divers).

Chandlery

Nowhere is better than St. Martin where everything is duty-free, for chandleries and boat shopping. The two giant stores, Island Water World and Budget Marine, both have marine catalogs and always offer a cash discount. If you are planning considerable shopping, both stores have various extra discount levels you can apply for, and these will be at their largest outlets in duty-free St. Martin. It is worth watching their ads in local papers for

extra special deals. Each store is different, and each has items not in the other, and both offer big catalogs of their regular stock, but it is more fun to visit. Both stores sell engine oil and batteries, and will recycle your discards. If you need some item not on the shelves, either store will probably be able to special order it for you.

Budget Marine is in a huge building with its own dinghy dock. It is the original store in an island-wide chain, with branches on many islands, including Trinidad, Grenada, and Antigua. Budget Marine introduced the first Caribbean marine catalog, and they can arrange delivery anywhere in the Caribbean. They have one of the widest ranges of equipment, so it is a good place to come when you are looking for some specific fitting or part, be it a windlass motor or a toilet pump. They stock almost everything, from cutlass bearings and zincs, to cables, pumps, alternators, ply, and resins, including a big range of stoves. They sell Tohatsu outboards and AB inflatables, along with other dinghies and kayaks. They have a range of superlight aluminum RIBS from Aquapro, starting at 57 lbs. Budget Marine is an agent for Harken roller furling. If you don't see what you want, ask, for they have several storerooms in the back. When approaching by dinghy, stay at least 150 yards off the shore between Budget and Lagoon Marina, as the water here is just an inch or two deep.

Island Water World is a magnificent and well laid-out chandlery, covering a vast area, with a dinghy dock outside. They have paints and resins, marine hardware, electrics and electronics, plumbing, charts and cruising guides, dinghies and outboards, fishing gear, ropes and ground tackle, safety gear, and back-saving seats. They are sales and service agents for Evinrude, Mercury, and Honda, Caribe Inflatables, and Boston Whaler. The sales staff is very welcoming and helpful. You can pick up their catalog and they can arrange delivery anywhere in the Caribbean. They have similar stores in Rodney Bay, St Lucia, and in St. George's, Grenada, as well as several smaller outlets.

RENAISSANCE ISLANDS

Isle de Sol   Chris Doyle

St. Martin Island Water World has now been expanded into the Caribbean's first full online shop: www.islandwaterwold.com. Your account status is stored on the computer, so if you are a big buyer with a big discount you will still get this, and see your price on line. You will be able to pick up online products from other IWW shops, which will save all the customs hassles, but this will affect your discount.

Marine Trading in is a small, friendly chandlery with two shops, run by Smiley and Elena. They spend time sourcing interesting stuff, and offer giant inflatable fenders top quality Fendersox covers from the UK, and they are agents for Bluewater Books. They keep an excellent selection of cleaning and polishing products, from special bilge cleaners to Barnacle Buster, a fair bit of hardware, as well as things you might not see in the other stores. They are very service minded and when a customer comes in, they source whatever they want quickly, if it is not in stock. The outlet in Isle de Sol caters almost exclusively to superyachts, usually Rose will help you. The other is in the Skip Jack fish market and restaurant, just north of the little bridge to Isle de Sol, with a convenient dinghy dock. This store has a more general appeal, with excellent tools and toolboxes, snorkeling, marine toys, and even fishing gear. They also have a crew house for those wanting to get off the boat.

Ace, a giant hardware store, is also of interest. Turn right out of Island Water World, turn left at the corner, and walk up Well Road. Ace is at the main road.

Technical Yacht Services
Electrics & Electronics

Just south of La Palapa, with its own dock in 20 feet of water, is Andrew Rapley's Necol, an excellent electrics, electronics,

Tradewinds Radio
The Sound Of The Tropics

FM 105.1 St. Maarten - www.tradewindsradio.com

and water-maker shop. On the electric and electronic side, they sell all kinds of equipment, from satellite telephones and navigation equipment to Westerbeke generators and Victron inverters and chargers. They are specialists at fixing gyros and integrated navigation systems on superyachts, as well as sorting out these large yachts' complex electrical problems. They can install and deal with all the AIS integrated security systems. They are agents for Furuno, KVH, Simrad, and B&G, among others. For racers, they like to set up complete integrated instrumentation. For cruisers they offer Iridium phones, with voice and reliable internet connection. For water-makers, they are agents for nearly all major brands from the US, Europe, and the Caribbean. Their service tender can reach everywhere in Simpson Bay and over into Marigot Bay in just a few minutes, or you can come to their service dock. Wander in and check them out, or call. Andrew is a pilot with his own plane, so is able to make down-island visits for big yachts in dire straits.

Electec (VHF: 14) are in a big new building next to the Lagoon Marina. This company is owned and run by Leslie Struthers and Derek Little. It is an installation and service shop for electrics and instrumentation, and they also repair all kinds of starter motors and alternators, and electronics, including VHF radios. They are agents for Onan, Northern Lights, Fischer Panda, Master Volt, and F. G. Wilson generators, but will repair other makes as well. They are authorized sales and service agents for Interstate batteries and their prices are good. Electec sells Spectra, Village Marine, Pur, and Sea Recovery water-makers, and they repair all makes. Leslie Struthers or one of his team will come to your boat for installation and repair work. Their showroom has a wide range of electrical components, both for yachts and shore power, and they sell Milwaukee and Makita power tools.

Altantis Marine is an electronics shop in Lagoon Marina run by two very personable guys, Gui from Brazil (electronics) and Andy from UK (electrics). Gui will fix any kind of electronics and is certified for installation and service of Raymarine. He is good with computers, networks, wifi, and audio and theater things (fancy a big waterproof screen outside that shows where you are, or movies, while your computer is dry below?) and will fix any kind of marine electronics. Andy will take care of your generators, starter motors, and all electrical problems. Their store has a stock of electronic accessories and also Phasor generators and VEI electronics. They have a reputation for excellent work and service at a reasonable price.

In FKG, Colin's Advanced Marine Systems specializes in cruise ships and the commercial application of gyros, radios, radar, and high-end satellite communications systems, mainly of the Sea Tel, Transas, and Sperry brands.

Shai Talmi, "The Wired Sailor," has an upstairs office behind Palapa. Shai is friendly, helpful, and knowledgeable. His specialty is with computers, wifi, Marine Information Technology, and other related systems. But he can work with all marine electronics, can design electrical systems, and is good with audio, video, and data systems.

Technical Yacht Services
Refrigeration

Perma Frost is a top refrigeration and air-conditioning specialist at La Palapa Marina, run by John and Ricarda. They are very good and can fix all brands. They design and build custom systems that work reliably, including variable speed compressors. They are very busy during the season with megayachts, but will try to help cruising yachts out. They can work on, and keep spares for, all makes, and are agents for many brand names, including Isotherm, Frigoboat, Dometik, Norcold, and Scotsman.

Rob of Rob Marine has a refrigeration and air conditioning shop at New Wave Marine Yard. He is agent for Technicold and Headhunter and works on all brands. His Headhunter expertise and stock includes all their big yacht toilets and pumps. Rob is very happy to work on cruising yachts as well as the larger boats, but no longer makes dinghy visits – you have to be at a dock.

Frostline is in the Lagoon Marina complex. Run by Glyn and Paul Frost, this is both a refrigeration air-conditioning shop, with lots of parts and accessories (including things to make your fridge smell good), and a repair shop. They keep all the parts necessary for superyachts with European systems, and much of their work is large yachts, but they also are happy to fix fridge systems on cruising yachts.

Ener Tech is opposite Fedex. It is a family-run refrigeration and air-conditioning business headed by Edward Kalna, aided by his son Michael. Uma in the office is very helpful. Edward is a qualified professional refrigeration engineer who used to work in the navy. They deal with everything from

Squeezing through the bridge

Chris Doyle

small yachts to large ships and can build systems to freeze many tons. They have a big water pump section and pull apart and rebuild all makes, including March/Scott and Calpeda. As distributers for many brands, their parts room is impressive and they are the authorized sales, installation, and service agents for Sea Frost, and Grunert, among others. Teamwork Marine are in Simpson Bay Yacht Club, and handle all refrigeration, air-conditioning, plumbing, and water maker problems.

Technical Yacht Services
Sailmakers, Canvas, Cushions

St. Maarten Sails & Canvas is run by Rob Gilders and his team. They have been doing this for 30 years, with excellent work and reasonable prices to a standard that has kept both cruisers and megayacht owners equally happy. They do all classes of work: biminis, canvas, cushions, and sails, from design and construction to modifications and repairs. For cockpit cushions they use Dryfast foam, which is soft and does not hold water. You will find them opposite Island Water World in a big loft with plenty of space and many machines to match

any job. This location makes it easy to bring your sails in, but if there is a problem you can ask about collection from all Simpson Bay Marinas. For new sails of any size they are very happy with their association with Quantum Sails. Rob finds that Quantum produces really top quality sails at some of the most reasonable rates in the Caribbean. It is well worth asking him for a quote.

Ernst's Tropical Sail Loft has a huge working area in the new Lagoon Marina complex. To go with this, Ernst has probably the biggest industrial sewing machine I have yet seen. He is a North Sails agent and works with Andrew Dove in Guadeloupe. You can get an instant quote for new North Sails. His loft is upstairs and he has a crane hoist and dolly to bring sails from your tender. During the season, much of his work is with megayachts (thus the monster machine). Ernst is helpful and knowledgeable and repairs all kinds of sails, as well as canvas work, and he sells lots of fabrics and sailmaking supplies, including sail needles.

Irene, at Tailor by the Sea, will repair or make you new clothes, but also she does all

Superyachts in Simpson Bay

Chris Doyle

RENAISSANCE ISLANDS

Simpson Bay Lagoon, south end   Chris Doyle

kinds of yacht upholstery work, including not only cushions, but curtains and bedding. She also offers a next day service for small jobs. You will find her in Plaza del Largo where she is open weekdays 0930-1830; Saturdays, 1000-1500.

Technical Yacht Services Motor Mechanics

Simpson Bay Diesel Services (VHF: 74), run by Armand Amato, has a fine, large workshop at New Wave Marine Yard, just north of Island Water World. Armand is the authorized factory service agent for Yanmar, Perkins, Volvo Penta, and Cummins, and can give you really excellent prices on new Yanmars, which he orders specially. Bring your broken Yanmars and Vovlo Pentas, and Perkins here to be fixed, as there is a good chance he will have the spares. Armand also works on all other brands of diesel and is at home with the big GM's, MYU's, and Caterpillars from superyachts. Armand's workshop is well placed for removing

engines for a rebuild. They also have a full mechanical machine shop.

Across the main road from Budget-Electec, you will see a row of shops. To the right of these is an alley of large workshop doors. One of these leads to Diesel Outfitters, owned and run by Ray Longbottom from Liverpool. Ray is a Perkins agent and worth checking with if you have a Perkins problem, as his price on spares can be good. In addition, he can supply new Perkins engines. Ray's second line of engines is John Deere, which makes 70-300 horsepower diesels, an excellent choice for those wanting the slightly heavier, last-forever kind of motor. Ray can also work on all brands of diesel. He makes boat visits to sort out your engine. Ray is often out and can be a little hard to find, the easiest way to find him is to use the phone (599-544-2320).

The Napa agent is just up Orange Grove Road. If you walk back from Budget to the main road and turn right, then immediately left, you should find yourself on it. They

92

sell many useful filters, engine parts, and spares and accessories, such as water pumps, batteries, and oils. They can make up hydraulic hoses.

Check also: Multiple and Other services.

Technical Yacht Services
Rigging

FKG Rigging (VHF: 71) is run by Kevin, Gordon, and Shag. They have a dock and room for 10 boats in front of their yard, with water and electricity (110 and 220-volt single and 3-phase),which they keep for boats having work done. The channel into their yard is dredged to 12 feet, and sometimes marked. If your draft approaches this depth, let them bring you in. If you have a draft of 6 or 7 feet, you may find it easier to come in via the Island Water World channel. Hug their dock very closely and then branch into the deeper channel. They can also bring yachts up to 20 tons into their yard that need hull work via a 20-ton trailer from Island Water World.

FKG Rigging is one serious rigging shop, with an endless stock of fittings of all sizes.

They can repair or manufacture just about anything, from making new compression fittings on rod rigging, to setting you up with a complete new mast and rig. Swages and wire are available up to 25mm, with rod rigging up to 170mm. Their technical chandlery has lots of rope and rigging-related hardware, including ropes, winches, quick release shackles, and general hardware.

They have a whole store dedicated to yacht hydraulics, including all big boat hydraulics. This store includes a large retail shop, mainly Aeroquip equipment, and this is also the place to come for any hydraulic work. They also sell and service hardware such as Antal and Lewmar, New England and Gleistein ropes, Recmann, Rondal, Furlex, and Profurl roller furling, and Barrett feathering propellers. In addition, they do SS tube work and lifelines. They have both a machine shop and all manner of welding facilities, and can do any kind of metal job and work on shafts up to 4 inches in diameter. They also build custom aluminum boats.

RENAISSANCE ISLANDS

Technical Yacht Services
Multiple and Other Services

Island Water World has its own crane for hauling yachts of up to 25 tons (9-foot draft), and there is room for five boats out at a time. You can do the work yourself or the marina can arrange it for you. They do their own fiberglass repairs, antifouling, and outboard mechanical work. For anything else, Simpson Bay Diesel Service is next door, St. Maarten Sails is across the road, and FKG is close by. Apart from doing all the regular work on cruising yachts, they have an excellent reputation for repair and maintenance of superyacht tenders. Should you suffer an engine breakdown, they have a towboat to bring you to their yard.

Budget Marine have their own one-stop shop for your tender or dinghy with their outboard engine and inflatable shop. They sell and do warranty services for Tohatsu and will try to help out with most other makes of outboard. They repair all makes of inflatables.

Several businesses operate in the FKG compound. Maintech, run by Roger, does cabinetry and woodwork, and, above all, fiberglass work. They have a gel-coat stripper and specialize in osmosis treatment. They also do serious carbon fiber and kevlar work, as well as all the laminates. During the hurricane season, they often undertake complete refits on boats, contracting any work that cannot be done in their yard. They also have a book swap.

Over in Lagoonies, E & MSC is an excellent metal working shop for welding and machining all metals. Peter, the owner, specializes in high quality work for large yachts, and keeps them happy by doing things fast and well.

Several other businesses are in New Wave Marine. Haresh has a custom metal workshop called Havin's. A couple of years ago, their main specialty was the design and construction of spiffy T-tops; aluminum and canvas marine hoods.

They have upgraded into one of the most advanced metalworking shops in St.

Martin. They have state-of-the-art equipment, including an automatic computer controlled lathe, which also does some milling, allowing complex parts to be drawn on a computer to your specs and then made with a superb polished finish. They can fabricate in just about any metal, including aluminum, stainless, and titanium. The shop is kept very clean, and they use only certified welders and machinists. In the summer they rely on the local market and resurface engine blocks, and build custom tanks. They are usually fast, reasonably priced and do excellent work, whether the job is big or just a simple weld. Rob McCall is very knowledgeable about yachts, including their electrical intricacies. His company, AtlanticSpirit.com, undertakes absentee yacht management and project management. He will look after your boat on dry land and in the water. If in the water, he can haul and paint it before you come and have it all ready for your departure.

Deon's Aquatic Solutions is a salvage and underwater shop. They have an underwater hydraulic hull cleaner and prop polisher, and can clean hulls, weld and cut, and they have a 600 h.p. tug for serious towing. They can easily raise sunken yachts, and do all kinds of underwater work, and can dredge in restricted areas anywhere in the Caribbean.

Eric Marine sells and services jet skis and big Mercury engines. Over in Palapa Marina, you will find Chris, a shipwright who originally apprenticed under Falmouth Boat Construction, and who now runs Palapa Shipwright. He does all kinds of marine woodwork, from re-planking a hull to the finest joinery and he replaces many teak decks.

John Gifford's Lagoon Divers (aka Amcon, (VHF 14) is based in Palapa and does all kinds of underwater work, from repairs to surveys. The good news for those that got stuck here a bit too long is that they scrub hulls and props for a reasonable rate. Kenny Awlgrip is a mobile operation. Kenny and his team will come to you by land or sea. They specialize in high quality Awgrip spray finishes, both paint and varnish. They also repair and touch-up paint, and do yacht names.

The bridge at Port de Plaisance

Chris Doyle

RENAISSANCE ISLANDS

Transport

When you need to get a plane ticket, Travel Planners are across the road from Palapa. When you need to rent a car, you will find many agencies close by. The most accessible are in or close to Palapa and Portofino Marinas, but if you have no luck here there are some more just south of Royal Village. Also in the area, Safari Car Rentals, on Airport Road, has cars, buses, and jeeps, which they will deliver. The Bertrand brothers' Aqua World in Palapa rents scooters both terrestrial and marine, they will provide a water taxi on request, and they rent inflatables. From time to time a water taxi service is available in the evenings. Ask around, or scan the radio.

Provisioning and Yacht Agents

Much of the provisioning is done by yacht agents, who not only provision but handle all the needs of their yachts, from fuel bunkering to concierge services. These include:

Lila Rosen's Dockside Management, a professional yacht and ship agency. Lila runs a VIP service for fuel bunkering, finding marina berths, provisioning, and arranging for air charters, scuba diving, and anything else. She does both yacht and airplane customs clearance and will work out visa problems. She has an island-wide network, so she can take care of her yachts throughout the islands. Her office is in the Laguna View block; it is best to call.

Jane Harrison's Mega Yacht Services is close by Simpson Bay Marina, opposite Z-Best. She is a full superyacht agent who does everything from full provisioning and organizing flowers to arranging car rentals or airline tickets. Jane is happy to use her local knowledge to get you the best seat in a local restaurant and she does quite a lot of crew placement work.

Super Yacht Services is in Simpson Bay Marina and run by Simon and Lucille. It is a professional agency, and Simon spends much of his time zooming out to customers in his tender. They handle everything superyachts need, from provisioning and cleaning to customs clearance and visa problems.

They have an agent in Anguilla, Gabi Gumbs. Super Yacht Services also arrange the St. Martin Charter Boat Show and have The Crew Network, an excellent crew placement service with dedicated staff.

Chris Doyle

You are welcome at the yacht club   Chris Doyle

Palapa Marina has dedicated staff for full provisioning, crew placement, and everything large yachts need. This service is available for all boats.

Provisioning

With the advent of megayachts, dedicated provisioning services have sprung up around Simpson Bay, catering to the luxury market. These businesses will get you fresh peaches, strawberries, and Russian caviar, as well as all the basics.

Simpson Bay Yacht Provisioning and Georgie's Gourmet Galley are a mother and daughter operation under one roof in Plaza del Largo. Georgie's Gourmet Galley is a wonderful European delicatessen that sells not only cold cuts and salads, but lots of meat, savory pies, roast chicken, French bread, and a fine collection of other goodies, including good wines and select fruits. There is always a beer in the fridge while you look around, or come for a coffee in the

morning and peruse the local papers they put out. Try one of their delicious meat pies for lunch. The full yacht provisioning side is handled by Danielle, who specializes in keeping super yachts topped up with everything they need. Gourmet Galley is open daily 0900-1930, except Sunday, when it opens 1100-1700.

Alan Dutka is probably the largest provisioner, and is especially geared to the megayachts. His IDS Yacht Provisioning is in Isle de Sol at the Sand Bar Restaurant. Alan will not only get anything you want, but will work with International Yacht Collection to deliver it to your yacht down island, so you never need suffer a miserable night in the Tobago Cays for the lack of the best Russian caviar or Cuban cigars.

Over in Yacht Club Port de Plaisance, Food Express is part of the large Lido chain. They offer full megayacht provisioning. They plan to reopen the pleasant walk-in shop, which is currently closed.

You can also go shopping for provisions and where you choose may depend to some extent on where you are anchored. For those in Simpson Bay, the Peli Deli over the Pelican Resort is a wonderful small supermarket, open daily from 0730 to 1930, except Sundays and holidays when they open 0800-1800. To get there, you walk upstairs through the resort to the next courtyard. Tie your dinghy inside on the west side of the westernmost dock.

Inside the lagoon, Gourmet Marché is a very nice, small supermarket behind Portofino. They have excellent fresh foods, deli meat, and fish, as well as a good variety of cans and packaged foods. They open daily 0800-2000, except Sunday, when their hours are 0900-1400.

If you get stuck on a holiday and everything is closed, dinghy to the St. Martin Yacht Club and walk across the road to the big Sunterra Hotel on the other side, where you will find the Royal Deli. They open from 0700 in the morning util 2100 at night every single day, including all holidays. In La Palapa, Connoisseur's Duty-Free is a comprehensive wine and liquor store. Special wines are brought in on request and they also stock beer and cigars. Opposite Palapa and Plaza del Largo are small supermarkets with most items.

Daily Extra is well worth checking out: it is a fairly big supermarket. Just go to the Budget Marine Dock and walk to the big main road (Welfare Road) and it is almost opposite. They have a good selection of everything, including fresh produce, and manager Wai Tin Chaong is happy to deliver orders you cannot carry back to the nearby docks. They open daily 0800-2000 except Sunday, which is 0800-1300. Do not leave your dinghy at the Budget Marine dock after they close. They lock their docks and gate.

The distinctive dinghy dock at Simpson Bay Marina

Chris Doyle

For a major provisioning, Le Grande Marché is about a 15-minute walk from Island Water World, on Union Road, close by the entrance of the main drive to Princess Casino. This is a fabulous, very-large supermarket, always spotlessly clean, with a big selection of everything. If you are buying a lot, they will deliver your groceries back to the dock.

La Sucriere is an excellent boulangerie/patisserie with its own dinghy dock next to Fedex. They make everything themselves, from great bread to delicious cakes. You can sit and have coffee or a sandwich on their big deck over the water. They open daily 0600-1900 except Sunday 0600-1315.

There are two drugstores run by the same company, which offer everything from prescription drugs to gifts, including all the regular vitamins and health care products. They are happy to give free advice and are especially helpful in topping up your yacht medical stores, including emergency dental kits. The Friendly Island Drugstore is at the Cole Bay Shopping Center, near Food Center, and the Simpson Bay Pharmacy is at Simpson Bay Marina. The Simpson Bay Pharmacy is open every weekday 0830-1930, Saturdays 0900 -1300, and Sundays 1700-1900.

Fun Shopping

Plaza del Largo does not have too many shops, but it does have good modern medical and dental facilities and Inter Coiffure, where you can get anything from a hair cut to full body massage. On the other side of the road, next to the bridge, Sunterra Resort has several gift shops.

La Palapa complex also has a variety of shops. These include Good Cards, owned by ex-yachty Janet Robertson, who not only stocks lots of cards, but souvenir items and books as well. Nearby is Xperts Hair and Massage Salon. Across the road, World of Electronics has good non-marine computers and cameras. At the Pelican Resort you will find sporty shops on the waterfront and more boutiques on the next level up.

RENAISSANCE ISLANDS

Chris Doyle

Restaurants

Bars and restaurants abound. We will mention just a few. Outside the lagoon, dinghy to the Buccaneer Beach Bar, with its 80-foot dinghy dock. This is a boater-friendly place, great for meeting people who gather at the big, round, open bar. You will probably meet the owners, Jill and Bernard. Bernard was once a yacht delivery skipper and still keeps his boat out in the bay. Their barbecue opens 1100-2200 every day, offering simple, inexpensive fare such as Caesar salad with fresh tuna, steak sandwiches, and burgers. The chef stands behind the barbecue pit and cooks everything perfectly to your specifications. They have daily selected shot drinks at a dollar and frequent entertainment. They also serve pizza from 1700-2200.

Next door, Picante is a big beach restaurant. It was closed for renovations when I went by, but will reopen in some guise.

Back inside the lagoon, La Palapa's Soggy Dollar is a crew bar open all day and until late in the evening. It has a nightly happy hour from 1700-1900 and the associated Palapa Dock Café serves snacks and good lunches. In the same complex, El Rancho is a fine steak house.

Heading towards the bridge, Ric's Place is an American Café and Sports Bar, just before the bridge, with its own good dinghy dock. The owner, Tamara is from California and creates a pleasant laid-back, open and friendly atmosphere. They offer free wifi as long as you spend $5, and you can find a power outlet for your computer for a dollar. They open daily from 0800 (American breakfast) through 2300, and later if big games are showing. Numerous TV screens, including three giants, bring you the action. If you want to escape the commentary, there is an outside open balcony with a great view of the superyachts berthing over at Isle de Sol. They have good American and Tex Mex food, with burgers, salads, snacks, quesadillas, and their famous nacho grande. Finish with a root beer float. Daily happy hour is 1800-2100.

The Sint Maarten Yacht Club has an Antillean-style club house and dinghy dock just on the southeast side of the entrance canal, with a deck that has a perfect close-up view of megayachts passing the bridge. It is a friendly place, but please do not abuse them by leaving and locking your dinghy where it says "no dinghies." At night, look down from the deck to watch a school of tarpon feeding on shrimps. You can catch up on yacht club news here, and check out the book swap. The bar and restaurant has some great food. The kitchen opens daily for breakfast, lunch, and dinner. The dinner menu offers a big range in price to suit all tastes with a variety of meat, vegetarian, and seafood dishes. Their Caesar tuna, done as you like it, is excellent. Happy hour is 1600-1830 daily, with two-for-one on beers and mixed drinks. A few steps from the Yacht Club, you cannot miss the brightly lit Lady C floating bar. Always full, lively, and fun, this is a popular watering hole for crews. Visit for happy hour from 1600-1800, hang about and try the "all you can eat ribs", and you can forget worrying about where to go to dinner. Next door, check out Halsey's. They have an interesting looking, fusion menu that will cater to sophisticated palettes. From here on down to the Boathouse, it is all waterfront seafood restaurants; take your choice.

A little farther down, Skip Jack's is a big fish restaurant and market, open to the sea, and they have "choose your own" live lobster.

Plaza del Lago is home not only to Simpson Bay Marina but has several really good, reasonably priced, eating spots. Dany and Tamela's Zee Best is an excellent Café/Bistro where you can get continental or a full American breakfast from 0700, plus French pastries, crêpes, fresh juices, and a great lunch. Jimbo's is right in the center of a shopping complex, but it has been cleverly designed to create a delightful open garden atmosphere. It is arranged around a small pool and waterfall, so when the heat of the food gets to be too much you can jump in and swim to the other side of the bar; kids love this. Jimbo, once an actor and playwright, came to St. Martin many years ago on holiday. He fell in love with the island, stayed and changed his life. Now he greets his customers and serves first-rate Tex-Mex food to the accompaniment of rock and blues music. He has a mesquite grill and offers excellent salads, enchiladas, fajitas, chimichangas, sandwiches, and burgers. With each drink you get a Jimbo dollar - collect five and next drink is on the house. Some of the crew collect them all season and splurge. The record: about 1500 Jimbos to spend. This is a good place to meet people and they have free wifi (no power outlets).

Piece of Cake is a pâtisserie/delicatessen and ice-cream parlor in one, where you can also get a good breakfast and reasonable daily specials for lunch or a light dinner, plus delicious desserts and goodies. They also sell good bread. They open daily 0700-2300. They are in Plaza del Lago, facing the road. Top Carrot Health food and vegetarian store is a wonderful place for fresh

RENAISSANCE ISLANDS

juice, gourmet health food items, and lunch. Saratoga is fancy on a luxurious patio over the sea. Head south along the shore from Simpson Bay Marina, and you will come to Simpson Bay Royal Village, with its own dinghy dock and a big collection of restaurants, ice cream parlors and shops. Pineapple Pete's is a happening place, with a friendly and cheerful staff. Domino's Pizza, which delivers to yachts in the marinas, is popular. Over in Isle de Sol, the Sand Bar Restaurant, with its own swimming pool and pool table, offers Caribbean seafood, steaks, pizza, and salad. They open for lunch and dinner, with live music and a barbecue on Saturdays, and are priced towards the yacht crews, rather than the owners.

Yacht Club Port de Plaisance has a French restaurant called La Guinguette, which has a bar area with wifi and daily happy hour from 1700-1800, and the food is reasonably priced. Across the bridge is a branch of Zee Best, open for breakfast and lunch, and up by the casino is Pegleg Bar and Restaurant. In the corner nearest the

airport, you will find a dock that makes a perfect place to pick up or drop off your guests. The $3 charge for this is a great saving over a taxi, but they don't want you to leave your dinghy more than half an-hour. You come off the dock into Jo's Steakhouse, a big restaurant open to the waterfront, serving high quality meat and seafood. If you are using the restaurant, you are not charged and usually there is no one collecting in the evening. Next door, served by the same dock, is Lal's Indian Cuisine, one of St. Martin's great and very friendly little bars. Lal, a local man of Indian extraction, presides over the bar, where you can just sit and enjoy a drink. When you get hungry, ask Lal for a menu, and he will serve you good traditional Indian food at a very reasonable price. There are tables, but most people eat at the bar. Lal also does take-out orders.

At the other end of the lagoon is Lagoonies — back in action. This favorite cruiser's bar is now run by Brad and Tara who spent many years running charter yachts. Lagoonies is informal and fun, with

Getting ready for the late afternoon bridge

Chris Doyle

Chris Doyle

a pool table, chess, and entertainment about five nights a week — a good place to meet other sailors. They have a happy hour every night from 1700-1900, except Sundays when they are closed. On Tuesdays, they keep happy hour going unt-til 2200, so you can socialize here on a budget. Most days they open at 1130, but Saturdays they open late afternoon. Daily specials are posted on the blackboard, with fish, fowl, and meat always available. They have lots of good Italian pastas, but are also famous for their cheeseburgers and seared tuna. They always have vegetarian dishes.

Ashore

Sunset Theatres is on the opposite side of the road to the boathouse, next to the casino. Three cinemas give you a choice of movies, the first showing is about 1815. Megaplex is another a little farther on the road to Philipsburg. Juan Pablo Piscione, an ex-sailor and a dedicated bike rider, runs Tri-Sport, where you can rent a range of bikes, from inexpensive models to high-tech mountain bikes. It is next to Necol. Upstairs in the same building is Mega Gym, the perfect place for your workout, whether you want to use their high-tech machines or take a class. Inexpensive daily rates work well for yacht crews.

Water Sports

There is good diving in this area. Dive sites include Explorers Reef in depths of 30 to 45 feet. You will see plenty of soft corals, crinoids, and anemones. Large fish, includ-ing barracuda, rays, and grouper, are often sighted. The Maze, which varies in depth from 25 to 45 feet, has good elkhorn coral. You will likely see turtles, rays, nurse sharks, and large French angelfish. You can also visit Proselyte Reef and Cable Reef from here, described in our Philipsburg sec-tion.

Scuba Shop, St. Martin's premier equip-ment sales and rental outlet, has a branch in La Palapa Marina run by Kim. This is

the best place to check out good deals on scuba equipment, much of it below list price, as they are the biggest Scuba gear dealer on the island. They run a very professional equipment rental service to charter yachts, and have their own guide booklet to dive sites that you can visit from your yacht (given free to customers). They have a complete service station for Sherwood, Scubapro, Mares, Aqualung, Sea Quest, and US Divers gear. Of special interest to yachts are tank adapters for blowing up fenders or blasting bits and pieces to clean them, extra long hoses so you can leave your tank on board while you scrub the bottom, and mini tanks for cleaning and quick jobs. They also sell some great yachting clothes, including some very fancy shorts and shirts, as well as diving watches. They have made their reputation by offering excellent service and advice to the yachting community.

Dive Safaris work with Scuba Shop in the same complex. Dive Safaris are the ones who will take you out diving and snorkeling. They also have a branch in Philipsburg and are the island's largest dive shop, though from Simpson Bay they only run small groups. They have full Nitrox facilities, can do both hydro-testing and annual visual inspections on your tanks, and will fill tanks.

Luciana and Jefferson are now running Leroy and Dominique's Ocean Explorers (VHF: 16), a good, informal combination dive shop and store on the Simpson Bay Beach, outside the bridge. (If walking, cross the road by the Boathouse.) Ask for

their map showing all the diving and snorkeling sites in the area. They have a well-stocked retail shop full of diving gear and accessories, plus t-shirts, and a big selection of underwater video camera housings, and some of the prices are great.

This whole crew is into underwater photography and video, and Leroy still goes out taking underwater videos, so if you are an enthusiast, this is the place to come. If you dive with them, they can also make a video of your dive. They fill tanks and frequently rent equipment to charter yachts. If the weather is calm, ask about One Step Beyond, Leroy's hidden bluewater dive. Depths vary from 45 to 90 feet over a large rambling reef where there are hundreds of fearless fish.

The Pelican Resort can arrange sports fishing, has a dive shop, and is the place to take the ferry Edge over to Saba.

FROM SIMPSON BAY TO POINTE BASSE TERRE

You can follow this coast quite closely, passing white sand beaches and cliffs, adorned with condominiums and hotels. In light settled weather, you can get temporary anchorage behind the dramatic white cliff at the eastern end of Anse Longue. The beach here is superb and it is the home of La Samanna, one of St. Maarten's most expensive and prestigious resorts. If you decide to visit, you may want to wear something more elegant than shorts, t-shirt, and flip-flops.

NORTH COAST — WEST TO EAST

When approaching from the south, give both Pointe Basse Terre and Pointe Plum a few hundred yards clearance. Steep seas can build up off Pointe Basse Terre, and there is a shoal with a rock awash that extends out from Pointe Plum. The water is 18 to 25 feet deep up to a mile and a half off most of St. Martin's north coast. This makes for fine sailing in bright turquoise and green water. The coast from Pointe Plum to Marigot is fairly clear of rocks and a few hundred yards offshore clears all dangers. The coast from Marigot up to Pointe Molly Smith is similarly clear of dangers. However, Pointe Molly Smith not only has rocks close to shore, but there is a reef with a small, 5-foot patch on it that lies about 150 yards out to sea in a northeasterly direction. Either stay half a mile off this point or, if the light conditions are good, pass inside the reef. There is 19 feet of water inside it. To the north of Grand Case, you can see the 100-foot Rocher Créole off Bell Point. Pass outside this rock. In calm conditions with good light, you can explore the inside passage, where there is 8-12 feet. As you go north of Bell Point, pass outside Marcel Rock.

Marigot

Marigot is the capital of French St. Martin. It has the feeling of a picturesque and fashionable Riviera seaport, with an attractive waterfront market and handsome streets, bursting at the seams with boutiques and restaurants. Although there are usually many yachts in the anchorage, there is always plenty of room. The currency is the Euro, which can be worth more or less than a dollar. Some shops and restaurants give equivalence regardless of the rate.

Navigation

The approach is wide open and free from dangers during the day. At night you

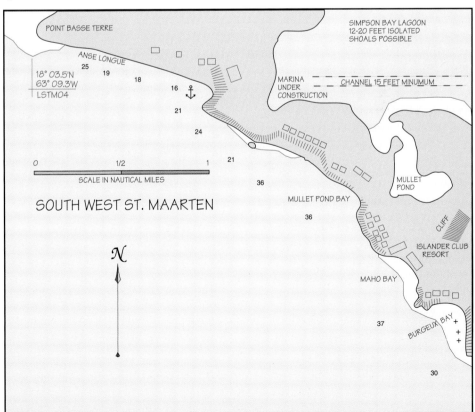

Map labels:
POINT BASSE TERRE
ANSE LONGUE
18° 03.5'N
63° 09.3'W
LSTM04
25
19
18
16
21
24
21
SCALE IN NAUTICAL MILES
0   1/2   1
SOUTH WEST ST. MAARTEN
N
SIMPSON BAY LAGOON
12-20 FEET ISOLATED
SHOALS POSSIBLE
MARINA UNDER CONSTRUCTION
CHANNEL 15 FEET MINUMUM
36
MULLET POND
MULLET POND BAY
36
CLIFF
ISLANDER CLUB RESORT
MAHO BAY
37
BURGEUX BAY
30

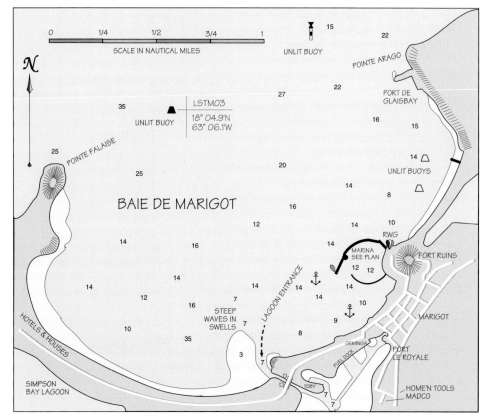

N

0   1/4   1/2   3/4   1
SCALE IN NAUTICAL MILES

15
UNLIT BUOY
22
POINTE ARAGO

27   22
PORT DE
GLAISBAY

35
UNLIT BUOY
LSTM03
18° 04.9'N
63° 06.1'W
16
15

25
POINTE FALAISE
25
20
14
14 △
UNLIT BUOYS
8
△

BAIE DE MARIGOT
16
10
RWG
12
14   16   12   14   MARINA
SEE PLAN
12 12
FORT RUINS

14
14   14   10
12   LAGOON ENTRANCE
14   14   14
14   16   7   14
STEEP
WAVES IN   7   10
SWELLS   9   MARIGOT
10   35   8
HOTELS & HOUSES
GEMINGA   PORT
LE ROYALE
3   7
FUEL DOCK
SIMPSON   TOBY   HOME'N TOOLS
BAY LAGOON   7   MADCO
7

need to miss some unlit steel buoys large enough to sit on after they have sunk your boat. One of these is a mooring buoy at 18° 04.88'N, 63° 06.35'W. On the other side of the bay, an unlit IALA buoy marks a 15-foot shoal at 18° 05.26'N, 63° 05.67'W.

The water starts shelving a long way offshore, but you can carry 8 or 9 feet right in close to town. Keep clear of the buoyed ferry channel. The wind can change here, so leave plenty of swinging room. During the winter months a swell or strong northeaster can occasionally make it uncomfortable. A green light flashes on the entrance to Marina Fort St. Louis, and a white light flashes on Port de Glaisbay. The fancy sector light to the north of the marina generally does not work.

You can also choose to go into the new Marina Fort Louis (VHF: 16), which now has all-around protection and is no longer troubled by swells.

Marigot has its own navigable corner of Simpson Bay Lagoon, and its own

entrance. To get into the lagoon, you must pass through Sandy Ground opening bridge, just west of the little cliff to the west of the town and hotels. The bridge opens Monday to Saturday at 0815, 1430 and 1730; on Sundays and holidays, 0815 and 1730. Sandy Ground Bridge can be contacted through Marina Port La Royale, (VHF: 16), T: 0590 87 20 43, or the bridge phone number (when it is manned) is: 0590-29-04-75 There is a large shoal area on the west side of the channel entrance. (See our Baie de Marigot sketch chart, page 106.) In northerly swells, steep waves build up outside this area, so you should approach from the east (town-side) of the bridge.

The channel has been dredged to 8 feet, but it silts up unevenly between dredgings. Seven feet is probably the maximum in the first part of the channel, and for going into the marina 6.6–foot draft would be more comfortable. Outside the channel are lots of shoals and finding an anchoring spot takes good light and local knowledge. When you come in through the bridge, aim for a round aerial on the hills ahead. Keep going until you are lined up with the channel, which is well marked.

To get into Time Out Boatyard, and the fuel dock, just follow the headland around, staying about 100 feet offshore. You have to go farther off just before the entrance, and then it is deep to go in. You need good enough light to be able to eyeball it.

Shoals separate the French and Dutch sides of the lagoon, but a channel takes you through. The channel's minimum depth in the center is about 7 feet and it was very well marked. If you go through the channel, leave the red buoys on your port side, until the last one, which you leave to starboard.

Port de Glaisbay is a new commercial deepwater port in the northeast part of Baie de Marigot.

Regulations

Your clearance procedures are done by the port authority, which handles all the official business. They are in a small office in the ferry dock complex. They open weekdays from 0930-1130, and 1400-1600; Saturday, 0800-1200. While Marigot is the only port of entry, they do not really mind if you take a taxi down to clear from one of the other French anchorages. If you need to clear outside office hours, contact Marina Fort Louis, and they may be able to arrange it. You pay an entry fee of 5 Eu, then, if you are staying in Marigot Bay (this does not apply to inside the lagoon), you pay a fee depending on your boat length.

The initial administrative fee, including first day's anchoring charges:

8-13 meters, 20 Eu, 13-18 meters, 30 Eu, 18-23 meters, 40 Eu, 28-33 meters, 60 Eu, 33-38 meters, 70 Eu, 38-43 meters, 100 Eu, 43-50 meters, 120 Eu, 50-75 meters, 130 Eu, over 75 meters, 150 Eu. Thereafter, non-resident boats pay 0.25 Eu per meter per day up to day 3. From day 4 on, they pay 0.35 Eu per meter. Resident boats pay 0.13 Eu per meter per day. You enter your own data on their computers.

There is a garbage depot just outside the Marina Fort St. Louis and another just outside the Port La Royale Marina exit, which is closest to the captainerie.

Communications

If you are out in the bay, you may be able to pick up Orange wifi or Marina Fort Louis. Marina Fort Louis also has an email

RENAISSANCE ISLANDS

Marina Fort Louis   Chris Doyle

station, as does Marina Port La Royale. Inside the lagoon, TOBY, Polypat, and Geminga have wifi to cover their yards. Signals out in the lagoon seem poor. You can find Cyberzone internet café opposite the tourist bureau, and another, called the Business Center, close to Madco.

General Yacht Services

Marina Fort St. Louis (VHF: 16) is run by Semsamar and efficiently managed by Etienne Taquin and several assistants. They all speak English well. This marina has the advantage over Simpson Bay of no bridge to bother with and also of being in the heart of an attractive town. The outer wall has been completed to give protection from seas all around. This marina has 185 berths with water and electricity (110-220-380-volts, single and 3-phase, 60 cycle). They also have showers, toilets, wifi throughout the marina, an email station, and communications, including courier. You will also find a laundry and laundromat, a full provisioning service, and a fuel dock that sells ice. There is plenty of room for small yachts and for about 17 superyachts of up to 200 feet or more. The controlling factor is usually depth, which the marina conservatively rates at 12 feet. Call the marina as you arrive and they will come with a tender to help you tie your mooring line and get you into the dock. Access to the marina is by a magnetic card. If you are anchored out, you can rent a card (good for a year) for 40 Eu, plus a 30 Eu deposit, which is refunded when you return it. This enables you to leave your dinghy at their guarded dinghy dock, a big plus in a town where dinghy thefts happen from time to time. You can also use the marina facilities, although some charges apply. The marina is home to Anchorage and Antisail.com charter companies, Caraibes Yachts (brokers), and 02-Limits Dive Center. This marina helps organize Le Course d'Alliance, three days of racing in November, going from Marigot to St. Barts and Anguilla, before returning. If you just want water, you can come in on the entrance dock outside the office.

Much of Marigot's waterfront is a long dock. The ferries and day charter boats use its northern end; dinghies should be left at the southern end. You can also dinghy into the lagoon and park at the dinghy dock in Port La Royale. This is convenient for the tourist office, which is in the car park, just west of this marina.

Marina Port La Royale Marina (VHF: 16) is very protected and welcomes visitors. Usually you will find a place, but call Regine, the captain, to make arrangements. In addition to docking, they have 50 bow and stern rental moorings. The maximum draft is 6.5 feet. They sell ice and water and have electricity on the docks (220-volt/60 cycles, 110 volts possible). They also offer showers, and a laundry. Marina Port La Royale is home to several charter companies and brokerage houses, most a few steps from the marina office. If you are ready for a change of boat, whatever the kind, big or small, visit Montaine at Must, near the marina office. They have plenty of people looking for boats and many on offer.

Next door, Anyway Marine Charter Company are sales and service agents for Lagoon, Nautitech, Beneteau, and Fontain Pajot, and can sell you one of these, or if you have one, they can sort out your problems. They also have a charter fleet, mainly catamarans, both bareboat and with skipper. They sell new and second hand yachts – mainly the brands they represent. If you buy a new suitable boat, they can charter it for you.

Pascal's Rêve Marine can rent you a little run-about; he has a good range on hand, some parked right in front of his office.

Just outside Marina Fort Louis, Emeric Monnier has a charter company, called MP Yachting, that charters power boats by the day. He is also the sales and service agent for Jeanneau and will take care of all their problems. Other services are on the north shore of the lagoon on the way to Sandy Ground. Geminga is a haul out yard just southwest of the marina. They haul yachts with an 18-ton trailer (good for cats and monohulls) and can store about 200 boats.

You can work yourself, bring in help, or they can find contractors to help you. They also have a 15-boat docking facility with water and electricity (220 volt).

JMC Marina and Boatyard is a little farther down the road. They haul boats with a 70-ton marine hoist that takes up to 23-foot beam, or otherwise they have a 135-ton crane in the yard. JC Constanzo, the owner, insists that masts come out for storage, and in the summer he digs boats down into the sand for security. He also has a small docking facility. You can do the work yourself, bring in people from outside, or choose from several services that are available on his premises.

TOBY, the new name for the old Time Out Boatyard, is in Sandy Ground, on the north side of the entrance channel, inside the lagoon. This slightly disorderly but cheerful place is owned and run by Englishman Michael Butterfield. They have a stern-to (with moorings) docking facility on the north side, offering water and 220-volt electricity. There is a large area for haul out and repair. They haul boats up to 15-tons, using a 40-ton crane. Hot showers, washing machines, toilets, email service, and storage lockers are available. Free wifi covers the yard. You can do your own work or use the workshops on the premises.

Jean Claude, the prior manager runs a marine flea market at TOBY on the first

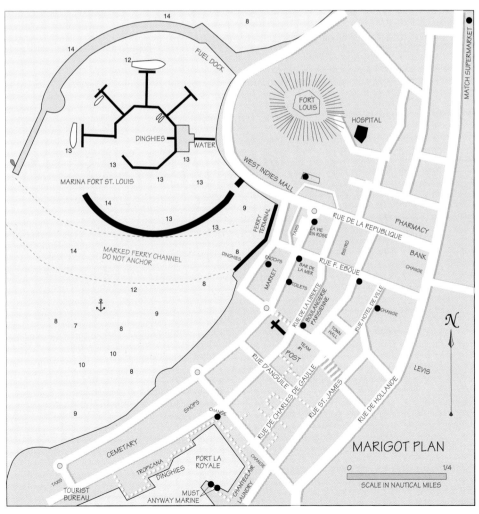

MARIGOT PLAN

Saturday of each month, starting about 0830. If you have a lot of old gear to sell, you can get a stall for free, but you must book it in advance. Otherwise, come see what others have to sell. The market takes on a carnival atmosphere, with the addition of bars and roadside barbecues. Time Out also runs an annual crazy craft race towards the end of the hurricane season.

Jean-Claude is the coxswain for the French SNSM and the rescue boat is berthed at the marina. Rescue efforts are coordinated by MRCC in Martinique. They stand by on VHF: 16, (0690-76-75-00) and their repeaters cover the entire French territory and beyond. Polypat Caraibes is a haul out yard on the south side of the bridge run by Fred Wojcik, who, despite his name, is French, and he speaks good English. They haul with a 60-ton crane, which also makes removing masts easy. You can do the work yourself or they can do it for you, especially painting and fiberglass repairs. They are a registered

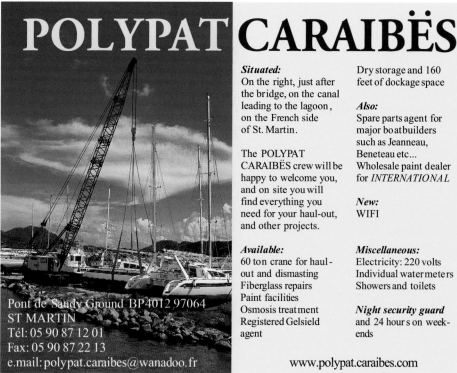

THE FRENCH SIDE OF SIMPSON BAY LAGOON

Gelshield agent for osmosis treatment and they can also do airless spraying of antifouling. If you want to bring in outside contractors, you need to discuss it with Fred. The yard has showers, toilets, 220-volt electricity, water to all the boats, wifi, and 24-hour security.

On one side of this compound, TMTT has a small docking facility for about 6-boats. Services are planned. Ask for Terry the metal-working guy (see Technical yacht services section). Apart from Marina Fort St. Louis, three other fuel docks are available, all with shops selling beer, oils, and accessories. Gess Marine is at the outside entrance to the canal, is open daily 0630-1800, and has over 9 feet at the dock. Boat Services fuel dock is to the north of Time Out is run by David and Virginie. They open daily 0700-1800 and have 9 feet of water on their dock. Cadisco is a fuel dock with easier access next to JMC Marina, open daily 0700-2000.

Chandlery

Right at the entrance to the canal, with access to the water, is L'Ile Marine, a full chandlery shop, the main yacht chandlery for the area. They work with Budget Marine, and can quickly bring in anything from the catalog. In addition to the Budget stock, they are also agent for Maxsea software, Dessalor water makers and Iridium communications. They carry alternative brands of antifouling and all the French emergency equipment.

Madco is the biggest marine store, and heavily geared to fishing and sports boating, with yacht gear as well, and they are are a major Mercury agent. Upstairs is a department geared to swimming pool and garden equipment.

Madco is a great place to come for fishing gear up to a professional level, and you can find some kayaks and other crafts. They carry an excellent fastener section, all in 316 stainless, including new kinds of hinges and hex head fasteners, plus you will find general boating accessories and some yacht gear, including Plastimo. To get there, start at the marina office and head away from the water to the road. Turn right, and when you come to a big shopping area, you will see it down a street to your right.

Close to Madco, but out on the main road, is Home n' Tools, a large DIY, houseware, lumber, and hardware store, perfect for those with a project boat. They stock exterior grade ply, cut to any square size you need. Boat Paint and Stuff, in Time Out Boatyard, sells paints, resins, and cloth, with good deals on antifouling.

Team Number One, opposite the Town Hall, is a water sports shop, with fishing, snorkeling, and diving gear. Around the corner, Surf'ace sells surfing, sailboarding, and water skiing wear and gear.

If you need personal protection, check out Carib Arm, a gun shop that stocks CS gas canisters and flare guns, as well as lots of fancy knives and survival gear. It is down a small alley off Avenue General de Gaulle, on the north side of Rue d'Anguille.

Technical Yacht Services
Sailmakers, Canvas, Cushions

Voile Caraibe is a large, full-service sail loft that also produces new sails of the Incidences brand. They are part of a Caribbean chain with two other stores in Martinique and can tackle any kind of repair job or order you a new sail. They can also do canvas and cushion work, as well as make biminis or cushion covers. It is also possible to order a sail in Martinique and pick it up here, or the other way around. They are behind L'Ile Marine. At SXM Sellerie in TOBY, you will find Stephanie who does all kind of canvas and interior upholstery work, as well as making awnings and biminis.

Jean Allaire's Grenadine SARL, is in JMC boatyard. They are sail-makers who also do canvas work. They are agents for Doyle Sails, sell new Delta Voile sails, and repair all sails and canvas.

Technical Yacht Services
Mechanics and Metalwork

Sandy Ground is the main area for yacht services in Marigot. Most of them are near the opening bridge. It is within walking distance of town but it is easier to visit by dinghy.

Ocean Xperts, the Yamaha agent is right on the corner by the bridge. This is a large store with its own waterfront area, and the only Yamaha agent on St. Martin. They work with the whole Yamaha line of products, including motor-bikes, as well as marine equipment. They offer sales, full service, and a big range of parts. In addition, they sell two lines of inflatables; Apex and the higher-end Prestige brand. They also sell runabouts by Hydra-Sports, Seaswire, and Glasstream.

In Time Out Boatyard, Greg Mechanique will take care of all your mechanical problems. Next to Time Out is Tony Parrondo's Minville Marine. Tony is the sales and service agent for Suzuki motors. He has small dinghy dock right by his office for yacht tenders wanting to shop at the US supermarket, and a direct walkway to it (See our Provisioning section).

At the entrance to the complex is an excellent general engineering shop called Mendall Engineering (VHF: 16). This family run business was started by Nuno and is now run by his daughters, Carla and Sandra, and his nephew, Mario. They are an excellent mechanical shop, with full machining and welding capabilities for all metals. They can work on electrics, and mechanics, including complete engine or

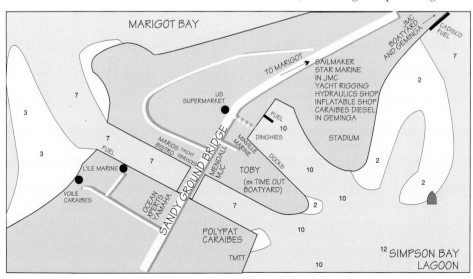

propeller rebuilds. They work fast and will fix all makes of engine, though they specialize in Detroit, Perkins, John Deere, Caterpillar, Dorman, and Deutz. They fix nearly all brands of generator. If they lack parts, they can easily order them. They speak French, Portuguese, and perfect English. In the same compound, Mark's MJC is a good welding and fabrication workshop. He works in all metals and does custom fabrication and can repair anything metal, including bent stanchions and bent propellers, but he leaves mechanical repairs to Mendall.

Just north, in part of the Polypat compound, you will find Englishman Terry, who will fix anything metal you break or bend. He can weld aluminum and stainless, and has a machine shop. He also does mast work and fixes many pushpits.

In Geminga, you will find an excellent diesel shop called Caraibes Diesel Services, owned by Erwan, who is also part of the SNSM lifeboat team. They are subagents for Volvo, through Frank Agren's Inboard Diesel Service in Martinique, and they are also agents for Caterpillar, which will be of interest to the large yachts. Erwin and his team will also work on any make of diesel and get you running again.

Also in Geminga is JMC, a hydraulics shop. They will handle all hydraulic problems and sell hydraulic equipment, including the Lecomble and Schmitt brand. In the same compound, Christiann's MGS is a metal fabrication shop. They weld in all metals and have a machine shop, and so can fix almost anything.

Technical Yacht Services
Fiberglass and Painting

Star Marine, run by Mathieu Yvon, is in JMC boatyard. He speaks English and does all manner of fiberglass repairs, including really large ones. He has a machine for osmosis and he spray paints topsides and antifouling. He also has several molds and builds runabout powerboats.

In Geminga, Pascal Register is the glass man and does most of the structural repairs on boats in the yard.

Technical Yacht Services
Rigging, Dinghy Repair, Carpentry

Patrick is the rigger. His shop, which is in Geminga is called Yacht Rigging, and he has a very professional, custom-designed workshop. Patrick used to work with, and still has connections to, Caraibes-Greement in Martinique. He can handle all rigging problems. He is an agent for Profurl, ACMO, Z-Spars, Facnor, Flexboat and Arimar. He can swage rigging to 16mm. In the same compound, you will find Patrick, who sells and repairs all inflatable craft. Away from the waterfront, down behind Match Supermarket, Philippe Caamano has an excellent wood-working shop, called Caamano Marine. He has good machinery, a computerized design office, and also a special dust-free varnishing and finishing room. He can do everything from interior design to beautiful cabinetry and veneer work. He specializes in marine work and can satisfy the most demanding super-yacht customers. You do

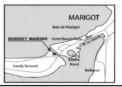
not have to drop by: he visits yachts all over Simpson Bay, just give him a call.

Provisioning

Yacht Services (normally open 0800-1730, but closed mid May to October) is next to the French bridge. It is a charming place, with a big patio open to the canal so you can come alongside in your tender. It is owned by Suzie Friedrich, who used to have a charter yacht and who offers first-rate megayacht services, including full provisioning. She handles everything from renting planes to port clearances. Some of what she does is also of interest to cruising yachts. Suzie offers excellent buys on cases of beer, has bargain as well as top quality wines, and she sells frozen vacuum-packed portions of meat and fish for easy storage. Suzie is very welcoming and willing to share information about the island. Drop by and pick up her provisioning list.

A water and bread delivery service had just started up; ask whether it is still going

RENAISSANCE ISLANDS

Marina Fort Louis

115

on the cruisers morning net (VHF:14, 0730).

The market is always colorful, with numerous stalls selling local handicrafts. Wednesdays and Saturdays are the main food market days, when fruit and fish sellers arrive from Dominica, and the waterfront is crowded with shoppers looking for bargains. US Supermarket (SuperMarché Import) is your easiest solution for a large shopping. It can be approached by dinghy. (Leave it by Minville Marine.) This is a big supermarket, good enough for a full provisioning for most yachts, with a big selection of duty-free liquors and tobacco, fresh produce, seafood, meat, delicatessen items, and ice, as well as all the staples. A special walkway allows you to take your trolley to your dinghy. They open every day 0730-2100. A café is just outside.

Match, on the outskirts of town heading toward Grand Case, is another, somewhat fancier, huge supermarket with everything for a major provisioning. It opens daily from 0900-2000, except Sunday when they close at noon. It is within easy walking distance of the waterfront, but when you return loaded, you will want to ask the receptionist by the cash register to telephone for a taxi.

For just a couple of items, liquor, or cases of beer, Krishna is just outside Marina Royale near the capitainerie and Waterfront Grocery is just across the road from the Marigot market. Marina Fort St. Louis has a full provisioning service. Upstairs in the West Indies Mall, Hediard is a very fancy champagne and gourmet store, where you can get caviar, foie gras, and smoked salmon for provisioning, or to eat there. On the entrance channel side of Time Out Boatyard, Gaetan sells live lobsters out of a pen. On the other side, outside the marina near the landing for the US supermarket, Michael Minville has a fishing complex. For boats going out, he sells baitfish and ice, for those needing fish, he sells both fish and lobster and has some huge freezers for holding it.

On the other side, if you walk from

Marina Royale a few steps towards Madco, you come to West Indies Lobster, where they bring lobster in from Saba.

Fun Shopping

When quality counts, Marigot is St. Martin's premiere shopping area. You can buy anything here from an inexpensive, brightly colored t-shirt to chocolates that cost more than precious stones. The shops are cool and you are far from milling cruise ship passengers. If you start in the main harbor, your first stop should be the fancy, new West Indies Mall, with all its stores and restaurants. Stroll up Rue de La Republique, renowned for its jewelry and precious ornaments. Next, wander down Rue Hotel de Ville and onto Rue Charles de Gaulle, where you can augment your wardrobe. Wander down and explore both sides of the marina, where there are many striking clothes shops. Also, inside the marina is an area where vendors set up stands selling all kinds of souvenirs.

In the same area as Madco, @utodeal is a big computer store, with lots of computers and accessories. The listed price of the computers is competitive with Philipsburg, though I suspect the Dutch side may offer a bigger discount.

You will find plenty of places to change money, though if you have US dollars, this is unnecessary, as everyone accepts the greenback.

Restaurants

If shopping hasn't given you an appetite, try walking up to Fort St. Louis. It is an attractive old ruin with a few cannons and a bird's-eye view of the marina, the bay, and Simpson Bay Lagoon.

Eating out is a pleasure in Marigot, well known for its restaurants, which span the range from cheap and cheerful bistros to gourmet wallet busters. Walking and looking is part of the fun, I mention just a few.

The market area includes a large building, which houses many worker-style cafés and bars, offering a local Créole lunch very inexpensively. A particular favorite seems to be Enoch's, which faces the waterfront. While on the cheap and cheerful, La Boulangerie Parisienne, near the post office, is a fine boulangerie/patisserie with a shady pavement seating area and a fine range of sandwiches and tasty pastries. Visit for a breakfast of fresh coffee and croissants: walk home with some excellent bread. There are several other equally nice boulangeries for breakfast or lunch, including La Croissanterie in the marina and Le Colibri on Rue de Charles de Gaulle. For a special night out, when you want really good French cooking, an excellent choice is La Vie en Rose looking out over the water. Expect first-rate French cuisine and attentive service. It is also a delightful place for coffee or lunch where you can sit outside and watch life go by in the best French manner. It is in a fine traditional building.

For the cheap and cheerful crowd, the Bar de La Mer and Bistro de La Mer are side by side with reasonable prices and food. In the West Indies Mall, Keops Café is a very fancy café where you can get a surprisingly moderately priced lunch, The marina is also a popular restaurant area, with some great restaurants looking out on the boats. Tropicana here is excellent, and it's a good value, but it gets full, so you may need to go early or book. La Belle Epoque is also inexpensive and very acceptable. Check out the more up-market Chanteclair for fine food. You might want to consider Mario's Bistro out by the bridge where you can arrive by dinghy. It opens at 1630, is fancy and excellent. He serves contemporary French cuisine. It is popular so you will absolutely need to make a reservation.

Water Sports

02-Limits Dive Center is in Marina Fort St. Louis. It is run by Paul and Cedric who dive four times a day.

Friars Bay

Friars Bay, just before Grand Case, is a popular day-time anchorage, with a fair beach and very active beach bar. The approach is easy, just head in and anchor in about 16 feet of water. Avoid this place in northerly or northwesterly swells.

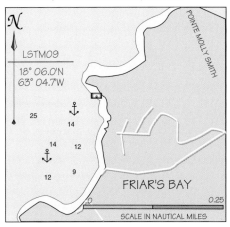

Grand Case

Baie Grand Case is a long sweeping beach-fronted bay and the town, built along the beach, is known as the gastronomic center of St. Martin, so be prepared to eat out. The anchorage is generally good for overnighting, though occasionally rolly.

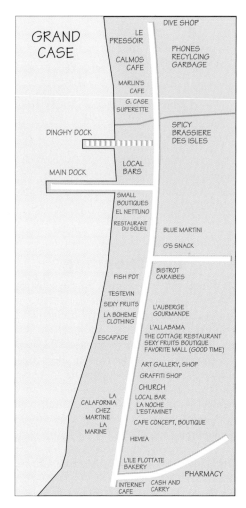

Grand Case is home of the French-side airport.

Navigation

At the southwestern end of the bay, about 150 yards northeast of Pointe Molly Smith, is a reef about 5 feet deep. There is 19 feet of water inside the reef. Pass inside in good light, passing between the reef and the headland, but note that there are also some rocks close to the headland. Alternatively, stay at least half of a mile off Pointe Molly Smith. The northern end of the bay gets some protection from Rocher Créole, a conspicuous rock island some 100 feet high. There are underwater rocks close to the island. It is best to pass outside

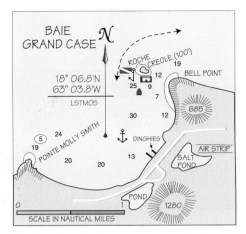

Rocher Créole, though you can find a passage some 12 feet deep between Rocher Créole and Bell Point, which is quite navigable except in bad swells. The bottom shelves to depths of 8 to 9 feet just before the passage on the Grand Case side, limiting the depth of boats that can use it. Anchor anywhere off the town docks in sand and weeds.

Communications & Services

The dinghy dock is convenient. A few dinghy thefts have been reported here, so take the normal precautions. However glass-bottom boats sometimes uses this dock and you need to tie up out of their way. This is not usually a problem in the evenings. The places to buy card phones and dump your garbage are opposite Calmos Café. If you come off the dock and turn right, the DVPRO Internet Café and Computer Store is towards the end of town. They are reasonably priced and have US and French keyboards set up. They also offer an onboard wifi, which covers Grand Case and Orient Bay. You buy a ticket from them; their signal is very good. They open Monday to Saturday 0930-1800.

You can top up on provisions or buy ice from any of the small supermarkets. Calmos Café offers free wifi.

Ashore

Grand Case is one long street of gaily-painted houses, most of them restaurants.

Many are elegant and serve first-rate French cuisine; others are cute and inexpensive. All restaurants have menus with prices posted outside, and half the fun is to get up an appetite by reading them while walking along. Several local bars look out over the sea between the two docks. Their barbecues go full time and you get inexpensive barbecued food in these bars, with plenty of beer to wash it down. They specialize in spare ribs, but also have fish, chicken, conch, and sometimes lobster. Since this is the area for fine food, you may choose to go up-market. If you stick with the restaurants that have been around a while, you will be happy – the reputation of the whole town depends on it! L'Auberge Gourmand, Testevin, L'Allabama, Fish Pot, Escapade, and The Cottage have all stood the test of time with a reputation for good food.

Le Pressoir, owned by chef Stephan, is set in an adorable Caribbean building, which has been tastefully decorated. Stephan offers good traditional French cuisine at moderate prices.

An excellent night to come is Tuesday for much of the season, when they have "harmony nights." They close off the street, bring out the music, vendors line the streets, and the whole town becomes a relaxing party. This augments rather than detracts from the fine dining. The best beach hangout is the Calmos Café, run by Alex (VHF: 16). It's open every day from 1030 to 2200, with tables on the beach, facing the sea. He offers free wifi, which you might pick up out at anchor, and hopes to have some computers. He has beach chairs and shade, and offers good salads, sandwiches, spare ribs, and local dishes. The barbecue runs most of the day to give you fresh fish and meats. It also has a good atmosphere at night if you are going for the less expensive, simpler food, and, in season, he has live bands twice a week. Currently the big night is Tuesday for Latin music. On Sunday it is a gypsy jazz band.

If you wake up the next morning with a terrible hangover, having spent all your money, you will be happy to hear that there

RENAISSANCE ISLANDS

is a large pharmacy in Grand Case that takes credit cards. If one of your crew wakes up early in the morning, send him down to the boulangerie (just before the internet café) to buy fresh croissants and pain au chocolat. They open from 0600.

Shoppers will find a row of vendors close to the docks, and a many little stores all along the main street, which specialize in art, elegant handicrafts, and clothing.

Water Sports

Snorkeling and diving are good around Rocher Créole. In most conditions you can anchor on the south side of Rocher Créole. Best treat this as a daytime anchorage only.

If you start at the northwest point of Rocher Créole, there is good snorkeling and diving around its northern end. Rocher Créole tumbles down into the sea and gives way to a large area of boulders at 33 feet. These are covered with both hard and soft corals and there are many small reef fish, including a giant school of sergeant majors, which live on bread handouts from visitors. Jacks and larger fish are often seen close by. There is a dive shop at the northern end of Grand Case called Octopus. They can refill your tanks and, if you don't have your own gear, you can join them on a dive at 0900 or 1400.

Port La Royale   Chris Doyle

Anse Marcel and Radisson Marina

Anse Marcel is a small, well-indented bay with a beach, two big hotels, and the exclusive Radisson Marina. Radisson Resorts own one of the hotels, the marina, and its surroundings. The outer bay anchorage is very pretty, with a white sand beach and turquoise water. Pelicans often dive together almost in formation and there are loud bird songs at dawn and dusk. Those who love to jet ski will find plenty of company here; those sensitive to their noise may be reduced to quivering wrecks from about ten in the morning to four in the afternoon. The Radisson Marina is small, peaceful, and very well maintained.

Navigation

You need to exercise caution when approaching from the direction of Marigot. After passing Bell Point, head way over toward Pointe des Froussards to go around Marcel Rock before turning into the bay. There is a small bay and beach before this rock, which sometimes causes confusion; Marcel Rock, about 15 feet high, has been mistaken for the118-foot Roche Créole off Bell Point.

Anse Marcel is reasonably well protected, though a surge does get in, especially in the winter months. Anchoring is not always easy, as the bottom sand is covered in thick weed. In addition, the wind swings from all directions. If you anchor bow and stern, you can cut down on the roll. Keep well clear of the mooring buoy in the southwest of the bay, as it belongs to the giant day charter cat Scubi Two, which swings all over the place.

The entrance to the Radisson Marina is by a clearly marked, narrow channel, about a quarter of a mile long, with only room for one yacht at a time, so sound your horn before going in. (There is a passing point half way down.) The channel is dredged to 9 feet. The marina is completely protected. The starboard marker and light was missing in January 2009.

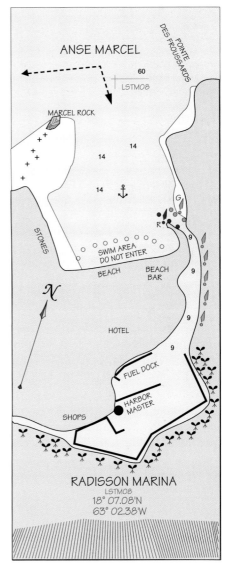

Regulations

You may clear in and out of the French side with Olivier, the port captain.

Services

Docking, water, ice, and showers are available at the 145-berth marina (VHF: 16, switch to 11). The fuel dock will be rebuilt shortly. Olivier, the harbormaster will drum up help, from a mechanic to an electronics expert, to work on your boat.

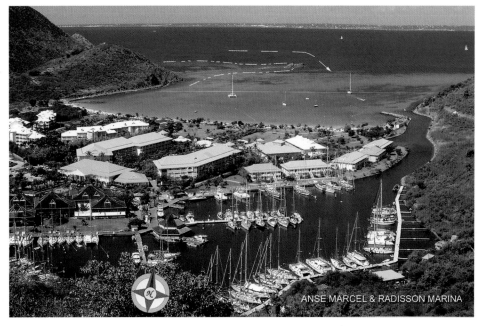

ANSE MARCEL & RADISSON MARINA

For much of the time they use Sun Maintenance, which is close by. It is run by a Dominican who speaks both English and French. Faxes may be sent. Wifi is available throughout the marina and you can make phone calls at Marina Presse. Do your weekly wash in the big washing machine in the port office building. You can rent a car through Olivier. Those anchoring outside but wishing to eat or shop in the marina will find a place to leave the dinghy. The marina is home to VPM Best Sail Charter Company.

Ashore

You can buy essentials at Picnic Superette. Boutiques sell clothing, elegant

Anse Marcel

Chris Doyle

122

household essentials and beachwear. The shop called Jocker has lots of games. You can look in the art gallery and pick up magazines and books or papers of your choice at Marina Presse. Given a little notice, Lili, the owner, will arrange any special paper you want during your stay. She also sells telephone cards and has a phone you can use to make calls.

Calypso is the main restaurant and is open from breakfast though to dinner every day, with both a café area and a more formal dining room. They specialize in seafood and make a special "fish pot calypso." In the same block, you will find La Locanda, a wine bar and trattoria. You can wander down to the beach for a beach bar and you will find a couple of other restaurants among the hotels.

Water Sports

Ready to go diving? Try Scuba Fun Caraibes, a full scuba shop in the marina. In the morning they take out certified divers, reserving their afternoons for resort courses and snorkeling, though some days they go all day to St. Barts. Scuba Fun rents gear to those going on charter and sells a good assortment of diving and snorkeling gear, including tanks and BC's from the Scuba Shop at well below American list price.

When the weather allows, Scuba Fun visits one of their prime local sites, Spanish Rock. This underwater reef varies in depth from 7 to 45 feet and includes a wall. Being in the middle of nowhere, the water clarity is usually excellent. Lobsters are common and it is a feeding ground for doctor fish. There is also a chance of seeing rays, turtles, and nurse sharks.

The Circus at Tintamarre is another of their popular sites. The dive here goes to 55 feet and includes lots of small caves and hiding holes which house the huge profusion of reef fish that gave it its name.

Sports fishing trips can be arranged on large comfortable fishing yachts. Ask at the marina.

RENAISSANCE ISLANDS

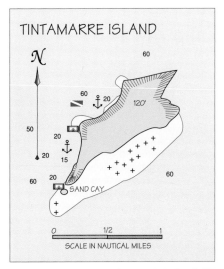

TINTAMARRE ISLAND

SCALE IN NAUTICAL MILES

FROM ANSE MARCEL TO TINTAMARRE

You can sail around the northern coast, staying a few hundred yards offshore. Spanish Rock is an offshore danger. It lies a good three-quarters of a mile off Pointe Nord, just north of a line joining the northernmost parts of St. Martin and Tintamarre. From Spanish Rock you can just see Rocher Créole, looking like it is part of the mainland. Spanish Rock is about 7 feet below the surface, which is too deep to see easily and too shallow to pass over. It breaks in heavy weather. If coming from the west, do not try to go outside it; it is so far off that you might hit it, thinking you had gone around it. Pass inside, sailing safely anywhere from a few hundred yards to half a mile off Pointe Nord. If you are coming from the Scrub Island Channel in Anguilla, head for Tintamarre Island and thus stay outside. Make sure the current does not set you down onto it.

Tintamarre

Tintamarre is a flatish island about 120 feet high and just over a mile long. There is a superb beach along its western shore which you will see very clearly if you are approaching from the west. The southwestern point of Tintamarre has a reef extending from it, which is easily identified by a small sand cay. The reef extends well beyond the sand cay, so give it wide clearance. A bank of sand and weed suitable for anchoring extends several hundred yards from the beach. Depths start at 24 feet and slowly shelve toward the shore. Normally, you can anchor here for lunch and overnight in calm conditions, though it can roll. In heavy swells you may want to give it a miss as landing the dinghy can be risky. The beach is fabulous and paths lead over to the southern shore where another long beach lies protected behind a barrier reef.

TINTAMARRE

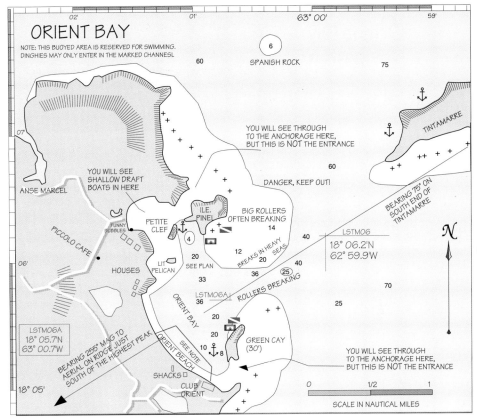

ORIENT BAY

NOTE: THIS BUOYED AREA IS RESERVED FOR SWIMMING. DINGHIES MAY ONLY ENTER IN THE MARKED CHANNESL

6

SPANISH ROCK

60

75

TINTAMARRE

YOU WILL SEE THROUGH TO THE ANCHORAGE HERE, BUT THIS IS NOT THE ENTRANCE

60

YOU WILL SEE SHALLOW DRAFT BOATS IN HERE

ANSE MARCEL

DANGER, KEEP OUT!

BEARING 75° ON SOUTH END OF TINTAMARRE

PICCOLO CAFE

FUNNY BUBBLES

PETITE CLEF

ILE. PINEL

BIG ROLLERS OFTEN BREAKING

14

4

40

LSTM06

18° 06.2'N 62° 59.9'W

HOUSES

LIT PELICAN

SEE PLAN

12

BREAKS IN HEAVY SEAS

20

36

40

25

70

33

36

LSTM06A 36

ROLLERS BREAKING

25

ORIENT BAY

20

LSTM06A 18° 05.7'N 63° 00.7'W

BEARING 255° MAG TO AERIAL ON RIDGE JUST SOUTH OF THE HIGHEST PEAK

20

20

10

8

GREEN CAY (30')

YOU WILL SEE THROUGH TO THE ANCHORAGE HERE, BUT THIS IS NOT THE ENTRANCE

SEE NOTE

ORIENT BEACH

SHACKS

CLUB ORIENT

0   1/2   1

SCALE IN NAUTICAL MILES

18° 05'

N

02'   01'   63° 00'   59'

07'

06'

Water Sports

If you snorkel north of the beach, you will find lots of colorful reef fish and the water is generally very clear. You can also do a photogenic dive here in 37 to 50 feet. Farther out, a sunken tug is encrusted with sea fans and other soft corals and there are lots of angelfish, sergeant majors, sennets, and snappers. To find the tugboat, take your dinghy around the northern end of the beach and head northeast. As you go, look behind you and line up the end of the rocky point north of the beach with the easternmost tip of St. Martin. The tugboat lies on this transit line. A buoy sometimes marks the site, but if it is missing, look for a large oval patch of turquoise water with a dark patch in the middle. Bring a good 100-feet of dinghy anchor line to anchor in the sand to the side of the wreck, not on the wreck itself.

ST. MARTIN'S EAST COAST

This windward coast can be rough and dangerous, but it does have several good anchorages. These should only be approached in moderate sea and wind conditions, and even then with caution.

There are reefs and rough water down most of the east coast, so give it a wide berth, unless you are entering a harbor. The offshore rocks at the south end of the east coast (Cow and Calf, Molly Beday, Pelikan, and Hen and Chicks) should be given good clearance. They can all be seen in normal conditions. Molly Beday and Pelikan are 100 feet high and make good landmarks. The others are low, but the mariner who keeps a good look out and is not sailing right into the sun, should have no difficulty. For specific instructions for sailing to Orient Bay from any direction, see Orient Bay, below.

Orient Bay
Navigation

Orient Bay can be both dangerous and difficult. Read all parts of this navigation section and the sections on Green Cay and Ile Pinel before you approach. Orient Bay is a large bay open to the east, and subject to rolling onshore seas. However, there are reasonably protected anchorages in both the northern and southern ends, behind Ile Pinel and Green Cay (Caye Verte). As winds approach 20 knots or more, the waves are steep and consistently breaking in depths of 20 feet or less. It is unwise to enter in these conditions. Do not enter during the afternoon, when the sun is in your eyes. This is the area in which charter boats have the most serious problems. About six were lost or badly damaged in one year alone, either trying to enter south of Green Cay, or being rolled in the big seas east of Pinel. (See our sketch chart, page 125.) Once inside, take care when going into Ile Pinel. Many charter yachts try to go around the wrong side of Petite Clef and run aground. If you follow the directions carefully and approach with a little apprehension, you should be fine. Keep the following things in mind: whether you come from north or south, you should have at least 25 feet of water all the way into Orient Bay and for much of the time the depths will be 30 to 60 feet. If you find yourself in less than 25 feet for more than a few moments, then turn around and head out again. The gap between the two islands is about a mile wide. If you approach an entrance that looks about a quarter of a mile wide, it is wrong. Turn around and go back out. If either of these things occur, or you are unsure of your position, sail over to Tintamarre and follow our approach directions from there. (See also "From Anse Marcel to Tintamarre," above, with instructions on how to avoid Spanish Rock.)

Approaching from the North. Between the north coast of St. Martin and Tintamarre, you will see the Ile Pinel anchorage through the gap between Ile Pinel and the mainland. Do not mistake this gap for the entrance.

If you look at our sketch chart of Orient Bay, you will see that there is a shoal bank, 12 to 20 feet deep, over the northern half of the bay that extends a long way offshore. This shoal, also clearly visible in our aerial photo, is missing from most other charts. Huge, dangerous, breaking seas build up here, so it must be avoided. If you follow our safe approach, you will be in 30 to 60 feet most of the way, with the occasional short bank of maybe 25 feet. If the depths are less than 25 feet, head back out again. The safest and easiest route is to sail right over to the beach at Tintamarre and start from there.

From the beach at Tintamarre, steer a course of 230° magnetic, which will take you in the direction of Green Cay. As an added aid, the entrance channel is on a line between the southern tip of Tintamarre and some aerials on a high ridge just to the south of the highest mountain you can see. The bearing is about 255°

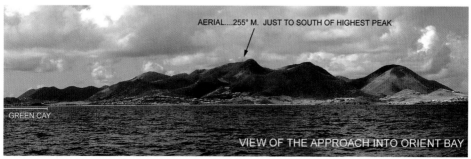

View of the approach into Orient Bay.

Chris Doyle

Tintemarre

Chris Doyle

magnetic to the aerials going in and 75° magnetic to the south of Tintamarre coming out. As you approach the bay, you will see two new conspicuous developments onshore on your starboard bow. One of them has mostly green roofs, though there are some red ones as well, and the other has mainly white buildings.

As you get closer, you can identify Green Cay and you will see breaking water on the reef around it. Sail in around the north of this reef and Green Cay. If you like using waypoints, we give a couple on our sketch chart that might prove helpful.

Approaching from the South. The problem when sailing from the south is to correctly identify Green Cay. It is low lying (30 feet high) and merges perfectly into the background. The headland at the end of Orient Beach looks like an island, which adds to the confusion. It is important to read the following directions carefully.

After you leave Oyster Pond, keep a quarter to a half-mile offshore. The next landmark, just under a mile from Oyster Pond, is a group of large rocks that extend from the southern end of Baie des Flamandes. Sail for almost another mile past these rocks, passing Baie des Flamandes. Try to identify the false entrance to Green Cay as you sail by. You will see a big sweep of beach and probably some anchored yachts. At some point, you will see the big pink housing development. You will see what looks like a clear entrance about a quarter of a mile wide. Do not mistake this for the entrance! You cannot even approach it for a look without running into danger. The water shelves very suddenly and skippers who wrecked themselves here approached cautiously, keeping a good lookout, but found themselves aground before they spotted the shallows. You will get no warning from your echo sounder before you are aground. The island on the right-hand side of this false entrance is Green Cay, and you have to sail on another half mile or so to round it. You may see breakers extending for what seems like a very long way out from Green Cay. The reef does come out a long way here and you may well have to head farther offshore to stay outside it. (Stay in at least 35 feet of water.) As you pass Green Cay, you will see the beach and the yachts disappear behind it.

Once you have passed Green Cay and the reef to its east, you can head on in. You will notice that when you are coming in the correct entrance, the bay is so wide (nearly a mile) that it doesn't have the feel of a channel at all. As you come in, you will start to see masts of the boats in and behind Pinel, almost a mile to the north, and when you get farther inside, you will see the boats off Green Cay. Note the bearings on the radio mast and the south end of Tintamarre given on our sketch chart. Keep the following rule in mind: if you are coming from the south and you are not absolutely sure where you are, sail over to Tintamarre and approach from there instead (see above).

Approaching Orient Bay from St. Barts. Sail to the beach at Tintamarre and enter as from the north (above).

Ile Pinel Anchorage

The Ile Pinel anchorage is good for an overnight stop, though it does sometimes get rolly. Ile Pinel is a park and a perfect

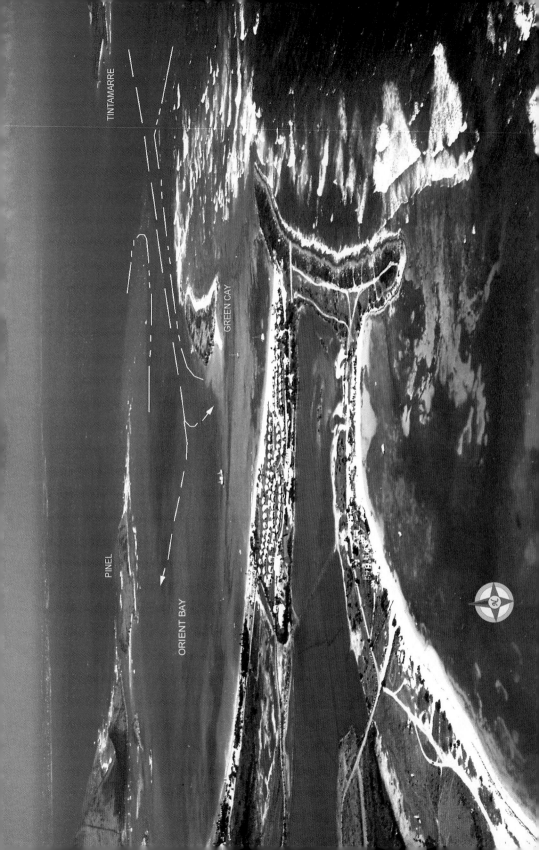

TINTAMARRE

GREEN CAY

PINEL

ORIENT BAY

Robinson Crusoe island with sandy beaches, waving palms, and a couple of hills, the highest one rising to about 100 feet. Closer to shore, Petite Clef is rocky, wild, and inaccessible. The anchorage is between these islands. It is a delightful spot, but there is barely room for a dozen boats, and it often gets crowded. St. Martin Marine Park may one day put in moorings. Until then, ignore any no anchoring signs.

Navigation

Approaching Pinel from Green Cay. Many yachts have a problem here because

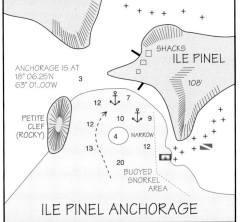

ANCHORAGE IS AT
18° 06.25'N
63° 01..00'W

SHACKS
ILE PINEL
108'
PETITE CLEF (ROCKY)
NARROW
BUOYED SNORKEL AREA

ILE PINEL ANCHORAGE

the anchored yachts cause confusion. Besides the boats in Ile Pinel, you can see many more anchored well to the west of Ile Pinel, in an anchorage behind Petite Clef. This mainly shoal anchorage is reached through a twisty reef-strewn passage to the north of Ile Pinel. It is strictly an anchorage for local boats with intimate knowledge of the reefs. However, the presence of these yachts leads many a navigator to try to enter this bay to the south of Petite Clef – and run hard aground.

Once inside Orient Bay, do not head into Pinel until you are alongside Green Island and can see right up into the lee of Ile Pinel. Make sure you can distinguish boats anchored here from those inside Petite Clef. And make sure you have correctly identified Ile Pinel and Petite Clef. Do not attempt to go inside Petite Clef or Little Pelican from the south, as it is all shallow and dangerous. There is also a 4-foot shoal right at the entrance to the Ile Pinel anchorage, marked with a small buoy. Leave it to starboard and you will arrive in the anchorage facing the wind, ready to anchor.

Ashore

The island is great to explore, with little footpaths everywhere. There are several

ILE PINEL
PETITE CLEF
DO NOT TRY TO ENTER HERE
LITTLE PELICAN

little beaches and the view from the hills is worth the easy climb (take shoes). On the shore are three attractive small restaurants (lunch only), with lots of beach umbrellas for day visitors, of which there can be many. They never venture far from the beach and are always gone by night. You might be able to leave your dinghy on the Karibuni dock across the spit, but ask first. If you take your dinghy around Petite Clef and back to the head of the big bay, you will find some small dinghy docks in very shallow water. If you walk back down the road, heading out as if to the main road, you will come to a few restaurants and shops.

Water Sports

For snorkelers and scuba divers, there is a reef around the southern end of Ile Pinel. It is easily accessible from your yacht and only about 25 feet deep. Swim out inside the snorkeling zone marked by buoys and carry on around the reef. Much of the reef is an interesting skeleton, full of caverns and holes, which make hiding places for reef fish. It is decorated by lots of soft corals.

Green Cay Anchorage

Green Cay is a low-lying island with a sandy beach at one end. To its south is the long and lovely Orient Beach, the liveliest beach in St. Martin, and the eastern part is well known as the spot where holidaymakers come to get a tan free of bikini marks. You can sail into the lee of Green Cay and anchor, or go on a bit farther and drop hook between Green Cay and Orient Beach. It shoals as you go in. This is not a particularly well protected spot, and you would not want to be here in a heavy northerly swell, but on a normal day it makes a good lunch time stop, and you can anchor overnight in settled weather.

A series of yellow buoys protects swimmers from jet skis, speedboats, and dinghies. Make sure you dinghy in through the marked channel at the eastern end of this area.

Ashore

The long beach here is cheerful and lively, packed with colorful beach brollies, bars, boutiques, and bodies, some more naked than others. A carefree holiday atmosphere abounds. You will also find water sports facilities with catamarans, sailboards, parasailing, and jet skis. Kon Tiki is probably the classiest of the restaurants, but also one of the most expensive. Any of them make a pleasant place to sit and watch the world go by. When you tire of the social scene, take a walk down the road and visit the butterfly farm, where you can wander in a large

GREEN CAY

screened garden amid hundreds of brightly-colored butterflies.

Water Sports

It is hard to imagine a better bay for dinghy sailing or sailboarding. At the eastern end you can rent sailboards and 15-foot fast beach cats from Orient Water Sports. They also sell ice. As you wander down the beach, there are many other stalls offering everything from parasailing to snorkeling trips around Green Cay.

The snorkeling around Green Cay is excellent with many sea fans and other soft corals. The easiest place to start is along the north coast of the island. You can wade around from the beach or anchor your dinghy nearby. Scuba divers can also enjoy this site. It is only about 20 feet deep, a good, easy beginner's dive.

Oyster Pond

Oyster Pond is a completely protected lagoon, surrounded by hills. Peaceful, pleasant and small, it makes a great base for seeing St. Martin. You will quickly get to know the staff in all the bars and restaurants and be treated as one of the family. On the outside a superb beach offers good swimming and acceptable snorkeling. It is an easy walk up Fife Hill, with its decorative cactuses and panoramic views. Inside, you can watch pelicans and terns diving, and when you tire of that, there is a good collection of restaurants. Captain Oliver's Marina (VHF: 67), The Moorings (VHF: 77), and Sunsail (VHF: 74) are all here. You can carry about 10 feet of water to the first docks.

Navigation

The approach into Oyster Pond can put hair on your chest. Sometimes you have to run downwind through steep seas onto a lee shore dotted with reefs. Occasionally, the seas get so bad that they break right across the entrance, and at such times it would be foolhardy to go in. At other times, the entrance is straightforward but, even at the best of times, this is no place to make a mistake, and you must be absolutely sure you have everything correctly placed before you enter.

The entrance is marked by an outer blue and white buoy and three red posts. These are privately maintained by Sunsail and Captain Oliver's Marina. Until you see them, do not even think about going in.

From the north you will notice Fife Hill with many buildings below. Keep well outside the reef off Fife Hill until you can identify the markers. Go first to the outer blue and white buoy and leave it close to port, then identify the red posts and head in. Once you are in the channel, stay within 30 feet of the red markers, leaving them to starboard.

From the south you can identify Oyster Pond from the row of many prominent square shaped buildings on the low land, which are part of Oyster Pond Beach Hotel. This is the most built up part of the coast. If you are coming from the south, keep well out in deep water, as if you were going to sail right by Oyster Pond. Turn in when you can enter as if from the north. You must leave the outer blue and white marker to port. A quick glance at the sketch chart will show that cutting the corner toward the channel from the south

would at best take you through the very rough 21-foot patch with the 10-foot shoal in the middle, and at worst land you on the reef.

Keep in mind that this entrance is downwind and down sea. If you are towing a dinghy, take precautions. (Some people like to have their dinghies on very long lines; some like to keep them so short they touch the stern protected by a fender.) If you plan to drop your sails before you enter, do it before you start your approach.

Once you are safely in the inner harbor, you can go into a marina or anchor, if you can find the space. There is a 2-foot shoal right in the middle of the harbor, but shoal draft yachts (3-5 feet) can feel their way in to find anchorage on its west side. Charter companies have placed moorings over most of the available anchoring space so anchoring room is very hard to find.

The band of deep water between Captain Oliver's outer dock and the shallows is so narrow that boats can only tie alongside this dock. If you are passing them, you need to stay very close to them.

When you leave Oyster Pond, you will be doing so against the wind into steep seas. You must power or motor-sail out. If you don't have a large auxiliary, then you

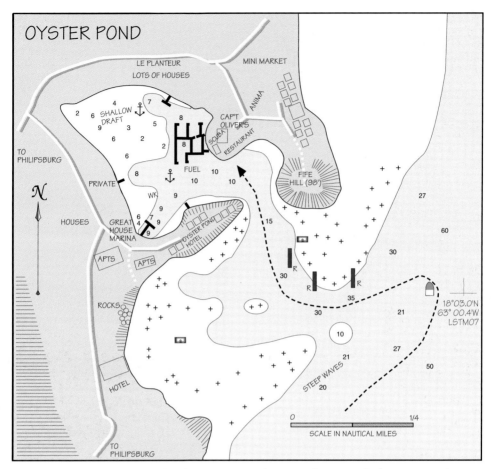

will need the mainsail to help the engine. Have a plan of action should the motor fail on take off.

Communications

Inside the main lobby of Captain Oliver's Hotel is a good little internet station; Anima has one also.

Services

Captain Oliver's 160-berth marina has fuel, water, ice, a grocery store, laundry, dockage, telephones, and fax. He also has garbage facilities for yachts staying in the marina. Car rentals are available. Captain Oliver's stands by on (VHF: 67).

This is a good place to leave your yacht and a boat care program is available. Pascal Erik is the dock master and will help in any way he can. Captain Oliver's fuel dock is open every day, 0815-1645. A laundry will

take care of your wash, leaving you free to visit the activities desk, which offers all kinds of tours.

The charter companies Moorings (VHF: 77) and Sunsail (VHF: 74) are based here. They do not offer any specific outside services, but they are knowledgeable about the area and are happy to give good advice.

Harel Yacht Brokers is in Captain Oliver's marina. Apart from selling boats, they will give you good advice on any kind of repair or service you need.

Great House Marina has a lovely dock for about 14 yachts up to about 8.5-foot draft. They have toilets, water, both 220 and 110-volt electricity, cable TV, and 24-hour security. Great House Marina is part of Brokaar Marine Services. This company, run by John Brokaar, is the best place to come to for commercial diving and salvage.

The man in charge of the fuel dock also

APPROACH TO OYSTER POND

runs a water taxi, on demand, between Captain Oliver's and Great House Marina (for the beach). The hours are the same as the fuel dock's.

Provisioning

Mom and Pop's is a small but fancy market at Great House Marina and they open 0700-2230. They have a good stock of wines, a fair selection of foods, gourmet ethnic sauces and spices, good coffee, ice, and more. For cash, visit the ATM in the lobby of the big Oyster Pond Hotel.

Restaurants

When Captain Oliver first sailed into Oyster Pond in his Gulf Star 50 on a cruise from Florida some 15 years ago, there was not much here. He marveled at the beauty of this perfectly quiet anchorage and decided this had to be the spot for his new enterprise. He sold his two restaurants in Paris and opened "Captain Oliver's" in Oyster Pond. Today, Oyster Pond has become a real estate hot spot, with fancy houses shooting up faster than bean sprouts. Captain Oliver's hotel has beautiful bedrooms, an exercise room, restaurant, and marina. The restaurant is perched on

a platform on the lagoon, overlooking the sea to St. Barts. You can select your own lobster from the pool and, while you have a cocktail, admire the aquarium-like view of the glass-sided swimming pool, as well as view fish through the glass floor. The restaurant is open every day from breakfast to dinner and features nightly entertainment. During the season you can eat a full meal any time of the day.

Matt and Pierre run the Dinghy Dock Bar at Captain Oliver's. Their two-hour happy hour is from 1700-1900, when you can mix your own drinks as strong as you like, making this a potentially dangerous place in a safe harbor. They are open all day and offer not only snacks such as burgers and sandwiches, but also several daily specials that sometimes feature inexpensive lobster and steak meals. They keep about 15 different beers and work hard to make their music the best in the bay. They serve food up until 2200.

You will also find the Yacht Club Piano Bar next door. Just past the Sunsail workshop is a little restaurant that changes owners and names each time I come by. Its present incarnation is Quai Oeust: check it out. The Iguana Bar at Oliver's features

a pleasant platform looking out to sea and open to the breeze. They have a happy hour from 1700-1900, and in the evening, long trousers are appreciated. Iguana Bar serves good Indonesian food. Between the Iguana Bar and the restaurant is an open fish pool with a shark and turtles. For a change of scene, try Anima, a tapas bar right outside the marina gates, or the fancier Le Planteur, farther down the road, with a view over the marina. Or, on the main road north, are a mini market, an art gallery, and two little snack/restaurants: Lolo and Eden. Further attractions are over on the south side, by Great House Marina. On the dock, the Mom and Pop store also has a very nice restaurant, which serves organic fish and meat; open from 1700 onwards. Just across from the dock, Mr. Busby's Beach Bar is open from 1000 and serves both lunch and dinner. The beach location is unbeatable. Indeed, the gorgeous Dawn Beach is one of St. Martin's fairest. You can reach it by passing though Mr. Busby's Beach Bar, right behind Great House Marina. Next to the Great House Marina is the fancy new Oyster Pond Beach Hotel. Behind the lobby, Infinity Bar and Restaurant has a pleasant location with a big menu and lots of special nights. On the grounds is also a Shipwreck Shop. Westin have built a big hotel on Dawn Beach and have restaurants and beach bars.

Water Sports

Snorkeling at the entrance to Oyster Pond is not bad. You can dinghy out or walk over to the beach and swim from there. The best snorkeling is to the south, as far away from the entrance to Oyster Pond as you can get. This also has the advantage that the current usually takes you north along the beach.

Divers setting out on a cruise should contact The Scuba Shop, run by Peter Frye. This excellent shop both sells and rents all kinds of scuba gear. Most of it is priced well below US list and is one of the better duty-free bargains in St. Martin. Scuba Pro, Mares, Shearwood, and Aqualung are all on sale. Peter will also fill

tanks. You can dinghy right up to the shop. Peter has put together an excellent little book, with maps that describes dive sites around the area that are easily accessible by yacht and dinghy. He will give you one of these at no charge. In addition to diving gear, The Scuba Shop sells some great yachting clothes, including some very fancy shorts and shirts (Columbia brand). Both quantity and crew discounts are available. Peter has another shop in Simpson Bay, which is also their gear-servicing center.

The dive sites near Oyster Pond are not easy to do in your yacht. Molly Bidet, the large rock you see right outside, is one of them. This dive is from 30 to 70 feet and has a large elkhorn garden on top. You then go down a wall with dramatic overhangs and there are some impressive coral pinnacles. You are likely to see some large pelagics, as well as all the usual reef fish.

Sports fishing enthusiasts should ask at the activities desk about fishing charters. A big ferry called Voyager makes quite a few runs to St. Barts.

PASSAGE BETWEEN ST. MARTIN AND ST. BARTS

St. Barts lies to the east-southeast of St. Martin. The sail from Philipsburg is usually a 12-mile romp to windward. The relatively shallow water, for the most part less than 100 feet deep, makes the sea a lustrous deep blue. A popular route is to pass between the Groupers and Table Rock, taking a lunch break at Ile Fourchue. If you plan your departure from the north end of St. Martin, rather than from Philipsburg, you can usually make the 15 odd miles in one exhilarating fast tack.

People usually give up sailing and motor after Anse de Colombier, as the winds get very fickle. The return trip is usually a run. If the wind gets dead behind, you can always tack downwind to make for an easier sail.

Gustavia from Fort Gustav Chris Doyle

St. Barthelemy (St. Barts)

FOR THE SAILOR, ST. BARTS has the allure of a small island whose economy and well-being have always been intricately bound up with its picturesque port. The island itself had little to recommend it for settlement in the early days, as the rainfall is insufficient to support agriculture. However, St. Barts is strategically placed in the middle of the Lesser Antilles. Its fine small harbor and several sheltered bays made it important enough to be fought over by the British, French, and Spanish. It prospered under the French in the late 1600's when it was used as a base by pirates who came here to spend their quickly-gained fortunes. The most famous of these was Captain Montbars, a Frenchman who was so horrified by what the Spanish had done to the native populations that he decided to avenge them, doing well while he did good. He took on an indigenous crew who, no doubt, felt somewhat bitter, and did so well he became known with some terror as "Montbars the Exterminator." He finally disappeared in a hurricane and it is thought that his treasure is still buried on the island, though it is more likely that it was spent on the island.

In 1784 the French gave St. Barts to the Swedes in exchange for free port rights in Gothenburg. The Swedes made it a free port, which it remains today. It had a second period of prosperity as a trading center during the American war of independence, when American rebels came here for supplies.

During the hundred years following 1852, its fortunes fell owing to changing trade patterns and several hurricanes. The Swedes sold St. Barts back to France in 1878 and it remains part of France today, though, like St. Martin, it is a free port and so somewhat special. Over the last 30 years this free port status has resulted in an astonishing economic recovery. At first it was mainly inter-island trade. Small motorless sailing sloops would arrive here from down island and load themselves to the gunwales with alcohol and cigarettes to be smuggled back home. Although the customs officers in their homeports were properly taken care of, the return journey was nonetheless a long and hazardous sail to windward. The smugglers' biggest problem was to evade the customs men in St. Kitts and Nevis who would happily confiscate their cargo, no matter its destination. To keep out of their way, many would sneak by night through The Narrows, the reef-filled passage between St. Kitts and Nevis.

Today St. Barts is going through an unprecedented renaissance. With its

St. Barts

Regulations

Clear in and out with the port captain's office in Gustavia (VHF: 12). They do immigration for you. No one seems to worry too much if you visit a few anchorages on your way in or out. Entry procedures and mooring fee are given under Gustavia.

There is a 3-knot speed limit on all craft, including dinghies, and no water sports of any kind are permitted inside Gustavia port limits. Water skiing and jet skiing are forbidden within 300 meters of all coastlines. Large areas of St. Barts are a marine park (St. Barthelemy Natural Marine Preserve), managed by Franciane Le Quell These are marked by large yellow buoys that flash yellow at night. We have marked these areas on our sketch chart. Both Ile

Fourchue and Anse de Colombier are part of this park, as are Pain de Sucre and Les Gros Islets to the west of Gustavia. In these areas you may swim and snorkel. You are not allowed to fish, spearfish, jet ski, waterski, hun lobsters, or take anything from the seabed, and there is a 3-knot speed limit. You should never take coral or thro garbage in any coastal waters. More stringent restriction apply to other areas; we will mention these where appl cable. All commercial operators, and this includes private yachts on charter, must visit the marine park office, g a permit, and pay a fee ($2 Eu per person per visit). Use the yacht moorings in Ile Fourchue and Colombier wh they are available. They are all yellow and all take boats up to 75 feet/25 tons. Some are small buoys attached t a line with a loop; others are large buoys with a line going right through them. Put your lines though the loop a the end of the line and leave a minimum of 10 feet scope.

You may also scuba dive in the marine park, but to do this you need to visit the park office next to the port. They open Tuesday to Saturday 0800-1200, Wednesday also 1400-1700. They will give you a plan of 20 dive sites, and you will a pay a fee of $2 Eu per person per dive. There is no anchoring on the dive sites, but mooring are provided for dinghies and tenders, which you may use for a maximum of 2.5 hours. Thirteen scuba divers is the maximum allowed for one boat. No anchoring is allowed in Anse du Marigot.

Pass divers slowly, giving them at least 100 yards clearance. Do not chase or try to grab onto turtles!

Telephones

You will see card phones on many streets and cards are on sale at the post office and various shops. To use them, pick up the phone, put in the card, close the door (if applicable), wait till it shows credit, then dial. To c out of the country, dial 00, and then the code of the country you are calling (for the US 1, for UK 44). Most of the phones also work with credit cards. French pay phones have numbers posted so you can call someone and have them call you back. You can also call from some businesses in town, as well as send email (see communica tions section).

All St. Barts numbers now start 0590 (regular) or 0690 (cellular). You must dial this prefix, even on a local call. If you are dialing into St. Barts from a non-French territory, you have to dial the country code first, which also 590, then leave off the first 0 of the number. Thus if calling from the US, for regular numbers you will dial: 011-590-590, then 6 digits.

Transport

Taxis are on the waterfront opposite Quicksilver.
Rental cars and scooters are available for hire. Use your own license and drive on the right.

Shopping hours

Opening hours are from 0800-1200 and 1500-1800, but many shops stay open over lunch. Some shops open when the first day charter boat arrives (0900) and close when the last one leaves (1500).

Holidays

- Jan 1st
- Carnival Monday & Tuesday (46 days before Easter: Feb 15-16, 2010, March7-8, 2011),
- Good Friday and Easter Monday (Easter Sunday is April 4, 2010, April 24, 2011)
- May 1 (Labor Day)
- May 8 (V.E. DAY)
- Ascension Day (39 days after Easter: (May 13, 2010, June 2, 2011)
- Whit Monday, (50 days after Easter Sunday, May 24, 2010, June 13, 2011)
  Corpus Christie, (June 3, 2010, June 23, 2011)
- July 14 (Bastille Day)
- July 21 (Victor Schoelcher Day)
- August 15, (Assumption Day)
- Nov. 1 (All Saints Day)
- Nov 11 (Remembrance Day)
- December 25 (Christmas)

St. Martin, Admiralty Leisure Folio 5641-1, 5641-2

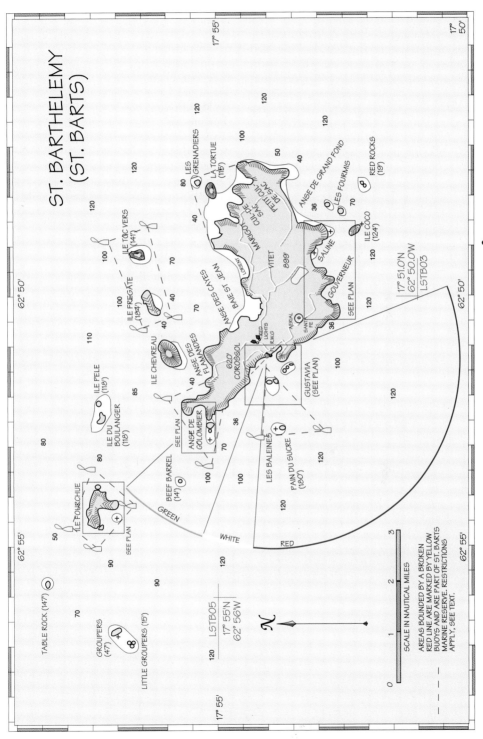

ST. BARTHELEMY (ST. BARTS)

RENAISSANCE ISLANDS

TABLE ROCK (147')

GROUPERS (47')

LITTLE GROUPERS (15')

ILE FOURCHUE
SEE PLAN

ILE DU BOULANGER (118')

ILE PELE (118')

ILE CHEVREAU

BEEF BARREL (147')

ANSE DE COLOMBIER
SEE PLAN

ANSE DES FLAMANDES

ANSE DES CAYES

BAIE ST. JEAN

ILE CHEVREAU

ILE FREGATE (184')

ILE TOC VERS (141')

LES GRENADIERS

LA TORTUE (115')

ANSE DE GRAND FOND

LES FOURMIS

RED ROCKS (191')

ILE COCO (124')

SALINE

GOUVERNEUR
SEE PLAN

VITET
898'

MARIGOT

CUL-DE-SAC
PETIT CUL
DE SAC

LORIENT

COROSSOL
620'

RED
LIGHTS
FL R.W.G

SANTA FE

AERIAL

GUSTAVIA
(SEE PLAN)

LES BALEINES

PAIN DU SUCRE (180')

17° 51.0'N
62° 50.0'W
LSTB03

GREEN
WHITE
RED

17° 55'N
62° 56'W
LSTB05

SCALE IN NAUTICAL MILES
0 1 2 3

AREAS BOUNDED BY A BROKEN RED LINE ARE MARKED BY YELLOW BUOYS AND ARE PART OF ST. BARTS MARINE RESERVE. RESTRICTIONS APPLY, SEE TEXT.

sharply contoured rocky hills, a picturesque port, and gorgeous beaches, it has become a world famous chic destination; the favored hot spot for the good looking, well-to-do "in" crowd, seasoned with a sprinkling of acting, singing, and sports stars: the Riviera of the Caribbean. Sociability reaches a crescendo around the New Year when a hundred or more superyachts arrive for festivities which include a spectacular fireworks display. St. Barts has some excellent cultural events. These include a music festival (classical and jazz) towards the end of January, and many art shows, as well as carnival (visitors are welcome to join in). The day after carnival they have a mock funeral and bury an effigy of all the evil sprits.

The Caribbean film festival in April is excellent and there is a festival of music and food in August, and a Flamenco workshop and show in October. November has both Swedish week (music and dance) and November 1st is All Saintes, when everyone decorates the graves.

St. Barts has extricated itself from Guadeloupe and is now an independent commune of France.

Navigation

St. Barts is surrounded by a host of small islands and rocks – some large and obvious, and others just awash. You can pick your own deepwater channels between these rocks, but study the charts well and keep a good look out. Do not try to go between groups of islands that lie together, such as

Groupers and Petite Groupers, or Boulanger and Ile Pele. The southeast coast can be very rough, so it makes sense to stay outside Red Rocks and Ile Coco. A marine park is marked by yellow buoys. (See our chart of St. Barts, page 139.) These are large and a collision with one could ruin your whole day. Being yellow, they are easy to see by day; at night they have flashing yellow lights. However, be warned that the lights have been known to go out, and the buoys have occasionally been known to go off station. The locations shown on our sketch charts should be treated as approximate. They are not navigational buoys.

Ile Fourchue

Ile Fourchue lies conveniently between

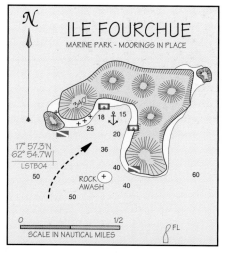

ILE FOURCHUE

St. Martin and St. Barts and makes a perfect stop. It is dry and rocky, with several steep hills and craggy peaks. Some of the hills are an attractive red color and their steep contours add interest to the view. For a long time, this island was left to the goats. They ate all the vegetation, including the prickles, causing huge eroded gulleys. Eventually, they ate themselves out of house and home and the population crashed. The remaining few were removed. Four years later, in the deepest of the gullies, trees have grown to over eight feet. Vegetation is slowly gaining a hold elsewhere on the island, with beach morning glory leading the advance.

Navigation

The island has a good-sized bay, protected from the north and east. A swell occasionally creeps in and makes it somewhat rolly. There is a rock awash off the southern headland and it is best to leave this to starboard when you enter. Tie up to one of the yacht moorings (no charge). They can all take yachts up to 25 meters or 25 tons. Superyachts should anchor to the south and west of the moorings in deeper water. If there are no moorings left, anchor on sand, south and west of the moorings. Ile Fourchue is part of the St. Barts Marine Reserve and they maintain the moorings to

protect the seabed: spearfishing, jet or water skiing, and damaging corals are strictly forbidden.

Ashore

Scrambling around this island affords excellent views, but take cactus-proof shoes. Ile Fourchue is privately owned. The owners do not want people lighting big fires and throwing a major party, but I am told they do not mind yachts people taking a quiet stroll, so do not worry about any "no trespassing" signs the goats failed to eat.

Water Sports

Snorkeling and diving here can be interesting when small fish are massing, especially if pelicans and boobies dive right close to you. Snorkel along either side of the bay, close to the rocks. The best dive spot is around the island that forms the western corner of the harbor. Anchor your dinghy on sand in the bay between the island and Ile Fourchue and work your way out around the island and back. The depth starts at 25 feet and goes to 60 feet or more. You will have sand on one side, an intricate reef on the other, and a chance of seeing not only reef fish, but rays and turtles as well. If sea conditions make this dive unsuitable, try the other side of the harbor, along the eastern shore. It is a little shallower there, but

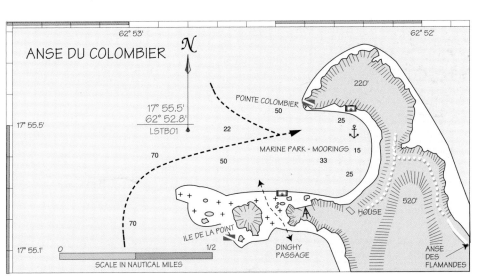

ANSE DE COLUMBIER

still interesting, with plenty of fish. The rock awash, just off the southern point, is quite pretty, but too small to be worth a dive on its own. If you have a compass, you can dive there and swim back to Ile Fourchue underwater.

Anse de Colombier

This secluded bay lies at the bottom of a steep, craggy hill. The village of Colombier peeks down from way up at the top. The bay has a perfect beach, backed by a smattering of palms. There is no road access and the only way to get here is by boat or a mile-long trek over the hills. Anse de Colombier was originally owned by the Rockefellers, who built the house on the southern hill. Farther out on the headland is a conspicuous turquoise summerhouse that looks like it was lifted from the top of the Eiffel Tower. Anse de Colombier is part of the St. Barts Marine Reserve. Fishing, spearfishing, jet or water skiing, and damaging corals are strictly forbidden. In addition to yacht moorings, moorings for divers and snorkelers have been placed among the southern islands and rocks. Since the marine park took over and put down yacht moorings, the grass beds have returned, attracting many feeding turtles, which has become a great attraction.

Navigation

Anse de Colombier is a well-protected anchorage and a good overnight spot. During the winter months northerly swells occasionally find their way in. Ile de la Pointe lies just to the west of the southern headland and a series of rocks extends out beyond the island. Some of these are quite visible, others are awash, and some lie just beneath the surface, so pass outside all the visible rocks by a good 300 feet when running between Anse de Colombier and Gustavia. Enter in the middle of the bay and pick up a park mooring (no charge). They all take yachts up to 25 meters or 25 tons. Superyachts, and other yachts, if there are not enough moorings, should anchor in the middle of the bay away from the moorings and grass beds.

Ashore

If you cross over the ridge by the steps at the north end of the beach, you will find a tiny trail leading over to Anse des Flamandes. This takes you on an adventurous half-hour walk over hills with panoramic views of some of St. Barts' rocks and offshore islands. Sweet smelling lilies grow along parts of the path. You will pass hills of cactuses and hollowed out cliffs and see butterflies and birds. The path ends at Anse des Flamandes, another appealing beach where you will find some small stores.

You can also hike from the beach to the village of Colombier – the collection of houses on top the hill that you can see from the anchorage. The path starts above the beach at the beginning of the path to Anse des Flamandes. It follows the ridgeline much of the way up, with some great views. It is surprisingly shady.

Water Sports

The snorkeling in Anse de Colombier is excellent. For starters, there are turtles in the grass beds all around, and you can watch them feeding. However, do not molest them, chase them, or try to approach closer than 10 feet. For reef fish,

start along the calmer northern coast. The bottom is rock with coral growths, teeming with brightly colored reef fish, including grunts, angelfish, parrotfish, bigeyes, and jacks. If the weather is calm, you can try the rougher water out by Ile de la Pointe and the rocks. Scuba divers have a choice of two sites, depending on conditions. You can dive on the western edge of Pointe Colombier in 25-50 feet. If you are anchored in the north part of the bay, start from your yacht and work your way out. There are many rock ledges and boulders. An even better site is on the south side of the small island, south of Ile de la Pointe. You will need to tie your dinghy to one of the small dive buoys put in by the marine park. You have a chance of seeing turtles and rays, as well the smaller reef fish.

Gustavia

Gustavia, St. Barts' main town, has the inherent charm of a small port. Red-roofed buildings are tucked around the protected

RENAISSANCE ISLANDS

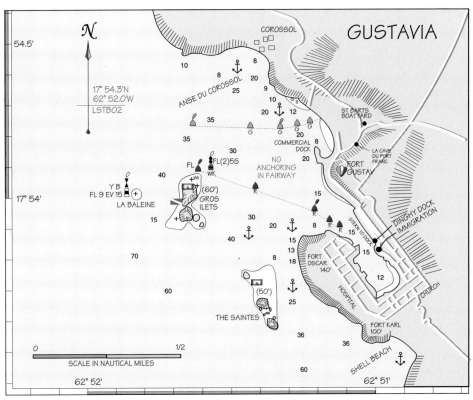

harbor. Yachts are tied up along the shore and anchored outside the harbor, so a steady stream of dinghies and small boats goes in and out of the port. The waterfront has recently been improved and expanded, and now has a pleasant walkway most of the way around, with flowers and plenty of places to sit and watch life out on the water.

The tourist office is next to the port office. Go there for a free copy of the latest tourist magazines and ask about evening live entertainment. Above the tourist office you can also visit the marine park and get the most up-to-date information.

The port is a basin with hills all around, which you can climb for great harbor views. The lighthouse at Fort Gustav affords one of the best panoramas and is an easy walk. Fort Karl has steps going all the way up and gives a view, not only of the harbor, but also of Shell Beach.

Navigation

There are several offshore rocks and islands. If you are approaching from the north, the easiest thing is to come inside them. La Baleine is marked by a flashing buoy (9 flashes every 15 seconds). To be on the safe side, avoid going between this buoy and Gros Ilets. If you are approaching from the south, there is enough water to pass between The Saintes and the mainland, but shoal water extends well out from The Saintes, so follow along the mainland shore. When you approach Gustavia, be prepared to thread your way through anchored boats, unless you come in the official buoyed channel. If you do come through the main channel, note that there is an isolated danger marker on the southern side of the channel by Gros Ilet. This marks the wreck of a freighter in about 12 feet of water. Gustavia is so popular that anchoring can be a problem during the winter season. Moorings are laid in the harbor in rows, according to boat length. (See our sketch chart, page 147). You need to call the Port of Gustavia to see if they have one available. Sometimes it helps if you check first, then dinghy in, and then

tell them which ones you saw empty.

The next most popular spot is northwest of Fort Oscar. You must anchor seaward of the red channel buoys. Keep in mind that the wind switches and yachts swing through 360 degrees. The boats close to shore are required to have stern anchors; those farther out are not. This creates a tempting hole between the two that cannot be used, for if you put down a stern anchor those that do not have them will swing into you, and if you not use one then you will swing into those that do. You need to dive on your anchor here, as the bottom is weedy. You can also anchor anywhere from here down to Shell Beach. Another anchorage is behind the marked area between Anse Corossol and the fairway to the public dock. There is no problem being there, but it is a longer dinghy ride into port. All outside anchorages can be pretty rolly. Anchoring in the fairway is strictly forbidden.

A good option is to go stern-to one of the long new sections of dock built especially for visiting yachts. They now have these on both sides of the harbor. This requires considerable skill, as it has to be done in a crosswind. In the winter it is also subject to swells, so you must tie your boat well clear of the dock. The secret is to set your anchor a very long way out, toward the far side. Add extra line if necessary. Plunking your anchor down in the middle of the channel is likely to result in an embarrassing drag. Accidents can happen, and the port insists that yachts have liability insurance.

Gustavia is a well-protected harbor under normal conditions, but winter swells creep in and it is often somewhat rolly. Gustavia is no hurricane hole, and you should evacuate at the first warning.

Regulations

If you plan to come into the docks, you should call St. Barts Port Authority on VHF 12, preferably an hour before arrival. Once in the port, take your passports and ship's papers to the port office. (If you have pets, take their vaccination certificates.)

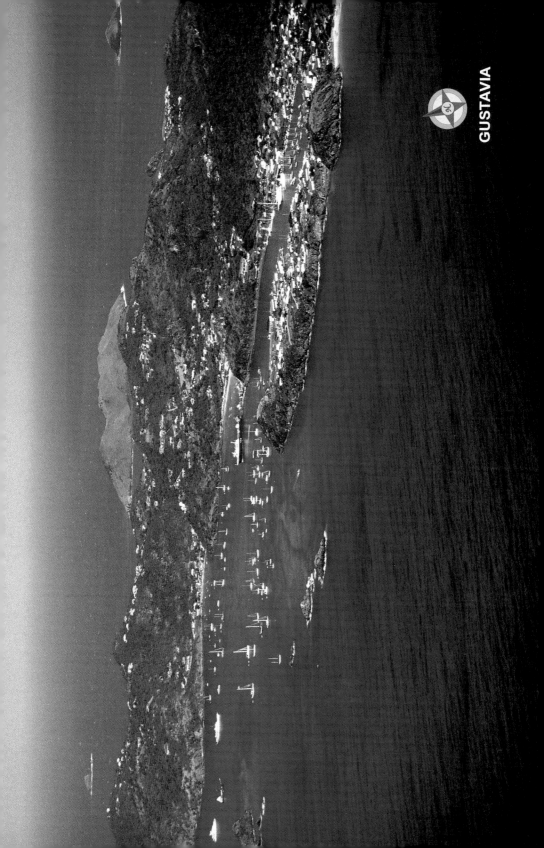

GUSTAVIA

The port system here is simple and efficient. You can clear in and out in one step for stays of 24 hours; otherwise, clear in and return to clear out. A harbor boat patrols the yacht anchorage daily.

The Port du Gustavia stands by on (VHF: 12) and is open from 0700-1800. Get there half an hour before closing to clear.

Yachts over 30 meters should dock or leave the dock between 0730 and 1530. The maximum length for docking is 60 meters (sorry, Bill Gates).

You will be charged in Gustavia according to your location, and pay when you clear in. The charges are by the square meter (length times beam). Outside the inner harbor, charges are 0.2 Eu per m^2 per day for private yachts and 0.25 for charter yachts. There is usually room to go stern-to, where in season charges are 0.8 Eu per m2 per day for private yachts, and 1 Eu for charter yachts. From June to November the rates are 0.3 Eu per m^2 per day for private yachts, 0.5 for charter yachts. If you manage to get a mooring, charges are 0.5 m^2 for private yachts and 0.7 m^2 for charter yachts. You can ask about longer term rates.

The speed limit in the harbor is 3 knots – not only for yachts, but also for their tenders, and all water sports, including water skis, jet skis, windsurfers, fishing, swimming, and diving, are not allowed in the port zone. Barbecues are not allowed on the dock. You need proof of liability insurance to be in the port

Communications

You can have mail or faxes sent to the Port Captain. It must have the name of your yacht and then: BP 695, Port du Gustavia, 97099 St. Barthelemy. Mail not clearly sent to a yacht is returned. Port de Gustavia has bay-wide wifi – a bit weak in some areas, but that should be improved soon. It is included in your port fees. Ask for a ticket when you check in.

For email, go to Center Alizes in an office upstairs next to Loulou's. They offer complete communications, with phone, fax, and a large bank of computers for email and internet connection. (They have QWERTY keyboards.) This is an easy place to make an international call and for cheaper calls they offer special phone cards that are quite inexpensive, though you do have to punch in a lot of numbers. In addition, they offer business services, including photocopying and laminating, and they sell top ups for French cell phones. They open Monday to Saturday from 0830 to 2000; Sundays and holidays 1500-2000.

L'Entracte offers free wifi if you take your computer in.

General Yacht Services

Water is available on the yacht docks. Toilets and showers are available to all yachts (opposite the port office) from Monday to Saturday 0800-1700. You will find garbage bins, please recycle into the appropriate bins; glass, tin cans, used oil, and general garbage. There is stern-to docking and 60-cycle, 3-phase electricity, 220 and 380 volts, is available up to 20 amps right outside the port office with 220 volts farther along the quay. Telephone lines are planned. New berths have been added to the western side of the harbor; these have water and will get electricity shortly. The weather is posted daily at the port office.

The port also runs the commercial port, with full security. It is most used by cargo vessels, but they open it to big yachts over the New Year holiday. The fuel station sometimes works, though is often put out of action, sometimes for years, by hurricanes. Ask in the port office.

Getting US style propane tanks filled is not possible, though Loulou tells me that if you are desperate, Martin Greaux, in Anse de Cayes, may be able to help.

St. Barth Boatyard is set back from the water. They take yachts up to 15 tons with a crane, lifting them in the port and then trailing them back to their yard. They have storage for 40-60 boats on concrete standing with tie-down rings embedded every 12 feet. They also have a large forklift for yacht tenders and powerboats up to 35 feet.

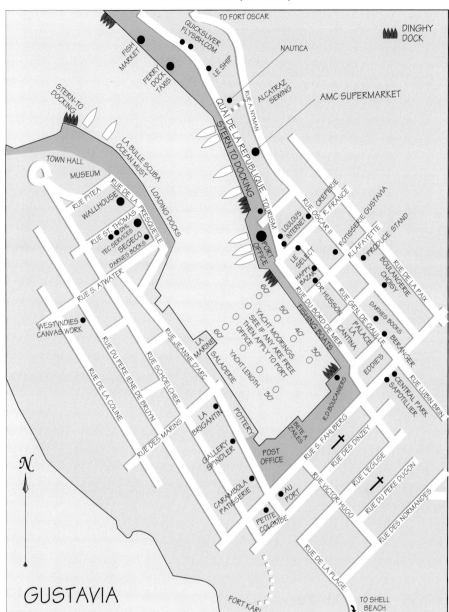

GUSTAVIA

Because of the road, they cannot store cats, but they can lift them for emergency work in the port. They also repair them (see Technical Yacht Services).

Ice is available from AMC supermarket. Superyachts should make use of Wendy's Nautica FWI. This is in the back of the Carre D'Or shopping mall, behind the fancy store, Black Swan. Nautica is a superyacht agent, and a charter agency

handling crewed yachts up to superyachts and bareboats for experienced sailors. They are also brokers. Any taxi will help you fill up your outboard gas tank.

Dr. Husson is an excellent G.P. just a few steps into town, and he usually sees patients without an appointment in the mornings. If it is out of hours, a holiday, or weekend, we give the number in the directory of the "Dr. on call". You can also find

View from Fort Karl   Chris Doyle

good dentists. One of these is Dr. Acheache (0590-52-80-32). St. Barts also has a well-equipped small hospital.

Chandlery

Le Ship, run by several brothers in the Magras family, is a great general and technical chandlery, offering lots of product lines not available in St. Martin, and many of their prices are excellent. They sell and service Mariner and Mercury outboards and stock a wonderful range of yacht gear, from dinghies and outboards through to hardware, stoves, and fridges, and including oil filters, pumps, electrical fittings, spare parts, and a fabulous collection of nuts, bolts, stainless fittings, and pipe fittings. They have an impressive range of lures and fishing gear, so if your catch has been down, wander over and chat with them. This is also a good place for yachting shorts, fancy shoes, and replacing the hat that blew over the side. They stand by on (VHF: 16) and you can also buy cold drinks. Le Ship is also a yacht broker.

Technical Yacht Services

Le Ship (VHF: 16) is part of a fairly large organization that covers many aspects of yachting. They have a full rigging shop, and they do both stainless and aluminum welding and fabrication. Boat signs and numbers are computer generated at the chandlery.

The St. Barth Boatyard is run by two Swedes, Per and Alf, along with more Swedish helpers. (They call themselves 2-Swedes Marine.) Apart from hauling and storage, they specialize in marine woodwork: anything from laying a teak deck to fitting fine cabinets. They also do excellent glasswork, from patching minor blemishes to doing major structural repairs. They have done many factory repairs for Nautor Swan, and can work in exotic materials like carbon fiber. They can handle rigging problems that don't involve swaging tools over 12mm, and they would be excellent people to use for a complete refit. They are good at re-spraying and have sheds to take boats up to 45 feet. They can do small welding jobs, and have a mechanical shop for Vovlo Penta for whom they are agents for St. Barts, St. Martin, and Anguilla. Ask anyone for the 2- Swedes, and you will be in good hands.

For serious stainless welding jobs, see Regis at his company, Boatinox, over in

RENAISSANCE ISLANDS

149

Clock tower, Gustavia Chris Doyle

Lorient. Taxi your broken bits over to him, but call first to make sure he is there. He does a good job.

Ledee Beranger is the Yamaha agent, offering full sales and service. He helps with all mechanical problems and fixes any kind of outboard. His store is one of the best places to rent a car, scooter, or van. They can also handle phone calls, faxes, and ship provisions. They stock some marine hardware and fishing gear.

Moviegoers may wonder whether Alcatraz Sewing is offering a hot line of striped crew uniforms. Nothing of the kind. Alcatraz means "pelican" in Spanish and this workshop, owned by Englishman Gordon Murray, does sail repairs, makes bimini frames and covers, keeps closed cell foam for cockpit cushions, and stocks a good selection of fabrics for covering berth cushions. You will find him just up a side road on Rue August Nyman.

Hughes Marine is a company that repairs and services inboard and outboard motors, as well as fixing electrical problems, and taking care of hydraulics and water makers. You will find them on Rue Victor Hugo.

West Indies Sails also has a shop. They do lots of kite sails and are agents for EH kites. They make cushions and do canvas work and can help with small sails or surf kites. Marco's La Voilerie du Port, is upstairs, on the left side of the road that leads to the 2-Swedes. He is the Incidence agent and can fix sails, but check to see that they have time before you bring them in.

JCG fixes electric tools, starter motors, and alternators. His mobile is (0690-55-32-40). Superyachts that need anchors untangling or moving can call Kuka (0690 58-77-59), (VHF:12), or Big Blue, 0690-35-86-35

When we sailed to St. Barts way back when, Loulou's chandlery was one of the major stores. Loulou is still around, and owns many properties, including the art gallery, Porta 34, which opens for special shows. If you are a sailing artist, you can rent it for a show (0590-27-72-81 – speak to Jean-Pierre). If you can find Loulou, he can be very helpful to long distance cruisers with general and marine information about St. Barts. Look for his double ender, Pluto, or watch a fleet of small yachts that sails through the port just before sunset. He is on the folkboat.

Transport

The taxi stand is right by the ferry dock opposite Quicksilver. For hiking or driving tours, contact Helene Bernier (0690-63-46-09) (see ashore section).

Provisioning

The glitterati eat well and you won't lack for much at the AMC Supermarket, which is conveniently placed across the road from the yacht dock. This is a fine place to provision your yacht. It has a super cool air-conditioning system and good fish, meat, and deli sections. They open 0800-1850 except Saturday, when they close at 1450, and Sundays when they are closed. You can phone or fax orders a day in advance and they will prepare them for you. They keep just about anything you may need for charter. Those with elaborate tastes should check their fine wine and liquor store directly across the road. They keep a few open bottles for sampling. They do not offer bags, so bring your own or take one of their boxes (they have plenty).

La Cave du Port Franc is just a few steps northwest of the commercial port and is run by the same family that runs the chandlery. They offer yachts very good prices on wines and spirits.

Christian Greaux's Segeco is on the northwest side of the harbor, to starboard as you enter. They stock a wide range of wines, spirits, beers, and cigarettes, as well as non-alcoholic drinks, groceries, and food. It is a very convenient location for loading the dinghy.

Above AMC is Tom Foods, a big wholesale place. They will deliver to the docks. Access to their store is from the street behind.

American Gourmet on Rue de Gaulle is both a very fancy specialty food market and a full yacht provisioner. Wander in, and you will find something you have really been missing. You will find a small fish market at the very end of the dock on the northeast corner, beyond the taxi stand.

Fun Shopping

Not since Montbars the Exterminator, has there been so much treasure loose in St. Barts. Gold, silver, fine jewels, and rich fabrics abound. You no longer have to risk losing your limbs to cannons while you pry it loose with a cutlass and blunderbuss. A small plastic credit card is quite sufficient. Yes, Gustavia is a major duty free shopping spot, with about two hundred shops all packed in a few small streets. The emphasis is on exclusivity and quality rather than quantity. It is a place where the exotic is commonplace. Just the name "St. Barth" adds glamour and ups the price. Instead of boutiques, you find collections. Many have simple names, like Dior. Most are in the streets behind the waterfront on the northeast side of the harbor, behind the main

QUIKSILVER
BOARDRIDERS CLUB
GUSTAVIA HARBOR ST.BARTH Tel 0590 29 69 40
roxy   Eyewear   Surf Board Rentals · Surfwear
Beachwear · Footwear
Surf Boards:
Al Merrick · Surftech

docks, but others are scattered all the way round the port. All the famous names are here, including Little Switzerland, Cartier, Lacost, La Perla, Hermes, and United Colors of Benetton. Indeed, it is de rigueur for high fashion shops to be able to include St. Barth on their fancy shopping bags. Art galleries are also popular.

Chistine and Stephanie's Quicksilver Boardriders Club is a great surf and relax shop. It is a good place to look for sailing and nautical clothing, good shorts, smart shirts, sandals, fine sunglasses (including polarized), swimwear, and accessories, like waterproof bags. They include a lot of kid stuff, which can be good for gifts, and when you have shopped over your luggage limit, check out their range of fancy bags. On the surf side, they have a ton of boards both for sale and rent and they have all the Naish kite surfing gear, and can arrange for lessons if you need them. Service is good; they look after you well. Jean-Paul and Didier run two establishments in St. Barts. Happy Bazaar on Rue General de Gaulle has two shops: one with elegant beachwear and jewelry, the other a collection of objets d'art, many collected by Jean-Paul and Didier on their travels. They are agents for the distinctive work of Thomas Hopman, who hand paints on sculpted pieces. You will find something you like here and prices are often reasonable. Gallery Spindler on the Rue Jean D'Arc is wonderfully crammed with two floors of Didier's striking original paintings, intermingled with large ornaments and pieces of furniture from all over the world.

The St. Barts Pottery has closed, but check it out, it sometimes reappears as an art gallery. Owner Jennifer May, who originally hailed from Cornwall in England, has a school of arts up on the hill behind Fort Gustav. She also knows all the local artists. If art interests you, give her a call at 0590-27-82-34.

On both sides of the harbor, Librarie Barnes has stores with lots of French and some English books, but also paper, stationary, painting supplies and more.

Restaurants

Gustavia is a great place to eat out. About two-dozen restaurants are dotted around the picturesque streets. They are always changing names and owners, so the best bet is to wander around and look.

For somewhere inexpensive, try Jean-Louis' La Cantina on the waterfront. It opens at 0715 for French breakfast, and for lunch you can get salads, as well as peruse their more elaborate menu. It has a group of dedicated customers and stays open as a bar until 2230.

Le Select is a popular, informal bar that is now the fashionable place to gather for an evening. There is always plenty of life here and you never know when Jimmy Buffet might pop in to give an impromptu rendition of "Cheeseburger in Paradise."

Eddie is a well-known St. Barts restaurateur. His dad originally owned Le Select and Eddie ran it for a long time. His next venture was Eddie's Ghetto, and, finally, he built Eddie's. It has an open courtyard, typical of the old Swedish houses, though the

RENAISSANCE ISLANDS

153

finished product is reminiscent of the Far East, with a high, open, woven roof, attractive wooden furniture, and many plants. The stonewalls date back over 100 years. Food is elegantly simple: perfectly prepared fish or meat with an appropriate sauce, and many prices are reasonable.

Nearby, The Palace (formerly Eddie's Ghetto) offers a good French meal at a reasonable price. Le Repaire is also not too expensive and overlooks the harbor. Take a bunch of cozy spaces on different levels, add a big statue and fountain, have it overseen by an ageing parrot, and you have the quaint atmosphere of Central Park. This place is curious and fun and can be peaceful or hopping, depending on the night. They often have music on weekends.

If you want to spoil yourself with some fancy food, check out Adam Rajner's Le Sapotillier (closed May to October) and Au Port, on the same road.

The Wall, right at the end on the southwest side of the harbor, is a good restaurant whose excellent lunchtime specials, at about 10 Eu, are the best value for money on the island.

L'Entr'acte on the waterfront is inexpensive. They serve pizzas, sandwiches, and tasty Créole meals. They also offer free wifi.

Restaurants have been built out over the waterfront along the end of the port – a prime location. Le Bête à Zailes has sandwiches or sushi for lunch, and salads and smoked and marinated fish for dinner. La Route des Boucaniers has a mixed menu and is not too expensive.

La Petite Colombe and Carambole Pâtisserie are great little places for breakfast coffee, patisseries, and lunchtime sandwiches. La Petite Colombe sells good bread. Carambole Pâtisserie make their own fresh juice and ice cream.

Another good boulangerie/patisserie is Choisy, and they keep bakers' hours – open every day from 0530, so come for breakfast. In fact, early morning is a special time in Gustavia. There is not too much traffic, the beautiful people are still in bed, and the locals are out. Take a stroll and have a

Gustavia's anchorage   Chris Doyle

breakfast of French coffee and warm, freshly baked croissants.

Maya's (dinner only, closed Sunday) is a good restaurant on the beach, behind the commercial dock. They are open to the beach, and although the view is good, the real draw is the imaginative menu, with inspiration from the Orient as well as France and St. Barts. The menu changes daily.

If you need a little exercise to work up an appetite, hike up the road leading south out of town till you come to the big aerial on the hill. Santa Fe Restaurant is on the right. When visibility is good, the view is superb. This is a fine restaurant (closed Mondays) that feels miles away from the harbor. They serve a mixture of Caribbean, French, and Oriental dishes, and the cooking is good.

Ashore

Those who have been having a hard time finding shells can take the short walk over to Anse du Grand Galet, otherwise known as Shell Beach, and pick to their hearts' content. It is sign-posted from town.

If you buy Jenny Stening's book on Gustavia, you can follow a walking tour of the town, which will introduce you to its early history and architecture. On the southwest side of the harbor, next to the fancy new Mairie (town hall), is the municipal museum of St. Barts, with an eclectic collection of pictures and artifacts, showing St. Barts' history. There is a small entry fee. It is open until 1800 most days, mornings only on Saturday, and closed Sundays.

The interior of St. Barts is by far the prettiest of the Renaissance Islands and you can derive great pleasure from renting a moke (or a scooter if you dare) and driving around the countryside. The roads are often cut into the sides of the mountains. It takes some nerve, but feels like the closest thing you can get to flying on wheels. In one day, you can cover just about every road. Highlights include the wonderfully rugged southeast coast along Grand Fond, winding along the tiny mountain roads in Vitet, scrambling around the rocks at the end of the Colombier Road and buying intricate straw work from barefooted women in traditional dress in Corrossol. Anse de Grande Saline makes a great stop for a walk and a swim. Among other roadside attractions are a shell museum in Corrossol and the Allée du Manoir Perfumerie in Lorient. Baie St. Jean (including the airport) is a tourist hot spot, with lots of shops and restaurants, which often become crowded when cruise ships come in. You might like to visit Anse des Cayes. Part of the beach is good for body surfing, or you can watch others doing the real thing. Behind the beach, the New Born Restaurant offers good French and Créole cooking and they have a lobster pool.

If you prefer to be more active, call

RENAISSANCE ISLANDS

155

Helene Bernier (0690-63-46-09) and go hiking with her. She has transport and knows of tiny trails, mainly on private land, that take you way up in the mountains to the highest peaks where you sit on a rock with the island laid out below you. Sometimes Sebastian comes along and plays music on the mountain top. For two people, a 3-hour hike costs 50 Eu per person; less per person for larger groups. She has hikes at all levels and her difficult climbs involve some serious scrambling up rocks with precipitous drops close by. Such hikes are really great, but you need to discuss your experience level. She also does cultural and historical walks. Helene also does full day and half day island tours by cab or by cab with hiking.

Water Sports

Before you go diving, visit the marine park office at the port for a diving map and to pay the two-euro fee per dive. Use the moorings provided for diving, do not anchor. Diving on the rocks just outside Gustavia harbor is good, with plenty of hard and soft corals, sponges, and colorful reef fish, on such sites as Les Petit Saintes, Gros Ilet, La Baleine, and Pain de Sucre. In addition, between Gros Ilets and La Baleine (closer to La Baleine), lies the wreck of Non-Stop, a 210-foot power yacht that sank in 60 feet of water. La Baleine is one of the best sites. It is a small, rocky pinnacle that just breaks the surface. You can dive down to 57 feet and will see giant barrel sponges, a variety of hard and soft corals, and plenty of fish.

There are several excellent dives farther off St. Barts. These are beyond the range of most yacht dinghies, so are best done with a dive shop. The Groupers includes two dives and they are considered among the best in the area. Little Groupers, the more southern group of rocks, make one dive. This dive is 20-70 feet around the southwest side. There are lots of rocks and gullies and there is a good chance of seeing turtles and barracudas. The larger rock and associated rocklets make another dive. If you go down on the small rock close by the large one, there is a tunnel that goes right through that you can swim through in calm weather. There are many walls and gullies, with lots of reef fish.

Table Rock is a dive for calm weather only. You can swim right around this island, which has a wall dropping to about 60 feet. Ile de Boulanger is another dive for calm weather only. Depths are between 30 and 60 feet, with lots of fish. Ile Coco offers good diving for both novices and experienced divers. In one part, a wall drops to 60 feet with a sandy bottom littered with rocks, where you find stingrays, turtles, jacks, and nurse sharks. There is also an area with pretty caves in 20 feet of water. The colorful reef fish include parrotfish and trumpet fish.

La Bulle can help get you underwater. It is in Ocean Must Marina. This is a small and friendly operation, and they are happy to fill your tanks or take you diving. They are the most convenient to dinghy to, and they only take small groups. The

Fort Oscar
Chris Doyle

best sailboarding spot is in Baie St. Jean, where there is plenty of wind and some protection from the sea. For those who want waves, it is not far to the ocean. There are two rental agencies on the beach.

Baie St. Jean

Baie St. Jean is on the northern side of St. Barts, just at the end of the airport runway. When planes take off, they need to bank to the north and anchored yachts can be a real hazard. Therefore, the only permitted anchorage is outside the line between the headlands shown on our sketch chart. You will notice one or two small boats tucked up in the southeastern corner of the bay inside this limitation.

These relatively small local boats with no live-aboards are allowed there.

The permitted anchorage is normally rolly and uncomfortable and not recommended. However, a few years back the winds were consistently from the south, and in these conditions it proved one of the better anchorages on the island. These were somewhat exceptional conditions. People were also anchoring in Anse des Flamandes, which is normally very rough. In such unusual conditions, there is no problem anchoring in the area shown, and it is convenient for enjoying the popular beach ashore. However, do not anchor farther in the bay, as it will force the police to make a special, and possibly expensive, trip to ask you to move.

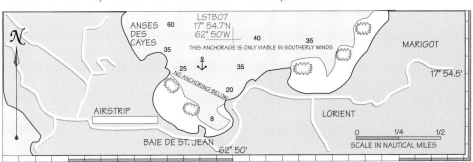

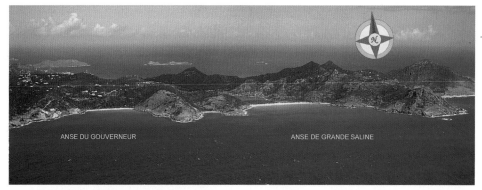

ANSE DU GOUVERNEUR   ANSE DE GRANDE SALINE

ANSE DE GRANDE SALINE AND ANSE DU GOUVERNEUR

Anse de Grande Saline and Anse du Gouverneur are two fabulous secluded beaches, surrounded by scenic cliffs. They are not really anchorages and are totally untenable in strong winds or in any southeasterly wind. However, on a calm day with a light easterly or north-easterly breeze, it is possible to hang in here for lunch. Do not try to anchor unless it is calm and do not stay overnight, as conditions could change. Beaching the dinghy could be hazardous.

Anse de Grande Saline is the larger and more protected of the two. You can anchor off the rocks that lie in the north-eastern corner. There is another small hidden bay a little farther toward the headland. Although small, this is per-haps the most protected spot, but take care, as the wind can swing around onto the shore.

Anse du Gouverneur is also accept-able as a lunch spot on calm days. Anchor off the western end of the beach. Do not attempt to get too close to shore, as the rollers get worse.

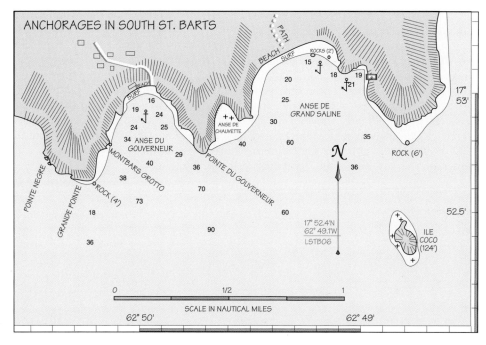

PASSAGES BETWEEN ST. MARTIN, ST. BARTS, SABA, STATIA, ST. KITTS AND NEVIS

These islands are well placed for pleasant passages that are easily sailed in a day. Approximate distances and courses are given in our chart. If sailing directly from St. Barts to Nevis, it is usually faster to sail down the northeastern side of St. Kitts and then pass through the narrows to Nevis. The reverse route is a good way to get back. Keep in mind that you will want to traverse the narrows in good light. (Some charter companies do not allow this.) Passages between St. Martin or St. Barts and St. Kitts, in either direction, are usually good reaches, though when you are heading south you will have to beat 10 miles to windward along the south coast of St. Kitts. St. Barts is considerably closer to St. Kitts than St. Martin, so sailing from St. Barts makes an easier passage. Passages between St. Martin or St. Barts and Statia in either direction are good sails that do not usually involve tacking. Although the sail from Statia to St. Kitts is generally hard on the wind, the sailing is pleasant and the distance across open water only about 10 miles, so it is very practical to visit Statia and then carry on to St. Kitts or Nevis. The passage from either St. Martin or St. Barts to Saba is easy, and if you are lucky, you will make it back to St. Martin in one tack. Normally, getting back to St. Barts from Saba will involve beating to windward; so if you are not in a hurry, why not sail to St. Martin first?

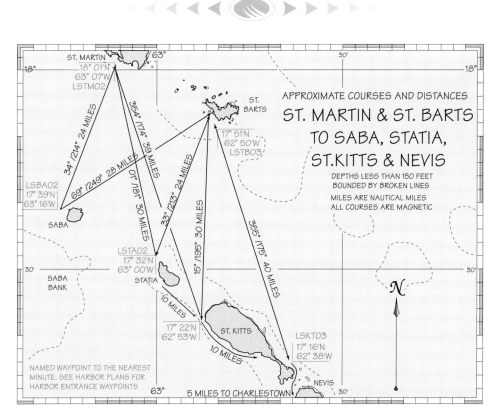

APPROXIMATE COURSES AND DISTANCES

ST. MARTIN & ST. BARTS TO SABA, STATIA, ST. KITTS & NEVIS

DEPTHS LESS THAN 150 FEET
BOUNDED BY BROKEN LINES

MILES ARE NAUTICAL MILES
ALL COURSES ARE MAGNETIC

NAMED WAYPOINT TO THE NEAREST MINUTE. SEE HARBOR PLANS FOR HARBOR ENTRANCE WAYPOINTS

ST. MARTIN
18° 01'N
63° 07'W
LSTM02

ST. BARTS
17° 51'N
62° 50'W
LSTB03

LSBA02
17° 39'N
63° 16'W

SABA

SABA BANK

LSTA02
17° 32'N
63° 00'W

STATIA

17° 22'N
62° 53'W

ST. KITTS

LSKT03
17° 16'N
62° 38'W

NEVIS

5 MILES TO CHARLESTOWN

354° / 174° 39 MILES
34° / 214° 24 MILES
69° / 249° 28 MILES
01° / 181° 30 MILES
33° / 213° 24 MILES
15° / 195° 30 MILES
355° / 175° 40 MILES
10 MILES
10 MILES

RENAISSANCE ISLANDS

159

the anchorages of the islands that
BRUSH THE CLOUDS

saba • sint eustatius (statia) • st. christopher (st. kitts)
nevis • redonda • montserrat

Southern peninsular, St. Kitts

Chris Doyle

The Anchorages Of
The Islands that Brush the Clouds

Saba, Statia, St. Kitts, Nevis and Montserrat are five small volcanic islands that rise steeply from the sea until their peaks touch the clouds. St. Kitts, the largest and tallest, is nearly 4000 feet high. Statia, the lowest, rises to nearly 2000 feet, although the island is merely 5 miles long. The high mountains trap passing moisture, which keeps them lush and green. For the most part they are surrounded by deep water, but to the southwest of Saba, the Saba Bank is about 600 square miles of sand and reef, 15 to 180 feet deep. It is fascinating to sail over this bank in gentle conditions, watching the reefs below. In heavy weather the shallow water can cause turbulent seas and it is best avoided.

These islands span some 90 miles and provide convenient stepping-stones between Guadeloupe and St. Martin. The anchorages in the smaller islands can be rolly to untenable in northerly swells, and St. Kitts was impossible in southeasterly winds until the marina was built. This lack of secure harbors has put them somewhat off the beaten track and kept them unspoiled. The passing sailor can be sure of a warm welcome.

While one or two of the anchorages are spectacularly beautiful, the main attraction of these islands is to explore on land. Ashore they feel like five completely separate countries. Saba and Statia are both parts of the Dutch Antilles, though each operates to some degree autonomously. St. Kitts and Nevis jointly form a single independent nation, and Montserrat, famous for its volcano, is a British colony. English is the accepted language throughout, though many people in Saba and Statia also speak Dutch.

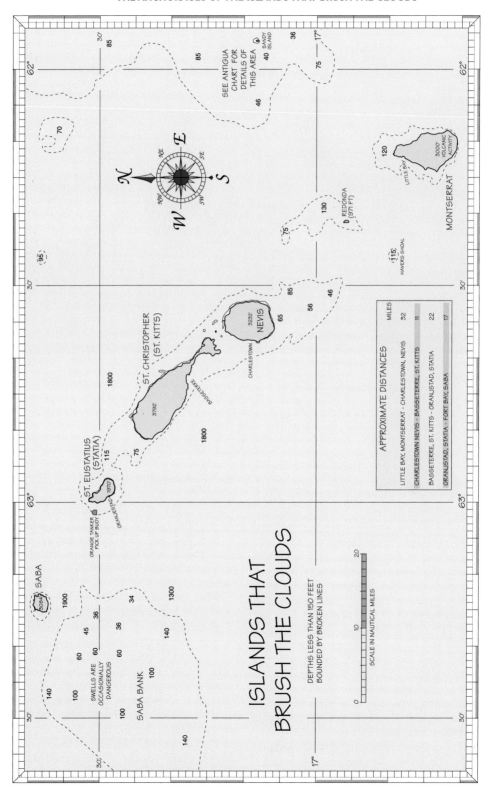

ISLANDS THAT BRUSH THE CLOUDS

DEPTHS LESS THAN 150 FEET BOUNDED BY BROKEN LINES

SCALE IN NAUTICAL MILES

0   10   20

APPROXIMATE DISTANCES	MILES
LITTLE BAY, MONTSERRAT - CHARLESTOWN, NEVIS	32
CHARLESTOWN NEVIS - BASSETERRE, ST. KITTS	11
BASSETERRE, ST. KITTS - ORANJSTAD, STATIA	22
ORANJSTAD, STATIA - FORT BAY, SABA	17

SABA

SABA BANK

SWELLS ARE OCCASIONALLY DANGEROUS

ST. EUSTATIUS (STATIA)

ORANJESTAD

ORANGE TANKER PICK UP BUOY

ST. CHRISTOPHER (ST. KITTS)

BASSETERRE

NEVIS

CHARLESTOWN

MONTSERRAT

LITTLE BAY

3000' VOLCANIC ACTIVITY

REDONDA (971 FT)

HAYERS SHOAL

SEE ANTIGUA CHART FOR DETAILS OF THIS AREA

SANDY ISLAND

162

Regulations

Those who have not visited Saba before and are unfamiliar with the anchoring and mooring system should stand off Fort Bay and send a dinghy ashore to clear with the port authority and Marine Park. Others may go and moor or anchor, then return by dinghy to check in. All the waters around Saba are part of a national marine park. Anchoring even a dinghy is prohibited, except in the anchoring zones shown on our charts. Littering or discharging foreign substances in the water is forbidden.

Eleven overnight moorings for visiting yachts (up to 60 feet) with one for larger vessels (up to 150 tons) lie between Ladder Bay and Wells Bay, and four are off Fort Bay. (Servicing can sometimes reduce the number). You are welcome to use these at no charge, other than the park fees. They are yellow or yellow with a blue stripe. (See Navigation, below.)

The white buoys and the orange buoys are for diving only and you may not use dive buoys for your yacht. You may tie your dinghy to the one at Torrens Point for snorkeling.

The park is self-supporting and there are charges that help pay for park maintenance. These are payable to the Marine Park and are currently $3 US per person per week for those on board yachts less than 100 feet. Vessels greater than 100 feet pay $0.10 US per gross ton.

Clear into Saba with Travis Johnson. He is open every day 0730 to 1800. There is a charge of $20US (most regular yachts) up to $150US (larger superyachts). Then clear in with the marine park office.

When passing dive groups, stay 150 yards to seaward. (This includes dinghies!)

Spearfishing or taking coral is strictly forbidden. Anyone wishing to dive must do so with one of the dive shops. Gloves are not allowed for snorkeling or diving. The marine park also maintains the land parks and the nature trails. You are encouraged to make a $1 per person per day contribution.

Telephones

You can make calls from the telephone office or a hotel. Card phones are available. Dialing 00 gets you out of the country. Then dial the country code (1 for the USA, 44 for the UK). Cell coverage is like Sint Maarten.

Shopping hours

Shopping hours depend on the proprietor, but try 0800-1200 and 1400-1600.

Transport

Saba is linked to St. Martin and Statia by several daily flights. Sit up front on the starboard side of the plane for the exciting landing on Saba, which resembles arriving on an aircraft carrier.

The Edge, a fast ferry, connects Pelican Resort in Simpson Bay, St. Martin with Saba Wednesday-Sunday, departing at 0900 and returning at 1700.

On Saba you can rent a car or take a taxi. Garvis Hassell (599-416-6114) is happy to go on roads deemed too scary by other drivers. Taxi rates in $US are:

Sightseeing tour (up to 4, then $10 per head)	$50.00
Fort Bay to Windwardside	$14.00
Airport to Windwardside	$12.00
Airport to Ecolodge	$14.00

Holidays

- Jan 1
- Good Friday and Easter Monday (Easter Sunday is April 4, 2010; April 24, 2011)
- April 30 (Queens Birthday)
- May 1 (Labor Day)
- May 5 (Liberation Day)
- Ascension Day (39 days after Easter: May 13, 2010, June 2, 2011)
- Whit Monday, 50 days after Easter Sunday (May 24, 2010, June 13, 2011)
- July 1 (Emancipation Day)
- Last Monday in July (and the next Tuesday) Carnival
- October 22 Antillean Day
- First Monday in December (Saba Day)
- December 25- 26

The Bottom.

Saba

SABA LOOKS LIKE A fairytale picture of a forbidden land. A mere 5 square miles, it reaches a lofty 3000 feet. Tall cliffs of red, pink, and brown rise almost vertically from the sea. Houses sit perched in seemingly impossible positions on the edges of precipices. Ashore, it lives up to its image, for, if there was ever a hidden Shangri-La in the Caribbean, it is Saba.

Until the early 1940s Saba was almost inaccessible. Everything had to come and go via Ladder Bay. This extraordinary landing on the leeward shore provides scant shelter from ocean swells. Some 800 steps are cut in the rock. The steepness of the steps and their elevation can be appreciated from the sea by looking at the old customs house, which is only half way up. Boats could only land when the sea was calm and even then men had to stand waist deep in water to handle the cargo.

Everything from the outside had to be carried up, including, at different times, a piano and a bishop. The Sabans were able to prevent unwanted invasions by keeping piles of boulders stacked behind wooden supports that were cut down when attackers were half way up the hill. A road was built to Fort Bay in 1943, but with no port to shelter the bay, the island was still impossible to reach much of the time.

The 1500 inhabitants are descendants of hardy Dutch, Scottish, and English settlers, along with a few Africans who originally came as slaves. They have worked hard, side by side, to derive a decent living from this rugged land. They became great seafarers, fishermen, farmers, cobblers, boat builders, and, in more recent times, women have become skilled in lacework. Sabans take great pride in their work and are unimpressed by obstacles. The two main villages in Saba are named Bottom and Windwardside.

Up until the 50s, the only way to get between the villages was to walk along a steep mountain track. Engineers came from

Holland and said the steep terrain precluded the possibility of a road. So Joseph Hassel, born in 1906, took a correspondence course in road building and the Saban people hand-built their road. It took them several years and was finished in 1958. Dutch engineers were similarly disparaging about the idea of an airport. The Sabans called in Remy de Haenen, a pilot from St. Barts. He looked over their one flat-topped rock and figured landing might be possible. The Sabans flattened the area as much as they could by hand, removing big rocks and filling in holes. Remy landed, proving the feasibility of flying in.

Today Sabans have their airport (it's like landing on an aircraft carrier), a road to the sea, and a tiny harbor. Despite its lack of beaches, Saba attracts visitors. Some come to try the diving, rated among the Caribbean's best. Others come for a glimpse of this remote island, which devel-

oped in isolation, away from the mainstream of Caribbean life. The first surprise is the beauty of the island. From the sea it looks like a rock, but up high in the hills the mountains and views are spectacular. The island is spotlessly clean, with villages of whitewashed, green-trimmed, red-roofed cottages that look like they were plucked from Europe sometime in the 19th century. There are cobblestone streets, low stonewalls, and small stone churches. The people are honest, straightforward, industrious, and cheerful. They have a strong sense of community and there is very little crime. The facilities for the sick, aged, and handicapped are amazing, considering the small population. Many of the new projects have been carried out with aid from their mother country, the Netherlands, but every cent has been wisely used. The Saba community has a perfection all its own. Unique in the Caribbean, a tour of Saba

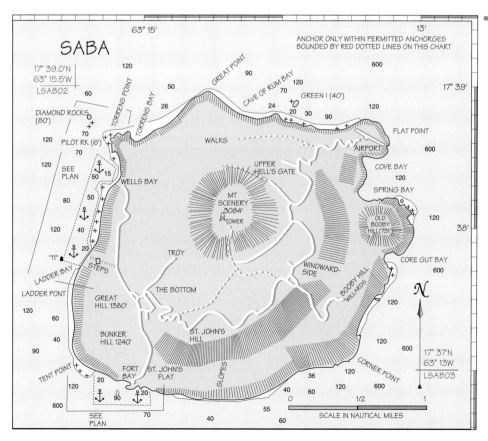

165

should be high on your agenda. The hike to Mt. Scenery on a clear day offers awesome views.

Industries include a small amount of tourism, the mining of gravel and sand from one of the hillsides near Fort Bay, and a new international medical school whose students, when in residence, add about 30-50 percent to the population. This, plus the arrival of a few more visitors and the building of a few more hotels, has brought some changes: there are more shops and their stock is much more plentiful; restaurants are excellent and booming. There are even a couple of discos.

Saba is not the easiest of anchorages, though the addition of yacht moorings helps. Many bare-boat charter companies make it off-limits for their guests. Those who cannot visit by boat should consider going by air or ferry as a side trip. The least expensive way is the Edge Ferry from Pelican Quay, Sint Maarten (Wed-Sun, $75US round trip), or Winair will fly you for about twice that.

Navigation

Like all good hidden kingdoms, Saba doesn't come easily, and the cruising sailor who wishes to visit must be prepared to pay the price of possible frustration in the face of the elements. The trick is to listen to the weather reports and avoid visiting if heavy northerly swells or strong northeasterly winds are forecast.

Approaching is no problem, as the island is steep-to and a quarter of a mile offshore clears all dangers, except for Diamond Rock and Green Island at the north end. A quick flashing white aerobeacon sits on top of Mt. Scenery, but is usually obscured by clouds.

For much of the time, the west coast offers excellent anchorage in either Ladder Bay or Well's Bay. Up to eleven yacht moorings are spaced along this stretch of coast. They are yellow with a blue stripe or plain yellow, (do not mistake them for the red or white dive moorings) and are suitable for yachts up to 60 feet or 50 tons; the southernmost one is suitable for yachts up to 150 tons. They are available on a first-come basis at no extra charge as a service of the Saba Marine Park. Each mooring has a tie up line attached to its top. This is easily recognized as it has a plastic-sheathed loop at the free end. Pass your own dock line through the loop and let out plenty of scope. It is best make a bridle with two lines, fastening one to each side of your bow. (Do not use one continuous line for this, or it will chafe as the boat swings.) Superyachts wishing to anchor should do so outside the line of moorings in about

FORT BAY

Chris Doyle

100 feet. The swell here is often comfortably long and gentle, though if the tides are running strongly, you can lay beam-to the swells for a few hours on the rising tide. While the coast is totally open to the north, the moorings are fairly deep, so unless a northerly swell is huge, you should be able to stay on the mooring OK. However, in a northerly swell it will roll. (Saba is probably a little better than Statia in northerly swells because of the depths.)

With four moorings off Fort Bay you can also tie up here. It is close to the harbor but usually much rougher (except in northerly swells when Fort Bay is better). You can tie here on a Fort Bay mooring during the day where it is closer to get ashore, and move over to the west coast for comfort at night.

Cruising to Saba in earlier days could be frustrating because, having arrived, one might sit for days waiting for conditions calm enough to land. Now you can take

your dinghy inside the harbor and climb ashore dry. It is less than 2 miles from Well's Bay to Fort Bay, so even with a 2-horsepower outboard you can make it in half an hour, though parts of the journey can be rough for a small tender, so do not overload it. The port has security that keeps an eye on dinghies.

Sabans are intent on keeping their waters as pristine and beautiful as their land. Anchoring is restricted to sandy areas where coral will not be damaged. We show these on our sketch chart. Check in with the park office when you go to Fort Bay. (See also Regulations and Water Sports).

Communications

Island Communications Services in Windwardside offers internet, phones, DVD rentals, US mailing, copying, and printing. They also rent cell phones, rent cars, and arrange airline tickets. They open

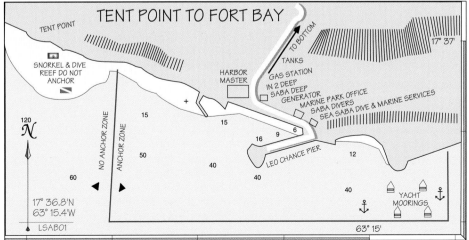

weekdays 0900-1099, Saturdays 1000-1700.

Services

You can get diesel, and gasoline in jerry jugs from the gas station open 0800-1500, Monday to Saturday. There are garbage bins on the dock. Ask the Harbor Master about filling jerry jugs with water, and if that does not work, talk to Saba Deep. If you need to make a phone call, the telephone office is in Bottom.

Sea Saba has a yacht services department at their dive shop in Fort Bay. They can help out in emergencies and their mechanical shop includes light fabrication, TIG welding (all metals), and mechanical services.

Matthew Dorm's Laundry is above Bottom. If you are doing an island tour, get your taxi driver to drop it off first thing and collect it before you go back.

Fort Bay Anchorage

The Marine Park has four moorings here and you may also anchor (see chart). It is usually uncomfortable and you would not want to be here in a southeast wind or large southerly swells, but this anchorage is OK in calm weather or when the wind is well to the north, and it is better to be here in northerly swells. You can also come by day to go ashore, as the ride into the harbor is very short, then return to the northwest coast when you get back.

Ladder Bay Anchorage

This is the best all round anchorage in Saba. The only available shallow anchoring space is off the steps. However, small yachts can anchor farther out in 50 feet of water up to Well's Bay or, better yet, use the yacht moorings that are spaced all the way to Well's Bay. Superyachts should anchor outside the moorings. The flattest bottom is towards the northern end. The southernmost mooring has heavy rope and is suitable for up to 150 tons. When you want to go ashore, do as any of today's Sabans would; use Fort Bay. Several yachtsmen have tried to follow in the footsteps of

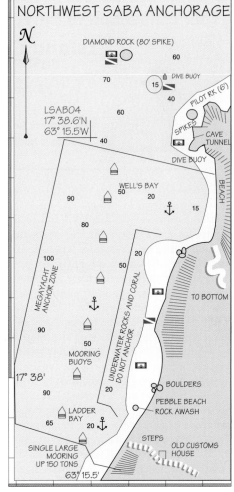

Sabans of old and use Ladder Bay. The high attrition rate indicates that modern cruisers lack the skill and patience of old time Sabans, so take the safe way. However, when ashore a taxi can take you to the steps, which are maintained as a monument, and the walk down and up is delightful and gives you a feel of Saba's history.

Well's Bay Anchorage

This is a spectacularly beautiful anchorage below high cliffs with huge rocks embedded in them. Tropic birds wheel and chatter above, and below you can find some of the Caribbean's best snorkeling. There is plenty of room to anchor in sand in 15 to 50 feet of water. Make sure you

WELLS BAY

NORTHWEST SABA

MOORINGS

stay clear of the reef and boulder areas at either end, and close along the shore. Do not use this anchorage in northerly swells. During the summer months there is a beach here, but in the winter the sand washes away, leaving boulders. There is a road leading to Bottom. The road from Bottom to Windwardside is known as the "road that couldn't be built", and some taxi drivers think that the road to Well's Bay is the "road that shouldn't have been built," as it is so steep they cannot make it up with a full load. Taxi driver Garvin Hassell is happy to use this road. (It is occasionally closed due to landslides.)

If it's exceptionally calm, you can land here to explore the beach. But if you head inland, swells could arrive while you are gone, and maroon you ashore for a few days. So, I would not advise it, especially as several people have hurt themselves in the attempt.

When leaving, most yachts can pass between the amazing Diamond Rock pinnacle and Torrens Point. Deep draft yachts should note the 15-foot-deep Man O' War Shoals in the middle, as well as underwater rocks extending from both sides, so do this in good light. You can tie your dinghy to the diving/snorkeling buoy at Torrens Point for snorkeling.

Provisioning

You can find a surprising variety of food on Saba, but don't expect the fancy supermarkets and provisioning available in St. Martin. The easiest place to provision is at My Store in Bottom. This is an impressive-

ISLANDS THAT BRUSH THE CLOUDS

ly large supermarket by Saban standards, but in keeping with the scale, rather than being a single big area, it flows through several small rooms. In Bottom you will also find the Saba Self-Service Supermarket.

Big Rock Market is in Windwardside, and this is also a sizeable shop with a good range of groceries of all sorts. D&A is another supermarket at Windwardside, opposite the tourist office. It is a bit smaller than Big Rock, but has a good selection including fresh produce.

Fun Shopping

You will find ATM machines in both Bottom and Windwardside. Saban women are artistic. About 120 years ago Gertrude Johnson learned to do a special kind of embroidery from nuns in Venezuela. She brought this dying art back to Saba and the Saban women have been improving on it ever since. It is known as "drawing thread handwork" or "Spanish thread work". The largest selection is at the Hellsgate Community Cottage, though you may enjoy buying from a lace maker's home.

There are elegant shirts, aprons, and household items. Lace is not the only Saban art. You can find great local arts and crafts as well as causal clothing here.

An interesting cluster of shops surrounds the tourist office. Sea Saba Shop has elegant t-shirts, casual wear, diving accessories, local books, souvenirs and more.

El Momo sells clothing, lots of handicrafts and t-shirts downstairs, and ornaments, decorations, candles, and art upstairs. Much of the work is made on Saba, and they also specialize in a large selection of excellent molas from the San Blas islands.

The Peanut Gallery (closed Mondays), is owned by Judy Stewart, who is a potter, and the gallery shows work of many talented local artists at very reasonable prices; also some of Judy's pottery. One of the artists, Heleen, has a beautiful book of her art called Saban Cottages available here (if you want to see more of her work, call Heleen for a visit to her studio in Troy: 416-3348).

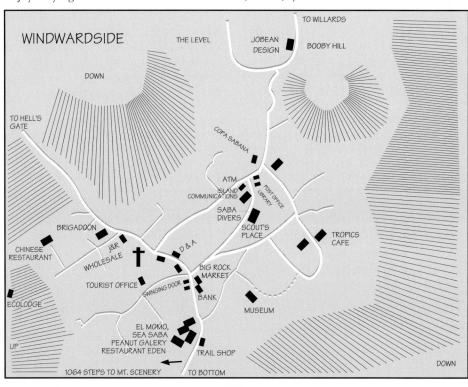

Across the road, the Trail Shop is part of the Saba Conservation Society (closed Mondays). A new national park has just been created and in the Trail Shop you can buy maps, nature books, t-shirts, and other eco-friendly souvenirs whose purchase benefits the society.

While you are shopping, try the special Saban liqueur called Saba Spice. It is made with lots of herbs and spices. The first sip reminds the uninitiated of cough medicine, but apparently it is possible to acquire a taste for it.

Take a pleasant short walk just out of town to Booby Hill, where you will find Jobean Designs, a wonderful working glass studio. Jo works with rods of glass to produce elegant jewelry, small glass sculptures of tree lizards, frogs, turtles, mermaids and more. She also makes many glass beads. These include imitations of (but you won't be able tell the difference) the famous slave beads once used in Statia and Heineken beads made from the bottles.

You can watch Jo at work creating handsome designs with different colored glass. She will even design something especially for you. She also sells silver jewelry and other gifts collected from her trips to far away places. Jo runs glass work classes on request. She is active in the turtle protection program, Widecast, and helps provide alternative employment for the turtle fishermen of St. Kitts.

Restaurants

Eating out in Saba is a pleasure, with plenty of choice. Willard's of Saba on Booby Hill is the last word in casual elegance and has the best view in the Leewards. It would be impossible to beat this fancy hotel, which has seven rooms – each one bigger than many Saban homes – a Jacuzzi, and a gym. It is perched with a swimming pool on the edge of a 2000-foot precipice that plunges down to the sea. On a clear day you can see Statia, St. Kitts, Nevis, St. Barts and Montserrat. Superyachts should make this their first choice. You do need to book in advance. Manager and chef Corazon de Johnson will welcome you warmly and feed you excellent Asian and European delicacies. She likes the challenge of working with those who have special dietary needs and can cook kosher food.

The Queens Garden Resort in Troy is within fairly easy walking distance of Bottom, and is also casually stylish. The courtyard is half-surrounded by a lush tropical garden that climbs the hill, the other half affords a panoramic view to Bottom and the ocean far below. This is also a sizeable hotel and Ron Mohlmann, the manager, keeps an attentive staff. They serve good international and local food, and have a tank for live lobster.

Wolfgang and Barbara Tooten have an unusual dive shop that is also Scout's Place, a guesthouse perched half way up a mountain in Windwardside. You do your pool training with a view 2000 feet down to the sea. They have a fine bar and restaurant, the food varying with the nationality and temperament of the chef. This is a very friendly place and the outer limit of their

dining room is a tiny balcony with a spectacular view. Pop in for lunchtime specials or make reservations for dinner. They also open for breakfast, and if you need a good place to stay ashore for a reasonable price, this is it.

Tropics Café (closed Mondays) is open from breakfast through dinner with a great view and a pool. Chris and Paul, the owners, have different menus for each meal, with a wide and imaginative choice. In the evening they offer seafood and a variety of steaks and meat. Sunday brunch is a big event.

Saba's Treasures has a pub-like atmosphere and bakes excellent pizzas. The Swinging Door also has a pub-like atmosphere and serves world-class hamburgers with ice-cold beer for both lunch and dinner (plus a Tuesday barbecue). Farther down the road, Brigadoon, with a view over the north side of the hill, is run by Michael Chamma. He opens evenings only and closes on Tuesdays. He varies his menu to use the fresh food that is available, and has a

Saturday sushi hour. He also likes to cook seafood, steaks, and rack of lamb.

Restaurant Eden has pleasant dining areas with the feel of a garden. Owner's Norbert from Holland and Nina from Norway are serious about their food, which is French in style, with some Italian other European influence. You can expect to eat well here, whether it is a sashimi sandwich for lunch or full evening meal. Before you eat too much, take a look at the tempting desert menu. They open every day for lunch (1200-1600) and dinner (1730-2130).

Copa Sabana is an informal little restaurant with a roof-top eating area owned by Hensley from Curacao. He does a lot of local specialties, including curried goat as well as burgers, salads, wraps, and more international dishes. He is open every day for lunch and dinner.

On the road from Hell's Gate to the airport is the Gate House. It is open for dinner only by reservation.

The perfect place for a meal before or after climbing the mountain is the Eco

Lodge run by Tom Vant Hof, Bernt and Dana. It is a 5-minute walk from the junction where the top road joins the hiking trail. Good salads and sandwiches for lunch and daily specials for dinner, though for dinner reservations are important. This is also a great place to stay, with little artistically painted cottages tucked into the forest.

Lollipop's, up the hill from Bottom, offers a bar, a restaurant serving good local food and a disco.

Closer to Bottom, near the new medical school building, Campus Corner does local meals and snacks and is open every day from morning right through until after dinner. In Bottom, the Family Deli is both a bakery and restaurant. Lime Time is a new authentic Chinese Restaurant.

Saba Deep operates an entertaining bar/restaurant called In Two Deep on the top half of their dive shop in Fort Bay. Sit and relax in cool air-conditioning. You will be greeted by Cheri and Tony Waterfield, originally from Virginia and royally fed by Joani, the chef, who is part Carib and is originally from St. Vincent. She cooks delectable hot lunch specials, including first-rate Créole fish. Or you can enjoy a sandwich while trading underwater stories. In Two Deep opens with the dive shop at 0830 and is a great place for breakfast or morning coffee and muffins and then lunch. They will open in the evening for large groups wanting dinner and are open on some special nights.

Ashore

Bottom is built on a shelf, with steep slopes above and below, it is Saba's capital and administrative center, and has the medical school. The other village, Windwardside, is up the mountain. Both are charming and photogenic. A full taxi tour is the best way to see the island. This can be a very flexible arrangement. Whatever you want to do will be fitted in. Time for shopping, photography, climbing the mountain, making a phone call, or having lunch, can easily be arranged. You can stay on the island as long as you want. The drivers are excellent guides. The roads are narrow and steep, facing many a sheer drop. Bring your camera. The tour rate is very reasonable and based on about a

Joani, the chef at In Two Deep

Chris Doyle

ISLANDS THAT BRUSH THE CLOUDS

Windwardside   Chris Doyle

three-hour ride. Your tour can last much longer than that if you are being dropped off and picked up, so the driver does not have to be with you all day. But if you go way over what you would think reasonable for a short tour, you might want to pay some extra.

Hiking in Saba is excellent and trail maps are available at the tourist office. The walk to the top of Mt. Scenery, which is about 3000 feet high, is world class. The trail begins in Windwardside, but you can get a taxi to drop you off from a road that meets the trail higher up. Like everything else on Saba, the path is well maintained and it includes some 1064 steps. The cloud forest vegetation of giant philodendrons, clusia, and tree ferns resembles a magnificent garden. Clouds passing below sometimes will give you a weird sensation of sitting on a cloud. If you are lucky enough to make it on a clear day, follow the path past the aerial to the end. You will be treated to one of the Caribbean's most spectacular and terrifyingly precipitous views, about 1500 feet straight down to Windwardside. A new trail goes the other way to the very highest point of the island, and for this some agility is required and you have to pull yourself on a rope that has been placed on the trail. The views here will probably also be amazing, but usually you will be in the mist. Allow 2 to 3 hours for the round trip hike, starting at the higher road. If you make it, the tourist office can issue you an award certificate. If you want a hiking guide in Saba, ask in the Trail Shop.

Water Sports

The snorkeling is fabulous and the diving stupendous. The self-supporting marine park was for many years the best in the Caribbean. Current laws forbidding independent diving have lost it this accolade in my opinion, but the diving is still great. Go to the marine park office next to the generating plant to get a brochure that describes all the dive and snorkel sites. The park maintains diving buoys on all the good sites, and will freely tell you anything you might want to know. Tom Van't Hof's book, *Guide to the Saba Marine Park*, describes all the dives. In addition, the Saba Marine Park keeps a recompression chamber for diving accidents.

The snorkeling at Well's Bay is first rate. Tie your dinghy to the diving buoy at the north end of the bay. There are two tunnels and a cave to explore in waters packed with fish and turtles. The first tunnel is easily seen from the mooring and looks like a cave. You find the cave by going through the tunnel and turning right. The third tunnel is beyond the cave and is underwater.

Saba plunges down into the sea as rapidly as it rises. There are excellent dives at all levels. Diving here is diving on the Caribbean's outer edge, and you might meet the unexpected anytime. Giant rays and hammerhead and whale sharks have been sighted; turtles and stingrays are fairly common.

Any of the three dive shops will be happy to take you diving and meet you at your yacht. You can try to call them on the radio, but you have to call before you arrive in Saba or get one of the dive boats when it is going out or returning, as it is impossible to reach Fort Bay by radio from the anchorage (some cell phones may work). Better still; make your dive arrangements when you go in for your tour of Saba. If you have your own dive gear and tender, you can arrange with one of the dive shops to supply a dive guide. All dive shops now do nitrox.

Saba Divers brings a European approach to diving in Saba. It is run by Barbara and Wolfgang Tooten. They are relaxed and friendly, and generally expect to be able to teach in English, German or Dutch. Their dive shop is in Fort Bay, a pleasant area with a shower and seating for after dive chitchat. They have two large, solid, covered dive boats. They listen to VHF: 16, but even up in Windwardside are out of range of the anchorage. It should be easy to contact them on your sail over. Courses and pool training are done in the pool at Scout's Place.

Saba Deep (VHF: 16) is the original dive shop and easy to find where the road leaves the bay. It is owned and run by Toni and Cheri Waterfield and they dive at 0900, 1100, and 1300. Saba Deep is a Padi and Naui facility. Toni and Cheri and their staff like to work with small groups and can train at all levels and do many advanced courses up to divemaster. They do a lot of nitrox diving and are very experienced with it.

Sea Saba (VHF: 16) is based both at Windwardside and in Fort Bay. It is owned by John Magor and Lynn Costenaro, who have been on the island over 25 years. John is an excellent underwater and land photographer. Sea Saba is a full Padi instruction facility with nitrox diving. They have two 40-foot covered dive boats, and usually take a maximum of 10 with two crew. They can teach in French, German, Dutch and English. Their workshop in Fort Bay

ISLANDS THAT BRUSH THE CLOUDS

Saba's small port

Chris Doyle

Chris Doyle

ered and they are curious and unafraid of divers. Margates, snappers, sole eyes, durgons, and doctor fish are just a few of the species you will see. The dive site is not large, so swim slowly. As you swim around the rock it seems that each new vista is more dramatically beautiful than the last. Occasionally there is current.

Man O' War Shoals lies between Diamond Rock and Torren's Point. It consists of a large rock whose twin peaks come to within 15 feet of the surface. This is another dreamy dive that makes me feel I am swimming in a perfect underwater painting. The rocks are well covered with a profusion of hard and soft corals and multi-colored sponges. This forms the perfect backdrop to a cast of thousands of fish who are completely unafraid. A few even stare in your mask, as if hoping to find some kind of intelligence. We saw a school of large and very tame jacks, a pair of tuna, and many margates, besides the usual reef fish. The area is small, but so beautiful it is easy to relax away an hour.

helps out with marine problems and is next to Pop's Place, which is great for a snack, cold beer, and the latest Saba gossip.

Diving is varied in Saba: from startlingly dramatic walls to serenely beautiful coral on white sand. Here are just a few of the 26 dives:

You can see Diamond Rock rising dramatically out of the sea from Well's Bay. It drops down to a sandy bottom 80 feet below. The rock is covered with colorful sponges and many hard and soft corals; the fish life here is staggering. It seems that all the brightest colored reef fish have gath-

Torren's Point forms the northern point of Well's Bay and many spiked rocks stick up above the water. We have already mentioned the caves with reference to snorkeling, but this is also a shallow dive area, rarely getting deeper than 40 feet. Large boulders and rock formations rise from the sand, leaving sandy channels, gullies, and pools between them. The rocks have been well colonized by corals and sponges and there is a profusion of smaller reef fish.

There are several dives off Ladder Bay, starting at around 20 feet and dropping to

176

Chris Doyle

about 90 feet. Here you will find many rocky ridges about 10 feet high, with sandy alleys between. There is an abundance of hard and soft corals, colorful reef fish, crabs, and shrimps.

Tent Point, just west of Fort Bay, is 30 to 80 feet deep, with pillar coral, colorful soft corals, and sponges, among which are lots of reef fish, some French angelfish, and the occasional turtle. Tent Reef Wall is a dramatic drop off, with purple and yellow tube sponges and black coral.

The next dives are perhaps Saba's most famous adventure dives: pinnacles that rise from 1000 feet deep to within 90 feet of the surface. They lie together about half a mile offshore.

Third Encounter consists of a plateau about 100 feet deep with a deep drop off on most sides. Coral mounds rise above the plateau. The climax of this dive is the Eye of the Needle. As you swim into the blue unknown, an amazing slender pinnacle appears before you, rising from great depths to 90 feet below the surface. It is so pretty you may want to hold your breath – but keep breathing! There is a painting of it on the backside of the marine park brochure.

Twilight Zone is in the same general area. A series of rocky outcrops rise to 80 or so feet below the surface from a ledge that in some places drops away as far as you can see. There are many deepwater gorgonians and sponges and many tame fish, including groupers and jacks.

Outer Limits is the third dive in this area: a long narrow ridge at 90 to 100 feet and over the edge of it a dramatic drop off to nowhere – and another dramatic profusion of fearless fish.

ISLANDS THAT BRUSH THE CLOUDS

View of St. Kitts from Statia's botanical garden   Chris Doyle

St. Eustatius (Statia)

STATIA IS A SMALL ISLAND with a large history. From the anchorage you will see a long cliff just behind a sandy beach. At the base of the cliff a couple of buildings are nestled between old stone ruins, which tumble into the sea. On top of the cliff the present small town peeks out through trees. To the east a perfect volcanic cone rises to 1800 feet. Ashore, a donkey grazes peacefully; little movement breaks the tranquility.

Imagine now, the Golden Era during the mid to late 1700s, when Statia was the trade capital of the Indies, and one of the world's busiest harbors. Up to three hundred sailing ships lie at anchor. All along the shore a sea wall protects a long street of shops and warehouses. Goods are available here from all over the world: fine fabrics, silver, gold, household supplies, slaves, guns, sugar, tobacco, and cotton. Thousands of tons of commodities are traded daily in a colorful, noisy, bustling town, with hundreds of small boats going from ships to shore. During these years, the European powers were fighting each other; in addition, England was unsuccessfully trying to put down the upstart American rebels. The major powers wrapped their colonies in a mass of red tape and taxes, stifling trade. The Dutch, who owned Statia, remained neutral and opened Statia as a free port. It became possible to buy or sell anything here, along with the appropriate papers. Countries not allowed to deal with each other could deal with Statia, so Statian papers were attached to many things produced elsewhere. For example, in 1770 Statia produced about 600,000 pounds of sugar, but exported 20 million pounds. It was officially approved smuggling, and the inhabitants, some 8000

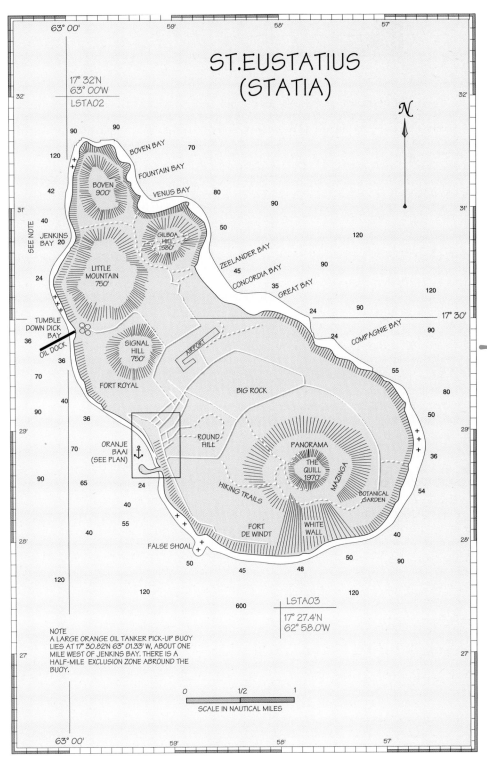

ST.EUSTATIUS (STATIA)

17° 32'N
63° 00'W
LSTA02

N

90

90

BOVEN BAY   70

120

FOUNTAIN BAY

+ +

42   BOVEN
            900'   VENUS BAY   80

90

40

JENKINS
BAY 20   GILBOA
             HILL
             1580'

50

120

24   LITTLE   ZEELANDER BAY
             MOUNTAIN
             750'   45   CONCORDIA BAY   90

35   GREAT BAY   120

+ +

24   90

TUMBLE   24   17° 30'
DOWN DICK   COMPAGNIE BAY
36   BAY   24   90
     OIL DOCK
36   SIGNAL
                  HILL   AIRPORT
                  750'   55

70   FORT ROYAL   80

40   BIG ROCK
90   50
     36

70   + + +
             ORANJE   ROUND   36
             BAAI   HILL   PANORAMA
90   (SEE PLAN)
65   THE   54
                    24   QUILL
                                     1970'
40   HIKING TRAILS   BOTANICAL
     55   GARDEN
40   + +   40
                FORT   WHITE
                DE WINDT WALL
FALSE SHOAL +   90
            50   45   48   50

120

120   120
            120
                     600   LSTA03
                            17° 27.4'N
                            62° 58.0'W

ISLANDS THAT BRUSH THE CLOUDS

NOTE
A LARGE ORANGE OIL TANKER PICK-UP BUOY
LIES AT 17° 30.82'N 63° 01.33' W, ABOUT ONE
MILE WEST OF JENKINS BAY. THERE IS A
HALF-MILE EXCLUSION ZONE ABROUND THE
BUOY.

0   1/2   1

SCALE IN NAUTICAL MILES

Regulations

On arrival, check with the harbor- master and immigration at the head of the town dock. Normal office hours are 0800-1600 weekdays, 0800-1100 weekends and holidays. Charges are according to size and the number of passengers and typical rates are $15 for a small yacht up to 105US for a big superyacht. There is also a $1 per passenger fee, which fee is good for three days; renewal costs $5. All Satia coastal waters are part of the the National Park, and they charges $10 US per night (or $30 US per week), a fee that includes theuse of their moorings.

Scuba diving is only allowed through the local dive shop. You can snorkel on your mooring or around your boat, otherwise see the Park about snorkel sites, and pay the snorkel/dive fee.

Telephones

Telephone calls are easily made from any of the credit card phones placed both in the harbor and in town, or see Eutel in town, who have a bank of phones, and they can also put money on telcel phones and some others. Dial 00 to get out of Statia, then the country code (1 for the USA; 44 for the UK).

Shopping hours

Shopping hours depend to some extent on the proclivity of the proprietor; try 0800-1200 and 1400-1800. Some food stores are owned by 7th day Adventists, and they close Saturday until after sunset, and then open to 2100. On Sundays some supermarkets open 0900-1300.

Transport

Statia is linked to Saba, St. Martin, and St. Kitts by several daily flights. For transport within the island, both car rentals and taxis are available. Typical taxi rates in $US are:

Sightseeing tour (up to 5 people)	$40.00
	$5.00 per person extra charge
Airport to Town	$5.00 per person
Harbor to Quill	$4.00 per person

The National Park office will arrange a cab for you.

Holidays

- Jan 1
- Good Friday and Easter Monday (Easter Sunday is April 4, 2010; April 24, 2011)
- April 30 (Queen's Birthday)
- May 1 (Labor Day)
- Ascension Day (39 days after Easter: (May 13, 2010, June 2, 2011)
- Whit Monday, 50 days after Easter Sunday (May 24, 2010, June 13, 2011)
- July 1 (Emancipation Day)
- Carnival takes place over the last two weeks in July; only the last Monday of this time is an official holiday.
- October 21 Antillean Day
- November 16 (Statia/America Day)
- December 15, Kingdom Day
- December 25- 26

ORANJE BAAI ANCHORAGE

mixed Dutch, English, and Jewish merchants, got very rich. Statia became known as the Golden Rock, but the prosperity was not to last.

In 1776 the Andrew Doria, an American vessel, came into harbor and gave a salute. Governor de Graff, not sure what to do, decided to fire a return salute, but two guns less. He didn't realize that, although Andrew Doria was a merchant ship, she was under the command of an American rebel navy captain. Thus Statia became the first nation to salute an American naval vessel. British officials didn't think much of this, and even less of the fact that an American ship later captured a British ship in the area and took it back to the States. This, plus the fact that Statia sold weapons to the rebels, led to war between England and Holland.

Admiral Rodney arrived and Governor de Graff, who did not know what to do about the salute, knew exactly what to do about Rodney; He surrendered. Rodney confiscated all the ships and warehouses, but found less cash and valuables than he expected. Rodney noticed that for a small population the merchants were having a lot of funerals. He ordered one to be stopped and looked in the coffin. It was full of coins and jewelry and a little digging in the graveyard revealed much more. He rounded up a hundred Jewish men for deportation. When his men searched them and ripped open the lining of their clothes, they found another 8000 pounds sterling. Rodney stole this too, before sending them to St. Kitts. He then held a giant auction that netted him and his crew a fortune. This was not too popular with British subjects who lost property. He was sued and questions were asked in parliament. Luckily for Rodney, he won the crucial "Battle of the Saintes" just in time and all was forgiven.

By the late 1700s Statia was again Dutch and trade was flourishing, but in the early 19th century the changing political and economic climate in the Caribbean ended Statia's role as the Caribbean's first shopping mall, and there followed a long decline and massive emigration. The sea wall, which had been built on sand, slowly sank and subsequent hurricanes destroyed the lower town. The last ruins can still be seen.

Every time I return to Statia it looks better. The historical society, with funding from Holland, has done an excellent job of restoring many of the ruins and old build-

ISLANDS THAT BRUSH THE CLOUDS

ings. It is also getting busier – traffic for the first time is noticeable. The American medical school helps stimulate the economy, as does a big oil storage depot in the north of the island. The 3400 inhabitants welcome visitors with genuine warmth. Statia is so far off the beaten track that the very few visitors you meet are likely to be interesting. To put icing on the cake, the scuba diving is impressive and there is a selection of enjoyable restaurants.

Navigation

Statia is steep to. A quarter of a mile offshore clears all natural underwater dangers, but there are several rocks and reefs within 100 feet of shore and some extend considerably farther. In particular, False Shoal rises to within 2 feet of the surface, 300 yards offshore.

White Wall is conspicuous from the south. It is a massive limestone slab that has been thrust up from under the sea.

A long fuel loading dock lies about a mile and a half north of Oranjestad, the main town. Northwest of this, about 1 mile off Jenkins Bay, is a large orange oil tanker terminal buoy, which flashes at night. Numerous tugs and barges are anchored and moored around the dock, and often

floating fuel lines go from them to shore, so you must pass outside the terminal buoy and give it a half-mile clearance.

The National Marine Park has also put in many unlit dive moorings (and one lit one). Oranje Baai is the only real anchorage. Most of the time it is acceptably calm, but it is no place to be in a hurricane or other disturbed weather system, including a really bad northerly swell. Regular easterly swells normally bend round the island to arrive in Oranje Baai from the south. You can get protection from these swells by anchoring behind the new breakwater. The Statia Marine Park charges $10 US a night and has put 12 moorings in a long row off the beach. They are designed for yachts up to 30 tons; the three deeper moorings at the northern end have heavier rope and will take boats up to 250 tons. Use of the moorings is included in the fee. Look for the round yellow buoys (a few have a blue stripe). Each has a looped pick up line attached to a smaller buoy. Pick up the loop and put your dock line though the eye at the end, and give it at least 10 feet of scope. It is best to use two separate lines, one to each side of the bow. Never moor with a single line from one side of the bow,

The harbor wall gives some protection to moored boats.

Chris Doyle

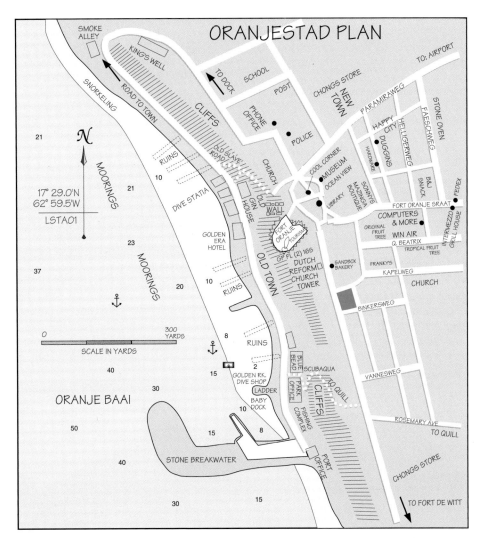

through the mooring to the other side of the bow. Your boat's motion will saw through the line. A surge often does find its way in from the south, and you can keep your boat a lot calmer by attaching to the mooring and then taking out a second anchor well to the east. Use this second anchor to bring your stern to the swells. Those on cats will not have to worry about any of this as they hardly roll.

The moorings in 2009 were good – each had a double seabed anchor, but still it is a good idea to snorkel and check your mooring, the water is very clear, it is not an onerous job – I usually see something inter-

esting – a ray, crab, or barracuda.

The National Park office covers both the marine park and the land park. Check in after you clear in. They open weekdays 0700-1700.

The marine park eventually plans to put in a system of reef balls (hollow concrete balls full of holes), which they hope might protect the beach by breaking the swells. These will be about 400 feet off the beach and will come to within a foot of the surface, so they should be visible in good light.

The Statia Port Authority sometimes stands by on VHF: 16/14; Statia Marine Park on VHF: 16/17. The port offers no

ISLANDS THAT BRUSH THE CLOUDS

protection from the occasional northerly swells. Moderate northerly swells are not too bad, especially if you are not too close to shore. In exceptionally bad swells, you won't want to be here. The port has a dinghy docking area on the shore side of the main ship dock. You can also tie your dinghy to the baby dock.

A light on the fort sometimes flashes 3 every 16 seconds. Several red lights on the hills just to the north of Oranjestad mark the airport, and a red light that flashes about once a second has been placed on top of the Quill. The port sees a lot of activity from tanker tenders bringing crew ashore.

Communications

The National Park office on the waterfront has a good internet station. They also sell postcards and stamps and will mail them for you. In town, Computers and More, run by Carlos and Cindy Lopez, is the place to check e-mail, send faxes, and buy some computer accessories. Look for their office in a trailer. The local library also has a bank of internet computers. They open weekdays 0800-1200 and 1300-1645, but they do not open on Monday mornings. King's Well has wifi for the customers, and you might get a hook-up to some station from your boat. You will also find a telephone office and a post office. Credit card phones are in several locations and there is a bank of card phones outside the telephone office.

Services

Sun Rain Laundry will collect and deliver from the dock - call 318-1644 or 1647, or ask the marine park to do it for you.

The Park office has toilets and showers ($2 a shower), they give out tourist information, have an internet station and tell you how to get ice. They are open 0700-1700 Monday to Thursday, 0700-1600 Fridays, closed weekends and public holidays. Manager, Nicole Eseban, was bought up in England and she and her staff are helpful.

The Quill over Oranjstad

Chris Doyle

The old gin house   Chris Doyle

You can arrange with the port office to come along side to take on diesel. The minimum is 100 gallons. For smaller quantities, or gasoline, you will have to take a taxi and jerry jug it from town.

Golden Rock Dive Center (VHF: 16/11) acts as the local representative for Sunsail and Moorings. In an emergency, Golden Rock Dive Center can supply water via a long hose if you go bow-to the baby dock. This is labor intensive for them, so there is a $45 US charge. For any yachting problems, call them on the radio or try their office by the baby dock.

Reynaldo is a good mechanic and diver who helps out with most yacht problems. He can take care of untangling anchors or undertake underwater repairs. He is most often called in to fix charter boat problems. Ask for him in Golden Rock Dive Center.

Ask Win and Laura at King's Well how to contact Carti, if he is around. He is a skilled diesel mechanic, who will have your knocking and smoking engine purring again.

Energetic people can walk over most of the island; others can take a taxi or rent a car. You will find garbage dumps inside the port, outside the fisheries complex, and farther along the road towards the Golden Era Hotel.

Shopping

Statia is completely duty-free, so prices of liquor and luxuries are competitive with St. Martin. If you are low on cash, take your credit card to the ATM machine opposite Mazinga Gift Shop, or the one by the airport. You can change money commission-free at the First Caribbean Bank.

185

Statia has some good supermarkets. Duggins is one of the best, complete with fresh produce, frozen meats, and delicatessen items, as well as an upstairs department store. They open Monday to Thursday 0800-1930, Friday 0800-1800, Saturday 1830-2100, and Sunday 0900-1300. They will deliver your order to the dock. The Chinese-run Happy City is a mini-market close by. Chon's Store is another Chinese market, near the post office. The Chinese stores open Saturday mornings when the others are closed. Check also the Sandbox Tree Bakery; if you want fresh hot bread, go at 1600.

Mazinga Gift Shop is a bit like a mini-department store, with sportswear and beachwear, stationary and books, a selection of English language magazines, office supplies, toys, a wide range of gifts, and they are also a full liquor store. If you buy too much to carry, they will deliver it to the dock before 1100. Mazinga is an ideal place to run off all those promised postcards. Ask them to sell you the cards with stamps. Buy a cold drink, too, and a pen if you forgot yours. You can write your postcards outside where they have a shady sitting area with tables. Afterwards, you can deliver them back to the Mazinga mailbox.

For souvenirs, remember to check both dive shops as they have interesting small shops with books, gifts, and more.

Restaurants

I suspect Statia has as many restaurants per capita as Washington has lawyers – at least 22 for a population of 2700. I will mention a few, mainly those close to the water. The first restaurant you will see is the Blue Bead, which is cheerful and open with a view right over the water. Ronald and Laurence, the owners, used to own Scubaqua, and have turned the same professionalism to the restaurant. They serve French food and pizzas, have live music on Mondays, and close Tuesdays and Wednesdays.

The modern Golden Era Hotel has a convenient bar and dining room that almost hangs out over the bay. It is clean, cheerful, and offers both local and international dishes. Rooms are available.

The Old Gin House is set in an elegant historic stone and brick building. By Dominique and Walter and is Satia's fanciest restaurants, with first rate food. They open the beach bar at 0630 for breakfast, and lunch (salads, fish 'n chips, burgers) is also served there, as is dinner on Wednesdays, which is a barbecue with live music. The beach bar also serves tapas from 1430 until late. Otherwise, dinner is in the fairly formal Gin House dining room, and they serve mainly seafood, including lobster as well as steaks and other meats.

If you follow the main road up to town, rather than taking the Old Slave Road, you will come to Smoke Alley on the corner. It is open to the bay and the breeze with a great view. This bar and restaurant is run by Manuel and Michelle, who come from Las Vegas. They open Monday through Saturday for both lunch and dinner. Friday night they blast the neighborhood with live music or a DJ, so this is the place for action lovers to be. The menu is hearty American with ribs, steak, local fish, sandwiches, salads, burgers, and daily specials.

A little farther up the hill is Laura and Win's King's Well. This is a great place, a home-away-from-home, rather than a formal restaurant. Different enough, it would make a good subject for a novel – come to think of it I have met a novelist hanging out there. Laura has an Irish background, and Win comes from northern Germany and the back end of their restaurant has a wonderful cliff-hanging view down to the bay. Win loves yachts and yachting people. He is a cruiser at heart, and currently owns a high-speed power boat which could be used as a water taxi to St. Kitts.

Laura loves animals and keeps a flock of macaws, countless iguanas, three dogs, (two of them the size of ponies, watch they don't step on your toes) and other interesting creatures. They open in the evening from 1800-2000, but if you pour your own drinks at the bar on the honor system, it is okay if you arrive early for sunset. Laura bakes beautifully and Win produces excellent German cuisine. His smoked barbe-cued ribs are famous, as are his steaks, schnitzels, rostbraten, and fresh fish. Plenty of cold beer is on hand. You eat very well here, and they will be delighted to tell you all about the island. If the anchorage gets too rolly, you can ask them about rooms (they have 15). You do need to book meals in advance. Laura often listens on VHF: 16 late afternoon to early evening. If you can-not get through earlier in the day, call Dive Statia (VHF: 16), and they will help out by phoning King's Well.

In town, ask about the current hot spot for local food. Ocean View Terrace right opposite the Fort, is quiet and relaxed with good food. A Santa Domingan runs the Fruit Tree. Places for Chinese food include the Chinese Restaurant, Cool Corner, and Sonny's. In the heat of the day, the air-con-ditioning at Super Burger will cool you out while you enjoy good burgers, milk shakes, or ice cream.

Frankey's (closed Wednesdays) often has live entertainment on Sundays and at any other excuse. Other local restaurants include the Stone Oven, and Local Cuisine.

Intermezzo Coffee Shop (closed Saturday) opens weekdays 0730 to 1400; on Sundays and holidays 0800- 1200. This is the place for great coffee (several vari-eties) and a good breakfast. Statians like a party and the odds are if you are here on a weekend, something will be going on. It could be a roadblock, when cars are stopped and every-one jumps up in the street. Check with the tourist office or follow the sound of music.

Ashore

Statia has a quiet charm, which quick-ly grows on you. The walk to Oranjestad is a good introduc-tion. Climb up the old cobbled Slave Road. Above, flow-ers are as colorful as the picturesque gingerbread houses, many beautifully restored. Day-old chicks forage safely along the edge of the road. You can visit the main attractions in the first hour. Fort Oranje has been beautifully restored and is the site of the tourist office. The nearby museum is in the house in which

Chris Doyle

ISLANDS THAT BRUSH THE CLOUDS

Chris Doyle

Admiral Rodney lived during his stay and you can get a sense of how pleasantly cool living in it must have been. Different rooms show ancient history, recent events, and part has been furnished as it might have been long ago. The museum gives out an historical walking tour map and sells an illustrated book to go with it. The tower of the Dutch Reform Church has been rebuilt, and when it is open you can climb up onto the roof for an all-round view. An interesting old Jewish cemetery lies at the end of Princesweg Street. For maps and information, check the marine park office, the tourist office, or the museum.

Hiking is tranquil and easy on Statia. The trails have been well laid out and posted. Visit the National Park office, which is also the Marine Park office. A $6 US yearly pass has been instituted for their upkeep, and they give you hiking maps. Guides are also available for the very reasonable price of $8 US per person, minimum 2. But they do need two day's notice (you can email: info@statiaprk.org).You can go with or

without a guide and set your own pace. One of the most rewarding hikes is up the Quill volcano. The quickest way up is to follow the path that starts between the marine park office and the Blue Bead, which brings you to a road. Turn right on this road then take the next left. Walk right to the top of the road then follow the signs. At the rim of the volcano, you have a choice of paths. One goes down into the Quill crater; another up to the panoramic view. The path into the crater may be a bit tough in wet conditions, because it can be muddy and slippery. You will see massive silk cotton trees here, with buttress roots 6 or 7 feet high. The base of the crater is home to many strangler fig trees. These trees originate when one of their sticky seeds germinates high in the branches of another tree. The seedling roots grow to the ground and then fatten, strangling the host and producing incredibly convoluted wooden sculptures. Other things to look for include black and yellow striped heliconid butterflies, purple-clawed hermit

crabs, and harmless red belly racer snakes (Alsophis rufiventris), which are only found here and in Saba. Doves abound in the Quill. Look for the red-necked pigeon (dark blue with a red neck) and the bridled quail dove (light brown belly and white stripe under the eye). You might also meet a couple of feral chickens. The panorama trail is a scramble and you will have to use your hands to pull yourself up the steeper parts. You need somewhat of a head for heights, as the final view is precipitous and spectacular, straight down over town and the northwestern part of the island. Morning light is best and don't forget your camera. Other trails to explore in this area, include the Mazinga Trail, a path around the mountain, and a trail to White Wall and the new Botanical Garden. From the dock it takes about an hour to climb to the ridge and then you need another half hour to get up to the panorama or down into the Quill.

Other hikes are in the northern part of the island. Signal Hill is a really nice hike, not too long, but it includes private land so you must have a guide. You will see an old fort and get a view of the anchorage (afternoon light the best). Gilboa Hill is a much longer hike, especially if you walk to the trail head. You walk in semi-open dry scrub and hike to great views (afternoon light) and will see endless old stone wall ruins, including primitive fort ruins and a distillery.

Water Sports

The water is often clear. You can snorkel in the anchorage along a ledge close to

shore, and on the ruins of the old walls under the water. Some old cannons are still off Golden Rock Dive Center. Snorkeling here is passable, and occasionally exceptional, as on the day I set my anchor and saw a stingray, several jacks, a baby angelfish, and a stone crab, all within a few minutes.

Divers will not want to miss Statia, as there are exceptional reefs and hundreds of fish of all types, from the smallest wrasses to large black-tipped sharks. Dive moorings have been placed on the dive sites. Since the advent of the marine park, a study has shown a tenfold increase in fish diversity. The National Park (Marine side) controls the diving and snorkeling around the entire island to a depth of 100 feet. There is a fee of $4 per dive/snorkel or $20 for a year diving/snorkeling. You can dinghy to some of the sites to snorkel on your own, but you need to check with the National Park to find out where you may go. All diving must be done with a dive shop, If you want to dive with just your own boat group, talk to the National Park, as there are a few dive moorings where, with a suitable guide, you could tie up your yacht. Dive Statia (VHF: 16) is owned by Rudy and Rinda, who came here from Texas via the Caymen Islands. They are professional, keen divers whose idea of a day off is to look for new dive sites, of which they have found plenty. They are the oldest dive shop, having been here over 16 years, they have a lot of practical experience. They welcome yachts people, and will happily give you information on

ISLANDS THAT BRUSH THE CLOUDS

Chris Doyle

the island. Their shop is a Padi gold palm 5-star facility. Like all three dive shops, they offer nitrox diving. They have a dive boat with shade, plus an inflatable for short trips. They can pick you up and drop you off from your yacht. They have underwater electric sleds that pull you along and you can rent these for snorkeling, which is fun. They also offer kayaking. Their shop sells diving and snorkeling gear, t-shirts, and local publications, and has a book swap. For boats arriving with all their own gear and a dinghy, they can arrange a dive guide for a reasonable fee.

The Golden Rock Dive Center (VHF: 16/11) has its office at the head of the baby dock. Glen and Michele Faires and their crew have a relaxed easy manner. Their shop is a National Geographic Padi Center and they have a 30-foot dive boat with a big swim platform, plus a custom catamaran dive boat with a cover. They are happy to pick up people from yachts, and they do snorkeling as well as diving trips. Glen will arrange island tours and fill jerry jugs with water. They have good small boutique.

Scubaqua is a CMAS/Padi shop based in the Blue Bead Restaurant and run by

Ingred and Menno. They run a professional shop and speak French, German, English and Dutch and are welcoming and friendly in all of them. This is one of the bigger shops, and they have plenty of staff, so they can usually afford one as a yacht guide.

The Marine Park includes 34 dive sites and snorkel sites. Some are close to the big drop-off and start at 80 feet, with a wall that seems to go down forever. Rock ridges form others with sand valleys between. In the north of the island, there are reefs and rocks on a sand bottom, with many rays, turtles, and sharks. It has been estimated that a turtle is seen for every 55 minutes of diving.

Statia has two dramatic new wreck dives. The Charlie Brown is a 300-foot long cable-layer. It lies on its side to the southwest of the island in about 100 feet of water; the top is about 48 feet deep.

It is still in whole and perfect condition, and for the experienced, penetration dives are no problem. The Chien Tong is a Taiwanese fishing vessel about 200 feet long. This one is sunk upright in about 75 feet of water at the edge of the anchorage. It has already attracted lots of fish.

Stenapa Reef is unusual – a manmade reef of old wrecks, including a cut-up World War II victory ship, a tugboat, and a large barge. This site attracts lots of fish, including large jacks, grunts, stingrays, flying gurnards, and snake eels. Turtles are sometimes seen; garden eels live in the surrounding sand. Interesting animals are found on the wrecks themselves, including tunicates, a variety of corals and sponges, and frogfish.

The Cliffs are near the southern end of the island. This site starts in a coral garden at 65 feet, and then falls away in a wall. You can go down as far as you feel comfortable, but you won't make the bottom as it drops to 1200 feet. The wall is encrusted with coral and sponges and is home to black-tipped sharks, turtles, groupers, and angelfish.

Hangover Reef is also toward the south of the island. This reef is 40-60 feet deep and well decorated by sea fans and anemones. There are lots of cracks and crevices, where you see elegant spotted drums and high hats, and on lucky days, seahorses and frogfish.

Double Wreck has the remains of two boats that sank in 60 feet of water. For some reason, this site attracts an unusually large number of fish. Hundreds of grunts use this as their daily resting place. Big barracudas patrol the waters above. Moray eels, southern stingrays, and flying gurnards hang out on the bottom.

Grand Canyon (70-130 feet) is Statia's most dramatic dive. A series of volcanic fissures separate this large sloping wall into a series of smaller walls. Superb visibility and a variety of large animals, combined with the Grand Canyon backdrop, make this dive unforgettable.

The medical school has a decompression chamber, which is a convenient facility for the diving community.

Chris Doyle

ISLANDS THAT BRUSH THE CLOUDS

Port Zante

St. Christopher (St. Kitts)

ST. KITTS IS GREEN AND pleasant, with a dramatically steep central mountain range rising to 3,750 feet. Much of it is covered in rainforest, which is often shrouded in passing clouds. Up in these heights live many thousands of African green vervet monkeys, descendents of a few originally bought over by planters. The land between the mountains and the sea is gently sloping and fertile, relatively flat, and easy to drive on. It is planted mainly in sugar cane, and though sugar cane is no longer harvested, the plants still persist.

The Caribs called St. Kitts "Liamuiga," which means "fertile isle." Columbus renamed it after his patron saint, and nowadays it is known either as St. Christopher or by the abbreviated St. Kitts. Sir Thomas Warner landed here with a group of settlers in 1623, making it the first British Caribbean colony. A French group joined them, and the two nations teamed up to massacre the 2,000 Carib inhabitants before they fell out between themselves. After 150 years of fighting and uncertainty, St. Kitts, with its sister isle, Nevis, became British under the treaty of Versailles in 1783. Today they are a fully independent, twin-island state with a British tradition and about 50,000 inhabitants. In graciousness and outstanding visual beauty, these islands have not changed too much from the old plantation days. Most of the large estates have been converted to small luxury hotels and restaurants. The economy is based mainly on tourism.

A railway, built for collecting the sugar cane, used to run right round the island, passing through perfectly scenic countryside. Part of this has been converted to tourism; you can take a luxury train ride, which offers spectacular views. This is the only surviving railway in the eastern Caribbean. Call St. Kitts Scenic Railway for details (465-7263)

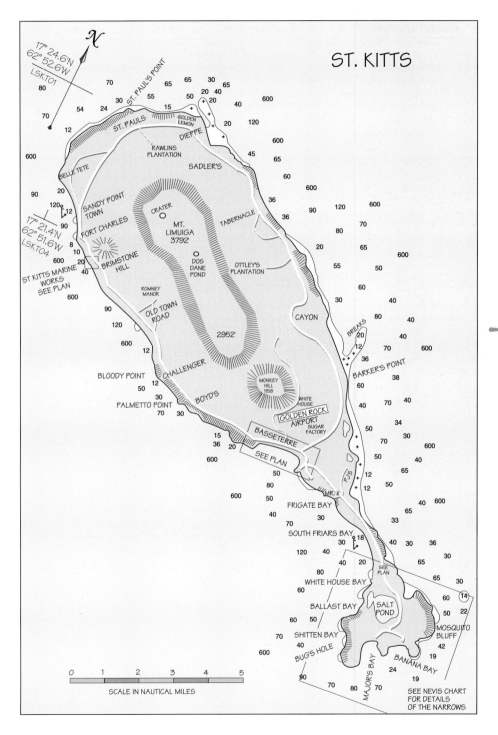

ST. KITTS

St. Kitts

Regulations

St. Kitts and Nevis are one country, though Nevis has considerable autonomy. Basseterre is the main port of entry in St. Kitts. Procedures are given under Basseterre.

Visiting yachts may not use any jet-skis or similar craft. Importation of such vehicles is banned. Scuba diving may only be undertaken with a local dive shop.

Telephones

There are card phones outside Cable and Wireless, in The Circus, outside Shoreline Plaza, and on the deepwater dock. Cards may be bought from Cable and Wireless on weekdays. To call the USA and Canada, dial 1 + the number. For other countries, dial 011, then the country code (44 for the UK).

Shopping hours

Weekdays 0800-1200 and 1300-1600. Many shops close on Thursday afternoons and all day Saturday.

Transport

St. Kitts has a large international airport with daily flights to San Juan and flights to New York several times a week. It is also linked to other Caribbean islands by LIAT and Nevis Express. Taxis are plentiful and many of them stand by on VHF: 16. The following rates are what you might expect to pay for up to four people <u>during the day</u> in $US:

Tour of Brimstone Hill	$50
Brimstone from White House Bay	$76
Island tour from Basseterre (3 hours)	$80
over 3 hours +$30 per hour	
Island tour from White House Bay	$130
Basseterre to White House Bay	$26
Basseterre to Deepwater Port	$10
Basseterre to Frigate Bay	$10
Basseterre to the airport	$10

Rental cars are available. You will need to get a local license that costs $24 US and is also good for Nevis. Drive on the left.

Buses run up the west coast to Dieppe and the east coast to Saddlers. They run about once an hour and the last bus returns at about 2200. In the mornings they leave from the waterfront (see our town map). Fares are very reasonable (no more than about $6EC).

Airport departure tax is $22US.

Holidays

- Jan 1
- Jan 2 Carnival
- First Monday in May (May Day)
- Good Friday and Easter Monday (Easter Sunday is April 4, 2010; April 24, 2011)
- Whit Monday, 50 days after Easter Sunday (May 24, 2010, June 13, 2011)
- Second Sunday in June, Queen's Birthday
- First Monday in August
- Sept. 19 (Independence Day)
- December 25-26

Navigation

The leeward (southwest) coast is fairly steep-to, and a quarter of a mile offshore clears all dangers. Give the northeast coast good clearance because of the reef off Dieppe Bay in the north and the shoals off Barker's Point farther south. Stay inside the 14-foot shoal to the northeast of Mosquito Bluff, as waves break here in heavy weather. See the Nevis section for details of The Narrows that separates St. Kitts from Nevis. There is a small anchorage behind the reef in Dieppe Bay. At present it is only of interest to those staying in St. Kitts for a long time. Locals use it as a hurricane hole.

Sandy Point Town, just northwest of Brimstone Hill, is an official port of clearance, though there is neither dock nor facilities. It is just an open roadstead that is fairly protected in easterly winds. (It can be calmer than Basseterre on occasion.) You can beach your dinghy and try to clear in with the local police station (walk north). They may tell you take a bus to town.

St Kitts Marine Works

This new project, already working as we go to press, lies under the southeastern flank of Brimstone Hill. The setting is scenic and rural with old chimneys and sugar cane fields. It belongs to Reg Francis, a very able, pleasant, and straightforward Kittian with lots of experience in salvage and heavy equipment. (If you ever run aground or start sinking, Reg is an excellent person to contact). Reg has already built the outer walls, and just has some final filling to do. He has yet to put in the proper travel lift docks, though he hauls and launches boats on temporary ones.

The Travelift is 150 tons, extended to take a beam of 35 feet. There is about 14 feet of water to the slip. Digging keel holes, tying down cats and securing yachts against hurricanes is easily arranged. Reg has a crane for removing the masts. The yard will be eco-friendly with a container pit under the wash-off area

Boat building services are provided by

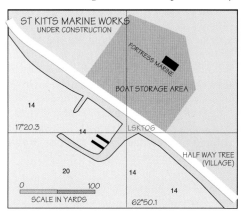

ISLANDS THAT BRUSH THE CLOUDS

Welcome to St. Kitts

St. Kitts offers its visitors a wide range of attractions, from Brimstone Hill, the most impressive historic fortress in the Caribbean to sparkling clear waters, beautiful beaches, breathtaking coral reefs, enchanting rainforests, great golf and tennis, super sports and endless activities.

Port Zante is a sparkling port facility of twenty-five beautifully landscaped acres of land, reclaimed from the sea, where you will find duty free shops, spacious plazas, elegant restaurants, a casino and a wonderful marina.

All this is just a short stroll away from the 18th century charms of Basseterre-capital of St. Kitts, the "Mother Colony" of the British West Indies.

Port Zante Marina
Inside the marina, yachts up to 70 feet in length and up to 12 foot draft can be accommodated with all the usual facilities of water, electricity and also cable TV. The Western Bulkhead can accommodate up to a 22 foot draft, or one to two larger vessels. Refuelling of both gas and diesel are also available.

Tel: (869) 466-5021

Fax: (869) 466-5020

The facilities of Port Zante have now made St. Kitts must-see on all yachtsman's itineraries.

Email: udccorp@sisterisles.kn

Website: http://www.portzante.com

Dougie Brooks and his team at Fortress Marine. They construct beautiful strip-plank cats to Dougie's designs, and can repair any kind of wooden or glass boat, however major the job.

Reg himself has a metalworking team and can weld and repair all yacht materials.

Contact Reg directly for more information (662-8930).

Basseterre

Basseterre, the capital, is the site of the original French settlement in St. Kitts. It is a delightful old town, built on the waterfront with architecture that varies from solid British to fancy French. It was largely rebuilt after a fire in 1876, and The Circus is modeled after Piccadilly in London. The Circus area and surrounding blocks contain handsome old buildings with decoratively painted shutters that make this one of the Caribbean's more attractive capitals.

The lovely old treasury building is the nation's new museum, with several artifacts and great old photos showing how it was long ago. The St. Christopher Heritage society has an office here. You can visit them and check out their selection of books and maps for sale; also, this is the place to come for serious research.

Port Zante is an ambitious project that extends the town's waterfront by some 25 acres and includes a marina and cruise ship dock. It stood empty for some years and is now undergoing a tremendous building boom; many businesses from St. Martin have built and opened stores here, and it feels more like an outpost of Philipsburg than part of St. Kitts.

Navigation

Be cautious when approaching Port Zante at night: there are quite a few cruise ship berthing piles, some of which are lit.

Basseterre is open and faces south. It is protected in easterly or northeasterly winds, but when wind and swell shift to the southeast, it becomes uncomfortable to dangerous, and at these times it is not unusual to have short seas over 3 feet high

BASSETERRE

rolling in. You can anchor or use the new marina. In settled conditions when the wind is northeast, the best anchorage is just outside the new marina. If there is any chance of the wind turning southeast, the calmest spot is close to the deep-water harbor, just in front of the coast guard dock. You will still get a surge in southeasterly winds, but nothing like being farther out. If there is any chance of a southerly swell, keep in water at least 14 to 20 feet deep. For comfort in these conditions, it is best to anchor bow and stern, facing into the swells. A marina is a wonderful asset, and it is great to have the protected new Port Zante Marina working. The outer wall has been extended, and it completely cuts out

the swells and allows for secure, calm berthing inside. This is the best place to stay and from which to view and tour St. Kitts. You should also cruise down to the south coast bays. A good road connects Basseterre to the south end of the island, so it is also possible to organize your sightseeing from there. White House Bay and Major's Bay have the easiest road access. There are several very large ship moorings placed well offshore in the area of Frigate Bay. They look more like fish traps than anything else. Keep a good lookout.

Regulations

Basseterre is the only manned port of entry in St. Kitts. Customs are both at the

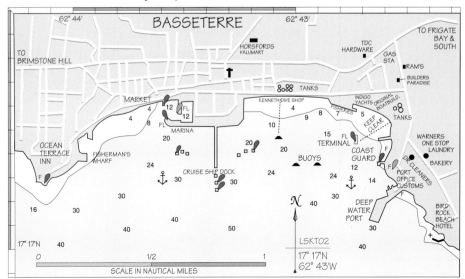

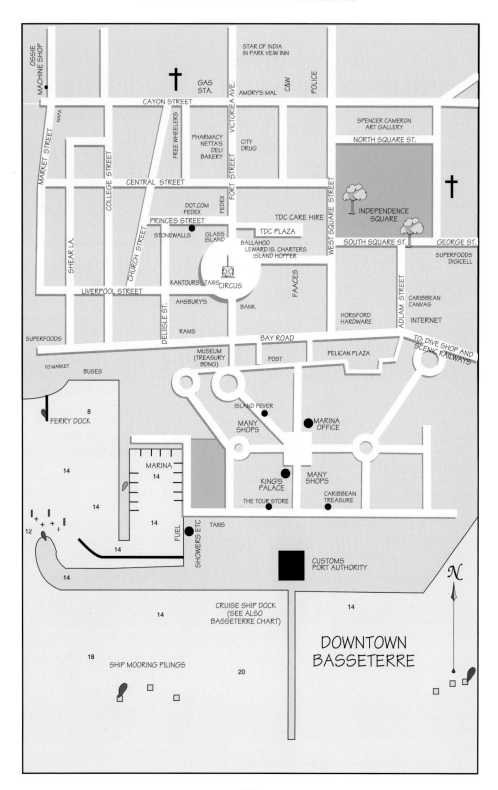

cruise ship dock near the marina and at the deepwater harbor, and they stand by on VHF: 16. The customs regulations are yacht-friendly. If you plan to visit both St. Kitts and Nevis, ask for a coastwise clearance to Nevis when you check in. This is valid for up to a week and means you can visit other anchorages in St. Kitts and Nevis on your way over. You must present the clearance to Nevis customs within a week. If you are just staying in St. Kitts you can get a cruising permit when you check in. List on it all the places you may want to visit. This permit is also valid after you have cleared out – so if you want to overnight in Major's Bay on your last night to shorten the trip, make sure your cruising permit includes that night.

Customs use the Eseaclear.com system, so you can do the paperwork before you arrive. Customs hours are 0600-1900 daily. Usually there is a customs officer in the Cruise Ship complex (a few steps from the marina) from 0800-1545. Outside those hours you may have to go down to the Deep Water Port. The boarding officers who do the clearance stand by on VHF: 16. Weekend clearance involves overtime charges (normally $10EC). There is a $10EC customs charge ($50 if you are over 100 tons) and $20EC yacht charge. In addition, port dues are collected in the port office, across the hall from customs. For yachts: $6EC up to 20 tons, $10EC for 20-30 tons, $12EC for 30-50 tons, $24EC for 51-100 tons, $49EC for 101-150 tons, $73EC 151-500 tons, and $98EC 501-2,000 tons. In addition, yachts of 100-499 tons must pay $220EC pilotage, and yachts 500-1,999 tons pay $440 pilotage. Fare-paying passengers are charged $6.50US per head ($5 immigration, $1.5 environmental fee). You need to make sure customs lists all the anchorages you wish to visit. Frigate Bay is reserved for swimmers so not normally allowed. Sometimes there is an immigration officer in the Cruise Ship complex, otherwise you will also have to visit immigration at the police station in town. When the police station is closed, you can find immigration at the airport – but make sure a jumbo jet has not just arrived. Large yachts wanting an agent can contact Rickie Browne at Serviz or Jason at Delisle Walwyn (662-4872, VHF: 16).

Communications

The Tours Store opposite the cruise ship terminal in Port Zante has internet access and wifi. They will also help yachts with whatever else they need.

NR Internet Cafe is opposite the Pelican Mall. They open daily 0800-2000 except Sunday, when they open occasionally, and they have many computer stations. They also do phone calls, faxes, and copying. Stonewalls restaurant has wifi and may lend you a laptop in a pinch. Ballahoo Restaurant also has wifi. Dot.com sells a good range of computers and accessories.

Chandlery

David at Indigo Yachts is the best bet for chandlery items. He has a large stock on hand for his boat yard and can sell to occasional visitors. He can also source, clear, and deliver parts duty free, including both

ISLANDS THAT BRUSH THE CLOUDS

cruising boat and specialty superyacht gear. Just out of town, giant hardware stores like Horsfords and Builder's Paradise sell housewares, tools, paints, fillers, plumbing parts, lumber, electronics, and occasionally some rope and stainless fasteners.

General Yacht Services

The marina basin is dredged to 14 feet and is designed to take about 56 boats with a maximum length of 150 feet. Larger boats (up to 250 feet) can arrange to lie outside the western wall. This is not a fancy marina with lots of services, but it is quite functional and run by the Port Zante management team, the people who developed this area. In 2009 the long pier was being expanded to make more space for visitors. Arriving yachts should call Port Zante on VHF: 68. A fuel dock with diesel, gasoline, and ice is inside the marina, duty-free for yachts. (The profit on fuel is tiny, so if you pay by credit card, there will be a sur-

charge; to avoid this use the cash machine in the port). Water and electricity are available on most docks, but limited to 30 amps on many (60 amps on a few). There is a garbage dump. The marina has probably one of the fanciest marina toilet and shower blocks I have seen. The overall manager is Keith Phillip and Indira manages the office. The staff are very friendly and helpful. They will sell phone cards and can help with car rentals or other services. This is the best and calmest berth for your visit to Basseterre.

Superyachts that cannot get in can take on water and fuel by arrangement with the marina on the outside dock, or by arrangement with the port authority on the cruise ship dock (when available). Overnight stays on the cruise ship dock are possible with water, fuel, electricity, and phone. Prop polishing can be arranged. There is security both on the cruise shop dock and in the marina.

Chris Doyle

If you are in the marina, there is man named Ras (to locals) Wayne (to his customers), who comes from a family of seamen. He lost the use of one arm in a mugging some years back, but will lend his good hand to any job you have, including scrubbing the bottom, polishing topsides or stanchions, or carrying beers from the supermarket. He is cheerful, helpful and good. He is always around, but if you want to call him before you come, his home number is 465-7192.

You can get your laundry done by Warner's One Stop. They will collect and deliver from your yacht in the marina or the docks at the deepwater port. They are very helpful and will do their best to meet your needs, including a fast turnaround. If you have special requirements or if you need laundry done on a Sunday, contact them a couple of days in advance to make arrangements. You can also try Trinity, 465-9603.

Unfortunately, for those anchored out, the deepwater port is not yacht-friendly. The agile can find a place to tie a dinghy up, and scramble up the rocks. If you have non-agile crew, drop them off at the roll-on dock. It is probably better and easier to dinghy down to the marina and leave your dinghy there for a fee of $10US. The garbage bins on the docks in the deepwater harbor are not really for yachts, but they do not mind you using them if you bag the garbage well. Sol EC can fill your cooking gas cylinders.

Leeward Island Charters [VHF: 16] runs the day-charter cats Eagle, Caona, and Spirit of St. Kitts. Their office is in the Ballahoo restaurant. Karen, in the office, is very helpful and will answer any questions

you may have, and if you need a local chart, they may be able to help. In addition, they sell t-shirts, and a few accessories, and should you want to see how it feels to sail at 16 knots, these are the people to talk to. (They recently clocked a full boat at 26 knots!)

The St. Kitts-Nevis Boating Club has its base in the Ballahoo, where the latest club bulletin is posted. Founding members include Phillip Walwyn, Peter Dupre, and Douglas Brooks. You can ask if there are any upcoming events.

Technical Yacht Services

See also St. Kitts Marine Works above. Two boatbuilders are neighbors on the waterfront near the deepwater harbor. Both Densil and Mike own Original Boatbuilders. They are Kittians who have built boats for many years and worked on such beauties as the Spirit of St. Kitts, Eagle, and Caona. They have a carpentry shop and can be very helpful with any woodworking job you may have. In addition, they will help with any boat problem or build a new boat. Cats in wood and glass are their specialty.

An excellent place to go with boat problems is Indigo Yachts, run by David, who has worked in the design office of Camper and Nicholson. Now he has his own yard, with full design capabilities, and he understands all kinds of yacht systems, up to superyacht. He works with a team of up to 18 employees and can haul multihulls up to 80 feet. The large yard has excellent vacuum-bagging tables, as well as a carpentry shop, and they can do any kind of techni-

cal construction. They keep marine ply, glass, cores, and lots of hardware in stock. David can do a surprising amount here on St. Kitts, and if a problem is out of range, he will have the right contacts to bring someone in. They can also help you source and import parts. Superyacht skippers might want to note they manufacture a sweet and light 24-foot cathedral hull craft, which would make a good tender. Indigo Yachts is agent for Yanmar diesel and Balmar electrical products, and they can fix all Edson steering problems.

Mark Theron's Caribbean Canvas Company has a small outlet on Adlam Street, not far from the marina. But all their work is done in Nevis, so it is better to see them there.

In town, Ossie is a good machinist. Though he does not have specific boating experience and would not normally keep exotic materials like stainless in stock, he can fix most things.

TDC is an agent for Yamaha outboards, with full sales and service. They can also help out with other brands. You can call them on VHF: 18.

The Tours Store in Port Zante, is owned by yachtsman Anthony Abourizk. His store has a full internet service and will arrange any kind of tour or taxi you require. In fact, being yachts people, they will organize anything you need, including getting laundry done, provisioning, getting a weather report, or finding a mechanic; just ask.

Transport

Most taxi drivers have VHF radios, and the taxi channel is VHF: 13. However, several of them have made yachts an important part of their business and also listen on VHF: 16. Quality Time Taxi stands by on VHF: 16 and 19, and owner Ashton Sampson is reliable and friendly; as one of my readers says: "Ashton is incredibly cheerful and helpful at all times." He has lived in both the Virgin Islands and St. Martin. He also works quite closely with Elvis Williams (Gibraltar Tours) who is also reliable and friendly and will work out a tour to suit both your personality and pocket. He likes historical tours like Brimstone Hill Fort.

If you want to go hiking, get in touch with Set Up Taxi by phone or VHF. Owner Henry Whyte runs both a regular taxi and does island tours, hiking with customers himself. He is an excellent man for the rainforest and the volcano. He was originally a plumber and carpenter, and he enjoys visitors and will keep you well entertained.

George Richards of Unique Taxi and Tour Service, is another good, reliable and courteous taxi driver who listens to the VHF. He loves to take people on scenic and historical tours of St. Kitts.

Ready to party? Call Christian Rameshwar at Tangerine Tours. Christian is from Trinidad and likes to get his passengers in fine spirits with an open bar of lots of beer and four types of rum. He wears very brightly colored clothes and a beard tinted to match. His tour vehicle is a big open bus, where you sit with the breeze and the view. Christian, who loves having fun, will jolly along anyone with Eeyoreish tendencies. He is knowledgeable and eloquent on historical tours.

TDC has car rental agencies in both St. Kitts and Nevis (Thrifty Rentals). If you wish to see both islands, they'll give you a free swap when you go from one to the other. This makes it particularly easy if you intend to spend most of your time in one island and just hop over to the other for a day. You can also take your car over on the Sea Bridge ferry.

TDC Travel (VHF: 18), right next to

TDC Plaza, is agent for UPS and Quick Pack; they are also travel agents who handle all airlines except American, and they arrange all kinds of island tours. The FedEx office is on Fort Street, close to The Circus. Kantours is the local American Express agency.

Provisioning

Ram's or Superfoods are close by the marina and acceptable for topping up stores. For a big provisioning, take the short taxi ride to the big supermarkets outside town: Horsfords Value Mart and Ram's are both good, and each will have a few things missing in the other.

Horsfords is large and modern, on the edge of Basseterre in a big mall. You could walk there, but probably not back with the shopping. It is vast, with a deli and bakery. They are also open on a Sunday morning.

Ram's is the closest to the deepwater port and has just about anything you could want at reasonable prices. They open 0830-1900 Monday through Saturday.

Fun Shopping

Port Zante has the closest shops. Judging by the shops, many of which are geared to cruise ship passengers, and the architecture, you might think you were in Philipsburg. This changes as you wander among the old buildings in the main part of Basseterre, with more traditional Caribbean architecture and many more shops.. In Port Zante, Island Fever, owned by Gigi offers artistic sports wear, beachwear, t-shirts, hats, jewelry, ornaments, and handicrafts. Island Fever has its own

Chris Doyle

ISLANDS THAT BRUSH THE CLOUDS

screen-printing business, so many designs are unique to this shop, and they print their own t-shirts in all sizes.

Also in Port Zante, Barry's Caribbean Treasure is fun to visit, because you can get to taste many of the rums made in St. Kitts. Then you can buy the one you like the best or anything else from their vast selection of spirits, wines, and jewelry.

The Circus is picturesque and well worth looking at for a moment or two. From here you can go up Fort Street.

Glass Island is Italian-owned, locally run, and they use a closed-kiln method of heating glass; they have created everything on display in the store. The impressive selection includes fused-glass ornaments and pictures, stained glass, and glass jewelry. Hardened yachties will need one of their ashtrays made out of molten Carib

Chris Doyle

bottles. They were moving so I am not sure exactly where you will find them. Island Hopper, below the Ballahoo, has a great selection of Caribelle batik and silk-screened clothes, as well as colorful jewelry and ornaments.

The TDC Plaza has shops selling the most elegant lines of jewelry, clothing, and souvenirs.

The Spencer Cameron Art Gallery is in an elegant old building, with a selection of local art, old maps, and prints. The gallery's owner, Rosey Cameron Smith, has a room full of her own works on display – both lovely island houses and a lot of studies of the local monkeys.

Faaces is a store owned by Ken Ballentyne. He has spent a lot of time in Africa and imports really beautiful sculptures in stone along with carvings and other artistic pieces. Lorenza Smith, who was running the store when I was there, was very helpful.

Restaurants

Eating out in St. Kitts is a real pleasure. The Ballahoo [VHF: 16], run by Peter Dupre, is an airy upstairs restaurant with tables on a long balcony overlooking The Circus, and it is a wonderful place to sit and watch the world go by. It is the best lunch spot in town and a gathering place for local business and yachting people. They serve good Créole food and inexpensive snacks. They also open for dinner, when they have a reasonably priced but more elaborate menu. Peter Dupre is a yachtsman and can help answer any questions you may have. He has free wifi and posts a daily weather chart during the hurricane season.

Circus Grill, has an equally attractive spot on the opposite corner of The Circus. They specialize in grilled seafood, steak, and lamb.

StoneWalls on Princes Street is set in a charming courtyard full of trees It is one of the Caribbean's great little restaurants and the perfect place for a drink or meal, very popular with locals, expats, and the few

Chris Doyle

visitors lucky enough to find it. Although small and intimate, they were discovered by Newsweek, who voted them one of their best bars in 1996 – the only Caribbean bar to get that honor. The owner, Simone, comes from a family of cooks and restaurants. They have a big menu, with a large selection for breakfast, lunch, and dinner. In addition, they offer daily specials, and with luck this may include some traditional Caribbean cuisine, which runs in the family. It is a very friendly place and you will soon feel at home here.

Reservations are a good idea for dinner, especially on a Friday, though you will usually get in (they close Sundays). They have free wifi, and if you forget to bring in your computer, Simone might lend you her laptop for a quick email- check.

Caribe Café is worth a quick mention. They sell a variety of good coffees, and

ISLANDS THAT BRUSH THE CLOUDS

serve several different kinds in a breezy room upstairs in Sands Mall.

The Ocean Terrace Inn (OTI) is a large hotel that cascades down the hill to the waterfront, with many pools and bars and different levels. The OTI is part of the TDC group, so you can always call TDC on VHF: 18 for reservations. OTI offers special room rates for yachts on a space-avail- able basis, and both restaurants offer occasional entertainment. The Fisherman's Wharf (dinner only) is a pleasant fish restaurant that comes complete with water lapping at the edge and nautical decor. The menu is large enough for all tastes and pockets, with everything from fresh lobster and swordfish to soup and a hamburger. You can beach your dinghy next to the

Port Zante

Chris Doyle

206

restaurant. Higher up, the OTI's Waterfalls Restaurant aims at fancy, gourmet cooking, where food becomes an art form.

Next door to OTI, Serendipity is another gourmet restaurant where you eat looking out over the harbor.

King's Palace is an authentic Chinese restaurant upstairs in port Zante; inexpensive, clean, and air-conditioned, with lots of dishes using local seafood. In the same area, Pride of India is a good Indian Restaurant.

Larkland Richard's Bird Rock Beach Hotel (VHF: 16) has its own sheltered dinghy dock, a short ride east of the deepwater harbor. The bird rocks are near the entrance, so I would advise going in by day before you try it at night. This makes a pleasant daytime hangout. Their Rocky's Beach Bar serves grilled seafood and steak at a reasonable price, right on the waterfront, and has musical entertainment on Saturdays. They also have a restaurant for the gourmet – it is called Diana's and hangs out over their little harbor. Chef Jeffrey Hanning creates great food from 1800.

Frigate Bay is a holiday area with great beaches, a golf course, and a casino, all of which are open to visitors. It is just a mile south of the deepwater dock. You can find all the activities you might want here, from Mr. X Watersports, who has everything from lounge chairs to Hobi cats, including windsurfers. He offers water-skiing, snorkeling, and boat trips, and is also very helpful with local information. Mr. X also offers food in the evenings at Frigate Bay out of his little food caravan (called Shiggidy

Shak). Among other things, he serves barbecued lobster and chicken.

Frigate Bay is a great place to eat out, be it for a lunchtime snack or an evening meal. The most popular spot is PJ's Bar and Restaurant, which has been owned since 1978 by Pat and Jude, two gregarious ladies who are famous for their pizzas. Local favorites include Garbage Pizza (everything but the kitchen sink – ideal for hungry sailors) and Mexican Pizza. Dinner specials on their ever-expanding menu include chicken rollantini, penne with shrimp, and seafood pasta. Pat and Jude are active in the St. Kitts Boat Club, and PJ's is very popular on Saturday nights. Also, check out also the Sunset Cafe, which is part of the Timothy Beach Resort. It is built on an unbeatable spot on the beach with a perfect sunset view.

Ashore

St. Kitts is a rewarding island for those who like to explore ashore. It has an unmapped network of small farm roads that criss-cross the cane fields and wander into the hills and up to the edge of the forest. These offer great mountain biking and hiking.

As you head north, the first interesting small stop is about a mile out of town. You pass a funeral home on your right, and on your left is a turnoff by a swampy area of trees that are packed with nesting and roosting egrets. Turn down this road and bear right, and you come to the home of talented potter Carla Astaphan, who will show you her studio and some of her work. A good landmark is the tall chimney of the

Chris Doyle

been built on the old foundations. Here you can watch as white sea-island cotton, as soft as silk, gets covered in a riot of lively colors. Caribelle Batiks are for sale in the Island Hopper shops in both Basseterre and Nevis, but it is much more interesting to come to the workshop and enjoy the magnificent manor grounds. Try to visit on a day when there are no cruise ships.

In the same town, Sprat Net is a beachfront restaurant just at the beginning of Old Road. It is owned by fishermen who decided they could do better by selling their fish as meals. They fish some days and open the restaurant most evenings, but always on weekends. It has become very popular.

Camps Estate, right opposite her house.

Clay Villa Plantation House and Gardens is about 4 miles west of Basseterre just before Challengers. It is a spectacular old plantation house that has been in the Matthew and Gumbs families since 1763. At only 10 acres, it was never a slave plantation. You can wander around immaculately maintained gardens with fruits, flowers, and rainforest vegetation, where you will see butterflies, hummingbirds and rabbits, and which also has a menagerie of monkeys, tortoises, and cockatoos.

The estate house interior is bright and artistic, and full of just wonderful old furniture, wall-hangings and artifacts. A museum has ancient pre-Colombian pottery. You have to call and arrange to visit (465-2353). The charge, which is eight US per person, with a minimum of four, is a great bargain.

Romney Manor is set in a beautiful old 10-acre estate garden dominated by a giant saman tree, which covers nearly an acre. It is in Old Road Town, off the road between Basseterre and Brimstone Hill. Romney Manor is the headquarters for Caribelle Batik. Originally there was a beautiful estate house, but it burned down, and three new workshops and display rooms have

Brimstone Hill has a wonderful old, strategically-placed fort, which is a lasting monument to the old enmity between the British and the French. British-built, it was captured by the French in a siege during which 1,000 British soldiers held out for some months against 8,000 French. Eventually they arranged surrender with full honor. The fort is being painstakingly restored. You may be lucky and spot a troop of monkeys that live here; they are a little less nervous than their mountain brethren. The Western Place of Arms offers an outstanding view down to Fort Charles and out to sea. On a clear day you can see six islands, from Montserrat to St. Martin. The fort twice suffered unprovoked attacks from above by lightning that blew up the powder room and did considerable damage. Several small museum rooms depict life in the old days and illustrate the Battle of St. Christopher, in which Hood gave DeGrasse such a thumping that he had to retire to Martinique for a couple of months. This gave Admiral Rodney sufficient time to come out and join Hood for the decisive "Battle of the Saints." At that time France and Spain were poised to drive Britain from the Caribbean, but this victory gave

England undisputed mastery of the sea. D.L. Matheson's informative booklet on the fortress is available in the souvenir shop.

St. Kitts' 3,700-foot mountain range is a completely different world of cool, dark rainforest, elfin woodlands, volcanic craters, and lakes. Several guides specialize in hikes here, as well as plantation and other walking tours. Check out Set Up Taxi; Henry likes to hike. You might want to opt for a long day to make it to the top of Mount Liamuiga (Mt. Misery), where you look down on the neighboring mountainous island of Statia before descending into a 1,000-foot crater that puffs steam from several vents.

The Royal St. Kitts Golf Course, recently taken over by Marriot, offers 18 holes, and all equipment is available for rent. Advance booking is essential during the winter season.

When touring, plan to stop for lunch at the north end of the island. Rawlins Plantation, owned by Kevin from England and Zai from Trinidad, is one of the Caribbean's very special places. Kevin is a yachtsman and enjoys sailing visitors. It is approached by a long, narrow cart track between fields of sugar cane. Suddenly you emerge in a wonderful oasis of lawn, trees, and flowers: a true English manor in the midst of the Caribbean. To the east, the view takes you across the flower gardens through fields of sugar cane and distant palms to Statia rising out of the ocean. To the west, rainforested mountains give a backdrop to the pool. These views are exceptional; so do not forget your camera. The buffet lunch costs $30US and is served on the patio overlooking the pool and view. The food is a wonderful assortment of local dishes. I can think of no better way to enjoy a Caribbean meal.

While here, drop by the Kate Design Gallery next door. This is a great place to look at Kate's Spencer's original art. She has originals and prints on sale, and even if you are not in the market for art, you should come by to check out her placemats, note-cards, and silks, all beautifully

ISLANDS THAT BRUSH THE CLOUDS

designed. In addition her husband, Philip Walwyn, is often building some interesting boat at Pleasant Boats Co. in the same place. His last project was Kate, a beautiful replica of an historic gaff-rigged 12-meter.

Otherwise there is the Golden Lemon, which belongs to Arthur Leaman, a designer from New York who has lived on St. Kitts for some 40 years and has put his energy into turning this old seaside estate into a hotel of flawless elegance. They have a simple lunchtime menu, including sandwiches. Don't forget to stroll on the beach and admire the reef-protected bay that is used by locals as a hurricane hole.

If you are not going all the way around the island, Ottley's Plantation Inn, a 20-minute drive from town on the windward side of St. Kitts, makes an excellent destination for lunch or dinner, with excellent cuisine. It is a lovely old family-run estate, with fancy lawns full of royal palms. Behind the hotel is a pleasant, shady walk in an area that was once cultivated and has been allowed to return to forest. Meal

guests are welcome to relax in the garden. They offer light lunches except on Sundays, when they do a big champagne brunch from 1100-1400. Reservations are advisable for dinner.

Close by the turn off to Ottley's, on the other side of the road, Fun Bikes is in another lovely old house. They have a great garden and do ATV tours. To see the island by bike, check out Free Wheelers; they rent mountain bikes and arrange tours on them.

Water Sports

Divers will want to explore St. Kitts' extensive reefs, which start around 40 feet deep and slope down as far as you can go – the fish getting bigger as you descend. Local laws insist that all diving be done with a local dive shop. There are three to choose from. Kenneth Samuel, a Kittian Padi dive master, is the most experienced and knowledgeable. Kenneth used to be a fisherman and would free-dive down to 120 feet for lobster. His love of diving turned him toward sports diving, and he has now

been teaching and taking groups diving for over 30 years. He runs two purpose-built catamaran dive craft and collects people from yachts and hotels. He hires several Padi instructors. He also specializes in private groups from yachts who want to go on their own and he has a 34-foot speedboat for them. Kenneth is also happy to act as a dive guide for big yachts with large tenders, who want to do it all with their own equipment. Another great thing Kenneth does is help anyone with special needs who would like to dive. Call Kenneth's Dive Center on VHF: 16 before 0800, between 1300-1400, or in the evening after 1700 to arrange a pickup, or phone anytime: 465-2670 or 664-6809. Kenneth will fill tanks if you need to work on your boat, but keep in mind that all scuba diving must be done with a dive shop.

Austen MacLeod's Pro Divers is based at the OTI. Two Padi instructors are available, and full-certification courses can be taken. They stand by on VHF: 16. Bird Rock Beach Hotel also has Dive St. Kitts. They have a good dive boat and sometimes listen to VHF: 16.

Among the many dive sites is Sandy Point Bay, which lies at the north end of St. Kitts. This is a superb dive. The reef starts at 40 feet, and the coral formations are beautiful, with both hard and soft corals and giant sponges. The reef teems with fish. The MV Talata was wrecked in 1985 and lies off the west coast of St. Kitts on a reef with depths of 30 to 60 feet. The River Taw was a 144-foot vessel that now lies on sand in about 50 feet of water. This is a good dive site for novice divers. Coconut Tree Reef, not far from Basseterre, is a lovely reef that starts at 40 feet and plunges to depths of 300 feet or more, with plenty of reef fish. See also Monkey Reef and Nag's Head, described in the Nevis section.

SOUTH ST. KITTS

The southern part of St. Kitts is connected to the main island by a long, narrow peninsula. The formation is both attractive and unusual. Hills of yellow, brown, and green surround several large salt ponds. It is dry with cactuses, century plants, and flocks of sandpipers that feed in the shallow ponds. It is the easiest place to see monkeys. A road runs right down to the end.

An alternative to being in the marina in Basseterre is to anchor in White House Bay or Major's Bay and sightsee by rental car or taxi. Many taxis stand by on VHF: 16.

South Friars Bay

South Friars Bay makes a fair lunchtime anchorage. It is easy to approach. The attraction here is a lovely and lively beach and many small beach concessions. (See our chart of St. Kitts on page 216.) On the Saturday nearest the full moon, all the locals gather here for full-moon party at the Shipwreck Bar. It is towards the south end of Friars Bay. In reasonably calm weather, anchor off and go to the party.

White House Bay

White House Bay and Ballast Bay are both well-protected. The only navigational hazard is a long reef between them that sticks out from Guana Point. Give it good clearance. White House Bay is much smaller, but it is nearer the road if you want to tour the island. Anchor in the middle of the bay in 18 to 20 feet of water. It is sandy close to shore, rocky farther out. There is a reef to the south of the of the bay decorated by an interesting old wreck, and there are a few underwater rocks that come out a couple of hundred feet from the shore in this area.

Ashore

If you look from the bay south east you will see a building overlooking the salt pond, This is the office of Christophe Harbour, developers who own much of the land in this area, and who will trasnform the whole of the salt pond into a marina and homes, with an entrance in Ballast Bay. They are also putting a golf course on the hill. They have put a small dinghy dock in White House Bay that you can use, and the road is right behind. It is unlikely any of this will be finished in the life of this

ISLANDS THAT BRUSH THE CLOUDS

guide, but if you anchor here you will see the construction in the distance.

Apart from pleasant hiking and snorkeling, there are two nearby attractions: a beach hangout called Reggae Beach (see *Cockleshell Bay*) and a very fine restaurant called The Beach House. The Beach House is in Turtle Bay, and owned by the Christophe Harbour Development. It

opens every day from 1130 and serves lunch till 1630 and dinner from 1700 to 2130. It has a lovely, casually elegant, open dining room facing the sea. You will not find a better ambience or food on St. Kitts. The food is the inspiration of George, the executive chef, an Anguillan, who has cooked all over the world in the finest restaurants. He loves to use local ingredi-

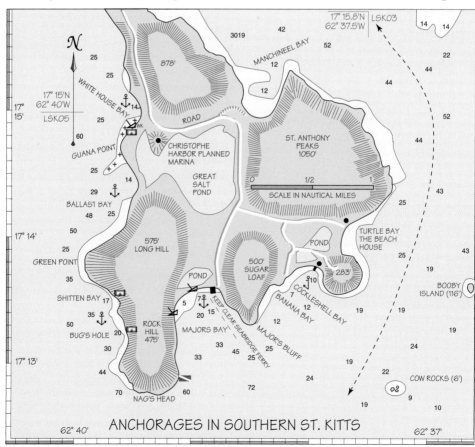

ANCHORAGES IN SOUTHERN ST. KITTS

ents so there is plenty of fresh fish as well as the best imported steaks for meat eaters Everything is artistically served in the best gourmet style. The cheerful and efficient ambience is maintained by Guish, the managing director. If you give them a call, they will come and collect you from White House Bay and take you back afterwards. The Beach House is perfect for a special meal out.

Ballast Bay

Ballast Bay, right next door, is much larger with a long, stony beach and lots of century plants. Once you are clear of the reef off Guana Point, you can anchor anywhere. It is very peaceful with no road. The walk behind Ballast Bay along the old salt trail, which leads out over a narrow bank built across the salt pond, is good for birders. You will see plenty of wading birds, but take insect repellent and avoid the heat of the day.

Shitten Bay and Bugs Hole

Shitten Bay and Bugs Hole are two bays whose rather unappetizing names belie their quiet beauty. Both are backed by cliffs and are deep except for the occasional rock close to shore. They make a fair lunchtime anchorages and offer excellent snorkeling.

Major's Bay

Major's Bay, on the south side of St. Kitts, is deep, and you can carry 14 feet close on the eastern side. The northwestern part of the bay is 5-7 feet seep with two wrecks ashore. A giant concrete block, an old mooring, is about 4.5 feet deep. I mark it as a rock. The Sea Bridge Ferry runs to Nevis from here, and you have to leave a clear channel into the dock. But there is room to anchor fairly close to shore between the channel and a conspicuous beached barge.

You can land on the beach and are within dinghy range of Banana Bay and Cockleshell Bay. The seabed is mainly sand covered in weeds. Once the hook has penetrated the weeds, holding is good. It can be a little rolly in here if the wind is from the south, but this the best-protected bay for northerly winds and a good choice should a cold front threaten.

Banana and Cockleshell Bay

If you come in close to the Cockleshell's Bay's eastern headland, you can find calm enough anchorage for a day stop and can even overnight there in light easterly or northeasterly winds. How far you can come in will depend on your draft, but you can usually find a calmish spot in 11 feet right off Reggae Beach.

Ashore

Reggae Beach is a popular local hangout owned by Gary Pereira and managed by Sonia Dyer. It is open seven days a week for lunch, with a dining room right on the beach. It is a popular place to spend beach time. Ocean kayaks and deep-sea fishing are available, and they can also arrange a fast ferry service to Oualie Beach in Nevis. Reggae beach serves everything from hamburgers to seafood meals, and you can visit the boutique. They have a landing/dinghy dock.

MAJORS BAY

Nevis Peak attracts the clouds.

Chris Doyle

Nevis

FROM SOME ANGLES NEVIS looks like a sombrero, peaked in the center and low around the edges. Clouds usually cap Nevis Peak, which is over 3000 feet high. On occasion they cling to the summit and fall down the sides, looking just like snow. Some say this is why Columbus named it "Nuestra Senora del las Nieves" (Our Lady of the Snows), after one of his favorite churches. Early attempts were made to settle the island from St. Kitts in 1628. The first town, called Jamestown, was built near Fort Ashby, but it sank into the sea after an earthquake and tidal wave in 1680. Various battles between the British and the French hampered development until 1783, when Nevis became British for an extended time. It flourished as a plantocracy and there are many old plantations and sugar mills on the island. The old mills are crumbling, but the plantations have been converted into hotels where visitors can relive those gracious old days without the evils of slavery upon which they were built. Two historical figures associated with Nevis are Alexander Hamilton, who was born here, and Horatio Nelson, who married Nevisian widow Fanny Nisbet.

Nevis, with a population of around 12,000, is quiet and peaceful, with lovely views, picturesque houses and delightful people. Exploring the island is highly recommended. Nevisians have been careful to preserve their architectural heritage and many traditional Caribbean-style buildings survive.

The mountain is clad in dense forest and with a suitable guide you can make it all the way to the peak. The less energetic should visit the Golden Rock Estate, buy a trail map, and take a stroll or hike. Going at 1530 hrs will give the best chance of seeing wild greenback monkeys. Return for tea in the majestic garden setting of the estate.

Several people lead historical, plantation and forest tours. Information on these, bird books, and trail maps are all available

214

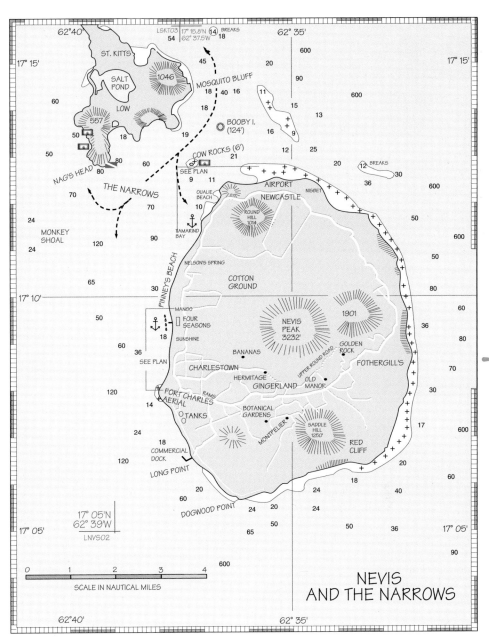

NEVIS
AND THE NARROWS

SCALE IN NAUTICAL MILES

ISLANDS THAT BRUSH THE CLOUDS

at the Museum of Nevis in the Hamilton House.

Navigation

Nevis's west coast is relatively free of dangers and a quarter of a mile offshore keeps you in deep water. A long commercial L-shaped dock extends from the shore off Long Point, a couple of miles south of Charlestown. Streetlights line the dock. There is also a navigation light that looks like a flashing red and white sector light at its outermost point. Unlit barges and buoys are often anchored close to shore, between the port and Charlestown.

Stay well off the east and south coasts

Nevis

Regulations

Nevis, together with St. Kitts, is one country (though every few years Nevis talks of succession). Visiting yachts may NOT use jet-skis or similar craft. Scuba diving may only be undertaken with a local dive shop. The best port of entry for yachts in Nevis is Charlestown. Customs procedures are given under Charlestown. All the officers I have dealt with have been very helpful.

Telephones

Card phones are all over town and cards are for sale in Cable and Wireless and instructions are posted on the phones. To call the USA, dial 1 + the number. For other countries, dial 011+ the country code (UK is 44). If you need assistance, the telephone office is open weekdays from 0800 to 1700.

Shopping hours

Weekdays 0800-1200 & 1300-1600. Some shops are also open on Saturday mornings. Bank hours: Weekdays 0800-1300. On Fridays they are also open from 1500-1700.

Transport

Taxis are plentiful and available at the head of the dock in Charlestown. Add 50% to the following rates between 2200-0600. They are for up to 4 people in EC:

Charlestown to Golden Rock	$46
Charlestown to Gingerland	$41
Charlestown to Botanical Gardens	$41
Charlestown to Airport	$54
Charlestown to Newcastle	$54
Island tour (3 hours)	$200
(For more than 4 people, add $50 per person)	
Rates between 2200 and 0600 are plus 50%	

There is an inexpensive and infrequent bus system. We give points of departure on our Charlestown map.

There are plenty of rental cars available. You will need to get a local license, which costs $20 U.S. It is also good for St. Kitts. Drive on the left.

Ferries link St. Kitts and Nevis., often once an hour in Charlestown harbor.

Superyacht owners with private planes will love the new Nevis Airport with its fine modern facilities.

Airport departure tax is $22US.

Holidays

All the same holidays as St. Kitts (see St. Kitts), in addition, the first Tuesday in August is Culturama holiday.

Nevis, Admiralty Leisure Folio 5641-2, 5641-3, 5641-9

Sail to a safe harbour
the crowds haven't found...

...and discover the magic of Nevis.

*W*hen you sail to Nevis you'll be welcomed into a serene, almost enchanted setting. Where anchorages and moorings dot the blue waters off our golden sand beaches and Lush hillsides beckon with the whisper of breezes, the chirping of birds. You'll be welcomed by gracious people who greet and treat you as friends. Enjoy great food, golf and tennis, or just laze the days away with a cool drink and spectacular views. Come, let Nevis cast its spell on you. Then, sail away if you must.

NEVIS TOURISM AUTHORITY
Main Street
Charlestown Nevis, WI
869.469.7550
866.55.NEVIS Toll Free
869.469.7551 Fax
www.NevisIsland.com

NEVIS AIR & SEA PORTS AUTHORITY – P O Box 741 • Charlestown, Nevis • West Indies
Tel: 869 469-2001 • Fax: 869 469-0441/2004 • nevports@sisterisles.kn

from which reefs extend almost half a mile. The north coast is separated from St. Kitts by The Narrows, which are 15 to 20 feet deep. Two visible rocks are Booby Island, some 125 feet high, and Cow Rocks, which are only 6 feet high. A mile and half east of Booby Island there is a large shoal with patches of coral that reach the surface.

While it is easier to stay on the western side of both islands, it is not hard to traverse The Narrows. If coming from the north, round Mosquito Bluff on St. Kitts and pass midway between St. Kitts and the islands in the middle (Booby and Cow). Reverse the procedure for leaving. See also the St. Kitts navigation section.

Charlestown

Charlestown, Nevis's only town, is a picturesque country town with many historic buildings of stone and wood. The renovated waterfront area has a pleasant open area facing the dinghy dock. Great little shops abound and there is a choice of restaurants.

Navigation

If approaching from the south, stay a few hundred yards off Fort Charles, as it is shallow some way out. Yachts of less than 90 feet must pick up one of the one hundred moorings that have been laid in varying groups from town to Oualie Beach. The main visitor moorings are white with NPA

on them. Each has a pick-up line with an eye. Put your lines through the eye. Never run a line from one side of your boat through the eye to the other – the boat movement will abrade the line. The charges for these moorings are reasonable and listed under regulations. Larger yachts may anchor in deeper water. The moorings were excellent in 2009, but it is always good to snorkel on your mooring to check it.

If approaching from the south at night, watch out for the new commercial dock off Long Point. The mooring area at the north of town, just off Pinney's Beach, was fabulous. Behind a strip of pale ochre sand were miles of palm trees, whose slender trunks and waving lacy leaves catch the sunlight. Mt. Nevis ascends into the clouds behind. Gliding pelicans fold their wings and crash boldly in the sea. St. Kitts lying to the north, appears to be part of Nevis in a sweeping panorama. The anchorage is still lovely, except most of the palm trees are dying from a bacterial infection.

The Four Seasons Hotel on Pinney's Beach (currently defunct) makes a conspicuous landmark. Four Seasons built four stone breakwaters in front of their hotel about 100 yards from the beach. They maintain entrance red and green navigation lights for their own tenders, and all the breakwaters were originally marked with flashing orange lights – these no longer seem to be there. These breakwaters make for interesting snorkeling and seabirds roost on them.

Regulations

Charlestown customs open weekdays 0800-1600, and weekends 0900-1300. The customs office is upstairs in the Cotton Ginnery, just behind the dock. New customs regulations have made things more yacht-friendly. If you plan to visit both Nevis and St. Kitts, ask for a boat pass to St. Kitts when you check in. This is valid for up to a week and means you can visit other anchorages in Nevis and St. Kitts on your way over. You should present the boat pass to St. Kitts customs when you arrive in Basseterre and within the week, and also clear out from there.

In my experience, the Nevis customs officers are among the best. Nevis is fully integrated into the Eseaclear.com system, so if possible do the forms online before you arrive. If not, they will do them with you in the office. Once you have cleared here, your boat details remain on the computer for your next visit. You also have to visit the port authority. As you come downstairs from customs and head back a few steps towards the dinghy dock, you will see it; a door just around the corner from the toilets. After checking in with customs and port authority, walk down the road to the police station and get your passports stamped. You do not have to repeat immigration entry procedures for St. Kitts. At customs you pay a yacht entry fee of $20EC, a customs charge of $10EC, ($50 if you are over 100 tons).

Port dues as follows: $6EC for up to 20 tons; $10EC for 20-30 tons; $12EC for 30-50 tons, $24EC for 50-100 tons. Fare paying passengers are charged $5 US per head. In addition there is a $4EC per head environmental levy, and a $3EC a night harbor fee. The moorings fees are for set time periods (not per day) as follows:

Up to 35' $10 US for up to two days; $15 for 3-7 days

36' - 60' $15 US for up to two days; $20 for 3-7 days

61' - 90' $20 US for up to two days; $25 for 3-7 days

In addition, there is a daily port charge based on tonnage. Up to 20 tons the charge is $3EC, 20-30 tons is $5EC, 30-50 tons is 6EC, 50-100 tons is 12EC, 100-150 tons is 25, 150-500 is $36EC, 500-2000 tons is 36EC. In addition, boats of 100-500 tons pay $218EC for navigation lights, and over 500 tons the charge is $436EC.

Fees are not collected again if you visit St. Kitts.

ISLANDS THAT BRUSH THE CLOUDS

COMMERCIAL DOCK OFF LONG POINT

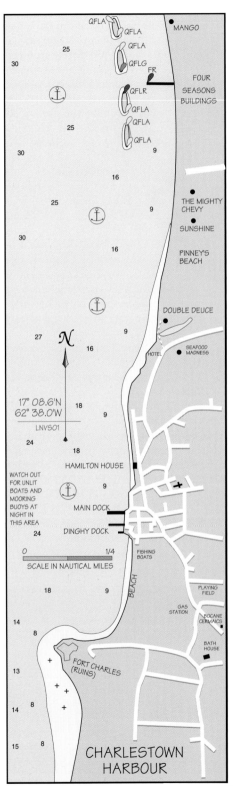

Communications

Double Deuce is a great beach bar and restaurant, which has wifi that you can sometimes get from your yacht. If you use it, pop in have a drink or meal and say thanks, it is a great place anyway.

The Public Library has two internet computers for a very reasonable rate. You walk a little further to Info Systems Security Designs (IDS). They open Monday to Saturday 1000 to late, Sunday 1700-1900 and in addition to internet you can rent DVDs. Cable and Wireless sells telephone cards. The Digicel office is across the road from customs.

Services

Water is available on the dock, currently $20EC for up to 1000 gallons, and so is fuel. The latter has to come by truck, so there is usually a minimum. Smaller amounts can be carried in jerry jugs. Call Nevis Port on VHF: 16 for permission to come alongside. Keep in mind that it is a dusty ferry dock, not designed for yachts. Inexpensive blocks of ice are occasionally available from the fish part of the market.

Annette Morton at A & M Enterprises is a yacht and ship agent. She can deal with fuel bunkering, and arrange water, customs clearance, and garbage disposal for large yachts. For all yachts, she can be a big help bringing parts in through customs and arranging taxis. A & M has offices both in Charlestown and the deep-water port.

CCC, owned by Mark Theron is a good, fully professional canvas and sail repair shop near the waterfront. Mark and his team, can fix all your sails, or build you a complex awning or bimini, and they also weld in aluminum and stainless, so they can build frames or fix anything you have broken. There are garbage bins just off the dock. You can fill most cooking gas bottles; ask any taxi.

Sunshine's Beach Bar can handle your laundry. Fedex has an office on Main Street. Jimmy Simmons, at Kustom Airbrush and Signs, can do any kind of boat name from computer transfer to airbrush. If you have any questions about the island, ask at the Nevis Tourism Bureau opposite the D.R. Walwyn Plaza. They love yachting visitors, wish to encourage yachts, and are very helpful. Ask for a copy of the Journey Map. This is one of the best visitors' maps I have seen in the islands. It includes hiking and biking trails and the newly redone Old Round Road.

Provisioning

The fresh food market has a good variety of produce. You can occasionally find fish in part of the market, fresh when the boats come in, otherwise frozen, and block ice is sometimes available.

The biggest and most modern supermarket in town is Superfoods, with a good selection of dry goods, cans, frozen foods, along with some meat and fish. It contains a deli section run by Annelise who used to be the pastry chef at Montpelier. If you want a treat, go in the morning, sit at the table and have some coffee and one of Annelise's scrumptious baked goodies. I had a delicious scone with homemade jam. You can go at lunch for sandwiches and pies. Superfoods is open weekdays from 0800-2000, Saturdays from 0800-2100, and on Sundays and most holidays they open 0900-1200. If you are buying a fair quantity, they will deliver it for you to the dock. You will also find smaller markets. If there is something you cannot find in Superfoods, take a cab or catch a bus out to Ram's new mall south of town (or it is a longish walk).

This is the biggest supermarket in Nevis, with a good fruit and vegetable selection. They open Monday to Friday 0830-1900 and Saturdays 0830-2000. Nevis Bakery on Happy Hill Drive will supply you with fresh bread and other great baked goodies, in small or charter-sized quantities. Or just pop in and pick up a snack.

TDC and Horsford's Nevis Center are both excellent large hardware stores just out of town that stock everything from housewares to rope

Fun Shopping

Henville's Plaza is right opposite the ferry dock. Here you will find a branch of Gigi's Island Fever, which Fodor's called "the most elegant boutique in Nevis." Their stock of artistic sportswear, beachwear, t-shirts, hats, jewelry, ornaments,

ISLANDS THAT BRUSH THE CLOUDS

CHARLESTOWN & PINNEY'S BEACH

handicrafts, and books will ensure that you find something for everyone. Island Fever has its own screen-printing business; so many designs are unique to this shop. Knick Knacks, in the same plaza, has attractive wooden boxes, artistic ornaments and souvenirs, art prints, and t-shirts.

The Cotton Ginnery is right opposite the dinghy dock. This is a plaza with many small boutiques. Chapter 1 Bookstore is here, with the latest bestsellers, magazines, and newspapers. You will also find a good little handicraft store selling basketwork.

The TDC Plaza houses Island Hopper, the outlet for Caribelle Batik. They sell many beautiful clothes and wall hangings, as well as handicrafts, leather craft, and souvenirs. Mildred Williams at Caribco has managed to gather an interesting collection of t-shirts, souvenirs, and ornaments, all with a Caribbean flavor. Pemberton's, a duty-free shop, sells perfumes, jewelry, and baubles with a tropical flavor.

Bocane Ceramics is on the edge of town as you head towards Gingerland. It is well within walking distance, just past the second gas station on the left hand side. Cheryl Liburd is the proprietor and a talented potter; she produces all the pottery

on the premises. She works with white clay and her pieces are all brightly colored and highly decorative – also reasonably priced. She makes everything – from plates to candlestick holders and big decorative wall hangings and will pack for traveling. In addition she hand paints t-shirts and her shop has some local teas and jams, jewelry, and art. Nevis Handicrafts Cooperative sells crafts, honey, jams, and chutney, all made on Nevis. You will find more crafts at Crafthouse, located a mile or so out of town on the road behind Pinney's Beach.

Restaurants
Charlestown

Café des Arts is a tiny building in a lovely garden setting close to Hamilton House. Elizabeth Smith, the owner, opens at 0830, has lots of different coffees, and serves cakes and muffins, as well as sandwiches, salads and quiche for lunch. She will happily give you any local information.

Unella's is just down the road from the main dock, on an open deck with a great view of the bay from its upstairs perch. Open for lunch or dinner, they serve plenty of fresh seafood, as well as ribs and steak. The view makes this a great lunch spot, and they serve good sandwiches and salads, as well as tasty local meals. They open all day Monday to Saturday, and on Sundays after 1800.

Eddy's is in a gracious old Caribbean town building open to the square. It opens on Wednesday and starts with half-price happy hour from 1700-2000, when you can also eat simple fare such as mahi mahi on a bun or hamburgers. Entertainment cranks up and goes late. Everyone on the island turns up for this, so it is a great place for people watching. Eddie also opens on Fridays, and you can ask about Mondays.

The Patio (closed Sunday) is run by the same people who have Superfoods and is in the same square. It opens daily from 0800 till 2000, serving breakfast, lunch and dinner. They have a lovely big patio so that you can sit outside – great when there is cricket playing at Warner Park, because it's right next door. They offer a local buffet lunch served daily, cafeteria style.

V's Courtyard Cafe is in a lovely hidden spot in a big courtyard, with lots of trees and plants. Wayne, who runs it, is welcoming and friendly. It is more of a bar and nights spot than anything else, but food is often available in the evenings and this is a good place for private parties.

The little open food shack, called Nite Moves, downstairs outside the Cotton Ginnery is run by Roger Cozier and does good local food, including rotis and fish sandwiches.

On the road to Pinney's Beach, Seafood Madness, owned by Freddy and Andy, serves a wide variety of fresh seafood on a large screened porch.

Then there is a special restaurant just a short taxi ride out of town straight up into the hills in Hamilton. Set in a typical Caribbean house with a lovely garden, including many fruit trees, Banana's offers elegant eating in a peaceful country atmosphere. You sit on a big balcony overlooking the garden. Gillian, the owner, offers upmarket, inventive cuisine. She has lots of fresh local fish and occasionally has fresh mussels and salmon flown in. It opens every day except Sunday for lunch and dinner. Lunches are lighter with lots of salads, burgers and grilled meats and seafood. There are occasional theme nights with entertainment.

Chris Doyle

ISLANDS THAT BRUSH THE CLOUDS

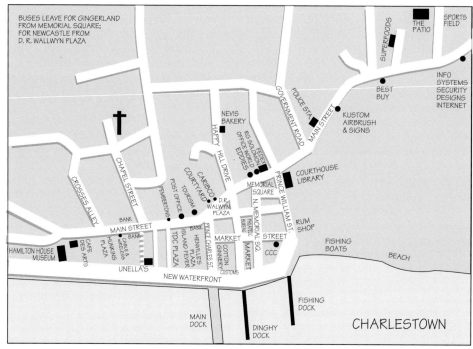

Banana's is also an art gallery with paintings both on the walls and in a separate gallery, which also sells jewelry and a few artistic handicrafts. If you want to visit there is usually someone around from 0830 onwards. If you come for the art, also check out Patricia Art (imaginative mosaics), Carolity Cantirll (paintings) and Iziah (sculpture). They are all close by.

Reservations for dinner at Banana's are essential, as it is very popular.

Restaurants
Pinney's Beach, South End

Pinney's Beach is so gorgeous you may want to laze away days here. Most yachts anchor here. Several excellent bars are open for lunch or dinner.

Sunshine's attracts escapees from the Four Seasons Hotel, locals, and yachts people, who eat under the palm trees. It is run by Sunshine, whose cheerful manner keeps people coming back and makes it an entertaining hangout. Sunshine's is is the biggest bar on the beach and recognizable by the many flags he flies. Pull your dinghy up right outside. One of Sunshine's "killer bee" drinks will get your mood up and make you ready for his daily barbecue of fresh fish, lobster, and chicken, cooked as you like it. Pull in for a swim and lunch, or come for a sunset drink and stay for dinner. Sunshine

also does yacht laundry, sells fresh fruit and vegetables, and will help dispose of yacht garbage. He will also keep an eye on your dinghy while you explore ashore.

Next door, Calysonian The Mighty Chevy and his wife Amelia run Chevy's Calypso Bar, which is open from 1000-2200. Chevy lived and sung in England for 18 years where he met Amelia. They cook local and international food, with the emphasis on fish, lobster and shrimp. Friday night has a happy hour from 1700-1900 followed by seafood specials with 20% off all seafood dishes including their coconut curried shrimp. Sunday night is party night with live reggae music, Monday night is Karaoke night with a bonfire and buffalo wing specials as well as all the other dishes. It kicks off with a happy hour from 1800-2000.

Continue down to the town end of the beach, and you will come to Lyndeta's Double Deuce. This was always a happening beach bar, but it shifted up a gear when Lyndeta's boyfriend Mark, who was the executive chef for Montpelier, gave that up and went to work with her. A special

advantage of this bar is that it is on the edge of town and if the swells are running, walking here from the dinghy dock is no sweat. If it is calm, this is a good place to leave your dinghy. The atmosphere is pleasant, relaxing and quiet. This changes on Thursday nights when they have Karaoke, and on other occasional music nights.

It is a great hangout, and you can borrow games like chess and scrabble from the bar, or browse their old yachting magazines, or use the fresh water shower. They have darts, table tennis, a pool table and wifi. Lyndeta and Mark produce perfectly grilled fresh local seafood, including tuna wahoo and whole red snapper. Also, chicken, and steak with local vegetables. Double Deuce is open every day from 1000 to late every night. Walk in for lunch, but make reservations for dinner.

The giant resort, which was run by Four Seasons, took a beating in Omar, and it is far from operational. The property owners (not Four Seasons) have said it will reopen, but the future at this point is unclear. This is a terrible loss for Nevisians, as it created about 600 jobs. (See also the section on

Gingerland.)

Transport

Ferries run about once an hour between Nevis and St. Kitts from the ferry dock. In addition, St Kitts Sea Bridge runs a car ferry from Cades Bay to Major's Bay. It starts at 0800 and runs every other hour until 1800. The return ferries start at 0900 and run every other hour until 1900. This makes it quite practical to take a rented car over for a day.

You can take a taxi, walk, or rent a car. Taxi tours are reasonably priced. Keep this in mind if you want to do something specific, as making it part of a tour might be the answer. For example, the rate to Long Point Port to clear customs and back is pretty outrageous, but you could make it part of a tour and get to see the whole island for just twice that fare. Also, I cannot fathom why taxis charge $3US more to visit the Botanical Gardens than the adjoining property of Montpelier.

Mountain bikes are another good way to see the island and rentals are available from Winston's Nevis Mountain Bike Center at Oualie Beach. Cars are few enough that you can still feel comfortable on the roads. In addition, newly opened trails such as the Upper Round Road are a natural for mountain bikes. Try renting one, taking a taxi up to Golden Rock, and coasting all the way back down (after you have dragged it along a few trails).

Fitzroy Williams, otherwise known as "Teach" because of his earlier profession as a schoolteacher, runs an excellent taxi, tour, and car rental agency called Teach Tours. He is friendly and informative and is happy to show you the island by car or organize hiking, rainforest tours, and other tours. You can call Teach on VHF: 16 or 09, or use his cell: 662-9022. Should you need a shore base, ask Teach – he manages rental properties. A reader also highly recommended Abba's Guided Tours.

Three other places you can rent cars from are Strikers Car, TDC and Noel's Garage. They all give good service, and these days with the new ferry going over to St. Kitts, you can use the same car for both islands. However, if you are moving your boat from one island to the other, talk to TDC as they might be able to have you return your Nevis car and pick up one in St. Kitts.

You can also rent scooters from 3 KB's Scooter Rentals.

Ashore

The Nelson Museum puts Britain's famous hero into the natural and cultural context of Nevis as it was in his day. Americans who have never heard of Nelson can find out who he was. For those of us who remember him as a dry lesson in history, the museum brings him to life. It opens weekdays 0900-1600 and Saturdays 1000-1300, but ask in Hamilton House to make sure it has not moved.

The Hamilton exhibit is in the house where Alexander Hamilton was born. Both the museum and the garden are charming and open weekdays 0800-1600 and Saturdays 0900-1200. The museum contains a library devoted to history and natural history, including the island's archives. Ask about horse riding as Director John Guilbert owns the Nevis Equestrian Center. You can also ask about guides, eco-tours, and trails.

Gingerland

The choice land in the old days was "Gingerland," just south of the mountain. Here, on fertile soil, one is elevated enough to be both cool and graced with a pleasant view. It is here that most of the large old plantations were built and some have been converted to small luxurious hotels with exceptionally fine dining rooms. These are grand old places, oozing with class, and absolutely perfect for sampling the fine style of the island. You can dress up as much as you want. Ties are not essential, but shorts and flip-flops do not go down too well in the evening. Most serve a set evening meal and the prices, which run at $50-$70US, make them top value for elegant dining. I can think of no other island where I would prefer to have that special night ashore. Reservations are essential. Most have some form of weekly entertainment, though not in the summer. You can visit without reservations for lunch, when they generally serve sandwiches and light meals.

Golden Rock Estate is approached by a long drive lined with old stone walls. Handsome historic buildings are set among bright flowers. This magnificent old estate covers some 96 acres on the edge of the rain forest. Pam Barry has ably run Golden Rock for some decades, and had just overseen one a major renovation, brightening up colors, and generally making it a wonderful place to visit, when they started on an even more ambitious plan. This is a new colonial style dining room patio and large walking area with numerous decorative formal ponds. It was nearing completion when I visited and should be open by the time you visit.

Yachts people are always made very welcome and lunch guests are invited to enjoy the swimming pool. (Most other estates reserve their pool for resident guests.)

Dinners here are excellent value. You can book on VHF: 16 or through the following taxis: Barry's Taxi, Libra One or Gentle A.

The extensive grounds also make Golden Rock Estate a delightful choice for lunch (sandwiches, salads, and grilled foods) or tea. Monkeys are often in evidence, and during lunch you can feed crumbs to the birds and lizards. You can follow the marked circular hiking trail (30 minutes). If you want to hike into the rainforest to the water source (a 4-hour round trip), this is the place to start. Consider coming here for lunch and walking back to town by the Upper Round Road. This newly finished trail is along paths that follow both old and new roads that follow the route of the early agricultural roads. It only takes a few hours to walk back to town along roads and trails with beautiful views. The trail continues all the way to Nisbet

Plantation. Pam will give you maps to help you on your way with any of these hikes. She can also put you in touch with Lynell or Larla Liburd, good guides.

Lupinacci's Hermitage is charming. It is made up of many small old buildings, all beautifully painted. Peacocks grace the lawns and you will probably see their Belgian carthorse and a donkey walking around. Before-dinner drinks are served in a friendly old living room. The meal (à la carte) is served on a patio overlooking the garden courtyard. On Wednesday nights they roast a suckling pig and have a string band.

If you fancy horse riding, this is a good place to start. They have a good selection, from Belgians to race horses. They ride in the hills every day from Monday to Saturday at 0930. There are horse races on Nevis about once a month.

The Lupinacci's are also sailing folks and have Gremlin, a 27-foot sailing boat, which their son Richie enjoys, as well as Intermezzo, a 34-foot power boat, which they charter as a water taxi to St. Kitts.

Montpelier has a grand entrance gate and heavy stone walls. It is owned by the Hoffman family from the USA. Drinks are served in an impressive living room; you repair onto the balcony with a great view over the lights of Charlestown for dinner (served 1930-2030). Janice oversees the food; the nightly set menu has three courses, as well as snacks and coffee. The choices always include meat, seafood, and vegetarian dishes.

For an even grander meal, ask to eat in the Mill. This is an exclusive setting with just a few tables inside the historic old stone mill. Here they offer a very elegant four-course champagne dinner.

Janice's cuisine is a blend of European and Caribbean flavors, using all fresh local ingredients. Everything, including the bread, is made on the premises. A la carte lunches are also available in the mill courtyard. While here, you can check out their small boutique. Reservations are essential for dinner.

Old Manor has the most impressive buildings, with a lot of wood, tall chimneys, and farm machinery, all amid a pleasant garden. Owners John and Margaret Carson, an English couple, were home owners in Nevis for some 12 years before this venture. Lynn Williams manages it on a day-to-day basis. They are open for breakfast, lunch, and dinner. They have a large front balcony with a view of Montserrat that is particularly pleasant for lunch or dinner under a full moon. Dinner is a reasonably priced à la carte menu, or a fixed menu, with everything from salmon to rack of lamb and is served from 1830-2100.

Another attraction in Gingerland is the Botanical Garden of Nevis, a creation of Dr. Joseph Murphy, a marketing genius from the USA who became so attached to Nevis that he became a citizen. The botanical garden covers 8 acres, with many artificial rivers and pools and includes a shaded rainforest conservatory. The centerpiece of the gardens is the teahouse and boutique, set in a gorgeous building that faithfully resembles an old estate house. The gift shop is worth a look.

There is no charge for visiting the restaurant and boutique, though there is a charge for wandering around the gardens. A guide is included and worth taking for his knowledge.

The gardens contain plants from all over the world, including orchids, cactuses, and palms. The collection is already impressive and the lower areas are tall and shady. They open to Monday to Saturday, 0900-1700.

The restaurant in the Botanical Gardens is called 1787 and is run by Montpelier, which is just down the road. It has an airy upstairs balcony where you can have coffee, tea, or lunch overlooking the gardens and right down to the sea. You can get a pleasant and elegant lunch here from 1130-1430.

Water Sports

Nevis has pleasant diving, with big fish and good visibility. Local laws stipulate

ISLANDS THAT BRUSH THE CLOUDS

that divers must go with a dive shop. Dives include Thermal Vents Reef, from 35 feet to 95 feet with lots of black coral. Overhangs and small canyons provide good hiding places for spotted drums, high-hats, arrow crabs and large lobsters. At 90 feet you can see the hot vent where 100°F water fizzes upwards.

Coral Gardens begins at 50 feet and has lots of tube sponges, sea fans and anemones. Packed with hard and soft corals, this area seems to continue forever. It is home for schools of Atlantic spadefish and large schools of horse-eyed jacks.

Monkey Shoals is a 2 square-mile reef, 5-miles offshore. The depth varies from 40 feet to 100 feet. Visibility here is usually over 100 feet. This is home to French and grey angelfish, nurse sharks and black tipped sharks, glass-eyed and yellow-tailed snappers and much more. You will see majestic stands of pillar coral, large brain coral and elkhorn coral.

Nags Head plummets to 75 feet. Here the large boulders are stacked on top of each other making great hiding places for crustaceans, crinoids and parrotfish. Eagle rays cruise past divers in formation.

Booby Island Dive is in the Narrows. This almost circular reef is packed with lobster, French grunts, horse-eyed jacks, southern stingrays, hawksbill turtles and large nurse sharks.

Those wishing to dive should contact Scuba Safaris' Ellis Chaderton, a NAUI and PADI trained instructor, who comes

from the island and knows his waters well. Ellis is brother-in-law to Derek Perryman from Dive Dominica. If you are visiting both islands, you can arrange for a package of dives split between them. Scuba Safaris stands by on VHF: 16 and is at Oualie Beach. A good time to call is about 0800, but you can often get them at other times of the day. Ellis will pick up divers from yachts in any of the Nevis anchorages. (See also Water Sports section under Oualie Beach.)

ANCHORAGES NORTH OF CHARLESTOWN
Northern Pinney's Beach to Oualie Beach

After you leave the first cluster of moorings off Four Seasons and head north, there is a second cluster starting at Nelson's Spring, with the large modern buildings ashore. These continue right up to Tamarind Bay, and you can also anchor in Oualie Beach. In general the whole northern area is calmer than Charlestown, though much of it is susceptible to north westerly swells. The very calmest spot is tucked up in Oualie Beach, the next calmest tucked up in Tamarind Bay.

This whole area covers about two miles, so it is all within dinghy, and energetic

Chris Doyle

walking range. Some excellent restaurants and bars make it a good place to hang out and enjoy Nevis.

Navigation

If coming from Charlestown, follow Pinney's Beach north, staying about 900 feet offshore. The moorings start at Nelson's Spring and continue up to Cades Bay. At the northern limit of Cades bay is a dock used for the Sea Bridge car ferries. There is a gap in the moorings to allow for the ferries and then more moorings are up at Tamarind Bay. As you go north from Tamarind Bay to to Oualie Beach you have to give a couple of hundred yards clearance as it is shoal closer towards the shore. There are also depths of about 7 feet outside the shoals which can be rough and break in a large swell. If you make a sweep well outside the bay and come in close to Hurricane Hill, there is about 9 feet of water close to the hill. There are three moorings up in Oualie Beach, but they are permanently taken by local boats, so if you want to be here you will have to anchor. It is the most sheltered spot, but he holding is poor on thick sea-grass. You can look for the odd spot of sand.

Services and Communications

Oualie Beach Club has an excellent dock, lit at night, which you are welcome to use. Make sure you tie up clear of the end part that is used by the dive and fishing boats, and a stern anchor is necessary.

Oualie Beach Club will help out with water in jerry jugs or shallow draft boats (probably 3.5 feet for comfort, but you could get in with another foot if you worked the tides) can come alongside the dock. This is an excellent service for powerboats and cats. The Oualie Beach Club sells ice, and the staff also helps dispose of garbage and organize car rentals and arrange anything you need. There is an internet station in the reception area. The dock here is the most protected and the best in Nevis.

A big new dock is also planned for Nelson's Spring, a couple of miles south of Oualie Beach. If for some reason that is not complete, The Yachtman's Grill, their restaurant, plan to put out a floating one. They also rent Polaris 4x4 vehicles in varying seating sizes, for touring the island even on the smallest trails. They also hope to offer laundry, trash disposal, small quantities of gas or diesel, complimentary hot showers, and wifi, which you will get from your yacht on a close mooring. They sell cases of cold beer and even have a shopping service. Greg, the owner, also rents power tools and plans to import inflatables. A full spa is in the same compound.

Crichi Beach Club also has a small floating dock that you are welcome to use.

Shopping

On the main road opposite Nelson's Spring, Deli by Wendi is a handy shop with cheeses, frozen meats, fish and lobster. They also do good sandwiches and snacks.

Farther up the road, opposite Chrichi, Mansa is a good local grocery with fresh local produce, as well as some cans and bottles, and some imported produce. In addition, they have a big seating area, sell excellent homemade local juices by the bottle, and they run a grill and cook chicken, ribs and more.

Restaurants

The Yachtsman Grill is a new restaurant at Nelson's Spring. It is owned by Greg, helped by Adrian. Greg is a yachting person and Adrian was in shipping, and they more than welcome those on yachts. The restaurant is bright, airy, open to the beach, the pool, and the breeze.

The kitchen, with its grill, smoker and giant lobster pots, is completely open so you can watch the chefs at work. They serve quality seafood and steak, with a lobster tank in the front, and this will be a great place for lobster. (It was just about to open when I was there.) Lunches are lighter, with salads and sandwiches as well as grilled foods. They offer a special southern pulled pork sandwich.

They also want it to be a hangout for yachts, so they offer wifi, hot showers (rent a towel). Customers can use the adjoining pool and they rent vehicles, help out with groceries, and even have a tender so they can take stuff to your boat or bring you in for dinner. It will open daily at 1100 for lunch and stay open for dinner with the kitchen closing around 2100.

Next door, The Coconut Grove is a very fancy beach restaurant built of poles supporting a giant thatched roof. Gary Colt, the owner, was a professional wine specialist, so they have a huge international cellar with about 400 carefully selected wines. On the food side, you will get an excellent meal beautifully served.

Ricky, the chef, is local. He trained under a French chef and has worked in fancy restaurants in the Dominican Republic and Anguilla. The basic cuisine is French, but Ricky has infused some Caribbean flavors, and uses local fresh ingredients, especially fish. The restaurant was awarded the top new table in the world

in 2006 by Condé-Naste.

They open every day for lunch (by the pool) and dinner (upstairs in the big open building). Lunches are lighter and include panini, salads and grilled fish. This is a choice place to come for a special night out.

As you head north, you will come to two local beach bars. The first is Island Life Beach Bar, and it has a reputation for good music in the evenings. The other is the Sunset Beach, which has an interesting location near a river as well as the beach, with egrets hanging out in the trees.

Just past Sunset Beach is Crichi Beach Club (closed Monday). Owner Christian is from Norway and he opens at noon, and this is a great (and popular) lunch place.

The food is light, but really excellent, with salads, pastas, sandwiches, seared sesame tuna, and delicious brownies or sorbet for dessert. They also open for dinner on Wednesdays and Sundays. If you are interested in property, Christian is building villas on the waterfront, he has a small floating dock, and you are welcome to use it, swells permitting.

The Gallipot (VHF: 16) is between Tamarind Bay and Oaulie Beach and within easy walking from both, just where the road runs right next to the sea, and it is visible from the sea. This is a lovely and friendly little bar/restaurant, where you can get to meet other yachties and locals. Owners Julian and Tracy Rigby used to run the deep-sea fishing at the Oualie Hotel, are also yachting people.

They open Thursday to Saturday, 1200-1500 for lunch and 1800-2100 for dinner. They also open on Sunday from 1000-1500. You can get brunch or a traditional roast beef and Yorkshire pudding lunch. Come early, as half the island sometimes turns up. Naturally they like to serve fish, usually mahi mahi and wahoo caught that day and perfectly barbecued right in front of you. Steaks, salads and chicken are also on the menu, which is very reasonably priced. The lunch menu also includes quiches and lighter fare.

The Oualie Beach Club, owned by John and Karen Yearwood, is a little waterfront hotel with a restaurant and bar. Both the location and service are good and they open daily for breakfast, lunch and dinner. The menu is wide-ranging, but always includes local fresh fish, perfectly cooked and everything is artistically served under the direction of Chef Webbe-Walter. During the season they quite often have musical entertainment.

In the same complex you can find Alistair Yearwood at Oualie Realty. He is a goldmine of information and well worth talking to should you be interested in property.

Ashore

Nevis is quiet enough to cycle around in reasonable safety; most of the roads are around the coastal plain and are relatively flat. This makes a bicycle a very pleasant way to get to know the island. You can do the whole island loop road in a morning or afternoon (the good guys can do it in an hour and half) or take a day and really relax. There are also many dedicated and slightly more difficult (up and down) trails

ISLANDS THAT BRUSH THE CLOUDS

in the area. You can rent mountain bikes at Nevis Windsurfing and Mountain Bike Center (see below). They will rent you bikes by the week, and you can also call them from Charlestown and they will deliver, though you might be better off anchored here, as shore access is easy, the prettiest rides are close by, and town is not a very long ride away.

For those who would like to ride horses, the Equestrain Center is not far from Nelson's Spring.

Water Sports

Nevis Water Sports is owned and operated by Ian Gonzaley. His water sports operation includes by far the best sports fishing trips on the island. You can sit in the bar and watch them haul the catch ashore. He also operates a water taxi between St. Kitts and Nevis, which can be very handy when you have guests arriving in, or leaving for St. Kitts and you don't want to take the yacht over. Rentals include fishing gear, snorkel gear, and sunfish. This is the base of the Nevis Yacht

Club Sports Fishing Competition, a major sports fishing event that takes place sometime in October. Call them on VHF: 16.

Next door is Winston's Nevis Windsurfing and Mountain Bike Center. Winston was born in Birmingham of Nevisian parents and has returned to his roots. He has a great sense of humor and was once the Caribbean mountain bike downhill champion. He does an excellent job at fostering running, sailing and biking with kids; he organizes the Nevis Olympic Triathlon and the Nevis to St. Kitts Cross Channel Swim (both in March), among many others. As you can imagine, this is a great place to meet other enthusiasts or discuss the next Caribbean Cup.

Apart from renting mountain bikes, Winston rents windsurfers and ocean kayaks, and all levels of instruction are available. He also does biking and kayaking tours.

Oualie Beach is also the home of Scuba Safaris, which we have written up under Charlestown water sports.

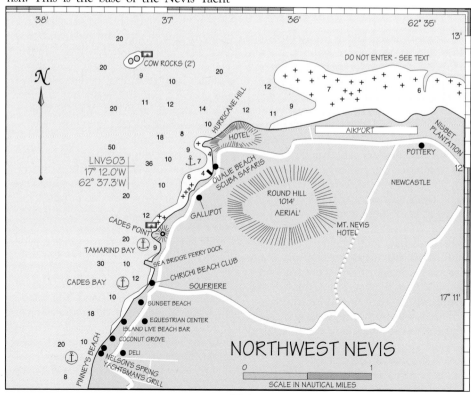

OUALIE BEACH

TAMARIND BAY

North of Oualie Beach

Newcastle, on the north coast of Nevis, used to be an important harbor. There is an almost impossible entrance amid breaking seas through a channel in the reefs. The reef, known as Carpenter Reef, is reputed to work equally well on fiberglass. The harbor is now shoal, windy, and totally unsuitable for yachts.

There are two beach facilities here. Pizza Beach operated by the Mount Nevis Hotel, serves pizzas and other snacks mainly on weekends and holidays. Then there is the local eatery Shirley's Place. Prices in both are reasonable. The new airport is very close by.

Newcastle has several other restaurants. These can easily be visited by land from the other anchorages. The Mount Nevis Hotel serves top-notch food on a comfortable balcony overlooking The Narrows.

The Nisbet Plantation Hotel is a lovely historic house set in a coconut grove leading to the beach. You can relax with a drink on the massive veranda with both a lounging area and a separate dining area.

There is also a beach restaurant for lunch. Thursdays is the most popular day, weather permitting. The manager holds his rum punch party at the beach restaurant, followed by dinner with a calypso

ISLANDS THAT BRUSH THE CLOUDS

band for entertainment.

They bring in fresh seafood for this event and serve it as a buffet. Dress is somewhat formal. If you come by day you can visit their boutique.

There is good clay in Nevis and the Newcastle Pottery is a cooperative of five local potters who make attractive and inexpensive unglazed earthenware.

REDONDA

Redonda lies between Montserrat and Nevis. It is a handsome rock, one mile long and almost 1,000 feet high. There is no proper anchorage, and climbing on the island is in any case difficult and potentially dangerous.

Redonda has a strange history: phosphates were discovered here in 1865 and mining began. In 1872 the British decided they had better take over Redonda before the Americans did and they annexed it as part of Antigua.

Phosphate production grew, 100 people worked on the island, and personnel and equipment were pulled up and down on a two-bucket cable car

designed so that the weight of the up-going load was balanced by seawater, which was first pumped into a reservoir at the top, then used to fill the descending bucket. In those days there were houses on the top and a wharf.

In 1914 the phosphate production stopped, and the mining lease was finally given up in 1930. In 1978, Antigua, now independent and keen to confirm ownership of the rock, set up a post office and issued a series of stamps to commemorate

100 years of phosphate mining. There was talk of reopening the mine. The post office was abandoned a year later and subsequent landslides and hurricanes have destroyed it.

There is also the story of the Kingdom of Redonda. In 1865 Matthew Dowdy Shiell, an Irish-Montserrat merchant, had a long-awaited son after eight daughters. Being a sexist, he wanted a kingdom for his son (the daughters could go marry) and, as no one had yet claimed Redonda, he did. In 1880 when Shiell's son, "M.P.," was 15, they took a day trip over to the rock with the Bishop of Antigua and other friends and Shiell had the Bishop crown his son King Filipe I of Redonda. They all had a good time and consumed much alcohol.

M.P. Shiel (he dropped the second "L" on his name) moved to England and became a brilliant writer of Gothic romance and science fiction. Although never hugely popular among the general public, he was held in the highest esteem by literary figures of his day, including H.G. Wells. He maintained his title and held court in London, creating several literary duchies to the realm. In his later years M.P. Shiel spent some time barraging the British government to get recognition of his title as King of Redonda. First they ignored him and then, to keep him quiet, gave him a pension for his contributions to literature.

Shiel died in 1947, but not before passing his crown to fellow writer John Galsworth (King Juan I). Juan I ended up taking to drink, bestowed titles in exchange for beer and tried unsuccessfully to sell the kingdom on several occasions.

Before he died in 1970 he passed the title on to Jon Wynne-Tyson (King Juan II). In 1979 a group of Shiel enthusiasts, including King Juan II, paid a visit to the island and planted an ecological flag on top.

King Juan II, tiring of his royal role, abdicated on April 1st 1998, and Robert Williamson, a writer and artist who lives in Antigua announced it had been passed to him (he claimed he had to be on the short list as he was only 5ft 2inches). King Robert (Bob the Bald) kept a flamboyantly colorful royal yacht (used in Pirates of the Caribbean), he mounted an expedition to Redonda with 16 loyal sub-

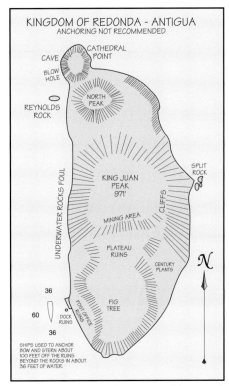

jects, and appointed many nobles to the realm. Since no country recognizes the king, anyone can claim it with impunity, and Bob is the best and most entertaining pretender to the throne.

However, the king, according to the Antigua and Barbuda Museum, and as directed in a letter written by Jon Wynn-Tyson, is Javier Marius, the Spanish novelist. Javier may, at a literary level be more deserving, but Bob was around and fun and made the whole thing more local.

Interestingly both Bob and Javier have or had a Redonda Literary award, but Bob's was geared specifically to the Caribbean.

In the meantime Redonda is left to its own devices. A tantalizing vision on the horizon, it is very much for the birds, and if you sail close by you will see them wheeling high over the peaks. A few boobies will probably accompany you for a short while.

You get a magnificent view of the cliffs and can see the remains of habitation. There are just a couple of trees and lots of cactuses and succulents.

ISLANDS THAT BRUSH THE CLOUDS

237

Chris Doyle

Montserrat

MONTSERRAT'S first European settlers were Irish who arrived from St. Kitts in 1630, having experienced problems with the Kittian Protestants. A second wave of Irish settlers arrived in 1649, after Cromwell conquered Ireland. They began as small farmers growing mixed crops, but the economy of the island slowly changed. Sugar became the main crop, slaves were introduced, and over the years the smaller farms became uneconomical. Many of the Irish returned to their homeland. They left behind smiling eyes, Irish names such as O'Brian, Dublin, and Ryan, and an Irish stew called "goat water". Today Montserrat, like Ireland, is known as the Emerald Isle.

As you sail past Montserrat, it is like two different lands. The southern half is starkly beautiful, a harsh terrain dominated by the awesome Soufriere Hills volcano, barren and smoking against the skyline. The remains of the ruined capital, Plymouth, are a humbling reminder of nature's power over years of human endeavor. On the southeastern coast, you can see historic windmill towers and buildings buried to their roofs in volcanic ash, and boulders the size of large houses spewed out by the volcano lying miles below the summit. By contrast, the island's north is lush and green, with verdant mountains and handsome modern houses perched on the hills.

What you cannot gauge from the sea is the extent and beauty of the northern part of Montserrat. Most of the habitations follow the road that runs from Little Bay in the north, along the west coast to Salem in the south. This area is protected from the volcano by the Center Hills mountain range, and what you see is an island of almost picture book perfection. On one side, lush dark green mountains are steep and convoluted. On the other, the land falls away to the coast, offering a perfect panorama of the Caribbean Sea with views of the islands of Redonda and Nevis to the west. At nearly every turn, coconut palms

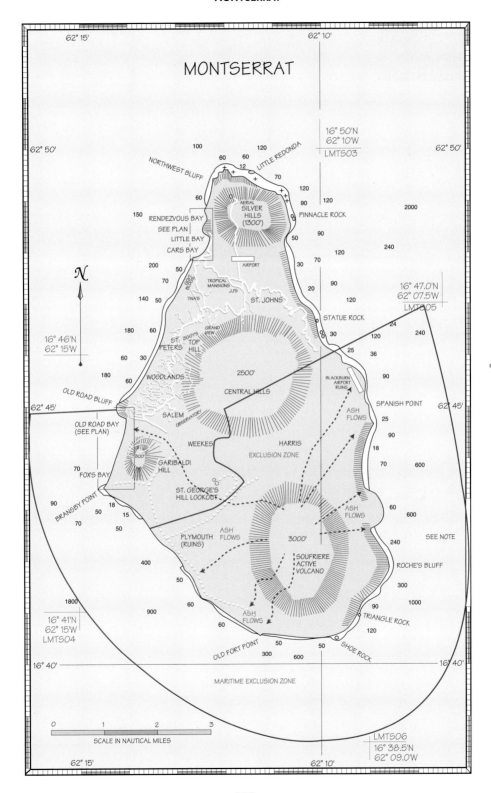

MONTSERRAT

62° 15'

62° 10'

16° 50'N
62° 10'W
LMTS03

62° 50'

62° 50'

NORTHWEST BLUFF

100   120   LITTLE REDONDA
        60   60
                12   70
                                120
        60   90   120
AERIAL   2000
150   SILVER
        HILLS
RENDEZVOUS BAY (1300')   PINNACLE ROCK
SEE PLAN   90
LITTLE BAY   50   240
CARS BAY   120

200   50   AIRPORT   30   70
                                            120
70   20   90
        TROPICAL
140 50 MANSIONS JJ'S   90   120   240
        TINA'S
                ST. JOHNS   STATUE ROCK

16° 47.0'N
62° 07.5'W
LMTS05

180 60 GRAND   30   24
        ST. VIEW   120   240
180 PETERS TOP
        HILL   25   36
60   30
                2500'   90
180   BLACKBURN
60   AIRPORT
WOODLANDS   RUINS
        CENTRAL HILLS   SPANISH POINT
                                ASH   25
16° 46'N   SALEM   FLOWS
62° 15'W   90
        OBSERVATORY
                WEEKES   HARRIS   18
OLD ROAD BLUFF   EXCLUSION ZONE
                                70   600
62° 45'   62° 45'
OLD ROAD BAY
(SEE PLAN)
                        800'   60
                GARIBALDI   ASH   600
70   HILL   FLOWS
FOX'S BAY
                ST. GEORGE'S
90   HILL LOOKOUT   SEE NOTE
BRANSBY POINT   18   70   240
        50   15   ROCHE'S BLUFF
70   PLYMOUTH ASH   3000'
        50   (RUINS)   FLOWS   300
                        SOUFRIERE
400   ACTIVE   1000
                        VOLCANO
        50   90
1800   TRIANGLE ROCK
900   60   120
16° 41'N   60   ASH
62° 15'W   FLOWS   SHOE ROCK
LMTS04   OLD FORT POINT 50   50
                        300   600
16° 40'   16° 40'

MARITIME EXCLUSION ZONE

0   1   2   3
SCALE IN NAUTICAL MILES

LMTS06
16° 38.5'N
62° 09.0'W

62° 15'   62° 10'

ISLANDS THAT BRUSH THE CLOUDS

239

Montserrat

Regulations

Yachts should proceed to Little Bay, the port of entry for clearance. For details see Little Bay.

Telephones

Use the card phones or make your call from Cable and Wireless. To dial to the USA or Canada, dial 1, then the number. For other countries use 011, plus the country code (UK is 44), then the number. For reverse charge and card calls dial 1-800-CALL USA. Only Cable and Wireless GSM phones work here.

Shopping hours

Weekdays (except Wednesday) 0800-1600; Wednesday and Saturday, 0800-1300. The Royal Bank of Canada & The Bank of Montserrat open Monday to Thursday 0800-1400, Friday: 0800-1500.

Transport

Montserrat has an airport with a 1700-foot runway and is linked to neighboring islands by Winair. Low clouds and windy and rainy weather can close the airport.

A ferry between Antigua and Monserrat runs during peak demand, periods like Christmans.

Taxis are available. Typcial rates in $US for up to 4 people are:

Little Bay to Aiport	10
Little Bay to Rams and return	40

Rental cars are available. You need to get a local license, which costs about $50 EC. Drive on the left. Departure tax is $55 EC

Holidays

- Jan 1st
- March 17 St. Patrick's Day
- Good Friday and Easter Monday
  (Easter Easter Sunday is April 4, 2010; April 24, 2011)
- First Monday in May (Labor Day)
- June (around the 10th), Queens birthday celebrations
- Whit Monday, 50 days after Easter Sunday
  (May Whit Monday May 24, 2010, June 13, 2011)
- August Monday (First Monday in August)
- December 25 and 26
- December 31 (Festival Day)

Montserrat, Admiralty Leisure Folio 5641-3

or brightly colored flowers provide the perfect frame for a photograph. Houses are typically modern day Caribbean, which means they can be small brightly painted wooden houses shaded by dark green breadfruit trees, whitewashed bungalows, or fancy modern mansions.

In 1995, the population was around 11,000 people who farmed, fished, and were employed in the tourist industry. Many Americans and Canadians bought homes here to escape the cold northern winters. The Soufriere Hills volcano first erupted in 1995, destroying the capital, Plymouth. Living and business conditions became very harsh with almost daily volcanic dust polluting the air. There followed an exodus of nearly two thirds of the population, and those who did not have homes in the north, had to resettle in the safe zone. The current population is around 4500.

In the summer of 2003 the huge volcanic dome collapsed, and the volcano showed every sign of going to sleep. This led to the reopening of many areas. The government removed the ash (some of it several feet thick) from many roads. People started repairing their damaged houses. You could go very close to Plymouth and up the hills behind it for dramatic views of the path of destruction and the ruined town. Then in the beginning of 2006 there was another spurt of dome growth, lots of activity and several major eruptions including one in December 2008. The exclusion zone has moved back up from Bransby Point to Old Road Bluff. The Vue Point Hotel, having been completely renovated and booked solid for the season, was evacuated. It is not easy living with a volcano.

The tone of the island is quiet and rural. There are hills with cows and goats, and few enough cars that you don't feel threatened as you walk along the roads. The mood is generally upbeat and very friendly. Most Montserratians living on the island today are delighted to be there and not in some tenement in London. The outlook is to the future: to bring in more tourists, to bring back Montserratians who fled: to create more jobs.

Just as the volcano in the south testifies to the power of nature, the northern end testifies to humans' ability to adapt and thrive in the face of adversity.

The ruined city of Plymouth   Chris Doyle

ISLANDS THAT BRUSH THE CLOUDS

Chris Doyle

Navigation

Radio Montserrat (88.3 or 95.5 FM), gives volcanic alerts about once a week. You can call the Montserrat Volcano Observatory at 664-491-5647, or see the volcano links on www.doyleguides.com. Both land and maritime exclusion zones remain in effect; we mark these on our sketch chart. The maritime exclusion zone extends 2 miles from shore around the southern half of the island. If dust starts falling, your yacht may be subject to falling ash, which is messy. If you sail around the south side of the island you can see an extra square kilometer of land that was formed by volcanic activity towards southern end of the east coast. It is marked on our chart. Considerable shoaling has taken place in the Old Road Bay area, where the beach has now grown to amazing proportions. Even without further volcanic activity, shoaling will continue for some years as effluent washes down. There has been considerable shoaling in the Plymouth area, where a significant part of the deepwa-

ter pier seems to have walked up the beach, though since a 2-mile maritime exclusion zone operates here, this shoaling is not likely to affect those sailing by.

Montserrat is steep to. A quarter of a mile offshore clears all shoals. A northwesterly current hits the windward shore, divides in the middle, and sweeps round both the north and south coasts at 1 to 2 knots. There is usually less than half a knot on the lee coast. Montserrat has no well-protected harbors and it is no place to be in a hurricane. It is also best avoided in bad northerly swells when the anchorages can be horrible and getting ashore is impossible.

The port of clearance and main anchorage are Little Bay. Little Bay is far from the volcano and considered safe. In regular strong northeasterly trades, Little Bay is often pretty uncomfortable as the easterly swell comes round the corner. You can radio the Montserrat Port Authority on VHF: 16 (or phone 664-491-2791) as you approach and ask for a report on the harbor conditions.

Little Bay and Cars Bay

Little Bay is the main port in Montserrat. It is set in beautiful country, which you can explore, given suitable anchoring conditions. There is now a grand scheme to build a town in Little Bay, expand the port, and build a marina and fishing port. Work had started on the town in early 2009, and the projected date for the port is 2011. The marina is likely to be much later.

Navigation

Little Bay and Cars Bay provide excellent anchorage when the wind is southeast or easterly at 10-20 knots, conditions that normally prevail from March to October. However, it is poor to terrible when the wind is from the northeast, or from the east and very strong (25 knots), or during northerly swells, conditions you find most often from December to February. Cars Bay and Little Bay both lie south of Rendezvous Bluff and are divided by Potato Hill. The best anchorage is in Little Bay. You can go to the north of the fishing boat moorings, or right up close to the beach. It is sometimes calmer further out in 40 feet of water close to the fishing boats. Leave clear access for the ships as shown, and make sure you have a good anchor light. There are the remains of a reef up to 30 feet deep in the area shown on our sketch chart. Avoid anchoring in this area, your anchor might get caught in a ledge.

Regulations

Little Bay is the port of entry. Montserrat Port Authority monitors VHF: 16. There is a port authority fee of $35EC (most yachts) up to $210 for some of the really big shiny ones (over about 200 tons). Passengers (not crew) pay a fee of $13.50 EC per head. Customs hours are Monday through Friday, 0800-1600. You will find customs officers out of hours and on weekends, but be prepared to pay overtime, which ranges from $70-100EC. Customs will give you an in and out clearance valid for 72 hours, so you can stay and enjoy. After you have cleared customs, you have to visit port authority and immigration. All the offices are right by the port entrance.

Communications

You might get lucky and connect with a wifi from your yacht. Otherwise you will have to carry your computer to one of the places that have wifi, which include the library and Tropical Mansions.

Ashore

You can leave your dinghy at the extreme inside (beach side) of the dock. You may find it easier to pull it up on the landing ramp. Little Bay is within hiking

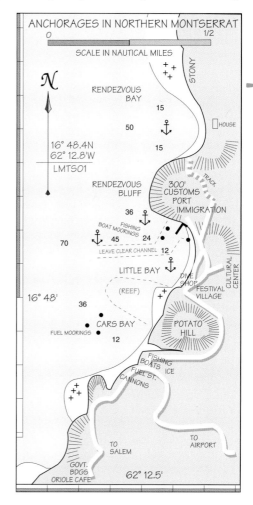

ANCHORAGES IN NORTHERN MONTSERRAT

SCALE IN NAUTICAL MILES

16° 48.4N
62° 12.8'W
LMTS01

RENDEZVOUS BAY

STONY

HOUSE

RENDEZVOUS BLUFF

300' CUSTOMS PORT IMMIGRATION

TRACK

FISHING BOAT MOORINGS

LEAVE CLEAR CHANNEL

LITTLE BAY

DIVE SHOP

FESTIVAL VILLAGE

CULTURAL CENTER

(REEF)

16° 48'

CARS BAY

POTATO HILL

FUEL MOORINGS

FISHING BOATS

FUEL ST.

ICE

CANNONS

TO SALEM

TO AIRPORT

GOVT. BDGS ORIOLE CAFE

62° 12.5'

ISLANDS THAT BRUSH THE CLOUDS

LITTLE BAY

Little Bay

Chris Doyle

distance of some restaurants and shops.

The closest supermarket is Victors, on the road to St. John's from Carrs Bay. The largest Supermarket is Ram's in Salem, and you will definitely need a taxi for this one. Ram's has a good selection of fresh produce as well as dry goods, cans, and frozen foods. There is also Ashok's and Angelo's near Tina's Restaurant, and Norman's farther down the road. The local market is near the cultural center and usually active on Friday and Saturday mornings. The Royal Bank of Canada has an ATM.

A taxi tour of the island should be a priority. When allowed. the view from St. George's Hill is spectacular. You look right down on the massive flow of volcanic efflu-ent, which sweeps from the Soufriere Hills Volcano and covers the central part of Plymouth, leaving just spires and roofs peeking through the ash. You can some-times visit Richmond Hill, right on the edge of town itself. A tennis court here looks fairly normal, until you notice that only the very top of the net is above ground. The volcanic ash is rich and fer-tile, and, except in riverbeds where it gets washed, you do not realize how much ash is

there, as it is quickly covered in vegeta-tion. In the rivers, where the soil gets washed away, the remaining sand and grav-el are now being sifted and exported. The observatory makes a good destination. It has a great overview of the area affected by the volcano and they have a vivid 20 minute movie, which they show at 15 min-utes past the hour on Mondays to Thursdays, starting at 1015 and finishing at 1515. ($10 EC per head)

Joe Phillip is a fearless, entertaining and knowledgeable taxi driver who seems to know everyone on the island and interacts with them all; he will give you a wonderful tour. He is a ham radio operator and has a scanner in his van, so you can call him on VHF: 16, call sign "Avalon". His ham call sign is VP2MBP, but he has no set listening hours. You can also call him on his cell: 664-492-1565. If you cannot get him, Sam (Sam Sword Taxi), is keen, keeps a radio watch and often waits near the port.

The Central Hills, apart from protecting northern Montserrat from the volcano, are a deeply wooded area with lots of wildlife, including the Montserrat golliwasp *Diploglossus montiserrati* a critically endangered lizard found only on Mostserrat. People have sighted over a hundred species of birds, as well as bats, agoutis, feral pig and more. You can arrange hikes with one of the two excellent guides. James Scriber-Daley, one of the foresters (496-1325), or Mappie, who works through the National Trust (491-3086). Both these guys are very enthusiastic and willing to hike at night with headlamps. If you prefer to go on your own, buy a trail map from National Trust or the tourist office

Restaurants

Oriole Cafe is within walking distance from Little Bay for the moderately energetic. It is at the entrance to the government offices andthey open from Monday to Saturday for lunch and dinner. You get first-rate local food at reasonable prices –dinners are a little more elaborate and expensive, especially if you choose lobster. Tina's is high on the hill on the road leading from Little Bay to Salem. You need a little more energy to hike to this one, which serves good-sized portions of local food at very reasonable prices and is open for both lunch and dinner. If you can't make it that far, you might reach the fancy new Tropical Mansions Hotel. They have a pleasant downstairs bar and restaurant. It is more expensive that than the others.

Ziggy's has been in operation from way before the volcano offering gourmet food, though they have moved from the3ir original location in town to the west coast. Their restaurant is a marquee in a delightful garden. See also Vue Point Hotel under Old Road Bay.

Royal Palm Club has pleasant and quite fancy surroundings. But one of the dinner party has to become a member ($100EC). Good, and inexpensive local restaurants include JJ's (You go up the road to the airport, but bear right at the Y junction. It is just beyond the conspicuous radio tower). La Collage (just where the final road to the airport turns off) and People's Place (on the road quite a long

Chris Doyle

ISLANDS THAT BRUSH THE CLOUDS

245

way past Oriole).

Near the dock, people tend to cook street-side in the area of the Festival Village on weekend evenings.

The action bar is Yvett's Lyme. It opens daily from about 1100, and serves a local lunch. In the evening it is a bar that also serves food such as burgers, chicken and fries. They have a big TV for sports and usually entertainment on the weekend. It could be anything – a show, live music, bingo, crab racing or karaoke. Check it out.For shoppers, the renowned silky sea-island cotton is still available on the island at Luv's Cotton store in Salem.

Water Sports

Montserrat has many good dives. One of these is called the Dome. It is an old volcanic dome covered in corals and sponges, with lots of big and small fish. Another dive is Lime Kiln Beach. This dive can be done from a boat or from the shore. It is an easy dive that goes down to about 50 feet, following various ledges with plenty of fish and coral.

You will find Troy and Melody's Green Monkey Dive Shop dive shop down in the waterfront area near the port.It also has its own bar. They will be happy to take you diving, but in addition to that they use their diesel custom boat to do touring trips over to Rendezvous Bay or to Plymouth

(depending on the state of the volcano). They keep a few essential boat parts and could help you get a little diesel fuel.

Rendezvous Bay

The half-hour walk along the track from Little Bay to Rendezvous Bay over the 300-foot Rendezvous Bluff is very pleasant. It starts in a quarry, on the left side. The path leads up a hill, along a fence, and then swings to the right. It is a bit of a scramble in places.

In calm settled conditions you can anchor in Rendezvous Bay to the north of Rendezvous Bluff. A reef extends a fair way out from the northern stony part of the beach, so eyeball your way in and anchor off the sand. Rendezvous Bay is Montserrat's only white sand beach. It is approachable only by path or boat. There is ahouse behind the beach. You will need to clear in at Little Bay and get permission to visit Rendezvous Bay before you go. Snorkelers can also dinghy round in suitable conditions

Old Road Bay

Navigation

When open, Old Road Bay is the most protected anchorage in Montserrat. It lies about 3 miles south of Little Bay. Before the volcano erupted, this was an area of

RENDEZVOUS BLUFF

RENDEZVOUS BAY

OLD ROAD BAY
SHOWING THE PROGRESSIVE
EXPANSION OF THE LAND

DOCK

SHORELINE 2001

SHORELINE PRE-VOLCANO

pretty houses and hotels, with a golf course in the valley. Since the volcano, rains have washed down enough volcanic sand and rocks to completely cover the golf course and encroach upon the sea, expanding the beach by a quarter to half of a mile most of the way along. Our sketch charts and photo show some of the changes in the coastline. When the anchorage is open, anchoring is easy, but approach cautiously as we have not acquired new information since 2001, when our depths were last measured. Considerable shoaling has taken place in the last few years, and will probably continue for years to come.

When the volcano is active, this area is very much in the danger zone. When the current situation quiets down, you may be able to anchor here again, but you need to clear into Little Bay and get a coastwise clearance before coming here. The danger zone often drops down to Bransby Point. With the disappearance of the

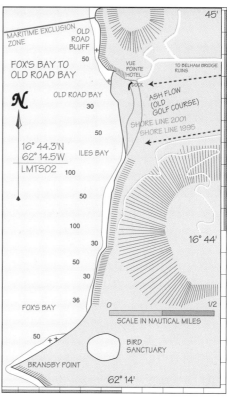

MARITIME EXCLUSION
ZONE

OLD
ROAD
BLUFF

45'

FOX'S BAY TO
OLD ROAD BAY

VUE POINTE
HOTEL

TO BELHAM BRIDGE
RUINS

𝒩

OLD ROAD BAY

DOCK

ASH FLOW
(OLD
GOLF COURSE)

30

16° 44.3'N
62° 14.5'W
LMTS02

50

SHORE LINE 2001
SHORE LINE 1995

ILES BAY

100

50

100

16° 44'

30

50

30

FOX'S BAY

36

0

1/2

SCALE IN NAUTICAL MILES

50

BIRD
SANCTUARY

BRANSBY POINT

62° 14'

harbor, getting ashore can be difficult in swells, as you have to make a beach landing.

Ashore

In 2005 was wonderful to see the Vue Point Hotel, the best in Montserrat, fully open again and looking great, with the gardens once again carefully tended. To achieve this the owners, Carol and Cecil Osborne had over 2,500 truck loads of volcanic ash removed. This included excavating the swimming pool, which had become a sandpit. I had hoped this was the final victory at the end of a long battle they waged to keep this hotel open in some form, whenever they were allowed in the area. But in 2007 it was back in the exclusion zone and has stayed there. Although fully booked, they had to close. The Vue Point Hotel has a great restaurant set around the pool and open to the view. If it manages to open again you will be sure of a good meal and friendly service. You can reach it by dinghy from Old Road Bay, or cab over from Little Bay.

Plymouth

Plymouth was destroyed by the volcano and a 2-mile exclusion zone is in effect around the town.

Passages Between Nevis, Montserrat, Antigua and Guadeloupe

Montserrat lies to the west of both Antigua and Guadeloupe, making for easy downwind passages to Montserrat and tougher sails in the other direction. Montserrat and Antigua are only 20 miles apart at their closest point, so with a weatherly boat one can easily slog over there in a day. You can sometimes make it into the lee of Antigua in one tack but when the wind is north of east, it is a tough beat.

A northeasterly wind gives a pleasant sail from Montserrat to Guadeloupe. It is

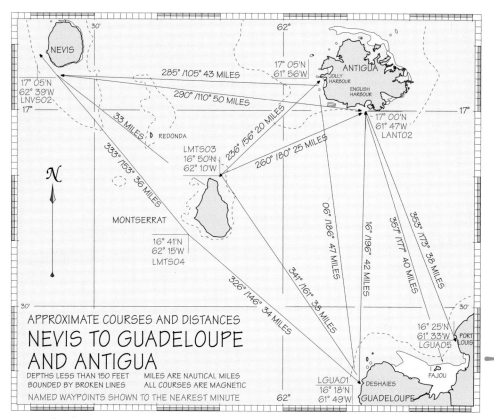

APPROXIMATE COURSES AND DISTANCES

NEVIS TO GUADELOUPE AND ANTIGUA

DEPTHS LESS THAN 150 FEET   MILES ARE NAUTICAL MILES
BOUNDED BY BROKEN LINES   ALL COURSES ARE MAGNETIC
NAMED WAYPOINTS SHOWN TO THE NEAREST MINUTE

more of a struggle when the wind shifts south of east, but it is not too hard to get into the lee of Guadeloupe and motor sail to the anchorage of your choice. From Nevis directly to Antigua is about 50 miles with the wind on the nose. (It is about 44 miles if you leave from Oualie Beach and get through the reefs to the windward side.) Although it is about 70 miles from Nevis to Guadeloupe, I have often found it more pleasant to sail to Guadeloupe, stop the night and then sail to Antigua the next day in strong northeasterlies.

As long as the volcano remains active, it makes sense to pass around the north side of Montserrat, so you don't get your boat covered in ash. When sailing from Guadeloupe around the north end of Montserrat, make sure you stay a good 2 miles off the southeast coast.

the anchorages of the islands of

MOUNTAINS &
MANGROVES

barbuda • antigua • guadeloupe • îles des saintes (the saintes)
marie galante • dominica

Chris Doyle

The Anchorages Of
The Islands of Mountains & Mangroves

T IS OVER 150 MILES FROM the south of Dominica to the north of Barbuda. This is the largest of the three areas we cover in this book and it has by far the greatest variety of scenery, as well as the largest number of anchorages.

Dominica and Basse Terre, the western half of Guadeloupe, like islands in the Mountains that Brush the Clouds, are relatively young volcanic islands. But in stature and size they are much more impressive, with mountains that climb to over 4,000 feet.

Both these islands offer spectacular hiking, with rain forests, rivers, waterfalls, crater lakes, and somewhat active volcanoes. I recommend spending considerable time hiking in both, but, for sheer natural beauty amid mountain scenery far from roads, you cannot beat the hikes you will find in Dominica.

Grande Terre, the eastern part of Guadeloupe, Antigua, and Barbuda are by contrast much older islands that have been largely eroded away. Like St. Martin and St. Barts, these have the spectacular beaches we have come to expect of the Caribbean, along with some very secluded and lovely anchorages.

Both Dominica and the country of Antigua and Barbuda are independent nations that used to be British colonies. Guadeloupe, on the other hand, is French and part of Europe. While Antigua is firmly in the British tradition, Dominica has lots of reminders of years under French rule. Many place names are French and Dominicans speak both English and a patois that is a sort of Africanized, Anglicized French. Both Antigua and Guadeloupe are major Caribbean yachting centers. As one may expect, English and American boats tend to gravitate towards Antigua, while the French often base their yachts in Guadeloupe. Both these islands are major charter centers and offer great cruising.

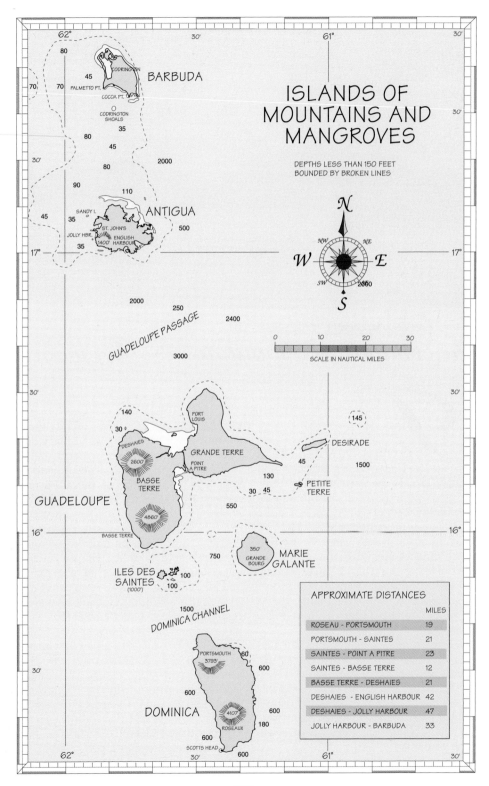

ISLANDS OF
MOUNTAINS AND
MANGROVES

DEPTHS LESS THAN 150 FEET
BOUNDED BY BROKEN LINES

BARBUDA

CODRINGTON

PALMETTO PT.

COCOA PT.

CODRINGTON
SHOALS

ANTIGUA

SANDY I.

JOLLY HBR.

ST. JOHN'S

ENGLISH
HARBOUR

GUADELOUPE PASSAGE

SCALE IN NAUTICAL MILES

GUADELOUPE

DESHAIES

BASSE
TERRE

BASSE TERRE

GRANDE TERRE

PORT
LOUIS

POINT
A PITRE

DESIRADE

PETITE
TERRE

ILES DES
SAINTES

MARIE
GALANTE

GRANDE
BOURG

DOMINICA CHANNEL

PORTSMOUTH

DOMINICA

ROSEAUX

SCOTTS HEAD

APPROXIMATE DISTANCES	
	MILES
ROSEAU - PORTSMOUTH	19
PORTSMOUTH - SAINTES	21
SAINTES - POINT A PITRE	23
SAINTES - BASSE TERRE	12
BASSE TERRE - DESHAIES	21
DESHAIES - ENGLISH HARBOUR	42
DESHAIES - JOLLY HARBOUR	47
JOLLY HARBOUR - BARBUDA	33

Frigate bird colony, Barbuda

Chris Doyle

Antigua and Barbuda

NTIGUA AND BARBUDA offers exceptional cruising. It has so many anchorages that you could cruise here for two weeks without stopping at the same place twice, and you would enjoy great variety. English Harbour, a beautifully restored naval dockyard from Nelson's time, has been adapted to modern yachting and commerce, and is the only Caribbean example of a Georgian naval base. Elsewhere, you will find a wealth of hidden anchorages where you can be on your own. This is unusual today, and they stay this way because they are difficult to navigate, and only those highly proficient in reading the water colors are going to feel comfortable on the eastern and northern sides of Antigua or sailing over to Barbuda. Polaroid sunglasses, always helpful in the Caribbean, are a necessity here. Barbuda is a special jewel, a wild country where horses, deer, and donkeys run free, where the beaches are longer and more beautiful than anywhere else in the Caribbean, and where you can visit a huge frigatebird colony.

Antigua has good medical facilities. If you are on the west side of the island, Dr. Nick Fuller (268-462-0931), with an office in Long Street, St. John's, has been treating yachtspeople for years and he is proficient and helpful. Out of hours you can call him on VHF: 16 or 68, call sign "Ocean View." On the English Harbour side, the Tree House in Falmouth has a visiting doctor on some days of the week.

If you need hospitalization, ask your doctor to get you into Adelin Clinic. Antigua has excellent lab facilities. Bell Labs and Belmont Clinic have the latest in medical testing between them, including MRI.

If you have a dental problem, visit Dr. Sengupta and Associates in the Woods Mall, 268-462-9312, Beeper: 409-3368.

Antigua and Barbuda have a marine rescue organization, ABSAR, with a large rib stationed at the Yacht Club Marina. You can contact them on VHF: 16 or phone: 562-1234.

Antigua and Barbuda is also a popular country for registering yachts through their department of Marine Services. The system is set up to be reasonably easy, though unless you are an Antiguan you will need to form a locally registered company to own the yacht.

MOUNTAINS & MANGROVES

Barbuda

Regulations

You can clear customs in Codrington. You can usually anchor anywhere and take a taxi to do the formalities; you have to visit port authority, customs and immigration, in three different locations. You cannot clear cargo here.

Spearfishing is forbidden in Antigua and Barbuda, except for residents with a license. Fishing is not permitted, except on a Barbudan boat.

For customs fees, see Antigua.

Telephones

You can buy phone cards and find card phones in Codrington.

Transport

Barbuda has a public airstrip and is linked to Antigua by several daily flights. There is also a private airstrip at Coco Point Lodge.

Barbuda Express is a ferry that runs between Antigua and Barbuda, (560-7978/464-2291).

Taxis are available; the rates in US are as follows:

One way:
Cocoa Point to Codrington	$35
White Bay to Codrington	$55
Codrington to Palmetto	$30

Round trip:
Codrington to Two Foot Bay	$80

Medical

There is a small hospital and one or two visiting doctors who will be able to take care of most emergencies. Contact any taxi and make arrangements.

Holidays

see Antigua

Barbuda, Admiralty Leisure Folio 5641-4, 5641-12

Barbuda

OR THE DEDICATED into-the-heart-of-nature diehard, Barbuda is heaven on earth. It is a low island whose highest point is only 125 feet above the sea. It is large, over half the size of Antigua, with a mere 2,000 inhabitants who live around the village of Codrington. Barbuda has so many miles of brilliant turquoise shoal water that, as you sail toward it, you can sometimes see a blue-green reflection in the clouds long before you see the land itself.

The area is dotted with coral, teeming with every kind of fish, and is excellent for snorkeling. You have a good chance of spotting decorative eagle rays, often swimming in pairs, or gently moving stingrays. There are endless pale pink beaches with nary a soul on them. The longest is over 16 miles long, broken only by the small boat harbor.

Ashore, donkeys, horses, and deer roam wild and there is a thriving and still growing frigatebird rookery, the largest in the Eastern Caribbean, and easily comparable to any in the Galapagos. Frigatebirds are masters of the air. At two to three pounds, they have the greatest wing area in proportion to their weight of any bird. This comes at the cost of being ungainly on their legs and they are unable to take off if they become submerged. For this reason, they avoid landing in the sea, and should they do so by accident, they have to struggle out immediately. They scoop their food from the surface of the sea, and have become masters at letting other birds do the fishing, then harassing them till they drop their catch; thus their common names: "frigate" or "man o' war" bird. During the mating season, the males display by blowing up huge, bright red pouches under their throats. They start mating during the late summer, lay one egg per couple, and most of the chicks have taken off by about the end of May. George Jeffrey, our guide, told

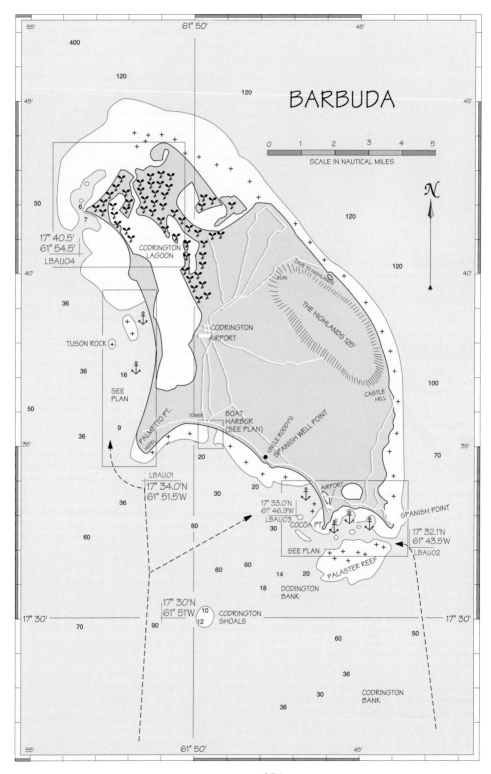

BARBUDA

0   1   2   3   4   5
SCALE IN NAUTICAL MILES

N

17° 40.5'
61° 54.5'
LBAU04

CODRINGTON
LAGOON

THE HIGHLANDS 125'

CAVE TO HIGHLANDS

RUIN

120

120

120

120

400

120

36

36

36

36

36

50

50

6
7

TUSON ROCK

16

SEE
PLAN

9

CODRINGTON
AIRPORT

PALMETTO PT.

HOTEL

TOWER

BOAT
HARBOR
(SEE PLAN)

UNCLE RODDY'S
SPANISH WELL POINT

CASTLE
HILL

100

70

20

20

LBAU01
17° 34.0'N
61° 51.5'W

30

20

AIRPORT

17° 33.0'N
61° 46.9'W
LBAU03

COCOA PT.

30

SEE PLAN

SPANISH POINT

17° 32.1'N
61° 43.5'W
LBAU02

60

60

60

14

18

20

DODINGTON
BANK

PALASTER REEF

17° 30'N
61° 51'W

10
12

CODRINGTON
SHOALS

17° 30'

17° 30'

70

90

60

50

30

36

36

CODRINGTON
BANK

us he once saw a frigatebird fall in the sea and then watched two others come immediately, one on either side, to lift it back into the air. Frigatebirds return to their nesting sites and Polynesians used them as homing pigeons. The Barbuda colony was featured in National Geographic magazine, and a visit to this colony is an outstanding experience, unique in the Eastern Caribbean. The colony is an unearthly spectacle. The frigates' strange cries and the noise of their clicking beaks come from all directions and the air above is alive with dark, wheeling birds. As far as the eye can see, clumpy mangrove bushes are full of little heads sticking out, looking like intelligent fruits from another planet. The guide's boat takes you right up to the birds, so if you bring a camera, you will surely get good pictures. While here have a look at the intricate upside-down jellyfish that litter the floor of the lagoon in this area. Like coral reefs, these jellyfish have plants (zooanthellae) growing in them, they turn upside down to offer these plants maximum sunlight. Intricate lacy tentacles maximize their surface area.

The Barbudan people were originally imported as slaves by the Codrington family who leased the island from England, beginning in 1685, for one fat sheep. Unlike most Caribbean islands, Barbuda was never a sugar plantation. Codrington used it for growing livestock and root crops for his estates in Antigua, and as a hunting ground for the Codrington family. Consequently, the Barbudans were not closely supervised and retained a tough independent spirit. They came to terms with the island environment, existing through cooperative efforts in fishing, subsistence farming, and hunting. When emancipation came, they stayed on the island, living in a cooperative way. Land is held communally and there is so much that no one fights over it. It has also been the key to the Barbudans keeping control over their own island. Since there is no individual land ownership, land cannot be sold to outsiders. England railroaded a reluctant Barbuda into joining Antigua when the two islands became independent. Since then there have been several ambitious projects to develop the island and "bring it into the 21st Century," an idea strongly resisted by many Barbudans, who see no benefit to changing their traditional lifestyle for one of being dressed up and employed to wait on tourists in exchange for the dubious benefits of better roads, more cars, and Kentucky Fried Chicken. Barbudans often have to fight other schemes that are dreamed up without their approval. One battle involved a plan to put in a big desalinization plant. Work started, but the Barbudans, fearing possible damage to their pristine, fish-filled lagoon, called a halt. Another time, the Antigua government allowed a huge hotel project to begin on Spanish Point. Mobile construction offices were erected. The Barbudan people wanted to keep this land as a park. They went en-masse to the project and shoved the offices over the cliff. It will remain a park. Many people would love to get their hands on Barbuda's beachfront real estate, but the Barbudans are resisting strongly. It is difficult to know how long they can resist McDonaldization. I've noticed a slew of fancy new cars over the last four years. The island has existed in part by selling sand, but that cannot go on forever, so the pressure for some income-earning development will become great. The community land ownership rule puts the local council in a unique position to direct and control such development for the good and profit of the community. To date they have proceeded cautiously; I wish them luck.

To get a feel for the island, take a bike or cab to Two Foot Bay. This bay is at the edge of the highlands. The road ends at an area of sculpted cliffs, huge boulders, and deep caves on one side and on the other is a fabulous white sand beach. A small, path leads back just where you see some bougainvillea. Follow this and you enter a large cave, climb up through it, and emerge 100 feet above on the flat top of the highlands, with magnificent views in all directions.

Another attraction is the Darby Sink Hole, a 45-minute walk from the ruins of

MOUNTAINS & MANGROVES

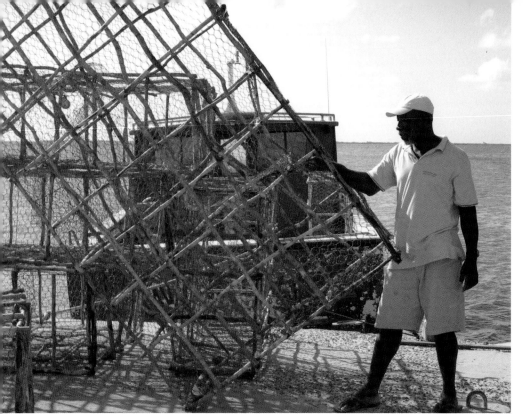

George Jeffrey loading traps.

the Codrington Estate house in the Highlands. The walk is surprisingly shady. Many of the plants in this dry area are 8 to 15 feet tall, enough to give a fair bit of shade. Darby Sink Hole is round and crater-like, about 100 yards in diameter, and about 100 feet deep. For the most part the sides are sheer cliff, but there is one place you can scramble down. It is completely covered in dense tropical vegetation, unlike the dry scrub above. Tall, wavy basket palms reach to the top. Inside it is cool, shady, and pleasant. The overhanging walls include the dramatic shapes of stalagmites and stalactites. While in Barbuda you will see many horses and donkeys, which are allowed to run free, are completely at home in the landscape, and look magnificent. Some of the donkeys are wild, but all the horses are owned.

One charming aspect of Codrington is that it has grown rather than having been planned. Roads meander, twisting this way and that. More and more of them are now

getting paved. It has a wonderfully rural feeling after dark. As you walk along at night large figures loom beside you – horses and donkeys that come in to graze. Every house has a fence, built to keep the animals out of the yard. Horses are an important part of Barbudan life, with horse races near Codrington many Sundays. This is a very popular sport, and on many mornings young men bring their horses down to the lagoon for a swim and grooming.

Transport

Exploring Barbuda is an outstanding experience, but all of the anchorages are a fair way from Codrington and many roads are not paved. If you anchor off Louis Mouth (Low Bay), you can drag your dinghy over the spit and get to Codrington on your own. (You will have to pass a sand control fence, but there are ways through.) You can also leave your dinghy on Louis Mouth, walk over to the lagoon side and take a water taxi to Codrington. You can do the same from about half a mile south,

258

off Barbuda Outbar Restaurant. They even have a dock on the lagoon side.

The Barbuda Council has a set a water taxi price of $40 US return or $10 a head over four people, which is almost as much as the frigatebird trip; absurd considering it is only two-miles and there is no guiding time. Luckily, George Jeffrey (see below) will do this for $3 US per person one way– with a minimum of $12 US.

You can also take a land cab from any of the island's anchorages, including Spanish Point. (There are no water taxis from these other anchorages as it is too far from the lagoon.) From these anchorages, a tour to the frigatebird colony and Two Foot Bay takes about four hours, longer if you stop in Codrington for lunch, or to shop and wander around. Since you are not using the taxi at this point, you can hang out in town as long as you wish at no extra cost. You might want to include the horse races or a fish fry. You can also combine clearing customs with a taxi tour if you need to. The tour cost breaks down as follows: The Barbuda Council charges $2 US per person. The cost of a boat ride to the frigatebird colony is also set by the Barbuda council and is $50 US for four, and $12 US a head over that. I find these rates quite reasonable, considering it is a 4-mile ride each way in a high-speed boat. If you want to start and finish at Low Bay, use George Jeffries as he will just add $12 US onto the trip price. Some of the others will add the $40 US crossing.

The return taxi fare from Cocoa Point to Codrington is $70 US; or $110 for White Bay. The caves are at Two Foot Bay, and the return fare from Codrington is $80, which includes waiting while you explore. There may be extra charges for over four people. Some drivers may give you a break on these prices when you combine everything into a day tour. Try John Taxi, 779-4652/788-1569.

For many years I have enjoyed the services of George Jeffrey. He does frigatebird trips and land hikes and he is the most knowledgeable of guides, as he knows nearly every plant and animal, including the birds. He is also well versed in the medicinal uses of many plants. George can organize day and hiking tours from any of the Barbuda anchorages and he uses taxi drivers who are reasonably priced. He will also help with anything else you need or want. Call him on the VHF: 16 ("Garden of Eden") or, better still, phone 460-0143 or 788-7067 a couple of days before you arrive. George is also a lobster fisherman and has a lobster boat called the Jenna J. This is usually kept down in the south of the island, and you can also try calling his boat on the VHF. He can often supply lobsters or fish.

Many Barbudans get around on mountain bikes. If you have one, this is a good island on which to use it. If not, contact Jonathon Pereira, who has a great bike rental shop in Codrington called Barbuda bike tours (268-773-9599/784-5717). He rents mountain bikes, and super-comfortable cruising bikes with high handlebars and no gears. He also rents ocean kayaks. It is a great and easy ride from Codrington to Two Foot Bay. If you want to go to some of the more adventurous places like the interior caves or Darby Sink Hole, ask Jonathon about a guide.

A call to "any Barbuda Taxi" will bring a response from one of the other taxi drivers. If you lack time to sail to Barbuda, take the Barbuda Express run by Greg Ulrwin (560-7978). This high-speed ferry visits Barbuda and returns to Antigua the same day; it takes about one and half hours one way. They sail out of St. John's every day except Sundays and Wednesdays.

Regulations

You can clear customs in or out in Codrington and get a cruising permit for Antigua and Barbuda. However, cargo has to go through Antigua. Customs, immigration, and port authority officials are in Codrington, so no one minds if you are anchored in one of the other anchorages. Taxis can be summoned on VHF: 16 or 68. Or you if you come to Louis Mouth, you can get a water taxi over. When checking in, visit the port authority (in the post

MOUNTAINS & MANGROVES

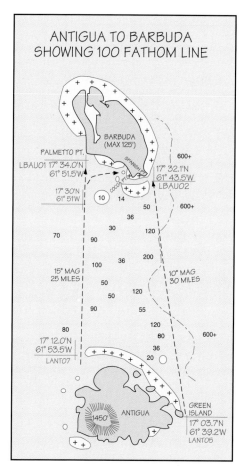

ANTIGUA TO BARBUDA
SHOWING 100 FATHOM LINE

Barbuda much easier. For a more detailed chart than those in this guide, you need the Caribbean Yachting Chart, which is excellent from the K-Club round the south coast, including the approaches to Cocoa Point. I think our sketch chart is the only chart that includes recent data for the northern part of the island. Most other charts are still very poor.

Nonetheless, you need to plan your arrival so the sun is behind or directly above and never ahead of you, and you need to keep a good lookout. The south coast is tougher to navigate than the west coast, as is the west coast north of Low Bay.

There are several ways to approach Barbuda. The easiest and safest is from the west, which is the obvious route if you are coming from the west side of Antigua. Plot a course to Palmetto Point that will take you clear of all the shoals. When you get close to Barbuda, Cocoa Point will appear as a small clump of pointed trees. On Palmetto Point you can see several buildings, including the Beach House Hotel. There is a water tower tucked among these. Also, to the east of Palmetto Point is the small boat harbor. Once you know where you are, sail over to Cocoa Point or head up to Palmetto Point and the anchorages to its north.

office) first, then customs, and finally immigration.

Spearfishing is illegal for nonresidents in Antigua and Barbuda. Fishing around the reefs may only be done on a Barbudan fishing boat.

Navigation

Barbuda lies 30 miles north of Antigua and some 200 shipwrecks attest to the hazards of its reef-infested waters. The island is often only visible 4 or 5 miles away, yet there are 7-foot shoals this far offshore. Barbuda's west side is open to northerly swells, and can be dangerous should these be bad. So it is wise to check on the general weather situation before you visit this coast.

Recent surveys of the reefs and the advent of GPS has made navigating

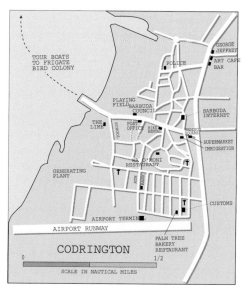

CODRINGTON

Many people sailing from Green Island, on Antigua's East Coast, like to take the shortest route and approach from the east. This involves passing between reefs in rough water, and you must set out early to arrive by noon. The course is approximately 10 degrees magnetic. If you have a GPS, use it; if not, take back sights and compensate for current. If you are equipped with a good log and echo sounder, you can keep close tabs on your position by noting when you lose and regain bottom readings as the 100-fathom line cuts your course twice (see our sketch chart).

You do not see Barbuda till the last 5 or 6 miles. Cocoa Point is distinctive, but Spanish Point barely stands out from the land behind it. To avoid the reefs, you need to approach Spanish Point from magnetic south or east of south. Do not let yourself get set to the west. Keep heading a little to the east of Spanish Point until the group of white buildings on Cocoa Point bears 300 degrees magnetic, and then head for the buildings. Reduce sail or switch to power in plenty of time to make your approach at a sensible speed, giving yourself room to spin around if you cannot see your way in. This allows you to eyeball your way between the two reefs. To starboard, the reef extending from Spanish Point usually breaks and you can see brilliant turquoise water behind. To port, the reef is in deeper water and harder to see. Stick in the deep water fairly close to the starboard-hand reef. The entrance is down wind and sea, but as soon as you pass

through, you find yourself on a vast, calm lake of turquoise, splattered with clumps of brown reef.

You can also sail from the east of Antigua over to the west of Barbuda, but make sure you plot a course to keep you clear of all the shoals. The huge Palaster Reef, a couple of miles south of Barbuda, should be given wide clearance on its south side, where patches of coral are hard to spot. It can be approached from the north side, either by dinghy or yacht. It is not a solid mass, and temporary anchorage can be found tucked among coral heads.

Keep well away from Barbuda at night. If you take the frigate bird tour, or take a boat over the lagoon to Codrington, you are likely to see a giant channel buoy anchored off the town. This was found floating off Barbuda and salvaged by some fishermen. It originated on the east coast of Canada, and to get to Barbuda would have likely taken a trip to Europe and then come back across the Atlantic - something to think about when you sail at night without a watch.

Codrington

Communications

You can check your email or surf the net at Barbuda Internet. They open most days from 1500 to 2100. In addition, they open in the mornings on Mondays, Fridays and Saturdays. But if you need help when it closed, call Polen (772-1809), and she will

Chris Doyle

LADY DAWN

MOUNTAINS & MANGROVES

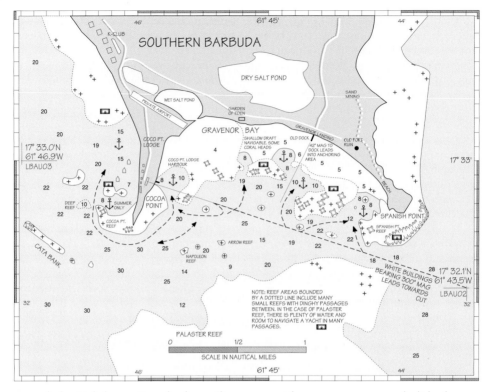

try to help. Lighthouse Bay also has wifi.

Provisioning, Shopping

Codrington is the main settlement. By day it is sleepy and hot, but as the sun drops below the horizon, people come into the streets. Some of the little shops are open till 2200. You will find many small stores, including a fair supermarket and many smaller shops and stalls where you can get most things, including ice and fresh produce. Few strangers spend time here, so you will find the locals very welcoming. From Friday to Sunday evenings several vendors cook up chicken, steaks, and more around Madison Square.

One store you should not miss is Claire and Mack Frank's Art Café. Claire, originally English, is both a photographer and an artist who does fine paintings on fabric, which are artistically framed. Her prices are reasonable, and if you prefer to wear art, she sells t-shirts. Claire or Mack can tell what is happening on the island, which restaurants are currently open, and also, if

you wish, rent you a car, or a holiday house.

Restaurants

There may be as many as four restaurants in Codrington, though it is doubtful all would be open at the same time. You can stop here for lunch as part of your tour or water-taxi across from Low Bay for dinner. All Codrington restaurants are local and reasonably priced. Jackie's Wa O'moni's Best (Wa O'moni is the original Kalinargo name for Barbuda) does good local meals featuring seafood – local fish and lobster as well as shrimp. She also has a snack menu. It opens Monday to Saturday 0700-2200, but call to make sure. They have a hair salon next door.

Cerene Deazle's Palm Tree Restaurant is reliable and open for lunch with good local meals at a reasonable price. She also does dinner on request. She was renovating in 2009, but should soon be open again. Carene also has a guest house.

Burton's Bar does chicken and simple fare from Tuesday to Saturday, and The

DEEP REEF

CATA BANK

COCOA POINT SHOWING
COCOA POINT REEF, CATA BANK
AND OTHER SHOALS

Lime, by the docks, is generally open on weekends, mainly for music.

It's a Bit Fishy, is a new restaurant owned by a local fisherman and his wife. They cook fresh local fish and lobster and have an excellent reputation, but it is essential to call in advance and find out if they will be open. They are a long walk from dinghy dock, just past the hospital on the opposite side of the road; best to get a taxi.

Weekends are a good time to visit. There is often some sort of fish fry in the late afternoon that goes on into the evening. You can ask anyone. Local horse racing is really fun to watch, and it takes place about every other Sunday. The racecourse is just south of the airport on the same side. Turn by the ruined government guesthouse. Races usually begin at about 1600.

When sailing to Barbuda, keep in mind that Codrington is far from many anchor-

ages, so plan your provisioning accordingly. Lobster and fish are often available if you talk to your taxi driver in advance.

Cocoa Point

Navigation

This anchorage faces miles of pristine creamy-pink beach and is a favorite among visiting yachts. If you are approaching from the south coast, head over to Cocoa Point and follow the reef closely. Once you are clear of the reef, head in toward the beach between the two hotels. There is a line of buoys in front of the Coco Point Lodge, from the reef right up to the yacht anchorage. The Coco Point management lays these to try to reserve the area for their water sports. They do not like yachts anchoring inside these buoys when the hotel is open (November to April), but at other times they do not mind. Be careful of

MOUNTAINS & MANGROVES

SPANISH POINT ANCHORAGE AND
APPROACH FROM THE EAST

the extensive reefs that start off at the K-Club, at the north end of this anchorage, and continue all the way to beyond the boat harbor.

If you are approaching from the west, note the reef marked on our sketch chart about half a mile offshore. Many boats have had a problem with this one. If you are coming from the southwest, you also have to avoid Cata Bank, which is not easily visible in some lights.

Ashore

There are two hotels, the Coco Point Lodge at the south end of the beach, and the K-Club, about a mile to the north. The Coco Point Lodge is clubby and has an excellent chef, but it is not open to even well-heeled yachtsmen.

The K-Club used to be happy to charge high prices to visitors for somewhat indifferent food. It has now collapsed and been abandoned.

Luckily there is a new local establishment, Uncle Roddy's Beach Bar, at Spanish Well's Point in a part called Coral Groove Bay. You probably will not see it from the sea as it is set back on the other side of the old sea road. This is a small, local, and fun little place. Uncle Roddy cooks up rice and local vegetables and uses them to accompany lobster, fish, or chicken. He opens every day from 1100 to sundown, and he will likely stay open for dinner if you give him a call. Better still, call him and he will come down to Cocoa Point and pick you up in his truck for lunch or dinner (785-3268, 460-0021). It is a bit far to walk. The dinghy is a possibility during the day; you have to find your way through the reefs. Uncle Roddy's son-in-law is building a guest cottage next door.

The Beach House at Palmetto Point used to be a fancy destination for super -yachts with high-speed tenders. However, it was closed in 2009. New owners may open soon. Those with helicopters can fly down to Lighthouse Bay Resort (see

Palmetto Point to Low Bay).

SOUTH COAST OF BARBUDA

The south coast between Spanish Point and Cocoa Point, called Gravenor Bay, has several good anchorages. These are the best anchorages in the winter months, when there is a chance of northerly swells. However, only experienced reef navigators should consider it. Unless you proceed with your heart in your mouth, you may be getting overconfident. It should be approached with the utmost caution. You need to plan your arrival so the sun is behind or directly above, and never ahead of you. A sharp-eyed lookout wearing polarizing sunglasses should be stationed in the bow. Even then it is not easy, for when the sun goes behind a cloud the whole seabed becomes black and unreadable. If you cannot clearly see underwater where you are going, wait or turn and go back. This is no place to press ahead regardless. The Nautical Publications (CYC) chart is the only good chart for this area. Our sketch chart is also pretty good and outlines the major reefs and reef areas along with the main passages. It was made using George Jeffrey's local knowledge and a GPS on WG84 datum.

Navigate from the Cocoa Point anchorage around the south coast as follows: Head towards Cocoa Point Reef. Deep Reef is just off Cocoa Point Reef. It looks shallow, but is about 12 feet deep. You can pass between the two in about 20 feet of water. Follow Cocoa Point Reef round to the east. To go into the Coco Point Lodge Harbour, follow the reef right on around. Otherwise, when you are on a line between Cocoa Point and Spanish Point, head for Spanish Point. Dodge south around the reefs to the west of Spanish Point when you get to them. The other anchoring area off the old dock is easy enough to find. Eyeball your way in past the reefs. If you can see the few remains of the old dock, then an approach of 42° magnetic should help you in.

White Bay

This quiet anchorage under the lee of Spanish Point is tucked among the reefs in brilliant turquoise water. Ashore there is a small beach. You can just see the ruin of an old fort to the north. The nearest habitation is Coco Point Lodge.

The approach is inside the reef that extends southwest from Spanish Point. Inshore, there are numerous patches of brown reef. Anchor outside these in 10 feet of water, about 150 yards off the beach. This anchorage is especially easy if you enter by the eastern route. You come through the channel and then follow the reef around into the anchorage.

Chris Doyle

MOUNTAINS & MANGROVES

Ashore

There are marvelous walks here, especially up the windward coast that has an endless spectacular beach. You will normally see quite a few horses and donkeys. Trade winds and salt air have shaped the vegetation in this area. Most plants are low lying; those that do reach up tend to get swept into curious shapes. If you take a close look, you will find many delightful small flowers. Prickles are common, so take good shoes. A road of sorts leads up to a former sand mining operation. The mining created an interesting crater that broke through the water table, so there is small pool of fresh water, much used by the animals. A rough road leads to Cocoa Point. For walking a ways up the east coast, it is best to start your hike in the area of the old fort.

Wherever you anchor, you will be within easy swimming distance of at least one reef. Snorkeling on the small isolated reefs is excellent for beginners; the reef off Spanish Point will satisfy the enthusiast. Remember, spearfishing is forbidden, and as a result you see lots of fish.

Old Dock Anchorage

To the west of the ruined tower are a few crumbling remains of the Gravenor Bay Dock, the island's original landing site. There are two anchoring areas. The outside one is in a large basin with a clear sand bottom in about 10 feet of water, with reefs all around you. Or pass inside to the inner passage for the second spot. Here there is a basin, 8-9 feet deep, just inside reefs. Depths gradually shoal as you go farther in.

The approach is easy from Spanish Point. Just follow the reefs around into the bay. A bearing of 42° magnetic onto the old dock can help.

Ashore

Snorkeling is good and there are two little beaches by the dock. You are also within dinghy and walking range of both Cocoa Point and Spanish Point. This dock is a good starting point for an east coast walk, and makes a good rendezvous point to meet

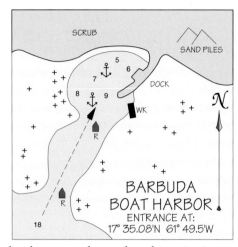

BARBUDA
BOAT HARBOR
ENTRANCE AT:
17° 35.08'N 61° 49.5'W

local taxis, as the road to this point is not too bad. From here on out to White Bay, it is terrible.

If you have a bike on board, a road of sorts runs about 4 miles north along the salt pond and continues to Castle Bay under the highlands on the east coast. This is an area of interesting cliffs and remote beaches.

Anchorage East of Cocoa Point

There is a small basin of water, 11 feet deep, just opposite the dock on the back side of Coco Point Lodge. The entrance is a narrow cut between two reefs. It is best to identify the reef adjoining Cocoa Point and follow it down to the opening. Once inside, you have reef protection from all around. It is an easy walk to the main beach on the west side. At the same time, you are close to the reefs for snorkeling. The dock and land ashore are all part of the Coco Point Lodge and they would prefer not to see you around during the winter months.

WEST COAST NORTH OF COCOA POINT

Navigation

Navigating the west coast of Barbuda is not hard. There is extensive broken reef along the shore from K-Club up to the Boat Harbour. This extends in places over

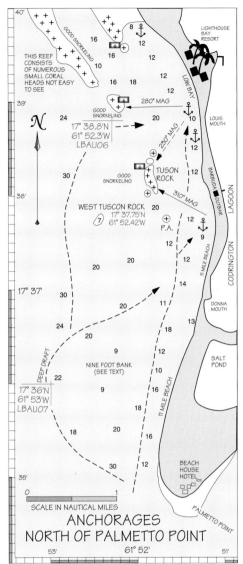

ANCHORAGES
NORTH OF PALMETTO POINT

half a mile offshore and should be given good clearance.

Boat Harbour

This small harbor lies about two miles east of Palmetto Point. It is used to import supplies to Barbuda and to export sand. There are also a couple of buildings and an old tower to its west. A red buoy marks the entrance to the harbor. You should see it if you approach the dock at 40° magnetic. Leave the buoy to starboard and head for the dock. A small basin starts just outside

the dock, opposite an old wreck. Depths here are 8 to 9 feet and they shelve gradually to about 6 feet opposite the loading bay.

This small harbor is the least attractive anchorage in Barbuda. It is susceptible to northerly swells and you will roll when the wind is south of east. The only reason to come here is to go to Codrington, which is nearly 3 hot miles away. It is easier to visit Codrington from Low Bay.

There are plans to modernize and improve this harbor.

Palmetto Point to Low Bay

From Palmetto Point northwards the coast is a wild, 11-mile beach. From afar, it appears white, but if you walk ashore, you will discern a pinky hue. Right along the water's edge, where waves reach in to brush the sand, there is a rich coral-red line. Since it is seldom visited and not commercial, no glossy brochures proclaim it to be the "most beautiful beach in the Caribbean," but it probably is.

For much of the way, the land is no more than a thin strip separating the sea from Codrington Lagoon. Codrington Village lies across the lagoon and those with a light dinghy could manhandle it over the land and get to the village by water. The easiest and closest place to do this is Louis Mouth, a bare stretch of sand about 300 yards south of the hotel at Low Bay. Louis Mouth is so called became it became a channel into the lagoon for some months after Hurricane Louis. Further

Lighthouse Bay   Chris Doyle

MOUNTAINS & MANGROVES

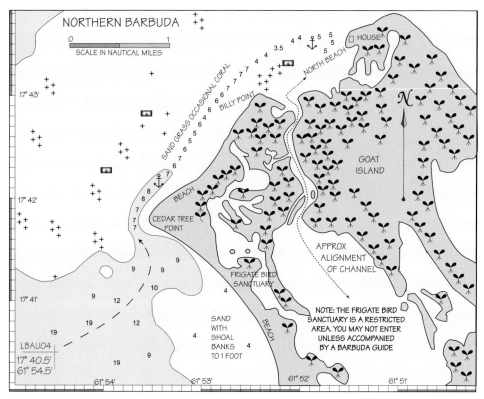

south is Donna Mouth, created after hurricane Donna, but the anchoring off this area is rocky and foul, so not advised. Do not approach the frigate bird colony by dinghy. It is a nature reserve and you need a local guide, who you can find in the village.

The coast north of Palmetto Point can be dangerous in northerly swells, so listen to the forecasts carefully, especially in the winter months. The area is not well charted. There is a broad bank some 3 miles wide that is less than 30 feet deep. The bottom is sand and it is quite possible that depths could change during northerly swells. Nine Foot Bank extends over a mile offshore and breaks in moderate to heavy ground seas. All yachts should avoid it. There is an inside passage which normally has a minimum of 10 feet over it and for much of the way is 12-17 feet deep. This is the easiest way to navigate this coast. You just follow the beach, keeping an eye on your depth, while staying 100 to 200 yards offshore. You can anchor almost anywhere

along here, though there is an indented spot just south of Tuson Rock that is particularly good. It is easily identified by a local restaurant (Barbuda Outbar) that has sunshades. You can also carry on up inside Tuson Rock and the surrounding shoals to Low Bay, an anchorage off the coast's only stand of palm trees and hotel. In moderate surges (seas breaking only occasionally on Nine Foot Bank), the calmest anchorage is found by feeling your way north of the hotel, where you begin to get some protection from the north of Barbuda and its offshore reefs. In choosing you spot, keep in mind Lighthouse Bay has a generator clearly audible by those anchored close by. Deep draft yachts must go outside Nine Foot Bank and approach these bays from the west. We show the positions of the reefs up to Low Bay on our sketch chart. There is plenty of room between them.

Ashore

This is a place to enjoy the beach, snorkel and organize a boat tour to the frigatebird colony (call Garden of Eden on VHF: 16). This is the least expensive way to see the frigatebirds, as you will not need a land taxi. George Jeffrey will pick you up on Louis Mouth, which is the bare patch of sand about 300 yards south of the hotel, or Barbuda Outbar You can also visit Codrington by dinghy or water taxi.

Lighthouse Bay is in the new, fancy, conspicuous yellow buildings with red roofs right on the water's edge at Low Bay. This is a beautiful and very fancy mini-resort with nine luxurious rooms. They also have a delightful bar, restaurant, and upstairs lounging/ viewing area, including the lighthouse deck. Managers John and Peggy welcome yachting visitors. Walk in for a drink, but for lunch or dinner you need to give them about 24-hours notice. There may also be rush times when they cannot take more guests.

Barbuda Outbar, about a mile south, is a very local bar/restaurant hangout owned by Jala. Jala opens normally to take care of ferry passengers, but given a bit of notice he will open for a groups of four or more, and may just be open anyway if enough boats are in. They barbecue fresh local fish and lobster, and have a meal price that includes a beer and soft drink. (Call: 721-3280/460-1509.)

Water Sports

There is excellent snorkeling on any of the reefs, with turtles and copious fish, including eagle rays, and stingrays. The reefs are rather a long way from the beach, though you can often see them at low tide through binoculars. We have given approximate bearings from the anchorages and GPS coordinates. If you do not have a suitable dinghy, you can find temporary anchorage in the lee of the reefs. Beware of outcroppings that extend well beyond the main structures. The reef off the point at the north end of our chart is the closest to shore and you can anchor to its south. While there are plenty of fish here (we once had a following of 10 barracudas), a lot of the coral is dead. If a surge is running, the water is murky.

NORTH BARBUDA

This area is probably mainly of interest to adventurous skippers of shallow craft (3 feet or less) who can get as far as North Beach, which is a pretty anchorage. Yachts with a draft of 6 feet can get some of the way in. The snorkeling is good on the surrounding reefs, and there is endless beautiful beach to walk on. This is for experienced reef navigators only. Navigation Charting of this area is out of date, so you have to feel your way in very slowly in good light. Shoals along the west coast south of Cedar Point come out to around 61° 54'W, so approach from west of this, then head for Cedar Tree Point, varying your course to stay in the deep water as you get close. Once you pass Cedar Tree Point, you get a lot of protection from northerly swells from the shoals and reef that lie to the west and north. After Cedar Tree Point, follow the coast northeast. At first you will need to be very roughly 200 yards off the beach; farther up you will need to be a quarter of a mile or more. Follow the curve of depths we show on out sketch chart. How far along you can go depends on your draft. Vessels of no more than 3-foot draft can make it to North Beach, where there is a good anchorage in about 5 feet of water. Some areas have grass banks and sand. Stay in the sand, as the grass banks are shallower. You also have to avoid the odd coral head. A grass shoal extends quite a way north of Billy Point, and you must stay outside this. You can easily recognize North Beach as a handsome lodge is built there. Rueben James, who owns it, is planning to rent it to visitors and to have a restaurant; a great place to bring some boats and friends. Call him for details (721-3317 or 727-0017).

If you want help coming in here, George Jeffrey (Garden of Eden VHF: 68) could pilot you in. He could also pilot craft of 3-foot draft or less right into Codrington. You should not attempt Codrington on your own, except in a dinghy.

MOUNTAINS & MANGROVES

Jolly Harbour   Chris Doyle

Antigua

ROM A YACHTING point of view, Antigua's most famous attractions include more beautiful, protected anchorages than most other islands, the famous and historic English Harbour, and Antigua Sailing Week. These are all covered in the text that follows. Amid Antigua's highest hills are areas of mixed forest, mainly dry-forest. Fig Tree Drive winds through this area and offers several attractions. Wallings Reservoir is along this road and many trails start here. You can hike up to Signal Hill where you will find an open area of small ponds and great views. You can also hike down to Rendezvous Bay. Along here you also find the Antigua Rainforest Canopy Tour. This is a misnomer as Antigua does not have a rainforest, and this is not a conventional canopy tour, but it is exciting, good exercise, and something you will really remember. Much of it has been built by Bernard

Nichols and it is a combination of walking on well-designed trails and steps, and flying back and forth across a gorge strapped to a harness on a series of wires. The longest of these rides is 300 feet over a drop of 350 feet. This takes you down hill and you walk back up some amazing steps to a bar with a great view of the forest.

Navigation

When approaching Antigua from the south or southwest, the light on Shirley Heights has a visibility of 20 miles. It has been known to go out of action.

ENGLISH AND FALMOUTH HARBOURS

In the old days it was hard to find secure ports that were easily defensible, with immediate access to the trade winds, yet protected enough to careen a ship and be safe in a hurricane. Falmouth Harbour and English Harbour sit side by side, almost touching at the closest point, and they meet all these requirements. Their potential was recognized as early as 1723 and

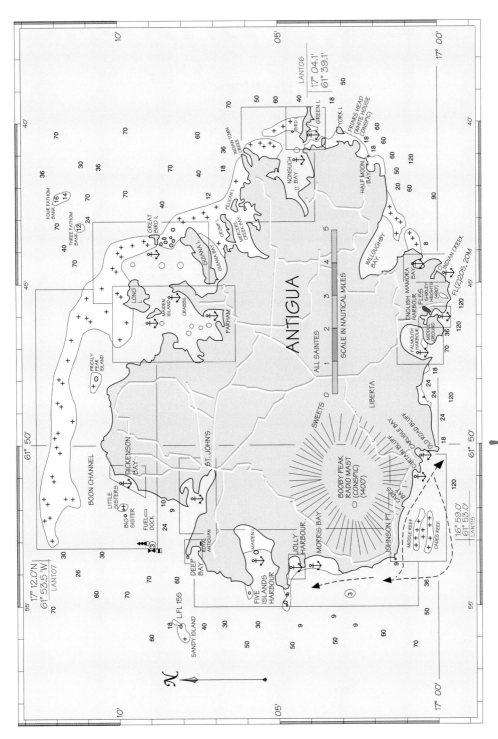

ANTIGUA

MOUNTAINS & MANGROVES

Antigua

Regulations

Antigua has customs stations at English Harbour, Jolly Harbour, and in St. John's. Once you have cleared in, you will get a cruising permit, which enables you to go anywhere in Antiguan waters, including Barbuda. We list the entry fees and other fees under the regulations section of English Harbour.

If your vessel is over 100 tons, you may need to send advance notice of your crew and passengers to immigration, which you can arrange through your agent.

Spearfishing is forbidden in Antigua and Barbuda, except for residents, and they need a license.

There is a 5-knot speed limit in all harbors. This includes tenders and dinghies and this automatically prohibits jet skis in these areas.

Telephones

Using a GSM mobile is the easiest way to phone in Antigua. Cable and Wireless and Digicel give good coverage. The rates here tend to be higher than in other islands. You can also use phone cards, which are widely sold.

Shopping hours

Opening hours are weekdays 0800 to 1200 and 1300 to 1600. Bank hours vary. Nearly all banks open at 0800, some close at 1300, and some stay open as late as 1500. Most stay open later on Fridays, till 1600 or 1700. A few banks open on Saturday mornings.

Transport

Antigua has good links to the USA, with daily American Airlines flights to Miami and then on to other destinations. BWIA has daily flights to New York and Miami, and British Airways has several weekly flights to London. Air Canada also has regular flights to Canada. LIAT provides the main link to other Caribbean islands.

Taxis are plentiful and sample taxi rates for up to four people in $US are:

St. John's to English Harbour	$30	English Harbour to Jolly Harbour.	$45
Woods Center to English Harbour	$35	St John's to Dickenson Bay	$12
St. John's to the St. James Club	$30	By the hour	$30
English Harbour to the airport	$31	For late and early rides, add approximately $10	

There is also an inexpensive bus system and our town maps show bus terminals. Rental cars are available, but you need to get a local license, which costs about $50 EC. Drive on the left.

Holidays

- Jan 1
- Good Friday and Easter Monday (Easter Sunday is April 4, 2010; April1 24, 2011)
- First Monday in May (Labor Day)
- Whit Monday, 50 days after Easter Sunday (May 24, 2010; June 13, 2011)
- Second Saturday in June (Queens Birthday)
- First Monday in July (Caricom Day)
- First Monday and Tuesday in August (Carnival)
- October 7 (Merchants holiday)
- November 1st (Independence Day)
- Dec 25th and 26th

There is a jazz festival, usually in late May, and a hot air balloon festival at the end of October.

Antigua, Admiralty Leisure Folio 5641-2, 5641-3, 5641-4, 5641-10, 5641-11

The old sail loft pillars   Chris Doyle

work was begun on the English Harbour Dockyard. It was completed much as it stands today in around 1745 and was Britain's main naval station in the Lesser Antilles. Nelson was stationed here in 1784 under Sir Richard Hughes, who had recently blinded himself in one eye while chasing a cockroach with a fork. Nelson eventually took over as naval commander. He did not enjoy Antigua and did not get on well with Governor General Shirley (after whom Shirley Heights is named) or the plantocracy, who resented the boring

way in which Nelson insisted on enforcing the Navigation Act. This meant he kept the port closed to trade for all but British ships. Nonetheless, the dockyard is now generally known as Nelson's Dockyard in deference to Britain's favorite hero.

When former commander Vernon Nicholson sailed into English Harbour in 1947, the dockyard was in ruins. The arrival of Nicholson's Charter Company in 1949 and the restoration of the ruins into a beautiful yet functional monument gave momentum to the development of the yachting industry here. Today these harbors are managed by the Nelson's Dockyard National Park, part of the National Parks Authority. They are not only the yachting capital of Antigua, but also a major Caribbean yachting center.

English Harbour and Falmouth Harbour attract hundreds of cruising yachts and are the winter home of many gold-plated charter yachts of sail and power. In particular, they have become the Caribbean's main base for sailing superyachts, and these make a grand spectacle on the docks. English Harbour is prettier; Falmouth Harbour is more convenient for most yacht services. Many businesses are set up to sell duty-free goods to yachts, and yachts can order duty-free parts through these businesses. A wide range of marine services and a convivial social scene are found here, complete with happy hours and jump up nights.

In the summer this area has a quiet village atmosphere and many businesses and restaurants close. Antigua is a good base for the hurricane season as it is uncrowded and has many secure hurricane holes. Even in Hurricane Luis, losses were much less than in other affected islands. There is a yachting committee in English Harbour that supervises the tying of yachts into the mangroves in the approved manner should a hurricane threaten.

The recommended method is bow to the mangroves, grounding in the soft mud as you get in close. Tie off many lines into the mangrove trees and use two stern anchors, not too far apart, to keep you from riding right into the mangroves. Use all available fenders and tie off to next-door yachts if appropriate.

The haul out facilities all take special measures to ensure that boats do not fall over. The whole of Nelson's Dockyard has been beautifully reconstructed to house hotels, restaurants, and businesses. It is an outstanding historic monument, all the better for being used, and a fitting scene for Antigua's main port of arrival for yachts. Falmouth Harbour is considerably larger and surrounded by hills. It has more facilities than English Harbour and is favored by most of the charter yachts, superyachts, and larger cruising yachts. Most places of interest are strung between the Dockyard and the eastern part of Falmouth, all within a few minutes stroll. However, the Catamaran Hotel and Marina and several important services in the northern end of Falmouth Harbour are a mile down the road. The road is hot, but buses run about every half hour. They start outside the Dockyard gates and pass Falmouth on the way to St. John's.

Several delightful walks have been laid out in this area. Everyone should take the short path out to Fort Berkeley Point, following the trail from just behind the dinghy dock. A second, really delightful trail forks right off this trail and takes you along the ridgeline past lots of old foundations to Pigeon Beach. You will enjoy magnificent scenery all along the way, with plenty of century plants, cactuses, acacias, and other dry site vegetation. You can return by road.

Across the harbor, all adventurous souls should take the hike up to Shirley Heights,

English Harbour

Chris Doyle

Antigua & Barbuda
Department of Marine Services & Merchant Shipping

- Registration of Ships under the Flag of Antigua & Barbuda
- Permanent Registration
- Yacht Registration
- Bareboat Charter Registration
- Incorporation of Offshore Companies under the International Business Corporation Act (IBC) or the Companies Act
- Worldwide Coverage of Safety Inspections
- Issuing of Endorsements & Seafarer's Books for Seamen on A&B Vessels and Yachts in accordance with STCW 95 Convention
- Qualified 24-Hour After Office Hours Service for Maritime Emergencies

For Registration & General Enquiries

Mr. D. C. R. Gardiner - Director and Registrar General
Captain J. A. Gillis - Senior Deputy Director and Registrar
Ms. N. E. Stewart - Deputy Director and Deputy Registrar

PO Box 1394 • St. John's • Antigua • WI
Tel: +1 268 462 1273 • Fax: +1 268 462 4358 • Email: marineserv@candw.ag

which affords magnificent views of both English Harbour and Falmouth Harbour. The path is in shade for much of the way, with good examples of many local plants adapted to dry conditions: dinghy to the Galleon Beach Club dock, turn left, and follow the road.

You will see the footpath on the right posted "To the Lookout." This takes you to the top. Sensible shoes are essential.

The main wall at Nelson's Dockyard has been rebuilt, with additional services put along the wall.

English and Falmouth Harbours each have their own section below. The two are close together and most services, restaurants, and shops work for both. Most service providers are members of the Antigua Marine Trades Association. This association has worked for yachts to ease regulations and would like to get input from visiting yachts. They will also be happy to give advice on services. Their trade directory and the Antigua Marine Guide are widely available.

Regulations

There are plans to make the whole of English and Falmouth Harbours a duty-free zone.

There is a 5-knot speed limit in both English Harbour and Falmouth Harbour. This applies not only to yachts, but to dinghies, tenders, and inflatables. Thoughtless speeding has already led to several terrible accidents, including one whaler that imbedded itself deep into the cabin of an anchored yacht and a death from another speeding craft. Fines for a first offense are up to $1000.

Those arriving from overseas should hoist a yellow flag and anchor in English Harbour or Falmouth. The skipper only should come ashore and take the ship's papers to the customs office where complete entry procedures involve customs, immigration, and the port authorities. These three offices are side by side in Nelson's Dockyard and are all open daily from 0800 to 1600. If you just need customs or port, they are open slightly longer: customs daily from 0700 to 1700; port 0700 to 1700 weekdays, 0800-1700 on weekends. However, when you want to clear out, make sure you go between 0900 and 1545 to be sure of catching everyone. The following fees are due anywhere in Antigua or Barbuda:

Entry charge:

    up to 20 ft: $10 US
    21-40ft: $12 US
    41-80ft: $16 US
    81 100ft: $20 US

Cruising permit:

    21-40ft: $8 US
    41-80ft: $10 US
    81-100ft: $14 US

Yachts of over 200 tons pay an alternative rate that includes all the above and starts at about $200 US.

The cruising permit is compulsory (not optional) and good for one month or until you leave the country. There are no overtime charges, even on holidays and Sundays at the Dockyard customs, but you may be charged overtime fees in the other ports of entry. In English Harbour, Nelson's Dockyard National Park collects the fees, and is to be congratulated for accepting major credit cards.

Immigration will stamp you in for 60 days. If you need to stay longer, extensions are possible at the immigration office in Nelson's Dockyard.

NELSON'S
DOCKYARD

ANTIGUA SLIPWAY

FORT BERKELY POINT

CHANNEL
NO
ANCHORING

CHARLOTTE POINT

MOUNTAINS & MANGROVES

ENGLISH HARBOUR

There are also port charges for staying in English Harbour or Falmouth Harbour, which go toward the maintenance of the park and toilet facilities. We give the rates in $US below, figures in parenthesis are low season (summer), the others are for the rest of the year:

($US)

.06 (.04) per foot per day

.30 (.20) per foot per week

1.15 (.75) per foot per month

You pay these fees whether you are at anchor or in a marina, unless you are staying in Nelson's Dockyard Marina, in which case they are included in the docking fee.

There is a onetime fee of $4 US per person entering the dockyard, which is valid for the duration of your stay. All yachts pay a garbage fee that averages about $1 US dollar per person per day, but this is quite variable, depending on many factors. If you are stern-to, there are also electricity and water fees.

English Harbour

Navigation

Entering English Harbour presents no special problems. Avoid the rocky shoal off Charlotte Point. Do not anchor in the channel marked on our sketch chart. You can anchor in Freeman Bay, or way up in the harbor, or stern-to the Dockyard Marina or Antigua Slipway. If you anchor in Freeman Bay, be warned that the wind can swirl around in this bay, particularly towards the southern end. Boats often drift stern to stern in the middle of the night and unplanned midnight meetings occur. You need far more swinging room than normal.

If you are entering at night, there is a range using quick flashing red lights, which sometimes work.

One of the less fortunate aspects of this harbor's long history is that anchors occasionally get wrapped round 200-year-old artifacts, not least of which are several massive chains known as "hurricane chains." We put the ones we could find on our sketch chart. Cautious sailors could use a trip line. When all else fails, call "Sea Pony" or "Dockyard Divers."

If you are going into the Dockyard Marina, call in advance and the marina will send out a boat to help you tie up to the buoys and come stern-to. Some of the yellow buoys are really far off the dock to accommodate large yachts and it may look like you can pass between a yellow buoy and a boat at the dock. Do not try and navigate between these yellow buoys and the docks! Some boats are hooked to them with underwater lines. They will also want you to drop an anchor.

Communications

The Image Locker is in the old Signal Locker building. Gaye and Arnold will get you hooked up to the internet. You can come in to their bank of computers, though more and more people are opting for the onboard wifi connection (called HotHotHotSpot if you do an automatic search from your boat). This system works right from the harbor entrance through Falmouth Harbour with numerous relay points. If you buy access by the week, month or season, it is also good for their system in Guadeloupe, the Saintes, Dominica and many other islands. This is the place to come to rent a digital phone or to buy a new sim (Lime or Digicel), or to buy time on these phones. They also do yacht name transfers, digital photo printing, passport photos, photocopies, and scanning. Here, too, you can buy cruising guides, courtesy flags, historical nautical jewelry (replicas), postcards, and small gifts. They also sell and custom-print t-shirts, coffee mugs, and other things using your photos and designs and di-sub printing. The Image Locker opens 0600-1800 daily (often later), the wifi works 24/7. In addition they have an excellent fresh food café (see restaurants).

As you walk down towards Falmouth, on your left is a big building, Anchorage Center, with offices and a couple of restaurants, including a pizzeria and Club Havana. Walk into the courtyard for Caribit, an internet station and computer

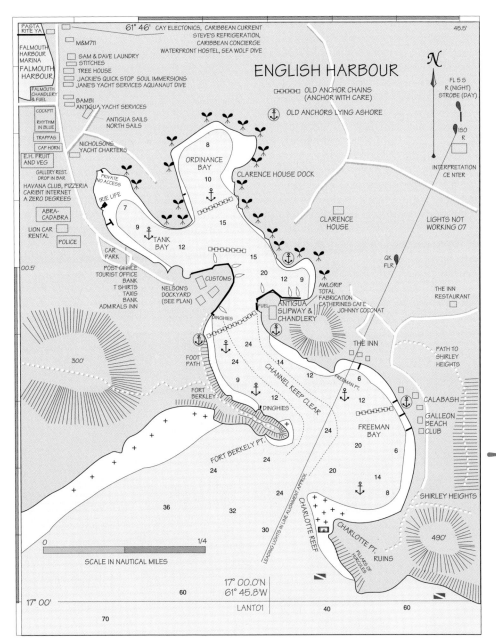

ENGLISH HARBOUR

store owned by Lorenzo. This is the main computer repair and sales outlet in the area. Caribit sells Apple and Acer computers, Hyperlink wifi and equipment by Dlink, Lexar, and Buffalo. Lorenzo repairs all brands of computers. He also does onboard consulting for yacht computer systems. They open weekdays 0900-1700.

General Yacht Services

There are garbage depots down a side road in Nelson's Dockyard (see our plan, page 281) and near the Falmouth Chandlery in Falmouth Harbour. Oil disposal is available. You have a choice of two docking facilities in English Harbour, both stern-to, and both supplying shore power at

MOUNTAINS & MANGROVES

60 cycles. The park authority has rebuilt the dockyard walls and refurbished the area, which is called Nelson's Dockyard Marina. It has 30 docks with bow moorings, electricity with 380/220/110-volt outlets, and water, phone, internet, cable TV, and 24-hour security. The dockyard has shower, toilet and laundry facilities open daily (to everyone) from 0800-1730. Take laundry in the morning and get it back in the afternoon - a reasonable and efficient service. A bank and post office are both near the t-shirt stands. Nelson's Dockyard is presently home to Sunsail and they stand by on VHF: 68, switching to 72.

If you use the Dockyard Marina, you do not have to pay the daily charges. The marina charges are: Stern-to ($US) Daily rate - 0.80 per foot day Fortnightly - 0.70 per foot day Monthly 0.460 per foot day Over 150 feet - 1.20 per foot day Multihulls pay double.

On the other side of the harbor is Antigua Slipway, managed by Mike Goldworthy, which has been offering yacht services since 1967. It is a full service marina, with a chandlery and an alongside fuel dock and a dock shop that sells fishing gear, motor accessories, and sundries. This is open in season weekdays 0700-1700, Saturdays, 0800-1600, and Sundays 0800-1200. There is a stern-to visitors' dock with water and 3-phase electricity (110/220/380 volts) that takes yachts up to 150 feet long.

Antigua Slipway is a major haul out facility, using a railway that takes yachts up to 14-foot draft and 200 tons and cats up to 40-foot beam. They also have a hydraulic lift, allowing for the hauling and storing of 50 yachts with a maximum draft of 9 feet. The Antigua Slipway is a popular place for summer storage. Mike Goldworthy is very

English Harbour

Chris Doyle

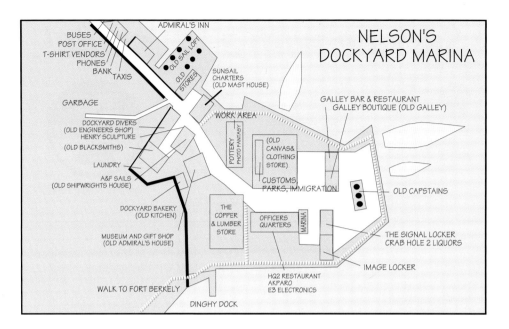

NELSON'S DOCKYARD MARINA

knowledgeable about yachts and their systems, so you are in good hands. The yard is geared up for yacht storage in the hurricane season. The storage area is concrete, the newer part having tie-down rings. All stored yachts are propped on stands, which are welded together using one-inch water pipe to create a rigid cradle. They have a crane that is used not only for pulling masts, but engines, big appliances, and the odd piano. You can work on your boat above the water line, or independent contractors can undertake the work for you. The yard or contractors do everything below the waterline and can do anything from an Awlgrip or bottom job to a complete refit, including woodworking, mechanical, fiberglass, refrigeration, mast, and rigging replacement or repair. New engines and other gear can be imported through them duty-free. Antigua Slipway has customer showers, a laundromat, garbage disposal, and is home to several small businesses. There is often a ferry around that runs to and from the dockyard, and will also run out to your yacht.

When Commander Nicholson first sailed into the ruins of English Harbour, it was on his yacht Mollyhawk, a yacht that had been sold to him by Archibald, Reid & Co., a well-established yacht broker from Eire. Well, now Archibald, Reid & Co. has a branch in the Signal Locker run by Nichola Long and Jolyon Menhinick.

Chandlery

Antigua Slipway Chandlery (VHF: 12), upstairs at their yard, is an excellent duty-free marine chandlery with a vast stock of stainless and bronze fastenings and pipefittings. They have very good buys on the best antifoulings, plus pumps, marine hardware, ropes, anchors, charts, and guides. This chandlery has a second outlet downstairs in the Yacht Club building in Falmouth. They open weekdays 0800-1700; Saturdays 0800-1200.

Technical Yacht Services Sails and Canvas

If your sails get blown out or you need new awnings or biminis, A&F sails (VHF: 68) has a loft right in the dockyard and they are agents for Bruce Banks Sails. They can repair your old sail or build you a new one, as well as doing all kinds of canvas work, including awnings and biminis. They pick up sails from Jolly Harbour on

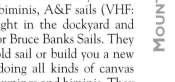

MOUNTAINS & MANGROVES

Wednesdays, and from Antigua Yacht Club Marina any day. If you are stuck somewhere else on the island, give them a call and they will help you arrange something.

North Sails and Antigua Sails have their lofts on the road leading up a slope from Nicholson Yacht Charters. North Sails is run by Andrew Dove, This is the highest tech sail loft in the Leewards. They maintain direct links to North Sails in the US, and have a chain of agents through the Caribbean, including St. Martin, St. Barts, Guadeloupe, Martinique, St. Lucia, Bequia, Grenada, and Trinidad. It is a fully computerized loft and they build most sails from panels cut by automated laser cutters. They offer performance cruising versions of the new seamless molded sails from the US. Quotes for new sails can be given immediately and you can see your sail on the computer before it is made. They will be happy to fix your old sails, even those made of the most exotic materials. They have made some special adaptations for the winter superyacht fleet; they can come to the dock to collect the sails with a special trailer where sails can be loaded and repaired without removing the battens. For the local racing fleet, they have an air-conditioned storage room for keeping high tech sails between events.

Antigua Sails (VHF: 68), upstairs above North, do not sew sails, but specialize in new canvas work and repairs. They will make awnings, specialty covers, biminis, and anything else you might need. Rena runs the Select Crew Agency from the gate cottage and will help find you a crew or a job. Rena can set you up with health insurance and she also has a gallery of art by water colorist David Cadogan, who arrived in Antigua by yacht. He paints yacht portraits and does commissions.

Technical Yacht Services Electronics

Cap Greene's Signal Locker (VHF: 68) is the oldest electrics and electronics firm in the area, and by far the most experienced. Cap Greene has run it since 1973. They are agents for a huge range of brand name products and whatever they don't have in stock they can bring in for you duty-free. This includes the Iridium phone system, which provides worldwide communication at a not-too-excessive cost, and even works with email, and the Skymate work-anywhere email system. Besides selling new gear, they can fix anything from starter motors to radar, including wind generators, and they do quick repairs on that faulty VHF. You can buy Deka and Prevailer batteries here. Also part of the same company, but with separate technicians, is Signal Refrigeration, a complete refrigeration and air-conditioning shop. They fix all makes and sell Grunert, Marine Air, and Cruisair, among others. Boats needing work in both areas will be happy to find these services under one roof.

E3 is a new electronics company devoted to large yacht electronics. You will find

them upstairs in the Officers' Quarters. This is part of a big group, with offices through the Med, and they are geared to giving top-quality service, including communications and being an air-time provider. They do satellite TV conversion, v-sats, radar, integrated navigation systems, and all manner of high end electronics.

Technical Yacht Services
Refrigeration

A Zero Degrees Refrigeration is on the right side of the road outside the dockyard. Marlon Hunte is the owner and chief technician, helped by his wife Tavia. Marlon designs, installs, and repairs all refrigeration and air-conditioning systems. He is used to big commercial and large yacht marine systems, as well as smaller units for cruisers. He also does ice-makers. His office is open weekdays 0900-1500.

Rob Steel runs Steel Refrigeration, which is in the back of Sea Wolf Dive shop (they share the space). He will repair all refrigeration and AC systems. (See also Signal Refrigeration above.)

Technical Yacht Services
Other Services

In the Antigua Slipway compound is Phil Hopton's Awlgrip Antigua. Phil and his team are specialists in glass and paint and they handle minor and major repair jobs and work in all the exotics and composites. They can fabricate tanks or parts, repair small nicks with a perfect color match, or they can Awlgrip your whole yacht. Next door is Richard Tillotson's Total Fabrication. Here they do welding, machining, fabrication, and mechanical work on diesels. Richard can weld stainless, aluminum, and all yacht metals. He can build you a stainless tank or davit and will repair your broken diesel engine. For yachts in storage, he offers to make sure the engines are properly stored and batteries kept charged and, when you return, he has everything running smoothly. Awgrip Antigua, Total Fabrication, and Chippy work together as a team called the Antigua

MOUNTAINS & MANGROVES

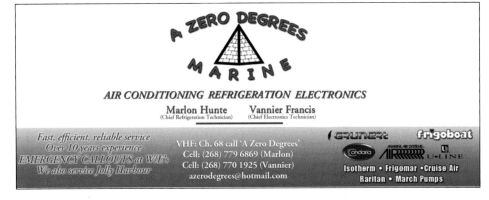

Refit Group. They joined together to be able to offer complete refits and to be able to quote insurance companies as a single unit for complex repairs.

Above these businesses is the woodwork shop, which is a workshop offshoot of Woodstock, used for doing jobs in this yard (see Falmouth Harbour).

Charter yachts needing a brochure, or owners wanting a yacht picture, can get photographs from Alexis Andrews, the specialist in marine photography. He often arranges helicopters for overhead shots. Alexis now works out of his home (460-1175). His photographic book about Antigua is elegant.

Some yachts also need promotional DVD films, and the person to contact for this is Roddy at Aqua Films (725-7873). He also works closely with Alexis.

Another person you need to know is Lucy Tulloch. Lucy is both a graphic artist and layout whiz who will put your photos into a perfect brochure. Lucy is also the Caribbean Compass rep and a well-known artist who is happy to paint pictures of boats on commission.

Transport

Dockyard Taxi (VHF: 68) is a group of official Dockyard taxi drivers. They maintain high standards of reliability and you can always get them on the radio. They are happy to take visitors on local tours, including Shirley Heights, or for a visit to the Interpretation Center.

Lions Car Rental is right outside the gates at English Harbour, next to the police station. You can also enquire in Dockside Supermarket in Falmouth. Try also Ti Ti Rent-a-Car, Bigs Car Rental, or, if in a daring mood, Cheke's scooter rentals – all close to the Temo Sports complex.

You can also contact Tropical Rentals, who have a big selection of cars, a good reputation, and will deliver and collect.

Provisioning

In Nelson's Dockyard, the good little Dockyard Bakery (closed Sundays) is tucked behind the small museum. They have excellent modern equipment, produce a good variety of breads, and will take orders on VHF: 68 for bread, Danish, chocolate cake, and carrot cake, as well as

savory patties, sausage rolls, and sandwiches. They can produce in quantity for charter yachts. They serve coffee, too, so this is a good place to come for breakfast or a snack lunch (open 0800-1700).

Crab Hole Liquors (VHF: 68) has two shops dedicated to replenishing your liquor locker and wine bilge. One is in the Dockyard and the other is about halfway between English Harbour and the Catamaran Hotel. It, too, has the full range of drinks, but has also grown into a supermarket.

English Harbour Fruit & Vegetables is a basic mini mart, open weekdays from 0800-1900, Saturdays 1830-2100, and Sundays 0800-1800.

Aubrey is an excellent place for local fresh produce, which he sells from 0900-1500 daily near the phone bank, just inside the Dockyard. If you want fish or something special, he will organize it for the next day. During the summer he works shorter hours and takes Sunday off.

Both Jane's Yacht Services and Antigua Yacht Services offer a full provisioning service.

Fun Shopping

There is plenty to satisfy shoppers looking for local treasures, from the t-shirt stands outside the post office to fancy shops. Janie Eastern started the Galley Boutique over 30 years ago, making her stock on a treadle sewing machine. Today the shop, under new management, imports an impressive array of elegant clothes and artistic gifts and usually stocks those vital polarized sunglasses.

Things Local is next to A & F Sail loft and is owned and run by Carl Henry, a sculptor who works with local wood. He produces many works, from abstracts and African game boards to fish and dolphins. He had the honor of carving a sculpture for the queen. Below, in the old work area, are two shops to peruse. Photo Fantasy is a photo studio and shop. You can get passport or fun photos here, and they also print photos on t-shirts and mugs. They stock

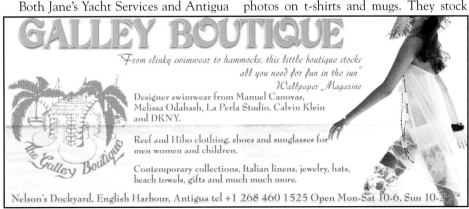
MOUNTAINS & MANGROVES

The beach bar at The Inn   Chris Doyle

photos by the owner, Ed Martin, as well as local gifts. Next door, Dockyard Pottery is more than just a pottery shop. It has a wide array of gifts and handicrafts, with lots of souvenirs.

Check also the Dockyard Gift Shop at the museum and see our section on Falmouth Harbour.

Restaurants

English sailors used to be called Limeys because they ate limes to ward off scurvy. When their ships were in port they had ample time to lounge around, thus the local verb 'to lime' came to mean 'hang out.' Today's yachtspeople keep pretty busy in port, but still find plenty of time to make merry. So much so that it can be harder to survive the active English Harbour social scene than the offshore reefs. Between them, Falmouth and English Harbour have lots restaurants and you can eat well.

Be sure to get up to Shirley Heights Lookout, with its fabulous view over English Harbour. The easiest way is to take a taxi, but the walk up is quite delightful and will help you work up a thirst. Take the tiny path that starts on the road leading out of Galleon Beach Club. If you are returning after dark, bring a flashlight. The Shirley Heights Lookout is a bar and restaurant, with a perfect sunset view. Don't miss the Sunday night hot party – it's a Caribbean institution. It starts at 1600 with a steel band and they switch to reggae at 2100. They cook an inexpensive barbecue and you will see lots of action. They also have entertainment on Thursdays from 1600-2000. Take care on the way back as some people still drink and drive.

The Calabash (lunch only) is the restaurant at the Galleon Beach Club and has its own dinghy dock. This is a special place for a long, relaxing lunch, sitting on a deck under the palms right beside the beach. Owners Mike and Pam are both yachting people, but it is Pam's cooking that draws all the local homeowners to gravitate here. Pam cooks wonderful tarts, local seafood, and curries, as well as her famous carrot cake and coconut cheese cake for dessert. On Sundays they often feature rack of lamb. On Sunday evening the Tot Club meets at 1800.

The Inn at English Harbour is on the next beach, with lands that lead up the hill. The Beach Bar is a very pleasant spot to relax, enjoy the beach, and look out over the bay. They serve breakfast and lunch daily, and occasional evening barbecues. For a relaxing evening meal in style, try the restaurant, which is up the hill. You can walk, or if that is too much work, give them a call and they will collect you from the beach bar.

Over at Antigua Slipway, you will find Catherine's Café (closed Tuesday), open from 0900 to about 1800, and on Fridays for dinner. This is an informal French café/restaurant where the food always smells fresh and appetizing; it is among the very best in the area. It is owned by Guillaume and Claudine from Brittany, and the staff are all very friendly and helpful; the atmosphere relaxed and pleasant, with seats outside on a large covered deck area. A new menu is posted every day. The lunch menu features salads and light things like quiches, as well as main dishes for the hungry. They often have shellfish: mussels at the beginning of the week and clams much of the time. In addition, they feature fresh fish, lobster, and prawns.

Next door, Johnny Coconut was named in honor of that famous Caribbean character John Caldwell who planted coconut trees all over the Grenadines, and the owner, Nat. Nat and his chef are Italian, and they have a big wood-fired pizza oven for wonderful, tasty, Italian thin-crust pizza, including the "Johnny Coconut". They make their own ravioli and taglioni, serve a lot of fresh fish and lobster, and also make good salads. You sit outside under cover, Mediterranean style, and their prices are reasonable. They open daily from 0930-2130, except Wednesday. They sometimes have evening entertainment.

In the dockyard, The Image Locker is not only an internet café, but a great hangout with fresh, healthy local snacks and lunches as well as a few decadent desserts and pastries. The serve fresh local fruit juices and smoothies, excellent coffee of all types, wonderful wraps, sandwiches, and pastries. Open every day in the season from 0600-1800.

The Admiral's Inn is very romantic and quiet. It has a superb location, with a lovely garden leading to the waterfront, next to the photogenic sail loft pillars. It is a perfect meeting place. They are famous for

Chris Doyle

MOUNTAINS & MANGROVES

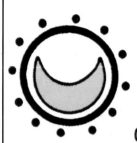
their pumpkin soup and have fresh fish and lobster daily. They have a subdued happy hour from 1800-1900, and occasionally they have a local string or steel band. If you would like something a little less expensive than the regular menu, ask for the "Yachtsman's Special." The setting makes the Admiral's Inn also perfect for a coffee or afternoon tea.

The Galley Bar is a pleasant place to sit with a view of the docks, and the closest watering hole for those in the marina. Manager Devan Baltimore is local and welcoming and opens from 0800 till late at night. Come for breakfast, a coffee break, or for lunch. Sunday afternoon is big, with live jazz and blues music from about 1600, and a barbecue dinner afterwards. Ask about music on other nights.

The Copper and Lumber Store is an artfully upgraded historic hotel. Their Mainbrace Pub has been beautifully renovated and has a mellow atmosphere of old stone and cheerful goodwill. It opens for breakfast and lunch and the food is good, with all kinds of burgers, steak, and barbecued spare ribs. They close at 1700. HQ2, upstairs overlooking the marina, is the area's most upmarket restaurant. It is owned and run by Parisian Anthony Ricart who specializes in French cuisine using fresh fish, often caught by his father Francis, a professional sports-fisherman. HQ2, opens for dinner every day and is the happening place musically on Sundays, when Anthony, who is a drummer, holds a jam session. The music can be anything from jazz to reggae.

As you walk out of the Dockyard area and head to towards Falmouth, you come into the main restaurant area. Want to know which ones are good? Stop by Drop in Bar (no sign outside), and ask the experts who gather here.

Abracadabra is a café, restaurant, and nightspot, where you will get good food and service. The Café is called Cloggy's. It is a great little hideaway for a quiet coffee and a good lunch. Abracadabra opens a couple of hours after Cloggy's closes at about 1830 during the season to serve authentic Italian food, including homemade pasta. They have musical entertainment most nights, including jazz and Latino groups, and guest DJ's from Europe. Both businesses close on Sundays (except during special events). Just down the road, The Gallery opens every evening except Mondays. You eat on a big open deck, which is very pleasant at night, and you can watch people walking by on the road. The food is excellent and artistically served at a price that makes it good value.

Restaurants can be found in the Anchorage Center: Club Havana is a big, open, relaxing place offering Anglo-Mexican food along with some local specialties and lobster. The Pizzeria has good authentic pizzas and is Italian-run by the same people that have The Inn at English Harbour. CG's café is the place to come for your morning coffee fix and a toasted sandwich.

Opposite, Life is built out over the water on stilts. There is a bar for hanging out and the food is wide-ranging with an eclectic menu. They sometimes show movies, special TV shows, and have other entertainment.

Caribbean Taste Native Restaurant is another local restaurant, pleasantly stylish and upmarket in presentation. You find it on the back road that runs from English Harbour (Turn by English Harbour Fruit and Veg.). Many more restaurants line the roads as you walk into Falmouth. We cover them under Falmouth Harbour.

Ashore

To prep for that great meal out (or repair its ravages), visit Akparo upstairs in the officer's quarters in Nelson's Dockyard. Akparo is run by Patricia and staff, who believe in having fun as they make you beautiful. They do all kinds of hair dressing for men and women, as well as facials, manicure, pedicure, waxing, and body massage. They have a printed price list of all their services, so you can drop by and pick one up.

Nelson's Dockyard National Park covers a large area, from west of Falmouth all the way to Indian Creek. It is a department of the Antigua National Parks Authority. Apart from preserving the buildings, maintaining trails, and running the museum and shop, they have an Interpretation Center on Dow's Hill, to the east of English Harbour. It is a 15-minute walk up the hill from Colombo's, or a $5 US (per head) taxi ride, and it is open seven days a week. There is a $6 EC entrance fee if you are staying in English Harbour or Falmouth. It is well worth paying this to see their 15-minute multimedia production on the history of Antigua. Afterwards you can enjoy a view of the entire park from the Belvedere viewing platform. There is also a shell and artifact display, a gift shop, and a restaurant. In the dockyard itself you can join an interpretation tour with many guides who are easily recognizable in their period dress.

Falmouth Harbour

Navigation

Falmouth Harbour is so well buoyed you could feel you were in a minefield of reds and greens. If you familiarize yourself with our sketch chart before you enter, it will be a big help. As you enter, leave the first two red buoys to starboard, which keeps you clear of Bishop Shoal. The next buoy is a red and green divided channel marker. To head up into the Yacht Club and Falmouth Harbour Marina, leave this to port, and head towards those marinas, leaving all the

Chris Doyle

MOUNTAINS & MANGROVES

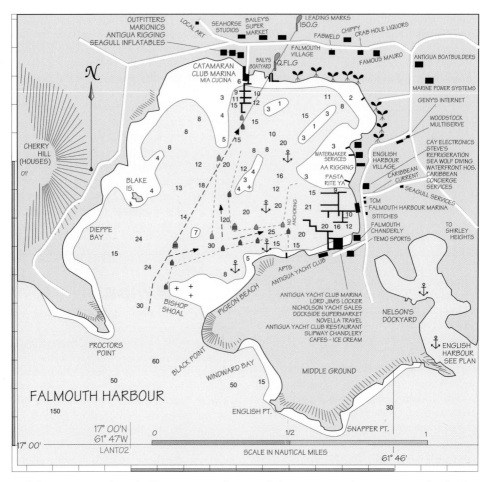

OUTFITTERS
MARIONICS
ANTIGUA RIGGING
SEAGULL INFLATABLES

LOCAL ART
SEAHORSE
STUDIOS
BAILEY'S
SUPER
MARKET
LEADING MARKS
150.G
FABWELD
CHIPPY
CRAB HOLE LIQUORS

FALMOUTH
VILLAGE

FAMOUS MAURO

ANTIGUA BOATBUILDERS

CATAMARAN
CLUB MARINA
MIA CUCINA
BAILY'S
BOATYARD
Q.FL.G

MARINE POWER SYSTEMS

GENY'S INTERNET

WOODSTOCK
MULTIISERVE

CHERRY
HILL
(HOUSES)
01'

CAY ELECTRONICS
STEVE'S
REFRIGERATION
SEA WOLF DIVING
WATERFRONT HOS.
CARIBBEAN
CONCIERGE
SERVICES

WATERMAKER
SERVICES
ENGLISH
HARBOUR
VILLAGE
CARIBBEAN
CURRENT

AA RIGGING

BLAKE
IS.

PASTA
RITE YA

SEAGULL SERVICES

TCM
FALMOUTH HARBOUR MARINA
STITCHES
FALMOUTH
CHANDLERY
TEMO SPORTS

TO
SHIRLEY
HEIGHTS

DIEPPE
BAY

APTS
ANTIGUA YACHT CLUB

ANTIGUA YACHT CLUB MARINA
LORD JIM'S LOCKER
NICHOLSON YACHT SALES
DOCKSIDE SUPERMARKET
NOVELLA TRAVEL
ANTIGUA YACHT CLUB RESTAURANT
SLIPWAY CHANDLERY
CAFES - ICE CREAM

NELSON'S
DOCKYARD

ENGLISH
HARBOUR
SEE PLAN

BISHOP
SHOAL

PIGEON BEACH

PROCTORS
POINT

BLACK POINT

WINDWARD BAY

MIDDLE GROUND

FALMOUTH HARBOUR

ENGLISH PT.

SNAPPER PT.

17° 00'N
61° 47'W
LANT02

SCALE IN NAUTICAL MILES

61° 46'

red buoys to starboard. To go into the Catamaran Club, leave this red and green and buoy to starboard and head down towards the Cat Club. You will see the next green buoy a long way away towards the marina and there are two bright orange triangular beacons you can line up to keep you on the channel. This channel is good for yachts up to about 14-foot draft. Deeper draft boats (16-18 foot draft) can use the deeper alternate channel. To find this, start following the channel towards the yacht club and then look for the second red and green divided channel marker. Leave this to starboard and head for the Cat Club, leaving the next two red buoys to starboard.

If you prefer to be at anchor, there is tons of room; just leave the channels free

and choose a spot that suits your depth. Do not anchor in the exclusion zone in front of the Yacht Club Marina and Falmouth Harbour Marina. Falmouth Harbour Marina has had problems with yachts anchoring too close. If you keep west of the closest of John Bentley's mooring buoys, you will be okay. Large yachts using the marinas sometimes end up with entwined anchors. Sea Pony (VHF: 68) solves these problems. If you arrive in Falmouth Harbour from abroad, walk over to English Harbour to clear in.

Communications

Card phones are dotted throughout the area. You can top up your phone at the Dockside supermarket.

The cafés Skullduggery and Seabreeze

have internet stations and provide wifi. Mad Mongoose offers free 24-hour wifi with electric plug-ins. The next nearest station is Caribit, on the road to English Harbour.

Geny's Internet Café, out beyond Woodstock, is run by Cecilia Hunte. Cecilia cooks an excellent and inexpensive local lunch that you can eat there or take away. She also has a beauty/stationary store that is open daily 0830-2030, except Sunday when it is 1500-1930.

General Yacht Services

If you are going to a marina, book early, as all the marinas get full during the season. In Falmouth Harbour, Antigua Yacht Club Marina and Resort has room for about 60 yachts, and during the winter months the docks are packed with a magnificent array of fancy charter yachts and superyachts (maximum draft 24 feet). Water, electricity (110, 220, 380 volts, 60 cycles up to 400 amps), phone, wifi, and duty-free diesel are available anywhere on the dock. Full communications are available in the office.

Antigua Yacht Club Marina is integral with the modern resort opposite. Here you find 49 modern rooms, suites, and apartments. Twenty-four-hour security is provided throughout. The hotel includes a spa, a modern gym, and a Turkish Bath (Hamam). These are only open to their marina and resort guests.

The marina is in a large two-story building out over the water, which houses cafés, a supermarket, shops, a travel agent, internet stations, and is perfectly placed for the local restaurants. They are host to the Antigua Classic Yacht Regatta and they stand by on VHF: 68/09. Call them if you want to come alongside for fuel and water. They can deliver fuel anywhere on the dock at 250 liters a minute.

The nearby Falmouth Harbour Marina (VHF: 68 switching 10) is owned by a consortium of Antiguans, including Hugh Bailey. It is designed for large yachts, superyachts, and even small cruise ships (maximum draft is about 21 feet), and can take up to 60 of these. There is water and electricity (110, 220, 380 volts, 60 cycles,

MOUNTAINS & MANGROVES

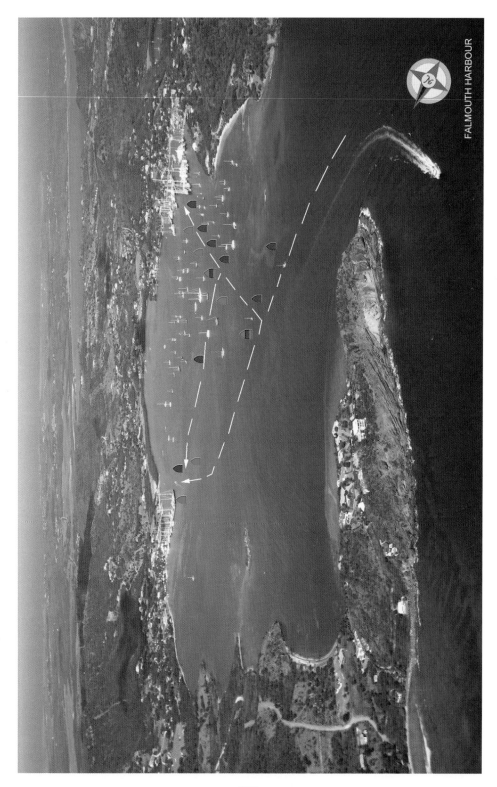

FALMOUTH HARBOUR

3-phase), along with cable TV and telephone lines on the docks and wifi. Duty-free diesel fuel can be supplied to any berth. The staff, including Janice and Ilene in the office and David and Troy on the docks, are all very helpful and friendly. They will help with faxes, and you can receive email here, as well as snail mail (Falmouth Harbour Marina, P.O. Box W792, English Harbour, Antigua). You can also come in just to take on water and fuel. Call the office so they can direct you to the easiest spot.

Across the Bay, Hugh Bailey's Catamaran Hotel and Marina (VHF: 68) has secure berthing in pleasant, peaceful surroundings for about 60 yachts, stern-to and alongside. The docks are kept in tiptop condition, with water at all berths and fuel and electricity (220/110 and 3-phase 380 volts) available at nearly every berth. They sell ice and rent storage rooms. If you need to leave your yacht, this is a good place to do it, and you can arrange to have it looked after. For nights ashore, there is the hotel. Several deep-sea fishing boats are based here. You can ask Hugh, a well-known Caribbean sportsman, about yacht racing and fishing competitions.

Hugh also has Bailey's Boat Yard close by. This is a haul out yard for work and storage. They use a 70-ton marine hoist and can haul boats up to 12 feet deep. They have a dock next to the travel-lift in case you need to get anything done before hauling. This is a small, quality yard, very clean and well laid out, and properly geared up for hurricane storage. They have six con-crete keel holes for absolutely secure storage, then 20 huge and solid cradles that you can leave your boat in. They will pull the mast for storage if you request it. They only store about 30 yachts, and all of them are well looked-after. All work must be done by the yard and Ken is the project manager. He has a team of guys to do painting and some repair; the rest he subcontracts out and supervises.

Moorings are available in Falmouth Harbour. They are orange and tagged with a label. Call Sea Pony on VHF: 68 for details.

Over in the Antigua Yacht Club Marina, you may meet Jol Byerley, another person closely associated with Antigua yachting since its beginning. Jol navigated through the early days of the grand charter yachts with the schooner Lord Jim, and he is well known as a racing yachtsman, humorist, and author. He and Judy start the day at 0900 with the "Not the nine o'clock news," on English Harbour Radio (VHF: 06) giving the weather forecast and local happenings. It is the best forecast in the Leewards and is done as a community service. During the day you will find Judy and sometimes Jol upstairs in the Yacht Club Marina building at Lord Jim's Locker, Antigua's best nautical bookshop, with a big selection of nautical books, cruising guides, charts, nature, travel, novels, biography, history, and cookery books. They also carry children's books (one written by Jol himself), courtesy flags, jewelry, Weems and Plath instruments, film, model sailing boats, and more. I want to call it Lord Jim's

MOUNTAINS & MANGROVES

Emporium, because it has expanded to take up two more storefronts and you can now buy anything from shorts to a yacht. Lord Jim's His & Hers Boutique adjoins the bookstore and stocks very elegant, casual wear, hats, sailing gloves, soft luggage, skipper's brief cases, Rainbow sandals, deck shoes, and more. This is the place to come for crew uniforms. They offer the Smallwoods line and can get overnight delivery.

The last department is Nicholson Caribbean Yacht Sales, the Caribbean's most prestigious yacht brokerage. They specialize in Swans, Hinckleys, and the cream of the custom-designed yachts. It is managed by Ian Mconnachie. In addition to yacht sales, Ian has Yamaha outboards in stock, and you can order Artigiana Battelli rigid inflatables that are delivered duty-free to your yacht, though supply can be a problem at times. Ian, Jol, or Judy are also the people to see for that new sail. As agent for North Sails, they have an efficient system for rapid competitive quotes and can deliv-

er your new computer-designed sails within two or three weeks.

Upstairs in the Yacht Club Marina is the good little Novella's Travel Agency. They will not only organize your next ticket, but also take care of car rentals, hotel accommodations, local lodgings, and sending faxes. They have a plain paper fax machine, can do photocopying, and are Western Union agents.

Laundry is no problem. You can use Sam and Dave's Laundry, opposite Falmouth Harbour Marina. Those on a budget can just have their laundry washed, or you can get the complete service with wash, dry, and fold. They are used to working large loads quickly for charter turnarounds. For convenience regardless of price, you really cannot beat the laundry ladies, Mavis, Maude, and Mrs. Baltimore, who sit outside the Yacht Club Marina or over in the Dockyard. You leave your laundry with one of them and it comes back the next day nicely folded. They stand by on VHF: 68.

Manix is an old Antiguan salt with years

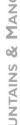

MOUNTAINS & MANGROVES

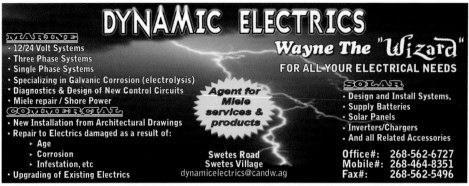
of sailing on yachts in both the Atlantic and the Pacific. You usually find him by his new convenience store, M&N 711. This store is clean, with some fruits, vegetables, ice, and frozen food, as well as basics. Call in an order and he will deliver it to your boat. He also has rooms for rent. Some of the varnishers, such as Yankee (772-6430) and Leonard (724-2590), hang out here. Manix runs a ferry in English Harbour.

Behind the Catamaran Marina, Outfitters Brokers and Sales has an efficient purchasing service for all kinds of parts and equipment, which they source worldwide For those in a hurry, parts can be brought down overnight or arrive in a few days by courier. Less urgent and larger items come regularly once a week by sea. Prices are often not much more than you would pay retail in the US, as Outfitters usually gets good discounts. They handle all the customs clearance, so it is a hassle-free way to get stuff, duty-free for most yachts. Outfitters also can supply duty-free fuel bunkering in several locations for those buying over 200 gallons. Ask for Arthur Thomas or Joan Bailey.

Falmouth Harbour Chandlery and Fuel Dock sells diesel and gasoline to both cars and boats. Upstairs they have a chandlery.

Jane's Yacht Services fill propane tanks on Tuesdays and Thursdays; bring them before 1000 (see Yacht agents).

General Yacht Services Yacht Agents

A few steps down the road and you come to Nicholson Yacht Charters and Services, a name almost synonymous with English

Harbour. They are the people who started the whole ball rolling when they arrived in 1949 to start the very first Caribbean charter business. They were major contributors to both the restoration of English Harbour and to Antigua's yachting boom. They operate the oldest yacht charter service and open from 0830-1600. Their office is just a few steps toward Falmouth Harbour from Nelson's Dockyard, on the right-hand side of the road. Nicholson Yachts listen to VHF: 68, "English Harbour Radio." They provide a mail drop (c/o Nicholson Yacht Charters, Antigua), phone and fax, crew placement and shore support, medical insurance, bookbinding, laminating, and photocopies.

Farther down the road, Jane's Yacht Services (VHF: 68 "Yacht Services") and Antigua Yacht Services specialize in yacht communications and professional yacht and crew services. They are past Nicholson Yachts, just about where Falmouth Harbour begins. Both have email stations. Jane's Yacht Services is a friendly informal place with a book swap. You can have your mail sent here (Jane's Yacht Services, English Harbour, Antigua). They have a full communications service. They supply island information, arrange crew placement, run a provisioning service, send FedEx's, do absentee yacht management, and they fill propane tanks on Tuesdays and Thursdays (bring them before 1000). They also can arrange secretarial services, and organize yacht deliveries. You can arrange a marine survey with Canter de Jage at Dutchman Surveys here.

Antigua Yacht Services (VHF: 68) can

also be used as a mail drop (Antigua Yacht Services, Nelson's Dockyard Post Office, English Harbour, Antigua), they have full communications and a crew placement service, and are agents for FedEx. Apart from superyacht services, they do absentee and project management and will put you in touch with qualified technicians. They organize varnishing, cleaning, laundry, provisioning, courier, and parts procurement. They also work with Peters and May for shipping yachts.

Caribbean Concierge Services is an agency that organizes anything and everything that professional yachts need. Tina, who runs it, will book your berth, organize your fuel and provisions, arrange for technicians, and even work things out with the airport so the owner's private jet landing goes smoothly.

Chandlery

Falmouth Harbour Chandlery and Fuel Dock has duty-free prices on a supply of stainless steel fastenings, hoses, cleaners, lubricants, and a big range of starting and deep cycle batteries.

Antigua Slipway Chandlery has a branch downstairs in the Yacht Club building in Falmouth.

The selection at the Yacht Club outlet is more general and a little less technical than over in the slipway. But you will find what you need to keep your teak decks in trim. If you need something not at hand, ask Gay. She is very helpful.

The Catamaran Marina has a good, small chandlery with hardware, ropes, fenders, the best deep-sea fishing equipment, and Sebago Shoes.

Technical Yacht Services Electrics/Electronics

Dynamic Electrics (VHF: 68) is run by Wayne Ross, a whizz at sorting out any electrical problems on boats, aided by his energetic young team. Wayne is prompt and offers good and expert service to both large and small yachts. He can handle all the usual problems be it fault finding in wiring, a malfunctioning alternator, or problems with inverters and chargers. He also repairs faulty appliances like washing machines and microwaves. He is an agent and can supply or repair all the Miele line of appliances. In addition to being an electrical engineer, Wayne is also a specialist in galvanic corrosion. His business is in Swetes (on the hill on the road as you head out for St. Johns), but give him a call and he will come visit (464-8351).

Cay Electronics has a duty-free concession and is part of a marine electronics chain, with shops in Antigua, BVI, and Rhode Island. They service, sell, and install everything from radars to alternators, including the modern satcom systems, and, being part of a chain, supply good backup as far as the US. Andrew Ford owns the Antigua branch and he is pleasant to deal with. He has Vann, a good general electronics man working with him. You can call them VHF: 68.

Caribbean Current is almost next door to Cay Electronics. Caribbean Current specializes in electrics, from starters and alter-

MOUNTAINS & MANGROVES

nators to rewiring and batteries. They do any kind of troubleshooting, as well as complete rewire jobs, and they install solar systems. They also do some electronics.

Marionics is behind the Catamaran Club. Owner Arougoo Adams has also been in the marine electrics/electronics business for a long time and he is good. He sells and repairs a wide range of equipment, including the newest VHF radios, SSB radiotelephones, autopilots, Vsats, and TVs. He is agent for Seatel. He also repairs generators, regulators, and inverters, and he keeps VHF radios in stock. Most new gear is by special order, so you can get exactly what you need, duty-free. Marionics is an agent for Atlas shore power systems and Xantrex charger/inverter systems.

Technical Yacht Services Rigging

Stan Pearson's Antigua Rigging Service is behind the Catamaran Club. This is Antigua's largest rigging company and they work in close association with FKG Rigging in St. Martin. This makes for a flexible arrangement whereby everything available in St. Martin can be brought over quickly. It also means that if you need something measured in St. Martin and fixed in Antigua, or vice versa, it's no problem. On-site swaging goes up to 16mm and they have a machine to handle rod-rigging terminals up to large sizes. Their new office has space for a retail section, which includes deck hardware and a big rope selection. They provide warranty and service for some major European builders, such

as Oyster and Swan, and are set up to undertake complete refits and project management.

A & A Rigging is on the left hand side of the road before Watermaker Services, as you walk in the direction of the Cat Club from English Harbour. It is run by Ashley who graduated from the Antigua Yacht Club's Youth Sailing program and stayed with the marine industry. For many years he worked for Antigua Rigging Service and is now doing very well in his own business. He will do anything from replacing a swage fitting to getting a brand new mast and rig. He will be happy to come to your boat and sort out your problems. He maintains a very good relationship with his former company and so can subcontract big swages or rod terminals if he does not have the equipment.

Technical Yacht Services Woodwork

Woodstock (VHF: 68) is farther down the road than A&A Rigging, on the right. This shop is run by qualified shipwright Andrew Robinson from the UK. He is a wooden boat enthusiast who likes to restore old wooden boats. His business started as a woodwork shop, doing anything from replanking to fancy interior joinery, but has expanded to include painting (Awlgrip, Stirling), glasswork, including carbon fiber, and an engineering shop for stainless and aluminum fabrication. For teak decks they use Teak Decking Systems. This combination of skills puts them in an especially strong position for complete refit

and restoration work, including classical restoration. Their expertise sometimes has them going to the US for a job, and sometimes working for big US companies down here. Andrew works with a flexible team, so there are plenty of people on hand for large jobs.

The next businesses are on the final stretch of road that runs to the Catamaran Club. On the right side, Jerry Bardoe runs Chippy (VHF: 68). He has been around since the days when most boats were built of wood, and no one has more experience in Antigua at running an excellent woodworking shop. He will build or rebuild anything from a rub rail through to the liquor locker, matching the fanciest charter yacht cabinetry. He and his team are good at teak decks and make gratings to fancy shapes. These are the people to come to for acrylic repairs; they can renew the crazed Perspex or Lexan in your aluminum hatches. They are also part of Refit Antigua, with Awlgrip Antigua, and Total Fabrication. In addition, you can arrange to buy all your teak

and exotic lumber through Chippy.

Antigua Boatbuilders is on the main road, between Woodstock and Chippy. Oliver Greensmith, the owner, has worked in Antigua for some years and made a name building some small, classic wooden day-sailors, which look fabulous. He does all kinds of woodwork on yachts, from replacing teak decks to interior cabinetry. He will also undertake full refits, contracting and supervising any work he does not do himself. His partner Lynn Roach, runs the metal-working side of the business. He machines, welds, and fabricates all metals and some plastics. He can undertake both small and large jobs.

Technical Yacht Services Mechanics/Welding

Steve Miller's Marine Power Services (MPS, VHF: 68) is on the right hand side of the road heading from English Harbour Village to Falmouth. It is a big building, easy to spot, set back a little way from the road. Steve, originally from England, heads

Chris Doyle

MOUNTAINS & MANGROVES

an enthusiastic team, which does all kinds of fabrication, welding, and mechanical work; they are very professional and experienced. They have portable equipment for onboard welding of all types. MPS sells and repairs all makes of diesel engines and generators and they are agents for Caterpillar and Yanmar marine engines and Northern Lights generators. They have become very good at hydraulics and are importing the special pipes and fittings used on superyachts. Another specialty is designing and making bimini frames, spray dodgers, and davits.

Seagull Services Center is run by Flemming Niehorster. It is on the right side of the road, a few steps up the hill on a road locally known as Crack Alley. Turn up right by Caribbean Current. Flemming fixes diesels, generators, gear boxes, and hydraulics systems and is agent for Northern Lights generators, MTU, Hurth, Man, and Borgwarner. He is also a full Perkins dealer for sales and service. He also represents Lewmar, Navtec, Harken, Parker, and Rondal.

Multiserve (VHF:68) is a mechanical workshop specializing in maintaining and repairing diesel engines, pumps and all plumbing installations. It is owned by Wesley, who has over 20 years experience in the field including time as a diesel engineer for MPS. Wesley has now opened his own shop in his specialty, and you will find him in the same building as Woodstock Boatbuilders. Fabweld is about a kilometer down the road from English Harbour towards St. James's Club. It is owned by Handle Warner, an Antiguan who was brought up in England, where he spent many years welding high-pressure gas pipes. He is now back home running his own company, which specializes in machining and onboard welding. He has excellent mobile equipment. Handle welds all metals, including stainless and aluminum, and is good at doing jobs in place on the fancy new superyachts, as well as on cruisers. Greg Outboards (VHF: 68) will fix your outboard if you give him a call (775-7576). (See also Seagull Inflatables below)

See also Antigua Boatbuilding for metalwork in the woodwork section.

Technical Yacht Services other specialties

Watermaker Services (VHF: 68), is run by Julian Gildersleeve, a watermaker specialist originally from the UK. He sells and services all kinds of watermakers and efficiently fixes any watermaker problem. This is an excellent place to buy a watermaker, as Julian knows exactly which systems break down and how often, and which are reliable. He keeps a good selection of spares in stock for most makes, and can quickly bring in anything he does not have. You will find him down the main road, heading towards the Cat Club, well past Cay Electronics.

Dino's Carpet Care does complete carpet cleaning, but more than that, Dino can clean mattresses, sails, even running rigging – anything that has gotten grungy. He can even get diesel fuel out of a Persian rug. So if the owner is coming tomorrow, and

the carpets are a mess after a wild crew party, give him a call. You can also seek him out at his workshop, which is on the left side of the road about halfway between English Harbour and the Catamaran Club.

Seagull Inflatables is owned by Canter de Jager (in partnership with Dino). Canter has vastly increased the scope of the company to cover all tenders, outboards, and safety gear. They do all liferaft and inflatable repair work. They are certified for inspecting and repairing Avon, Zodiac, Plastimo, Givens, Switlik, Revere (RFD), Ocean Safety, Autoflug, and BFA liferafts. They repair all makes of inflatable and are agents for the sale and warranty work on AB, Avon, Caribe, and Zodiac. They can tackle the really big jobs, including re-tubing large ribs. In an emergency, they can even send a team down-island for a repair. They now also sell and repair inflatable fenders, so essential for the big boats, as well as flexible fuel and water tanks. They also cover the full range of safety gear, from fire extinguishers and suppression systems to lifejackets and ACR

and McMurdo Epirbs. In addition, they have become one of the Caribbean's foremost tender-care centers, for all yacht tenders, whether fiberglass or inflatable. They can haul out, repair, and service your tender, whatever the make. They also service and repair all outboard motors, and they can sell you a new one.

Canter de Jager is also a qualified marine surveyor (USSA member) under the name Dutchman Marine Surveys and Services. He can do insurance, damage, and condition surveys, and he can oversee repairs and refits and look after your yacht while you are away.

John Shears' Seahorse Studios is across the main road, just above the Catamaran Club. John and his assistant Roxanna have state-of-the-art equipment for computerized designs. They generate beautiful boat names, custom silk-screened t-shirts and caps, and embroidered caps can be arranged.

Other services in this area are probably best contacted by radio or phone. John Bentley (VHF: 68, "Sea Pony") has been

doing commercial towing, salvage, and diving work in Antigua for years and he is the best for these operations. His tug, Sea Pony, is also available for commercial, survey, and film work. He looks after yachts when owners are away and is an excellent choice for this job, especially in the hurricane season, when real expertise is essential. He rents secure moorings in Falmouth, handles yacht deliveries, and untangles superyachts' anchors from one another on a daily basis. Sallie Harker at Nauti-Signs (VHF: 68) does beautiful traditional sign painting, including gold-leaf work, the only answer for a classic yacht.

Jane Coombs has a first-rate yacht soft furnishings studio called Comfort Zone. The best way to get in touch is by phone (720-3926).

Provisioning

Falmouth Harbour has two decent supermarkets. Dockside Liquors and Supermarket is owned by the same Antiguan family that owns Lion Car Rental. They are conveniently placed on the waterfront in the Yacht Club Marina Complex. They stock all manner of drinks – spirits, wines, beers, soft drinks, snacks, and ice – as well as having a complete supermarket with deli items and fresh produce. They open Monday to Saturday 0800-1900, and Sundays 0900-1700. You can dinghy right up and put the cases on board, or they will help you drop your goods to English Harbour before 1600. They will also top up mobile phones.

Bailey's Supermarket, near the Catamaran Club, is reasonably priced, takes orders over the radio (VHF: 68), and will deliver large orders. They open 0900 to 1900, Monday through Saturdays. Apart from a wide selection of canned, packaged, and frozen foods, they keep a good stock of local vegetables, and the best day to go for fresh produce is Thursday. If you need some flowers to decorate your yacht, there is a flower shop next door, and for an ice cream try their Sweets Store. Bailey's also stocks household and hardware items, including cooking pans, engine oil, and duct tape. Brits can get their Marmite here. Bailey's is

302

easy to get to by dinghy, via the Catamaran Club, from anywhere in Falmouth and just a short bus ride from English Harbour. If you are stocking up there, you will get a lift back with your shopping.

If you want someone else to do it all for you, there are professional provisioning services. Trans Caribbean Marketing (TCM) is opposite the Falmouth Harbour Marina. You can drop by and pick up a provisioning list. They fly in all their produce to keep it fresh.

Shore Solutions is another good, dedicated provisioning agency for the professional yachts, and they are right in Falmouth Harbour Marina.

Coffee lovers should visit the Carib Bean Coffee Company, owned by Tim and Nora Wall. The turn off is just at the brow of the hill as you leave Falmouth on the left hand side. You will like the coffee smell as you enter their little Caribbean house, and they will give you a cup of espresso as you enjoy the view and order your coffee supply. They offer an outstanding range of flavors and you can have your own special blend mixed

and labeled with your yacht name.

Why spend hours in the galley baking a birthday cake when you can visit Tony's Cake Shop opposite Bailey's Supermarket? Cakes are made to order, or can be bought from their stock items.

For a really big supermarket, take a taxi to the Epicurean at Woods. (See our St. John's section, page 330.) You can also get there by taking the bus to St. John's and then the dollar shuttle from the West Bus Station. I noticed an even bigger supermarket was under construction on the road from St. John's to Dickenson Bay. It should be worth checking out.

For the biggest variety of fresh Caribbean produce, take the bus to the local market in St. John's. It is good any weekday and best on Saturdays.

Also, a fair taxi ride away, in the same place, you will find a trio that combine to make Antigua's oldest, best and most complete provisioners. Best Cellars is an excellent wine and Liquor that provides wines to many of the charter yachts. Island Provisions, do the main wholesale provi-

MOUNTAINS & MANGROVES

sioning for both the hotel and the yacht industry, and if you like to nose around personally, Gourmet Basket is an upmarket supermarket for the discerning customer.

However, for major provisioning, you only need to get in touch with them, and they can arrange everything and deliver.

Shopping

Souvenir shoppers will find several shops of interest. Portobello in the Yacht Club Marina sells colorful pareos, souvenirs, and smart swimwear and ornaments. Rhythm of Blue is an art gallery featuring the work of Nancy Nicholson, Scrim, and several others. It opens Monday to Saturday 1000-1800. Nancy (daughter of Desmond of English Harbour fame) digs all her clay from local deposits and uses freehand glazing and scraffito techniques to decorate bowls, plates, vases, and more. The colors and themes are of the ocean: deep blues to pale turquoise, with fish, dolphins, and early Amerindian designs. Mike Scrim, her partner in the shop, is a master of the art of scrimshaw, but you will also find his silver jewelry and the work of other jewelers and painters.

Next door, Jason Pickering's photo studio does all kinds of photography, including passport photos, and they sell art photos.

We be Stitching (by English Harbour Fruit and Veg) and Stitches are two shops that specialize in finely embroidered hats and sports shirts, customized with names and logos for yachts. We be Stitching is very reasonable, but with limited base stock. Stiches is run by Chris and Elizabeth, who have good quality polo shirts, caps, and hats. The shop always looks closed, but they work behind the shop and it is best to call them. A little farther down the road, Island Life Boutique (in the Sam and Dave Laundry building) has a wild selection of wind chimes, some handicrafts, and women's clothing.

Restaurants

As English Harbour turns into Falmouth, the restaurants continue along the road. Trappas Bar (VHF: 68) is one of the hot eating places in Falmouth. The atmosphere is very informal and unpretentious, with wooden seats and bottles of soy on the tables. It is open to the kitchen where you can see your dinner being cooked. The blackboard menu is always

Party at Shirley Heights.

Chris Doyle

Chris Doyle

changing and they offer an amazing variety of dishes that will suit all tastes, including fresh fish when it is available. Their simple pricing has all main dishes the same price. Trappas is fair value and fills up fast. Make reservations early.

Le Cap Horn (open from 1900, winter season only, closed Thursdays) is a perfectly charming family-run restaurant where you can enjoy good French food or genuine Italian pizzas from a wood oven in their pizza parlor. You will be made to feel welcome by Helene from France, who will come and explain all the daily specials she has dreamt up. Her husband, Gustavao, from Peru, is an inventive chef who blends many delightful and light sauces into his cuisine, using herbs from their small garden. Like all first class restaurants, they bake their own bread. They offer many seafood and meat dishes. Save room for dessert.

On the other side of the road, Bambi is a small Italian Restaurant in a sweet local house run by Armando, who makes his own fresh pasta and is open from 1830-

2200 nightly. He also cooks seafood and other dishes.

The Cockpit, right at the turn off to Antigua Yacht Club Marina, is a bar known for lively and good-looking staff, and a happy your from 1900 (when it opens) to 2100. It is a late night place, open till 0200 any day and 0300 on weekends. Angie, the owner (who also has the foredeck bar in Jolly Harbour) plans to be serving food for the coming season.

Next come some local restaurants that offer good value for money, with tasty local food at reasonable prices. Tax and service will not be added and you will appreciate the cheaper beers. Next to Cap Horn, Grace before Meals serves very tasty rotis, local meals, and very tender conch. It is small, with just a few tables inside. Farther down the road, Jackie's Kwik Shop faces Falmouth Harbour, with front-view seats outside on the balcony as well as a sizeable dining room. Jackie opens all day and her meals feature Creole conch, curried chicken, local fish, rotis, and more. Farther towards Falmouth, Collin's Place offers the

MOUNTAINS & MANGROVES

Falmouth Harbour   Chris Doyle

very best value for money and good local food. It is owned and run by Sandy, with help from her mum, Vera, and the name is a tribute to Collin, Sandy's brother who works on yachts.

Farther down the road, above Cay Electronics, The Waterfront Hostel, is run by Julia and Dennis Compton. This is an inexpensive place for crews to stay ashore between jobs, but they also do very inexpensive food, from breakfast through to a light lunch menu, and then a single-dish dinner, which changes daily. It has a relaxing, clubby atmosphere, but you may need to let them know you are coming in the evening so they cook enough food. While there, you can enjoy a Sam Adams beer.

The Mad Mongoose is in a brightly painted building on the road to the yacht club. It flows through several rooms to a pretty garden with tables and chairs. Their offer of 24-hour free wifi usually keeps a few people sitting here even when it is closed. The action gets going at happy hour, which is 1600-1900. It is popular spot for dinner, when an ever-changing menu features dishes like steak and kidney pie, stir-fry, and fresh fish. They are closed Mondays and they go on holiday from August to October.

The Antigua Yacht Club Marina restaurant is spacious and elegant, and takes up a large portion of the upstairs in the new Yacht Club Marina complex. The view is great – you sit and look down some of the most exclusive yachts in the world. They open every day for breakfast, lunch, and dinner. The location is perfect for a sunset cocktail, followed by a dinner of good, straightforward Italian food, including homemade bread and many fresh pasta and seafood dishes. (Try the lobster pasta.)

Skullduggery is downstairs in the Yacht Club Marina building. This is a coffee bar where you can get coffee that will jet-launch you into the new day, as well as croissants, donuts, lunchtime sandwiches, and more. They have several internet stations so you can buzz on the internet. Seabreeze, next door, is a European style café run by Manny. They serve great coffee, wonderful gelato, have lunchtime sandwiches, and of course, a little wine to help them go down.

The Antigua Yacht Club is a two-story building, normally for members only, except after races. Although they have no reciprocal arrangements, if you walk in with any yacht club card and look pleasant, you have a good chance of being accepted. Those planning to stay for a long time should become members. Pasta Rite Ya (closed Sunday) is a pleasant small bar and restaurant next to the water, with a dinghy dock outside. It is run by Laurence and Florence from France. They open Tuesday to Friday for lunch and Monday to Saturday for dinner. Florence, who used to be the chef at HQ2 does the cooking, and her cuisine is a fusion of Italian, French, and Caribbean flavors. You will eat well in a relaxed, intimate atmosphere.

Famous Mauro is on the road between English Harbour and the Catamaran Marina. The pleasant, open-air room has a huge wood-fired brick oven as its central feature and Mauro and Roberta will whip out the most excellent pizzas for dinner. Salads and extra items are available. The downstairs part of the business is a bakery, offering fresh bread, croissants, and Danish. You can come to their hole-in-the-wall window open 0700-1400; otherwise they sell through the Falmouth supermarkets daily.

La Mia Cucina is the Catamaran Club restaurant. It is a fine Italian restaurant run by Davide and Barbara Anfi who used to run Harmony Hall, as well as other restaurants. It opens Monday to Saturday for lunch and dinner, and breakfast is also planned. They have lots of local seafood, lobster, and pasta. You will eat well here.

It is worth noting that if you stroll way down the beach to the west, a local lady called Wendy cooks up good food for beachgoers on Fridays and Saturdays, starting around lunch.

Ashore

If, after all that food, you need to get fit again, then Temo's Sports Center rents everything necessary for tennis or squash. Their Chez Maman Restaurant opens for breakfast and lunch Monday to Saturday, with a blackboard posted with salads, burgers, steaks and daily specials. They also open on Thursday nights for mussels in wine and cream sauce, and on Friday nights for a traditional bouilabaisse. Lots of other things go on at Temo, including include chess nights, darts tournaments, pool tournaments, and yoga classes. The best thing is to go and have a drink and ask about the current schedule of events. They also have a great book swap, and if you like it all so much that you want a permanent home, English Harbour Realty is in the same compound.

If you prefer to work off your calories by horse riding, then you should contact Sarah Scott at Spring Hill Riding Club. This is the home of the Antigua Horse Society, a member of the Federation Equestre International. Sarah's rides are grand fun, covering beautiful and unspoiled country. A full-day or half-day trip makes a perfect break from the varnish, and for those with ambitions to learn dressage, this is the place. If that sounds too energetic, there are two beaches for swimming. The one in Freeman Bay is pleasant and used by both hotel guests and yachtspeople. However, many prefer the more informal Pigeon Beach where topless sunning is acceptable. Snacks and cold drinks are sometimes available from stands on the beach.

While on the subject of health and beauty, everyone should know about Tree House group, who are easy to contact on VHF: 68. Tree House is a complete body shop for men and women, run by a friendly and enthusiastic group. On the beauty side, they do hairdressing and have a complete beauty shop, with everything from facials to pedicure. On the health side, you can get ten types of massage, including

MOUNTAINS & MANGROVES

Swedish, Shiatsu, deep tissue, and Hypertonics. If you put out your back pulling one anchor too many, two osteopaths are on hand. For medical problems, Dr. Patricia Miller-Nanton makes regular visits.

Sacred Space offers a variety of massage, beauty, and meditation services.

Water Sports

It is amazing how many calories you lose diving, and right outside English Harbour there are dives with a variety of hard and soft corals and reef fish, to say nothing of old anchors and artifacts.

Soul Immersions Dive Shop is in a cute local building in Falmouth Harbour. It is run by Sawn and Kamesha. They do a morning dive at about 0900 and an afternoon dive around 1300 or 1400. Apart from taking you diving, Soul Immersions is an equipment service center, with hydro-testing and full equipment repair.

Sea Wolf Diving School is a professional Padi dive shop where they teach diving and have a very flexible program for yacht crews. Bryan Cunningham, the owner, dives once a day at 1000. In addition, he has a good retail shop with Cressi and Shearwood diving gear and occasional good deals on bulk snorkeling gear for outfitting yachts. You can also call "Aquanaut" on VHF: 68 to go diving. John Charlesworth will be happy to collect you from your yacht. Aquanaut Divers is in the same building as Jane's Yacht Services. They also offer all kinds of courses.

Tony Fincham came here on New Freedom many years ago and one of his claims to fame is the "Fincham Follies" show at Agent's Week. Tony stayed to get involved in diving and archeology and sometimes restaurants. He is an agent for Sea Quest and Shearwood, and he can import duty-free to those on yachts. Tony's is a one-man operation and he specializes in small groups and special requests. He is an avid photographer, both under water and on land. He will fill tanks and repair equipment. He can do commercial work for those with underwater problems. You can call him on VHF: 68 or find him at Dockyard Divers, in Nelson's Dockyard.

The dive shops maintain buoys on most of the dive sites that you can use if you are going in your own dinghy.

The Pillars of Hercules (20 to 48 feet) is an easy dive, accessible by dinghy, at the mouth of English Harbour. Just anchor off the Pillars or look for the dive buoy. There are several reef ledges, lots of small reef fish, and an old anchor. If you continue east into the next small bay, you come to Nanton Point. This is still within easy dinghy range in calm weather, and a much more delightful dive among huge boulders and ledges that slope from 20 to 70 feet. They are well decorated with soft corals and sponges. Some boulders make caverns and tunnels large enough to swim through. A delightful variety of reef fish swim by, including porkfish, hogfish, angel fish, and many in the grouper family.

If you continue into the next bay, again you will notice some big boulders at the eastern end. Diving is good all over this

Chris Doyle

bay and local operations use it as three dive sites. Anchoring can be tricky, but with luck you can find a dive mooring.

If you keep going east, you will come to Cape Shirley, right below Shirley Heights. This dive goes from 55 to 120 feet and is amid giant boulders that have tumbled down the cliff to form tunnels, gullies, and caves. There is also an overhanging wall. You will see a profusion of hard and soft corals and rich fish life, including spadefish. There is a good chance of seeing spotted eagle rays and sharks.

Stingray Alley (40 to 80 feet) is in the entrance channel to English Harbour. Coral grows along the rock sides, including a handsome stand of pillar coral with many reef fish and lobsters. In the sand between you will find whole families of stingrays.

At Barracuda Reef (55 to 120 feet), the dive is among a series of deep ledges and caves. Barracuda hang out here, sometimes whole schools of them. You will also see giant barrel sponges, coral formations, lobsters, and reef fish, and there is a good chance of seeing nurse sharks.

Yacht Racing

The Antigua Yacht Club has local racing from time to time, as well as well-attended Laser and Optimist races.

Everyone is welcome to participate. Ask for a program at the yacht club. Anyone can join the yacht races, and if you don't have a rating, you will be given one.

No mention of this area would be complete without mentioning Antigua Race Week. In days of old, the residents had mixed feelings about the Dockyard, regarding it as a wicked place: "The Sabbath was unknown. The yard bell rang on Sundays for people to labor. Ships of war were anchored here and acts of immorality of the worst description were perpetrated." In some ways it hasn't changed much, especially during the riotous aquatic carnival known as "Antigua Race Week," when there is a lot of hard sailing and partying and everyone has a marvelous time. This is the Caribbean's premier regatta and it starts on the last Sunday in April. It has been going for well over 30 years and attracts some 270 racing yachts from 20 countries, and at least as many onlookers. All the races take place along the coast, and make a magnificent spectacle, which is enjoyed by visitors and locals alike.

A week before Antigua Race week, there is the more genteel Classic Yacht Regatta, organized by Kenneth and Jane Coombs. This provides a magnificent spectacle of exquisite traditional yachts. To be

MOUNTAINS & MANGROVES

a classic yacht is not a matter of age or material, it is a matter of style: the right sheer, a straight keel, billowing sails, and long bowsprits all help. Anyone interested in any of these events should contact the Antigua Yacht Club. Another feature around Antigua Race Week is the Megayacht Regatta for the really big boys (over 100 feet long). It includes a race from Guadeloupe and an ocean triangle race. The sheer sizes of the boats make it quite a spectacle.

Antigua is now home to the new RORC Caribbean 600 – a 605-mile race that has participants weaving in and out and around all the northern islands from Barbuda to the Saintes to Saba and St. Martin. It has to be completed in 4 days.

If you do not have a boat to race in, Falmouth is the Caribbean base of On Deck, a charter company that specializes in regattas and races, both bare and crewed yachts. They are also an RYA training center and you can train to Yachtmaster Ocean.

Indian Creek

When the English Harbour social scene gets so much that you cannot stand anoth-er happy hour, set sail for Indian Creek, which lies less than 2 miles to the east. This perfectly charming little hideaway winds back between cactusy hills and is currently so deserted that you will see more goats and birds than people. Eric Clapton owns the house on Indian Creek Point.

Navigation

Sunken Rock lies in the entrance to Indian Creek. It is just below the surface and makes a great scuba site. The sea usually breaks over the rock and it can be seen in good light. However, it is a definite navigational hazard, so do not forget about it. You can pass on either side, but there is more room on the southwest side. Once past Sunken Rock, carry on down the middle of the creek. Close to shore, the channel takes a sharp turn to the west and is somewhat narrow. It is about 9 feet deep at the turn, and once inside, there is a fair-sized basin in which to anchor. Our soundings showed it to be 10 to 12 feet for the most part. It shoals rapidly past the fence on the north side and the end of the road on the southern hill. Yachts drawing less than 5 feet can get well up in the mangroves. Indian Creek is so protected that

INDIAN CREEK

you have the feeling of being completely landlocked. It feels cozy enough to ride out a storm, though I am told that the sea level rises significantly in hurricanes.

Mamora Bay

Mamora Bay is a well-protected lagoon and is the site of the aquatic activities of the prestigious St. James's Club. It may be the only place in the Caribbean where you can tie to the dock and get room service on board. It is popular during the season with large luxury power yachts.

Navigation

The entrance is down wind. There are no markers, so you will have to find the channel entrance on your own. This is not hard, but do it in good light. Approach close to Standfast Point and follow the headland up into the channel, staying outside any shallow water. You should also be able to see the barrier reef on the north side of the channel. Once past Sober Island, stay in the middle of the channel. If you approach from the north, stay well clear of Willoughby Bay, which has reef most of the way across the entrance. Some people have mistaken Willoughby Bay for Mamora Bay. Do not try to go in until you are sure of your position.

The inner lagoon was dredged to 15 feet, and the sand from the dredging was used to create the inner beach. Depths have been a bit up and down since. Current depths allow entry of a vessel drawing 11 feet with no problem. The bottom is sand and mud. Once inside, you can go stern-to the dock or anchor out in the lagoon. Anchor on the west side of the bay, well clear of the beaches and the water sports. A strong southeasterly can make the bay somewhat uncomfortable, but this seldom happens.

Services

The St. James's Club stands by on VHF: 68/11. You can get water and ice on the dock and the electrical outlets provide 220

volts at 60-cycles, 50 amps. You will also get hooked up to a telephone line and cable TV. Laundry can be arranged. There is space for 15 yachts on the dock, but for large yachts advance booking is advisable in season. There are no customs or immigration facilities, and you must clear in before coming here. Captain Noel (764-8903) is in charge of berthing, but anyone on the dock will help.

Room service is available on the dock, and you can make arrangements for the club to cater your party.

On the road outside the St. James's Club, behind the generator, is a food wholesaler called Horizons Supplies. Yacht customers value them for fresh meat, portion-controlled frozen meats, seafood, and produce.

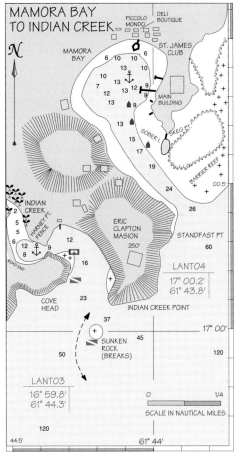

MOUNTAINS & MANGROVES

MAMORA BAY

Ashore

The St. James's Club provides a whole gamut of activities. Larger yachts get automatic membership, which enables them to many of the same privileges as the guests, including all non-motorized water sports. Those anchored can buy a day pass. At a price, additional options open to everyone include horseback riding and a hair and beauty salon.

Evenings at the St. James's Club are on the formal side and require at least slacks and a sports shirt or equivalent. Most of the restaurants have some kind of nightly entertainment; they are not usually all open at once. The most popular for yachtspeople is the Docksider, a waterfront grill where you can eat lobster, fish, steak, and more. Others include Piccolo Mondo, Coco's, and the Rainbow Garden.

After dinner you can enjoy wandering up to the Jacaranda Bar, which sometimes has a disco. When the hotel is full, the restaurants sometimes stop accepting outside meal guests from anchored yachts, though those paying dockage are assured of a table.

The Hideout is a reasonable walk down the road. It is a creative place, owned by a Dutch family of two artists and a chef. The chef, Max Freling, is an excellent cook and the meals are reasonably priced. Plus, you can admire a room full of his mother Norae's imaginative work. She paints and sculpts, using a variety of materials, and her papier mache models are attractive and inexpensive. Some paintings by her husband, Bill, may also be on show. They open Tuesday to Saturday nights from 1900.

Water Sports

The Mamora Bay Dive Shop, a Padi facility, is close to the dock and run by Linda. You can join a dive, take a course, or reserve a private dive charter.

Willoughby Bay

Willoughby Bay is next to Mamora Bay, to the northeast. It is over a mile wide and 2 miles deep and a reef runs most of the way across the entrance. Yachts occasionally enter through the channel and anchor behind the reef. Since there is nothing very special here and as it has claimed more than its fair share of keels, I recommend giving it a wide berth.

NONSUCH BAY AND GREEN ISLAND

Green Island is Antigua's easternmost tip. It is the gateway to Nonsuch Bay, a reef-protected expanse of water covering several square miles. This is a wonderful gunkholing area, with a wealth of good overnight anchorages in settings that vary from protected mangrove creeks to open vistas, where only a reef lies between you and the Atlantic Ocean, rolling unbroken from Africa.

Navigation

The easiest approach is from the south. Expect a brisk 9-mile beat to windward from English Harbour. Make sure you stand well clear of the reefs that cover most of the entrance to Willoughby Bay. About a mile and a half south of Green Island, on Friars Head, is a conspicuous white house that looks like a lighthouse. Pass outside the 127-foot-high York Island to its north, by which time Green Island will become obvious. There are two bays on Green

Island's south coast: Tenpound Bay and Rickett Harbour. The headland that separates them has a big reef extending both to the south and east. Give it good clearance.

Green Island

Green Island is unspoiled by buildings. There is abundant bird life, including red-billed tropicbirds, white-crowned pigeons, ospreys, night herons, and pelicans. The island is under lease to the Mill Reef Club and only members are allowed behind the beachline. (All Antigua beaches are public.) The Mill Reef Club uses Tenpound Bay and Rickett Harbour. Please avoid going ashore, making noise, or zooming around in a dinghy when you see these bays in use. They do not mind yachtspeople going a little way inshore in the northwestern part of the island.

Tenpound Bay

Tenpound Bay is a charming spot to sit and enjoy the view. The surrounding land is a natural rock garden. Low cliffs give way to dark green shrubby trees. You see tall

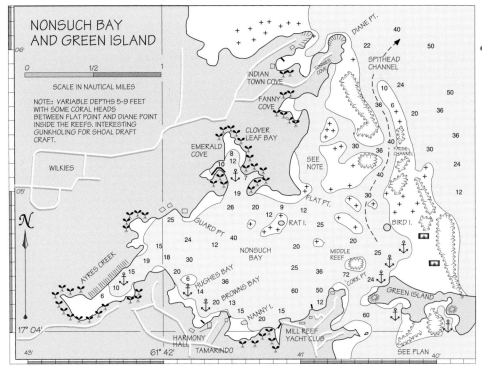

cactuses and a generous sprinkling of century plants with their lofty stems and bright yellow flowers. When sitting palls, there are two small beaches and some fair snorkeling. Marked trails take you to the southeastern part of the island.

Navigation

Unfortunately, the anchorage is so tiny that two boats are a crowd. As there is barely room to turn round inside, it is tricky, especially for yachts of 35 feet or over. Drop your mainsail before you enter, as there may not be enough room to come head to the wind in the channel. The anchorage may be rolly in southeasterly winds. Approach close to the eastern headland and eyeball your way in past the reefs. It can be very rough at the entrance, but it gets steadily calmer as you go in. You first pass a small bay with a pretty palm-lined beach. There is a narrow cut of deep water going into this beach that is used by the Mill Reef Club, and makes for easy access to the beach with the dinghy. Carry on past this and anchor in about 9 to 11 feet of water at the entrance to the inner bay. You will almost certainly have to use a stern anchor to keep clear of the shore in case the wind shifts.

Rickett Harbour

Rickett Harbour is a perfect, quiet spot with two lovely white sand beaches. A hill rises on one side and low rocky ledges with plenty of cactuses and century plants lie along the shore. Snorkeling is fair on the reefs on both sides of the harbor.

Navigation

As you sail up from the south, pass a few hundred yards off York Island and Neck O'Land, then head in toward Submarine Rock till you can make out the reef extending south from Rickett Harbour. Pass to the west of this reef and follow it right up into the harbor. You will find good anchor-

age with plenty of room in 10 to 18 feet of water, sand bottom.

North and West Green Island

The north side of Green Island is protected by a barrier reef. You can find comfortable anchorage inside the reef anywhere between Green Island and Bird Island, in a vast expanse of turquoise water. The open ocean is just a reef away, giving a great feel of being out on the edge of the world. Impending squalls look majestic as they sweep in across the sea. There are two beaches: one is on the northwestern tip of Green Island, and the other is in West Bay. Snorkeling on the barrier reef is interesting.

When approaching from the south, keep halfway between Green Island and Cork Point, as a reef sticks out a good way off Green Island's western tip. Then stay fairly close to Green Island to avoid the big Middle Reef. This is no problem in good light, as it is clearly visible. The water immediately north of Green Island tends to be shallow, about 5 to 8 feet. The water is deeper toward the reef as you get closer to Bird Island. You can see this in the color of the water. If strong winds create a chop out

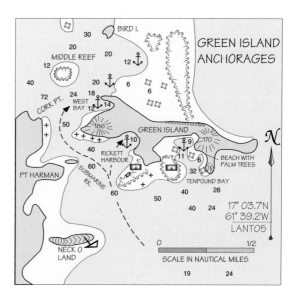

in the open water, you can tuck up close to the beach in West Bay, where there is 12 feet of water almost up to the sand beach.

Nonsuch Bay

This bay was named after the first visiting "yacht," a ship called the Nonsuch, which in 1647 found its way in through the small entrance and dropped anchor. Some 2 miles deep by one and a half wide, protected from the east by Green Island and the barrier reef, Nonsuch Bay is a gunkholer's delight. You can anchor almost anywhere in the bay, though the fetch is so long that in strong winds some places will get choppy. Let us take a clockwise tour from Cork Point.

Cork Point to Nanny Island

Most of the land from Cork point to Nanny Island is owned by the Mill Reef Club. This very exclusive resort has members who are likely to look on yachtspeople as unwelcome intruders. The Mill Reef Yacht Club is definitely not open to visitors, though it is based in a very pleasant

creek that has 8 feet of water up to the beginning of the mangroves. You might be a bit in the way here if there is a lot of sailing activity going on. However, just outside you can feel your way in to a pleasant spot between Nanny Island and the shore; you cannot go too far in as it shoals.

One advantage of this spot is a restaurant ashore, which is sometimes open. It has a great location with a dinghy dock, but when I visited in 2009 the restaurant was in one of its defunct stages. Check it out, it will probably come back to life.

Browns Bay

Browns Bay is easy to find. Pass Nanny Island, go around the next headland, and you are there. If you have a GPS, 17° 04.24'N, 61° 41.75'W should get you there. There is about 4 feet close to the head of the bay, but you can find comfortable anchorage outside this in 10 to 15 feet of water. Ashore you will see a dock and an old sugar mill up on the hill with a curious hexagonal shingle roof perched on top. From offshore trees hide the mill.

This is all part of Harmony Hall (VHF: 68), an elegant art gallery, boutique, restau-

Tenpound Bay

Chris Doyle

Chris Doyle

rant, and bar, owned by the Antigua Yacht Club Marina and Resort, headed by Carlo Falcone and managed by Jana. The bar is in the mill and you should bring your camera for the bird's eye view from the platform on top. The art gallery has an eclectic selection of work, featuring artists as varied as Jonathon Roulth (of Candid Camera fame), Graham Davis, Claire Frank, and Frane Lessac. Their boutique has the most artistic of local handicrafts and some exclusive dresses.

The restaurant, which has been mentioned in *Gourmet Magazine*, is in a delightful garden setting among flowers and hummingbirds, with a view over the bay. Lunch guests are welcome to use the swimming pool. Harmony Hall is open daily for lunch and for dinner on Fridays and Saturdays. They often open the restaurant on other nights for large groups when asked. The food is excellent, a combination of Caribbean and Italian flavors, and it gets so busy that reservations are necessary for Sunday lunch. They welcome

yachts and you can use their dinghy dock. They also run the ferry Luna for lunch and can pick you up from your yacht near Green Island. Luna picks up at about 1100 and drops back around 1400.

Charter yachts can use Harmony Hall as a pick up point for guests as it saves the guests the 9-mile beat to windward from English Harbour. Taxis can be arranged, and rooms are available. Harmony Hall owns a fleet of Dragons for racing.

Hughes Bay to Ayres Creek

There is a pleasant deserted spot off Hughes Bay in about 10 feet of water. You cannot go too far into the bay, as it is shallow. Some thin strips of beach invite exploration. Deep draft boats will need to watch out for the shoal to the north of Hughes Bay. For the most part, it has 7 to 9 feet over it, but there are one or two spots only 6 to 7 feet deep.

Development looks likely here in the

Caribbean 600 yachts beating up Antigua's east coast.

Chris Doyle

near future. Ayres Creek, at the head of Nonsuch Bay, is private and quiet. Apart from one new house, there is nothing here but limestone hills covered in scrub and little mangrove-lined bays. You can find an anchorage in 7 feet of water tucked up some of the way into the first mangrove-lined bay on the southeast side of the creek. This is a calm spot, perfect for anyone who has had too much sea time. You are surrounded by land and have the feeling of being in a river.

Ayres Creek to Clover Leaf Bay

There is not much between Ayres Creek and Clover Leaf Bay, though you could find anchorage just south of Guard Point near some new houses. It is deep here, with 25 to 30 feet quite close to shore. A big development is rapidly rising ashore, outside and around Clover Leaf Bay.

Clover Leaf Bay

Clover Leaf Bay, sometimes called Guynais Bay or Ledcoff Cove, is a deep mangrove-lined waterway, shaped like a clover leaf. You can explore all around the bay. There is 7 to 10 feet of water halfway up the western arm; 8 feet of water halfway up the northern creek, and 7 feet of water halfway up the eastern creek. There may be some shoaling as a result of construction. In case of a hurricane, you would find excellent shelter tucked up in the eastern creek.

Inside the Reef: Flat Point to Diane Point

You can eyeball your way through the reefs between Flat Point and Rat Island, where there is a passage about 9 feet deep. You can then turn north and, according to the charts, there should be 7 to 9 feet of water all the way inside the reef as far as Tonnies Cove. We found depths at the entrance to be shallower than the chart suggested and felt there was not enough safety margin for the average yacht drawing 6 to 7 feet. However, it looks like an intriguing area to explore in good light with a shoal draft craft.

Heading North: The Spithead Channel

Yachts heading north can leave via the Spithead Channel. You might want to proceed under motor and main as it is quite narrow. However, in good light conditions the reefs are clearly visible and the first part is in calm water. Start over by Bird Island. There is one little reef as you go north, almost in the middle of the channel. After you have passed that, just follow the deepwater channel between the reefs. As you get out toward the open sea, you have to resist the temptation to head out too soon, as the reef continues a long way down toward Diane Point, with 6 to 10 feet over it and big waves rolling in. Avoid the false channel that tempts many navigators. Unless you know the area exceptionally well, it is not worth trying to use this channel to get into Nonsuch Bay from the north as it is hard to see and it would be easy to get into trouble.

ANTIGUA'S NORTHEAST COAST

There are good anchorages inside the reefs along Antigua's northeastern coast, but these should be approached from the west side of Antigua via the Boon Channel. Otherwise, the whole of the northeast coast of Antigua is dangerous. The land is featureless and shoals extend up to 5 miles offshore. It should be given a very wide berth. If you have a shallow draft boat, Indian Town Cove can be a good anchorage (The bar is a little less than 6 feet.) The entrance is scary. Inside, the Long Bay Hotel has a good restaurant and dive shop.

Having said this, those staying in Antigua for a long time might like to know that there are some anchorages tucked into this coast, but the approaches are hairy enough to warrant a trusted companion with local knowledge. They include Mercer Creek Bay and Guiana Bay, which are both remote protected anchorages. The

Chris Doyle

MOUNTAINS & MANGROVES

largest community in this area is Seatons.

NORTHERN ANTIGUA
Boon Channel to Guiana Island

Northern Antigua has several anchorages dotted among reef-protected islands. Some of them are out-of-the-way spots where you can enjoy solitude and snorkeling. A shallow reef-studded bank provides some protection to Antigua's north coast. There is a navigable channel some 25 to 50 feet deep between this bank and the coast. It is called Boon Channel and it is the best way to approach northeast Antigua. The reef is not solid, but the many unmarked twisty passages through are best left alone. The easiest is Horse Shoe Reef Channel, above Prickly Pear Island, passing close to the east side of Horse Shoe Reef, but even this would be safer to negotiate going out rather than coming in. A dry coral patch has appeared on the western side of this channel, which is some help. If you are coming from or going to Barbuda, you have to pass around the western end of the reef at Diamond Bank. This bank is unmarked and dangerous. We give a GPS reading for the outer edge. The safest way to negotiate this bank is to keep Sandy Island due south until you are safely past the bank. When coming from the north, this means keeping Antigua well on your port hand until you can identify Sandy Island, then approach with Sandy Island magnetic due south. This gives you about 2 miles clearance from Diamond Bank.

You should only navigate through Boon Channel in good light so you can see the reefs. There is plenty of room to tack up the channel, staying between the coast and the reef system. It is possible to pass either side of Prickly Pear Island. The deepest water is outside, but you have to avoid many reefs to its north and west. There is room for most small yachts to short tack between Prickly Pear Island and the shore, but stay near the middle of the channel. A small ferry links Prickly Pear to the main-

land and tourists come out to snorkel and play Robinson Crusoe in luxury for a day. Once you are east of Prickly Pear, head toward Maiden Island on a bearing of about 143° magnetic, staying west of all the reefs off Long Island. Parham Channel is dredged to 16 feet and runs past Maiden Island to Crabbs, the big docks, buildings and tanks between the desalination plant and the cement factory. These big docks are a small ship/ large superyacht facility just built by Stanford. Crabbs has a 32 foot wide, 150-ton travel lift, a giant painting shed, and enough tanks to keep Antigua in fuel and water for a few days.

The future of this facility is uncertain. The channel is marked, but the buoys are not clearly colored and are unreliable. Sail down the western side of Maiden Island, staying a couple of hundred feet offshore, eyeballing your way through the shallows. Stay close to Maiden Island at the southern end, as there is a wreck within 5 feet of the surface to the west of the channel.

As you sail up the Boon Channel, you may well find yourself among a colorful

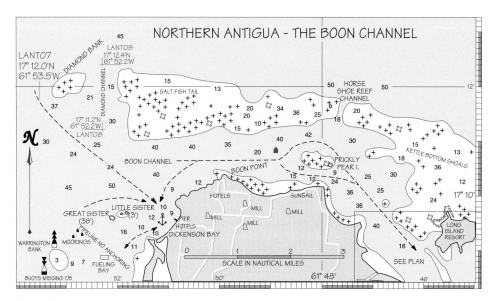

NORTHERN ANTIGUA - THE BOON CHANNEL

fleet of small sailing craft, para-surfers, and windsurfers. This is Sunsail's Club Colonna, an excellent sailing resort for those wanting to learn. If you pass by on land, they have a good restaurant.

Shell Beach Boatyard and the Airport

This facility is used by superyacht owners arriving by private jet. With careful navigation large yachts can stay in over 30 feet of water into Parham Sound and find an anchorage according to draft. Shell Beach Boatyard is only a few hundred feet from FBO 2000 at the airport. FBO have an exclusive facility for looking after private jets. They park nearby, the crew and passengers don't go anywhere near the main airport, customs and immigration are done in privacy at the plane or in the pleasant FBO office, and then FBO will drop the crew and baggage the few hundred feet to the waiting tender at the marina. It is elegantly smooth and stylish.

Michael Josiah's Shell Beach Boatyard has a fuel dock and offers diesel, gas, and water. They also have a 25-ton marine hoist. The approach is straight in from the red (sort of) buoy less than half a mile to its northeast. There is 8 feet of water as you

approach the marina, and then it shoals to 5-6 feet alongside the fuel dock, though you could bring in a 7-foot draft boat at high tide. Cats and powerboats can take on fuel and water here easily; monohulls of suitable draft can make it with care. If a yacht is much over 40 feet long, it might be a good idea to drop anchor and bring just part of the boat alongside the 40-foot dock.

Long Island Anchorage

Long Island is a large exclusive resort in a setting of pale green water, sprinkled with snorkeling reefs. There is an exquisite anchorage off the beach in Jumby Bay. When you are half a mile northwest of Maiden Island, look to the east for the buoy that marks the shoal extending north from Maiden Island. (The buoy has recently been white.) Leave this to starboard and head in toward the beach. Anchor well out from the beach, south of all the reefs. You can also pass between Long Island and Maiden Island and anchor in Davis Bay on the south coast. There is nearly 8 feet of water in the channel between the islands. It is not as pretty as Jumby Bay.

Ashore

Long Island is a private resort (Jumby Bay) with several private houses on the

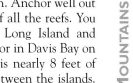

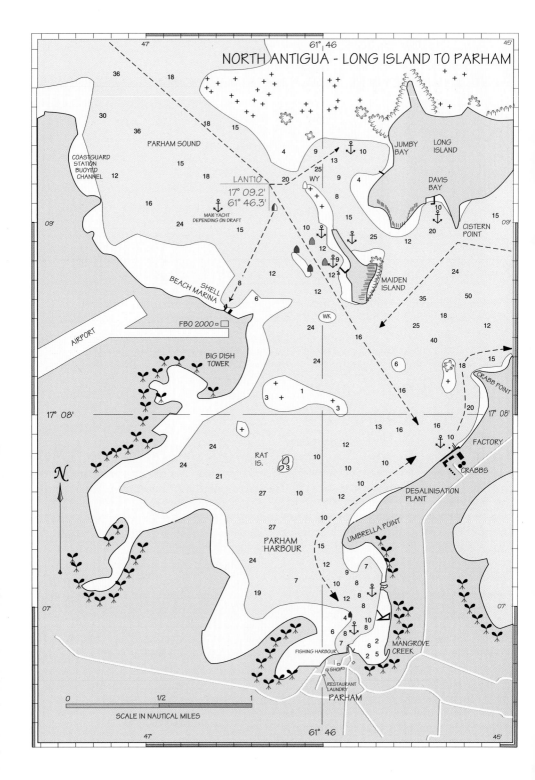

NORTH ANTIGUA - LONG ISLAND TO PARHAM

61° 46

47'

45'

36
18

30
18

36
15

PARHAM SOUND

4
9
JUMBY BAY
LONG ISLAND

COASTGUARD STATION BUOYED CHANNEL
12
15
18
18
20
WY
9
4
13
25
10
DAVIS BAY

16
LANT10
17° 09.2'
61° 46.3'
MAXI YACHT DEPENDING ON DRAFT
15
8
10
15
20
CISTERN POINT

09'
24
15
10
12
25
25
12
09'

12
12
9
12
MAIDEN ISLAND
24
50
35

SHELL BEACH MARINA
8
12
WK
24
16
25
18
40
12

6
FBO 2000

AIRPORT
24
24
6
16
18
15
CRABB POINT

BIG DISH TOWER
3
1
3
13
16
16
20
17° 08'

17° 08'
24
10
FACTORY
10

24
RAT IS.
3
10
10
10
CRABBS
DESALINISATION PLANT

21
27
10
12

N
27
10
UMBRELLA POINT
10
PARHAM HARBOUR
15
12
9
7

24
12
8

7
10

19
12

4
10
8

6
8
2
MANGROVE CREEK
8
2
5
7
6

FISHING HARBOUR
SHOP

RESTAURANT LAUNDRY
PARHAM

0
1/2
1

SCALE IN NAUTICAL MILES

47'
61° 46
45'

island. The two restaurants are open to visiting yachts, but you must give them a few hours advance notice and there is a limit to how many extras they can take. When the resort is really full (usually Christmas/New Year), they may have no extra tables. In the winter 09 they were remodeling. The exclusive Estate House restaurant was still open, and a new restaurant in the main building will come on line. In either case the dress code is at least slacks and a sports shirt. This is a fancy place and prices are on the high side, but not excessive. Telephoning or walking in early in the day are the surest ways to reserve, but you can also try calling "Jumby Bay Resort" on VHF: 18.

Maiden Island Anchorage

Maiden Island is a handy little anchorage. Anchor on the lee side, making sure you are well out of the channel. You will find good holding in 9 feet of water with a sand and weed bottom. Some people also like to anchor on the northeast side of Maiden Island, just out of the channel. It does have a pleasant view of the islands. Maiden Island now has two big houses and lots of shoreside construction is going on, so keep a good lookout.

Parham

Parham was once the second most important port in Antigua and home of the Governor. Nowadays, it is a pleasant but sleepy waterfront town, decorated with trees and flowers. The churches and one or two old walls are relics of its bygone glory. The anchorage is very well protected and, like the town, it has an air of great peace: you will see more chickens in the roads than people. There are buses to St. John's.

To get to Parham from Crabbs, follow the coast, pass around Umbrella Point, and head toward town. If you want to visit Parham town, anchor to its northeast off the dock in 10 feet of water. The holding is good in mud. You can also anchor closer to town. However, if you try to go there on a straight line from Umbrella Point, you will run hard aground. As you come around Umbrella Point, you have to make a swing into the general mangrove anchorage, then head to the town dock before heading up into town. (A red buoy currently marks the offending shoal.) If you want to be farther away, you can anchor in toward the mangroves, anywhere between Parham and Umbrella Point. In the southeast corner of the bay, there is a cut into the mangroves that makes for interesting dinghy exploration. There is a good 5.5 feet at low water

MOUNTAINS & MANGROVES

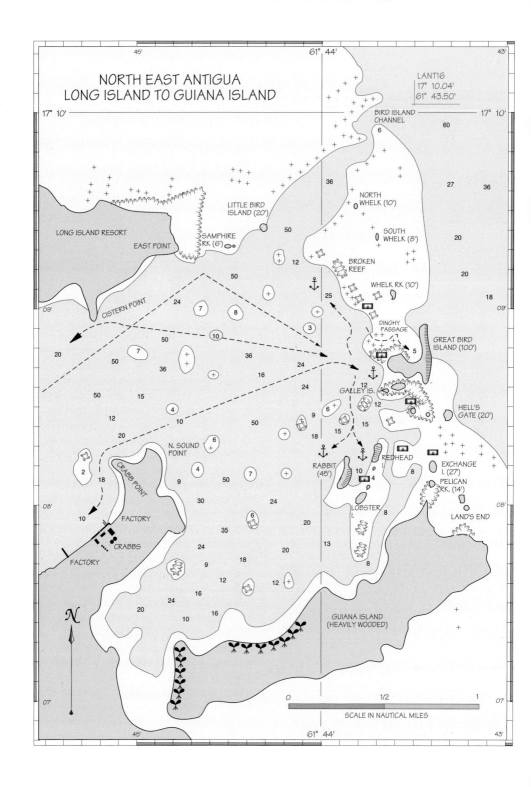

NORTH EAST ANTIGUA
LONG ISLAND TO GUIANA ISLAND

LANT16
17° 10.04'
61° 43.50'

17° 10'

BIRD ISLAND
CHANNEL

60

LITTLE BIRD
ISLAND (20')

NORTH
WHELK (10')

36

27   36

LONG ISLAND RESORT

SAMPHIRE
RK (6')

SOUTH
WHELK (8')

20

EAST POINT

50

12

BROKEN
REEF

20

WHELK RK (10')

CISTERN POINT

09'

50

24

7   8

3

DINGHY
PASSAGE

25

18

GREAT BIRD
ISLAND (100')

20

50

10

7

36

16

24

5

HELL'S
GATE (20')

50

36

50

24

12

GALLEY IS.

15

50

15

12

6

9

15

50

N. SOUND
POINT

4

6

18

15

RABBIT
(45')

10

REDHEAD
I.

EXCHANGE
I. (27')

2

18

CRABBS POINT

9

4

50

7

8

4

8

PELICAN
RK. (14')

08'

10

FACTORY

30

24

20

LOBSTER
I.

8

LAND'S END

CRABBS

35

20

13

FACTORY

24

18

8

9

12

12

24

16

16

GUIANA ISLAND
(HEAVILY WOODED)

20

10

16

N

0   1/2   1

07'

SCALE IN NAUTICAL MILES

61° 44'

most of the way up. Some shallow draft boats like to sneak in here and tie themselves into the mangroves when hurricanes threaten.

Regulations

An immigration officer is usually at the fisheries complex 0600-2000 daily. They normally only clear cargo vessels, not yachts. If you want to find out if that has changed, call them: 562-6693.

Services

A new fishing port has been built here. You can carry about 7 feet to the dock, but you have to come in pretty straight to stay in the deep water (bow or stern-to is an option). Ask whomever you can find in the fisheries, and you should be able to arrange to take on water and ice. Snow White is a fair-sized modern laundry, just down the road from Sugar Apple Alley.

Ashore

You can tie your dinghy to the town dock and wander into town where you will find two tiny basic stores, and maybe a restaurant.

Sugar Apple Alley restaurant is very local and was good with a few tables outside under the trees. It is owned by Troy who has been opening it for barbecue on weekends. Last time I was there he was rebuilding, so who knows. There is always a chance of a meal, but don't count on it.

Great Bird and Other Outer Islands

To the east of Long Island and North Sound Point is a large bay protected from the east by a series of reefs, barrier islands, and rocks. Rather than the usual Caribbean backdrop of beaches and palms, there are oddly shaped rocks and deserted islets, bare or covered in scrub, with mangroves developing in the calmer spots. The shapes of the rocks provide drama to the view and one of them, Hell's Gate, has a hole right through it. This is a wild, uninhabited area, with delightful anchorages full of seabirds when they decide to nest. The snorkeling is good, and the sense of being in a remote area, completely at peace, makes this one of Antigua's really great anchoring areas.

The largest island is Great Bird Island, which is the only one to attract any tourists. One or two day-sailing cats arrive about 1000 and leave about 1600. This whole area is very sensitive environmentally and is now part of a park area. The nesting bird populations used to be immense. I don't see any now, though it may be later

GT. BIRD ISLAND

READHEAD

EXCHANGE

RABBIT I.

LOBSTER

GUIANA ISLAND

MOUNTAINS & MANGROVES

Among the outer islands   Chris Doyle

in springtime that they come. One of the main threats to wildlife is from rats. Food scraps encourage rats, so no food should be taken ashore and no scraps dumped from the boat. Don't walk on, or dinghy too close to islands if birds are nesting. Make sure not to anchor on coral, and don't spearfish or otherwise damage the marine life.

The whole area is a maze of reefs and shoals, so you have to proceed cautiously, with the light behind. There are several ways to reach Great Bird Island. If you are coming from Crabbs, follow close up the coast to Crabb Point, staying inside the off-shore shoals. Follow the coast around close to North Sound Point. From North Sound Point head toward the northern part of Great Bird Island, keeping your eye open for shoals. When you near the island, head into the anchorage. If you are coming from the north, work your way down to Cistern Point on the south side of Long Island. From Cistern Point, head just to the north end of the Great Bird Island anchorage. This route takes you over one reef, which currently has at least 10 feet of water over it. You can see it by the change in water color and it is possible to edge around its southern end. I found another route, rec-ommended by Eugene who works with Horizon Yacht Charters, helpful when tacking up, and would be even easier under power. From the south of Maiden Island you have plenty of clear water to tack up

the south coast of Long Island, heading in the direction of Little Bird Island. When you reach East Point, you can head over towards Galley Island, which, with a bit of luck, you can make in one tack.

The most popular anchorage is Great Bird Island. It is pleasant and peaceful, with a couple of small beaches easily reached by dinghy and a path to the top for a panoramic view of the bay. Just at the top are two 100-foot, well-like blowholes that fall straight to the sea. It is the only home (in the wild) of what might be the rarest and most endangered snake in the world, the Antigua racer (Alsophis antiguae).

A small shallow channel twists through the reef to the north of Great Bird Island, where there is another anchorage in front of a small northern beach. You can explore it with your dinghy and possibly take a shoal draft craft (3-4 feet) through here.

There are gorgeous anchorages to the south of Great Bird Island, tucked among the islets and rocks. How far you can go depends on your draft and ability to find your way through the maze of shoals. You can also leave your boat safely anchored in Great Bird Island and explore by dinghy. The anchorage between Redhead and Rabbit Islands is calm, picturesque, and not too hard to reach. From Great Bird Island you swing out round the shoal and head down between the islands. In spring you often see big baby pelicans. Do not climb ashore as you might upset the birds if there are eggs or young. If you pass west of Rabbit Island, you can go down to Guiana Island and work your way back up the coast towards Exchange Island, with many possible anchoring places en-route. The Nautical Publications chart is the one I use to search out new routes, though it is all eyeball navigation. In some cases hard enough that you might want to check it out with the dinghy before taking the yacht.

In good settled conditions you can eyeball your way up along the barrier reef and anchor about halfway between Great Bird Island and Little Bird Island.

Guiana Island is named after its first settlers who had to leave Dutch Guiana in 1667. There are plans to build a vast international resort here, which are greatly opposed by local environmental groups. The project is currently stalled, but the present government, staunch environmentalists while in opposition, changed their minds on taking power, and were going to revive it. It has now stalled again.

Bird Islet Channel is a narrow winding channel out to the open sea. This is best left to people with local knowledge, though someone really adept at reading reefs might like to try it as a way out, but not a way in, in very calm conditions. Follow the barrier reef up to Little Bird Island, then turn northeast down the channel. You can see the reefs on either side.

Water sports

This whole area is magnificent for snorkeling, as long as the visibility is good, which it often is. The area bounded by Great Bird Island in the north and Exchange Island in the south, between Red Head and Hell's Gate, is not all shallow reef, as it looks on the chart. It is a maze of reefs and deeper water, with magnificent coral heads that sometime rise to within 6 feet of the surface. Encrusting fire coral has made some intricate, woven fairy castles. There is a growing amount of healthy brain coral and star coral, as well as some staghorn and elkhorn areas. There are lots of fish, though mostly on the small side. I suspect the larger ones have been eaten. Occasionally, you get lucky and see a ray or some larger creature. The snorkeling is also good north of Great Bird Island.

THE WEST COAST OF ANTIGUA

Navigation

There are plenty of anchorages on the west coast of Antigua, with many hotels where one can enjoy a meal ashore. Many

Chris Doyle

MOUNTAINS & MANGROVES

anchorages are somewhat susceptible to northerly swells. The best overnight anchorages in the winter months are Jolly Harbour, St. John's, Deep Bay, and Five Islands Harbour.

The west coast is somewhat shoal, with several islands, reefs, and rocks. This makes the sea a wonderful lustrous turquoise; the color alone makes sailing on this coast a pleasure. For a normal draft yacht (under 7 feet), there are just a few to watch out for: Big Sister, off Dickenson Bay, is a conspicuous island, and next door, the rocky Little Sisters are easy to see. The shallow Warrington Bank must be avoided, especially as the buoys are often missing. (They were missing in February 2009.) Those following the coast would normally pass well inside it.

Sandy Island is clearly visible. Avoid the adjoining Weymouth Reef, named after HMS Weymouth, which was wrecked here in 1745. These are 2 miles offshore, well outside a normal coastal route.

There are little islands off the points at both the north and the south end of Five Islands Harbour. I would pass outside Barrel of Beef at the northern end. You have to give it a couple of hundred yards clearance as a reef sticks out a long way to the west. At the southern end, you can either pass right outside Five Islands (the safest route) or take the Five Islands Channel inside the outer islands. This is not too hard in good light and there is 11 feet in the channel. Look out for the rock that extends well to the north of the eastern island group. The shoreline along the Mosquito/Morris Bay area has been shoaling. You can pass just outside the bays (see the sketch chart, page 337), where depths jump between 8 and 14 feet. Otherwise, go farther out in about 12 to 18 feet of water. Return toward shore at Ffreys Bay to make sure of staying inside the 3-foot reef about 1,600 yards to its west. Those with deep draft yachts need to study the charts and choose their routes carefully, because there are plenty of 9- and 10-foot shoals well offshore along the west coast.

Dickenson Bay

The mile-long beach at Dickenson Bay is a lively holiday resort area with plenty of action. The beach is decorated with gaily-colored t-shirts hung out for sale. There are all kinds of water sports, from jet skis to glass bottom boats, beach bars, and a variety of restaurants.

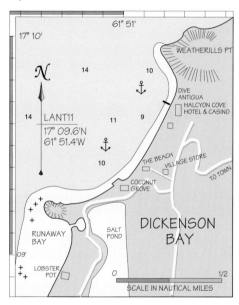

From the north, round Diamond Bank and head straight in, leaving Little Sisters to starboard. From the south, most yachts can pass inside Great Sisters and Little Sisters. (See Northern Antigua sketch chart, page 321.) Yachts of over 7-foot draft should take the deeper route, going outside these. Those coming from Crabbs Peninsula can follow the coast west and turn in round Weatherills Point. The bay is only about 10 or 11 feet deep in most places and it is susceptible to northerly swells. Anchor at least 100 yards offshore in the winter months. There is no dinghy dock, so you must pull your tender up on the beach. If you want to lock it, pull it up close to Warri Pier and use one of the posts.

Ashore

For a quick provisioning, check out The Village Shop, behind the Beach

DICKENSON BAY

Restaurant, which sells basics. Cynthie sells fresh vegetables from a van outside the store on Mondays, Wednesdays, and Saturdays from 0900 to 1800.

Souvenir hunters will enjoy the craft market up near the Halcyon Cove, as well as a variety of beach vendors.

Sneaky Pete's and Tony's are two beach bar grills where you can get lunch and sometimes dinner.

When evening comes, you can take your choice of restaurants. The Beach is about halfway down the beach. Come for their sunset happy hour at 1630-1830. The menu is international and on Friday nights they have a DJ from 2230-0200.

Just south of The Beach, the Coconut Grove hangs out over the water. It too has a sunset happy hour from 1600-1900. You can stay for good, fancy food in an elegant waterfront setting.

Rex Halcyon Cove Hotel has three restaurants: the Warri Pier, built right out over the water, the Arawak Terrace, set back in the hotel, and the Grill, out by the beach bar.

They also often have entertainment at night in the Ciboney Cocktail Bar. Also, at the back of Halcyon Cove, are several boutiques, including the Corner Store where you can buy US and UK newspapers.

If this is not enough, you will find more restaurants down at Runaway Beach, the next beach south and well within walking distance. One of these, the Lobster Shack, has a good reputation.

Chris Doyle

MOUNTAINS & MANGROVES

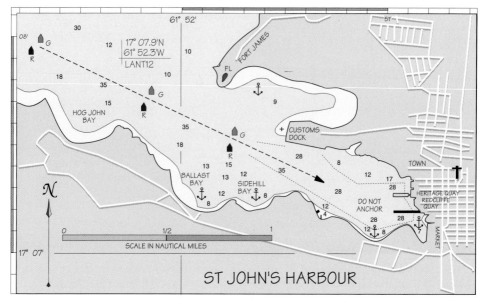

ST JOHN'S HARBOUR

Water Sports

Scuba enthusiasts can call Dive Antigua on VHF: 68 to arrange a pickup from the yacht. They are also happy to pick up off Deep Bay. The beach is lined with stands offering other water sports.

St. John's

St. John's is the capital of Antigua. It is an attractive city, with carefully restored old buildings, some modern buildings, as well as rougher old buildings full of local color. The shopping is excellent - you can buy beautiful jewelry, local crafts, fashions high and low, luggage, and accessories, much of it duty-free. This plus the convenience of major supermarkets, good restaurants, and a local produce market, have their appeal to visiting yachts. St. John's is a cruise ship destination, but also has facilities for cruising and professional yachts. It is a very easy bus ride from English Harbour.

Navigation

The main channel is dredged from 28 to 35 feet deep. It includes a large maneuvering area in front of Heritage Quay and Redcliffe Quay. It is buoyed according to IALA B (red right returning). Under no circumstances should you anchor in the channel. Go into Redcliffe and tie up stern-to, or anchor out of the main channel. If you want to be close to town, you can find an anchorage just south of the ship channel. Stay pretty close to the shipping channel and avoid anchoring by the huge culvert, which is a big drain exit, unless you are interested in exotic smells and garbage. You can also find a spot just east of the dredged area towards the fishing port. If you have a fast dinghy, there is no problem anchoring in Sidehill or Ballast Bays as these bays are scenic, pleasant and have plenty of room. There is 8 to 9 feet close to shore, except in the western side of Ballast Bay, which is shallow.

Regulations

All craft, including yachts, should keep clear of cruise ships by 150 meters. If you want to go between two cruise ships, try calling "Deepwater Harbour" on VHF: 16, their patrol boat may escort you in.

Customs are set up for ships rather than yachts, so yachts will find it easier to clear in Jolly Harbour. Should you have to clear here, there are two sets of customs and immigration. One is on the big deep-water dock on the north side of the harbor and the other is right at the head of Heritage Quay dock. You will end up having to go to the deep-water dock to pay the port authority, so it is simpler to stop there on your way in. Since you have to deal with port authority, you need to go when they are open: 0830-1630 (the others are open longer) Customs officers move between stations, and the Heritage Quay branch is often closed. Officialdom here may be closed on weekends.

Communications

The Best of Books on St. Mary Street has a special internet room with half a dozen stations and is a pleasant place to visit.

Kangaroo Express, another good internet station, is a short walk up Redcliffe Street. They open weekdays 0800-1900, Saturdays 0900-1900.

Koolnet has a bunch of email computers on Heritage Quay and is open 0830-1700 weekdays, plus Saturdays if a cruise ship is in.

Comnett sell a good selection of computer accessories. Fedex is on the other side of the same building.

Services

St. John's works well for the large professional yachts. Their agents can arrange berthing on either of the cruise ship docks, which are managed by the Pier Group. Here you can take on water and fuel, which is supplied by West Indies Oil Company (462-0552) and they can also take the waste oil. This is a good location for loading stores, as you can bring large trucks right alongside.

Redcliffe Quay is in the most charming part of town. All the good-looking historic buildings have been renovated and turned into restaurants and shops. They do have docks with room for visiting yachts right between the two cruise ship docks. If you want to come in, contact Chris White who is in the Key Properties office. His number is 562-1960, weekends; 720-8090. Water can be arranged.

Island Motors, on the corner of Independence Avenue and Queen Elizabeth Highway, has a good-sized modern machine shop that can undertake stainless and aluminum welding as well as all kinds of fabrication and repairs. They

CHANNEL AND TURNING ZONE
NO ANCHORING

ST. JOHN'S HARBOUR

MOUNTAINS & MANGROVES

can shave heads, re-bore and sleeve cylinders, work on shafts, thread a special nut, or fix winches.

The Yamaha dealer, Automotive Art, is on the Old Parham Road, a short bus or taxi ride out of town. You can expect good professional service here, whether they repair your old outboard, sell you some spares, or sell you a new engine. The Map Shop run by Miriam and her son is the official Admiralty Chart agent. Those moving to distant places should discuss their chart needs some weeks before they take off. They also stock a wonderful array of antique maps, prints, and a good selection of nautical and nature guides, as well as West Indian writers and educational books. This is the place to come for proper survey maps for exploring Antigua.

Provisioning

Food Emporium, more commonly known as Bryson's IGA Supermarket, because the old sign is still standing, is modern, and organized, with a wide selection of wines and liquors, frozen meats, fish, and many fresh vegetables, as well as dry goods and cans. It is adequate for provisioning. They open Monday to Thursday 0800-1900, Friday and Saturday 0800-2200 and Sunday 0800-1600.

For a big provisioning, visit the Epicurean Supermarket at Woods, just outside St. John's. It is Antigua's best supermarket and it is set in a modern shopping mall. They carry an excellent range of products, including luxury items such as smoked salmon, and you will find a good delicatessen section. They are open every day, including Sundays, from 0800-2200. A dollar bus runs to and from the West Bus Stop in St. John's. You might want to check out an even bigger supermarket that was under construction on the road from St. John's to Dickenson Bay.

Best Cellars keeps the island's biggest stock of wines, all carefully temperature-controlled out by the airport. You can also get all your spirits here. They are together with the best food wholesaler Island Provisions, and the supermarket Gourmet Basket. Both are a taxi ride from St. John's,

Chris Doyle

332

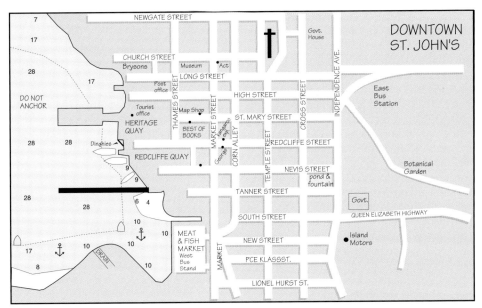

but you can also call to arrange an order with delivery.

The local market is in a pleasant building and has lots of fruits and vegetables, as well as some handicrafts. Opposite are the local fish and meat markets; you can dinghy right down there.

Fun Shopping

C & C Wines, on Redcliffe Quay, is run by two charming women, Claudine and Cutie. They sell wines from South Africa and are knowledgeable and enthusiastic about their products. The prices are good, too. They have a lovely little courtyard seating area where you can sit and sample, and, when you find the perfect wine, you can buy by the case. They also sell by the bottle or glass and you can get a cup of coffee, along with quite a few finger foods. They open Monday to Saturday about 1000 and stay open 'til quite late at night. Claudine and Cutie also own Australian Ice Creams and Chocolates a few yards away. This shiny, clean shop has a big selection of ice creams and sorbets, plus a big selection of delectable Belgian chocolates that make great gifts.

Boutique shoppers will have a field day here. Redcliffe Quay is old-world elegant with many excellent handicraft and arty

stores. Next door, Heritage Quay is much more modern with many jewelry and perfume stores downstairs and clothing stores upstairs. More stores continue up St. Mary Street and on other streets surrounding the Quays.

Aquasports is upstairs in Heritage Quay, opposite the Casino. It is duty-free and has an excellent stock of fishing gear, including deep-sea reels and many lures. They can make up a suitable trolling rig for those going on charter. They have a full range of snorkeling gear and accessories, including the Leatherman tool and Sperry Topsiders. They also sell tool kits, knives, flashlights, beach toys, waterproof boxes, and mace for personal protection.

Sunseekers in Heritage Quay is the best place to find a new swimsuit or bikini. They stock all sizes from baby to giant and cater to both sexes. You will find all the renowned brand names here, including Gottex, Jantzen, and La Perla. They also stock casual wear and good sailing shorts.

Between Heritage and Redcliffe Quay is a colorful local vendors market with lots of brightly colored garments and wraps.

In Redcliffe Quay, the Pottery Shop carries the work of several Antiguan potters, including small works that are easy to pack. Jacaranda has artistic Caribbean handi-

MOUNTAINS & MANGROVES

crafts. Upstairs, to the side of Hemingway's, is the Art Loft, run by six local artists. The work is good and the prices quite reasonable.

E.M. Graeme's Best of Books and Made in Antigua is in a lovely old building on St. Mary Street. This is an excellent bookshop on two floors with many interesting nooks and crannies and a large variety of books, US and UK magazines, and newspapers, as well as Antiguan-made souvenirs. This is the best place for stocking up on novels and new literature.

Island Photo is on Redcliffe Street. They provide a fast and high-quality photo processing service, as well as passport pictures and on-location photography. They also have a graphic design studio and can restore your damaged pictures. This is the place to come for ready-made frames.

Restaurants

There are several restaurants around the Redcliffe Quay complex. Café Napoleon is a delightful French-style coffee house where you can also buy fresh croissants and baked goodies or a good lunch. Mama Lolley's, owned by Maxine and Mary-Lee, specializes in a variety of vegetarian dishes and has a fresh fruit juice and smoothy bar during the day. They also open on Friday nights for Fish Fridays. You will also find Middle Eastern fast food.

Just up the road, Big Banana offers Pizzas in Paradise, in a modern, shiny atmosphere. Commissioner Grill on Redcliffe Street is open daily from breakfast to dinner and serves excellent Caribbean food.

Upstairs on St. Mary's Street,

Hemingway's Bar and Restaurant is a lively and popular place, with a balcony overlooking the street. Lots of salads and sandwiches are featured for lunch, with more elaborate dinners. They also open for breakfast.

Check out Café Bambula, hidden in a little courtyard on High Street, north of Market Street. This is a great little hideout for breakfast or lunch that will get you far from the cruise ship crowd.

For entertainment at night, check out The Coast, at the north end of the cruise ship docks.

Ashore

If you need a doctor, Nick Fuller has an office on Long Street, opposite the Museum. 462-0931, VHF: 16/68 "Ocean View". He is very good and is active in yachting himself. If it is your yacht rather than yourself that needs rescuing, he even has a salvage company "North Coast Towing and Salvage."

While in town, pay a visit to the Museum of Antigua and Barbuda. It is very well done, with lifelike exhibits tracing the history of Antigua from pre-Colombian times to independence. Some exhibits are meant to be handled, which makes it fun for the kids. Antigua's Environmental Association is in the same building.

Golfers will want to check out Antigua's Cedar Valley Golf Club, a few minutes beyond Woods Mall.

Deep Bay

Deep Bay is a charming anchorage with a long, sandy beach. It is the home of the mammoth Grand Royal Antiguan, a resort that is end on to the bay and does not affect the view.

The wreck of the Andes is right in the middle of the bay. The bow and a few mast stumps almost break the surface. You can pass on either side, but do not pass too closely. Anchor off the beach in about 10 to 12 feet of water. This anchorage is normally well protected, but it can roll in northerly swells, and a boat was once wrecked in really bad northwesterly swells.

Ashore

On the north side of Deep Bay, Fort Barrington stands with commanding views all around. It was a battery and observation post from Nelson's time. It is fun to scramble up. Walk back along the lagoon toward the fort as far as you can go and then follow the path up.

The Grand Royal Antiguan Resort has three good restaurants, and a boutique, and wifi. Their tennis courts and a gym are open to the public for a charge. The restaurants include the popular Andes, perched out over the water on stilts, the Lagoon Café, and the Barrington up in the main building. The Barrington is the most luxurious, and the one to choose for fine dining.

Water Sports

Snorkeling or diving on the wreck of the Andes is splendid. This three-masted iron barque was sailing from Trinidad with a load of pitch in 1905. When it got to Antigua, the crew noticed smoke rising from one of the hollow masts and suspected the motion of the boat had caused enough friction in the cargo to start a fire. Being a hazardous cargo, they were refused permission to go into St. John's, so they anchored in Deep Bay. When they opened the cargo hatches to deal with the problem, the infusion of fresh air caused the pitch to burst into uncontrollable flames. The wooden deck burned off the steel frames and the vessel sank. The Andes sits upright on the bottom, encrusted with sponges and coral. She provides shelter for big schools of small fish and many larger reef fish. Sometimes jellyfish mass here.

Deep Bay to Barrel of Beef

Galley Bay lies just to the south of Deep Bay. You will see a long wild looking beach, backed by a tangle of palms and seagrapes. Galley Bay Hotel peeks through the palms. There are lumps of coral close to shore and it is best to visit by dinghy from Deep Bay, surf permitting. You can get a light lunch in the pleasant open-air restaurant and eat to the sound of bird song.

The coast from Deep Bay down to Barrel of Beef is somewhat shoal, with scattered coral heads and rock ledges. Do not approach too closely. The 25-foot, aptly-named Hawksbill Rock looks just like a giant turtle head staring out to sea. Although it is not an anchorage as such, some people drop a hook outside Hawksbill Bay to lunch at the Hawksbill Beach

MOUNTAINS & MANGROVES

Chris Doyle

Resort. This is an immaculately landscaped place with wood-shingled roofs tucked amid waving palms and bright red bougainvillea. The hotel is spread between two beaches, with the main buildings and an old mill (now a boutique) on the headland between. There is a concrete dinghy dock under the southern side of the headland, but a dinghy anchor will be essential in a swell.

Five Islands Harbour

This magnificent bay is the best part of a mile wide and 2 miles deep, with beaches and mangroves. You will find good anchorage in the lee of Maiden Island, which sits in the middle of the bay. A lovely beach anchorage lies between Bakers Cellar and Stony Horn. If that is crowded, there is another in Hermitage Bay, which now houses the fancy Hermitage Hotel, all built of hardwood. Their beach bar and restaurant is lovely, but the hotel is all-inclusive and does not accept walk-in trade. They do accept occasional yachting visitors. Smaller groups have a better chance, a chance increased by giving them a couple of days notice. Call 562-5500.

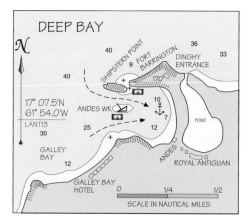

DEEP BAY

17° 07.5'N
61° 54.0'W
LANT13

SCALE IN NAUTICAL MILES

Navigation

From the north, pass well outside Barrel of Beef, as rocks extend about 100 yards to its west. You can then power or tack up to Maiden Island. There is good anchorage pretty close to its lee in about 10 feet of water. Watch out for an isolated coral head about 100 feet west of the island. About 14 years ago nesting birds here were densely packed and all calling together. You may still see a few, but not as before. Otherwise, anchor off the beach between Bakers Cellar and Stony Horn. If this is crowded,

WRECK OF THE ANDES

DEEP BAY

feel your way into the beach in Hermitage Bay, though this bay is more shoal, so take care. Treat these beach anchorages with caution in northerly swells.

From the south, you can either pass well outside Five Islands or, in good light, you can try the Five Island Channel, which goes inside the outer grouping of the islands. Note that one rock extends well north of the eastern group of islands (see our Jolly Harbour sketch chart). You can anchor off either of the beaches mentioned, but be wary of them as overnight anchorages if there is a chance of a big northerly swell. It is best to stay to the west of Maiden island, as the bay gets shoal and buggy farther in, plus a big garbage dump sits at the head of the bay.

Jolly Harbour

Jolly Harbour is a large, new marina and condominium development, with over 7 miles of dredged waterfront. It is very well protected and in several hurricanes has come through with little damage. There is a full-service marina, partly owned by Charles Kenlock, who is sometimes in the office, a shopping center with over 30 shops and seven restaurants, and 500 practical, two-story houses, each with its own waterfront space for docking a yacht. Some houses are still available for sale or rent. There is still room for expansion. Jolly Harbour Yacht Club organizes some major regattas and many informal races throughout the year. They host the Arc Europe Return Rally towards the end of May and are a featured stop on the Blue Water Round the World Rally.

Navigation

The marina channel was dredged to 17 feet. My soundings suggest that you now have about 11-foot at regular low tide. Boats of 11 feet draft or more should call the marina for the latest depth information. Deep draft yachts should come from the west, approaching Five Islands at about 105° magnetic, and then plot a course to take them north of Irish Bank before approaching the dredged channel. The

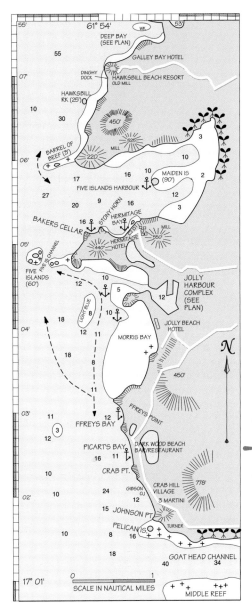

dredged channel is marked by beacons and buoys (red-right-returning). The outer red beacon and both of the channel turning marks are lit by flashing lights. There is always plenty of room in the marina (see page 338).

Those seeking anchorage outside the marina can feel their way out of the channel before the turning marks. The most pleasant anchorage is to the north of the

channel, off the beach. While most of this area is currently 7 to 12 feet deep, approach cautiously as depths have been known to change. You can also anchor just out of the channel after the first turning marks, but be careful of the depth. Moorings are available farther inside.

Regulations

Jolly Harbour is a port of entry. The customs and immigration station have an office and dock north of the megayacht berths. Call "Jolly Harbour Port Authority" on VHF: 16 before arriving to clear, or call Jolly Harbour Marina on VHF: 68. Yachts should tie to the customs dock for clearance (megayachts can go directly into their berths, which adjoin). If the customs berths are full, anchor outside or pick up a mooring and dinghy in. Customs are open from 0800-1600, including weekends. They may also want you to bring your yacht on their dock for clearing out.

Communications

The marina offers Hothothot Spot wifi stationed on the fuel dock. You can buy tickets in the marina or use a credit card online.

Jolly Services.com is in the marina, on the side of the building that faces the road. Here you will find internet access, TV, VCR, and video rentals, cell phone rentals and sales of cable and wireless sims and top-ups, a Money Gram agency, and they have a book swap (the selection is large but there is a fee). They open 0900-1800, except Sundays 1000-1700.

Melini's has a free wifi system for clients, as does Java Jo Jo. You can also buy digicel phone cards at the pharmacy and at Epicurian.

General Yacht Services

Jolly Harbour is a full-service marina, recently expanded, with berths for 152 yachts. These have water and electricity (110/220 volts, 60 cycles), and cable TV. . Ashore there are showers, laundry, and full communications. In addition, there is a new docking area near the golf club house with room for nine superyachts that has 3-phase, 50-cycle electricity, 125 amps at 380 volts. Also 60-cycle electricity: 600 amps at 415 volts, 200 amps at 208 volts and 50 amps at 110 volts. Both diesel and gasoline are available at a separate fuel dock, and duty-free bulk bunkering can be arranged.

JOLLY HARBOUR

MOUNTAINS & MANGROVES

The fuel dock opens weekdays 0800-1700, weekends 0800-1600.

About 12 moorings have been placed inside the entrance. You can use these if one is available for $15 US per night. No anchoring is allowed in the harbor area. Jolly Harbour has a 70-ton travel lift and storage room for 200 boats. An expanded area of hard standing means there is plenty of room for long-term storage on concrete for stability. Stands are welded for hurricane protection, and there are tie-downs. You can do your own work here or arrange it through the yard. They have people to scrape and paint and other services can be arranged. The marina manager is Festus Isaac, a yachtsman himself, who has a Dehler 36. A book swap is in the office (no charge). Two dinghy docks will help you get ashore. They are right inside the main docks on either side. The one to the southwest is very close to the supermarket.

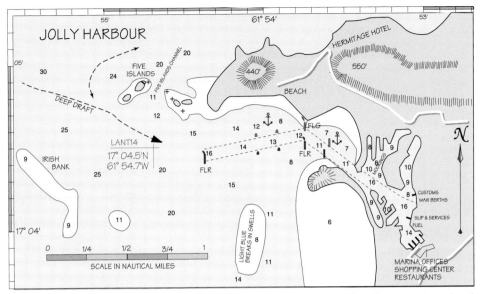

Burton's Laundromat, by the haul out, is good and reasonable. They open every day except Saturday.

Stuart Lockheart Legal Services is in the big new building beside customs. Stuart is the man to see if you want to register your yacht in Antigua (a very popular registration these days). He works in English and Spanish, and specializes in company and yacht registration. But if you need any legal help at all in Antigua, this would be an excellent place to begin.

Jolly Harbour is home to Anjo Insurance, a company that has been around for over 80 years. Yachts are a big part of this broker's business and if you are in the market for yacht insurance it is well worth asking them for a quote. You can do

MOUNTAINS & MANGROVES

341

this from their web page, anjoantigua.com

Jolly Harbour is home to Tradewinds Yacht Cruises, who offer holidays on a fleet of large catamarans, and Horizon Yacht Charters (VHF: 68), managed by Alastair and Jackie. This is an excellent bareboat charter company that offers many options, including one-way trips.

Chandlery

A large building in the haul out area houses most of the marine services, including a branch of Robbie Ferron's Budget Marine. This excellent technical chandlery is on two floors with lots of stock, including Tohatsu outboards at duty-free prices for visiting yachts. Ask for anything they do not have in stock, as it can be brought over from St. Martin quickly.

Technical Yacht Services

George Bridger's Star Tek houses several services under one roof. He is right on the waterfront in the haul out yard with his own dock, which you can use while he is working on your boat. This is the place to go for all your electronic and electrical repairs. George does not keep a stock of new electronics, but can bring in anything on order. George is a refrigeration man and can persuade recalcitrant systems to cool beer again. He also looks after boats when owners go away, and he is the Antigua agent for Doyle Sails.

Joseph George is the cabinet maker/shipwright at Harbour Woodwork. Joseph specializes in remodeling the interior of yachts with high-class cabinetry and he does lots of interior yacht cabin soles and enjoys any kind of ornamentation. He can also put in a new plank or fix a broken hatch.

Carl Mitchell's A-1 Marine is below Budget Marine. It is a full mechanical workshop where any kind of engine or boat mechanical system can be repaired. They have a large workshop for a full rebuild. Carl and his crew weld and fabricate aluminum and stainless steel and do some machining. They do a good job.

Antigua Yacht Paint is run by Tyndale Gore. As a paint specialist he does top quality spray painting (preferably Awlgrip) as well as varnishing and anti-fouling. Tyndale also does glass patching, hull peeling and osmosis treatment.

Tony Quinland is the fiberglass repair man and he can also fabricate anything in glass, as well as doing good gelcoat matching and repair.

Xtreme Marine is run by Ivan De Souza. His workshop is outside St. John's, but he will come to both Jolly Harbour and English Harbour to work if you call (464-4826). He fixes outboards of all makes, rigs their steering and gear controls. He also repairs diesel engines, outdrives, and all the associated electrical gear, including starters and alternators.

A&F sails visit once a week, usually Wednesdays, so you can get repairs, or order new sails, biminis, or awnings. A&F Sails, agents for Bruce Banks Sails, will be happy to come and do any necessary measuring. Give them a call to set up a meeting.

Shopping

The shopping center is complete. Change money or get cash on your Visa from the ABI Bank. Stock up your boat at the Epicurean Supermarket and Deli in its own building, which opens every day 0800-2000. This rates as one of Antigua's largest and best stores, good for a full provisioning. The packers will normally help you over to the dinghy dock, if there are none you can borrow a trolley for a $20 US deposit.

If you want to pay by credit card, take a photo ID. For wines and liquors, try Quin Farara's. You will also find soft drinks and a few food items in Sysco Pharmacy, as well as UK and US newspapers.

If you prefer to catch your food yourself, visit Aquasports, which has a good selection of rods, reels, lures, and live bait. They also sell good fishing/sailing shorts and shirts, beach toys, elegant knives, and more.

For the leisure-minded, the unisex Oasis

MOUNTAINS & MANGROVES

Hair Salon also does beauty treatments and massage. Chakra is a yoga and massage center, and there are about six boutiques. At Taino's you will find Antiguan artist Luis Jarvis hard at work. His mother is Haitian and this shows in the style of some of his work. He also sells paintings from the local Haitian community on consignment. It is a good gallery.

If you fall in love with Jolly Harbour, talk to ReMax, La Perla or Jolly Harbour Realty Ltd. They should have all the current properties for sale and know what is soon to come on the market.

Paradise Boat Sales rent scooters, mountain bikes, and boats, and are agents for Mercury and Honda outboards.

Restaurants

You have to walk a few steps to one of the nicer restaurants, Castaways, which is on the gorgeous long beach just a short walk from the marina. If the air is clear, you get a perfect sunset view of the islands of Montserrat, Redonda, and St. Kitts. They open every day for lunch and dinner, except Tuesday when they close for dinner (though this may change). Happy hour is timed for sunset, 1630-1830. The atmosphere is informal and it is on the beach, so you can bring the kids. They cook good West Indian food, including curries, coconut shrimp fritters, and jerk chicken, as well as authentic Asian and Chinese specialties. Friday night is Karaoke night.

Back in the marina, The Foredeck is Angie's bar right on the waterfront. Angie is from Canada and runs a lively and entertaining bar from afternoon till late, with good looking staff who will keep you cheerful. It is the place to hang out and meet other yachtspeople and it also doubles up as the club bar for the Jolly Harbour Yacht Club.

A fancy new Italian restaurant and pizzeria is under construction beside the customs dock, which should be a great addition. At least part of this is to be called Al Porto and to be owned by Angie from the Foredeck Bar. Angie always does a

Sheer @ Cocobay

Completely Unmitigated CAbsolute

Tuesday to Saturday 7pm -10pm tel: 562-2400 www.sheerantigua.com
Located 5 Minutes from Jolly Harbor

good job, so it is well worth paying a visit.

The Dogwatch Tavern, opens at mid afternoon. Expect a friendly atmosphere, good music, and two pool tables. They have a very stylish and long dining deck just outside the pub. The ambience is pleasant, the menu large and varied, and the food generally good. But cover well or bring plenty of Off, or the bugs and you will be dining at the same time.

Mark and Adrian's Melini's serves pizzas and mainly Italian cuisine in an open air dining room facing the marina. The chef's name is Jose, which makes you wonder about the Italian part, but he does a great job, and they are open every day for lunch and dinner, and have free wifi for their customers.

Peter's is owned and run by chef Peter Wagner from Switzerland and is open for lunch and dinner. Peter does wonders with steaks, smoked and spiced sausages, and shrimps over an open fire. This is complemented by a large salad bar. You can finish

MOUNTAINS & MANGROVES

Chris Doyle

346

with espresso and ice cream.

Java Jo Jo, offers good espresso, goodies, sandwiches, and wifi. B-Hive Sports Bar & Grill is in the sports complex and it caters to the energetic set, with a choice of squash, basketball, tennis on four courts, and a swimming pool. The restaurant is open for lunch and dinner and specializes in fresh local fish. Their occasional nightly entertainment often includes cabaret and reggae bands. For those working in the yard and covered in paint, Phill's is right there for soft drinks and a bargain lunch.

The vast Grand Princess Casino, over-looking the marina, is closed, but may reopen.

When you are in the mood for a really excellent and special meal, the place to go is the Sheer Restaurant at Cocobay Hotel way down beyond the south end of the beach. Take the short cab ride, rather than trying to walk. elegant and delightful restaurant is in six open, cliff-hung pavilions connected by a wooden walkway over-looking Little Ffryers Beach. Executive chef Nigel Martin, amalgamates South American, Asian and Indian flavors, in interesting and unusual ways. This is a very fancy place so men need to wear at least long trousers and a proper shirt.

Ashore

A new 18-hole golf club, with club-house, shop, lounge, and restaurant is open to visiting yachtspeople.

When you want to rent a car, contact Tropical Rentals (they are just down the road). They deliver and collect their cars, offer a very wide range of vehicles and have an excellent reputation for customer service.

You will find Caribbean Helicopters in the marina shopping complex. Jolly Harbour is in a perfect location for the Caribbean's most dramatic flight over Montserrat's volcano. Fly around the volcano and back, or stop and take a land tour for lunch. Charter for a lunch excursion to Barbuda, or to visit friends in St. Barts.

MOUNTAINS & MANGROVES

They also do Antigua sightseeing tours, photographic flights, and can deliver seasick charter customers close to their yacht as an alternative to a rough day's sail. They have great expertise working with photographers for perfect shots for brochures or boat portraits.

The road south from Jolly Harbour to the south end of Antigua is flat. Along it, several salt ponds are home to an array of water birds, including ducks, coots, herons, and egrets. Some lovely beaches lie along this coast. This is excellent biking territory and bicycles are available for rent from Paradise Boat Sales.

Water Sports

Snorkeling, skiing, and parasailing are available on Jolly Harbour Beach.

Indigo Dive comes into Jolly Harbour. This is a friendly Padi dive shop and they instruct and guide in English and German. They arrive at 0830 every day to pick up customers near the sports complex. Yachtspeople are especially welcome. If you want to rent an underwater digital camera, let them know in advance.

Jolly Dive is a full service dive shop, accredited by both Padi and Naui. They do full training and regular dives. Equipment is available for rent and they have a shop that sells diving and snorkeling gear and accessories.

Morris Bay

This whole area has been gradually shoaling. Yachts of about 6-foot draft can find a reasonable anchorage well offshore,

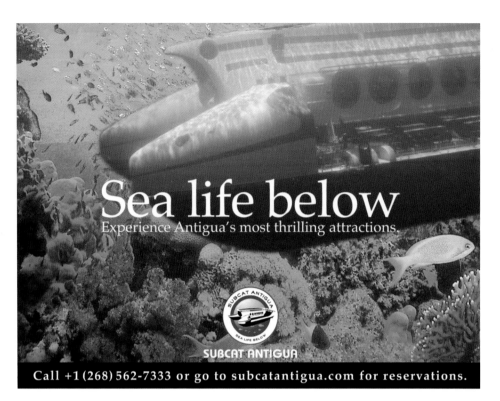

but only really shoal draft boats can get in close. You can edge in toward the hotel and anchor. Follow the coast up or down, staying well outside a line between the headlands. In rough weather, stay inside the large, clear, pale blue patch up toward the north end, which has some 8-foot patches and breaks in heavy seas.

Ffreys Point to Pelican Island

This stretch of coast is made up of three long beaches, separated by headlands. Ffreys and Picarts Bays are especially attractive for lunch stops. Keep in mind that there is a 3-foot shoal about three-quarters of a mile off Ffreys Bay and stay well inside it. You can find good temporary

anchorage in Ffreys Bay and Picarts Bay, but they are rolly and not safe for overnighting if there is a chance of a bad northerly swell.

Ashore

Behind Ffreys Bay, Dennis Cocktail Lounge and restaurant (closed Mondays) stands on Ffreys Point, whose small rise gives a great view over two beaches. It is pleasant and open to the view, with a big and varied menu.

The beach at Picarts Bay is called the Dark Wood Beach and there is a cheerful restaurant at the southern end that caters to visiting groups. From here south a few beach restaurants make a good lunch stop. Gibson's specializes in seafood and is open for lunch and dinner, Wednesday through

MOUNTAINS & MANGROVES

SOUTHWEST ANTIGUA

CADES REEF

Saturday and on Sunday for lunch. Just a few steps farther down, OJ's, open every day for lunch and dinner also specializes in seafood.

3 Martini is a great bar, restaurant, and apartment block on the left side of the road farther on. Lots of bareboaters use this for a stay at the beginning or end of their charter. They also have a friendly bar and restaurant and serve good food, both local and international, and they are open every day for breakfast, lunch, and dinner.

Turner's Beach Restaurant and Bar is on the long stretch of golden sand just north of Johnsons Point. The restaurant has a large, thatched, shady terrace, offers an interesting and reasonably-priced menu, and is known for good local lobster and

Chris Doyle

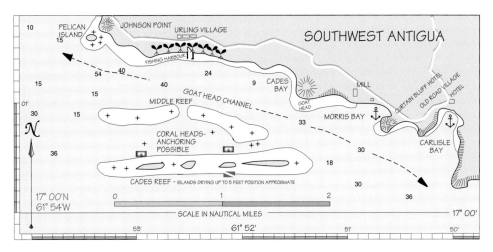

SOUTHWEST ANTIGUA

curried conch. They open from 1000-1800.

SOUTHERN ANTIGUA
Pelican Island to Falmouth

A 2-mile-long reef lies up to one and a half miles off the western part of Antigua's south coast, from Pelican Island up to the Curtain Bluff Hotel. The outer part of this reef is called Cades Reef.

In 1989 it became much more obvious when Hurricane Hugo turned it into a long string of shingle islands, which are still with us.

The inner reef is known as Middle Reef. There is about a half-mile-wide channel between Middle Reef and the shore. This channel is not hard to navigate in good light and the water is much smoother than outside the reefs. There is plenty of room to tack up through the channel, but keep in mind that the line of breaking water is Cades Reef, which is outside Middle Reef. Middle Reef is broken and harder to see, so tack before you reach any light colored water. There are also reefs close to shore, which are usually easy to see; they are widest around Goat Head.

Between Middle Reef and Cades Reef is a large area of water, often 12-20 feet deep, punctuated by coral heads. Middle Reef is also broken, and the experienced reef navigator can find channels through it to the outer reef. Here one can find good anchorage between Middle Reef and Cades Reef, perfect for snorkeling and windsurfing. Much of the bottom is covered with coral, which is easily damaged by anchors and chain. As the boat swings with the wind,

MOUNTAINS & MANGROVES

351

CARLISLE BAY

MORRIS BAY

the chain can destroy anything in its arc. You can avoid this by setting two anchors so you stay put. Snorkel on your anchor so you can see what is happening.

Two anchorages lie to the east of Cades Reef. Morris Bay is a good daytime stop, or, if you want to eat ashore, it may be worth the overnight roll. The Curtain Bluff Hotel makes a conspicuous landmark, sitting high on the point at its eastern end. The bay is about 20 feet deep and you can anchor off the dinghy dock. Carlisle Bay is more protected, though in southeasterly winds a surge will find its way in. Anchor off the middle of the beach in about 10 feet of water.

The coast between Old Road Bluff and Falmouth is exposed and rough. There are some reefs close to shore and a rock in Rendezvous Bay. Stay well outside all these.

Ashore

The Curtain Bluff in Morris Bay is one of Antigua's oldest and most prestigious hotels. It is exclusive and they expect male dinner guests to wear a jacket, but it is good enough to be worth the effort, and yachtspeople who do are very welcome. Reservations are recommended, as the hotel is often full. Lunch is more informal and you can have anything from a sand-

wich to the daily special.

Carlisle Bay is home to a fancy resort of the same name. Like Curtain Bluff, this is upmarket, don't expect to buy a beer for chump change. They have two fine restaurants; Indigo on the Beach is open lunch and dinner with a varied menu that includes plenty of seafood. East is next to the pool, and opens only for dinner to serve a fusion of Japanese, Thai, and Vietnamese foods. They have a substantial dinghy dock with a beach bar. Meal reservations are advisable, especially for large groups in high season.

PASSAGES BETWEEN ANTIGUA AND GUADELOUPE

It is about 40 miles between Antigua and Guadeloupe. You will often be influenced by a westerly current of up to one knot. Normally, you can make it in either direction on one tack. The run from English Harbour to Deshaies on 193° (all bearings magnetic) should be a good reach. Returning north at 13° is usually a reach, but close in a northeasterly. The course from English Harbour to Port Louis is about 168°, and to the channel into

Grande Cul de Sac Marin about 173°, which will be close to the wind if the wind is from the southeast. The passage into Grand Cul de Sac on the north coast of Guadeloupe takes good light and some concentration, so those coming from English Harbour might like to overnight in Port Louis and tackle it the next day. Sailing to English Harbour from either Grand Cul de Sac (352°) or Port Louis (348°) should be a fine reach. (See the chart in "Passages between Nevis, Montserrat, Antigua & Guadeloupe" on page 249.) When you look at Antigua from the south, the western end is hilly, and on a clear day it will rise above the horizon before the eastern part. From afar, the eastern part is lower and flatter. At first, Shirley Heights stands out as a bump on this stretch. The top of the bump dips slightly in the middle, but is fairly flat. As you get closer, Shirley Heights still stands out as the major cliff along the south coast. English Harbour is just under the western side of Shirley Heights.

Chris Doyle

MOUNTAINS & MANGROVES

Deshaies Chris Doyle

Guadeloupe

Guadeloupe, known by the Caribs as Karukera (Island of Pretty Waters), has a population of 330,000 and is part of France. It is partly agricultural, with the emphasis on sugar cane, and the local "rhum" is highly valued in France. Tourism is also important.

Guadeloupe is composed of two islands in the shape of a lopsided butterfly, with a river separating the two halves. Whoever named the islands had a sense of humor, because the larger mountainous one is called "Basse Terre" (low land) and the smaller, low one "Grande Terre" (large land). Grand Terre is a much older island. It once looked more like Basse Terre, but over millions of years its mountains have eroded. Basse Terre is a younger volcanic island. Yachts of up to 6.5-foot draft can navigate between the two islands on the Rivière Salée.

You should visit the interior, at least in mountainous Basse Terre, which has some exceptional views and sites. Route de la Traversée runs through the national park, smack in the middle of Basse Terre. The Crayfish Waterfalls are well worth a visit and swim, but make your way to the upper part to avoid too many tourists. If you are driving yourself, take the detour to Morne à Louis for the spectacular view from the top, overlooking Pigeon Island. Some buses that run between Pointe à Pitre and Pointe Noire take Route de la Traversée.

The most dramatic destination is the 350-foot Carbet Waterfalls in the south of Basse Terre. These are the tallest falls I know of in the Eastern Caribbean. If you rent a car, it is easy to find the car park and you reach the second falls by a beautiful 30-minute walk on a well laid out trail through the rainforest. But this is just the beginning, as many hikes have been well laid out in this area. Try the one-hour hike up to the first falls. This takes you above the rainforest through cloud forest. These first falls, which are equally as high as the second falls, are very red from the volcano. Whichever fall you hike to, remember to take your bathing things: they all have good bathing pools.

Other attractions in this area are several

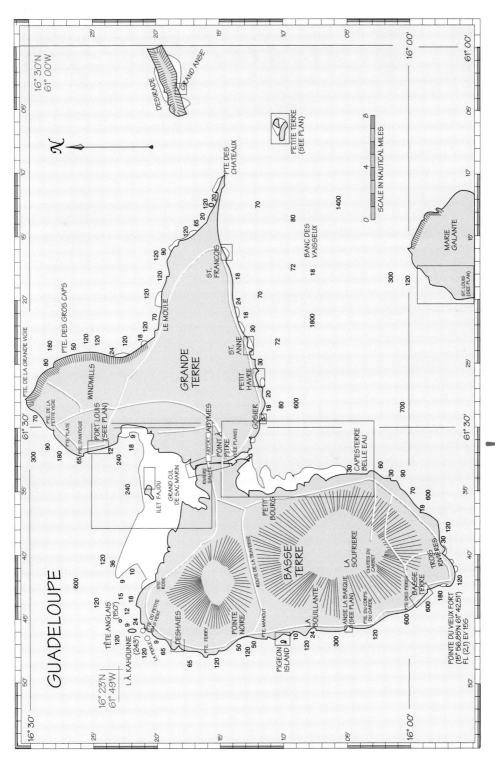

GUADELOUPE

16° 23'N
61° 49'W

MOUNTAINS & MANGROVES

Guadeloupe

Regulations

Guadeloupe is a department of France and it includes the smaller islands of the Saintes and Marie Galante. Customs clearance may be found in Deshaies, Basse Terre, Pointe à Pitre, the Saintes, and Marie Galante. You can sometimes catch the customs officer in Port Louis (not officially a station for yachts) and also in St. François . There are no yacht charges.

Under French law, visiting foreign yachts over 5 tons must have valid national documentation or registry. Original papers (no photocopies) must be on board. Those less than 5 tons can use a registration equivalent to that of state registration in the USA. There is no problem with cruising in Guadeloupe, nor, in general, with chartering. It is okay to pick up and drop off charters in a French territory. The only gray area is when you pick up passengers from one French destination and leave them in another. Commercial vessels (like ferries) doing this should be European flagged; however, pleasure vessels – those with the owner or friends or clients of the owner – are generally exempt. If you end up in the marina in Guadeloupe, you should have no problem. In case you run into an officer who does not understand the situation, talk with marina staff and they will sort it out. Foreign flagged vessels are allowed a stay of up to 18 months in French territory before they become liable for VAT. Foreign flagged vessels may buy duty-free fuel once they have cleared out.

Telephones

Most public phones take telephone cards. Buy these at the post office or any shop that advertises them. Lift the phone, insert the card, and dial the number. To get out of Guadeloupe, dial 00, then the international number (1 for the USA, 44 for the UK). Just dial the 10-digit number if you are calling within Guadeloupe or to St. Barts or to St. Martin. French phone boxes have numbers posted so you can use a card to call someone and have them call you back.

All Guadeloupe numbers now start with 0590 (regular) or 0690 (cellular). You must dial this prefix even on a local call. If you are dialing into Guadeloupe from a non-French territory, you have to dial the country code first, which is also 590, then leave off the first 0 of the number. Thus, if calling from the USA, for regular numbers you will dial 011-590-590 + 6 digits, for cellular numbers: 011-590-690 + 6 digits.

For reverse charge and collect calls, the ATT number is: 0800 99 00 11.

Shopping Hours

Normal shopping hours are 0800-1200 and 1500-1730, though many shops open later than this and most supermarkets stay open over lunch.

Transport

Guadeloupe has a large international airport. Air France flies once or twice a day to Paris, and serves Cayenne, and Caracas with several daily flights. They also have weekly flights to Bordeaux, Lyons, and Marseilles. The rest of the world is also well served by many airlines.

Guadeloupe is also linked to Marie Galante, Desirade, and the Saintes by ferry. Ferry times are designed so that whichever way you are going, you can get there and back in a day. It is best to ask about ferry times on the appropriate ferry dock, as they tend to change. Ferry docks are marked on our town maps. A high-speed ferry runs to Dominica, Martinique, and St. Lucia about three times a week.

There is an efficient and inexpensive bus system. Our town maps show bus terminals and details about routes are mentioned in the appropriate section. There are plenty of taxis in Pointe à Pitre. Try STI at 0590-83-13-65 or Tele Taxi, 0590-94-33-40. In Basse Terre taxis are in front of the customs building, or call 0590-81- 79-70. Taxis in Guadeloupe run by meter, so rates vary with the traffic conditions. They tend to be reasonable for short runs, but very expensive for long ones. The following rates in Euros are approximate:

Marina Bas-du-Fort to the Airport	20-30 Eu
Basse Terre to Marina Rivière Sens	10-15 Eu
Pointe à Pitre to Basse Terre	80 Eu
Deshaies to Basse Terre	80 Eu

For sightseeing, ask in a tourist office about tours. Renting a car is a reasonable alternative and there are car rental agencies in Pointe à Pitre and Basse Terre. You can use your own license. Drive on the right.

Holidays

- Jan 1st
- Carnival Monday & Tuesday (Monday -Tuesday, 46 days before Easter: Feb 15-16, 2010; March 7-8, 2011)
- Good Friday and Easter Monday (Easter Sunday is April 4, 2010; April 24, 2011)
- May 1st (Labor Day)
- May 8th (V.E. Day)
- Ascension Day (May 13, 2010; June 2, 2011)
- Whit Monday, 50 days after Easter Sunday (May 24, 2010; June 13, 2011) Corpus Christie, June 3, 2010; June 23, 2011
- July 14th (Bastille Day)
- July 21st (Victor Schoelcher Day)
- August 15th (Assumption Day)
- November 1st (All Saints Day)
- November 11th (Remembrance Day)
- December 25th (Christmas)

Guadeloupe, Admiralty Lesiure Folio 5642-1, 5642-2, 5642-3, 5642-5, 5642-7

crater lakes, including As de Pique, shaped like an ace of spades. By contrast, Grand Terre, has pleasant countryside of rolling hills, especially the northern part, with lots of sugar cane and picturesque, ruined windmills. Pointe à Pitre, the largest city, has a big marina, excellent chandleries, and you can get all kinds of boat work done.

Most French post offices have ATM machines, and these are sometimes easier to find than a bank.

Navigation

In addition to the IALA-B buoyage system, yellow buoys are used in the French territories to mark many different things. I have seen them used to mark no anchoring areas, limitation of fishing, an area where sand is being dredged, underwater pipelines, waterskiing runs, and as navigation buoys. If the buoys are in deep water, there is usually no problem in navigating through the marked area. If these buoys are placed near a beach or resort area, it is unwise to anchor inside them. Yellow and black buoys are always navigation buoys on the IALA-B system.

There is a lifeboat association called SNSM, which operates a 24-hour watch on VHF: 16/11 (Tel: (0590) 70 92 92) through MRCC-Fort de France relay. It covers the area from about Antigua to St. Lucia. If you call MRCC on VHF: 16, they can give you an English version of the weather.

NORTH TO SOUTH: GUADELOUPE'S WESTERN COAST

Guadeloupe's western coast is mountainous enough that winds on the lee side can be light and fluky, and you can get a wind acceleration effect at the ends of the island, particularly the north end.

From Deshaies, south to Pte. Du Vieux Fort, the coast is steep to and a quarter of a mile offshore clears all dangers. You can pass either side of Pigeon Island, which lies half way up the coast. A shoal called La Perle lies about a quarter of a mile offshore,

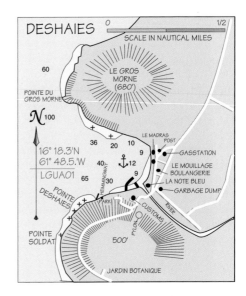

two bays north of Deshaies. In heavy surges it breaks dramatically. There is another shoal off the hotel to its north. You can pass inside Îlets a Kahouanne and Tete à L'Anglais, though the water is only 12 to 14 feet deep, so it is best avoided in large swells or rough conditions.

There are four anchorages spaced along the leeward coast. In calm weather you can tuck in almost anywhere else that appeals to you.

Deshaies

Deshaies (pronounced Day-ay) is a picturesque fishing village near the north end of Guadeloupe's west coast. Attractions include a tropical river and a spectacular Botanical Garden.

Deshaies is set in a deep, well-protected bay, surrounded by hills and mountains. A breakwater forms a harbor for small fishing boats close to the entrance to the river. A ferry terminal has been built onto the breakwater.

Enter the middle of the bay and anchor anywhere inside, leaving a channel into the fishing harbor. Be careful if you anchor within 50 yards of La Mouillage restaurant, as ruins of the old town dock lie underwater.

Guadeloupe acts as a giant windscoop

DESHAIES

MOUNTAINS & MANGROVES

Bougainvillea decorating Deshaies' main road

Chris Doyle

especially when the wind is east or south of east. Deshaies is a vent in this system and the winds here sometimes howl in an alarming manner, leading you to believe conditions outside are closer to the roaring forties than the Caribbean. If you are heading north, the winds get even worse as you sail to Ilet Kahouanne, but after you clear the island they return to normal. Strong winds usually comes from the town; lighter winds can be variable.

Regulations

Le Pelican, the internet café, tells me they are now authorized to check people in and out, which is perfect. If for any reason this does not work, the customs office is up the hill on the south side of town. It has no regular hours, and it is very hard to catch anyone.

Communications

Le Pelican, an attractive photo and art store that does color photocopies, also has a good internet café. They open 0830-1230 and 1600-1900 (closed Sunday). Cyber Foyer is the municipal onshore internet spot. It is upstairs over the police station and opens Monday to Thursday 0800-1200, 1400-1730, and in the morning only on Friday. They have lots of computers, but it can get crowded.

Several stores, including the post office, sell Orange or Digicel phone cards. A few card phones are available that take cards you can buy at the post office. It is possible that HotHotHot spot will get going again here soon.

Services

You can fill jerry jugs with water at La Note Bleu for a small fee. If you dinghy up the river beside the restaurant, the hose will reach your dinghy. Water and electric points have been put in among the fishing boats and close to the ferry dock. They are not yet operational. When they become so, getting water on the ferry dock is a possibility. Gas sold on the fuel dock is only for local fishing boats.

A garbage dump can be found on the road to the river, just off the main road.

Deshaies is on the main bus route to Pointe à Pitre and Basse Terre. Buses leave from early in the morning, and the last bus returns from Pointe à Pitre around 1700, from Basse Terre around 1530. They are both two-and-a-half hour journeys.

A gas station opposite the post office sells cube ice, as well as fuel, and they are often open till 2000. Spar Supermarket also sells ice, as does Alimentation Generale.

Since the demise of the town dock, the best bet for leaving your dinghy is up the canal on the left side after the pedestrian bridge. There is a metal structure people use for locking. You can also look in the fishing port. I have seen dinghies tied to a little wooden dock behind the fuel dock.

Provisioning

Spar is a modern new supermarket with a good deli section and a fair fresh produce selection. They open daily 0800-1300, 1530-2000, and Sundays 0800-1200. This is good for provisioning.

You may need to supplement your purchases with fresh produce from Alimentation General, Heliconia, or other small stores. For meat, try the Bonne Entrecôte butcher at the north end of town.

There are no banks, but you will find two ATMs. The one at the post office is the best. The pharmacy will often cash US dollars.

Daily life begins opposite Le Mouillage at the boulangerie/pâtisserie Amandine, which opens at 0630. You can sit at a little table on the street sipping coffee and eating croissants, Danish, and pain au choco-

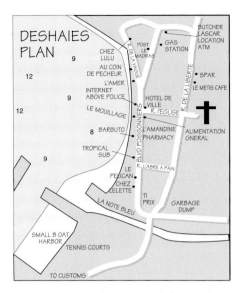

lat straight from the oven, while watching the town wake up.

On Wednesdays and some other mornings, fresh produce stands are set up on the roadside.

Fun Shopping

Browse around among the dozen little souvenir shops in town. If you need a haircut, try the stylist opposite the gas station at the north end of town.

Restaurants

Deshaies is an excellent place for a French meal ashore. There are many restaurants, most reasonably priced. Wander round and take your choice, I mention just a few to give you an idea. Le Mouillage restaurant has been in town just about forever and is both the best known and one of the best, with the largest menu. First-rate Créole seafood is their specialty.

L'Amer is very cute on a balcony hanging right over the beach. They specialize in fresh seafood, served with delightful French sauces. A new menu is posted each day. They close Sundays.

Barbuto is a new restaurant specializing in seafood with a menu that includes French, Créole, and Italian dishes.

Down the beach to the north, Le Madras has seats right out next to the

MOUNTAINS & MANGROVES

361

Deshaies   Chris Doyle

beach, as well as inside. It is inexpensive and, if you give them enough notice, you can choose from a wide variety.

At the other end of the beach, you will find La Note Bleue. It is open, airy, and inexpensive, with a pleasant atmosphere. It is next to the fish dock so you can be sure the seafood is fresh.

Edouard Da Court's Le Kaz, has a very inexpensive set menu and is good and friendly. Côte de Pecheurs, down towards Le Madras, is worth a look.

Restaurant/Bar Le Matis is a Tapas café next to Spar that does a two-for-one happy hour from 1700-1830.

Apart from these, Hemmingway is a beautiful restaurant, down in the Batterie Park on the south side of the Bay. Their dinghy dock is fine unless the swell is bad (take a long line to attach to the buoy). You climb just enough steps to get a great view over the bay from the dining area. The restaurant has a casual-elegant atmosphere with a comfy bar and lounging area,

and dining areas with a great bay view. They open every evening around 1900, and for lunch on weekends, specializing in seafood with a live lobster tank. They usually have live music on Friday and Saturday nights and for lunch on Sunday.

Ashore

This is a good spot from which to explore the mountains of Basse Terre and you can rent a car. Lascar Location is in the same building as the butcher. The hotel in the Batterie Park also rents cars, and I am told there are more car rentals out of town to the north.

There is plenty to do on foot. Anyone ready for a cool, shady, scramble should follow the Deshaies River as it winds its way into the mountains. A concrete road leads back a short way and after that you follow the river from rock to rock passing many a pretty pool. Continue for one to two hours and you come to another road that joins the river on the left hand side and which

Guadeloupe

JARDIN BOTANIQUE DE DESHAIES
Parc floral et animalier

Le site incontournable
Ex-propriété Coluche

05 90 28 43 02
Restaurant panoramique
Snack - Boutique - Aire de jeux

about a kilometer and a half walk straight uphill, heading out past customs. It is well worth the walk and the 14 Euro entry fee. (However, you do not have to walk: if you phone 0590-28-43-02, they will send a free car to pick you up). This is a perfect botanical garden – nature with a dash of theatre. Apart from a thousand species of plants, with everything from cactuses to orchids and big trees, they have built a 50-foot waterfall with rivers and ponds. A walk-in aviary has brightly colored parakeets; and rosy flamingos that hang out round a pool. Kids will love the brightly colored macaws in their Caribbean-style birdhouses. Hike up in the cool of the morning (it opens at 0900) and stay for lunch. They have a fancy restaurant with a great view, a snack bar, and an ice creamery.

Don't miss the huge horticultural sheds where they have lots of potted plants for sale. They even sell some that will eat flies for you.

On your way down you can visit Pointe Batterie, on the southern headland. (Directly from the bay it is a kilometer walk.) This park includes an old battery with a few canons and a picnic area, as well as a good restaurant. The park area has information on the forest, labels are on some trees, and there are lots of birds, including the endemic Guadeloupe woodpecker. Take the road leading south from town to the big radio mast and follow the signs to Pointe Batterie. You can reach the park by dinghy to Hemingway. There is also a full spa in the park.

There is a gorgeous beach in the bay north of Deshaies. Walk on the main road north out of town and look for a path to the beach on your left.

Deshaies boasts new sports facilities, including tennis. These are available to visitors for a small fee. Ask M. Mathieu at La Note Bleue.

will bring you back down to town in about 15 minutes. However, don't return yet. Carry on up the river for another 20 minutes and you arrive as far as you can go without a detour. Your path is stopped as the river comes out of a giant cave-like gully, with a waterfall at the back of it. Several readers have complained that this hike is difficult; avoid it after heavy rains.

The Jardin Botanique de Deshaies is

MOUNTAINS & MANGROVES

Water Sports

For divers and snorkelers there is a delightful coral garden in 10 to 50 feet, just inside the northern headland, under the last cliffs you see from the anchorage. Anchor your dinghy in the bay just east of it. Big rock ridges and coral-covered boulders rise from a sand bottom and are home to lots of fish. There are big schools of chromis, grunts, and doctor fish, and this is a good place to see sun anemones and porkfish.

For diving, check out La Note Bleue Dive Club behind the restaurant. Owner Thiebault speaks good English and dives twice daily at 0915 and 1430. Or, you can go down the road to Tropical Sub; they also speak English. Either will fill tanks.

Pigeon Island Anchorage

The main attraction here is the Cousteau Underwater Park, which includes the islands and the coast northwards for about a mile. If you like scuba diving, make a special effort to visit, as this is an excellent underwater site. You will find rocks, cliffs, corals of all types, octopus, and brightly colored fish. Fishing is strictly forbidden. I also find the snorkeling excellent here, as the water is generally clear and there are lots of fish and sea creatures. However, some snorkelers find it too deep and are disappointed.

Anchoring in the park is not allowed, but mooring buoys are dotted around the islands. The white and blue ones are for professional groups, the yellow ones are for

yachts, and sometimes these go adrift. The authorities only replace them occasionally. If there are no yellow ones, you can use one of the others, but just to snorkel and dive, not to use as a mooring as they are much demand by the dive boats. You can also leave your dinghy on them, but use plenty of line so a dive boat can come alongside. If there are no yellow moorings, you can probably overnight on a blue and white buoy if you go towards sunset when the commercial boats have left.

You may find it calmer to anchor overnight on the mainland shore, in the bay opposite Pigeon Island. The rocky shore is broken by two sandy beaches. The smaller one is more secluded, the larger one more popular, with many shacks selling snacks and handicrafts, not to mention dive shops and agents for glass bottom boats and restaurants. Enter the bay in the

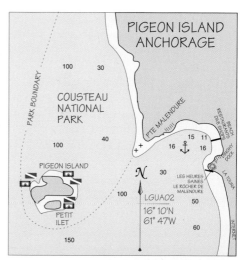

Chris Doyle

PETIT ISLE

PIGEON ISLAND

center and anchor in 12 to 16 feet of water. Holding is variable, so make sure you are well dug in. The wind can swing around, so those on rope are advised to use two anchors. A stern anchor can help cut down the roll if there is any swell. The view of the islands from the anchorage makes a perfect sunset photo.

Services

You can use the long dock if you keep your dinghy near the beach, away from the day-boats. A large concrete garbage bin is behind the dock facing the road. You can use the public fresh water showers which are open and on the beach.

Provisioning

A Match supermarket is about half a mile south from the dock (just over the river) in the direction of the village called Pigeon. It opens daily at 0830. On Sundays it closes at midday; the rest of the week it opens until 1945. However, Monday to Thursday they break for lunch from 1300-1530. Intrepid explorers can dinghy there (conditions permitting). A tiny fishing bay is just inside the mouth of the river; you can see it from the sea, and in 2009 a large wall was being built on the southern bank. This is also the bottom of the car park. Be prepared to paddle over the bar. A Leader

Price is across the road.

Ashore

Several snackettes and restaurants are built on the beach. The cheap mobile ones are excellent for sandwiches and drinks. For a good meal you would do better to walk just a few hundred yards south to either Le Touna or Le Rocher de Malendure. Both are first-rate seafood restaurants and both are reasonably priced. Le Rocher de Malendure is on top of a little headland, and has a great atmosphere. You sit up high in some cozy patio corners amid flowers, while overlooking the bay. They listen to VHF: 72. They open every day for lunch and dinner.

La Touna is right on the waterfront, looking at the islands. It has a nautical atmosphere and opens daily for lunch (1200-1500) and dinner (1900-2130). The staff are friendly and welcoming.

Pigeon is in the general area called Bouillante (meaning boiling). This is because of thermal springs that are hot enough to power electricity in the town of Bouillante, south of Pigeon Island. Those on smaller cruising boats without modern conveniences will be happy to learn that there is a continuous supply of hot fresh water from these springs on a small beach just south of Pigeon. It is on the headland

MOUNTAINS & MANGROVES

Chris Doyle

that separates Pigeon from Bouillante. You can find temporary anchorage off the beach. Look for a black beach with blue changing huts. A floating dock is sometimes installed on this beach. Inside the changing rooms is a ceramic tub with a pipe that continuously pours out a light stream of hot water. For a good wash, take along your dinghy bailer or a bucket, as the pipe is low to the ground.

Water Sports

Diving is very commercial in this area and the numerous beach dive shops continually take people out to the reef. If you have your own equipment, you can dive straight from your yacht when you are tied to a park mooring. However, you need to bring all your own equipment, as renting tanks and weights will cost you as much as a regular dive. You can get your tanks filled here.

Les Heures Saines is in Rocher de Malendure. It is probably the best shop and the most likely to have someone who speaks English. They have a dock off the rocky headland. It even has air piped down to the boats so they do not have to move tanks. The gear is fully up to modern standards and it is a NAUI and PADI resort with full nitrox capabilities. They also arrange whale watching and river canyon hikes, and stand by on VHF: 73. They will fill tanks if you bring in your dive card.

I love snorkeling around the islands. When you tire of finning, take turns being towed behind the dinghy. Non-divers can check out the glass-bottom boat or the semi-submersible.

Anse à la Barque

Anse à la Barque is a useful little hideout where you can find calm water when Pigeon Island and the offshore Basse Terre anchorages are too rolly. It is about 6 miles north of Basse Terre. It is easy on learner navigators because both lighthouses are clearly labeled. The white one is near a new dock built out of the remains of the old steamer dock. The yellow lighthouse

ANSE A LA BARQUE

stands on the northern headland. Enter in the middle of the bay, as there are big rocks on both shores. Two small buoys, which look like fishpot floaters, mark shoals on the southern side. One is red and one white. Anchor outside of the fishing fleet, off the dock ruins, in 30 to 40 feet in passable holding on a hard bottom. The main road running right around this anchorage stops it from being a real beauty.

Water Sports

The snorkeling along the southern shore is excellent and the outer part of the northern shore is well worth exploring.

Basse Terre

Basse Terre is conveniently situated

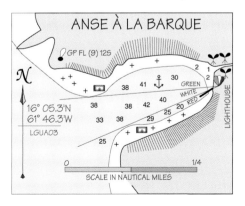

ANSE À LA BARQUE

GP FL (9) 12s

N

16° 05.3'N
61° 46.3'W

LGUA03

2 1
2
30 GREEN
38 41
38 38 42 WHITE
40 20 RED
33 38 29
LIGHTHOUSE

25

0   1/4
SCALE IN NAUTICAL MILES

toward the south end of Guadeloupe's west coast. It is the capital of Guadeloupe and the island's second largest town. The architecture is a blend of old and new. It lacks the flamboyant gaiety of the Pointe à Pitre architecture, being more serious in design, with handsome arches, large well-proportioned windows, and small balconies. There are many small shops, boutiques, and a good fresh food market. Basse Terre is ideally situated for exploring the mountains and the rainforest.

The approach to Basse Terre is deep; there are no shoals. The best place for yachts is by the Marina Rivière Sens about a mile south of town. It is sad to see the old part of the marina (in front of the capitainerie) in a terrible state – the old concrete docks are collapsing, a wreck has sunk alongside, and unfortunately this was the visitors section. It has just gotten worse over the last six years; it is a municipal marina clearly in need of new ownership. Despite this, it is a pleasant place. The marina holds about 300 boats and is full. You should call to see if they have space – you might be lucky. You can take on fuel at the fuel dock.

Hurricanes Lenny and Omar both destroyed the end part of the walls, including the lights, and stones fell into the

 MOUNTAINS & MANGROVES

channel, creating obstructions. It is best to enter in good light when you can see this underwater. From afar, the two shallow areas overlap, making it look like the entrance is blocked. But if you stay closer to the inside wall as you go past the end of the outside one, then swing closer to the outside wall as you go past the end of the inside one, you still have over 7 feet at the entrance Much of the rest is still easily accessible for boats of 6.5-foot draft.

If there is no room (often), or if your yacht is too deep to enter, the best anchorage is off the marina entrance on a shelf that varies from 11 to 45 feet, with good holding. Off the shelf, it is very deep. Or anchor south of the marina off the black sand beach in 20-30 feet of water. Use lots of scope as holding is poor in weed 'til you break through it. If the quarry is working, it creates some noise here, but has not been bad recently. You are welcome to leave your dinghy in the marina.

It is also permissible to anchor off town, at the north end of the large ship dock, in about 25 feet of water. There are low wharfs where you can leave your dinghy. It does roll, however, and the marina is a better option.

Regulations

Customs are in an office to the side of the post office. Official hours are 0700-1200 Monday to Friday, though they are occasionally off on other jobs. It is probably more reliable to clear in the Saintes.

Customs are also in Basse Terre, on the town edge of the big dock, next to the tourist bureau, but they do not like dealing with pleasure craft.

Communications

A Carte Orange mobile store is beyond the chandlery. Basse Terre had no internet stations when I visited, but Antilles Yachting Services has wifi if you take your computer in. (You can try getting wifi from your boat).

Services, Chandlery

You can get diesel and gasoline, at the marina fuel dock, along with cube and

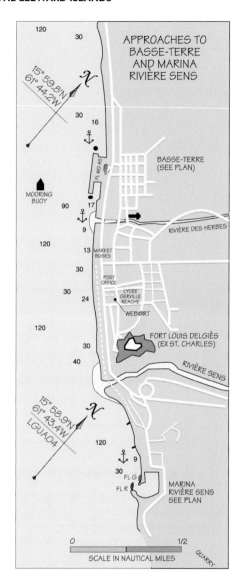

block ice. There is a place to leave your garbage by the main road. Talk to the marina about water.

Antilles Yachting Services (just down from customs) is part of Caraibes Greement and has an excellent and recently expanded yacht chandlery and fishing store, with a little of everything – from electronics to oilskins. They keep a stock of marine paints. They open 0800-1230, 1430-1800, closed Sunday and Monday morning. They have wifi if you bring your computer in.

Almost next door, Dulac is a first-rate

BASSE-TERRE

fishing store with nearly everything for the fisherman, plus a few tools.

Provisioning

8 à Huit is a good, medium-sized super-market. It opens 0800-1300 and 1500-2030 daily, except Sunday when it opens mornings only. In the same area is a great little traiteur/boulangerie/patissierie/glacier, which offers a whole array of dishes; you can eat there (pleasant seating) or take out. You will also find Pharmacy Bride J.C., which is both modern and good. If you want a good bottle of wine, Boutika Vins, is among the row of restaurants at the end of the marina. For a big provisioning, visit Cora (See Ashore in town). Also in the shops around the marina is a convenient laundromat and dry cleaner and two hair-dressers. Some small fishmonger shacks are behind the fuel dock. The post office has a single ATM that may work.

Restaurants

A row of restaurants faces the marina at the far end from the capitainerie. There are sometimes a few around the capitainerie, and you will find more among the shops and apartments across the road on the eastern side. They seem to have been changing rather frequently, so check them out; let your nose be your guide.

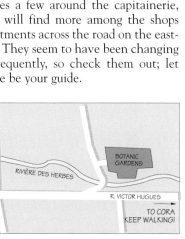

BASSE TERRE

MOUNTAINS & MANGROVES

MARINA RIVIERE SENS

Ashore

Marina Rivière Sens is a good base for exploring the rainforest. You can drive up behind Basse Terre to the Maison de Volcan, then hike to the top of the still active volcano. It is not far to the Chutes du Carbet. You will find a public warm-water bathing pool at Dole (above Trois Rivières).

Marina Sun rents cars. Manioukani, on the hill above the marina, is a large new thalasso therapy center.

For runners, walkers, and bikers, there is pavement for much of the way between Basse Terre the Pointe du Vieux Fort lighthouse, and not too much traffic. Fort D'Olives is small and rambling and is on the slope from the main road down to the lighthouse.

For current information, visit the tourist office downstairs in the marina building.

Water Sports

There is a wall off Fort Louis Delgiès, 66-130 feet deep. It has interesting overhangs and is decorated with sponges and is home to many reef fish. There are also several wrecks in the area.

A government-run dive shop, Departmental de Pleine Nature, is where you see all the dinghies, just northwest of the marina. They dive Wednesday, Friday, and Saturday at 1330, and will fill tanks.

Ashore in Town

A waterfront walkway runs from Rivière Sens to town. Parts of it are very fancy, with elegant lamposts, a red tile pathway, and well-spaced seats. To reach it from the marina, walk right past the post office and turn left to the waterfront. If you don't feel like walking, buses run to town about every half hour, but you may have to walk out to the main road to find one. If you dinghy from the marina to town, you will find a place to leave your dinghy on the ferry dock.

The big fresh food market is excellent.

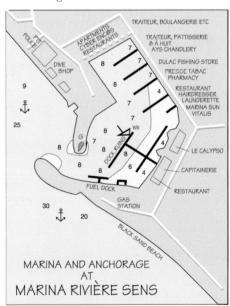

MARINA AND ANCHORAGE
AT
MARINA RIVIÈRE SENS

Just behind the market is a Champion supermarket. There is also a Leader Price and Ecomax. Probably you will find the 8 à Huit at the marina more convenient. For a large provisioning, it is worth paying the taxi fare to visit Cora, a giant supermarket in the hypermarché class, just east of town (going out by Rue Victor Hugues). It is huge and complete with lots of departments.

Basse Terre is full of interesting shops, a good place to buy fabrics, fashions, inexpensive jewelry, and more. The shops are geared to the local market, as few tourists visit. The post office has an ATM machine. You can change money at the change place on Rue Nolivos, which is on the right hand side as you approach the cathedral square. To change travelers' checks, visit Banc Populaire.

Town Center is right in front of customs. The tourist office, the taxi stand, and the Mairie (town hall) are all here around the main square. Most of the interesting boutiques and shops are within a few blocks east of this, toward the Rivière aux Herbes. Behind the market is an inexpensive and interesting area, which smartens up by the time you reach the big government buildings. Down by the waterfront, next to market, are bus stations from which buses go all over the island.

If the heat and crowds get to you, visit Minikebabs, a little air-conditioned snack bar right on the pleasant St. Frances Square, opposite the Cathedral. They offer a range of fresh juices and sandwiches.

Other attractions include Fort Louis Delgiès (0800 -1700), which is a massive old crumbling fort with good views. Check out also the well-ordered botanical garden to the east of town, where all the plants are carefully labeled. L'Artchipel is a very fancy new national theater. When in operation, tickets and programs are available at the theater.

Trois Rivières

Trois Rivières, on the south coast, overlooks the Saintes, and has a small harbor

MOUNTAINS & MANGROVES

that is used by the ferries heading in that direction. Set above this harbor, in a lovely tropical garden with a spectacular view over the Saintes, is Jardin Malanga, a small hotel created out of a large old colonial house. It has a highly-rated restaurant and coffee shop, and would be perfect as a stop on your tour round the island.

NORTH TO SOUTH: GUADELOUPE VIA THE RIVIERE SALÉE

Port Louis

Port Louis is a small but active fishing port on the northwest coast of Grand Terre. The surrounding land is low, with a long attractive beach to the north. It is wide and showy, with rolling waves breaking ashore in places. It can be popular with holidaymakers, with plenty of action on the weekends, including snack bars and

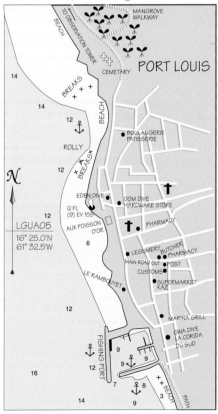

drink stalls.

The big new port is basically finished, though more docks may be added. It was designed for pleasure as well as fishing boats. The basin is mostly 9 feet deep. You can anchor inside (it can be buggy), but there are no services. The bar at the entrance is 6.5 to 7 feet deep. Check it, as this depth is prone to change.

If approaching along the coast from the north, keep clear of the reefs that partially fill the bay to the north of Port Louis. If you wish to visit the beach in this bay, there is a clear patch between the reefs just south of the cemetery. Eyeball your way in and anchor in about 12 feet of water. This anchorage can be rolly and is best as a daytime stop. A quieter anchorage is just west or south of the new fishing port at the south end of town.

This is convenient, as you can leave your dinghy in the fishing port. The outer anchorages at Port Louis are very rolly during bad northerly swells. In such swells, go into the port if you can, or carry on to Ilet à Colas.

The lighthouse in town is not too reliable. As one fisherman said: "It works about one day in five". New lights are under construction for the port, but not yet operational.

Regulations

To find the customs office walk up the main road to the post office, turn right and it is a few buildings down. There is a gate and it is marked "Douanes" on a notice on the wall. This is not an official port of clearance for pleasure boats, but, Paryse Tancelin, the usual customs officer, is very helpful at trying to clear people in and out. If you want to catch him, try going at 0730.

Provisioning

Port Louis has a pleasant front street, which parallels the waterfront and is lit at night by a row of old iron lampposts. There are several admirable old Créole buildings with wobbly balconies and faded gingerbread. In the center of town, there are several shops, including a boulangerie (Le Gourmand du Nord), two pharmacies, and

The Port at Port Louis   Chris Doyle

jungly vegetation lines the hardware store. The fishing port is the center of life, with brightly painted open boats tied to the docks. You can nearly always buy fish here – small spratts in the morning – big dolphin, tuna, and whatever else is running in the afternoon. Cars pull up from all around to buy fish. Supermarché Kaz à Prix is a good small supermarket where you can top up stores, buy French cheeses and wine, and they sell ice. For fresh produce, the Legumery is a first-rate greengrocer, open every day (including Sunday morning). You will also find a butcher.

Restaurants

La Corida du Sud is the fishermen's café. Give them a little notice and they will cook an inexpensive and first-rate Créole dinner, which you can eat facing the port. If you want something a little more elegant, walk down the waterfront to Aux Poisson d'Or, with its dining room facing the ocean. Try also Marina Grill and Le Rambouyant on the front street.

Ashore

An interesting and popular footpath heads north along the shore all the way to Anse Betrand. It starts in the beach car park north of town, and the path is drivable for about quarter of the way. A side trip is a mangrove path that includes some lovely wooden sections perched over swampland. The interesting part of this path starts just south of the cemetery. Close to the end of the path is a three-story wooden observation tower.

A tiny wild walkway, between beach and mangroves, also follows the coast south for a couple of miles. You can find rock pools, hidden small beaches, and a few places with interesting snorkeling. This path starts at the abandoned blue truck in the southeast corner of the marina.

Water Sports

You can arrange to go diving with GWA right next to Corrida du Sud, or Eden Plongée or Dom Plongée on the front street. All can fill tanks.

Grand Cul De Sac Marin

Large areas of Cul de Sac Marin, including Ilet à Fajou, Pte. De Grande Rivière, and most offshore islands, are protected national parks and fishing is prohibited.

MOUNTAINS & MANGROVES

Many park areas are marked by yellow buoys and small beacons, some of which show fixed or flashing orange lights at night. Some are outside the outer reef in deep water to the west of the Passe à Colas entrance buoys.

A system of reefs extends up to 4 miles from Rivière Salée and encloses miles of navigable water. Entrance from the north is not too hard in good light. First, spot the low-lying, mangrove-covered Ilet à Fajou. This island is about a mile long and stands out clearly from the land behind. Enter the channel between the red and green markers, which lie about a mile to the northeast of Ilet à Fajou. Once you have done this, the channel presents no problems. Follow the buoys, keeping the "red right returning" rule in mind. If you are coming from Port Louis, the channel entrance is almost on a line between Port Louis and the east end of Ilet à Fajou.

For those passing through to the Rivière Salée, our sketch chart gives a series of waypoints that will help you steer towards the next buoy until you can see it. The last two red buoys as you approach Rivière Salée can be hard to see against the mangroves in some lights.

Ilet à Colas Anchorage

There is a small anchorage beside the channel, close to Ilet à Colas and Ilet à Fajou, which makes a fine stopping place on your way north or south. There is a green channel buoy just south of Colas, and there are several hundred feet where you can anchor east of the buoy, out of the channel. You are protected by all the surrounding reefs. The water is generally clear, so you can see the reef and pick your spot. Anchor in about 14 feet of water and, if necessary,

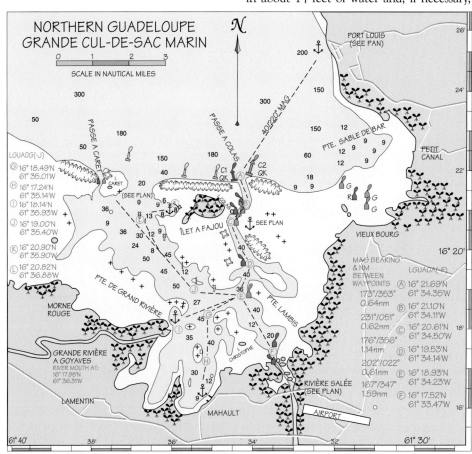

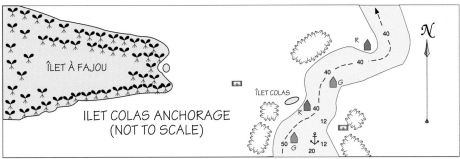

ÎLET À FAJOU

ILET COLAS ANCHORAGE
(NOT TO SCALE)

ÎLET COLAS

N

use a stern anchor to keep you from swinging on the reef. Holding is very variable – good to poor depending on the spot.

Water Sports

Plunge over the side of your boat with mask and snorkel, for you will see many coral heads and sponges with interesting small fish and creatures. This is a good place to see pencil urchins and big variety of sea cucumbers.

This is also a great spot to mess around in the dinghy. Near Ilet à Fajou, you can glide around on water so shallow and clear you might be on a cushion of air. Below, amid the turtle grass, are bright red starfish, lots of urchins, and the occasional crab, eel, or baby ray. Now and again, a pelican will make an ungainly splash in pursuit of a tasty morsel.

Dense mangroves cover most of Ilet à Fajou, but all around the western end are tiny beaches that you approach by wading around the shore. There are places to peek into the dark mangrove forest and listen to the birds.

Baie Mahault

Cul de Sac Marin is a wonderful area for gunkholing. The problem is, apart from the main channel, there are no navigation markers. However, good reef navigators with a GPS, a good chart of the area (try Caribbean Yachting Charts #C32A), our waypoints, and good visibility can find their way to the most obvious anchorages and leave by Passe à Caret or Passe à Fajou. Some of the markers on our sketch chart are of unknown reliability and are park marks, not navigation buoys.

Baie Mahault is deeply indented and very protected. Start at the green buoy, which lies halfway between Ilet à Fajou and Isle Christophe, and head toward Point de Grand Rivière. You can turn down towards the town when it bears true south, and eyeball your way through the reefs. The waypoints on our sketch chart will help. Just north of waypoint H is a very small white marker on the shoal to the west of the channel. Anchor anywhere off town. The town dock is usually full of powerboats, but there is a smaller dock where you can leave your dinghy.

Walk up to the town and pass to the right of the big modern town hall to start down the main road. Close by are several fair supermarkets. Farther down is a big boulangerie and a few small restaurants.

Come here to buy the last couple of things you forgot, to get your scuba tanks filled, or go for a dive on the outer reefs with La Bulle Diving, which is right on the waterfront.

Point Grande Rivière Anchorage

The anchorage off Pte. Grande Rivière is not too difficult to find and puts you in a convenient position to explore the river. Start at the green buoy that lies halfway between Ilet à Fajou and Isle Christophe. Steer straight for Pointe Grande Rivière (approximate course 250°). As you approach the point, you can get protected anchorage behind some reefs just to its northeast. Go in good light and bring out the polarizing sunglasses, because this is strictly eyeball navigation, and the reefs

MOUNTAINS & MANGROVES

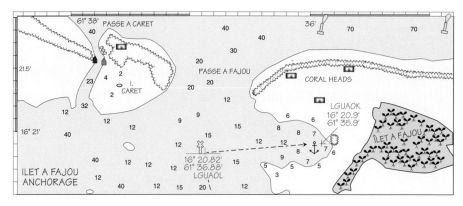

are not easy to see in the murky water. The anchorage is about 150 yards offshore, with the point bearing approximately 185°. Currents are quite strong, but holding is good in clay-like sand. The anchorage is isolated and surrounded by miles of open water, with occasional patches of low land and distant hills.

Ashore

The attraction here is Grande Rivière à Goyave, the longest navigable river in the Eastern Caribbean. You can dinghy or powerboat up for about 5.5 miles; big mangroves and jungly vegetation line the banks for the first mile or two. This gives way to pastoral scenes with grassy banks, cows, and pretty trees. It reminds me of a gentle river in the States or Europe, except that, instead of weeping willows, there are stands of bamboo and breadfruit; fields of sugar cane, rather than corn; and every cow has its attendant egrets, daintily picking their way. This river is the perfect antidote for a tough crossing and ideal for a picnic lunch. You can follow it almost up to the first bridge, though there is no great advantage to doing so unless you have forgotten lunch and need to buy bread and wine from the local store. In strong winds, the passage from the anchorage to the river mouth can be choppy. There is a shallow mangrove channel to the right before the river that could be mistaken for the river. The river is quite wide and has 3 or 4 feet of water at the bar. Inside, the river is from 6 to 15 feet deep for some miles. Do not swim in the river, as there is a danger of bil-

harzia (caused by parasitic worms and also known as schistosomiasis).

Ilet à Fajou Anchorage

On the west side Ilet à Fajou is a fabulous away-from-it-all anchorage on a vast turquoise sea. This part of Ilet à Fajou has several tiny beaches and it is moderately popular on weekends. The snorkeling out by the reef is good, but it is a long way from the anchorage. Snorkel anywhere around the anchorage to see lots of starfish and a big variety of sea cucumbers. The whole area is a marine park – no fishing or taking anything.

This anchorage is a little shallow, but monohulls of up to 7.5-foot draft can anchor here. Our sketch charts shows the depths I found, adjusted to mean low water. From the green buoy by waypoint E on our sketch chart, you should see a park marker with a cross on it. Leave it on your starboard hand. After this you will be able to pick up the white post on the isolated shoal, just south of the rest. (Waypoint J takes you just south of it.) Once past this, head towards Ilet à Caret. When you get to the yellow buoy, which is our waypoint GUAOL, head to our anchorage waypoint, GUAOK, feeling your way into the suitable anchoring depth as you go. (For the deepest water, try to stay over clear sand, rather than grass.)

If you make it here, leaving into the open sea by Passe à Fajou is not difficult. Passe à Caret is also not hard in good light. The channel is narrow and twisty but the

RIVIÈRE SALÉE

delineation of deep and shallow water is quite clear in good light. Ilet à Caret is a tiny sandy island covered in palm trees and surrounded by reefs. It has several thatch shelters and is very popular with locals on weekends, when it fills up with small powerboats. Shoal draft craft (up to 4 feet) can find temporary anchorage just out of the channel.

Rivière Salée

The Rivière Salée is not so much a river as a saltwater mangrove channel separating Basse Terre from Grand Terre. You can pass through with an overhead clearance of 80 feet. Maximum beam is 25 feet, and for this you will need lots of crew and fenders. For the most part Rivière Salée is 9 to 16 feet deep. The minimum (low tide) depth right in the channel is about 6.9 feet (north of buoy RS1). But to find the deepest part of the channel here is not easy, and on either side the depth drops another foot or two. My sounder showed a couple of feet of very soft mud that might give more navigable depth. You can certainly make it with 2 meters draft or more, but in the shallowest spot you might want to go carefully and, if you have a problem, sound ahead with the dinghy.

There are two opening bridges. (Technically three as Pont de Gabarre is two bridges close together – a pedestrian bridge and a road bridge that open at the same time. There is a bit of curve between them, but it is not too bad.)

Currents can be fairly strong in the river and maneuvering while waiting for a bridge can be a little tricky. Navigating Rivière Salée does vastly shorten the sail to Antigua, but bridge times are restrictive, so this route is best approached as adventurous fun rather than just a short cut.

The regular daily bridge times given below are Monday to Saturday. Heading North: Pont de la Gabarre is near Pointe à Pitre. The bridge opening time is 0500, though you should be ready about 15 minutes before. They usually let the southbound boats through first. The north bridge (Bridge l'Alliance) will open as you approach (0520).

Heading South: The north bridge (Bridge l'Alliance) opens at 0430, which gives you time to make it to the second bridge by 0500, when it opens. You must be geared up, lights on, and ready to go at 0420, for if the attendant comes and sees no yachts waiting, he wisely turns his car round and goes home for coffee.

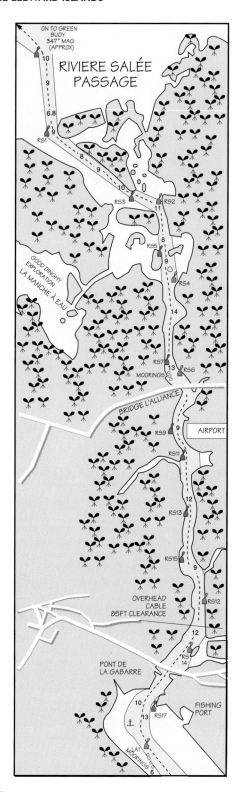

378

Luckily, whichever way you are going, you can anchor or moor close to the bridge, so you are all ready. All moorings were missing in 2009; we shall see if they are replaced. In the meantime you can anchor just north of the north bridge, and the water here is a good 9 feet. At the south end you will find lots of room to anchor in plenty of water, just south of the channel after the last green buoy.

Local powerboats ignore the 5-knot speed limit, and it is worth using an anchor light as people occasionally zoom through in the early hours.

The channel is well marked with flashing green and red buoys. Note that it is red-right-returning to the Pont de la Gabarre, and switches directly after that. You have to go between the two bridges in the dark, which is not too hard with the new buoys (a few buoys are sometimes missing). If you are heading north, it is more relaxing to anchor after the northern bridge, take breakfast, and continue when it is good and light, and you can enjoy the scenery.

For up-to-date bridge time information, call the marina: VHF:19 or 0590 93 66 20. They speak English.

It is hardest to stay in the deepest water at the two ends of Rivière Salée. At the north end, the shallowest part on my last survey seemed to be just at the entrance to the channel, just north of RS1. Start very close to RS1 and aim for RS2. Go slowly, and if it starts to get less than 6.9 feet deep, try edging slightly to the east.

The passage between the river entrance and Pointe à Pitre is a narrow channel at least 8 to 10 feet deep in a broad body of much shallower water. As long as all the buoys are in place, it is no problem. However, when heading north you cannot run straight from the last green to the red – you must follow the curve of the river around before heading for the red buoy (reverse for heading south). A look at our sketch chart will show this and help identify the places where you are likely to have problems.

If you reach a bridge the afternoon before, enjoy exploring the narrow man-grove channels either side of the river by dinghy. In places, they are so narrow that the mangrove branches meet overhead. There are times when you have to paddle, but it is very picturesque, with falling roots, broken reflections, and crabs running all over the mangroves. It can be buggy, so repellent is advised. Buggy also describes the anchorages either side of the bridges, so have a coil ready to burn. You may see lots of birds, including herons, egrets, and king-fishers. La Manche à Eau makes for interesting dinghy exploration.

Pointe à Pitre

Pointe à Pitre, Guadeloupe's largest and most important city, is a lively Créole town with a hodgepodge of old and new buildings. The huge, well-protected harbor has two acceptable hurricane holes: Rivière Salée and Port de Plaisance. Port de Plaisance, more properly known as Port de Plaisance de Bas du Fort, is inside the harbor entrance, about a 30-minute walk from town. This whole area is geared to yachts, and this is one of the best yachting service

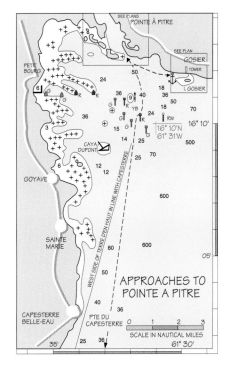

APPROACHES TO POINTE A PITRE

MOUNTAINS & MANGROVES

centers in the Leewards, especially for those with high-tech boats.

They are used to working on the outrageous racing machines that participate in the Rhoute de Rhum. They service motors of all types, from big units for power cruisers to rinky dink diesels and outboards used in fishing boats. You will find top-notch people here to help you, whether you need a new rig, a hull repair, or a perfect racing sail. The chandleries have a European slant, and you can find excellent buys on some things. A large residential area surrounds the marina and includes an active shopping district. The selection of restaurants within walking range, makes a visit a delightful prospect.

If you want to get to know some of the

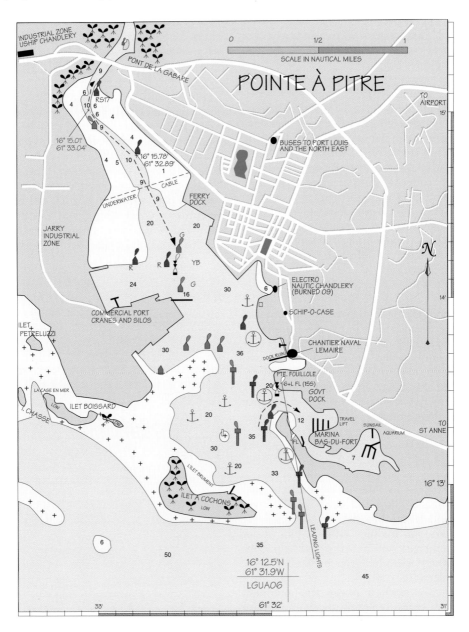

POINTE À PITRE

APPROACHES TO POINT A PITRE AND MARINA BAS-DU-FORT

MOUNTAINS & MANGROVES

locals, you can try joining some of their regular races. Wander over to the Cercle Sportif during the day and find out what is planned.

They also hold some great regattas where you will be welcome. These include the Tour de la Guadeloupe in May, where you stop in a different anchorage each night. Le Regate des Saintes in June, where you race to the Saintes, the Triskell Cup, in October with racing out of Pointe à Pitre and La Grande Galette, with racing to Marie Galante in December.

Navigation

(See also our section on sailing between Guadeloupe and the Saintes (page 418), and sketch chart page 379)

A deepwater channel is well buoyed for big ships going in and out of Pointe à Pitre. There is plenty of water to shortcut over the bank to its east, except for one shoal called Mouchoir Carré, which is only 9 feet deep and breaks in heavy swells. This shoal lies just east of the last red beacon of the shipping channel. The beacon southeast of that one is black and yellow and east of the channel line. If you pass to the southeast of this black and yellow beacon, you will stay in about 23 feet of water. If you follow the main shipping beacons, take care not to then follow the fishing boat channel right up into Petit Bourg, as it starts soon after the main shipping channel ends. This is most likely to be a problem at night or in a rainsquall.

You can tie up in the marina, take one of the marina buoys outside, or anchor nearer

town. You can also anchor anywhere between the channel and Ilet à Cochons.

When entering the marina, leave the red buoys to starboard. Leave both the yellow and black one and all the green ones to port. There is a shoal between the yellow and black buoy and the shore, despite the efforts of several erring yachts to grind it away with their keels.

Regulations

Customs and immigration are next door to the marina office. When they are not around (often), the marina will do the clearance for you for the cost of 2 Eu for the fax.

Communications

The marina's wifi system was not working in 2009, but they should soon have a new one. They also have an internet computer in the office that you can use. The marina offers a mail drop: Port de Plaisance, Marina Bas-du-Fort, Guadeloupe, F.W.I.

Adjoining the marina is a large area of businesses. One of these, Post Office Cyber Service, is an excellent communication center. You can email from here, with their fast connection or you can bring your computer in for wifi. Their phone booths will call anywhere, and have excellent rates to the US on a phone card system. Sending and receiving faxes is easy, and they will put stamps on your letters and packages and mail them. They also repair computers, design and install web sites, offer courier service, secretarial services, color photocopying, and they sell phone cards. If you are staying a while, mailboxes are available

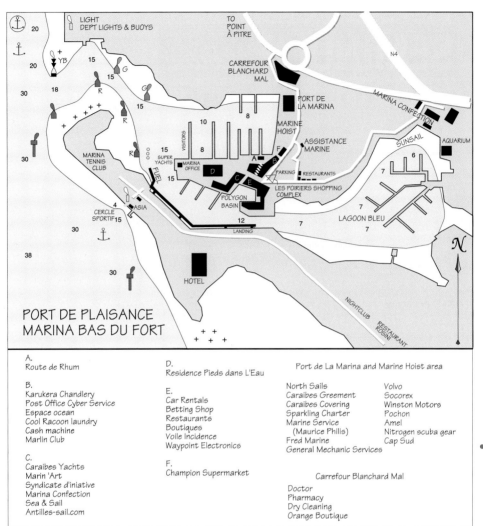

PORT DE PLAISANCE
MARINA BAS DU FORT

A.
Route de Rhum

B.
Karukera Chandlery
Post Office Cyber Service
Espace ocean
Cool Racoon laundry
Cash machine
Marlin Club

C.
Caraibes Yachts
Marin 'Art
Syndicate d'iniative
Marina Confection
Sea & Sail
Antilles-sail.com

D.
Residence Pieds dans L'Eau

E.
Car Rentals
Betting Shop
Restaurants
Boutiques
Voile Incidence
Waypoint Electronics

F.
Champion Supermarket

Port de La Marina and Marine Hoist area

North Sails
Caraibes Greement
Caraibes Covering
Sparkling Charter
Marine Service
 (Maurice Philis)
Fred Marine
General Mechanic Services

Volvo
Socorex
Winston Motors
Pochon
Amel
Nitrogen scuba gear
Cap Sud

Carrefour Blanchard Mal

Doctor
Pharmacy
Dry Cleaning
Orange Boutique

for a reasonable fee. They open Monday to Friday 0800-2000, Saturday, 0900-1400.

General Yacht Services

Marina Bas-du-Fort (VHF: 09) is a very pleasant full-service marina with 1080 berths. It is well run by a good local company (TAV-CGP). Guylaine, Chymene, and Akila behind the desk are all helpful and speak good English. Three port masters are on hand, to come with a dinghy and help you in with your boat. Ariane Graf speaks perfect English and runs the full gamut of superyacht services, from customs clearance to provisioning and duty-free fuel. For big yachts coming into the marina, Ariane is the best person to contact.

The main visitor's berth is right off the marina office, but if they ever run out of space here, they have plenty of room elsewhere. Most berths are stern-to, with pick-up buoys. Megayachts with depths of up to 14.5 feet and 75 meters long are welcome. The berths for these are outside the capitainerie.

Entering is very easy, even for single-handers. You radio when you are near the entrance, and one of the staff will come out with the launch and help you in. They have 24-hour reception at 0690-35-19-19.

MOUNTAINS & MANGROVES

The docks have water and electricity (220- and 110-volt and the big yacht docks also have 380-volts, up to 150 amps). The electricity is mainly 50-cycle, but some is switchable to 60-cycle.

Water, diesel, gasoline, and ice are available on the new fuel dock on the other shore, facing the marina office. Duty free fuel is available for foreign yachts that have cleared out.

Showers and toilets are available; they use magnetic cards that you get in the office, and these also work for the car park and dock gates. Large garbage containers are near the end of the visitors' dock, as are depots for used oil and fuel. The garbage contains full recycling, including metals, plastics, cardboard, and glass.

The marina has a service area with a 27-ton marine hoist. The surface is being upgraded, with holding tanks and a painting area for an ecological haul-out. More service shops will soon be built. The marina is also building an 800-ton, 45-meter dry dock, which should soon be just outside the marina entrance. Longer term plans

include rebuilding and enlarging the main office. There is no long-term dry storage at this time.

A dinghy dock is close to the marina office. On the other shore, you can tie up inside the fuel dock (take your magnetic card for access). New security arrangements, which include posted video cameras, guards, and gates, are good.

The marina also controls the water outside the marina, which has moorings. The fee for the moorings is 10 Eu per day or 150 Eu a month. The fee enables you to get a magnetic card for the facilities and also to take on water for free at the fuel dock. They have had problems maintaining the moorings, so if there are very few, and there is plenty of space, you may also anchor (no charge). You can also still anchor off Ilet à Cochons and by town with no charge.

French style gas bottles are available, but those with English-style bottles should take them to Sodexgaz over at Jarry (Sodexgaz uses propane which may affect some regulators).

Services are distributed around the

marina area. One major complex is Porte de la Marina in the north corner of the marina, others are in the marina shopping-complex and around the Polygon Basin. A few are at the head of Lagon Bleu. More services are between the marina and town and we list these separately.

The marina is home to many charter companies, which all have people who speak English and can help with general information.

Caraibes Yachts, run by Jean Paul, is a yacht brokerage and charter agent. Jean is a very pleasant person, speaks perfect English, and handles a wide range of new and used boats, both multihulls and mono-hulls, and he has offices here, in Marina Fort Louis in St. Martin, and in Marin in Martinique. You can list your current yacht with them, buy a secondhand boat (Jean Paul is the main Amel broker), or a new Jenneau or Lagoon. He also charters pri-vate yachts for clients. His office faces the Polygon Basin.

Cool Racoon opens 0830-1230 and 1400-1800, and will take care of your laun-dry. I find they have reasonable prices and friendly service. They will just wash, wash and dry, wash, dry and fold, or even iron if really required. They also have a major English language book-swap.

If you need dry cleaning done, 5 à Sec is in the Carrefour Blanchard Mall, and Espace Pressing is another laundry here.

Marten Barriel, Socarex, and Yves Cardan at Exmar are the local surveyors, and will do damage, condition, insurance, and other surveys.

In the next bay toward town from the marina, there is a large boatyard area. Shipyard Chantier Lemaire, the largest haul-out facility in the area, is at the head of the bay. It is actually three businesses in one, involving several members of the Lemaire family. One of these, Seminole Marine, offers very complete engineering, fiberglass, and carpentry shops. Their dry dock can take yachts up to 120 feet long, 42-foot beam, and 13-foot draft. They haul quite a few superyachts and have experi-

MOUNTAINS & MANGROVES

ence with these. They can also handle really big cats.

Their crane can pull masts or engines up to 10 tons, and they have tow boats for the engineless. You can do your own work, or they can arrange for a full team to tackle any job. Lemaire is agent for International Paints, Hempel, and Nautix, and keeps a crew to do topside spraying, as well as antifouling. Between them, the three businesses build commercial and pleasure craft, both outboard and inboard. At the yard with the two smaller dry-docks, they build excellent lightweight fiberglass dinghies, which make good yacht tenders, and their prices are reasonable. They can repair any kind of fiberglass problem, and find you anything you need. The Lemaires speak English.

Apart from Ariane in the marina, Gerard Petrelluzi (0690-35-31-58) and Jimmy at Caribbean Luxury Cars (0690-93-03-56) offer full concierge services for the big yachts.

For medical problems, visit Dr. Thierry Caussee (0590-93-64-01), who is a GP and also a sailor. His office is in the Carrefour Blanchard Mall outside the Port de la Marina, between the dry cleaner and the laundry. Next to his office is a new modern pharmacy. You will have a harder time finding the two good, modern dentists: Dr. Cardin, also a sailor (0590-93-62-62), or his partner Dr Alexis Sebrien (0590-990-79-00). Their office is in the big apartment block behind Plaisancier restaurant, but you have to find your way back into this area – normally done through a gate near Plaisancier restaurant and keep turning right, then when you come to the last steps, look up. They open weekdays 0830-1230 and 1430-1830, but you must call for an appointment.

Le Syndicate d' Initiative acts much like a tourist office.

Chandlery

Karukera Marine is in the marina shopping mall. It is the largest and best general chandlery in the marina. They are particularly strong on fishing and snorkeling gear, with a huge range and some good prices on rods. Karukera also stock regular yacht hardware – from lights to stoves – they have a fine selection of ropes, and you will find cruising guides, charts, and dinghies, plus a section of nautical ornaments. In their next-door shop, Le Ponton, they sell casual nautical clothing and French-brand yacht shoes, as comfortable and chic as those well-advertised American brands. If you have a language problem, ask for the general manager Jean Claude Guisbert. He speaks excellent English.

How about some monogrammed (embroidered) or photo transfer boat towels, crew caps, polo or t-shirts? You will enjoy meeting with Eileen Cookson from Blackpool, who enjoys answering any questions you may have about the area. Her shop, Marin 'Art, is in the Polygon Basin. She has an automated machine and a computer system with hundreds of logos and type styles, or you can scan yours in. Unlike many similar businesses, there is no minimum quantity. Her stock of towels, shirts, and caps are all top quality, and for the large yachts she can help with crew uniforms. Eileen also sells gifts, clothing, soaps, and lots of things for babies and kids.

Caraibe Greement have a first-rate chandlery at Port de la Marina, specializing in the technical side of yachting, with everything for rigging, You won't find a better selection of pulleys, rigging fittings, shackles, Spinlock equipment, and Goiot hatches and hatch spares. They also stock toilets and toilet spares, cooking stoves, pumps and pump parts, winches, ropes, and general marine hardware.

Caraibe Greement is also the Profurl agent and can sell you a new system or help with your old one. Visit them also if something ails your mast or rig. They handle all kinds of rigging problems, stock cable and swages for up to 16mm, and can even order you a new mast. Caraibe Greement are agents for Lewmar and Navtec. They do not have much time now for boat work, but Cedric, the manager, will help find you someone, He speaks good English and Spanish.

Schip-o-Case is between the Lemaire yards and Electo Nautic. It is within easy walking range of either. This is an intriguing second hand chandlery whose stock and price is fixed by those who own the items for sale. You will find rope, sails, outboard engines, dinghies, fixtures, fittings of all types, lots of fishing gear, and, occasionally, bicycles, as well as a selection of new bolts and a multilingual book exchange. The owner, Anke, is from Holland and speaks perfect English.

Electro Nautic, just opposite town, was one of the Caribbean's largest chandlery and appliance stores, also agent for Suzuki. The store was burnt to the ground by rioters during the general strike of 2009. If it gets rebuilt, it will be a fine new shop, so take a look.

Uship is a giant new marine store out of town in an industrial park heading west after the bridge over the Rivière Salée. (You have to turn right after the bridge into the industrial area and look on your left a long way down). It has lots of inflatables, sailing dinghies, beach cats, and

MOUNTAINS & MANGROVES

kayaks, as well as general chandlery, charts, safety gear, and marine accessories.

In addition to the chandleries, there is a good wholesaler in Jarry. West Indies Nautic Distribution (WIND) is managed by Pascal (who speaks English) and owned by Bruno Marmousez, who has a similar establishment in Martinique. The difference is that the Martinique store is both wholesale and retail; this one is only wholesale. They specialize in paint, epoxy system 3, polyester resins, fiberglass materials, and the latest cores, as well as all the applicators. They also sell Jotun and Seajet antifouling paint and supplies such as flashlight batteries, dust masks, and sandpaper. WIND is also the best flag outlet in the Eastern Caribbean. They have or can quickly get any kind of courtesy flag or ensign. For the most part, you will probably buy their products from the chandleries mentioned above. However, if you get involved in a big project, contact them directly, also for antifouling and specialty ship batteries.

For electrical stuff (especially hard-to-find 24-volt bulbs), check Waypoint Marine (see Technical Yacht Services).

Chris Doyle

Technical Yacht Services
Sails and Rigging

You will find that people in most services mentioned in our guide either speak good English or enough to sort out your problems and help you get by.

North Sails is at La Porte de la Marina. Ask for Bernoit Brillant, who speaks English, or Tony Elise. North Sails is the highest tech sail loft in the Leewards. They maintain direct links to North Sails in the US, and have a chain of agents through the Caribbean, including St. Martin, St. Barts, Antigua, Martinique, St. Lucia, Bequia, Grenada, and Trinidad. It is a fully computerized loft and they build most sails from panels cut by automated laser cutters, normally from South Africa. They offer performance cruising versions of the new seamless molded sails from the US. Quotes for new sails can be given immediately and you can see your sail on the computer before it is made. They will be happy to fix your old sails, even those made of the most exotic materials. North Sails stocks a good line of FSE ropes at reasonable prices, and they make catamaran nets, sail covers and lazy bags, but they do not do cushions, biminis, or awnings. The owner, Andrew Dove is also English, and he is occasionally here, but most often he is in his Antigua loft.

Caraibes Covering, next to North Sails, handles everything except sails – all your canvas, awnings, cushions, and soft furnishings. The staff is welcoming and they have an excellent stock of materials, including that hard-to-find closed-cell foam for cockpit cushions. They will make or repair whatever you need – from a bimini or windsurfer cover to new bunk mattresses.

Marina Confection, in a big shop down by Sunsail, specializes in yacht interior decor and they sew all kinds of cushions, sunscreens for windows, covers, and biminis. They keep a good stock of foam, including closed cell. This is also an excellent place to come for your own sewing projects. They not only sell a great selection of fabrics and webbings, but all the snap hooks, zips, and other little fitting you need to go with them. They open weekdays 0800-1300, 1400-1800.

Another general sailmaker, Voile Incidences GPE, run by Rudolphe Bizière, is by the Polygon Basin. He is friendly and helpful and works on sails and all other canvas products. He quotes on new Incidences sails from France. Whether these are a good buy or not will depend on the exchange rate.

Jean Paul Levert, known as JP, runs GPS Rigging Service and he has an excellent reputation. Call him on his mobile phone, 0690-58-18-04, and arrange for him to come see you at your boat. He can handle any job, however big or small, from replacing a stay or fixing a navigation light to getting a whole new rig.

CTA is a rigging shop run by Claude Thelier. He has moved it back in the area behind Lemaire. His brother has an advanced welding shop and you can always get any metal welded or machined, or new

MOUNTAINS & MANGROVES

389

bimini frames built. They can repair aluminum hulls or fix broken stanchions. As a mast and rigging shop, they can fix anything, from replacing a stay to getting a new mast and rig, and you will not find anyone better at difficult high-tech jobs. They are agents for Spar Craft, ACMO and JP3. In addition to purely rigging work, they can install and repair hydraulic systems. Claude can be busy, so you need to allow lots of time.

Technical Yacht Services Motor Mechanics

If your problems are mechanical, there are several marina workshops around the marine hoist and Port de la Marina. Fred and his team at Fred Marine are a first-rate mechanical and refit shop. On the mechanical side Fred Marine is agent for Yanmar inboards and Tohatsu outboards (you can also buy a Suzuki). They can sell you a new engine, or get your old one running again. They fix all brands of inboards and outboards, and do all engine-associated electrical repairs, including starters.

They have a good-sized shop, selling oils, filters, and other engine consumables. For a while Fred Marine has also been doing work on the slip preparation, sandblasting, and antifouling.

Now they have expanded to complete project management and boat care. You can leave your boat in their hands with a big list of jobs and come back and find it all done, the boat painted, and ready for sea. Or, if you just want them to keep an eye on it and run the motor, they do that too. If you prefer to do your own work, they rent equipment. They have a 24/7 breakdown service and have plans for an even bigger workshop in 2009.

General Mecanique Services is run Yves Hecq. He repairs many makes of diesel engine and has his own machine shop. He is agent for Caterpillar, Lombardini, and Cummins diesels. He also works on Onan, and most other brands. He does the precision side of mechanics: repairing and servicing both injectors and injection pumps. He also does a lot work on shafts and bearings and keeps a good stock of cutlass bear-

ings. He has a new store with lots of spare parts and accessories.

Guadeloupe now has a specialist for larger diesel engines. Assistance Marine is a first-rate mechanical shop run by Luc Casanova. He is the Guadeloupe agent for Nanni Diesel and the Caribbean agent for Baudouin Motors. Luc also works on nearly all makes of engine, including Caterpillar, Deutz, MTU, Volvo, MGO, AGU, Perkins, and Warsila. Luc keeps many of the ferries going and is pleased to work on yachts that have big engines. The only brand he does not work on (because of the specialized tools) is GMs.

Marine Service is run by Maurice Philis. Maurice is a good general mechanic and works on all kinds of diesel engines, including big GMs and Caterpillars. He is an agent for Volvo Penta and Motor 56. You can buy your new Volvo Penta here. His work includes electrical repairs, starters, and alternators. He also organizes bottom painting, shaft repairs, cutlass bearings, and more.

Those with malfunctioning Volvo or Perkins auxiliaries can seek help from G.M.D. who offer a full Volvo Penta and Perkins sales and service station, managed by Bernard Vonesch. His shop also sells small chandlery items and motor accessories. For outboard motors, check Winston Motors, the local agent for Suzuki, Mercury, Evinrude, and Yamaha. He can get your outboard running again, whatever the make, or sell you a new one.

Technical Yacht Services
Electronics

If you have problems with your electrics or electronics, visit Stephane's Waypoint. He has a good electrical/electronic chandlery, with everything from radars and instruments to lights and connectors, including windmills and solar panels. They have, or can get, a big range of 12-volt batteries, including the Optima line. They also stock some refrigeration compressors and spares. Stephane is agent for Simrad, Raymarine, Garmin, Furuno, Victron, and Aerogen, and he fixes just about every-

thing that uses electricity – from a starter motor to a depth sounder. In addition, they now sell and repair HP watermakers. Stephane speaks good English and his workshop is on site. If he is out, his assistant Jerome will help you. In addition to regular yachts, Waypoint can handle all mega yacht systems.

Over by North Sails, Pochon Marine, run by Philippe Mazellier, is a branch of a large French electronics company. They sell and repair Furuno, Icom, Garmin, Magellen, B&G, Raymarine, Cobra, NKE, Sharp, Hummingbird, and NaviControl products. For the big boats, they are agent for Kannad/Martec Epirbs, and they also sell and service Schenker water makers. They keep a good range of new electronics in stock, as well as all those electronic charts. They will also come and work on boat electrical problems, though not starters and alternators.

Technical Yacht Services
Inflatables

Espace Ocean has a store in the marina and a large workshop close to the airport. They repair, test, and are the exclusive agent for Zodiac/Bombard life rafts and inflatables. They keep these products in stock and also offer a good supply of safety equipment, including life jackets and flares. They repair all brands of inflatables and carry pumps and other spares. In addition, they sell fancy sunglasses, watches, and lycra shirts.

Eurosurvie is another specialist in life rafts and inflatable boats. Since the owner, Dominique Outil, has his workshop in the zone artizinal in Petit Bourg, you may find it easier to call him: 0590-32-24-51. He does testing, sales, and repair on Viking, EV, RFD, and Plastimo products.

Technical Yacht Services
Painting, Woodwork,
Cleaning, and Other

Several good technicians work out of vans. You have to phone them to get them to come over and see you. For example,

François Sebesi is one of the best people to see for fiberglass repairs. His company is called F-Systems. He has a plant in St. François where he does construction work, from wood to carbon fiber (he can make masts), but around the marina he works out of his van, so you will have to get him on his mobile: 0690-72-49-58. François is an excellent structural glass man for large or small repairs and is familiar with exotics. He can do good gel-coat matching or top-side spray painting. He also re-gel-coats boats as an alternative to painting. François is a good man to see for carpentry, cabinetry, and wood-epoxy systems.

Clean Boat Service and Coco Boats can do pretty much anything. Coco Boats is run by Pascal Poisson, who used to manage VPM. He is a good generalist and knows how to fix all boat problems. He will fix your heads, pumps, electrics, and engines, as well as polishing, painting, lending a hand, and keeping an eye on your boat if you leave it on anchor. The best way to get him is on his mobile: 0690-75-77-97. He works with Clean Boat Service who do partial or complete interior cleaning.

GRPro Clean uses high-tech chemicals to clean and protect your gel coat. They can renew a whole boat, or if you just have one bad stain, they can clean it and leave the glass around looking like new. It is not a very expensive service and you can call Olivier Preteseille and he will come and give you a quote: 0690-44-47-03.

MB Services, run by Matthew, is first-rate for external wood repairs or high quality internal cabinetwork. He also does glass repairs and gel-coat matching. He speaks good English and you can call him on his cell: 0690-39-41-82.

A good man to see for your failed fridge, freezer, or air conditioning unit is Richard Dupuis (Iceberg Refrigeration), who will come to your boat and get things working again. He will also install new US Dometic units, including Frigomatic. Richard speaks English. You can call his mobile: 0690-58-78-20.

Cap Sud are the main Caribbean agents for Beneteau , Four Winns, and Wellcraft yachts, and they also work with Lagoon Catamarans. You can buy a new boat through them and come here for any kind of warranty work or, if the warranty has expired, they can get the right replacement parts for your boat.

They also use courier services to get parts to owners anywhere in the Eastern Caribbean. They can have these delivered duty free in Guadeloupe. You are most likely to speak with Bruno Deverre, who speaks excellent English. Call before you arrive with a boatload of problems so he can set some time aside for you. This is also the place to come for a Weber grill.

If you happen to own an Amel, the agent, Laurent Colonna, is in the marina. Since he has to get his own boats repaired, he can direct you to various repair services available in the area.

Superyachts with tangled anchors, cruising yachts bugged by barnacles, or anyone needing underwater work should contact Frédéric Bernier at Sea'mpatic who will efficiently take care of the problem. It is best to

Chris Doyle

call him on his mobile: 0690-50-03-70, but you can also ask for him at the restaurant Asia as he is a member of the family.

Transport

If you want a car for a few days, several agencies are in the marina area. The most convenient is Hertz, right by the visitors dock. The others are not far away: Jumbo offers a line of cars from tiny to family-sized, and Cap Caraibes specializes in four-wheel drive vehicles.

Alain is a good English-speaking taxi driver and you can contact him at: 0690-35-27-29. Otherwise, you can order a taxi from DCL 0590-20-74-74 or the marina will call one for you.

Water Sports

Nitrogen, in Port de la Marina, is an excellent, modern, dive-equipment shop selling Mares and Scuba Pro brands, among others. It is part of Caraibes Greement. They also rent equipment to those going on charter, fill tanks, and repair equipment. They have Nitrox capability, but they do not take people diving.

Provisioning

Just down from Cool Racoon is an ATM that will help you get cash from a Visa or Mastercard. Many people take US dollars.

For provisioning, the Champion Supermarket is open daily 0800 to 1945, except on Sundays and holidays: 0830 to 1215. When you buy more than you can carry, they will deliver your groceries to the dock, though most people just run them down in the trolley. There is also an Economax in Carrefour Blanchard Mall.

For the fun of visiting a really enormous supermarket, go to Cora, a really vast and fabulous store that is part of a big mall. This supermarket has the best array of fresh food and frozen foods, seafood, and delicatessen items, along with computers, televisions, and clothing. They open 0830 to 2030 Monday to Saturday. You can call a taxi or, if you take your dinghy to the Aquarium, it is about a 10-minute walk. Get on the main road, turn right, take the first right turn, follow the road bearing left when you

MOUNTAINS & MANGROVES

have a choice, and you will see it on your left. You can ask the supermarket to call a taxi to take you back. While there, you can use the bank and teller machines and visit the many stores, which have everything from fashion and sportswear to car parts.

If you are here on a weekend, dinghy to the new fuel dock on the north part of the harbor. They have a dock shop that does excellent takeaway: fresh cooked quiches, pies and other goodies.

Fun Shopping

Back in the marina, boutique lovers will find t-shirts and souvenirs, and two good unisex hairdressers.

Restaurants Around The Marina

Eating out around the marina is entertaining. There are over a dozen restaurants and most of them are good and moderately priced. Many surround the Polygon Basin and are open to the water, boats, and passersby. Others are just outside this area. It is a pleasure to wander around. People flock here at night and there is always plenty to watch.

For the evening you might want to fire up a drink at La Route de Rhum. This bar was built in 1978 to welcome the first transatlantic race of the same name. They keep a gallery of sketches of outstanding sailors so you can recognize them. Work up an appetite by walking around, smelling good food, and perusing the menus. If you want something very simple, Pizza King turns out good pizzas very quickly. The Arizona Grill makes an excellent lunch stop. It is a fancy fast food joint with first-rate hamburgers, daily specials, and more. Lucky Asie has good, inexpensive, Asian food.

When it comes to dinner, or a special meal, there are lots of restaurants. Let us start at the Polygon Basin. For a fancy and special meal, try La Voile Blanche. It is a classy, family restaurant run by Marie and France and their son Alexander, who speaks good English. Look also at Coté Jardin, which is where important people

dine in air conditioned comfort when in this area.

On the way into the marina you pass Pirate Caribeen. This is a popular meeting place with free wifi and a big screen TV for sports and news; you always find people gathered here. It is a good place to eat lobster as they have a lobster tank, and offer a reasonable lobster menu. They also have daily specials and Créole food.

The inexpensive yachty hangout is Le Plaisancier (closed Sunday), a congenial restaurant, inexpensive enough that you can go whenever you cannot be bothered to cook. The food is good and excellent value for money. Lots of yachties come here in the evening and the bar is one of the main nautical hang-outs.

Little Buddha, is a simple, clean Japanese restaurant with inexpensive sushi and a fusion menu. Le Rose des Vents has some set menus, which are excellent value for money and their cooking is good. Check out also La Fregate and The New Port Côte to see if they appeal.

On the road side of the marina, the names seem to change a lot, but Rotisserie des Iles is an excellent traiteur where you can buy a good lunch and eat it outside, or take it home. There is also Ital Café, and for night life, L'Evasian bar.

Outside the marina, Rome des Isles is Italian with another pizza joint nearby, La Jana is a Moroccan restaurant, and Zoo Rock Café is beside it.

A short walk behind the fuel dock on the other side of the water is the Cercle Sportif, a combined sailing school and club, and on the grounds is a delightful Vietnamese restaurant called Asia. The location is wonderful: very open, with the waves gently lapping right outside, and a good view of the local boats and the passing ships. Asia is a family run restaurant headed by Pinpin Loan and both the food and service are very pleasant. (Closed Sunday and Monday)

Ashore

Are you a snorkeling enthusiast? I recommend a trip to the Aquarium in Lagon

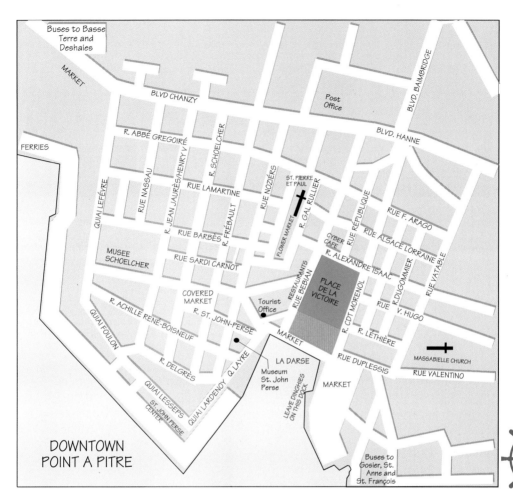

DOWNTOWN
POINT A PITRE

Bleu. They have a superb collection, including seahorses, turtles, and some rarer Caribbean fish and invertebrates that you don't often see. In addition, they offer a tantalizing glimpse of some Indo-Pacific fish. You can dinghy to the door. They also run a friendly little restaurant just outside.

If you need somewhere to stay, try Joel and Françoise's guest house, La Case en Mer. Not only are they sailors, they also speak excellent English. Their house is on Isle Boissard, just behind Jarry, a dinghy ride from the marina.

Ashore Downtown

The marina is so complete that it is easy to forget to go downtown, but this would be a mistake, for Pointe à Pitre has an intriguing Créole atmosphere. It is a fasci-

nating and varied town with lots of different corners and hidden surprises. If you arrive by dinghy, you can go up into La Darse, a bustling waterfront market with brightly colored umbrellas and gaily-dressed market women. To the west, they are surrounded by heaps of fruits and vegetables; on the eastern side, it is a souvenir and handicraft market. The fishing boats pull up on the northern wall and sell from their boats. Pointe à Pitre bursts with life and color.

There are several open markets and different kinds of shops, with street sellers out on the sidewalk. Don't get so absorbed in the shops that you fail to look up now and again, for here and there are the most fascinating old style Caribbean buildings, ele-

MOUNTAINS & MANGROVES

Government buildings off Place de la Victoire Chris Doyle

gantly built of wood with gingerbread, balconies, and overhanging roofs. A few years ago, some of the old buildings were replaced by featureless concrete blocks. I am happy to say new construction now seems more in keeping with the older style.

Leave the dinghy on the old ferry dock, which now no longer used. There are several tie-up rings.

A good place to start exploring is the tourist office, where you can pick up the latest maps and information. Pass by the museum of poet Saint-John Perse, even if only to look at the wonderfully restored old building in which it is housed. If you like museums, you could also look into the museum in memory of Victor Schoelcher who fought against slavery until it was abolished in 1848. Ironically, it is here that you can see mementos of slavery: slave collars, chains, and pictures of slave ships. On a more cheerful note, it has a pretty garden with a fountain.

When it is time to shop, the best general area is in the region of the old market. All around are fine shops with souvenirs and handicrafts.

Walking north, you will find the boutiques and clothes shops. The clothes here are light hearted, attractive, and mainly inexpensive, with lots of bargains. Try Rue Nozieres, Rue Frebault, and Rue Schoelcher. Don't miss the brand new Saint-John Perse center, with its elegant little boutiques and restaurants geared to cruise ship passengers. You can do emails there, at the tourist office, and at the cyber café at the top of the park. The flower market is really pretty. It opens every day, but is biggest on Fridays and Saturdays. The covered market, too, is very photogenic.

When it comes to lunch, you cannot do better than outside at one of the cafés that line the shady Rue Bebian, where you can watch the passersby and have the park as background.

In case you plan to travel farther afield, our town map shows the location of buses and ferries. There is one bus station beyond our map for buses that go to the northeast (Port Louis, etc.). If you go up Rue Freebault and continue on Blvd. Legitimus you will eventually come to it. You can get a larger map in the tourist office and ask them to pinpoint it for you.

THE SOUTH EAST COAST OF GUADELOUPE

Marie Galante and the southeast coast of Guadeloupe provide an off-the-beaten-track cruising area of small towns and pretty beaches. Some anchorages involve reef passages in quite large seas. These should always be attempted in good light.

The south coast of Grande Terre is mainly low lying, with small cliffs and beaches. Around Ste. Anne there are some very low sandy points covered in palms. There are reefs close to shore along much of the coast, and in the Petit Hâvre area the reef extends up to half a mile offshore.

Water usually breaks on the reefs. A bank of less than 100 feet extends up to 7 miles south of the coast. Fish traps are everywhere, usually two tied together by a floating line. Since this is open sea with sizeable waves, they are not easy to spot. Those missing their home video games will find avoiding these much more enthralling than Pac Man. A 21-foot bank about 7 miles south of St. François is particularly well covered in traps. The St. François light leads the fishermen to the bank. The white sector is right on it; the green and red to either side. If approaching Grande Terre from Marie Galante, it is easy to make out St. François and Ste. Anne. St. François is the easternmost town on Guadeloupe's south coast, and Ste. Anne is about 8 miles to its west. In between there is a conspicuous large block of white houses. The conspicuous giant windmills are on the east coast, well north of La Moule.

Ilet du Gosier

Ilet du Gosier is a tiny wooded island, partially surrounded by reefs, with soft white sand beaches, and a pleasantly old fashioned lighthouse. It is only 3 miles from Pointe à Pitre.

Navigation

From Pointe à Pitre it is simple to follow the coast down to Ilet du Gosier.

Sailing from the Saintes, you can see the town of Gosier, with smallish cliffs on the south. The feature that stands out most in sunlight is a very contemporary church spire, which is oblong and looks like an

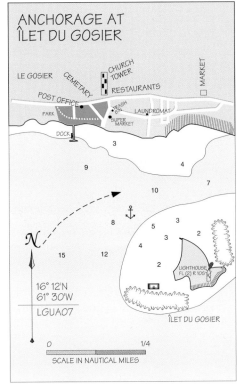

apartment building that has been through a French fry machine. As you get closer, the lighthouse becomes visible. Approach the anchorage from the Pointe à Pitre side and eyeball your way in slowly. Once you are well inside the reef, the seabed shelves gradually up to the island. You can anchor anywhere between Ilet du Gosier and the small town of Gosier in good-holding, clay-like sand. In theory, you can carry 7 feet through the pass between the island and

MOUNTAINS & MANGROVES

Chris Doyle

GOSIER

the mainland. In practice, it is not worth trying. The bottom is a patchwork of sand and weed and it is hard to tell the shallow spots from the deeper spots.

Ashore

This is a place to swim, laze on the beach, snorkel, and maybe patronize the tiny snack bar. You can climb one flight up the lighthouse to an outside platform.

Dinghy over to Gosier and tie your dinghy to the new dock off the park (tie to the ends of the dock, leaving the middle free for the ferries). The town has a post office, pharmacy, souvenir shops, a church, an Economax supermarket (opens 0830 till 1900 most days; on Sundays till 1230), and a bakery. It also has a laundromat open weekdays 0700-1800 and mornings on Saturdays.

Gosier is becoming a fashionable tourist spot, and if you want to eat out, there are several restaurants where you will get a meal. Some of them are on the waterfront by the park, others on the main street close to the modern church spire.

On Friday afternoons from 1600, the road next to the cemetery is closed to traffic and opened as a market. Go if you can; the local produce is fresh, wonderful and reasonable.

Petit Hâvre Anchorage

This south coast anchorage lies about 3 miles east of Ilet a Gosier and is protected from the sea by a reef. It has the beauty of being on the edge of the ocean. You get a feeling of solitude and privacy, far enough away from the houses on the hills ashore.

There is good snorkeling on the seagrass beds in the anchorage and out on the reef. The reef is vast and extends well beyond the part you can see. If the sea is very calm, the snorkeling is good around Le Diamant. The beach ashore has a conspicuous and curious concrete obelisk. It is popular with locals and there is a food shack that is most often open on weekends. There is another beach area, popular with tourists, with a snack bar and garbage facilities at the eastern end of the bay.

Navigation

You can identify the reef by the breaking seas and Le Diamant rock at its eastern end. Le Diamant is about 9 feet tall and shows up quite clearly, along with smaller rocks. If you are approaching from Marie Galante, try to gauge the 3 miles from Gosier, and then look for some noticeable semicircular cliffs partially covered in vegetation, just east of the anchorage. Give the reef good clearance on the seaward side

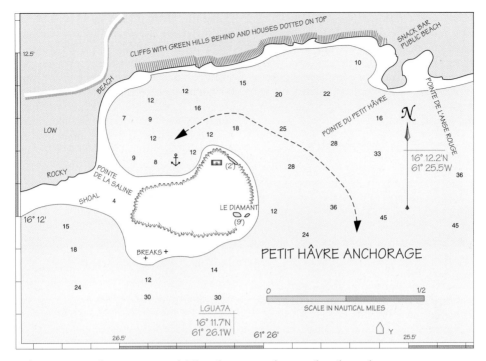

12.5'

CLIFFS WITH GREEN HILLS BEHIND AND HOUSES DOTTED ON TOP

SNACK BAR
PUBLIC BEACH

10

BEACH

15

12

20

22

POINTE DE L'ANSE ROUGE

LOW

12

16

7   9

12   18   25

POINTE DU PETIT HÂVRE   16

16° 12.2'N
61° 25.5'W

28

33

36

ROCKY

POINTE
DE LA SALINE

9   8   ⚓

12

28

LE DIAMANT
(9')

12   36

45

45

SHOAL   4

16° 12'

15

24

18   BREAKS +
+

14

12

30   30

24

LGUA7A
16° 11.7'N
61° 26.1'W

PETIT HÂVRE ANCHORAGE

0   1/2

SCALE IN NAUTICAL MILES

26.5'   61° 26'   Y   25.5'

and enter around its eastern end. The closer you can tuck up to the reef, the farther out of the swell you will be. Holding is good in sand and weed.

There are four or five yellow buoys laid out to mark a large area that starts at Petit

PETIT HAVRE ANCHORAGE

MOUNTAINS & MANGROVES

Hâvre and continues about a mile to the west and a mile to the south. Only one is close enough to appear on our sketch chart. These mark an area where sand is dredged to be used for commercial purposes ashore. The buoys do not affect navigation, but keep clear of any dredges operating in this area.

Sainte Anne

Ste. Anne lies about 3 miles east of Petit Hâvre. There are abundant coconut palms along the shore. The harbor lies in a bay protected by several reefs. From outside it looks enticing: a vast expanse of calm turquoise water, yachts at anchor, beaches, and a pretty town. This is a great anchorage for shallow draft yachts that can anchor close off town in about to 6 feet of water. Deeper yachts can find a safe, though often rolly, anchorage.

Enter Ste. Anne by the main entrance. You have to pass between two reefs in fairly large waves. Two red buoys mark the channel, but you should enter in good light so you can see the reefs. Make sure that you can see both buoys and that everything looks right before you attempt to go in.

Leave the first red buoy close to starboard and head to the second (approximately 330° magnetic). Most yachts turn in toward the town after the second red buoy and anchor between town and the small boat channel to the beach. However, unless you are shallow draft, there is not much space. An alternative for deeper boats is to go toward the fishing harbor and anchor between it and the reef. Although an enticing turquoise color, the water in this part is murky, and you should proceed with caution. Sometimes the shallow spots show as darker shadows. Holding is good in sand. Numerous yellow buoys mark the 300-meter line from shore, inside which the speed limit is 5 knots and anchoring is limited to approved areas (like the ones we mark). Yellow buoys also mark the small boat channel into the beach.

Just to the west of Ste. Anne, in an indented bay with a spectacular beach and several buildings on the eastern side, is the Club Med complex. This bay is partially protected by reefs. You can enter on either side of the central reef. In 2009 a line of yellow buoys lay offshore, including right along the outside of this center reef, and

STE. ANNE

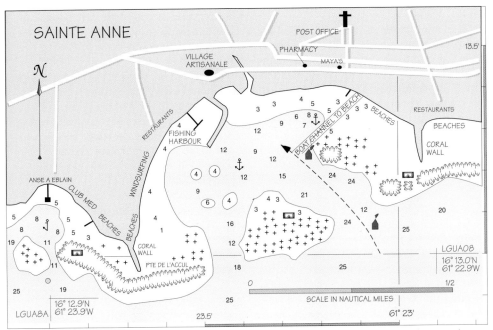

there was just one yellow buoy (hard to distinguish from the rest) marking the east side of the center reef. In good light you can eyeball your way in. However, it is quite small inside, and not all that deep. Monohulls will tend to roll enough to limit this to a lunch stop. Shallow boats can get a good overnight spot in 5 feet of water between the reef and the Club Med Moorings. Here, too, yellow buoys separate bathers from boats.

Services

Maya has a great little cyber-café right across from the beach. After from checking your email here, you can get coffee and

excellent non-alcoholic punches made on the spot from fresh fruit.

You can leave your dinghy on the beach or in the new Ste. Anne fishing harbor, which is well protected.

Ashore

The attraction here is the beaches: Club Med to the west and the town beaches to the east. These are photogenic, popular, and lively beaches, sculpted with dead coral and generously adorned with wavy palms. The shallow, turquoise water is protected by the reefs. There are always lots of people, including many kids, all having fun. The windsurfing enthusiasts hang out

In St. Anne market stalls line the waterfront

Chris Doyle

MOUNTAINS & MANGROVES

on the western side of the bay.

The atmosphere is that of a holiday camp, with restaurants behind the beach from one end to the other – a few of them double as nightspots. Shops or vendors cover the same area. You can buy pareos, vegetables, coconut hats, and art. The town itself is pleasant with a church, post office, pharmacy, supermarket, and a few other shops. Two boulangeries in the main square make good places for good coffee and some pâtisseries.

St. François

St. François lies 8 miles east of Ste. Anne. A well-protected reef anchorage lies between the town and some large hotels. Although the deepwater anchorage in this area is quite small, the reef encloses miles of turquoise water, giving a wonderful feeling of space. Add the municipal marina and you get an area that is attractive to yachtspeople, yet just far enough off the beaten track not to be crowded.

St. François has two harbors: a ferry and fishing port in front of the town and the yacht marina to the east. The outside anchorage off the yacht marina can easily take yachts of up to 8-foot draft. The entrance is a long, narrow channel between reefs. It is well buoyed, but enter

the first time in good light when you can see the reefs. Both wind and sea push you in, so you want to do it right. Pass to the southeast of the first yellow and black buoy. Green and red buoys mark the channel into the harbor (red right returning). Seas often break right up to the first buoys. Do not cut inside them! It is easiest to approach the entrance a bit from the east. Before you enter, make sure you can see the next pair of buoys. Once you pass these, the water is relatively calm.

The deepest anchorage is just north of the channel, behind the reef, in 8 to 10 feet. Many yachts go in a little more, past the next red buoy, (which is the shallowest part of the channel) and anchor in the deep water in front of the marina wall in about 7 to 10 feet. The deepest water is close the marina wall. You can find a berth in the marina, but make sure you leave the inside green buoys to port. Once you have made it to the harbor entrance, there is plenty of water inside, though it does get shoal in some places towards the edges. There is a single rock about 5 feet deep on the western end of the dock, right in front to the capitainerie – the dock you are likely to use to take on water. Tie up on the eastern end of this dock and you should be fine.

When you leave St. François, you have

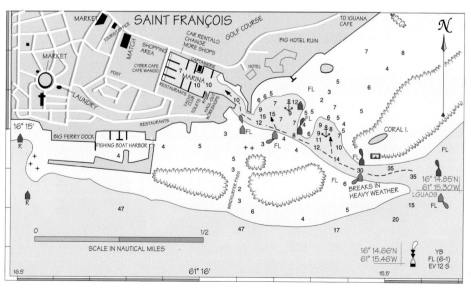

SAINT FRANCOIS

MOUNTAINS & MANGROVES

to power out into steep short waves with the wind dead ahead. Motor failure at this point would be unfortunate. Have a jib ready to hoist and back should this unlikely event occur.

Communications

You might get lucky and find a signal in the anchorage, otherwise you can check your email at Cybercafé le Pr@-net at the end of the marina or L'Arabas Café, one of the restaurants right next to the marina, or take in your computer and use the free wifi at Quai 17 in the same row, or Le Panier à Salade on the way to Match.

General Yacht Services

The St. François marina has been rebuilt with the doubling of marina berths to 200, many taken by long-term residents. The Capitainerie is in the fancy building on the north side of the marina and it opens weekdays 0830-1200, 1430-1800,

mornings only on Saturdays. They will accept yacht mail (Capitainerie Marina St. Francois, BP17 97118 St. Francois). There is a work area (not yet complete) with a ramp for hauling boats. When the trailer arrives, it will take yachts up to 14 tons, 1.7 meters draft, and 6.5 meters wide. Until they get a dinghy dock, you can lock your dinghy to one of the ladders, which is away from the slips.

Dominique Blain, the captain, will look after you and you can even call him after hours: 0690-50-85-15. Dominique will arrange a berth or for you overnight or to just to come alongside for water. He can also find you a customs officer, given time. In addition, if you need a taxi or any kind of technical help, Dominique will help. (Most of the technicians in Point à Pitre will come here, and François Sebesi's F-Systems workshop is close by.)

You can take your garbage to the bins on

Isles de la Petite Terre is an easy day sail from St. Franois.   Chris Doyle

the main road close to the Capitainerie. When the toilet/shower block is finished, it will include a launderette. In the meantime, you can find a laundry in town close to the circular market.

Eventually, St. Francois should have a fuel dock, probably in the fishing port. But in the meantime, fuel has to be jugged from the local gas station, a short taxi ride away.

The local yachting people belong to the Yacht Club de Saint François, and they were finishing their club house near the toilet/shower block when I went by. Check them out. The president, Claude Grasset, lives on a Catana 44 in the marina and you can call him on his mobile: 0690-30-62-52, (or: ycsf.gpe@gmail.com). The yacht club also arranges several racing events, including a week in November when the participants visit the Saintes, Dominica, and Marie Galante. The Trophy Gardel, a race around Petit Terre, takes place towards the end of March. Sports fishermen come for the Hemingway Trophy on the first weekend in May.

Provisioning

The big Match supermarket is excellent and includes produce and fresh fish sections, as well as a deli. You pass a Deli France on the way there, where you can buy fresh bread. The best local produce market is just beyond the Match. You will also find a flower shop there. Visit the fishing harbor for fish straight from the boats.

Fun Shopping

The marina area of St. François has now merged into the old town, with restaurants and shops filling most of the streets. Tourism here has intensified recently, though St. François is still pleasant and far from crowded. Most shops lie on the road behind the capitainerie. They line the road down to the Match supermarket. Here you will find Guadeloupe's largest assortment of boutiques catering to tourists from the hotels. Many have large stands on the pavement, giving a market atmosphere, which is pleasant and shady. The shops sell everything from the latest fashions and perfume to art and exotic handicrafts, in a relaxed and uncrowded atmosphere. Visit the outside circular market downtown, which has lots of handicrafts and people selling spices in bulk, giving it a pleasant aroma. Many more local tourist style shops are close to this market.

You will find some useful shops, including a pharmacy (with a medical and dental clinic), and an Orange mobile boutique on the road south of the marina that leads towards the post office.

Restaurants

The marina is surrounded by restaurants, which open for lunch and are still brightly lit and lively at night. Many restaurants are to be found on the seafront road that runs from behind the marina to the fishing port. They all post menus, so looking is half the fun. You will have a pleasant meal in most of them. When you want a really great meal, visit the Iguana Café, one of my favorite restaurants in the Leewards. It is French, with a touch of the East, and fairly pricey, enough to pay for a bevy of chefs

Chris Doyle

MOUNTAINS & MANGROVES

who spend all day creating and preparing new dishes for the evening. They work hard, and both the food and atmosphere tell you this is a staff that has fun while taking the job seriously. It is about a mile down the road heading northeast past the big hotels. Continue until the road stops then take the short footpath to rejoin the main road and turn right. It is on your left on the first small rise. You can also dinghy there by going just beyond all the breakwaters to the public beach. The main road is behind. Turn right on the road; the restaurant is on your left. Sunday is the only day they also do lunch, and they are closed Tuesday. If you are not making reservations, it is best to go early. (They open about 1900.)

Ashore

Car rental agencies line the road behind the capitainerie. On the other side is a stall renting electric bikes and scooters. You can take a day excursion to see Désirade by ferry. Golfers will be delighted to find there is a golf course right behind the marina.

If you are not going to make it to Petite Terre, you can arrange a charter in the marina, and if you want to visit La Desirade, the ferries leave from the ferry terminal. (You can also get ferries to the Saintes and Marie Galante.) The reef outside the anchorage extends endlessly in both directions, with beaches to the east. Great for dinghy exploration and snorkeling, and, if you happen to have a shoal draft yacht, there are anchoring possibilities.

You cannot help but notice many large windmills in the distance. They generate a fair bit of the local electricity.

Water Sports

You will find St. François Plongée at the end of the marina, and Noa Plongée behind the capitainerie. They will take you diving, and you can get your tanks filled. Back on the beach, watch or be part of a brilliant display of sail-boarding, including some spectacular jumps.

Iles de la Petite Terre

Iles de la Petite Terre are two uninhabited green islands, protected by reef. The whole area is a national park with no fishing, or taking of conch or anything else from land or sea. They are very low, though cliffs at the eastern ends are about 40 feet high. You see the lighthouse (108 feet) long before you see the islands. A calm, protected anchorage lies between the islands with clear water of turquoise, azure, and aquamarine. It is somewhat reminiscent of the Tobago Cays. Snorkeling is excellent, with brightly colored reef fish, turtles, and eagle rays. A path leads from the palm-backed beach on Terre de Bas to the lighthouse. From here you can explore the hilly eastern end of Terre de Bas. There are some magnificent tidal pools below the cliffs.

You can also follow the mile of beach to the western point of Terre de Bas. While ashore, you will probably see a few iguanas, which are abundant on both islands. You may not go ashore in Terre de Haut, because it is a very sensitive nesting area, easily disturbed by people. However there

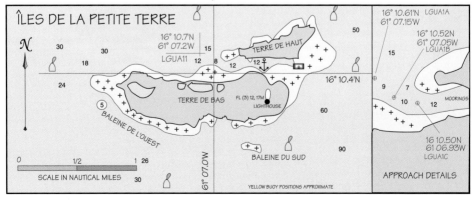

A large charter cat visiting Isles de la Petite Terre   Chris Doyle

is one small beach on its north coast near the moorings, which you can land on to rest if you are swimming from your boat or from the other island. A couple of large sailing catamaran day charter boats make regular runs here from St. François. By late afternoon you often have it to yourself and it is a great place to wake up in the morning.

Navigation

Iles de La Petite Terre should only be considered when the trades are moderate (less than 20 knots) and without big northerly swells. As you approach, you will notice the islands are surrounded with large yellow buoys that mark the park area. These flash orange at night. Depths and sea state limit the entrance to the anchorage. Depths are 12-15 feet outside the anchorage and 10-13 feet inside. Between

them is a bar of dead coral with a depth of 7-9 feet. Some swell builds on the bar in normal trades. You have to decide for yourself how safe it is to go in. You cannot eyeball your way in because the bottom depths are unreadable. I have taken many soundings on approaches varying from 130-140° magnetic to the lighthouse and I haven't got a reading less than 7 feet at low tide. Using a Garmin 162, I found the deepest approach as shown in our sketch chart with three waypoints to get you in, this should give you over 8 feet. I have visited with 6.5 foot draft, and you should be able to get in with up to 7 foot draft, except possibly at extreme low tide. You could take in a boat of 8-foot draft or more by working the tides, but you will need to anchor off and sound it out for yourself from the dinghy.

If the bar is breaking continuously and

MOUNTAINS & MANGROVES

all the way over, come back another day. If it is breaking just occasionally, it is your judgment call, but obviously the shallower your draft and the more power you have, the better your chances. Remember, the breaking seas are pushing you toward the shore.

Once inside, pick up one of the 14 park moorings. The white ones are for yachts up to 10 tons; larger yachts go on the white ones with a blue quadrant. Inside, you will have a 1-knot current setting to the west.

The entrance can be impassable in very large northerly swells, when waves break right across, so if you plan to stay overnight in unsettled conditions, bring a pot to cook iguanas.

La Désirade

As you approach La Désirade, it is etched starkly on the horizon: a 700-foot slab of rock rising from the ocean, 5 miles long by one and half wide, and much of that width is the mountain top plateau. The northern side is steep and inhospitable, the southern side has the only easily habitable land and this is protected for much of the way by a fringing reef. Seen by

Columbus's crew after a painful two-month crossing on his second voyage, it seemed like heaven on earth; they gave it the name Désirade.

This quiet and beautiful island is off the beaten track. The 1,700 local people, many whom fish for a living, are exceptionally friendly.

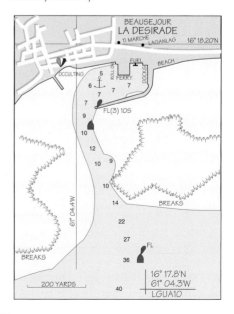

You can rent cars, scooters, or bikes and explore all the roads, including one that goes right along the mountain ridge. Up there, walks down little side trails will bring you to spectacular views. Swimming and beaching are excellent on several places behind the barrier reef.

The island provides all the electricity it needs from about 50 windmills perched on the mountaintop. They sell the considerable surplus to Guadeloupe. These windmills are the first generation; older and smaller than the newer ones on Guadeloupe and Marie Galante.

Navigation

The government built a protected fishing and ferry port with a dock at the end. The channel to the harbor through the rough water is at least 9 feet deep. At the harbor mouth, you can carry 6.5 feet fairly close to the outer wall into the fuel dock area. My soundings show the southern and inner part of the harbor is about 7 feet deep. But the northern and outer part, the main anchoring area, is only about 6 feet at low tide. Several people have assured me that boats with 6.5 feet draft do manage to anchor without a problem, possibly because the mud is very soft.

The channel is marked by two red buoys. Leave both to starboard, kissing them both. Swing up into the harbor after the second red buoy. Anchor close to the entrance and leave plenty of room for the ferries to turn round. On Fridays, there is an added complication as the roll-on boat comes in and needs a bit more space for getting out than do the ferries. But it is very maneuverable, so if you leave someone on board it should be all right.

Services

Garbage bins are on the dock. You can take on gasoline and diesel, as well as water, at the fuel dock. There is no harbor master, but the tourist office can help tell you if you have anchored clear of the shipping. People are very friendly and they want visitors.

Ashore

Ti Marche is a great little supermarket just behind the harbor. Marie Elisabeth, the owner, speaks excellent English, also Spanish and German. There is plenty here for stocking up on provisions, including fresh fruits and vegetables. There is also an 8 à Huit in town. You will also find a pharmacy where the owner, Christophe, speaks English, and there are several more stores.

The three main beaches have restaurants that are popular with tourists. For the best food, visit Lagranlag (closed all day Monday and Thursday evening; otherwise open 1200-1500 for lunch and 1900-2130 for dinner). It is on the main road, just east of the fuel dock. Mme Zamia Chantel will make sure you get a good meal. Her gratin vegetables and court bouillon are both very tasty.

MOUNTAINS & MANGROVES

Marie Galante

BY THE TIME COLUMBUS sailed into Marie Galante, he had run out of saints, so he named this island after one of his boats. From afar, Marie Galante looks as flat as a pancake, but when you get close you realize that, as pancakes go, it is quite substantial; over 300 feet in elevation in many places and over 600 feet at its highest point. The soil includes much clay, so the land retains the rain and is thickly wooded and green, with many palm trees along the coast. It is a quiet backwater, an unspoiled haven, an ideal place to wind down, eat good Créole meals, take quiet walks, and have a good chunk of perfect Caribbean beach to yourself.

Marie Galante is a great for touring by car or scooter. It is an island of dense dry forests, lots of fruit trees and big areas of sugar cane. The traffic is light so you do not fear for your life on a scooter and these have the advantage of being able to amble along the tiny farm roads that would challenge a car.

Some 50 high-tech windmills on the east coast produce electricity for Marie Galante. This is, in a way, a continuing tradition, because at one time some 600 sail-driven windmills ground sugar cane (still the most important crop). Seventy-three of the original windmills remain in various states of repair; none are commercially used, though ox-drawn carts still haul the cane. Le Moulin de Bezard has been completely restored to working order. They hoist the sails daily from 1030-1430 and crush a little cane for visitors. It is one of the few places to see an old-fashioned working windmill in the islands.

Look out for an exceptional beach at Capesterre, and a couple more to its south. A barrier reef lies quite close to shore along these beaches, creating beautiful turquoise shallow lagoons with good snorkeling just a short swim away. If this makes you hungry, Capesterre has several restaurants for your midday meal.

In the northeast of the island, you can visit Gueule Grand Gouffre, a round sinkhole with a rim about 200 feet high, smooth sides, and an arch at the bottom open to the sea. There are majestic cliffs around the east coast and a short walk in the area of Caye Plate will show you the best.

Marie Galante

Regulations

Marie Galante is part of Guadeloupe and Grand Bourg is a port of clearance. For procedures see Grand Bourg.

Telephones

Marie Galante has the same card phone system as in Guadeloupe. For details see Guadeloupe.

Shopping Hours

Shopping hours are normally 0800-1200 and 1400-1700.

Transport

Major airlines go in and out of Guadeloupe. Marie Galante is linked to Guadeloupe by both ferry and daily flights. Check for the latest ferry times; current ferry times from Grand Bourg to Point à Pitre are Monday to Saturday: 0600, 0900 and 1600. On Sundays: 0600, 1600 and 1800. From Point à Pitre they are Monday to Saturday: 0800, 1245 and 1715; Sundays: 0800, 1715 and 1915.

There is a regular and inexpensive bus service to all major villages. Rental cars, scooters, and bicycles are available in Grand Bourg and Saint Louis. Drive on the right.

Holidays

see Guadeloupe.

Marie Galante, Admiralty Leisure Folio 5642-3, 5642-5

MOUNTAINS & MANGROVES

From a yachting perspective, the beach at Anse Canot and those to the south of St. Louis will be major attractions. Hikers will be pleased to know that hiking trails have been laid out all over the island. If you speak French, you can go the tourist office and buy a good little booklet on these trails (including maps) put out by the forestry department.

Navigation

If you are approaching from the north, the cliffs and low lying Îlet du Vieux Fort stand out as landmarks. If approaching from the west, you can make out the huge old sugar dock and crane off Pte. Folie Anse and also the town of St. Louis. If you are heading from St. Louis to Grand Bourg, note that it is quite shallow up to half a mile out.

Anse Canot

This bay, just to the north of Baie de St. Louis, has an alluring beach in the northeast corner, protected by dramatic cliffs. One conspicuous, modern, two-story house is right on the beach. Anchor in about 12 feet of water. This bay is not as protected as St. Louis and a swell does enter in easterly and northeasterly winds, so it is best as a daytime stop, unless you enjoy being rocked to sleep. Take care beaching the dinghy in the surge.

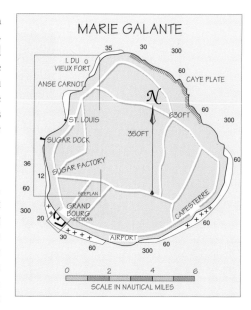

MARIE GALANTE

SCALE IN NAUTICAL MILES

Saint Louis

St. Louis is the main yacht anchorage in Marie Galante. It is huge, shallow enough for easy anchoring, with an excellent sand and weed bottom. If you are approaching from the north, give Pte. du Cimetière a wide berth. The bottom is shoal to its west a long way down and breaking waves often roll in. Anchor north or south of the large ferry dock off the beach, but leave room for ferries. Do not anchor between the yellow buoy and the fuel tanks ashore as there are underwater pipes. Depths in the bay are

ANSE CARNOT

PIPELINE DO NOT ANCHOR

SAINT LOUIS

mainly 8 to 11 feet, shelving as you approach within 100 yards of the shore. This shelving is not clear in the water colors, so approach the beach with caution. Moorings were laid down for the arriving racing yachts for the first Belle-Isles-en-Mer transatlantic race in 2007. They have not been maintained, but were still in use in 2009. The chain was very thin where it rubbed in the sand, so if you use one, snorkel on it before you leave the boat. If you prefer a more secluded atmosphere, anchor off the Kawann Beach Hotel.

In calm seas, Saint Louis is a spectacular anchorage with water so clear you can see starfish over the side in moonlight. In easterly winds, the swell may rock you gently to sleep. In a strong northeaster it can throw you out of bed. In these conditions, you will find it better at Plage de Trois Ilets or Grand Bourg. While here, don't miss the mile-long beach at Pte. de Folie Anse.

Communications, Services

M.J.C. de Saint-Louis has several internet stations and is open weekdays 0800-1200 and 1400-1800, Saturdays, 0800-1200. There is no sign, but the building is wide open and you can see the computers inside.

Kawann Beach Hotel has wifi near the bar. You can tie your dinghy to a very fancy floating dock, which is part of the ferry dock. If this is not in place, pull it up on the beach.

During school holidays kids love to swim off the floating dock and splash. If that worries you, take the dinghy down the dock or beach it.

The town has a church, post office, pharmacy, and public telephones. You will find bins for garbage. Sympa supermarket sells ice.

Saint Louis is a good base for exploring the island; several places rent cars and scooters.

The tourist office, which is combined with a craft shop, is on the dock, is helpful and sometimes open.

Provisioning

For breakfast treats and daily bread, visit Delice Saint Louisienne, just beyond the head of the dock.

Visit the market for fresh produce. A butcher next to the market opens Thursday to Sunday. Otherwise, several small supermarkets will have most basics. One of the

MOUNTAINS & MANGROVES

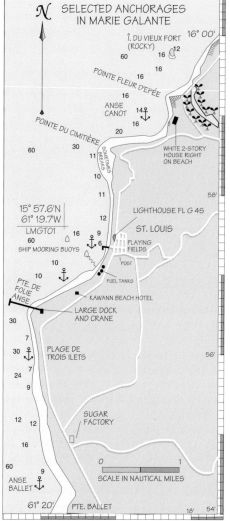

SELECTED ANCHORAGES
IN MARIE GALANTE

Î. DU VIEUX FORT
(ROCKY)   16° 00'
60   16   12
        16
POINTE FLEUR D'EPÉE
        16
ANSE   14
CANOT   16
        20
POINTE DU CIMITIÈRE
60   30
    11   SOMETIMES 3 AREAS
                    WHITE 2-STORY
                    HOUSE RIGHT
                    ON BEACH
    10
    11   58'
15° 57.6'N
61° 19.7'W   12   LIGHTHOUSE FL G 4S
LMGTO1   16   9   ST. LOUIS
60   6
SHIP MOORING BUOYS   PLAYING
                            FIELDS
    10   POST
PTE. DE 10
FOLIE   FUEL TANKS
ANSE
        KAWANN BEACH HOTEL
30   LARGE DOCK
        AND CRANE
7
30   PLAGE DE
7   TROIS ILETS   56'
24
9
            SUGAR
12 12   FACTORY
16
60   9
ANSE   0   1
BALLET   SCALE IN NAUTICAL MILES
61° 20'   PTE. BALLET   18'   54'

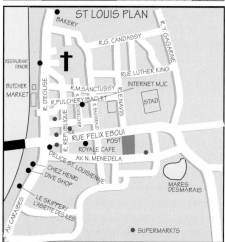

ST LOUIS PLAN
BAKERY
R.G. CANDASSY
R.Y. GAGARINE
RESTAURANT
DENIOR
RUE LUTHER KING
BUTCHER
MARKET
R. DÉGLISE
R. PULCHERY/BAGLET
R.M.SANCTUSSY   INTERNET MJC
R. SCHOELCHER   STAD
R. E. NAVIS
R. BASTARAUD
R. RÉPUBLIQUE
RUE FELIX EBOUI   POST
DELICE DES LOUISIENNE   ROYALE CAFE
AV. N. MENEDELA
CHEZ HENRI
DIVE SHOP
LE SKIPPER/
L'ASSETTE DES ILES
AV. CARAÏBES
MARES
DESMARAIS
SUPERMARKTS

biggest is the Potony, way down Ave. Nelson Mandela. A fishmonger (mornings only) is close by the internet station.

Restaurants

St. Louis is a delightful place to eat ashore. Le Skipper/Les Assiettes des Isles is a good choice, with tables set right out on a pleasant part of the beach. They serve Créole-style food, specialize in seafood, and do it well. The menu is posted on a blackboard and changes from time to time.

Chez Henri (closed Monday) is a serious nightspot with a large exterior on the beach. They do serve food but do not open for dinner until fairly late. They offer special jazz evenings and other entertainment. You can walk in ask what is happening.

Bar à Quai is pleasant, on the beach, and open usually for both lunch and dinner.

Le Royal Café is straight down the road that leads from the dock. The service is friendly, the food local and good, but it is only open for lunch.

Denior is another pleasant Créole restaurant open for lunch except Wednesday. Denior also does dinner on Saturdays.

Should you want a fancier meal, La Kawann Beach Hotel lies about three quarters of a mile down the beach at Pte. de Folie Anse; a long walk but a reasonable dinghy ride. It is cleverly set just behind the beach trees so it does not spoil the coastline. You can also anchor here, use their bar, wifi, and restaurant and rent a car or scooter through them.

Water Sports

Man Balaou is a dive shop right on the beach. They dive daily and one of their instructors speaks good English.

Anse de Trois Ilets and Anse Ballet

Heading south from Pte. Folie Anse is a long and beautiful deserted beach with a sugar factory two thirds of the way down. The northern part of the beach is called Plage de Trois Ilets and the southern part Anse Ballet. You can feel your way into a

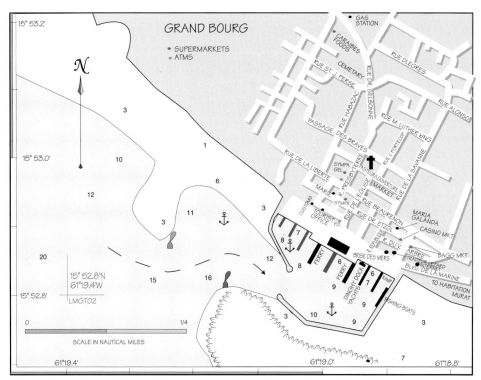

GRAND BOURG

• SUPERMARKETS
• ATMS

15° 53.2'

15° 53.0'

15° 52.8'

15° 52.8'N
61°19.4W

LMGT02

0   1/4

SCALE IN NAUTICAL MILES

61°19.4'   61°19.0'   61°18.8'

GAS STATION
CARAIBES FOODS
RUE ST. J. PERSE
CEMETARY
RUE D'LEGRES
RUE DR. SELBONNE
RUE ALONSO
RUE HABAZAC
RUE M. LUTHER KING
PASSAGE DES BRAVES
RUE DE PORTEOR
RUE DE LA LIBERTE
RUE DE LA SAVANNE
SYMPA GEL
R. PASTEUR/OUVERTURE
MARKET
CUSTOMS
MARIE
R. PRESBYTERE
RUE DE L'EGLISE
SYMPA
RUE DE BEAURENON
TOURIST OFFICE
P.O.
RUE DR. ETZOL
R. DU V.
MARIA GALANDA
CASINO MKT
ARBRE
BAGG MKT
BRISE DES MERS
THE LEZARD
FERRY
DINGHY DOCK
YACHTS
CAMP
FISHING BOATS
TROIT INTERNET
BLVD. DE LA MARINE
TO HABITATION MURAT

fair anchorage off this beach in 10 to 15 feet of water. When the swells are from the north, it is often calmer here than in St. Louis. The northern third of the beach is often as good an anchorage as the southern part, and at the south the steam-driven sugar factory can be very noisy, though it only operates a few months a year.

Grand Bourg

Grand Bourg is the main town in Marie Galante. Two large walls create a moderate–sized harbor, which is partially complete, about half the planned docks having been built. The final plan includes another ferry dock, and three more yacht docks. (The planned docks are shown in red on our sketch chart; the finished ones in black.) The whole harbor has been dredged to 7 feet. There is no problem in anchoring in either half of the harbor, or using the yacht docks that have been built, though currently there are no services. You will have to find a place on one of these docks for your dinghy.

Approach from offshore and enter between the two buoys. Holding is generally pretty good,

Regulations

Grand Bourg is a port of clearance. The customs are sometimes at the airport. The best time to catch them in the office is between 0900 and noon.

Communications

Pegases is a pleasant internet café/bookstore behind the harbor. They open 0800-1900, Tuesday to Sunday. Sandrine, the owner, speaks English and has some English keyboards.

La Brise des Mers has a free wifi system for customers if you take your computer in.

Services

You will see a fuel dock (gasoline) near the yacht docks. At the moment, this is detaxed fuel for fishing boats only, but there are plans for a full fuel dock. Mobile garbage bins are placed around the car park and road. There is no water on the docks,

GRAND BOURG

but there is a fresh water tap in the little fish market that you can use to fill a few jugs.

Provisioning Shopping

Grand Bourg is a typical country town, with a church, several pharmacies, banks, ATMs, card phones, and some fair supermarkets. Among the new houses are quaint old ones left from another era.

Caraibe Food is the biggest supermarket, but a bit of a walk. It has a good cheese and frozen food selection, including lots of seafood. Sympa and Supermarket Bagg are close to the port with a fair selection. For fresh produce, visit the open market. Sympa Gel on Rue du Presbyterre specializes in frozen foods. None of the food stores are open on Sunday.

Early morning is a good time to go ashore for breakfast or fresh bread. Boulangerie La Baoule faces the port. Le Soleil Levant Boulangerie is next to the market and another bakery is on Rue de Presbyterre, opposite Sympa Gel.

La Galante Des Iles and Ornata, at the head of the dock, are the best spots to sip a drink and watch the world go by.

If you want to stock up on beer, wine, olive oil, and other goodies before heading south, visit Bagg Cash, a wholesaler and retailer. Follow Boulevard de la Marine, and when you get to the crossroads, go straight across onto D9 to Capesterre. It is the first turn on the right and is signposted. The prices you see are the bulk prices.

Sowka Dance, is opposite Maria Galanda. It is packed full of interesting handicrafts.

Restaurants

A good reason to come here is to visit Maria Galanda, a magical little courtyard restaurant on Rue Etzol. You eat beside old stone walls, amidst plants and fish ponds, to the sound of tree frogs. They open for dinner at 1900 every day except Thursday. The food is good and the set menu is exceptional value, but they do not take credit cards.

La Brise des Mers is a hangout on the road facing the port. The owner, Frances, offers a variety of daily specials for lunch, and in the evening he has very inexpensive tapas.

Otherwise, you can check out La Moussan on Rue Presbyterre, or Le Footy beside the port. Several vans also serve meals in the port car park. . For lunch or takeout, visit the super little Lezard Traiteur, which opens every day 0930-1300 and also on weekdays from 1500-1700.

Chris Doyle

MOUNTAINS & MANGROVES

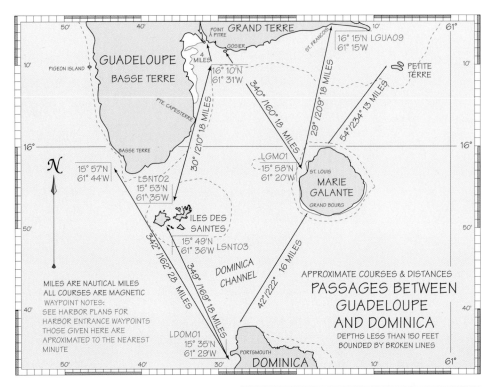

APPROXIMATE COURSES & DISTANCES
PASSAGES BETWEEN GUADELOUPE AND DOMINICA

DEPTHS LESS THAN 150 FEET
BOUNDED BY BROKEN LINES

MILES ARE NAUTICAL MILES
ALL COURSES ARE MAGNETIC
WAYPOINT NOTES:
SEE HARBOR PLANS FOR
HARBOR ENTRANCE WAYPOINTS
THOSE GIVEN HERE ARE
APROXIMATED TO THE NEAREST
MINUTE

There are quite a few other small restaurants, though some open only for lunch.

Ashore

You can rent scooters and cars right at the end of the dock. Grand Bourg also makes a great base for exploring the island.

There is a white sand beach used by fishing boats about half a mile east of town.

Habitation Murat is a gorgeous old plantation and distillery ruin. It is very picturesque, with a view of the sea in the background. An adjoining long hiking trail starts by the southern fence of the estate by the entrance (look for the signpost). Consider grabbing a taxi to Murat and walking back. Or just take the half-hour walk. To avoid the main road, follow Blvd. De la Marine, cross over onto D9 to Capesterre. Take the first right, pass Bagg Cash, and keep going straight. When the road turns to the right, keep straight on a footpath, which ends along the southern fence of Habitat Murat.

Chris Doyle

PASSAGES BETWEEN GUADELOUPE THE SAINTES & MARIE GALANTE

Sailing from Marie Galante to Pointe à Pitre or St. François, or returning is usually a decent sail without having to tack. Iles de la Petite Terre is more to the east and you often have to tack. Marie Galante to Dominica is a great reach, but the other way is hard on the wind and probably involves tacking. It is downwind to the Saintes, but directly into the wind to return.

The Saintes are about 5 miles from Guadeloupe at their nearest point. Sailing between Basse Terre and the Saintes is a pleasant short passage, even if sometimes hard on the wind when heading south.

Sailing from the Saintes to Pointe à Pitre is usually a windward passage, especially before Pointe de la Capesterre. The trip from Pointe à Pitre to the Saintes is generally very pleasant.

The only complications between The Saintes and Pointe à Pitre are the various shoals from Sainte Marie over toward the deep-water channel. (See our sketch chart,

"Approaches to Pointe à Pitre" on page 379.) The current can take you rapidly to the west, so it is easy to get taken down onto these shoals without realizing it. It is best to head well out and approach Gosier, rather than trying to cut the corner. The following procedure should keep you clear both ways: When close to Sainte Marie, keep a gap between the Saintes and Pointe Capesterre. Farther toward Pointe à Pitre, let Terre D'en Bas go behind the headland, but keep a gap between Terre D'en Haut and Pointe Capesterre. The deepwater channel in and out of Pointe à Pitre is well marked, but there is plenty of water to short cut over the bank to its east, except one shoal called Muchoir Carré that is only 9 feet deep and breaks in heavy swells. This shoal lies just east of the last beacon of the shipping channel. The beacon southeast of that one is black and yellow and east of the channel line. If you pass to the southeast of this beacon, you will stay in about 23 feet of water. If you decide to follow the main shipping beacons at night or in a rain squall, take care not to follow the fishing boat channel right up into Petit Bourg, as it starts soon after the main shipping channel ends.

As you arrive at Îlet à Cochons, pass between the red and green beacons, leaving red right returning.

Chris Doyle

MOUNTAINS & MANGROVES

The fishing harbor, Terre d'en Haut

Îles des Saintes

HIS IS AN IRRESISTIBLE group of islands with idyllic Gallic charm. They are small, dry, and steep, with red and brown cliffs. Mountains climb to over 1,000 feet and white beaches abound. After a hard day's sail, it is bound to be love at first sight.

The only small town, Bourg des Saintes, is on the largest island, Terre d'en Haut. The Saintes have been French since shortly after they were colonized, and have long supported a small community that used to rely almost entirely on fishing. There is a strong link to the north of France, especially Brittany, and some years ago you could see beautiful Breton-style fishing boats all along the waterfront. Boats are now designed to take the larger outboards. Since the islands were never agricultural, no slaves were imported, and the inhabitants that are of African descent have arrived fairly recently and, like you, by choice.

Bourg des Saintes is an adorable seaside town, sparkling clean and picturesque, with red roofs and a handful of those older Caribbean buildings that are all balconies and gingerbread. Flowers grow in abundance around the houses and no one is in a hurry. Local boats are anchored all along the waterfront.

In the last two decades, tourism has become a major industry. Many ferries arrive each day from Pointe à Pitre, bringing an influx of day-trippers. There is a sort of rush hour when they arrive at 0900 and another when they leave at 1700.

Locals make their living renting scooters, selling t-shirts, and feeding them. Terre d'en Haut is much quieter before they arrive and after they have gone. From a yachting point of view, the Saintes offer delightful choices: you can enjoy the restaurants, shops, and life in Bourg des Saintes, and then, when you want real peace, you can migrate to Ilet à Cabrit or

The Saintes

Regulations

Clear at the Mairie (see regulations in the main part of the chapter).

Personal watercraft (jet skis and the like) are not allowed in the Saintes, nor is the taking of conch.

Telephones

Telephones in the Saintes use the same area code and phone cards as in Guadeloupe. Cards are available at the post office and some tourist shops. See Guadeloupe for details on using phones.

Shopping hours

Shopping hours are variable. Most shops open at 0800, some close for lunch, and others open till as late as 1900.

Transport

Overseas transport is via Guadeloupe. The Saintes are linked to Guadeloupe by ferry. Most ferries are geared to bringing in tourists, rather than taking locals shopping. However, you can get to both Basseterre and Trois Rivière and back in a day. The easiest and best way to get around the Saintes is to walk or rent a mountain bike. They are available near the church. Drive on the right. If you prefer to be part of the pollution problem, you can rent scooters.

Holidays

See Guadeloupe

Les Saintes, Admiralty Leisure Folio 5642-2, 5642-3, 5642-6

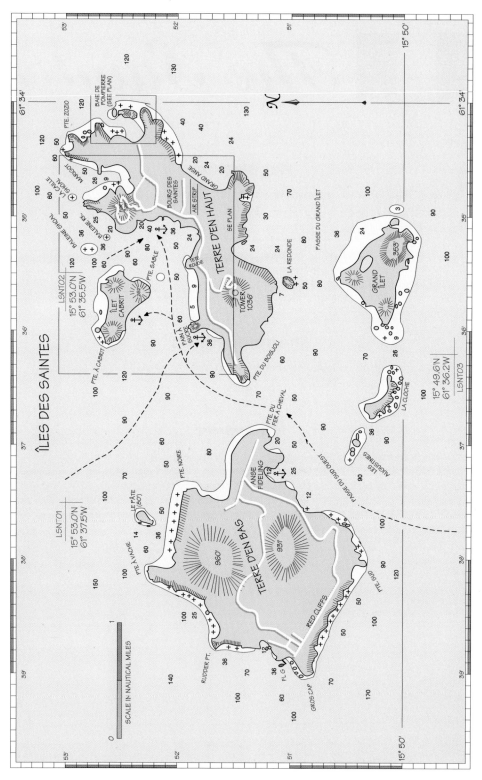

Terre d'en Bas.

Navigation

From the south, the easiest entrance is Passe du Sud Ouest. Some people use the smaller passage between Grand Ilet and La Cloche. If you do use this narrower passage, do so in good light.

From the northwest, it is easiest to enter between Le Pâte and Ilet à Cabrit. Besides several shoals along the coast, there are a couple of obvious dangers to watch out for. One is the coral patch between Pte. Sable (on Ilet à Cabrit) and Tête Rouge (on Terre d'en Haut). It is marked by an isolated shoal buoy. The shoal is visible in good light, and you can pass on either side. The passage is wider between the buoy and Tête Rouge. The other danger is Baleine Shoal as you pass between Ilet à Cabrit and Terre d'en Haut. This is marked by a large green beacon that flashes green twice every six seconds. The main channel is between this buoy and Ilet à Cabrit and this is the only sensible way to enter. However, if you are leaving, you might consider passing between the shoal and the 2-foot-high Baleine Rock, or between Baleine Rock and Terre d'en Haut, depending on sea conditions.

Anchor anywhere off the town, but leave a wide berth for the ferries. The sand close to the main ferry dock is hard and may prove difficult for some anchors. It is sometimes rolly by the fishing port, but holding is good. If the roll gets too much, there are two other anchorages within a mile or so and you can always move for the night.

Apart from the long ferry dock, a cruise ship tender dock is outside Le Genois, and a perfect floating dinghy dock extends from Café de La Marine. You can also use the very inside of the new commercial dock west of the fishing harbor if you can reach it. (Good for going to the dive shop, the Case aux Epices restaurant, or hiking to the west.) The outer small dock in the fishing harbor (keep clear of the swimmers) is good for loading provisions.

Do not block the channel to the new commercial dock or to the ferry dock.

The wreck of the ferry Lindy lies at 15° 52.3N, 61° 35. 07W. It is about 20 feet deep, but a potential anchor trap. Two large yellow buoys mark it.

You will see some huge mooring buoys. These are hurricane moorings for the ferries and bareboats sometimes tie to them.

Regulations

Clear in (or out) at the Mairie (town hall) just south of the church. Enter by the side entrance. The Gendarmerie Municipal does the clearance in the back office. They will have to fax the forms to Guadeloupe and wait to get them back, so you will probably want to fill in the forms and then come back later for the clearance. Their opening hours are weekdays 0800-1200 and 1400-1700; closed Wednesday afternoon. You cannot clear on weekends or Wednesday

Chris Doyle

MOUNTAINS & MANGROVES

THE SAINTES

TERRE D'EN BAS

LE PATE

ILET A CABRIT

PAIN A SUCRE

TERRE D'EN HAUT

BALEINE RK

LE CAILLE

BAIE DE MARIGOT

afternoon.

Communications

Internet communication is easy. Turn right off the ferry dock and look on your right. You will see the upstairs Terre de Haut.net. It opens daily 0900-1300 and 1400-2000. You will like this station as they have some qwerty keyboards. They also fix and sell computers and have accessories, do photo-printing, and have computer screens for sports events (they often open late on Saturdays) with a basic bar.

In addition, if you have wifi on board HotHotHot spot has an excellent signal from the roof of Maogany.

Chandlery

Saintes Brico is a marine and general hardware store in Bourg de Saintes. It has a good selection of fishing gear, snorkeling gear, and some marine hardware. They stock blocks and shackles, as well as a good stock of fiberglass, resin, and wood, including quarter-round hardwood. They also sell plumbing, electrical, and household products.

General Services

Jerome offers several services at his Yacht Club des Saintes (VHF: 68, call sign "Jerome"), open every day 'til whenever. He has a water buoy off his yacht club in about 12 feet of water, with a hose attached. You pay a set fee of 30 Eu, and take as much as you want. Jerome's wife, Valerie, will wash but not dry laundry, and they act as a help station for yacht problems, with a technician on call. They have a telephone, fax, and an internet station with free yacht club wifi. They also have a water taxi. The yacht club has an open bar

MOUNTAINS & MANGROVES

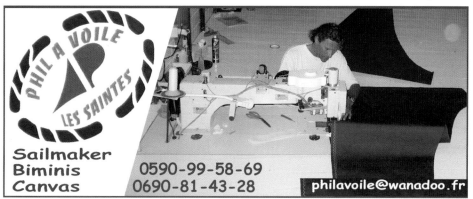

and restaurant where drinks and food are reasonably priced. They specialize in fish, lobster, and steaks. The meal price includes wine and coffee. They also rent kayaks. Jerome speaks English.

You can buy ice in some of the supermarkets.

The fuel station is in Baie de Marigot (see Technical yacht services, boatbuilders, below.

Technical Services
Sailmakers

The Saintes have a first rate sailmaker, Philippe Petit. His new Phil à Voile loft has a giant sewing machine for any size of sail. It is just outside town, near Marigot, on the road to Baie de Pompierre from the center of town. Philippe can also make awnings, covers, cushions, and any canvas work. He lives behind his shop. If you want to discuss a new project, wander over and talk with him. (It is a pleasant 10-minute walk, past 8 à Huit and keep going.) But if you have sails to repair, give him a call and he will pick them up from the harbor: 0690-81-43-28.(If you don't have a phone, Yves in the

boutique Maogany will help you.) Phil is an agent for North Sails and organizes the North Cup regatta, which takes place towards the end of May, with two days of racing in the Saintes.

Technical Services,
Boatbuilders,
Fuel Station

Other yacht services are in Baie de Marigot on the northern side of Terre d'en Haut. It is a lovely bay between rocks, cliffs, and Fort Napoleon, and makes a pleasant anchorage, except in northeasterly winds and swells. You can take your yacht there, or walk over. It is a long but lovely walk, the last half-mile being along a tiny path through the trees, for two of the boatyards.

If you are approaching Baie de Marigot from Bourg des Saintes by sea, eyeball your way between La Baleine rock and the shore, weather permitting. However, you must go well outside Le Caille shoal before heading into the bay.

It can be choppy as you enter Marigot,

but the seas diminish farther in. A long dock provides fair protection, with room to anchor in about 8 feet of water. The service area on the eastern shore might be part of a Conrad novel. Half-ruined buildings have been taken over by the encroaching jungle and it has a desolate, almost abandoned atmosphere: no road leads in; the only way to get here is by boat or a tiny footpath through the hills. But among the ruins are two well-equipped boatyards building fishing boats in wood and glass, and to make it even more surreal, this is the site of the island's only fuel station; all the fuel for the scooters and cars you see on the island comes from this station via jugs in fishing boats back to town. It is part of a community development that started, stalled, and now is in slow decline. There are still the remains of a marine railway that worked a few years ago but are now abandoned; the support buildings have been demolished.

The fuel station is in its own little harbor and sells both gas and diesel, but the harbor is tiny and suitable only for tenders or small open fishing boats. For a boat at anchor here, the two boatyards are easily accessible and they work in both glass and wood and can handle any repair or fabrication you need. The one nearer the sea is called Chantier Pineau and the one farther in is Chantier Judes.

If, on the other hand, you come by road, then Chantier Naval à Foy is much more accessible, with road access at the head of the bay. They build fiberglass boats – from tiny Optimists to 30-foot cabin cruisers.

They are also good wood boatbuilders and can help fix wooden boats.

Provisioning

Most food and some household items are available in one of the many small supermarkets around town. Most have fair delicatessen sections, with wines, cheeses, and meats. Keep your eye open for locally smoked fish; it is excellent. 8 à Huit is right in town, beyond Galerie Merchande, and opens 0800-1300 and 1500-2000. It is modern and clean and has the largest selection. Owners Bonbon and Luidgi welcome sailors and you will find everything you need here, including lots of French wine and cheese. If you buy a bunch, they will deliver to your dinghy dock. The others are just behind the fishing harbor, close to the dock on that side of town.

The Saintes has become one of the easiest places to stock up on beer, wine, and liquor, with Alexandra's Delco Distribution right at the head of the dinghy dock. They also sell juices from small bottles to 5-liter boxes, mixes, sodas, and bottled water. You can use their dolly to take it the few feet down to the dock or they will deliver it there for you. Stop by and pick up one of their price-lists, which include both retail and wholesale prices. Wine lovers will enjoy their selection, which ranges from the excellent to inexpensive box wines. They open Monday to Saturday 0800-1200 and 1430-1830.

Ti Saintes is an excellent boulangerie and café owned by the same people that have the Supermarché des Saintes. Fournil

MOUNTAINS & MANGROVES

de Jimmy's also bakes bread and pâtisseries, and you can get coffee to go with them from about 0500. For fresh fruits, try the market behind the fishing port, or Jardin De L'sle, the greengrocer.

The island's ATM is on the ferry square. Credit cards work well for boutiques and restaurants.

Fun Shopping

I remember the days when there were perhaps two boutiques in the Saintes; now they are wall-to-wall. And they are a great bunch, all very local and different, reflecting the interests and tastes of their owners. It is well worth pottering around and looking inside; you will get some pleasant surprises.

One of the oldest is Yves Cohen's Maogany (closed most of Saturday). Yves is an artist who sails and the Saintes have been his home for the last 40 years. He creates hand-painted and silk-screened clothes in themes reminiscent of the sea. The colors are those you observe when

lying on a beach looking at the water: turquoise, pale luminescent green, blue, and all the shades between. The shop is the most restful and elegant in town, but perhaps equally important from a cruising person's point of view is that Yves lived in the States for a couple of years, speaks good English, and will lend his local expertise to whatever problem you may have. Yves creates elegant, custom, hand-painted boat portraits on garments – the most exotic yacht shirts you can get. He also does yacht portraits on canvas, as well as other paintings. When he travels, he brings back a few small ornaments, which he sells. His work can be seen on his internet site. He also houses the Saintes' wifi, HotHotHot spot.

At the back of Maogany, with a cute garden corner, Yves' daughter Rachel and her Brazilian husband, Aou, run a family café called Agua na Boca. They open daily except Saturday from 0930-1800, and serve sweet and savory crépes, panini, smoked fish, and local cheese sandwiches, frozen fruit drinks, coffee, and Haagen Dazs ice cream. It makes a very inexpensive lunch.

Opposite Maogany, Café de la Marine looks out over the harbor. Their boutique sells silk dress pareos, swim and casual wear, brightly painted jewelry made from calabash, banana leaf art, river stone carvings, lacework, and plaster wall hangings – most of it locally made.

A few steps down the road is the Pharmacie des Saintes. This is an interesting, state-of-the-art pharmacy with a view of the sea. Gilles, the owner, likes helping yachting folks as he is a yachtsman himself and both he and his assistant, Cecile, (wife of Philippe the sailmaker), speak perfect English. Gilles' wife, Severine (usually in the back office), is a doctor of pharmacology, specializing in nutrition. They have a huge stock of prescription medications, and their computerized system can locate anything that is available in Guadeloupe and bring it in within a few hours. Their shop has full range of OTC supplements, plant extracts, herbal teas, and remedies, including some brand new ones recently discovered in the Caribbean. They also have sun screens, beauty products, and French perfumes. Since a small island pharmacy has to be inclusive, you can also get medications for your pets. French products look exotically different to those you may be used to, but Gilles or Cecile will

make sure you find what you need.

Nearby is the Saintes' own soap factory, Bruno and Françoise's L'Atelier du Savon des Saintes, where everything is made in the Saintes from vegetable extracts. They produce soaps, perfumes, eau de toilette, including aloe vera lotion, soap, and shower gel. You can watch the soap being made in the shop. They package them attractively in small baskets. Of interest to charter yachts, they can supply soaps with your yacht's name on them, and are happy to sell in bulk.

Opposite the ferry terminal is the Martine Cotten Art Galerie for prints and originals of Martine Cotten. Martine was born in South Finistère, in Brittany. She became fascinated by the Saintes, whose fishing boats and fishermen could have come from her birthplace, and she has painted here for many years, using pastels as her medium. You can now buy her art prints on bags and t-shirts.

There is a Saintoise artist called Pascal Foy who produces good models of house facades in the Saintes and related art. His creations are elaborate, with much detail work, and the hinges on shutters and doors all work. Each is a replica of an actual house that exists or existed. While he still does these, in recent time Pascal has started creating abstract constructions, many of

Chris Doyle

MOUNTAINS & MANGROVES

which use bits of old building material.

While on the subject of art, restaurants La Saladerie and Solo mio are also art galleries, carrying their owners' work, and several other restaurants have works of art for sale on their walls.

A new shopping block is on the right hand side as you walk towards the church from the ferry dock. You will find many clothing stores selling excellent sailing shorts, hats, and t-shirts.

Hervé Samson's CB is the Saintes' first jewelry store. CB is delightfully individualistic, with many of the items being made on the Saintes by Hervé. Just about every material is used, including wood and stone as well as silver and gold. The variety is impressive and the prices reasonable. Hervé also owns Ultra Marine, towards the fishing port. This surf shop has the latest bathing, beachwear, and casual fashions.

Tropico Gelato is a fancy new ice-creamery with lots of flavors and specials. They also serve sandwiches and pâtisseries. The owner, Sophie, speaks good English.

Galerie d'Art les Saintes, has a wonderful collection of art and all kinds of collectables and decoration from around the world. This is a combination of the art of Didier Spindler, and a collection of objets d'art acquired by him and his partner Jean Paul on their travels. You will find something you like here and prices can be surprisingly reasonable.

You don't have to go to Paris for a good hair-styling: try Ludo Coiff or Blanc Emeraude instead. Lud Coiff unisex hair salon is in a cute Caribbean style house on the back street, just north of the post office. You will be looked after by Ludo and Géraldine. They are busy enough that you won't be able to walk right in, but with luck you can visit and get an appointment for later the same day or the next. Blanc Emeraude, a new hair stylist, has opened next to Lo Bleu Hotel.

Restaurants

Eating out is one of the great pleasures of being in the Saintes. For a small community, Terre d'en Haut has an excellent selection of restaurants, be it for a long drawn-out lunch followed by a siesta, or for an evening on the town. I know of nowhere where there are so many places to choose from. Two- and three-course menus from 15-30 Eu are common, as are fancier establishments. Part of the pleasure is to wander round and choose the one that takes your fancy. We mention just a few.

Le Genois, has a delightful intimate ambience right on the waterfront, in front of the town tender dock, with some tables under the stars. Owner Carole, who is from the southwest of France, will most likely greet you. Le Genois has a wide-ranging menu that should please most tastes. You can get anything from a quiche and salad to a perfectly cooked fresh tuna steak, and they make an excellent fish pâté. Finish with an old rhum and pâtisserie. Le Genois is small, so come early or make a reservation.

Franck and Betrand's La Fringale is a charming bistro-style restaurant. Walk in and you will find yourself in a charming

Restaurant La Fringale — BRASSERIE

French and Creole cuisine
Live lobster tank
Draft beer
Magnificent mural by local artist Philippe Remaury

Reservations
0590-98-14-65

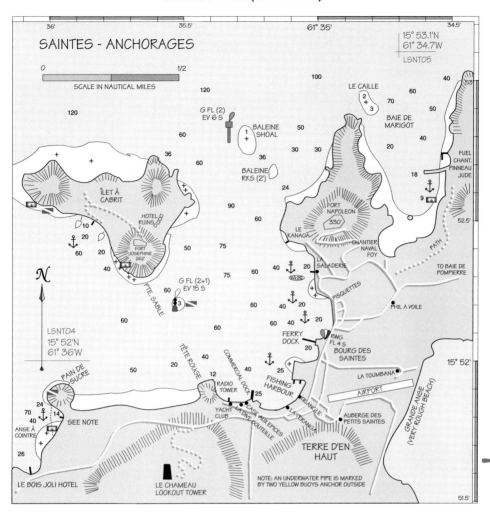

SAINTES - ANCHORAGES

SCALE IN NAUTICAL MILES

15° 53.1'N
61° 34.7'W
LSNT05

courtyard garden, which makes a nice change from the sea. They serve Créole food, as well as traditional French dishes. Fresh seafood is always on the menu, as are freshwater crayfish, and when the lobster tank is installed,, this should become the premier place for lobster. Prices are reasonable; they have both set menus and a full à la carte. It is closed Wednesdays.

On the back street, Kaz a Man Albe is owned and run by the Brudy family who run the travel agency and taxi service. It is a good Créole restaurant, with a warm, intimate atmosphere where they serve local meat and seafood, together with a really delicious and varied collection of local vegetables. Open Monday to Saturday for lunch and dinner.

Le Mambo, right on the main street, is a great place to watch the world walk by. It is a very inexpensive pizza, coffee, and snack joint. They open daily from 0700 for good espresso coffee and breakfast (fresh local bread), right through till the evening. Their tasty pizzas are popular and they also cook inexpensive local dishes. This is the place to come for a drink late in the evening. Alfred, the owner, has a 30-foot fishing boat and you can ask him about for local fishing trips.

Edouard's La Saladerie (Closed Monday and Tuesday, and mid-September to mid-October) is on a headland with its own dinghy dock. Edouard is an artist and his

MOUNTAINS & MANGROVES

431

restaurant is tasteful. You walk up steps from the dock to the open dining room with a charming view of the bay through tropical foliage, which gives the feeling of sitting on a deck amid the treetops. Food here is light and pleasant, with many wonderful salads (their smoked fish salad is great), as well as meat and seafood dishes. Leave room for their desserts, which include some wonderful ice cream concoctions. During the season, reservations are advisable, especially on weekends and holidays – or arrive early. Occasionally, Edouard has a jazz group come to play in the evenings. La Saladerie is also an art gallery. Edouard has evolved his own art form. He visits beaches, bringing back bits of old wrecks, driftwood, and metals, and cuts and glues them into quite magnificent designs. This has brought him quite some fame, with exhibitions in France and sales all over the world. (He can ship.)

For a gourmet dinner in a quiet elegant atmosphere, the place to go is Laurence Jean's Auberge des Petits Saintes (open from 1800, closed Mondays, and from mid-June and to mid-October). It is a seven-minute walk, just above town, with a flower garden, swimming pool, and a magnificent view of the harbor. You sit on a balcony, almost among the treetops, and the food is excellent; beautifully prepared and artistically presented. They always have fresh seafood and, if you wish for lobster, you need to call in the morning, so they can get a fisherman to catch some. If you do not make it for dinner, come for an evening drink and tapas, an inexpensive way to sample some wonderful flavors.

Couleurs de Monde (closed Tuesday and Wednesday), upstairs on the main ferry square, is special. You walk into an amazing jumble of riches in art, furniture, and decoration – a veritable Ali Baba's cave. The decor is a creation of Jean-Paul and the artist Didier Spindler, whose striking original paintings adorn the walls. These are intermingled with a collection of objets

d'art and furniture. The restaurant is owned by Melissa, Cedric and Maryline, it has seating on a balcony overlooking the square as well as inside. The staff are wonderful and the food inventive and excellent. It is small and intimate, and while you can walk in during the day, it is essential to book for dinner.

La Teranga is the restaurant for Lo Bleu Hotel. It has a perfect casual-elegant beach location in the fishing harbor, with a lovely view of the bay. They open for both lunch and dinner every day except Tuesday when they open only for dinner, and Monday when they close all day. Isabelle will welcome you, while her partner, Jean-Michel, runs the kitchen. Jean Michel is a Catalan who combines local ingredients and traditional Créole cooking with his own ideas to produce some new flavors.

3 Boat is a special find, a tiny, shiny-clean, air-conditioned restaurant across the road from Tropico Velo. The owner "Chicken" Georges is one of the Saintes best known chefs, and he always does a good job. He opens Monday to Saturday for lunch and dinner. Each day he works out his menu and posts it on a chalk board. He offers a 15 Eu three-course menu with three choices for each course.

Simple and fun, the Triangle (open for lunch and dinner, closed Sunday) is an inexpensive restaurant (a three-course meal starts at 17 Eu), right on the beach, facing the fishing port. You can just dinghy in and tie up right outside. If you walk in from the road, the entrance is a little funky, but the dining room is great: the tables charmingly set and completely open to the sea, giving the illusion of eating on the beach without having to contend with sand. Saintoise owner Pedro Foy specializes in Créole cooking, using the daily catch of lambi (in season), fish, and squid. He puts this with fresh local vegetables such as plantains and christophenes. Reservations are advised in season. Menus are available in English.

Le Café de la Marine, right by the long floating dinghy dock, is a boutique, a charming bar, and lunchtime restaurant

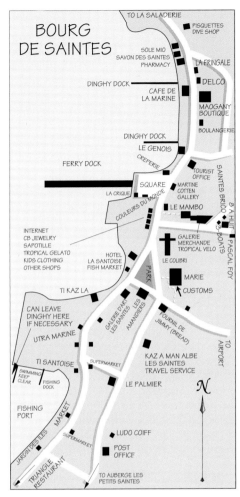

right on the waterfront. They open every day except Saturday. The menu always includes plenty of fresh seafood. They used to also serve dinner, and may do so again one day.

Les Amandiers, run by the Charlat family, is one of least expensive places to eat, with a choice of inexpensive set menus that give you a taste of typical Créole food. Try their court bouillon (fish poached in fish stock) or their colombos (stews), including lambi.

Le Palmier is a local restaurant on the back street. Back street ambience but great food; their dorado in a passion fruit sauce, if on the menu, is wonderful.

Patrick and Catherine's Sole Mio is

MOUNTAINS & MANGROVES

open all day, every day, except Sunday. It is a pleasant restaurant right on the water-front, and the owners will welcome you warmly and look after you well. They have a wide-ranging menu, including plenty of fresh local seafood. For cocktail lovers, they have a big cocktails menu, with a history of these elaborate drinks and, on Thursday, Friday, and Saturday nights, they have a variety of tapas menus for cocktail customers. People also come by in the afternoon for those delicious ice cream concoctions the French do so well. Between them, Patrick and Catherine speak good English and Spanish and get by in German and Italian. They both also paint, and their art adorns the walls and is for sale.

Ti Kaz La is a hangout, right on the edge of the water, and completely open to the sea. You can pull your dinghy up right outside, but watch out for all the fishermen's ropes. It is open and breezy, with enough space to accommodate the largest of groups. The setting is informal and entertaining. The owner, Philippe, speaks perfect English as he worked in England for 15 years, both in Park Lane's restaurant Gavroche and as pastry chef in Grosvenor House and Harrods. You can watch him at work on the open grill. The food is first-rate and they specialize in fresh local fish and have a live lobster tank. Philippe's wife, Sophie, runs Tropico Gelo, the ice cream store and lunch place.

La Case aux Epices is owned and run by Christine Sirvain, who has spent a lot of time in the south of France. It is on the beach, well away from the bustle of town, and opens for lunch daily. She and her partner make good salads, which may be enough on their own, or try a little of their fish mousse on the side. You can follow with traditional French and Provençal dishes: meat, fish, and vegetarian. They also offer a full lobster menu.

Chris Doyle

434

Chris Doyle

The hot bar of an evening among the young local crowd is Coconut's, behind the fishing harbor.

Bar La Crique is in a quaint old building adjoining the ferry dock. It opens from morning till 1800, and is popular with those waiting for ferries. They offer lunch and, like many restaurants, sell interesting paintings.

Gemaine and Henry's Restaurant La Toumbana is a good Créole restaurant, and also the cheapest, with a menu starting at 10 Eu. It is a 10-minute walk to get there, down the road to the airport. The dining room has a pleasant garden setting. They open from Monday to Saturday for lunch and dinner, walk in for lunch – you must reserve for dinner.

La Kanaoa is a hotel with its own dinghy dock, so it is easily accessible by boat. It is a fair walk, which is maybe why it can sometimes be very quiet. They do good Créole food at a reasonable price and the dining room looks out over the bay. Open every day for lunch and dinner.

Transport

The Saintes now has a travel agent: Monique and Brudy's Les Saintes Travel Services on the back street, part of Kaz a Man Albe They can book your flights, arrange your accommodation, and Brudy will take you around the Saintes in their taxi. Of interest to larger yachts, they can arrange charter flights.

Ferries are abundant; you can get to Guadeloupe (Trois Rivières) for the day and get back pretty late. There is a little ferry that will run you to Terre d'en Bas for lunch.

Terre d'en Haut is small enough that you can walk everywhere. Locals use scooters. Everything here goes by scooter. I have seen building irons, planks, cases of beer, and many a suitcase being buzzed around on these two wheelers. Tourists also like to rent scooters. They are noisy and smelly, and at one time a law was passed to make visitors' scooters leave town except during lunch. Things got much better, but the scooter operators took the matter to court and won, so for a while it was two-stroke mayhem again. Then the town blocked off the ferry dock and much of the main street to all traffic, which has created a very peaceful friendly atmosphere. You can rent a scooter or a mountain bike. Pedaling is much more eco-friendly. Unless you have recently done the tour de France, you will have to walk up some hills, but the distances are so short that this is no problem. You can rent bicycles from Jean Louis Cassin at Tropico Velo. In the mornings, you will see a line of them running from the church to his shop. Cycle on the right. Roads are mainly well surfaced, though small and twisty. Take your camera.

Ashore

The Saintes has a tourist office. You should go there as they have a useful map of the Saintes and current information on

MOUNTAINS & MANGROVES

435

Grand Bourg's fishing port

Chris Doyle

activities.

Fort Napoleon, built 1867, stands on a hill to the north of town, with a commanding view of the harbor. It is only open 0900 to noon, and there is a small (about 4 Eu) entry charge, which goes toward the upkeep of the fort. The fort has been magnificently restored. The whole of the top half is a well-tended garden of cactuses and succulents, which are labeled so you can identify all those plants that have been stabbing you. When the aloes bloom, they attract a horde of hummingbirds. Iguanas, fat from tourist scraps, will come right up to you. As you look down on town through your camera viewfinder, every shot will look like a picture postcard. Inside, the museum has early furniture and a section on the famous battle of the Saintes, when England's Admiral Rodney demolished the French fleet under De Grasse in 1782. You will also find some lovely examples of the

old Saintoise fishing boats, which are becoming very rare. It is not hard to walk up to the fort. Even gravitationally-challenged cruise ship passengers do it.

On the other hand, you do need to be reasonably fit to make it to the island's most spectacular view from Le Chameau, by the old Napoleonic lookout tower. The road is closed to traffic and you have to walk up. It is about 1,000 feet in elevation, road nearly all the way, and quite steep. Check out the rickety ladders in the tower, and if you think they will support you, climb them for a spectacular 360° view. You see over town, round to Ilet à Cabrit, and to the south. This is the highest point on the island, and from a photographic standpoint, much like being in an airplane. For photographing town, you will want the afternoon light. When the garbage dump is smoking, it detracts from this walk.

You can find a beach to suit your mood.

436

One of the nicest is Baie de Pompierre, which we write up in a separate section. If you like pounding waves, surfing, or body surfing, take the airport road and keep going on to Grand Anse. This long straight beach has rugged cliffs at both ends and is totally exposed to the easterly swells. Swimming can be dangerous in rough conditions. If you walk to the south end of the beach, you will come to another road. Follow it south to another small, secluded beach, where you can snorkel around the rocks.

There are many fabulous walks along marked trails on the hills between Marigot and Baie de Pompierre. Start in Marigot behind Le Paillotte restaurant and follow the marked trails to Fort Caroline. Fort Caroline is just an old ruin, but there are lots of great views and you are likely to see iguanas. Le Paillotte makes a convenient place for lunch afterwards.

For the really adventurous, Caraibes Escalade, has a beginners rock climbing ascent in Baie de Marigot, which is safe in as much as you are roped onto a series of fixed points. The climb affords spectacular views (0690-58-96-50)

Water Sports

Diving in the Saintes is easy and fun, with thousands of fish crowding walls and reefs, and the water is usually very clear.

The sites are varied and good. Turtle lovers will want to include Pte. Gouvernail on the lee side of Terre d'en Bas. This is a wall dive where you nearly always see several turtles, as well as barracudas. La Vierge, off La Cloche, got its name from a tall rock that looks just like a statue of the Virgin Mary. There are many interesting canyons and lots of fish, including ceros, chubbs, and spadefish.

You can choose between two dive shops, and both will fill tanks if you have a card. Cedric's Pisquettes is a PADI shop over by the doctor's house (the one shaped like a boat). They usually dive at 0900 and 1400. They have staff who speak English and they are also happy to do private dive charters for those who want to dive on their own, or to provide a dive guide to go with your tender.

Luc and Sylvie's Le Dive Bouteille is by Jerome's Yacht Club. Discuss diving with them. Their program changes each day, but they often dive at 0830 and 1330, and they rent gear.

The Saintes now has something new in Club de Kayaks des Saintes. Here, Canadian Sylvie (she speaks perfect English), offers guided tours on and sells completely transparent molded Lexan kayaks. These are great, you can see under water just as well as above, and the 90-

Baie de Marigot

Chris Doyle

MOUNTAINS & MANGROVES

ILET A CABRIT ANCHORAGE

PAIN DE SUCRE ANCHORAGE

minute tour will take you over all the wrecks and reefs in the bay. If you develop a taste for this idea, you can buy one to take with you. She also rents snorkeling masks with an attached 5-mp digital camera; perfect for some underwater stills or movies.

For those diving on their own, the most accessible sites are around Pain de Sucre, and toward the western end of Ilet à Cabrit. (Details are given under these anchorages.)

Anchorage Behind Pain de Sucre

Pain de Sucre is a 200-foot mini-piton. It is joined to the island by a low strip of land with exquisite beaches on both sides. There is one house surrounded by palms. You cannot anchor close to shore as an underwater pipeline carrying fresh water runs here. If the yellow buoys are in place (not always), they mark the limits of the anchorage. Anchor outside these buoys in about 20 to 40 feet. If you like this anchorage, you could use this as a base and visit the rest of the island from here.

Ashore

There is a track leading up to the main road, and those in good shape can hike up Le Chameau, to the old lookout tower at the top. In the other direction, past Le Bois Joli, is a small, secluded beach that is often used for nude bathing.

Hotel Bois Joli is a modern, fancy hotel, open every day, whose airy dining room has a spectacular view out over the bay. They offer traditional Créole and Saintoise food, and keep a live lobster tank.

For those who just want a moderate stroll, follow the signs behind the hotel to the cross, which is way up on the hill with a great view of Pain de Sucre and your yacht at anchor.

Water Sports

If you don a mask and snorkel, you will find things to look at along the reef between the Pain de Sucre beach and Le Bois Joli and also around Pain de Sucre itself. There is a pleasant dive around the base of Pain de Sucre in about 60 feet of water. If you are anchored close enough, you can go straight from your yacht. There are boulders encrusted in coral and sponges, with many colorful reef fish, and

438

the sand is dotted with sea pussies.

The Saintes has some spectacular wind-surfing and it is possible to rent a board or other small sailing craft from the Hotel Bois Joli.

Ilet à Cabrit

This is a pleasant spot and much more protected in northeasterly winds than Bourg de Saintes. With an outboard, it is not too far to dinghy between the two, though in strong winds it is a wet ride. Anchor anywhere along the beach. Some people go stern-to, which minimizes any roll from passing ferries. Do not obstruct the dock, as fishermen use it for preparing their nets.

Ashore

The ruins of an old road lead up to the remains of Fort Josephine. Wear good shoes as the goats have eaten everything but the prickles, and these abound. Each year the track gets more overgrown, if you have a cutlass, take it with you. Take the camera for grand views from some of the old ramparts. There are also the ruins of a hotel that didn't quite work out. Bird watchers can see kingfishers, yellow warblers, and a host of other small birds.

Water Sports

Snorkeling is bright and colorful along both ends of the beach. Big schools of chromis cluster in some areas and you are likely to see angelfish, spotted drums, trumpetfish, and parrotfish. If you go over the sand, you will almost certainly see flying gurnards. There is a chance of seeing the rather rare cornetfish in the grass beds.

Diving is very pleasant off the boulders toward the western end of Ilet à Cabrit's south shore. Follow a coral slope from the surface down about 25 feet at the eastern end and head west where the reef deepens to about 60 feet. Watch out for current. The reef is alive with brightly colored fish

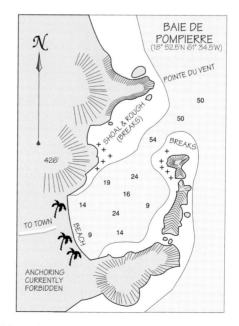

ANSE FIDELING

and sea creatures. Hundreds of garden eels live in the sand at the base of the slope. You sometimes see scorpionfish here.

Baie De Pompierre

In 1996 the Mairie banned yachts from anchoring in Baie de Pompierre. Yachts anchoring there have been asked to leave and some to pay a fine. The reason is that the wind is onshore, it is a very popular bathing beach, and the officials worry about pollution. You can visit by rowboat or sailing dinghy; otherwise it is an easy walk from town.

Baie de Pompierre is on the windward side of Terre d'en Haut. It is protected from the east by two rocky islands whose sheer cliffs rise to about 130 feet. Behind is a sweeping beach, shaded by palms, sea-grapes, and almonds. This beach is part of a national park and fills up during the day, but in the early morning and late after-noon, you will have it all to yourself, unless campers are in residence. It is a good har-bor, and is even used by some locals as a hurricane hole.

A pleasant little restaurant, Douceur de l'Isle, is a couple of hundred yards back up the road from the beach. It opens for lunch

and serves Créole specialties.

Ashore

The beach by the entrance gate gets very crowded during the day. A great thing to do (and it gets you well away from the crowds) is to climb the rocky islets that protect the bay. The windward sides of these are very dramatic, with sheer drops and breaking seas. Take your camera to catch the view back over the bay, past the beach to the dumpy hills behind. The snor-keling is good. Spearfishing is forbidden.

Terre d'en Bas

Terre d'en Bas is very quiet, with long walks away from habitation. Several hous-es had to be abandoned for rebuilding after the earthquakes of 2005. You will find sev-eral little Créole restaurants that some-times require an hour or two's advance notice. There are probably more iguanas in Terre d'en Bas than anywhere else in the Caribbean, except Isles de la Petit Terre, so this is a good place to look for them.

The anchorage at Anse Fideling is quite delightful in calm conditions. On shore you will see the ruins of an old pottery, which makes for interesting exploration.

Navigation

There are no suitable bays for anchoring on the lee side of the island, although there is a fishing harbor for the small local open boats. You can find temporary anchorage off the coast, but it is very exposed.

Anse Fideling is the best anchorage and well protected from the north and east, but southeasterly swells can creep in and make it roll, and strong southerly winds could be bad news. It is fine for overnighting in settled conditions.

Services

In the next bay to Anse Fideling there is a fuel station at the head of the ferry dock and, in a squeeze, fuel can be arranged, but it is not really suitable for yachts.

A regular ferry service runs to and from Grand Bourg. Terre d'en Bas is also within dinghy range of the other anchorages, conditions permitting.

Ashore

The old road that runs right over the middle of the island is scarcely used by cars anymore and makes for great walking. Near the top of the mountain, down a side trail to the right, is an area with a few small ponds called l'Etang. This was once farmed and there are many interesting old stone walls.

Many lovely marked walking trails are laid out all over the island, and the hiking is excellent. While here, don't miss a meal at Madame Joseph's à la Belle Etoile. It is local, simple, inexpensive, and right on the beach at Grand Anse. I doubt you will find better court bouillon or lambi anywhere in the Saintes. Choose these, rather than the barbecued fish, which may be overcooked. Try to give her a couple of hours notice.

PASSAGE BETWEEN THE SAINTES AND DOMINICA

(See sketch chart Passages between Guadeloupe and Dominica page 418) The sail from the Saintes to Dominica can usu-ally be done in one tack, but if the wind is southerly, it will be hard on the wind. If leaving from Bourg des Saintes, remember to avoid the shoal between Ilet à Cabrit and Terre d'en Haut. The easiest way out is by the Passe du Sud Ouest. If you use the passage between La Coche and Grand Ilet, be very careful and do it in good light. As you get closer to Dominica, the Cabrits and the 1,200-foot Barbers Block Hill, just behind Rollo Head, stand out as landmarks. The sail north from Dominica to the Saintes is usually a great romp with the wind abeam or on the quarter. The easiest way into the Saintes is to head for Terre d'en Bas (the westernmost of the Saintes). For a long time Grand Ilet will be merged with Terre d'en Haut, but as you approach, it separates into a distinct island. You may be quite close before you make out La Coche and Les Augustins. Le Passe du Sud Ouest between Les Augustins and Terre d'en Bas is the easiest entrance. Give plenty of clearance to the western side of Les Augustins to avoid the shoal that lies about 150 yards west of the westernmost visible rocks. Pass between Terre d'en Bas and Terre d'en Haut, round Le Pain de Sucre, and then head up into town. Favor the Terre d'en Haut shore to avoid the shoal over toward Ilet à Cabrit. See also the navigation part of our chapter on the Saintes.

Chris Doyle

Dominica

*T*F CHRISTOPHER COLUMBUS came back today, Dominica is the only island he would recognize. This is because Dominica is the region's most unspoiled country and its most exciting destination for spectacular natural beauty. When Columbus was before King Ferdinand and Queen Isabella of Spain, trying to describe the awe-inspiring mountains of Dominica, he had to resort to crumpling up a sheet of paper to illustrate the dramatic form of the land, with its valleys, gorges, and pinnacles. This gives an idea of its topography, but tells nothing of its amazingly lush vegetation. Greenery erupts everywhere, thrusting upwards, curling, stretching, climbing, and falling, till the whole land is covered in a verdant tangle of trees, vines, shrubs, and ferns. Add to this a plethora of birds, butterflies, and brightly-colored flowers, and you can begin to imagine its almost magical nature. In addition, there are such unusual natural phenomena as a

boiling lake and hot waterfalls, to say nothing of the more usual sulfur springs and crater lakes. The high mountains attract clouds, creating frequent showers interspersed with sunshine, and as a result the island is known as the land of many rivers. It could equally be known as the land of many rainbows. You are sure to see some, and, around the full moon, you might see a moonbow. Dominica also has some lovely beaches, but not in the profusion of the islands to the north and south, so tourism is low-key.

Dominica has 70,000 inhabitants who have a natural curiosity about outsiders and enjoy meeting visitors. Nature lovers and free spirits will likely rate this majestic land their favorite. Some of the island can be seen from the boat, but the best times are found walking inland. Light rain gear is advisable, as the island attracts frequent showers, which alternate with bursts of bright sunshine.

Exploring inland should be a priority. We will outline some attractions under the nearest anchorages, if you only stop at one anchorage, you can reach them all by road. It should be noted that many of Dominica's hikes, including the one to Trafalgar Falls, can cover slippery and muddy terrain and should only be undertaken by those who are reasonably agile and fit. The Dominica Forestry Department has laid out many hiking trails in the extensive area included in the island's national parks. They have done an amazing job, sometimes laying out miles of log walkways. These trails are a delight. You can get trail maps from the Forestry Department in the botanical gardens in Roseau. There are charges for visiting park sites and tickets can be bought by the visit ($5 US single site), or all sites by the week ($12 US). All the money goes towards park maintenance and is well spent. Right now they are working on the Waitikubuli National Trail, which goes from Scotts Head to the very north of the island, passing through the Trois Pitons National Park and Northern Forest Reserve. It should be noted that just about all of Dominica is spectacular, and there are numerous lovely hikes on small roads and paths that are not part of the park.

Dominica has seven potentially active volcanoes (most other Caribbean islands only have one). There is no expectation of an eruption anytime soon, but it helps explain the dramatic scenery. An undersea fault to the north of Dominica created an earthquake a couple of years ago and affected Dominica, the Saintes, and Marie Galante.

If you have any medical problems, call Dr. Fitzroy Armour (275-1804). He has his own yacht, is in charge of the decompression chamber, and if he cannot help you himself he can put you on to the best person.

Navigation

The leeward coast of Dominica is generally steep to. A quarter of a mile offshore will keep you clear of all dangers, from the north down to Scotts Head. If you are closer in than that, watch out for shoals off Toucari, the Layou River, the coast below Morne Daniel, and Anse Bateaux. Le Grand Maison is a shoal that extends between one and two hundred yards off the coast just to the north of Soufriere. As you round Scotts Head, keep clear of The Pinnacle. This large rocky peak rises to within a few feet of the surface. It lies about 300 yards west of the northern part of Scotts Head. You can see it when the sun is high and visibility is good, and on calmer days fishermen often anchor in the general area. Give it a wide berth at night or in

James Fine

MOUNTAINS & MANGROVES

Dominica

Regulations

Under Prime Minister Roosevelt Skerrit, the youngest leader ever elected in the Caribbean, Dominica has broken new ground in making customs and immigration procedures the simplest and best for yachts in the Caribbean and we hope it may start a trend in other islands. Under the new rules, as long as you are not changing crew members, you may check in and out at the same time for a two-week period. This means that you only need to make one visit to customs and, once you are checked in, you are free to visit any permissible anchorage in Dominica, and you do not have to return to customs before you leave. This should encourage visiting cruisers to stay longer, and make it a more attractive destination for the charter fleet based in Guadeloupe. Perhaps the best part of this is that, by giving a two week clearance to those who plan to stay less, the officials are presenting a clear message of "you are welcome," and those who cannot take advantage of it this time round probably will the next. Obviously, if you are changing crew members or plan to stay more than two weeks, you will need to clear in when you arrive and out when you leave.

Entry is simple. Visit customs with all passports and ship's papers and the clearance-from your previous port. They may handle immigration for you or they may ask you to visit immigration. If you are changing crew or have passengers, immigration will want to see you.

You currently pay a $4 EC environmental tax per person and a $5 EC stamp duty. If passengers are leaving in Dominica, there is a $46 EC embarkation tax and a $5 EC security tax.

Office hours are Mondays 0800-1300 and 1400-1700; Tuesday-Friday 0800-1300 and 1400-1600. Moderate overtime fees are payable at other times.

Fishing, including trolling, is only allowed with a permit. Anchoring is strictly prohibited in the marine protected areas. These include the Soufriere Bay/Scotts Head Marine Reserve that stretches from Anse Bateau through Soufriere Bay to Scotts Head Point, and the northern Cabrits Marine Reserve, which includes the coastal waters north from the Cabrits to beyond Toucari. Moorings have been put down for authorized dive boats and operators. Yachts and their tenders may not use these moorings. (See the relevant sections for more details.)

Visitors must dive with a local dive shop; independent diving is not allowed. Dominica's best asset is her environment. Spearfishing, anchoring on reefs, throwing trash in the water, or taking or damaging coral or live shells anywhere is illegal.

Sperm whales are a resource here for whale-watching trips (check out the whale skeleton in Anchorage hotel). If you see one, keep 200 yards away, and do not interfere with the whale watching boats.

The National Park areas charge a visitors fee. This is $5 US for a single site visit, or $12 US for a week and it is good for all sites.

Telephones

Dominica has some card type phones. Cards are available at the telephone office and in some shops and bars near the phones. Otherwise, you can go to a hotel to make a call. Mobile phones, Cable and Wireless, Digicel and Carte Orange work here.

Shopping hours

Normal shopping hours are 0800-1300 and 1400 to 1600. Many offices are closed on Saturdays.

Transport

Dominica has two airports. The smaller Canefield Airport, near Roseau, takes twin Otters with 19-seat capacity. The larger Melville Hall in the north will take larger inter-island planes. Connections to major international airlines are not hard to make, as the island is linked by several airlines, including American Eagle which flies to San Juan.

Rental cars are available, though you will need a local license, which costs $30 EC. Drive on the left. Taxis are abundant and happy to organize tours. All taxi drivers are trained in natural and local history, the good ones are also willing to hike with you.

Taxi Rates

Roseau to Melville Hall Airport	$170 EC
Portsmouth to Melville Hall Airport	$170 EC

Tours are usually quoted in $US for up to five persons and then a rate is given per person over five. A half day (4 hours) is $180 then (over 5) $40 per head. Tours included in this category include Calibishe with Chaudiere pool, Syndicate Forest with Milton Falls, or the Carib territory. Or, if you are in Roseau, Trafalgar Falls.

Day tours (8 hours) cost $250 then (over 5) $60 per person. These include a variety of island tours, a detailed northern tour (if you are in Portsmouth), or if you are in Roseau, Victoria or Sari Sari Falls.

There are some extreme tours – for example climbing Mt. Diablaton, Trois Piton, or the Boiling lake if you start in Portsmouth, which will cost more like $100 per person.

There is an inexpensive bus system that runs between most of the major settlements. It is strictly private enterprise and each driver sets his own schedule. Buses to outlying areas will often come in to Roseau in the morning and head out again in the afternoon. Before heading off, it is wise to ask what time the last bus returns. Bus rates vary from a couple of EC dollars to about ten EC dollars from Portsmouth to Roseau.

Holidays

- January 1st and 2nd
- Carnival Monday & Tuesday (46 days before Easter: Feb 15-16, 2010; March 7-8, 2011)
- Good Friday and Easter Monday (Easter Sunday is April 4, 2010; April 24, 2011)

- May Day (May 1)
- Whit Monday, 50 days after Easter Sunday (May 24, 2010, June 13, 2011)
- August Monday (First Monday in August)
- November 3rd (Independence Day),
- November 4th (Community Day of Services)
- December 25th and 26th

Dominica, Admiralty Leisure Folio 5642-3, 5642-8

MOUNTAINS & MANGROVES

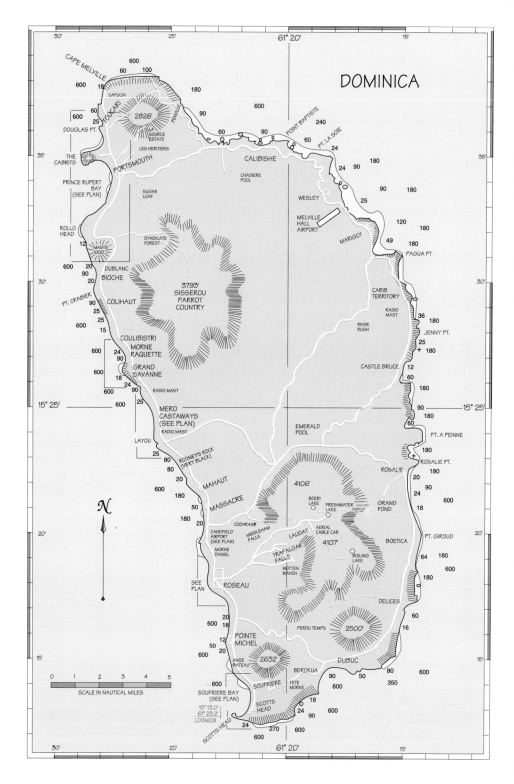

DOMINICA

CAPE MELVILLE
600
60 100
600
18
CAPUCIN
600 25
TOUCARI
2826'
DOUGLAS PT.
SOURCE
ESTATE
LES HERITIERS
THE
CABRITS
PORTSMOUTH
PRINCE RUPERT
BAY
(SEE PLAN)
ROLLO
HEAD
12
MASTS
1000'
SUGAR
LOAF
SYNDICATE
FOREST
DUBLANC
BIOCHE
PT. CRABIER
COLIHAUT
25
600
15
COULIBISTRI
MORNE
RAQUETTE
24
90
GRAND
SAVANNE
18
24
600
90
25
RADIO MAST
15° 25'
600
MERO
CASTAWAYS
(SEE PLAN)
RADIO MAST
LAYOU
25
80
RODNEY'S ROCK
(VERY BLACK)
80
20
MAHAUT
600
180
MASSACRE
50
180
20
COCHRANE
CANEFIELD
AIRPORT
(SEE PLAN)
MIDDLEHAM
FALLS
MORNE
DANIEL
SEE
PLAN
ROSEAU
20
600
18
12
50
600
POINTE
MICHEL
600
ANSE
BATEAU
2632'
SOUFRIERE
SOUFRIERE BAY
(SEE PLAN)
15° 13.0'
61° 23.2'
LDOM09
SCOTTS HEAD
SCOTTS
HEAD
24
600
180
90
180
600
60
90
120
60
90
PENVILLE
POINT BAPTISTE
PT. LA SOIE
24
CALIBISHE
24
90
CHADIERE
POOL
MELVILLE
HALL
AIRPORT
WESLEY
25
MARIGOT
49
PAGUA PT
CARIB
TERRITORY
3793'
SISSEROU
PARROT
COUNTRY
RADIO
MAST
36
180
RIVER
RUSH
JENNY PT.
25
+ 180
CASTLE BRUCE
12
60
180
90
180
60
EMERALD
POOL
PT. A PEINNE
180
180
ROSALIE PT.
ROSALIE
180
20
20
4106'
90
24
600
BOERI
LAKE
FRESHWATER
LAKE
GRAND
FOND
18
LAUDAT
AERIAL
CABLE CAR
4107'
BOETICA
PT. GIROUD
TRAFALGAR
FALLS
BOILING
LAKE
64
180
WOTTEN
WAVEN
600
180
DELICES
60
PERDU TEMPS
2500'
16
DUBUC
80
600
BEROKUA
90
50
350
TETE
MORNE
600
18
24
600
90
270
600

N

0 1 2 3 4 5
SCALE IN NAUTICAL MILES

heavy rain. Other rocks extend underwater from the Scotts Head side; so do not try to pass between Scotts Head and the Pinnacle. Be prepared for shrieking gusts that seem to come from nowhere off some valleys, especially in the Scotts Head area. These are worst on days when there are no clouds hanging over the mountains.

Prince Rupert Bay

This magnificent protected bay is over 2 miles long and a mile wide. Under normal conditions, you can anchor almost anywhere off the coast, from the Coconut Beach Hotel on the south shore right around to the Purple Turtle restaurant on the north. The best anchoring areas are outlined below. The harbor is so good that Portsmouth was picked to be the island's capital. However, this never came to be because of the extensive swamp below the Cabrits. In bygone days, malaria or yellow fever often afflicted people trying to settle the area, and so Roseau became the capital. Today, you can consider this area to be healthy. Elizabeth Pampo Israel, the oldest person in the world, lived here till her death at the age of 128.

Regulations

Clear in with customs in the dock area, about half a mile south of the town of Portsmouth. Their hours are Mondays 0830-1300 and 1400-1700; Tuesday to Friday 0830-1300 and 1400-1600. If you clear outside these times, you must pay a moderate overtime charge. Out of hours, you will find a customs officer in the cus-

toms residence, just on the town side of the customs area. Occasionally, you may be asked to visit immigration, which is in the police station in town. You will get a clearance that is valid for two weeks and is your departure clearance as well. You will not normally have to revisit unless you are staying longer than two weeks or changing crew. (See also Regulations in Dominica at a Glance)

You may not use or approach the cruise ship dock by yacht or tender when cruise ships are docked alongside.

Portsmouth Town Anchorage

Most yachts anchor off the beach a little to the north of town, in the general area of the Purple Turtle. This is the calmest spot in northerly swells. In this area, anchor in less than 40 feet of water, as there are some coral reefs in the deeper water. Occasional coral can also be found between the cruise ship dock and the Purple Turtle, close to shore in 9-15 feet of water. If you want to anchor in this shallower water, snorkel and take a look first.

Holding is quite variable. In some spots the sand seems mixed with coral rubble and your anchor may drag. I have found excellent holding in sand, as you get closer to the beach from the Purple Turtle south. Thirty moorings are now available for rent for those who would like one. They cost $10 US a night, $50 US a week, $90 US for two weeks, or $170 US a month. Maintenance is done by PAYS (see below),

MOUNTAINS & MANGROVES

and funds go to them. If you use a mooring, tie your docking line to the mooring loop and leave at least 15 feet of scope. You will receive an official PAYS receipt. From the anchorage it is easy to get to town or to the Cabrits National Park.

From November to May the security here is generally excellent. The Indian River Guides got together with other businesses and formed the Portsmouth Association of Yacht Security (PAYS). They run regular patrols at night in the anchoring area around the Purple Turtle, and since this has been active there have been no problems in this area. Jeffrey (Sea Bird), the current president of PAYS, invented a great way to help fund this. He started a PAYS beach barbecue on Sunday nights. It costs $50 EC and that includes fresh juice and rum punch. It became an instant success; a great way to meet other cruisers, eat well, and dance the early evening away. In the summer, security is not necessarily a problem, but ask about the current situation from one of the PAYS group.

Big Papas has loud music on Wednesday, and very loud music on Friday and Saturday. This can go on till 0300 or so. Great if you are in the party mood, otherwise you may wish to move anchor to the other side of the harbor for the night.

Communications

Wifi is available on the HotHotHot spot system out of Purple Turtle. Or you can try your luck ashore. Big Papa's has an internet station and downtown Computer Resource Center is an internet and computer shop open Monday to Saturday 0900-2200. Farther along, above the first gas station, Everland Internet Café has good rates and opens Monday to Saturday 0900-2100. On the back street, Variety Store has internet (and baked goodies) Monday to Saturday 0900-2030. Foneshack is a mobile phone store that sells phones, sims, and top-up for both Lime and Digicel. You can do Skype from Everland Internet café, or use a regular phone at Lime (ex Cable and Wireless).

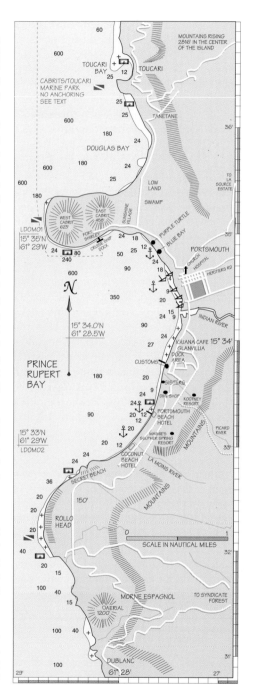

Chandlery

A small Budget Marine Chandlery is in town. It is part of Dominica Marine Center in Roseau. They keep a variety of marine

Chris Doyle

gear in stock and anything in the catalog can normally be delivered in three days.

General Services

You can tie your dinghy up at the entrance to the Indian River, either on the left side of the bridge or the right, as both have concrete platforms. Leave most of the steps area free for the river boats. PAYS also maintains the old town dock as a dinghy dock. For long stays on the town dock, tie a line off to one of the small moorings, or, if not in place, put out an anchor. You can also dinghy to the Cabrits dock – perfect for visiting the Cabrits. However, since 9/11 you cannot use it if a cruise ship is in. You can also leave your dinghy on board and use one of the water taxis. You can also use the dinghy docks at Purple Turtle, Big Papas, and Blue Bay Restaurants. You may need a stern anchor.

Water is available from the cruise ship dock. It is too big to be an easy dock for yachts, and, when the wind is blowing, it is often better to go onto the inside of the T dock, as the wind holds you off. The nominal charge for water is $15 EC for up to 500 gallons. The Dominica Port Authority has a 3,000-gallon diesel tank at the Cabrits Cruise Ship Berth for selling duty-free diesel fuel to all yachts. National Petroleum can, on request, deliver large quantities of diesel and gasoline to the customs dock.

Some river guides (Sea Bird and Eddison) have family members who do laundry. The rest of the guides will take it to town to one of the laundries for a delivery fee. You will also find laundries in town and many are just indicated by signs stuck up on the window of a small house. The two big ones are fairly close together near the market. One is opposite the market - you see the sign and the gate looks closed, but walk a few steps down the side street and you will see the door on your right. The other is a short walk away on back street.

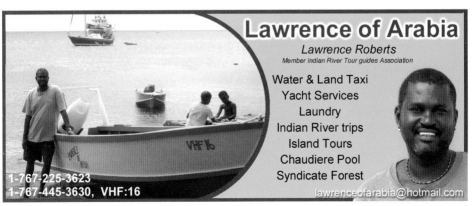
MOUNTAINS & MANGROVES

ROLLO HEAD

CABRITS

DOUGLAS BAY

PRINCE RUPERT BAY
AND APPROACHES
ANCHORING IS NOT PERMITTED
IN TOUCARI AND DOUGLAS BAY
WHICH ARE PART OF A MARINE PARK

TOUCARI

Ask about cooking gas refills in Duverney's little store on the road behind Blue Bay. They send tanks down mainly on Mondays and Thursdays. You need it in early in the morning to get it back that night. Check Budget Marine also for gas refills as they should be doing this soon.

General Services Yacht Helpers

Dominica has an exemplary group of young men who provide the main yacht services for yachts. Not only will they help you get fruits, bread, and ice, take your laundry, find a technician, and act as a water taxi, but they act together in the group called PAYS, which provides security, helps maintain dinghy docks, and tries to make sure yachts have a good stay. Their primary business is river and other tours, but they provide all the other services for their customers. PAYS also includes the shore businesses: Cabrits Dive, Max the taxi driver, Big Papa's, Blue Bay Restaurant, and Purple Turtle.

Many of PAYS' members have a few large yachts for which they act as agent: helping with clearance, arranging stores, fuel, and more. You will do best if you work primarily with a member of PAYS. They are each accountable to the group and have an excellent reputation.

When you arrive, you will likely be approached by a PAYS member as they

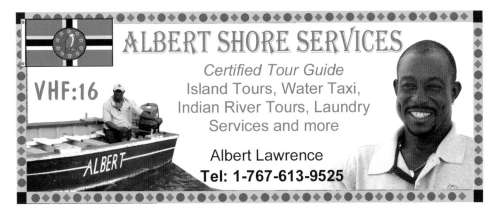

have a sharing system of approaching yachts. You will see a name painted on the side of the boat and current members with boats are Albert, Alexis, Charlie, Cobra, Eddison, Lawrence of Arabia, Providence, Sea Bird, Spaghetti, and Uncle Sam. They all listen to VHF: 16.

If you get approached by anyone else, I suggest you tell them you are dealing with one of the above (pick one at random; they are all good). PAYS members will give the same degree of professionalism as a good business ashore. Be wary of others, especially those that paddle out on surfboards. This is the way some young guys start up (I first met Jeffrey this way), which is fine, but one or two crack-addicts are also out there. It is all right to buy things from vendors that offer them, but NEVER give a vendor cash to go and buy you something. If you have any problems with any vendor, call Sea Bird (Jeffrey), the current president, or failing him, another PAYS member. They

will try to sort it out. For more information on the PAYS group, see ashore.

The PAYS group operates as water taxis and the rates are as follows: $26 EC to take you to clear customs and back. $10 EC in or out of town (up to five people) during the day when the water taxis are running around. If you are going out to dinner the rate will be more like $20 US return.

Technical Services

If you have any mechanical problems (diesel, outboard, or general), contact Igna Mitchell: 277-9406, who lives by the market. Igna keeps all the local outboards running. He is also a fully-qualified marine diesel mechanic, has been an engineer on several ships, and can probably fix any other boat problem you may have. If I didn't tell you now, it might come as a surprise to see that he only has one arm. However, Igna knows how to use it so well, that he does not consider himself, nor does anyone in Portsmouth consider him, in any way

different (except possibly better) than those with two. He has also now trained a couple of younger men to work with him, who are good mechanics. Igna is also an excellent diver (he was the marine park warden when they had one) and can help you out with any underwater problems you may have.

If you have any technical problems, it is a good idea to discuss it first with your PAYS member. They will help arrange the appropriate technician.

One they may suggest is Soso: 612-1886. Soso has endless boating experience, having crossed the Atlantic several times and he has sailed right through the islands. His specialties are wood and glass construction and repair and spray-painting. He can fix, or arrange to have fixed, almost anything that has gone wrong, and he is able to get good people to deal with any problems that he cannot repair himself. He also repairs inflatable dinghies and does rigging repairs. He can arrange to get your sails repaired or to have Irvin fix your refrigeration. While Soso keeps stocks of polyester resin and glue for inflatables, if you need epoxy or rigging wire or terminals, these will have to be brought in. This can be done fast via Budget Marine.

Provisioning

Portsmouth is a friendly and cheerful town – an enchanting mix of the old and new, the poor and the wealthy. Some of the smaller, older wooden buildings have great style and color.

If you tie up to the town dock, you will come out on Bay Street, which is dotted with small supermarkets, including Mini Cash. There are two gas stations: one is a few steps down the road leading inland from the town dock. The other is opposite the Indian River boat station. A bank with an ATM is next door to the Indian River gas station.

If you come early on a Saturday, you will get tremendous buys at the fresh food market. There is a smaller market on Tuesdays and Fridays. Rosalie's fruit shop has some fresh produce at other times and it is just

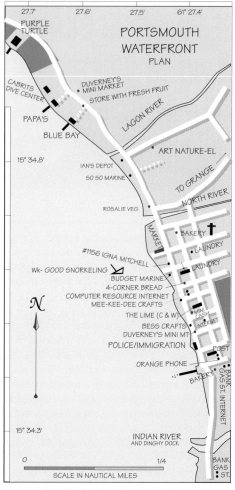

across the bridge heading north from the market. Several other small stores also display fresh produce.

Ian is a cheerful and pleasant baker who cooks excellent bread, cakes, and other things, including a very inexpensive fish 'n chips. He has an early morning job, but you often find him Ian's Depot (a tiny shack), in the afternoons, evenings, and on weekends. He will cook you a great cake to order.

The mini markets offer mainly staples: canned goods and chicken. One of the biggest, Mini Cash, is open 0800-2200. Their stock includes local fish, meat from the states, film, and basic pharmacy supplies. If you dock by the Purple Turtle, you

will find Duverney's little store on the road behind Blue Bay. It sells most basics. If you need more, it is a $10 EC bus ride to Roseau.

Fun Shopping

A few steps to the north of the police station, on Bay Street, are two excellent handicraft stores. Bess's is stacked with handicrafts and the owner, Earl Hector, who lived for many years in Scotland, is very welcoming. Here you will find endless Carib straw goods, tablemats, and postcards. Mee-Kee-Dee is great little craft shop on the other side of the road a little farther north. They have some elegant woodcarvings and art as well as small handicrafts.

If you do a tour, ask to stop at Don's Souvenir Shop, near the medical school. It has lots of locally made souvenirs, great fresh flowers, fruits, and vegetables.

Restaurants

Eating out is fun, Créole style, and very local. Some of the restaurants are on the waterfront and have a dinghy dock, or are close by one. The food is generally plentiful and well prepared. You can always walk in for a fish or chicken meal, but some local specialties, such as crayfish, lobster, conch, or goat, need advance notice. We mention a few of the bigger and better known restaurants.

The Purple Turtle Restaurant has a prime location, with parkland on both sides, and it is right on the beach, overlooking the bay. You can tie your dinghy to their dinghy dock (and leave it here when you explore ashore). Patricia Etienne has expanded the place to include an attractive large lounge at the top, with an open party area. They hold parties there from time to time and if you are traveling in a group and need a private conference area, it would be ideal. Downstairs, the open restaurant is a pleasant place to sit and hang out. Patricia Etienne welcomes yachts and helps her yachting customers in any way she can. She serves both snacks and full meals, and does tasty local fish, meat, and lobster dinners. Her meals are excellent value. To satisfy the demand of Portsmouth's many medical school students, they have good hamburgers. Patricia will fill jerry jugs with water for her customers, and she has a tap close to the beach.

Al from Switzerland owns Big Papa's Restaurant. The restaurant is quaint and artistic inside with a courtyard atmosphere of varnished bamboo, plants, and little hidden corners. It now also has a treetop hang out, good for party nights and it could be used for special functions. Big Papa has one of the better dinghy docks (these come and go), so is a popular hangout and meeting place. It also has internet stations and free wifi. You can get good fresh fish and other local meals here. Party lovers will want to come on Wednesday, Friday, and Saturdays nights for the late night maximum music.

The Blue Bay Restaurant is a few steps

MOUNTAINS & MANGROVES

The Blue Bay Restaurant is a few steps south. You can tie your dinghy right outside. This restaurant is a change from the others as it has a French Créole slant to the food, and the nautical décor is a distinguishing feature. River guide Charlie, who ran it for a couple of years, is often here of an evening as barman and will look after you well. Fresh fish, chicken, crayfish, and lobster are usually on the menu.

Quite a few small restaurants have sprung up in town, which you can check out, and one larger one, Adaj, has quite a fancy menu.

Keith and Evelyn's Heaven's Best is north, out of town, a short car ride away. A couple of readers fell in love with this place and sent me there. The restaurant is part of a reasonably priced guest house that has a swimming pool and garden in which Keith grows many of his herbs and vegetables. Keith and Evelyn are very pleasant and look after you well, Keith loves to cook and his food is different from the standard Créole dishes, influenced by his travels abroad. They do not serve alcohol, but you can bring your own wine. If you give them a call, they may well be able to pick you up in their truck or car: 277-3952.

Poonkies is an atmospheric restaurant and bar on the right hand side of the road in the same direction; it is built right on the edge of a river. I have not eaten here but they serve fairly upmarket fare, including crayfish and lobster. Take a group there and give it a try.

I write up other easily accessible restaurants under Portsmouth Beach Hotel anchorage and I write up the Cabrits Dive Shop Bar in Water sports.

Ashore

Several major attractions are easily accessible from Portsmouth. A trip up the Indian River is an amazing experience, unlike anything else you find in the Eastern Caribbean. The river quickly narrows and gets completely overhung by huge swamp bloodwood trees on both sides. Their massive buttress roots spread out above the soil and down into the water, twisting and tangling into interesting wavy designs. Here and there, long vines dangle into the river, and as you glide along you see fish below and crabs on both banks. Overhead, the trees form a complete canopy, so it is dark and cathedral-like. This, along with the occasional sounds of insects and birds, creates a magical quality. Many of the herons are quite tame, and there is a chance of seeing iguanas. Be sure to use one of the official guides we mention below. Outboards are not allowed on the river beyond the bridge, and you should not take your own dinghy beyond the bridge. One of the best times to go is early in the morning, before anyone else starts up. This is especially so in late February or early March when the swamp bloodwood trees are in fruit and attract groups of foraging parrots. Or go in the late afternoon, when most of the others have left.

Cobra has a Jungle Bar at the head of the river, great for a drink, lunch, or a special function, such as a birthday party or wedding. This trip nowadays takes over

two hours, and involves hiking as well as the boat ride. For this extended tour the price is $20 US and worth it (minimum four people). You also have to pay the national $5 US park fee, which can be done at the gas station across the road. (If you are staying a few days get the $12 US weekly pass for all sites: you will need it for the Cabrits.)

For going up the river and other tours, I recommend that you use one of the PAYS group. They will pick you up from your boat and drop you back afterwards, or later, if you want to visit town. They all listen to VHF: 16.

They will all arrange land tours, and many of them own land taxis and have professional tour guides to drive them. When you arrange a land tour with one of these guides, you should expect the following excellent service: pick up from your yacht, a qualified tour guide who knows about the local plants and agriculture and who will hike with you on any hiking parts of your trip. All of them are fully qualified and registered tour guides, with knowledge of local nature, culture, and history.

The PAYS group includes Max Taxi, who will not come out and meet you in a boat as he is strictly a land man. But he is a very experienced and a good taxi driver, and you can contact him directly. Some of the PAYS river guides also send their tours with him. The rest of the PAYS guys you will meet on the water, and in every case their favorite tour is the Indian River.

Albert Lawrence, who fishes in his spare time, has been taking people up the Indian

River for 28 years. If you want a tour he will arrange it with Max. He will also guide you in the Cabrits, or ask him about whatever else you want to do.

Cobra Tours is owned by Andrew O'Brian and you will meet him or his associate, Jerome. Cobra Tours is used to dealing with yacht problems. They act as an agent for some of the French bare-boat companies, they do their own land tours by bus or Landrover. Cobra Tours also owns the Jungle Bar on the Indian River.

Eddison is the man currently in charge of security for PAYS, along with Martin (Providence). Eddison's mother does laundry, so you can give him yours. He has his own taxi and offers first-rate tours; among his favorites: Chaudiere and the Carib reserve and a variety of island tours. He also likes to do snorkeling trips and set up beach barbecues.

Lawrence of Arabia (Lawrence Roberts) has a both a river boat and a taxi. In the high season, he stays on the water and has a friend do the tours; in the low season he does both. Ashore he likes Chaudiere Pool, Syndicate Forest, and the Emerald Pool.

Providence's owner is Martin Carriere, who is reliable and helpful and also has a bus, offers excellent tours, and will help with yacht problems. His favorite tours include Chaudiere Pool and Red Rocks. He likes the long northern hike, and his taxi does the mountain road to Penneville and Hampstead Beach, for those who want less hiking. Martin also organizes beach barbecues and live music.

Alexis Tours is run by Faustin Alexis

MOUNTAINS & MANGROVES

who also likes to take people snorkeling and on fishing expeditions. He has his own air-conditioned taxi. His favorite trips include the Syndicate Rainforest, the aerial tram, the boiling lake, and the Carib reserve.

Charlie, like all the others, is an excellent tour guide and water taxi. He ran the Blue Bay Restaurant for a couple of years and you may find him there of an evening tending bar. He does good Indian River Tours, will take care of all your boat needs, and can also arrange any land trips you may want.

Sea Bird, is owned by Jeffry, who I have known from when he was a young kid paddling a windsurfer. He is now the president of PAYS, has his own modern bus, and offers excellent land tours. His favorite tours include the Syndicate Rainforest and Milton Falls. He also likes to take people on fishing trips. He now works with Andrew, who greets boats for him.

Spaghetti's Erik Christopher has been a river guide longer than most and he also likes to take people on snorkeling trips. He arranges all kind of land trips, usually with Max or Jeffry's taxi.

Uncle Sam was one of the very first professional river boat men and he once worked for Sunsail. He left to work on cargo ships for many years, but is now back driving Lawrence of Arabia's taxi. He may soon set up his own river boat again.

All the PAYS boats will take you to the best snorkeling sites, and the current price is $20 US per person for about one and half hours.

The Cabrits National Park has well-marked trails. Fort Shirley, an old British fort dating from the 18th century, has been partially restored and there is a small museum. It includes a well restored large building which can be used for big events like weddings. The guiding light in this enterprise is Dominica's local historian Lennox Honychurch, whose book, *The Dominica Story*, is a delight to read. If you follow the trail to the top of East Cabrit, you will be rewarded by splendid views over the harbor and surrounding country, including the swamp. The proximity of the swamp makes for interesting bird life on the road leading to the park. You should also hike to the top of West Cabrits for great views of the Saintes and Guadeloupe in clear weather. A large dock and a building for craft vendors on the Cabrits caters to adventure-type cruise ships. Part of this is low enough to be accessible by dinghy, and you may use it as long as no cruise ships are here. When the gates are locked, you can normally walk through the building.

Horse riders or novices should check out Rainforest Riding Dominica, with both thoroughbred racers and local horses. Owner Valerie Francis, originally from Canada, has a degree in animal science and a minor in tropical agriculture. She can handle all levels of rider, from absolute beginners to advanced. Her optimal group size is around four but she can take up to eight. Her rides include beach, agricultural land, and rainforest. She is moving to a

Chris Doyle

Dominica's rain forest

Chris Doyle

convenient new location between the Purple Turtle and the Cabrits.

Indian River Source

Right close to Portsmouth are several attractive walks you can do on your own or with a guide. You should allow two to three hours for any one of them, though if you have less time, you can always go part way. An easy one is to an Indian River water source spring. Start at the main town dock, head past the gas station and keep walking on the main road east. After half a mile or so, you will see a big aerial ahead of you. Look for a minor road on the right with a big, disused shed on one side. Take this road. It crosses over a feeder river to the Indian River. Right by the bridge is a deep pool, perfect for a swim amid the big roots. Carry on up into the hills among fruit and cinnamon trees and flowers. You eventually wind into the hills and get a lovely view of Portsmouth and the anchorage. The road ends not long after. Once you see the view, keep walking and you will see a big rock on the left with a little copra house. You will also see a couple of boulders down

the hill on the right. Follow the small trail past these boulders and you will come to a lovely spring that gushes out of the hill; a source of the Indian River.

Heritiers

If you look at the hills to the north of Portsmouth from the anchorage, you can see a place where the hill line is broken by a clump of palm trees. This field of palms offers splendid views of the bay and the mountains to the south and the walk to reach it is delightful. Start on the same street as the market and just keep heading uphill. You start to get nice glimpses of views from about the big old water tank. The land you pass through is agricultural, with lots of fruit trees, including mangos, guavas, and cashews. At some point the road disappears and becomes a trail leading uphill (always head uphill if you have a clear choice). You will eventually see the field of palms on your right and you scramble up the bank and into the field to get the views. Continue up this trail into the forest. It is cool here, under the canopy. The top part of the path has become rough

MOUNTAINS & MANGROVES

and overgrown.

La Source Estate

The road through Grange to La Source Estate is the longest of these walks. The road is truck or wheel drivable all the way and it would not be a bad idea to get a taxi to take you up and then enjoy some time at the top and walk back down. To walk the whole way, start at the market, cross the bridge heading north, and take the next road on your right; keep going. You pass through the village of Grange and agricultural land. The scenery is pleasant, though not especially exciting, until you get to the top of the road and head downhill again to where it ends. The scenery for this short last part is really beautiful, and at the end of the road you come to a steep river gorge with a swimmable pool right below, and lots of vines dangling down into it. A rough trail leads up into the forest on the other side of the stream for some way.

Other major attractions in the north include the Syndicate Rainforest (part of a national park) and Milton (a.k.a. Syndicate) Falls. They can be combined into a long morning or afternoon trip if you use a car.

Moses serves Ital food in a calabash

Allow a whole day if you do it by bus and hiking. You can hike on your own, but to get to the falls you pass over private land, so there is a small fee to pay. The Syndicate trail is an easy walk, just under a mile long but, depending on the state of the road, you may have to walk a little farther. This trail traverses the best example of tropical rainforest in the Leewards. There are many huge and magnificent trees, including one with buttress roots about 35 feet across. The trees form a dense canopy high overhead and there is little undergrowth. If birds are your special interest, then make the effort to contact local forester, Bertram Jno. Baptiste (cell: 245-4768, home: 446-6358), the most knowledgeable bird expert. Bertram will want to start at the crack of dawn to give you the best chance of seeing the two parrot species, the sisserou and the red-necked, which live only in Dominica. He has a good four-wheel drive car to get you there. In the same park area, a rough hiking trail leads up Morne Diablontin and this is a great climb for the very fit and energetic.

The walk to Milton Falls takes you along a river, and through lush agricultural land with lovely mountain views. The falls are about 80 feet high and plunge into a pool. The river is used as a water source, so right now swimming is forbidden, but this may change, so ask one of the guides. The vegetation is so dense that the sun only reaches the falls at midday, but it is great to go anytime.

Calabishie is on the north coast, not too far from Portsmouth. This picturesque seaside village stands on a white sand beach with extensive shallows, and includes a couple of small restaurants. For those on a tight budget, the bus trip there takes you through some lovely countryside. If you rent a car or take a taxi, the surrounding countryside is delightful and many good beaches are hidden away. This is easy to do on your own. Martin Carriere took me to the Chaudiere pool, some miles east of Portsmouth. This is one of the Caribbean's most perfect tropical pools, set amid lush

Hanging out at Moses' Rastaurant

Chris Doyle

vegetation. It is fed by a small waterfall and surrounded by rocks. The water bubbles from the falls, reminding one of a cauldron. The pool is about 15 feet deep and swimming is part of the fun; the adventurous can jump from the cliffs. Part of the charm of this place is that you are likely to have it to yourself; it makes a perfect spot for a picnic lunch. You have to hike 20 minutes down slope. Martin usually combines this with Calibishe and the red rocks as a half-day tour. The red rocks are compacted mud that have been etched into strange gullies and shapes and feel impermanent under your feet. This is an interesting and photogenic area with good views.

There is a delightful road from Tanetane to Pennville. It also makes a very lovely, though long, hike. Buses run over here so if you start walking you can end up taking a bus one way or the other, depending on what comes along. Towards the summit you get excellent views over Toucari Bay, Douglas Bay, and Prince Rupert Bay. Right at the top is a lovely area between the hills. In this region is a "cold soufriere," a bubbling pool of cold water from a volcanic vent.

Martin combines driving this road with Hampstead Beach, as part of a tour for those whose hiking ability is limited. Hampstead Beach is a magnificent wild beach with a big river at one end. You can swim in both the river and the sea. It was one of the sets for *Pirates of the Caribbean*, part two, as was the Indian River.

If you prefer a long hike on a trail, there is a good one from Capuchin to Pennville, along the northern end of the island. Take the bus to Capuchin and ask to be put off at Bellevue. It is the end of the road and you just carry along on the path. The hike takes about three hours, through thickly wooded scenery with occasional great views. You can easily get lost at Grand Fond where a tree has fallen over the trail; the wrong turn takes you to a deserted village and orchards where you can find good oranges and grapefruits. We went with Martin and found two delightful small waterfalls with pools where you could swim.

You can rent a car or take a taxi through Calibishie and beyond to see the Carib territory. The Caribs were fierce warriors who predated the Europeans and for a couple of hundred years kept them at bay. They called the island "Waitikubuli," meaning "Tall is her Body." Caribs were still active here when European settlers colonized the other islands, and one of the hazards facing the settlers was Carib raiding parties. However, the tide of history was against them as the colonists flourished. Slowly, Caribs started trading with Europeans and even made friends with some missionaries.

MOUNTAINS & MANGROVES

War parties took a toll on their numbers, as did the curious events surrounding "Indian Warner." Warner was the son of the English governor of St. Kitts, and his mother was a Carib slave from Dominica. He was brought up with the other sons, but when his father died, his stepmother persecuted him, so he fled back to Dominica's leeward coast where he became a chief. He remained on good terms with his half brother, Phillip Warner, and did several services for the British. At this time there were mixed feelings among the settlers as to whether the Caribs should be exterminated or accommodated. The people of St. Kitts, victims of several raiding parties, were for extermination.

Phillip Warner came down with a troop in his command. What happened next is unclear. One version says Phillip held a feast for Warner and his tribe, plied them with brandy, then, as a signal to his troops, he treacherously stabbed his unsuspecting half brother to death, whereupon his forces massacred the whole tribe. Another version says Phillip's troop joined Indian Warner's and they went together and raided the windward coast Caribs, who were inclined to be Francophile. In the following victory feast Indian Warner got into a brawl and was killed, which led to a fight in which the Caribs were massacred. The village of Massacre stands on the site of the incident.

As a sequel to this, the surviving Caribs were so outraged they went on a revenge trip to Marie Galante and massacred all the settlers, sticking their heads on poles on the beach. This beach is also called Massacre.

As their numbers dwindled, some Caribs migrated to South America and the rest were forced into accommodation with the Europeans and given a territory on the windward coast, where you can visit them today. Pure Caribs are Native Americans, rather bronze in color, with Asian features. When I was at the Anchorage Hotel an amusing thing happened. A Carib came by to deliver vegetables and a Japanese tourist staying in the hotel walked up and started talking to him rapidly in Japanese.

In the Carib territory you can buy handicrafts and see dugout canoes being built by traditional methods. There is also a waterfall on the Crayfish River and you can probably arrange to have someone catch you a pound or two of freshwater crayfish (fisheries permitting).

A very special place called River Rush is in the heart of the rainforest. It is built on an island on the river, with cottages on the surrounding river banks. You get around on beautiful little winding garden paths. Sleeping in the rooms is like having your own luxurious platform in the middle of the forest; it feels very magical. Maureen (Mo), the owner, rebuilt it for the luxury

Chris Doyle

market and makes it available for functions like weddings or birthdays, for a week's retreat, or just an exceptional day of hanging out in the forest. Bring your own chef or have her supply one.

If you prefer to drive yourself around, Silver Lining Care Rental will fix you up, and if you want a guide for some particular trip, one of the PAYS guides will be happy to go along with you.

Portsmouth Beach Hotel Anchorage

The Coconut Beach Hotel (currently defunct) and the Portsmouth Beach Hotel lie on one of the prettiest beaches in Dominica. Palms and flowering trees edge the sand, many bananaquits and humming-birds can be seen. Behind, the land slopes up into dense green mountains. The anchorage affords privacy. When southerly swells make the Portsmouth town anchorage uncomfortable, this anchorage is fine. It is about a mile from Portsmouth, though you are not far from the customs dock. You can find a spot anywhere back from the customs dock. When you get to the Portsmouth Beach Hotel it is a bit hard to anchor and be sure you are not damaging either the inner or the outer reef. The only way to do this is to anchor a little bit farther out than the dock. If you are not sure, then put a snorkeler over to choose the spot.

One robbery with gratuitous violence occurred here in 2009, so I would ask one of the PAYS group about security. They were hoping to extend their patrols at least on party nights so people could escape the noise.

Services

The Portsmouth Beach Hotel is owned by the Armour family, who also run the Anchorage Hotel in Roseau. It has a long dock, currently wrecked, but they should be rebuilding it soon, and when that happens, you are welcome to use it. Services ashore include a bar and restaurant (see below), full communications, garbage disposal, a laundry, and island tours. Otherwise, you can use the customs dock, which is within reach of two good restaurants. You can also dinghy here from the other side of the bay.

Ashore

If you dinghy to the customs dock and turn right, the road reaches the river and follows it towards the main road. Riverside Restaurant is a new spacious restaurant where you sit on a big balcony hanging out over the river, making a scenic change from the usual seafront. Both food and service are very good. You can get anything from lobster or rack of lamb to a spring roll. They also do good hamburgers and sandwiches. They open every day from 1130 till 2400. Since you have to visit customs to clear, consider walking down for lunch. Come for a special dinner out.

Iguana Café is the other way, a short walk back towards town from the main customs dock. It is a Rasta restaurant run by Etienne and Jennifer who bring fresh food

MOUNTAINS & MANGROVES

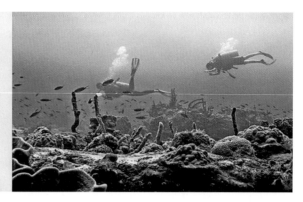
down from the mountains every day. They do excellent vegetarian and seafood, including freshwater crayfish. You need to call them and let them know when you are coming: 277-0815.

The Portsmouth Beach Hotel has the pleasant Le Flambeau restaurant, which is a popular watering hole for the medical students who rent apartments here. They open every day from breakfast to dinner and have a menu that includes Mexican specialties for lunch and more local/international food at dinner.

Sisters Sea Lodge is an open-air bar/restaurant, in the direction of the customs dock from the Portsmouth Beach Hotel. You walk down the beach and past two houses, one on the beach and one fronting the rocks. Sisters is next. You can also get there by taxi or rental car, but don't ask a water taxi to take you – the landing is rocky and bad.

Sisters is run by Harta and Elke from Germany. Behind the house is a garden where vegetables are grown for the restaurant. The restaurant has a lot of class, in an informal way, with artistic touches and handmade tables. They are open every day, but reservations are advisable. They specialize in barbecued fish and serve magnificent portions on banana leaves (couples share).

Cabrits Marine Park

Cabrits Marine Park starts at the reef north of Toucari Bay, includes the whole of Douglas Bay and the Cabrits, and continues south to inside the cruise ship dock. This magnificent park has some of Dominica's most wonderful snorkeling and diving.

Regulations

In creating this park, the government was attempting not only to conserve the reefs, but also to help provide employment for Dominicans as guides and small boat operators. Thus, as with the Indian River, yachts, dinghies, and yacht tenders are not allowed to anchor in the park, or use the buoys that have been placed at all major dive and snorkel sites.

A good way to visit the park is to hire one of the Indian River guides with a 40-hp engine to take you around. If you have this kind of water taxi, you can drift snorkel with the current, making life easier. If you want to spend a long time in the park, you could arrange to visit a few of the snorkel sites furthest from the beach, then have your guide drop you on one of the beaches and collect you later, or you could take a bus back. Remember, the money you spend with these guides helps the local economy. Snorkeling trips run at about $20 US per person, and there are also excellent sites off Rollo Head.

Snorkeling from the beach is also permitted (no guide necessary), and nearly all the good snorkeling is accessible from the shore at either Toucari Bay or Douglas Bay. Transportation buses run fairly frequently from Portsmouth.

Water Sports

Fish life varies from sparse to abundant for snorkelers, and is generally abundant for scuba divers. Colorful sponges and corals are found throughout the park. The snorkeling north of Toucari is over a large reef with the very scattered remains of an old wreck. A reef area on the south side of Toucari Bay with lots of corals and fish, is easily accessible from the beach. The headland between Toucari and Douglas Bay is a fascinating wall, with lots of gullies and a cave where a few bats hang out. Farther towards Douglas Bay, on the same headland, is a triangular cliff, which was much larger, within living memory, before part of it split and fell into the sea. The result is an area called the Canyons, with deep fissures between huge rock masses, making a dramatic underwater scene. At one point there is a 20-foot tunnel, which you can see right through. There is more excellent snorkeling on the outer part of the Cabrits, where two rocks jut out to sea. Currents here can be fearsome and you should pay attention to the current throughout the park.

The diving in this area is even better than the snorkeling, with walls, tunnels, pinnacles, and places where you see a huge number of fish in crystal clear water. They also have at least one curiosity – a big

Chris Doyle

MOUNTAINS & MANGROVES

patch of sea pens, a rather rare critter whose plumes sticks up from the sand.

To dive you must go with a local dive shop. There is an excellent one in Portsmouth called the Cabrits Dive Center run by Helen (from England) and Peter (from the US), along with lots of local help. This is a Padi 5-star center with two good custom dive boats. Their main dive shop is on the southern shore, but they also have a coffee shop (espresso, cappuccino, mokaccino), and bar, which is also a branch of their dive shop next to Big Papas. It opens daily 1000-1800. Helen will normally greet you and she is wonderfully friendly. They like to take fairly small groups (6-10), but can accommodate up to 15. They can teach up to Dive Master and do the popular two-day "Scuba Diver" course. They like working with those on yachts and will pick you up right from your yacht and drop you back there after. They even carry a portable credit card machine, so there is no reason to visit their office – unless of course you want to buy some snorkeling gear, t-shirts, or one of the souvenirs that they sell there. You can join one of their dives, or they are very happy to take out private groups and families, and they can supply a guide for yachts with really large tenders. They also do deep sea fishing.

Dominica has a Dive Fest every year about July. Many divers come for this, new equipment is shown, and there is lots of socializing. Contact any dive shop for details.

I only made four dives on the twenty or more sites and all were superb. At the pinnacle off Toucari Bay, we started at around 20 feet and descended slowly to about 70. The sand is another 30 feet down. At one point, we were looking up a sheer rock wall to the top of a huge boulder and on top schools of small fish swam around, watched by an almost motionless giant barracuda. Colorful corals and sponges made for some brightly painted areas, with many kinds of reef fish, including some giant dog snappers. Towards the end of the dive, we swam through two tunnels, well-adorned with marine life and offering dramatic views.

Off the Cabrits, the bottom curves downward in a slope that seems to get ever steeper. You can dive as deep as you want, but there is not much advantage to going below 60 or 70 feet. The sand bottom is covered with many shapes and sizes of boulders, which sometimes look like fairy castles. The boulders sport as vast a collection of different sponges as you are likely to see anywhere in the Caribbean. Hard and soft corals, anemones, lots of crinoids, scorpion fish, and reef fish abound. The sand between the boulders makes for a delightful contrast and reflects light, keeping everything bright and colorful. There are many sea pussies buried in the sand.

The Douglas Point Dive begins as you slowly wander over a large reef area about 50 feet deep with lots of reef fish, corals, corallimorphs, tunicates, and other sea

464

creatures. Igna Mitchell, my guide, pointed out the delightful and unusual sight of about half a dozen little jawfish bobbing up and down on top of their holes like ballet dancers. The canyons themselves are spectacular, with tunnels to swim through and a place where you drop down between narrow canyon walls decorated with bright sponges. Clear visibility, lovely large rocks bedecked with fish, and tunnels with dozens of cardinalfish and squirrelfish, make this dive memorable.

Igna oversaw the sinking of a new wreck on the north side of the Cabrits. This makes a good dive, with plenty of fish and photo possibilities.

A dive I have not yet done is right at the north end of the island and is called Kick Arse Reef. Dive Cabrits describes it as "an incredible dive on the high-energy Atlantic north side of Dominica". You see schools of margate, snapper and other fish, as well as turtles and rays, and occasionally sharks. There is also a wonderful coral archway at 80ft-100ft deep. This dive is not possible all the time, as sea conditions can be too rough, but when it's calm this is an incredible dive. The boat ride to the dive site is also breathtaking, as the boat travels along the cliffs of the uninhabited shoreline. Talk to Dive Cabrits if you are interested in whale watching, as they hope to soon also offer this.

Secret Beach and Barber's Block Bay

These are two small beaches on the north shore of Rollo Head. The eastern one is stony and the bay very rocky, with a small house ashore. Secret Beach, the western one, is wild and sandy with a big rock tunnel and sand dollar skeletons out in the shallows. There is excellent snorkeling farther round Rollo Head. You can find good anchoring in sand off the beaches for a temporary stop, but it may be easier to get one of the river guides to bring you. Be sure not to anchor on any of the coral. Another good temporary anchorage can be found just south of Rollo Head, in a small bay. Make sure you anchor in sand. You can dinghy from here to Rollo Head for snorkeling.

Batalie Beach, Coulibistri

The bay at Batalie Beach is home to the Sunset Bay Club, a quiet hideaway owned by both Roger and Marcella, originally from Belgium. Roger, the chef, offers a variety of seafood and meat with his own special sauces. The food is good and medical students come here for special nights out. Roger and Marcella speak English, German, French, and Flemish. Occasionally, yachts anchor stern to the beach while they visit for a meal. Roger now has a dive shop, and the anchored dive boats will give you a good idea where to drop hook. The water can be deep and you may need to take a line ashore.

Salisbury

Salisbury is currently the best place to stop in the middle of the island. The anchoring area is not large (south of the East Carib Dive dock), and there is some reef around you could harm. To help with this, East Carib Dive has put down four moorings which you are welcome to use (no charge).

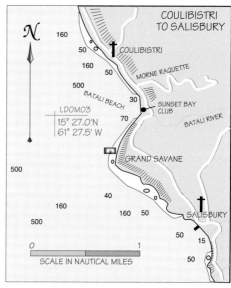

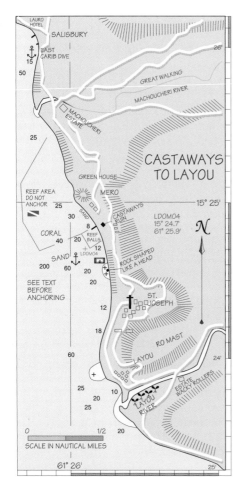

Map labels:
LAURO HOTEL
SALISBURY
EAST CARIB DIVE
26'
50
GREAT WALKING
MACHOUCHERI RIVER
MACHOUCHERI ESTATE
25
CASTAWAYS TO LAYOU
GREEN HOUSE
MERO
REEF AREA DO NOT ANCHOR
25
15° 25'
30
8
CASTAWAYS RUIN
LDOMO4
15° 24.7'
61° 25.9'
CORAL
40
REEF BALLS
12
N
SAND
LDOMO4
ROCK SHAPED LIKE A HEAD
200
60
20
SEE TEXT BEFORE ANCHORING
20
12
ST. JOSEPH
18
RO MAST
60
LAYOU
24'
25
10
ESTATE WACKY ROLLERS
20
25
LAYOU RIVER
20
0   1/2
SCALE IN NAUTICAL MILES
61° 26'
25'

Services/Ashore

Beatrice (from France) and Harald (from Germany), run both the Chez la Doudou bar/restaurant and the East Carib Dive Shop (VHF: 16). Between them, they speak English, German, French, Spanish, and Italian. Chez la Doudou is a tiny, cheap and cheerful beach bar with excellent prices. Snack type lunches are nearly always available and if you want to get a good local dinner, it is best to call them on the radio and let them know, because if there are no customers, they close up. They have a water tap on the beach so you can refill your jerry jugs, and also a power line, so if you need to repair your dinghy this might be a good place. You can use their dock for your dinghy.

One close-by local attraction is the Macoucheri rum factory and river valley, just down the road. The Macoucheri Estate, near the mouth of the river, is just off the main road. It is a rum factory where they crush the sugar cane with water-powered machinery. If you wish to see it in operation, go before 1500 when they close. A feeder road, which winds up the river valley behind the estate, makes a fabulous walk among sugar cane and mountain scenery. Take along a towel, as there are plenty of places to cool off in the river when you get hot. You are also in walking distance of Mero.

Chris Doyle

CASTAWAYS
ANCHORAGE

LAYOU

Water Sports

Beatrice and Harald will be happy to take you diving. They have a pleasant small dive operation (normally groups of half a dozen).

Castaways, Mero

You will also find a huge and pleasant anchorage farther down the coast in Mero, just off what we mark at the Castaways Beach Hotel ruins. There is a wide shelf of good holding sand that starts about 25 feet deep and slowly shelves into the beach. Avoid the weed patches. Anchor to the west or southwest of the dock ruins, as there are reefs and dive sites a few hundred yards to the northwest. Stay in water about 20 feet deep and you will avoid an artificial reef, made of concrete reef balls, that was placed right in front of the hotel, both north and south of the dock, in 12 feet of water. This leaves a clearance of about 8 feet of water over the balls. A few yacht moorings are placed in this area; you are welcome to use one.

Steep hills rise behind the hotel ruins and in the rainy season a small waterfall cascades out of the cliffs. The hotel beach has a curious feature – it is home to a rather unusual (non-stinging) beach wasp that can be seen in profusion burrowing holes in

the sand and chasing each other in and out of them.

There are no services, though you can pull your dinghy up on the beach. I have been told that what remains of the hotel has been bought by Blaise Carroz, who has a mansion on the loop road behind Castle Comfort. Mr. Carroz is a well-known Swiss developer, so you may see something happen here.

Ashore

Mero, just down the beach to the north, is quite active, with several small bars and the people are very friendly. Basic provisions are available in Mero, and Roseau is only a 20-minute bus ride down the main road.

Connie's on the Beach at the northern end of the beach is very popular as a Sunday hangout with a big local following.

In the same area, Augustus Mason will fix you up with a wonderful fresh local juice. Ask for the one called "heaven" and ask him to throw in little local rum for flavor. Head up towards the main road to the Green House. This is a local, very inexpensive restaurant where you can get good fish, chicken, and ribs. Jason, the owner, has a big screen TV so you can catch any important sports action.

The Layou River is within dinghy, or

even better, kayak range. This lovely river is sometimes navigable in a dinghy, past the bridge and a bit beyond the lovely old estate house on your left. You need to be very careful at the shifting entrance, which usually has small, steep waves were the river meets the sea. Once inside, you must row. Outboard motors are not allowed. The lovely old estate house is the home of Wacky Rollers, a tour organization offering a survivor-like challenge park where they have strung wires all through the tree tops. You hook on a huge bunch of safety hooks, climb a long ladder to a platform and are on your way walking on swinging bamboo, gliding from tree to tree on a pulley system or, in one place, swinging like Tarzan into a giant net. If your life needs some adventure, this will do it. For the more sedentary, they offer kayaking, tubing, and rainforest tours.

Canefield

Canefield lies a little less than 2 miles north of Roseau and is the site of one of the island's two airports. There is a spot to anchor, just north of a huge silo, off Donkey Beach, and opposite the Shipwreck Bar, in about 15 to 25 feet of water, sand bottom.

This anchorage is not particularly scenic. Ashore, it is industrial, with everything from concrete sheds to car wrecks, but there are a couple of things worth

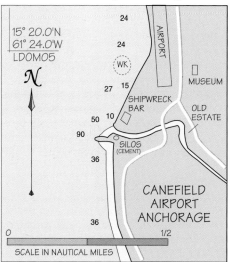

15° 20.0'N
61° 24.0'W
LDOM05

24
24
WK
27 15
SHIPWRECK BAR
50 10
90
SILOS (CEMENT)
36

AIRPORT

MUSEUM
OLD ESTATE

CANEFIELD AIRPORT ANCHORAGE

36

0   1/2
SCALE IN NAUTICAL MILES

knowing. Just down the road is a small fiberglass repair shop where you can also get engines repaired, both diesel and outboard. In addition, close by the beach, Michael's Marine Services is an excellent machine shop run by Norman. He can weld and machine any kind of fitting, fabricate parts, and repair pretty much anything that breaks.

This is also the place to get your gas bottles filled: a short walk up the small road brings you to Sukie's Cooking gas depot. They can usually do it on the spot. The Shipwreck Bar, owned by Patrick James, has been closed for years, and the beach is not great.

Roseau

Roseau is the capital of Dominica and the main town. Of all the islands, this city has the most wonderful assortment of authentic and very lovely Caribbean buildings, along with some new blocks. Many older buildings feature balconies and overhangs and intricate gingerbread trim. If you peek into gateways, you'll see interesting courtyards. Much of Roseau is being renovated and some of the refurbished older buildings are gorgeous. A few of the older, simpler wooden buildings are untouched and beautiful, just because of their weathered and aged appearance. Roseau is the only city in the Eastern Caribbean I know of in which many of the houses have cellars. These practical rooms allowed for cool storage and provided a place to shelter in a hurricane. At the Sutton Place Hotel one has been converted to a cozy bar called Cellars Bar.

The waterfront of the town has had a face-lift and is now a wide street, with a long walkway. A cruise ship dock stands at one end, a ferry terminal in the middle, and a fishing port towards the river. Roseau is the best place from which to explore the southern national park and surrounding attractions. It also has the best collection of shops and restaurants.

Yachting got a big boost recently with two new fuel docks, a new water dock, and the Dominica Marine Association, which

CANEFIELD

has brought all those dealing with yachts under one umbrella and who work together to try to maintain security (which is generally good). If you have any security problems, call the current president of the DMA, Hubert Winston, on his cell: 767-275-2851.

Roseau has several doctors and a good and reasonable optometrist at Harlsbro Medical Center on Hillsborough Street.

Navigation

Moorings are laid all the way from Fort Young to the Anchorage Hotel, as well as some beyond Anchorage, down near Aldive. This whole area is the main yacht anchorage. You are welcome to pick up a mooring yourself, or one of the waterfront boatmen will help you (see services). All moorings currently get charged out at $10 US per night – more for superyachts when one is suitable.

Dive Dominica, at Castle Comfort Hotel, and the Evergreen Hotel are between the Anchorage and the Sisserou Hotel. Avoid anchoring close to the docks or the mooring buoys used by the dive boats. These are off the Dive Dominica docks. Do not pick up any of their moorings.

The moorings at Fort Young and the Dominica Marine Center are very convenient for town, but they also tend to be a little more rolly for monohulls in normal conditions on the tidal turn, or in southerly winds. This may change in times of northerly swells, when the deepest mooring will probably be the best. Monohull owners sensitive to roll might want to

anchor stern to the beach, which is generally the calmest way to lie. Do not tie too close to the beach or you may find yourself in the surf line in case of a large swell from an onshore wind. Ask one of the boatmen to help.

You can also anchor wherever there is room clear of the moorings. If you anchor close to shore down towards Aldive, stay as far out as possible or you may be in the way of the fishermen.

Superyachts can anchor in deep water and use the Fort Young Hotel landing dock that they will find is the most suitable for their guests. Ashore, they have fancy shops and restaurants. This is the most attractive place to land in Roseau.

General Yacht Services

You are welcome to use the dinghy docks mentioned below. This means that wherever you anchor, it will not be hard to visit everywhere we mention from Roseau town down to Aldive.

In this description, I go from north to south. Fort Young, the most prestigious and interesting hotel in Dominica, is created out of an old fort overlooking the sea. They offer six moorings (currently gone, but just about to be replaced) and you are welcome to pick one up, let Fort Young Dive Shop (VHF: 16) know, and pay them the fee. It is a good idea to snorkel on any mooring you use to make sure it is in good shape. Fort Young's moorings offer the easiest access to Roseau. The shelf close to this hotel has many large boulders almost rising to the surface, making anchoring in

MOUNTAINS & MANGROVES

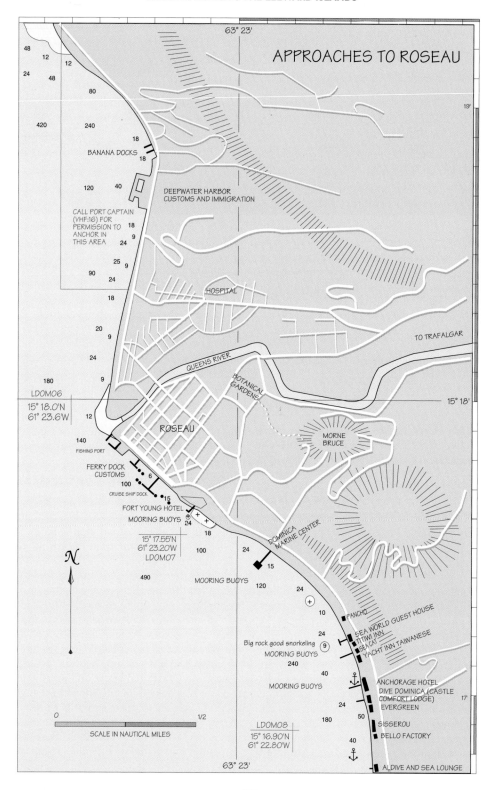

APPROACHES TO ROSEAU

63° 23'

19'

48
12
12
24
48
80
420
240
18
BANANA DOCKS
18
120
40
DEEPWATER HARBOR
CUSTOMS AND IMMIGRATION
CALL PORT CAPTAIN
(VHF:16) FOR
PERMISSION TO
ANCHOR IN
THIS AREA
18
9
24
25 9
90
24
18
HOSPITAL
20
9
24
TO TRAFALGAR
180
9
QUEENS RIVER
LDOM06
15° 18.0'N
61° 23.6'W
12
BOTANICAL
GARDENS
15° 18'
ROSEAU
MORNE
BRUCE
140
FISHING PORT
FERRY DOCK
CUSTOMS
6
100
CRUISE SHIP DOCK
15
FORT YOUNG HOTEL
MOORING BUOYS
24
18
15° 17.55'N
61° 23.20'W
LDOM07
DOMINICA
MARINE CENTER
100
24
15
490
MOORING BUOYS
120
24
10
PANCHO
SEA WORLD GUEST HOUSE
TITIWI INN
SEA CAT
YACHT INN TAIWANESE
24
Big rock good snorkeling 9
MOORING BUOYS
240
40
MOORING BUOYS
ANCHORAGE HOTEL
DIVE DOMINICA (CASTLE
COMFORT LODGE)
EVERGREEN
24
50
17'
180
SISSEROU
BELLO FACTORY
40
LDOM08
15° 16.90'N
61° 22.80'W
ALDIVE AND SEA LOUNGE

N

0   1/2
SCALE IN NAUTICAL MILES

63° 23'

470

shallow water tricky. (The snorkeling is fair, but watch out for boats!) Fort Young Dive Center manager Ken George Dill is very helpful; check with him and he will arrange whatever you need. They have a good landing dock, which is also a fair dinghy dock. Tie up on the north side by the low platform. Use a stern anchor or stern line to the outer T to keep yourself off the dock and arrange it so others can get in. They also have a bar and restaurant, shops, and other facilities of interest to yachtspeople. You can get water in jerry jugs or bring the boat alongside or stern to the dock for water, conditions permitting. Arrange this with the dive shop manager Ken George Dill. You should check with him anyway, as he can organize almost anything from island tours to duty-free liquor. Those in superyachts can use this to land their guests. Ken has his own bus, taxi and tour company and will be able to arrange tours and anything else you need.

The Dominica Marine Center has 11 moorings; some are very strong with two 3-ton blocks and capable of taking some superyachts. They also plan one monster

mooring for larger superyachts. It is run by Hubert Winston and connected with Sukie's. This is the most complete yacht service in Roseau, with a fuel (diesel and gasoline) and water dock, ice, cooking gas fills (takes a few hours), internet station and wifi, small supermarket, bakery, bar (restaurant planned), chandlery, and a laundry is close by. Decide for yourself how you want to do the fuel and water – the dock end is 20 feet square and 16 feet deep. If you feel you are too big for alongside, come stern-to. You are welcome to use the dinghy dock, but tie your dinghy off the dock to make sure the swells don't mash it. For fuel over 1,000 gallons, Hubert can arrange duty-free fuel on the main ship or cruise ship docks. Dominica Marine Center can also arrange local provisioning. If superyachts want a customs agent, they can supply that. They are also the best place to come for most repairs (see technical yachts services).

The Dominica Yacht Club is also here. They have a fleet of Optimists and a few sunfish to train young Dominicans in sailing, and to be ready to host any Caribbean

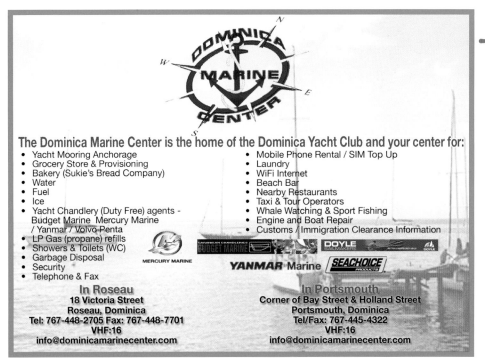

MOUNTAINS & MANGROVES

yachting events.

If you are taking fuel on the dock, you will pay a $7 EC service charge for activating the mobile fuel station. You do not pay this if you come for outboard gas and get it from their gas station above.

When you arrive, the dock reception and internet computer is just round the corner to the left of the gas station as you walk out. It is in the outboard shop. This is also where you can leave your laundry and cooking gas tank. The Dominica Marine Center stretches from here past the chandlery, right down to the bakery.

Sea World Guest House (VHF: 16) is run by a charming Dominican family, including Decima and her mother Philomen, and it will not be too long before Decima's daughter Malika will help. Decima studied business in Texas, and enjoys meeting all the visitors. They have a good dock, damaged in Omar, but soon to be rebuilt. A big expansion of the business was underway to include a swimming pool.

You can do your emails here, use their phone, and send faxes. You can also buy ice, get your laundry done, and arrange car rentals through a network of their relatives. They will dispose of your well-wrapped garbage and offer hot showers, change money, and have discounted rooms. They run a good little store in town called the French Deli, and a branch of this will soon be open here. Decima is also a fully qualified tour guide and has a bus. (see also restaurants).

Sea Cat (Cell: 245-0507) has half a dozen moorings, a house on the waterfront with a long dock you can use for your dinghy or to bring your yacht alongside for water. His staff representative (maybe Desmond) in the Sea Cat launch will happily bring you supplies and take you to customs for $40 EC and won't mind waiting if you need to do a quick bit of shopping at the same time. He can also arrange laundry, shopping, or anything you need. If you are using the dinghy dock, tie off to one of

ANCHORAGE OFF THE ANCHORAGE HOTEL

ROSEAU

THE LARGE DOCK, CENTER PHOTO, IS THE CRUISE SHIP DOCK.
THE SMALL DOCK TO ITS RIGHT IS THE FORT YOUNG HOTEL DOCK

the small moorings to keep you off the dock. Sea Cat is one of the best taxi driver/tour guides and you will be delighted if you take a tour with him. (see Transport). Sea Cat's house is almost next to to Titiwi Inn for internet, laundry, and a good place to cool out, drink and eat (see restaurants).

The Anchorage Hotel has one of the best docks in the calmest area. It has 19 feet of water at the end and they sell water, ice, and diesel fuel. You need to coordinate your arrival with their dive shop, and you can do this by phone (448-2639), VHF:16, or pay them a visit. You can also use this as a dinghy dock. They have some small moorings, so bring an extra line to keep your dinghy off the dock. You are walking right through the hotel, so it is a nice gesture to use some of their services, which include email and communications, a bar and restaurant, a dive shop, laundry, hot showers, and whale watching tours. You may also use the swimming pool for a small fee. They will help you dispose of well-wrapped garbage for a small fee. They have a good restaurant and organize tours (see ashore). Andrew Armour is the agent for Northern Lights generators (see technical Yacht services).

Several mobile yacht services patrol the area south of the Dominica Marine Center and they work hard to aid boats in a variety of ways. They hope that you will also take tours with them. They all stand by on VHF: 16, and offer moorings, some they own, others are government sponsored yacht moorings, funded by the European Union. In all cases, the mooring charge is currently $10 US. If you prefer to anchor and go stern to the shore, do so in the area from Sea Cat north. If you get help from one of the boat guys, $10 is an acceptable fee, but pay more at night or if you do it badly. I have already mentioned Sea Cat, who also has a dock and some shore facilities.

Pancho (cell: 235-3698), and his helper, Lenny, are the most ambitious and active of those offering these services, and usually are out front to meet you. Pancho has moorings both by his house and close to the government moorings. They will run a skipper to customs for $27 EC; for the whole crew and with some extra time thrown in and it will be $40 EC. Pancho will take your laundry and fetch any supplies you need. He offers tours with a number of taxi drivers, and both he and his wife Cecile are qualified tour guides and sometimes go along. Pancho usually has his customers use the Anchorage dock.

Harrison (Jason) Warrington (Cell: 614-3565) is a pleasant, young Dominican who spent some years as a roofer in Florida. He lives by the water, but his family comes from near Victoria Falls and for tours he works with Carl, a taxi driver from that area. Jason will often come along for the tour and he is a qualified tour guide. Jason will take you to customs for $10 US, and if you want to stay a little longer, you can tip him extra. He will deal with your laundry and garbage and any shopping you need. Jason works closely with Aldive and will

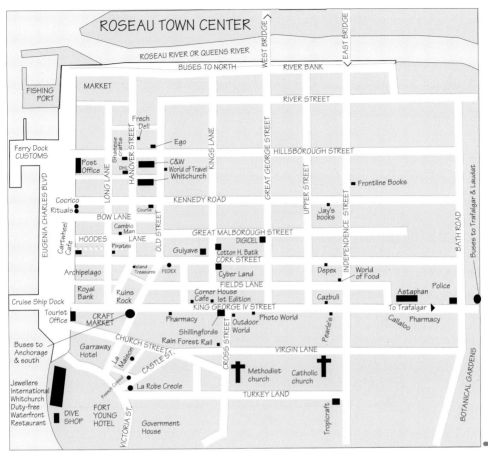

use their dock when it is finished. In the meantime, he uses Sea Cat's dock. For French people, Jason can put them in touch with a Frenchman, Michel, who can arrange tours.

You may find Roots (Cell: 315-6446) on the waterfront. He is very helpful will take you to town, to customs, get your shopping, and take your laundry. Roots also sends tours with a taxi driver. Nearby the Yacht Inn Restaurant and Bar offers both laundry and dry cleaning for a small fee One of the boat helpers will take it in and bring it back for you.

MOUNTAINS & MANGROVES

475

Chris Doyle

Billie and Samantha and Welden Lawrence together own Aldive towards the southern end of the anchorage. This family-run establishment has several moorings near the premises and they are are building an impressive dinghy dock. They also have a restaurant and wifi. They are right on the edge of the little village of Loubiere, which is a friendly and pleasant place with a local bakery, bars, and more. Ask about security when you use one of these moorings, as there were a few minor incidents last year.

Technical Yacht Services

For any mechanical or other problems, visit the Dominica Marine Center. They have a mechanical workshop and are agents for Yanmar, Mercury, and Cummins inboards, though they will fix any make. They will also fix any make of outboard, or sell you a Mercury. Go to the yacht reception in the outboard shop. They have access to full machining capabilities in the form of Norman (see Donkey Beach). They can fix most yacht problems, whether mechanical (a broken head) or electrical.

If you need a Northern Lights generator, or have a problem with one, contact Andrews Armour at the Anchorage Hotel as he is the agent.

In a real emergency (hurricane coming, no engine, or serious underwater damage), the deepwater port has a crane capable of hauling most cruising yachts and putting them ashore.

Regulations

A customs officer can be found on the new ferry terminal. You can dinghy to Fort Young Hotel and walk. Someone is usually on hand on Mondays 0800-1700, and other weekdays 0800-1600. They are sometimes open on Saturday mornings (0900-1130) and Sunday afternoons (1500-1730), depending on the ferry schedule. Even on weekdays, the officer does sometimes get called away when no ferry is expected. In this case, you will have to go to the deepwater port, just north of Roseau. Pancho, Sea Cat's rep, or Roots can also take you.

The two-week in and out clearance makes life very easy: only one round of officialdom. Customs were passing the crews list to immigration, so unless you are changing crew, you do not normally have to visit immigration. You pay a nominal environmental fee, and more fees to pay for security may be in place soon.

Communications

You can get on the internet at Fort Young Hotel, Anchorage Hotel, Titiwi Inn, and Sea World. Dominica Marine Center and Anchorage both offer free wifi, and Sea Cat has bay-wide wifi on the HotHotHot Spot system. Fort Young also offers a fax and copying service.

In town, the Corner House Cafe offers full email and internet connections and is just up the road from where the bus from Anchorage Hotel stops in town. Federal Express is on the corner of Cork and Old Streets.

Chandlery

Dominica Marine Center Chandlery is part of the compound at the head of their dock. They sell Tohatsu and Mercury outboards, safety gear, fishing and snorkeling gear, ropes, and boating hardware. They are part of the Budget Marine group and can supply anything from the catalog within three days, duty free, though transport may push the price a bit over list. If you need special parts for a breakdown, Hubert, the owner, is the best person to talk to.

Security and Outdoor World is a good fishing/marine store in Roseau. They have safety and fishing equipment and lots of useful oddments at good prices. They are near Shillingfords supermarket.

Roseau anchorage

Chris Doyle

MOUNTAINS & MANGROVES

Provisioning

You can provision reasonably well in Roseau, at a good fresh food market, or at several large supermarkets, of which Whitchurch and Co., Shillingfords, and Astaphans are the biggest. Whitchurch has been completely modernized and includes a good deli section. For cases of beer, cans, and heavy stuff, Sukie's supermarket at Dominica Marine Center is by far the most convenient place to pick things up. They keep fresh fruit, yogurts and many essentials. Dominica Marine Center also offers a full provisioning service for locally available foods.

For a few higher end products, try Archipelago. They are an excellent duty-free wine and liquor store with a few specialty foods. If you just need a few bottles, they will be delivered to the ferry dock customs for you to pick up when you clear out. If you are buying several cases, discuss delivery to the nearest dock after you have cleared out. (A customs agent will have to be present.) If you need to change money,

you can do so at the Cambio Man a bit farther back. Check out also Pirates on Long Lane. This is a wine and specialty food shop owned by Cocorico. Also check the tiny French Deli on Hanover Street. French Deli is owned by Philomen and Decima from Sea World; it has good French oils, yogurts, wines, and spices. A branch should soon open in Sea World.

Fun Shopping

The new waterfront and cruise ship dock in Roseau makes a pleasant place for a stroll. A tourist office stands at the head of the cruise ship dock, with a museum upstairs. Behind this are a craft market and a taxi and bus stand. This is where you catch a bus to the Anchorage Hotel and points south.

In town, the souvenir hunter will be delighted with the variety of Dominican handicrafts. Some are made by hand weaving roots, screw pine leaves, and grasses. The Caribs are specialists and produce the finest baskets, bowls, and bags in the Caribbean. Others souvenirs are created by

Chris Doyle

Chris Doyle

sculpting local materials and hand painting them in bright, clear colors. On cruise ship days, vendors outnumber shops, and many shops flow out onto the streets, making for a lively, colorful atmosphere. Tropicrafts sells hand-woven mats and baskets, as well as ornaments. Janic Jones' Cotton House Batiks has decorative batiks and tie-dye, as well as local handicrafts. They do all their own designs.

Ego on Hillsborough Street, where it crosses Old Street, has an elegant collection of clothing, cushions, and artistic handicrafts. For more local handicrafts, visit Shanese's Crafts close by.

On King George IV Street, the Cazbuli mini-mall is in a beautifully restored old building with a shady courtyard. Downstairs at Pages, Antonia will sell you paperback novels, books, and magazines. Upstairs is a beauty salon and a place to buy Levis and casual clothes.

Frontline and Jay's bookstores are the best for interesting local publications.

The smart shops are in the Fort Young complex. Here you will find Jewelers International for high-end watches, porcelain and jewelry, and Whitchurch Duty-Free for perfumes and elegant gifts. Check out also Land in the Archipelago Duty-Free Emporium for fine leather goods and luggage.

For art, check out Cocorico Café. They have works of Dominica's better-known artists, including Ellingworth Moses and Earl Etienne on their walls. Silverline has some excellent Cuban and Haitian art.

Down in Castle Comfort (by Anchorage), check out the Bello Plant. It is just a short walk south from Anchorage. They have lots of local products, including jams, hot sauce, chutneys, and sampler gift packs.

Restaurants

After hiking in Dominica, you won't have to worry about calories, and what better way to relax than a meal out. The

MOUNTAINS & MANGROVES

Roseau area has good restaurants at moderate prices. The food and choices are better than ever. The Anchorage Hotel has an excellent location, with its own dinghy dock. You have to come here sometime to see the great sperm whale skeleton that is on display. The bar area is downstairs and the restaurant upstairs, both have great views overlooking your yacht, and the bar offers fresh juices at unbeatable prices. You can ask for a menu and eat in either place. Come for happy hour from 1730-1900 and watch the sunset. The food is very good under the new chef, Floyd Bell. They do an excellent breakfast, including local saltfish, any day, but let it linger till noon on Sundays. On Thursday nights they have a buffet barbecue, often with live music in season.

Titiwi Inn, is the retirement project of Keith and Janet who have come back to their roots from England. Keith and Janet are great people who run a very friendly guest house with a bar and pool They will lend you their computer for checking the internet or using their wifi, and you can drop off laundry here. Their bar with a swimming pool is a pleasant place to hang out. They do meals to order, so wander over and talk to them. Janet likes to cook local food, but she is versatile and can probably cook up whatever you fancy. Coming from the UK, you can also get a good pot of tea here. Keith has a power runabout for fishing, coastal cruising, snorkeling or beach trips. You can use the Sea Cat dock just a few steps down the beach and walk over. You cannot see the entrance into the pool patio from anchorage as it is on the side wall.

Decima's Sea World Guest House has restaurant on a big balcony overlooking the anchorage (The balcony hangs out farther than all the rest); a swimming pool is under construction. Decima cooks really excellent local food. It would be a good idea to make reservations.

Right on the waterfront, the Taiwanese owned and run restaurant Yacht Inn has a pleasant dining room looking out over the anchorage. Julia Yang does the cooking and the food is very good, lighter and more delicate than many Chinese restaurants. The prices are reasonable. Julia also owns a laundry and dry-cleaning business, so you can take care of this at the same time.

Heading south, the Evergreen Hotel has the Crystal Terrace restaurant right on the water's edge, overlooking the bay. Come with a big appetite as they offer a set menu with several choices for each course. You won't find a more pleasant ambience or better service on the island. They also open for lunch – with a full or snack menu.

Castle Comfort Hotel, home to Dive Dominica, also has a very pleasant little restaurant. It is owned by the Perrymans, a Dominican family who have traveled extensively, and they serve local food with recipes that have been influenced by their travels. Dinner is from 1900-2030 and is a set menu with a choice of seafood, meat, or poultry. Plenty of local vegetables accompany the meal. This is a popular eating place for divers. Dominica Marine Center has a great outdoor bar as well as a dinghy dock, and this may be expanded to include a restaurant.

Sea Lounge is at Aldive, at the southern edge of the anchoring area – a 10-minute walk from Anchorage. When the Aldive dinghy dock is done, you will be able to dinghy there. This great new French restaurant currently only opens in the evenings, from Thursday to Sunday. However, they will often make a special opening for groups of 10 or more. It is the creation of Gilles and his chef, Vincent, who was once chef at the prestigious "La Maison," and reservations are a good idea. Gilles is very entertaining and looks after you well. Vincent cooks wonderful crepes, especially the "crepe de la mer." Start with a drink and the "amuses bouches" sampler menu while your order goes in. Vincent uses top quality meat and seafood, served with local organic vegetables, all cooked with French flair and fair bit of cream. They also offer frozen meals to take cruising.

Other restaurants are in town. Erika, from St. Vincent and Tony, from Cornwall, own and run La Robe Créole. This classy

Hike to the boiling lake

Chris Doyle

restaurant is set in a lovely old stone building, their food is excellent, and all their vegetables come from their active estates: Mount Lofty and Petit Coulibri. They also make chutney, which you can sometimes buy. They are among the few who succeed in growing strawberries in the Caribbean, though the season is short. Many travel writers rave about their wonderful calaloo soup. Daily specials may include local rabbit, octopus, and lambi, depending on the season. Shrimps, prime US tenderloin steak, and local fish are always available.

Fort Young was built to defend Roseau in 1770, when Sir William Young was governor. It saw many battles and changed hands between the British and French. It finished its service as a fort in 1854. The Fort Young Hotel has been created out of the original buildings. This is the most up-market establishment on the island, with good food and service, at Dominican prices. They have several locations for food and drink; Marquis de Bouille Restaurant,

the Waterfront Restaurant, and the Ballast Bar. They shift the location around from year to year, so ask. Their expansive week-day lunchtime buffet is excellent value for money, and this is also the place to come in the evening when you want to eat well in elegant surroundings. Try to make it on a Friday night for their happy hour from 1800-2100. It's a great place to mingle with visitors and local people, with a live band playing from 1900-2300.

One of the fancier restaurants in town is La Maison on Fort Street. This fancy French Restaurant is open in the evenings and does not take too many guests, so reservations are essential.

Cornerhouse Café, owned by Sarah, has a pleasant clubby atmosphere in a typical old Caribbean building. A narrow balcony looking down on the busy street provides entertainment. Good salads, sandwiches, and snacks are always available, as well as a big variety of daily specials, using all local produce. You can check the internet while

MOUNTAINS & MANGROVES

Chris Doyle

you are here. Open during the day and in the evenings Wednesday to Saturday, and Sundays on cruise ship days.

Cocorico is open at 0830 for breakfast and serve crepes, salads, omelets, sandwiches, and specials for lunch. It is French and good, and they have a continuous exhibition of local art (for sale) on the walls.

Rituals Café is part of a super Caribbean chain of coffee houses: good coffees, delicious baked goodies, fine sandwiches, in a clean, cool, and modern setting with free wifi.

The World of Food was a pleasant little courtyard restaurant in what was once the home of famous Caribbean novelist Jean Rhys. It was closed in 2007; I am leaving it on the map so Jean Rhys fans know where to look. At the Guiyave Restaurant, you can sit out on a balcony and watch the activity in the street below while you eat Créole food.

Curried goat, rotis, and fresh fish are always on the menu. Downstairs they have a sit-down patisserie, with good coffee, pastries, and pizza. Other local restaurants worth checking out include Port of Call and Pearl's Cuisine.

The Cartwheel Café is small and friendly and overlooks the sea from one of the oldest buildings in town. Seating is inside or out in the tiny courtyard. The lunch menu includes soups, local lunches, sandwiches, and snacks. The food is very good. They open for breakfast and you can stop by for delectable chocolate cake and coffee anytime. For something different, try Natural Livity Ital Restaurant: all natural ingredients, strictly vegetarian, fresh juices (no alcohol) served in calabash or on a plate. They open during the day and on Friday Nights with music.

Ruins Rock Café is a bar built out of ruins and offers local spices for sale. The setting is interesting.

Transport

The Dominica government is serious about educating its taxi drivers and tour-guides. All of them have to pass exams to be able to take people around, so whomever you go with, you can be sure of getting someone knowledgeable. They have to pass exams in history, nature, and first aid. Not all taxi drivers want to hike. Some will take you to the various sites and then leave you to hire an official guide, which can work out be expensive. You will not have this problem with the ones we mention below. These guys are reliable and personable taxi drivers, who are also official tour guides.

Sea Cat, whose other name is Octavius Luguy, is energetic, entertaining, and great for arduous hikes as well as for relaxing drives. He will walk with you wherever you are going, is always enthusiastic, and will

Moses cooking in his "rastaurant". Chris Doyle

be the first to jump under the waterfall. He is happy to do long hikes, such as the one to the boiling lake. Octavius knows people everywhere and knows some off-the-track sites, which you will not find for yourself. He has built up an excellent reputation over the years. I once went to a party where he was the guest of honor in New Hampshire (US). I was amazed to find myself amid about 40 people all of whom had been to Dominica, taken a tour with Octavius and had the greatest time. Call him on VHF: 16 "Sea Cat."

Pancho is entertaining and lively and arranges tours with a variety of taxi drivers. Both Pancho and his wife are qualified tour guides and sometimes lead a hike, especially long hikes like the boiling lake.

Decima at Sea World is a well-qualified tour guide. She is quite delightful, loves meeting new people, and when she has time, she is happy to hike to the boiling lake and such places. She has a tour bus. You can go to the restaurant to find her and discuss what you would like to do.

The Anchorage Hotel use good tour guides and will be happy to arrange tours for you. You can rent a car and explore on your own. I suggest you discuss the car rental with Decima at Sea World Guest House. She has a brother who rents cars, and he will work something out for both Roseau and Portsmouth.

Eddie Savarin used to work for Anchorage and relates well to yacht people. He is a good man to use for trips to or from the airport and he will also do good tours. You will have to call him: 245-2242

With plenty of time, most things can be done by bus and on foot. If you go this

MOUNTAINS & MANGROVES

483

route, start with a trip to the forestry office to buy their trail maps. In addition, buy all the interesting booklets they have on the plants and animals in the national parks. Check out also the Maps and Surveys department on Cork Street for a decent topographic map of Dominica. If you are hiking, try to get the really big one in three sections. It is 30-years out-of-date, with lots of roads missing, but the price is right, and it is the only map where you can clearly see the contour lines in detail.

Ashore

A fine botanical garden blends into the edge of the city. A map with a key to the plants is available in the forestry office. They can also give you information about the national parks and sell you hiking maps. For a bird's eye view of Roseau and the surrounding country, take the short hike in the botanical gardens up to the cross on Morne Bruce (it is marked on the plan). While in the gardens, check out the forestry department's other publications.

Roseau lies close to the Morne Trois Pitons National Park, and is central to many attractions. There are lots of exciting hikes that can be tackled in a variety of ways, depending on your proclivity and budget. For many sites, you will need a park permit. You can get a single visit ($5 US), or weekly pass ($12 US).

At many sites official guides will approach you. They have had training and are imperative for a few hikes, such as the boiling lake. Other hikes can be done with the trail maps, but you will learn more with a good guide.

Many of the more visited sites, including Trafalgar Falls and the Emerald Pool, really get overrun with tourists on cruise ship days. They are still lovely, but best visited early in the morning or late in the afternoon when the crowds have gone.

A modern attraction is the Dominica Rainforest Aerial Tram. You ride in a suspended open gondola that holds 8 passengers, together with a well-qualified guide. It is completely open and you are right in the trees – among the trunks and low growth for the first half, and amid the treetop canopy for the return. As part of the trip you can get off and walk from the top station down to the second; a walk that includes crossing a suspension bridge several hundred feet above the Breakfast River Gorge. This whole trip is breathtakingly beautiful, silent and about $78 US per person. They only open on cruise ship days, and it is best to go late in the day or over lunch when the cruise ship people have gone. You can catch a bus quite close to their base. A good alternative is to use one of the guides we mention and combine it with a hike to Titou Gorge or the crater lakes afterwards.

Victoria Falls, back from the east coast, is a tough enough hike to keep out the crowds. You get to cross the White River about five times. This is the highest falls in Dominica, with an impressive volume of water. The water is whitish with high sulfur content, as it comes from the Boiling Lake. It is lovely for a swim and the sulfur is considered therapeutic for many aches and pains. We went with Sea Cat who swam with us and coaxed us under the slight shelter of a rock on the edge of the falls, where we were treated to a really awesome view of the cascading water. Sea Cat arranged for us to eat Ital food with Moses and his family at their "Rastaurant". They live at the beginning of the trail to Victoria Falls and have a lovely garden which goes down to the river, and is full of local fruits and vegetables. The open dining area is just a shelter in the garden, you eat out of a calabash bowl with a coconut spoon; the food is wonderful.

Sari Sari Falls are also off the beaten track, farther to the north. You have a pleasant hike amid dense vegetation close to the Sari Sari River. The falls themselves are tall and form a crystal clear pool for swimming below. The area containing the falls is not huge and the falling water creates strong winds so the whole area is drenched in a fine misty spray. Keep your camera well wrapped.

Trafalgar Falls tumble high off the mountainside into lush rainforest. Visit by

Trafalgar Falls   Chris Doyle

taxi, bus, or on a tour. On cruise ship days this is madding crowd madness, but come on a non-cruise ship day, or late in the afternoon when the passengers are back on board sipping pink gins, and it is a wonderful destination, with just a few locals and stragglers. Jump in the big waterfall pool for a bracing swim (it is quite a tough scramble to get there), then, on your way back, look for the hot stream, close by the path, and luxuriate in its natural pools. If you come late, stay to see the moon rise. Also, for a small fee, you can luxuriate in a hot bath at the nearby Papillote Wilderness Retreat, which has an extensive tropical garden and is a pleasant place to stop for lunch.

Trafalgar is home Xtreme Dominica. Their headquarters is Cocoa Cottages, a cute guest house set in the forest. They specialize in canyoning and climbing in rivers, rappelling much of the way. Lots of fun for the adventurous and if you want to do something really crazy, like tightrope over the boiling lake, these are the guys to talk to. There are two crater lakes set high in Morne Trois Pitons National Park. At this elevation, mists and the coolness of the high mountains stunt the trees, but mosses, ferns, and epiphytes thrive, creating a dense, moist plant community called elfin or cloud forest. Freshwater Lake, the first one you come to, is the prettier lake, but the hike to Boeri Lake takes you on an enchanting path through the cloud forest. There are many open views down to the coast and the air is cool. The first lake is accessible by car, and you can make it some of the way by bus. This site is generally not crowded. There is also a lovely hike on a marked trail from Freshwater Lake to Grand Fond on the east coast.

For a long half-day Sea Cat took me to hang out in the valley of Perdu Temps

MOUNTAINS & MANGROVES

Chris Doyle

(Lost Time). Certainly this is an apt name for this area, which is probably as close to the Garden of Eden as you are likely to find. It is a broad valley, walled in by steep mountains. We wandered through agricultural and forestland, much of the time near a river (where you can easily cool off). Way up in the hills, a long way from roads, are several Rasta farms, each one beautifully kept and artistically laid out with flowers and fruit trees, and the odd chicken and donkey. The steep mountains provide the backdrop. To make a day of it, continue on the trail, way up, though a mountain pass, all the way over to Delices: a long but pleasant hike through forest and along rivers.

The hardest, best, and most unusual hike is to the boiling lake. A good local guide is essential for this one, at least for the first time. The hike there and back takes from five to nine hours, and it can be muddy, so tough shoes are essential. The path takes you steadily up through rainforest, then over a crest and down to the Trois Pitons River. You climb again, this time out of the rainforest into cloud forest to a mountain peak with great views. Now it is down through low vegetation with great mountain views to the last drop into Valley of Desolation, which is a steep, potentially muddy scramble. In this, the Valley of Desolation steam belches all around and the rocks feel soft and impermanent. You follow a hot river here for a while before winding your way up through some more hills covered in low vegetation to the boiling lake. This is the second largest boiling lake in the world and is in a 60-yard wide crater. It belches clouds of steam high into the air. You stand on a natural ledge right on the edge. From time to time, the steam clears and you see the boiling water. On the way back you can soak for a while in a piping hot pool in the river, but don't over-do it as you will become dehydrated and enervated, and find it hard to walk back.

Titou Gorge is at the beginning of the trail and a great place to swim on your return. It is a deep slot-canyon that winds back a couple of hundred yards into the mountain. The sheer walls are narrow and wind round into various interesting chambers. The bottom is a river, so you have to swim. The light coming from the forest above is dramatic as it lights up the sheer walls. At the head is a thundering waterfall. If you are not hiking to the boiling lake, you can make this one by bus and a short walk. It is just beyond the Aerial Tram.

Middleham Falls is probably Dominica's most beautiful waterfall, and since it involves a long hike, is somewhat secluded. The hike passes mainly through beautiful rainforest. You can go by tour, taxi, or bus. If you do not have a guide, take a trail map. If you start at Laudat, you can walk to the falls and continue onto Cohrane. If you then head back towards the coast, you will pick up a bus somewhere.

The photogenic Emerald Pool is set amid tall forest trees with a dense canopy. It is approachable by taxi, tour, or bus. Ask a Castle Bruce bus driver to let you off where the trail starts. You can ask about several restaurants not too far away. There are also a few private falls where good trails have been built and you can visit for a small fee. Any one of these falls is delightful, though not as dramatic as the major ones. You may meet other hikers, but probably no cruise ship passengers. Sea Cat can tell you how to get there.

Champagne is close to shore, north of Soufriere Bay. Warm bubbles ascend in about 10 feet of calm water, good for beginning snorkelers. You can snorkel in shallow coral, around boulders and back to the amazing underwater thermal spring. The bottom is warm to the touch and you can hear an eerie sigh as mother earth releases a stream of bubbles. Close by, brightly colored corals, sponges, and huge schools of tiny fish reflect the sunlight. You can catch any Scott's Head or Soufriere bus to get

Chris Doyle

MOUNTAINS & MANGROVES

Chris Doyle

there. Clement Johnson has Irie Safari at the entrance. They have a bar, rent snorkeling gear and do snorkeling trips. There is also a $2 Marine Park fee.

Wotten Waven is a pretty and very rural village in an area of high thermal activity. There is a small spot in the road where you can stop and look at bubbling, slurping water and steam. Since the government put a road from there through to Trafalgar, it is more on the tourist route and several roadside natural hot tub areas have sprung up. You can catch a bus here, or walk or cycle from Roseau – Once you start seriously climbing, the road up to Wotten Waven is heavenly and shaded. Pink and mauve impatience line the roadside, a rainforested hill rises on one side, the valley falls on the other. When you get to the top, refresh yourself with a water nut from Brenda's store, and prepare to laze away some time in hot water. Tia's Bamboo cottages is one the nicest hot tubs with a delightful restaurant (you have to let them know you are coming). They have a won-

derful bamboo enclosed private hot tub along with several public ones ($10 EC for a half-hour), and rooms if you want to stay the night. Screw's Sulfur Spar has numerous public pools ($10 US per hour) and a bar. Shangri-la Resort is the wildest, with a belching cave (no wonder people thought there were dragons), a crystal cave, boiling mud, and about 7 small baths dotted in the open around the land. Fred, the owner, and his team also do serious therapeutic massage and have rooms for stay-overs. For about $10 US a head he will let you loose on his land to use the tubs, jump in the river, and all those good things. Massage and meals need to be arranged in advance.

You can get in training for hiking by working out in the Anchorage Hotel's squash court ($10 EC an hour).

Water Sports

There are three excellent dive shops, all run my locals, and all stand my on VHF: 16. (Remember, to dive in Dominica you must go with a dive shop.) Andrew and his team run Anchorage Dive Center at the Anchorage Hotel. They are very good, take small groups, and there is usually no problem joining them for a dive on short notice. They dive daily at 0900. Next door, Dive Dominica is run by owner Derek Perryman, a Naui instructor and ex-LIAT pilot. He discovered many Dominica dive sites and is very knowledgeable. He works with cruise ships and holiday groups that come down from the US. He runs big groups, is busy, and advance contact is advisable. The third shop, Aldive, is of interest to yachts. This is a family-run shop with Billie and Samantha, and Welden Lawrence. They use smaller boats (thus smaller groups) than the other dive shops and aim for a more personal service. They will pick you up from your yacht, are happy to arrange private group dives, and are flexible on times. They also offer waterskiing, and kayaking. Aldive is both a Padi and Naui shop.

Superyachts should note that a super-yacht tender must not be put on a park mooring for diving, even if you have a local dive instructor on board. Unfortunately, you have to be in one of the local dive boats. However, most dive shops will be happy to provide a private one for you.

All the dive shops run whale-watching trips. Dominica is home to quite a few sperm whales, as well as many species of dolphins, including pilot whales. These are outstanding trips, and both whales and many species of dolphins are often encountered. Dolphins may play around the bow for over 40 minutes, if the boat is kept at their preferred speed of 7 knots. The whale watch leaders are informative and educational. When you next see dolphins at sea, you will be better able to identify and understand them. Andrew at Anchorage has an almost-tame sperm whale that often comes to see him, and he also has the whale skeleton in the bar, a great start to understanding their form and relationship to us. You can easily join a whale watch on short notice. Anchorage runs them at 1400 on Wednesdays, Saturdays, and Sundays.

Chris Doyle

MOUNTAINS & MANGROVES

Remember to take your camera.

You can also arrange your diving and whale watching trips through Fort Young Dive Center, and they will see that you are picked up at their dock. Dominica's rugged topography continues below the sea. Walls drop farther than you can dive, towering pinnacles rise from the seabed, and underwater hot springs bubble. The most popular dives are in Scotts Head Marine Park, written up below.

The Canefield Wrecks lie off the river mouth at Canefield. A 60-foot tug lies upright on a sandy bottom at depths of 55 to 90 feet, attracting schools of squirrelfish, soldierfish, sergeant majors, and even the odd barracuda. The current is sometimes strong, making this dive more suitable for experienced divers. However, not far away is an overturned barge lying in 5 to 40 feet of water, with a reef at one end. There are many small reef fish and this is an easy dive; good for beginners and snorkelers.

Scotts Head Marine Park

Navigation

When approaching or leaving Dominica by Scotts Head, give a wide berth to the underwater pinnacle that lies about 300 yards west of Scotts Head. Coast huggers should beware of La Grand Maison, a large reef that comes to within 2 feet of the surface and lies 100 to 200 yards off the coast, west of Soufriere. There are several other rocks and shoals fairly close inshore as you go north. The wind often shrieks down the valleys in this general area, with short intense gusts. These are worst in clear weather, when few clouds hang over the island. There are frequent shifts in direction.

Regulations

The entire area from Scotts Head up to Anse Bateau (just south of Pointe Michel) is a marine park. Yachts must not anchor in this area or use any of the moorings, unless specifically authorized by fisheries to do so. Yachtspeople can and should enjoy the area, which is beautiful, but they should leave their yachts near Roseau and visit by bus or taxi. Charges are now being levied for snorkeling and diving in the park.

Ashore

Scotts Head is some 250 feet above sea level and the view back to the rest of Dominica is of a spectacular array of green craggy peaks and majestic mountains. The steepest peak, just north of Soufriere, appears to almost lean out over the sea. In one spot there is an underwater wall that local divers say goes 1,000 feet down. The rock above is reputed to be where Caribs with tender egos punished their faithless wives by hurling them from the top. To the south, the bay is protected by a narrow strip of land – the rim of an extinct volcano: frigatebirds wheel in the air. At the base of Scotts Head an underwater shelf starts at 6 to 25 feet deep and then falls into the crater, dropping rapidly to over 100 feet. This area has some good snorkeling for experienced swimmers. The surrounding countryside is a scenic wonderland, and hiking anywhere will be rewarding. The two fishing villages, Soufriere and the village of Scotts Head, are both picturesque. On Friday nights they often have a party with some seafood for sale, sometimes they do a much bigger and more impressive version of this called Koné Konla, with lots of seafood stalls and a live band.

This is a wonderful place to hang out for a day and there is plenty to do and explore. Scotts Head village is a colorful local fishing village. Several little bars and rum shops line the street where people relax and play dominos.

One of the nicest is Scotts Head Hotel, run by Annette and John from Denmark and Holland. Their restaurant hangs out over in a lovely little dining room. The food is very good with local, Danish, and all kinds of other interesting dishes, which are nicely served. Fresh local seafood is always available. They have fresh juices and coconut water. If you come here for lunch with snorkeling and hiking gear, you could probably get them to look after one while you did the other, and make this your

SOUFRIERE TO SCOTT'S HEAD MARINE PARK

THE PINNACLE

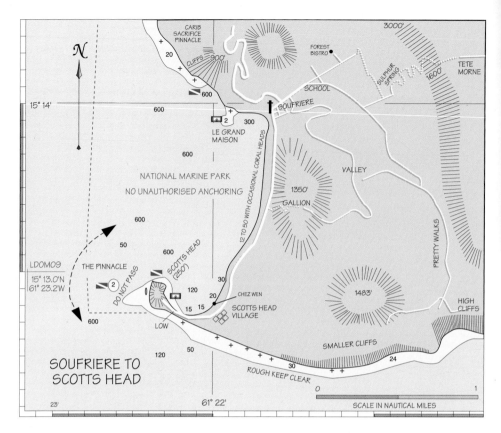

SOUFRIERE TO
SCOTTS HEAD

base for the day. They open every day except Monday for lunch and dinner.

Chez Wein cuisine, is another nice little restaurant on the same side of the road offering good Créole seafood. You will also find a bakery and several small stores. Sometimes fresh fruits and vegetables are for sale.

You can rent mountain bikes from Nature Island Dive in the village of Soufriere. Rent one for a day or half a day; the cycling at this end of the island is great. Follow the old road out to Coulibri and Petit Coulibri Estates, which takes you through lovely scenery, including some picturesque old estate ruins. When you finally get to the south end, you will see the ocean, and on a clear day, Martinique. If you cycle along the road to Galion, you will have magnificently precipitous views down to Soufriere.

Alternatively, you can hike, and for hikers Galion can be done as a round trip. A small steep trail leads up to Galion from about halfway between Soufriere and Scotts Head village. Relax and enjoy the view from the top before taking the longer hike back by the road. This hike takes you through lovely hidden valleys and mountains and there is very little traffic. The round trip will take about two and half hours.

Another spectacular hike is the main trail from Soufriere over the mountain to Tête Morne (about 2 hours). You can catch a bus back to your yacht from Tête Morne. On the way you pass a small sulfur spring and hot water source, part of the national park system. A pool has been built so you can take a bath, but, unfortunately, the design is such that the water is pretty cold by the time it fills the pool. The best hot water is in the sea, at Soufriere, where you see some reddish rocks on the beach. You can find some hot underwater thermals to sit in really shallow water.

Chris Doyle

Water Sports

This area has some of the best diving in Dominica. Nature Island Dive, in the village of Soufriere, is run by an enthusiastic and international group of young people. Karen Moise is the operations manager. They generally run fairly small dive groups and they run snorkeling trips and rent kayaks. The Pinnacle, an underwater spire, rises to within a few feet of the surface, about 300 yards west of Scotts Head. It has plateaus, ledges, and caves. You can swim through a tunnel where shifting light patterns and a huge school of red fish make a perfect picture. You will probably see schooling fish, barracudas, and rays. Dramatic forms and a superabundance of fish make this a very exciting dive. Sea conditions can be tricky and it is for experienced divers only.

Scotts Head Drop Off, on the northern shore of Scotts Head, is thought to be part of the rim of an old volcanic crater. A plateau of coral lies about 5 to 15 feet deep, then a steeply shelving slope drops to over 150 feet. The drop-off is adorned with a wonderful array of brightly colored sponges, corals, tunicates, and anemones. You will see plentiful reef fish, including large schools of resting squirrelfish, and have a chance of spotting larger ocean fish. Frogfish and seahorses are not uncommon. The water here is relatively sheltered and good for all divers. The plateau is good for snorkelers.

FROM DOMINICA TO MARTINIQUE

The passage from Dominica to Martinique covers about 26 miles in open water. The course going north is about 357° magnetic and south about 177°. The sail usually is a good reach in either direction. If you are sailing north, remember the shoal 300 yards off Scotts Head. The islands from Martinique to Grenada are covered in *Sailors Guide to the Windward Islands*, by Chris Doyle, available from www.CruisingGuides.com.

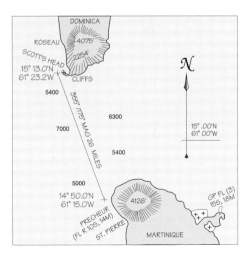

MOUNTAINS & MANGROVES

The Cruising Guide Directory

This directory is arranged by island in alphabetical order. The following abbreviations have been used:
F = Fax, VHF = VHF radio channel.
With restaurants we also give an approximate price guide in $US which is what you would expect to pay for dinner including a drink. (Lunches are usually less.) **$A** = over $50, **$B** = $25-50, **$C** = $12-25, **$D** = under $12

ANGUILLA

Anguilla phone numbers work like the USA with an area code of 264, dial 1 plus the number, within Anguilla just dial the last 7-digits

ANGUILLA SERVICES
EMERGENCY/OFFICIAL
General, 911
Hospital, 264-497-2551/2
Dr Hughes, 264-497-3053
Dr. Brian, 264-497-0765
Police, 264-497-2333
Road Bay Customs, 264-497-5461, VHF: 16

AIRLINES
Air Anguilla, 264-497-3643/2643
Airport manager, 264-497-2384
American Eagle, 264-497-3501
Anguilla Travel Services, 264-497-3613
Malliouana Travel & Tours, 264-497-2431
J.N. Gumb's Travel Agency, 264-497-2238/9, travel agent
LIAT, 264-497-5000
Winair, 264-497-2748

CHANDLERY - FISHING GEAR
Anguilla Techni Sales, 264-497-2419

COMMUNICATIONS
Roy's Beachside Grill, 264-498-0154
Syd-An's, 264-497-3180/235-7740/729-1738
sydans@hotmail.com

GENERAL YACHT SERVICES
Harry's Taxi, 264-497-4336, VHF: 16, fills cooking gas bottles
Richard West, 264-497-2095, registration surveys
Stott & Co., 264-497-2744, F: 264-497-3350, yacht registration
Super Yacht Services, 1-268-497-5438/476-7972

MISCELLANEOUS
Marine Park, 264-497-2871
St. Regis Golf, 264-498-7000
Tourist Board, 264-497-2759, F: 264-497-2710, atbtour@anguillanet.com

TRANSPORT
Connor's Taxi Service and Car Rental, 264-235-6894/497-6433, F: 264-497-8410, VHF: 16
Fedex, 264-497-2719
Steven's Taxi, 264-581-7183/772-5194, VHF: 16

TECHNICAL YACHT SERVICES
Bobcat, 264-497-5974, electrical repairs
Anguilla Techni Sales, 264-497-2419, welding, installation, Evinrude/JohnsonOMC

ANGUILLA SHOPPING
FUN SHOPPING
Anguillan Handicraft Shop, 264-497-2200
Pyrat Rum, 264-497-5003
Savannah Gallery, 264-497-2263, F: 264-497-4017, savannah@anguillanet.com, art gallery

PROVISIONING
Three-C'S Supermarket, 264-497-2067, F: 264-497-5066, proct58@yahoo.com
Albert's, 264-497-2115, lakear@anguillanet.com
IGA Food Center, 264-497-3877
Proctors, 264-497-2445/2446, jwproctors@anguillanet.com

ANGUILLA HOTELS & RESTAURANTS
Barrel Stay, 264-497-2831, F: 264-498-0161, barrel-stay@aol.com, $A-B
Da Vida, 264-498-5433, info@davidaanguilla.com, $A
Deon's Overlook, 264-497-4488, $A-B
Elvis Beach Bar, 264-772-0101/498-0101, $D
Jacquie's Ripples, 264-497-3380, ruan@anguillanet.com, $B-C
Johnno's, 264-497-2728, F: 264-497-8406, info@jonnos.com, $C-D
Mala's Roti Hut, 264-497-5030, $D
Nico's, 264-497-2844, $D
Prickly Pear Bar & Restaurant, 264-235-5864, pricklypearanguilla@yahoo.com, $D
Pumphouse, 264-584-3826, Pumphouse@anguillanet.com, $B-C
Reggae Reef, 264-461-7333, $B
Sammy's Bar, 264-235-5001, $D
Sandy Island, 264-476-6534, mysandyisland@hotmail.com, $D
Roy's Beachside Grill, 264-497-2470, 264-497-5428, royboss1@anguillanet.com, $ B
The Café at Veya, 264-498-2233, $D
Veya, 264-498-8392, $A
Yard Style, 264-772-7741, $B-C

ANGUILLA DIVING
Douglas Carty, (Road Bay) 264-497-4567/8438/235-8438, dcarty@anguilla.net, Dive shop

ANTIGUA

Antigua phone numbers work like the USA with an area code of 268, dial 1 plus the number, within Antigua just dial the last 7-digits
Abbreviations: FH = Falmouth Harbour, EH = English Harbour, JH = Jolly Harbour

ANTIGUA SERVICES
EMERGENCY/OFFICIAL
General emergency, 911
Absar, 268-562-1234, F: 268-460-1444, absar@candw.ag VHF: 16
Adelin Medical Center, 462-

0866

General Emergency numbers:
999 or 991

Antigua Medical emergency,
Nick Fuller, 268-462-0931. Out of
hours call on VHF: 16 or 68, call
sign "Ocean View." Dermatologist:
Dr. Maira Pereira,268- 481-5210,
Woods Complex: If you need
hospitalization, ask your doctor to
get you into Adelin Clinic.

Dental Emergency
Dr. Sengupta and Associates,
(Woods), 268-462-9312,
Beeper: 268-409-3368

CUSTOMS

Barbuda, 268-460-0085, VHF: 16
English Harbour, 268-460-1397
Jolly Harbour, 268-462-7929,
VHF: 16
**St. John's Deepwater
Harbour**,
268-462-2401
St. John's Heritage Quay,
268-462-6656

PHARMACIES

Sysco Pharmacy, (JH),
268-462-5917

AIRLINES

Air Canada, 268-462-1147
American Airlines,
268-462-0950/2
BWIA, 268-480-2900
British Airways, 268-462-0876/9
FBO 2000, 268-462-2522, VHF:
131.4, fbo2000@candw.ag,
agent for private planes
LIAT, 268-462-0700
Novella's Travel, (JH),
268-460-1209, F: 268-462-3352,
VHF: 68, novellas@candw.ag,
travel agent, car rentals
Virgin Atlantic, 268-560-2079

CHANDLERY –
FISHING GEAR

Antigua Slipway, (EH),
268-460-1056, F: 268-460-1566,
VHF: 68/12, antslipway@candw.ag,
chandlery with two locations at
English and Falmouth Harbours
Aquasports, (Heritage Quay),
268-462-5620/1, F: 268-462-0183,
(Jolly Harbour) 268-462-6320,
fishing and snorkeling gear plus
beachwear and toys
Budget Marine, (JH), 268-462-
8753, F: 268-462-7727,

sales@budmar.ag
Catamaran Marina, (FH),
268-460-1503/1505/464-6538,
F:268-460-1506,
catamaranmarina@candw.ag,
chandlery and fishing gear
**Falmouth Harbour
Chandlery**, 268-463-8081,
F: 268-463-8082, SS fastenings,
resins, hoses and more

COMMUNICATIONS

Antigua Yacht Services,
268-460-1121, F: 268-460-1123,
VHF: 68. USA, 207-236-4378,
F: 207-236-2371, ays@candw.ag,
communications, sourcing of yacht
parts, refit and yard work
arranged both in Antigua and USA
Caribit, 268-562-6424,
info@caribit.com,
computer repair, internet
Falmouth Harbour Marina,
268-460-6054, F: 268-460-6055,
falmar@candw.ag
P.O. Box W792, English Harbour,
Antigua, VHF: 68,
falmar@candw.ag, mail drop,
receipt of emails and faxes
Jane's Yacht Services,
268-460-2711, F: 268-460-3740,
VHF: 68, antyacht@candw.ag, full
communications including email,
crew placement, propane filling,
yacht provisioning and absentee
yacht management
Kangaroo Express, (St. Johns),
268-772-4837, internet
Jolly Harbour Marina, P.O. Box
1559, St. Johns, Antigua, WI,
festus@jollyharbourantigua.com
268-462-3085/6041/2, F: 268-562-
7703, mail drop, telephone, fax
Jolly Services.com, (JH) 268-
562-2377/2357, F: 268-562-2409,
nenayola@hotmail.com internet
access, Western Union
Outfitters, Falmouth,
268-460-1966/720-3773, F: 268-
460-3490, VHF: 68, out-
fit@candw.ag, Ft. Lauderdale, FL
33313, 954-523-4301, F: 1 954-
523-3048, shipping, sourcing, customs clearance
The Image Locker,
268-460-1246/560-1178, VHF: 68,
wifi@image-locker.com

GENERAL YACHT
SERVICES

Antigua Pier Group,
268-562-1960, apg@candw.ag,
superyacht docking in St. John
Antigua Slipway, (EH),
268-460-1056, F: 268-460-1566,
VHF: 68/12,
goldswothy6@hotmail.com,
full service marina, berthing, hauling, all kinds of repairs, water, fuel,
laundromat, chandlery
Antigua Yacht Club Marina,
(FH), 268-460-1544,
F: 268-460-1444, VHF: 68,
aycmarina@candw.ag, marina with
fuel, water, and electricity
to docks. Well designed to
service superyachts
Bailey's Boatyard, (FH),
268-460-1503/460-1506,
catamaranmarina@candw.ag, VHF:
68, travel lift, work and storage
(concrete keel holes)
Burton's Laundry, (JH),
268-462-7595, laundry
**Caribbean Concierge
Services**,
268-726-2271/462-2271, 401-662-
3360, VHF: 68,
tina@ccsantigua.com, professional
yacht agent
Carpet Care Antigua,
268-729-0511/464-1702, VHF: 68,
carpetcareantigua@hotmail.com
Catamaran Hotel & Marina,
(FH),
268-460-1503/1505/1036/1339,
F: 268-460-1506, VHF: 68,
catamaranmarina@candw.ag,
pleasant marina, yachts of any
size, water and fuel on most
docks, telephone and fax services
Dutchman Marine Surveys,
(EH), 268-773-2457, F: 268-460-
3740,
dutchmanmarine@hotmail.com
**Falmouth Harbour Fuel &
Chandlery**,
268-463-8081,
F: 268-463-8082, fuel dock
Falmouth Harbour Marina,
268-460-6054, F: 268-460-6055,
VHF: 68, flamar@candw.ag.,
Marina with berths for 44 supery-
achts, sale of duty free fuel
Jolly Harbour Marina,
268-462-6042/1, F: 268-462-7703,
VHF: 68,

Directory

festus@jollyharbourantigua.com
Full service marina, for yachts and super yachts, haul out facility, dry storage and all kinds of technical services
Nelsons Dockyard Marina, 268-481-5022/5035, F: 268-481-5030, natpark@candw.ag, marina run by the National Park
Nicholson's Caribbean Yacht Sales, (EH), 268-460-1093, F: 268-460-1524, nicholsoncy@candw.ag, yacht brokerage, North Sails agent, Yamaha agent, AB dinghy agent
Shell Beach Boatyard, (Parham Sound) 268-562-0185, F: 268-563-5255, fuel dock, small hoist
Sam and Dave's Laundry, (FH), 268-463-1266, VHF: 68,
Snow White Laundry, (Parham) 268-463-2061
The St. James's Club, (Mamora Bay), 268-460-5000, F: 268-460-3015, VHF: 68/11, SJCadmin@candw.ag, marina, superyachts especially welcome

MISCELLANEOUS
Akparo, (FH), 268-460-5705, VHF: 68, akparo@candw.ag, massage and beauty treatment
Antigua Rainforest Canopy Tour, 268-562-6363/4
Antigua Tourist Board, 268-462-0029/0480
BBR Sportive, (JH), 268-464-6969/268-462-6260, F: 268-462-3084, rpool10405@aol.com tennis, squash, swimming
English Harbour Realty, 268-764-2493
Jolly Harbour Realty, 268-562-5333/464-6327, joehutchens@ hotmail.com
Museum of Antigua and Barbuda, 268-462-4930
National Parks Authority, Nelson's Dockyard Park, 268-481-5021, F: 268-481-5030, natpark@candw.ag
Remax Antigua, 268-462-1873, properties@remax-antigua.com,

realtor
Springhill Riding Club, 268-460-7787, VHF: 68, horse riding
Temo Sports, (FH), 268-460-1781, 463-6376, boutique, 268-463-9372, VHF: 68, sports center with tennis & restaurant
Tree House Body Shop, (FH), 268-460-3434, VHF: 68, treehse@candw.ag, massage, health and beauty center; over ten types of therapeutic massage

MISCELLANEOUS MARINE
Alexis Andrews, 268-460-1175 F: 268-460-1176, VHF: 68, photography, brochures
Anjo Insurance, 268-480-3050, jhall@anjoinsure.ag, insurance
Antigua Marine Trades Assn., 268-562-5085, VHF: 68, office@antiguamarinetrades.org
Department of Marine Services, 268-452-1273, marineserv@candw.ag
Lucy Tulloch, 268-720-6868, lucy@thelucy.com, brochure design, graphics, yacht portraits
Seahorse Studios, T&F: 268-460-1457, VHF: 68, seahorse@candw.ag, yacht names, customized t-shirts and hats, brochures
Stitches, (FH), 268-560-1838 723-6994/464-2645 stitches@candw.ag, embroidered hats and sports shirts for yachts
Stuart Lockheart Legal Services, 268-562-6209, clerks@sallegalservices.com
We Be Stitching, (FH), 268-779-0368, webestitching@yahoo.com

SAILMAKERS, CANVAS, CUSHIONS
A&F Sails, (EH), 268-460-1522, F: 268-460-1152, VHF: 68, afsails@candw.ag, sail makers, canvas work, collection from Jolly Harbour
Antigua Sails, (EH), 268-460-1527, F: 268-460-1526, antsails@candw.ag VHF: 68, sail makers

Comfort Zone, 268-460-1879/720-3926, comfortzone@actol.net marine upholstery, interiors
North Sails, 268-562-5725, Andrew@sales.northsails.com

TRANSPORT
Bigs Car Rental, (FH) 268-562-4901/727-1732, VHF: 68
Caribbean Helicopters, (JH), 268-562-7333, subcatantigua@gmail.com, helicopter charter and sightseeing service, marine photography
Cheke's Scooter Rental, (FH) 268-562-4646/773-3508
Dockyard Taxi, VHF: 68, reliable taxi drivers
Europcar (JH) 268-460-1400
Hyatt's Car Rental, 268-460-6551
Lion's Car Rental, 268-562-2708, F: 268-562-2707, VHF: 68
Paradise Boat Sales (JH) 268-460-7125/5760, F: 268-462-6276, paradise@candw.ag, bike, scooter and small boat rentals, Mercury sales and service agent, some second hand boats.
TiTi rent-a-car, (FH) 268-460-1023/3336 Car rentals are also to be found in the Jolly Harbour Marina shopping center
Tropical Rentals, 268-562-5180, tropicalrentals@candw.ag, car rentals

TECHNICAL YACHT SERVICES
A-1 Marine Services, (JH), 268-462-7755, mechanics, outboards and inboards machining and fabrication
A & A Rigging, 268-464-9962/562-5616, rigging@candw.ag
A Zero Degrees Refrigeration, (EH), 268-462-6624/779-6869, F: 718-360-0748, azerodegrees@hotmail.com, VHF: 68
Antigua Boatbuilders, (FH), 268-772-6621/782-7321/775-4361, info@antiguaboats.com
Antigua Rigging, (FH),

268-562-1294/562-2651/2,
F: 268-463-8575, VHF: 68,
antrig@candw.ag, full rigging service
Antigua Yacht Painting, (FH),
268-774-1461
Automotive Art, 268-460-7211,
automotive@candw.ag
Awlgrip Antigua, (EH),
268-562-4243, VHF: 68,
awlgrip@candw.ag, fiberglass
repairs, Awlgrip paint
Caribbean Current, (FH),
268-460-7670, F: 268-460-7671,
VHF: 68, yachts@candw.ag,
all electrical systems
Cay Electronics, (FH),
268-460-1040/728-6091, F: 268-
460-1227,
VHF: 68, cayelec@candw.ag, all
electrical and electronic systems,
sales and repair
Chippy, (FH), 268-464-2447/460-
1832,
bardoe@candw.ag,
VHF: 68, woodworking
E3s, 268-562-5797, F:268-562-
5836,
Antigua@e3s.com, big boat electronics
Dynamic Electrics, 268-562-
6727, 464-8351,
dynamicelectrics@candw.ag,
electrics and appliances
Fabweld, (JH), 268-463-9578/
772-4658,
SS and aluminum fabrication
Harbour Woodwork, (JH)
268-723-1108, shipwright, joinery
Island Motors, (St. John's),
T&F: 268-462-2138, VHF: 82,
full machine shop
repairs and fabrication.
Marine Power Services, (FH),
268-460-1850, F: 268-460-1851,
VHF: 68, info@MPSantigua.com,
complete marine engineering
shop, machining, mechanics,
hydraulics, generators also construction of dodgers and bimini
frames
Marionics, (FH),
268-464-1463/460-1780/,
F: 268-460-1135, all electrical and
electronic systems
Multiservice, 268-764-
5525/560-9789,
multiserv@hotmail.com, diesel
mechanics, pumps, plumbing

Nautisigns, 268-460-1234,
VHF: 68, yacht signs
Paradise Boat Sales (JH)
268-460-7125/5760,
F: 268-462-6276,
paradise@candw.ag, Mercury
sales and service agent
Seagull Services, 268-460-3050,
mechanics, generators, hydraulics
Seagull Inflatables, (FH),
268-773-2957/ 460-1020, F: 268-
460-3740, VHF: 68,
info@seagullinflatables.com.
com, repair and service inflatables
and liferafts, safety gear, tenders.
Sea Pony,
268-460-1154/464-3164/726-
3164,
F: 268-460-1524, VHF: 16/68,
johnbentley890@hotmail.com,
towing salvage, commercial diving,
moorings available
Star Marine Tech, (JH),
268-729-7828/720-7827, F: 268-
560-2356,
yachting@candw.ag, all electrical
and electronic systems, refrigeration and air conditioning
Steel Refrigeration, (JH), 268-
725-7586
The Signal Locker, (EH),
268-460-1528, F: 268-460-1148,
VHF: 68, lockers@candw.ag, electronics sales and repair, Prevailer
battery sales, refrigeration and air
conditioning sales and repair
Tony Quinland, 268-772-5836,
fiberglass repair
Total Fabrication, 268-464-
1700, totalfabrication@actol.net,
welding, fabrication, diesel
mechanics
Watermaker Services, (FH),
T&F: 268-460-1156, VHF: 68,
info@watermakerservices.net, full
watermaker sales and service all
brands
Woodstock, T&F: 268-463-6359/
727-2345, F: 268-562-6359, VHF:
68, office@woodstockboats.com,
woodworking, metal fabrication,
painting, complete refits
Xtreme Marine, 268-464-4826,
xtrememarine@actol.net, outboards, diesels, electrics.

ANTIGUA SHOPPING

BANKING

American Express, Antours

Agency, 268-462-4788/9,
F: 268-462-4799
Bank of Antigua, 268-480-5347.
Visa group
Barclays Bank, 268-480-5006/7

FUN SHOPS

Bailey's Country Side Florist,
(FH), 268-463-1142, flowers
Best of Books (St. John's),
268-562-3198, F: 268-562-3198,
bestofbooks@yahoo.com
Dockyard Pottery, 268-562-
3035, pottery, handicrafts, souvenirs
Galley Boutique, (EH), 268-460-
1525,
info@galleyboutique.com, clothing, souvenirs
Harmony Hall, (Nonsuch B),
268-460-4120,
Harmony@candw.ag,
art gallery, some artistic gifts
Island Photo, (St. John's),
268-462-1567, photoshop@candw.ag
Lord Jim's Locker,
268-460-1147, F: 268-460-4093,
VHF: 68, lordjim@candw.ag, cruising guides, charts, local and international books of interest to the
yachting community, novels
Map Shop (The), 268-462-3993,
F: 268-462-3995,
cesmpa@candw.ag, cruising
guides, Admiralty chart agent
Portobello, (FH), 268-460-5851,
boutique, pareos, souvenirs
Rhythm of Blue, (FH), 268-562-
2230, pottery, scrimshaw, art, jewelry
Sail Loft Studio, and crew
placement, 268-562-5335,
F: 268-460-1562,
sailloftstudio@candw.ag
Sunseakers, (St. John's),
268-462-3618, F: 462-2705,
sunseakers@candw.ag, swim wear
The Art Den, 268-460-3012,
F: 268-460-1531, dddsa@candw.ag
Things Local (EH),
268-461-7595, sculpture

PROVISIONING

Small food stores are also available in Dickenson Bay, Parham,
Crabbs and there is a good local
market in St. John's
Bailey's Supermarket, (FH),
268-460-1142, F: 268-468-1847,

VHF: 68, supermarket, delivery to docks

Best Cellars, (Airport & EH), 268-480-5180, T&F: 268-480-5185, psold@bestcellars.biz, wines and liquors, free delivery to marinas

C& C Wines, (St. John's), 268-460-7025/464-3975, F: 268-561-0221

Carib Bean Coffee Company, 268-462-5282, F: 268-462-2326, VHF: 06:"Coffee Roaster", caribcoffee@candw.ag, Caribbean coffees

Crab Hole Liquors, (FH), 268-460-1212, VHF: 68, and Crab Hole 2, (EH), 268-462-9082, VHF: 68, wines, liquors, party essentials, free delivery

Dockyard Bakery (EH), 268-460-1474, F: 268-460-1472, VHF: 68, shmeena_86@hotmail.com, baked goodies, bread, charter boat quantities available

Dockside Supermarket and Liquors, (FH), 268-463-9000, VHF: 68, opens late, wine, liquor and supermarket

Epicurean Supermarket, (Woods & Jolly Harbour), 268-481-5400, F: 268-462-3846, Antigua's largest supermarkets.

Famous Mauro, (FH), 268-460-1318, VHF: 68, bread, baked goods

Horizons Supplies, (Mamora), 268-562-1582/1581, F: 268-463-3807, horizons@candw.ag, wholesalers

TCM, (FH), 268-462-3428/764-1198, F: 268-462-3429, tcm@candw.ag, provisioning service

ANTIGUA HOTELS & RESTAURANTS

ACCOMODATION ONLY

Catamaran Hotel, (FH), 268-460-1503/ 1505/1036/1339, F: 268-460-1506, VHF: 68

RESTAURANTS

3-Martini, 268-460-9306, 3martini@apuainet.ag, $B-D

Abracadabra, (EH), 268-460-1732/2701, abra@candw.ag, $B

Admiral's Inn, (EH),

268-460-1027, F: 268-460-1534, admirals@candw.ag, $A-B

Antigua Yacht Club Marina, (FH), 268-460-1545, F: 268-460-1544, aycmarina@candw.ag, $A-C

Bambi, (EH), 268-562-5517, $B

Café Bambula, (St. John's) 268-562-6289, $C

Calabash, (EH), 268-562-4906, $B-C

Carlisle Bay (Indigo and East), 268-484-0000, $A-B

Castaways, 268-562-4446, castaways.antigua@gmail.com, $B-D

Catherine's Cafe, (EH) 268-460-5050, mestipho@candw.ag, $A-B

Caribbean Taste (EH) 268-562-3049, VHF: 68, $B-C

Cloggy's at Abracadabra, 268-263-8083, café

Cockpit Bar, 268-764-9395, angidickinson@shaw.ca

Collin's Place, (JH), 268-561-1354, $D

Chez Maman, (FH), 268-723-5005, $B-D

Curtain Bluff Hotel, (south coast), 268-462-8400, $A

Drop-in Bar, (EH), 268-560-8086

Dennis Restaurant, (Ffryes Bay), 728-5086, $B-C

Dogwatch Tavern, (JH), 268-462-6550, dogwatchtavern@aol.com, $B-D

Dry Dock, (FH), 268-460-3040, $B-C

Famous Mauro, (FH), 268-460-1318, VHF: 68, $D

Foredeck Bar, 268-764-9395, angidickinson@shaw.ca

Galley Bar and Restaurant, (EH), 268-460-1533, VHF: 68, $C

Grace Before Meals, (EH), 268-460-1298, $D

HQ2 Restaurant (EH), 268-562-2563, $A

Harmony Hall, (Nonsuch B), 268-460-4120, F: 268-460-4406, VHF: 68, harmony@candw.ag, $A-B

Jackie's Kwik Stop, (FH), 268-460-1299, $D

Johnny Coconut, 268-562-5012, $B-C

Le Cap Horn, (FH), 268-460-

1194, VHF: 68, $B

Life, (EH), 268-560-3525, VHF: 68, $B-C

Long Bay Resort (Jumby Bay), (Parham), 268-462-6000, VHF 18, mccameron@rosewoodhotels.com, Estate House, $A

Grand Royal Antiguan, (Deep B.), 268-462-3733, F: 268-462-3732, $A-C, reservations@grandroyalantiguan.com

Mad Mongoose, (FH), 268-463-7900, $B-D

Mainbrace Pub, 268-460-1058, $B-C

Mio Cucina, 268-562-2226/764-4639, $A-B

Pasta Rite Ya, (FH), 268-764-2819, flochief@hotmail.com

Peter's, (JH), 268-462-6026, $A-C

Rex Halcyon, (Dickenson B.), 268-462-0256, rexhalcyon@candw.ag, $B

Seabreeze Café, 268-562-3739

Sheer Restaurant, 268-562-4446, cocobaycandw.ag, $A

Shirley Heights Lookout, 268-460-1785, VHF: 68, $B-D

The Beach, (Dickenson B.), 268-480-6940, $A-B

The Gallery, (EH), 268-562-5678/724-1640, thegallery@apuainet.ag, $B, good food

The Hideout, 268-460-3666/7, VHF: 68, hideout@candw.ag, $B

The Inn at English Harbour, 268-460-1014, 268-460-1603, $A,

The St. James's Club, (Mamora B.), 268-460-5000, VHF: 16, $A, about four different restaurants

The Waterfont, 268-460-6575, $D

Trappas Bar, (FH) 268-562-3534, VHF: 68, $B

Yacht Club Marina Restaurant, (FH) 268-640-1797, $B-C

ANTIGUA SCUBA DIVING

Antigua Divers, (EH), 268-729-4698

Aquanaut, (Falmouth), 268-460-2813/728-7688, VHF: 68

Aquarius, (Long Bay), 268-460-9384, Cell: 727-9384, rmronan@candw.ag

Dive Antigua, (Dickenson Bay), 268-460-3483, F: 268-460-7787, dai@candw.ag
Dockyard Divers, (EH), 268-460-1178/1179/729-3040 VHF: 68, dock-divers@hotmail.com
Indigo Divers, 268-562-3483, infor@indigo-divers.com
Jolly Dive, (JH), 268-460-3550/462-8305, maiter@jollydive.com,VHF:68
Mamora Bay Divers, (Mamora), 268-464-4905, mamorabaydivers@candw.ag
Sea Wolf Diving School, (FH), 268-460-3550, bryan@seawolfdivingschool.com
Soul Immersions, (EH), 268-728-5377, VHF: 68, soulimmersions@hotmail.com

BARBUDA

Barbuda and Antigua are the same phone system, which works like the USA. dial 1 plus the number. Inside Antigua/Barbuda just dial the last seven digits.

BARBUDA SERVICES

CUSTOMS
Barbuda, 268-460-0085

MEDICAL EMERGENCY
Call any taxi on VHF: 16/68 and

ask them to get you to the doctor

COMMUNICATIONS
Barbuda Internet, 268-561-1651

TRANSPORT
Barbuda Bike Tours, 268-773-9599/784-5717, jonatpereira@hotmail.com
Barbuda Express, 268-560-7989/764-2291
George Jeffrey, 268-460-0143/788-7067, VHF: 16, "Garden of Eden" or "Annella J", tours, frigate bird trips, lobster
John Taxi. 779-4652/788-1569

BARBUDA RESTAURANTS
Barbuda Outbar, 268-721-3280/460-0509
Beach House, 268-764-4042,

info@thebeachhousebarbuda.com , $A
It's A Bit Fishy, 268-772-0262/3525, $B-D
Lighthouse Bay, 268-562-1481/720-9156, $A
PalmTree Restaurant, 268-784-4331/722-5496, $C-D
Uncle Roddy's, 268-785-3268/460-0021, $C-D
Wa O'mani's Best, 268-724-3715, $C-D

DOMINICA

Dominica phone numbers work like the USA dial 1 plus the number, within Dominica just dial the last 7-digits

DOMINICA SERVICES

EMERGENCY/OFFICIAL
Police Fire & Ambulance, 999
Coastguard, 767-266-3072
Customs, Portsmouth: 767-445-5340, Deep Water Harbour, 767-448-4462
Dr. Fitzroy Armour 767-616-1804
Optical Services Ltd., 767-449-9099, optiserv@cwdom.dm

AIRLINES
Air Caraibe, 767-448-2181
American Eagle, 767-449-2153
Cardinal Air, 767-449-8923
LIAT, 767-448-2421/2
Whitchurch & Co., 767-448-2181, F: 767-448-5787, travel agent

CHANDLERY - FISHING GEAR
Budget Marine, Portsmouth, 758-445-4322
Dominica Marine Center, 767-448-2705/275-2851, F: 767-448-7701, info@dominicamarinecenter.com
Security and Outdoor World, 758-440-3475

COMMUNICATIONS
Computer Resource Center, Portsmouth, 767-445-3370, F: 767-445-8370, office@crcdm.com
Anchorage Hotel, P.O. Box 67, Roseau, Commonwealth of Dominica, 767-448-2638/9, F: 767-440-2639, VHF: 16, anchorage-

dive@cwdom.dm, mail drop, phone and fax, internet
Cornerhouse Cafe, 767-449-9000, F: 767-449-9003, cornerhouse@cwdom.dm, internet
Everland Internet Café, 767-445-5013, everlandinternet-cafe@hotmail.com
Federal Express, 767-448-0992, F: 767-448-0993
Foneshack, 767-445-0970, Portsmouth@thefoneshack.com
Variety Store Internet, 767-445-4305 Internet also available at Fort Young, SeaWorld and Green Flash Hot Hot Hot Spot available in Roseau (Sea cat) and Portsmouth (Purple Turtle)

GENERAL YACHT SERVICES
Anchorage Hotel, Roseau, 767-448-2639, F: 767-440-2639, VHF: 16, anchorage-dive@cwdom.dm, Fuel and water dock, laundry, showers
Dominica Marine Center, 767-448-2705/275-2851, info@dominicamarinecenter.com, Fuel and water, dinghy dock, laundry, provisioning
Fort Young Hotel, Roseau, 767-448-5000, F: 767-448-5006, fortyoung@cwdom.dm, moorings
Lin's laundry and dry cleaning At Yacht Inn, Roseau anchorage, 767-448-3497/616-8988
National Petroleum, 767-448-7423/449-2415, F: 767-449-2477, fuel
Pancho, 767-235-3698, VHF: 16, moorings
Portsmouth Beach Hotel, 767-445-5142/445-5130, F: 767-445-5599, laundry, showers, Ice. Picardbeach@candw.dm
Providence Boating, Portsmouth, 767-245-2700/445-3008, VHF: 16, Carrierre@hotmail.com, Martin Carriere, help with provisions, cooking gas, laundry and shopping.
Sea Cat, 767-245-0507, VHF: 16, moorings
Sea World, Roseau, 767-448-5068, F: 767-4408-5583, seaworlddominica@yahoo.com

Directory

laundry, showers, car rentals

MISCELLANEOUS

National Development Corp., 767-448-5710, F: 767-448-5840, tourism@discoverdominica.dm, tourist office

Xtreme Dominica. 767-448-0142, cocoacottages@cwdom.cm, waterfall rappelling

Irie Safari, 440-5085, iriesafari@cwdom.cm, snorkeling at Champagne

River Rush, 767-295-7266 or 599-553-3702 (St. Maarten)

Shangri-la Resort, 767-440-5093, shangrila@cwdom.dm, hot baths

Rainforest Riding, 767-265-7386/445-3619, rainforestriding@yahoo.com

Tia's Cottages, 767-448-1998/225-4823, hot baths

Wacky Rollers, 767-440-4386, wackyrollers@yahoo.com, Challenge treetop course, tubing, kayaking

TRANSPORT

Anchorage Hotel, Roseau, 767-448-2638/9, F: 767-448-5680, tours

Bertram Jno. Baptiste, Portsmouth, 767-448-4562, DrBirdy2@cwdom.dm, best bird guide

Eddie Taxi, 767-245-2242, eddietours2001@yahoo.com

Max Taxi, Portsmouth, 767-285-6774

Nature Island Dive, Soufriere, 767-449-8181, F: 767-449-8182, walshs@cwdom.dm, bike rentals

Providence Boating, Portsmouth, 767-445-3008, F: 767-445-5181, VHF: 16, Carrierre@hotmail.com, Martin Carriere, taxi and tours.

Rain Forest Aerial Tram, 767-448-8775, site: 767-440-3266, USA: 305-704-3350, reservations.dom@rfat.com

Sea Cat Tours, Roseau, 767-448-8954/245-0507, VHF: 16, seacat55@hotmail.com, good taxi, will hike anywhere

Silver lining Car Rental, Portsmouth, 767-445-3802, F: 767-445-3802 silverlining@cwdom.dm, car rentals

INDIAN RIVER GUIDES

All of them stand by on VHF: 16

Albert, 767-317-5433/613-9525, abertshoreservices@hotmail.com

Alexis Faustin, 767-317-0901/277-0013

Charlie, 767-225-5428

Cobra Tours, (Andrew O'Brien), 767-445-3333/245-6332, F: 767-445-3333, info@cobratours.dm

Eddison, 767-225-3623/6/445-6978, eddisonlaville@hotmail.com, VHF: 16

Lawrence of Arabia, 767-225-3632/445-3680, VHF: 16, Lawrence-of-dominica@hotmail.com

Sea Bird, (Jeffrey Frank), 767-245-0125, seabird123@hotmail.com

Spaghetti (Eric), 767-445-4729,

Providence Boating, (Martin Carriere), 767-445-3008, F: 787-245-2700, VHF: 16, Carrierre@hotmail.com

TECHNICAL YACHT SERVICES

Igna Mitchell, 767-315-7209/445-3466, Portsmouth, good general mechanic diesel and outboard also other yacht systems

Michael's Marine Services, Canefield, 767-449-1526, machining, fabrication, all metals welded

So So Marine, 767-612-1886, boatbuilding, rigging, sails

BANKING

American Express, Whitchurch and Co., 767-448-2181

Barclays Bank, 767-448-257, Visa Group

FUN SHOPS

Archipelago Trading 767-448-3394, F: 767-448-5338, yvorn@cwdom.dm

Cotton House Batiks, 767-245-3955,

Dive Dominica, 767-448-2188, VHF: 16

Ego, 767-448-2336

Frontline Bookstore, 767-448-8664

Mee-Kee-Dee,

767-445-3225/235-3727, meekeedees@yahoo.com

Ti Kai, 767-614-5886

Tropicrafts, 767-445-5956/448-7126/2747

PROVISIONING

Archipelago, 767-448-3394, F: 767-448-5338, cocori-co@cwdom.dm

Ian's Depot, 767-277-4689

Pirates, 767-449-9774, pirate@cwdom.dm

Mini Cash, 767-445-4453

Shillingford & Co., 767-448-2481/5, F: 767-448-6681

Whitchurch Supermarket, 767-448-2181

RESTAURANTS, ACCOMODATION

Anchorage Hotel, Roseau, 767-448-2638, F: 767-448-2639 VHF: 16, anchorage-dive@cwdom.dm, $B-C

Big Papa's, 767-445-6444/245-1673, $C

Cartwheel Cafe, Roseau, 767-448-5353, F: 767-448-5905 $D

Chez Wen Cuisine, Scott's Head, 767-448-6668, $D

Cornerhouse Café, 767-449-9000, F: 767-449-9003, cornerhouse@cwdom.dm, $D

Evergreen Hotel, Roseau, 767-448-3288, F: 767-448-6800, evergreen@cwdom.dm, $B-C

Forest Bistro, Soufriere, 767-448-7105, $C-D, special, check first

Fort Young Hotel, Roseau, 767-448-5000, F: 767-448-5006, fortyoung@cwdom.dm, $B-C

Green House, Mero 767-285-3333, $C-D

Guiyave, Roseau, 767-448-2930, $C-D

Heaven's Best, 767-445-6677/277-3952, reservations@heavensbestguesthoue.com, $B-C

La Maison, Roseau, 767-440-5287, $A-B

La Robe Creole, Roseau, 767-448-2896, F: 767-448-5212,

$B-C
Papillote, Trafalgar 767-448-2287, papillote@cwdom.dm, $C
Pearle's, Roseau, 767-448-8707, $C-D
Poonkies, 767-285-6774, $B
Portsmouth Beach Hotel, 767-445-5142/ 445-5130, VHF: 16, picard_beach@candw.dm, $B-C
Port of Call, Roseau, 767-448-2910, $C-D
Purple Turtle, Portsmouth, 767-445-5296, $C-D
Riverside Restaurant, Portsmouth, 767-445-5888/613-1888, stevenjiamg_992@hotmail.com, $B-C
Sister's Sea Lodge, Portsmouth, 767-445-5211, $B-C
Sea Lounge, Roseau anchorage, 767-225-9473, gilles@dominica-discovery.com, $B
Sea World, Roseau anchorage, 767-448-5068, F: 767-448-5168, seaworlddominica@hayoo.com, VHF: 16, $D
Sunset Bay Club, Coulibistrie, 767-446-6522, F: 767-446-6523, sunset@cwdom.dm, $B
Titiwi Inn Roseau anchorage, 767-448-0553, info@titiwi.com, $B-D
Yacht Inn Roseau anchorage, 767-448-3497/616-8988, $D

DOMINICA SCUBA DIVING

Aldive, 767-440-3483, info@aldive.com, also do whale watching
Anchorage Dive Centers, Anchorage Hotel, Roseau, 767-448-2639, F: 767-440-2639, VHF: 16, anchorage-dive@cwdom.dm, also do whale watching
Cabrits Dive Center, Portsmouth, 767-445-3010, F: 767-445-3011, Lagoon Branch, 7 67-295-6424, USA: 347-329-4256, cabritsdive@yahoo.com, cabrits-dive@cwdom.dm
Dive Dominica, Roseau, 767-448-2188, F: 767-448-6088, VHF: 16, dive@cwdom.dm, also whale watching
East Carib Dive, Mero, 767-449-6575, ecd@cwdom.dm

Fort Young Dive Center, 767-448-5000, F: 767-448-8065, fyhdivecenter@cwdom.dm,
Nature Island Dive, Soufriere, 767-449-8181, F: 767-449-8182, walshs@cwdom.dm

GUADELOUPE

Guadeloupe numbers are ten digits, starting with 0590 (fixed phones) and 0690 (mobile units). From French territories dial this ten-digit number. If you are calling from outside French territory, dial the international exit code (usually 011), then 590, then the full number we give but leave off the first 0. Thus, from overseas if we give 0590-71-92-92, you dial 011-590-590-71-92-92. This doubling of 590 is a little confusing, but absolutely necessary.

GUADELOUPE SERVICES

EMERGENCY/OFFICIAL
COSMA, 0590-71-92-92, VHF: 16, 11, French lifeboat association. Also give weather and navigational warnings on the VHF.

MEDICAL EMERGENCY
SAMU (medical emergency), 15
Police, 17
Firemen (also pump out sinking boats) 18
Dr. Theirry Caussee, 0590-93-64-01 (GP near Marina Bas du Fort)
Dr. Cardin, 0590-93-62-62 & **Dr. Sebrien**, 0590-90-79-00 (dentists near Marina Bas du Fort)
Medical Emergency Service, 0590-91-39-39
Hospital, (Basseterre), 0590-81-71-87

CUSTOMS
Basse Terre, 0590-81-17-28.
Deshaies, 0590-28-41-19.
Marina Bas du Fort, 0590-90-87-40
Marina Riviere Sens, 0590-81-85-33
Pointe a Pitre, 0590-83-30-22
Port Louis, 0590-22-97-16
DDE , 0590-83-61-48, information on navigation markers
DDE , 0590-21-26-50, information on the opening bridges

AIRLINES
Air Canada, 0590-21-12-77
Air Caraibes, 0590-82-47-47
AOM, 0590-21-14-84
Air France, 0590-82-61-61
American Airlines, 0590-21-13-68/21-11-80
LIAT, 0590-21-13-93
Nouvelle Frontieres, 0590-90-36-36

CHANDLERY - FISHING GEAR
Antilles Yachting Services, (Caraibe Greement) (Marina Riviere Sens) 0590-94-54-86, caraibesgreement@hotmail.com chandlery, fishing gear
Caraibe Greement, 0590-90-82-01 F: 0590-90-97-50, caraibe.greement@hotmail.com, Rigging shop good technical chandlery, winches, blocks, stoves, everything for rigging, marine hardware
Dulac (Riviere Sens), 0590-92-61-50, fishing store
Karukera Marine, 0590-90-90-96/8, F: 0590-90-97-49, karukera.marine@wanadoo.fr, big selection of chandlery, fishing gear, snorkeling gear, fancy deck shoes and more
Marin 'Art, 0590-90-83-80, Mob: 0690-32-29-31, marinart@wanadoo.fr, embroidered towels, hats and t-shirts
Schip-o-Case, 0590-83-17-75, anke.beunis@wanadoo.fr secondhand shop
Uship, 0590-26-20-20, big marine store.
W.I.N.D., 0590-99-27-69, F: 0590-99-27-70, windguadeloupe@wind-flag.com, resins, batteries, work supplies, antifouling, flags
Waypoint, 0590-90-94-81, F: 0590-90-92-63, Waypoint.gp@outremer.com, electrical and electronic marine hardware

COMMUNICATIONS
Fedex, 0590-26-85-44, courier
L'Arobas Cafe, (St. Francois), 0590-88-73-77, arobas.bar@wandoo.fr, internet

Directory

café
Le Pelican, (Deshaies),
0590-28-44-27, internet
Maya Cyber Cafe, (St. Anne),
0590-47-87-20,
maya@mediaserv.net, internet
cafe
Post Office Cyber Service,
(Marina Bas-du-Fort)
0590-28-09-88, easynetmari-
na@gmail.com,
email, internet access, phone and
fax, secretarial services, courier,
mail drop, email, computer repair

GENERAL YACHT SERVICES

Caraibe Yachts, (Marina Bas-du-
fort) 0590-90-81-61,
F: 0590-90-80-13, VHF: 72,
jp.bahuaud@caraibeyachts.com,
absentee yacht management,
yacht broker
Cool Racoon Laverie, (Marina
Bas-du-fort) 0590-90-84-80, laundry (Marina Bas-du-fort)
Gerard Petrelluzi, customs
agent, superyacht agent,
0690-55-86-62, petrel-
luzi.gerard@wanadoo.fr
Marina de Riviere Sens,
0590-81-77-61, F: 0590-99-00-01,
VHF: 16, marina, water, fuel
Marina Bas du Fort,
0590-93-66-20, F: 0590-90-81-53,
Info.marinabf@loret.net, 1000-
berth marina, fuel dock, haul out,
all manner of repairs available.
Major yachting center
Marina St. Francois, 0690-50-
85-15, marina, water
Martial Barriel, 0590-28-14-41,
0690-55-42-78,
expert.maratime.barriel@wanado
o.fr, surveyor
Press'Net
0590-81-50-99/99-04-74,
laundrette, dry-cleaner in Marina
Riviere Sens
Seminole Marine & Shipyard
Chantier Lemaire, 0590-26-67-10,
23-18-60,
F: 0590-91-96-52, y.kimel@ool.fr,
large haul out facility with four
dry docks any size of boat up to
1300 tons. Do it yourself or technical staff available including
mechanics and machinists
Socarex, (Marina Bas Du Fort),

0590-90-89-30, F: 0590-90-89-21,
christian.mir@wanadoo.fr, marine
surveys

MISCELLANEOUS

Aquarium de la Guadeloupe,
0590-90-92-38, seawater aquarium, near Marina Bas du Fort
Bagage Plus, 0590-93-60-91,
F: 0590-93-61-05,
bagageplus@wanadoo.fr
**Cercle Sportif Bas du Fort
(CSBF)**, 0590-90-93-94,
csbf.guadeloupe@wanadoo.fr
**Conseille General Yachting
Rep**: Olivier Souilhac,
0690-31-18-13
Jardin Botanique de Deshaies,
0590-28-43-02, F: 0590-28-51-37,
info@jardin-botanique.com
L'Artchipel, (B.T.),
0590-99-29-13, F: 0590-99-29-20,
theater
Tourist Office, Basseterre,
0590-81-24-83
Tourist Office, Pointe a Pitre,
0590-82-09-30/89-46-89,
F: 0590-83-89-22
Triskell (yacht racing club), 0690-
49-57-57,
organization@triskellcup.com
0590-88-48-74/40-01
Syndicat d'Initiative, (Marina B.
du F.),
0590-90-70-02, F: 0590-90-74-70
Yacht Club de Saint Francois,
(Claude Grasset), 0690-30-62-52,
ycsf.gpe@orange.fr

SAILMAKERS , CANVAS, CUSHIONS

Caraibes Covering,
0590-90-94-75, F: 0590-90-94-22,
caraibes.covering @wanadoo.fr,
canvas, cushions, everything but
sails
Marina Confection,
0590-90-85-04, F: 0590-90-77-64,
marinaconfection@wanadoo.fr,
interior cushions and fabrics,
awnings etc
North Sails, 0590-90-80-44,
F: 0590-90-89-76,
gavin@sails.northsails.com, new
sails and repair of old. Excellent
for high-tech work
Voile Incidences,
0590-87-06-04/90-87-65/0690-74-
54-00, i.voiles@business.ool.fr,
sailmaker, canvas and cushions

TRANSPORT

Alain Taxi, 0690-35-27-29
Cap Caraibes, (Bas du Fort),
0590-93-61-86, F: 0590-93-62-86,
cap-caraibes@caramail.com,
4-wheel drive rental
CDL, (P.A.P), 0590-20-74-74,
taxis on call
Europe Car, (St. Francois),
0590-88-69-77, car rental
Jumbo Cars, (Bas du Fort),
0590-90-86-32/-91-55-66,
F: 0590-91-22-88, car rental
Lascar Location, (Deshaies)
0590-28-55-98
Marina Sun, (R. Sens),
0590-99-03-13/56-11-18, car,
scooter and bicycle rental
Tele Taxis, 0590-94-33-40
TSGR, (B.T.), 0590-81-79-70,
Taxis on call

TECHNICAL YACHT SERVICES

Assistance Marine,
0590-84-59-40/0690-45-52-84,
F: 0590-90-07-03,
assistance.marine@wanadoo.fr,
large engine repair and maintenance
Atelier Maurice Philis,
0590-90-88-77, 0690-35-32-47,
F: 0590-90-83-79,
philis.maurice@wanadoo.fr good
general marine mechanic, also
shafts, bearings and props and
application of antifouling paint
Cap Sud,
0590-90-76-70, F: 0590-90-76-77,
info@capsud.net, agent Beneteau,
Lagoon, repairs and warranty
work.
Chantier Amel,
T &F: 0590-90-85-83,
0690-38-10-21,
amel.caraibes@wanadoo.fr, Amel
agents
Clean Boat Service,
0690-75-77-97, 0690-54-54-97, F:
0590-90-80-13
coco@caraibes-charter.com
general fix it, painting etc.
CTA, 0590-38-78-98,
F: 0590-95-67-42,
ccthelier@wanadoo.fr, all kinds of
rigging repairs also stainless and
aluminum welding plus hydraulic
repairs of all types and machining
Espace Ocean, (Marina Bas-du

fort) 0590-90-75-48/90-34-14, F: 0590-90-31-88, espace-ocean@wanadoo.fr, sale and testing of liferafts, inflatables and safety gear

Eurosurvie, 0590-32-26-51, F: 0590-32-26-52, eurosurvie@wanadoo.fr. liferafts, safety gear

F System, 0590-84-06-58, 0690-72-49-58, F: 590-84-13-28 fsystem@wanadoo.fr.

Fred Marine Mecanique, 0590-90-71-37,F:0590-90-86-51, 0690-35-66-11, fredmarine@wanadoo.fr, Mechanical repairs of all types both inboard and outboard

GMD,Volvo Penta, (P.A.P), 0590-90-94-03, F: 0590-90-96-23, gmdvolvopenta@wanadoo.fr, repair of Perkins and Volvo

General Mecanique Marine, 0590-90-70-51

GPS Rigging Service, 0690-58-18-04, 590-22-76-23, jplev-ert@wanadoo.fr, Rigging

MB Services, 0690-39-41-82, F: 0590-84-06-73, Mathieu.bonvoisin@wanadoo.fr

Pochon, 0590-90-73-99, F: 0590-90-90-51, pochon.antilles@wanadoo.fr, sales and repair of electronics in Marina Bas-du -Fort

Richard Dupuis, 0690-58-78-20, iceberg.refrigeration@wanadoo.fr, refrigeration and aircon repairs

Sea'mpatic, 0690-50-03-70, fred.bernier@wanadoo.fr, under-water work, hulls cleaned

Waypoint, 0590-90-94-81, F: 0590-90-92-63, waypoint.gp@wanadoo.fr, electri-cal and electronic marine hard-ware, complete repair service for all electrics and electronics

Winston Motors, (P.A.P.), 0590-90-82-73, F: 0590-90-82-73, winston.turney@wanadoo.fr, good general outboard mechanic, also new outboards

GUADELOUPE SHOPPING

BANKING

American Express, Petrelluzzi Agence, 0590-83-03-99

Visa Group, Credit Agricole, Marina, 0590-90-91-54, their 24-

hour ATM machines will also take your card

PROVISIONING

8 a Huit, (St. Francois), 0590-85-20-97, F: 0590-85-53-17

Bolangerie Patisserie Amandine, (Deshaies), 0590-28-45-98.

Champion Supermarket, (marina), 0590-90-80-40, F: 0590-90-75-80

Desirade Ti Marche, 0690-50-89-15/50-69-79, capcaraibeshdg@wanadoo.fr

Cora, Basse Terrre, 0590-81-20-68

Spar, (Deshaies), 0590-28-36-69, F: 059-068-4840, ephile-tas@hotmail.com

GUADELOUPE HOTELS & RESTAURANTS

RESTAURANTS

Au Poisson D'Or, (Port Louis), $B-C

Asia, (P.A.P), 0590-93-60-88, $B-C

Barbuto (Deshaies), 0590-8789-87-28, barbuto971@orange.fr, $ B

Cote Jardin, (P.A.P), 0590-90-91-28, $A-B

Hemmingway, (Deshaies), 0590-28-57-17, F: 0590-28-57-03, $B-C

Iguana Cafe, (St. Francois), 0590-88-61-37, $A-B

L'Amer, (Deshaies), 0590-28-50-63, F: 0590-28-50-43, valerie.robein@wanadoo.fr, $B-C

Lagranlag, (Desirade), 0590 -20-01-00, $B-C

La Note Bleue, (Deshaies), 0590-28-50-39, F: 0590-28-55-03, mathieudrouot@wanadoo.fr, $C

La Touna, Pigeon, 0590-98-70-10, $B-C

La Voile Blanche, (P.A.P), 0590-90-25-79

Le Mouillage, (Deshaies), 0590-28-41-12, $B,

Le Plaisancier, (P.A.P), 0590-90-71-53, plaisanci-er@wanadoo.fr, $B-D

Le Pirate Caribbean, (P.A.P), 0590-90-73-00, $B-D

Le Rocher de Malendure, (Pigeon), 0590-98-70-84, $B-C

Marina Grill, (Port Louis),

0590-22-93-44, F: 0590-22-98-63

GUADELOUPE SCUBA DIVING

Centre Departmental de Pleine Nature, near Marina Riviere Sens, 0590-81-39-96, F: 0590-81-61-21

Eden Plongee, (Port Louis) 0590-22-87-27, dive shop

GWA Dive, (Port Louis) 0590-22-86-47, dive shop

La Bulle, (Baie Mahault) 0590-26-22-71, apouget@mediaserve.net, dive shop

Noa Plongee, (St. Francois), 0690-15-03-49

St. Francois Plongee, (St. Francois) 0590-85-81-18/0690-56-51-79, bescales2@wanadoo.fr

Les Heures Saines, Rocher de Malendure, Bouillante, 590-98-86-63, F: 0590-98-77-76, heu-saine@outremer.com

Nitrogen, 0590-90-78-26, F: 0590-93-62-58, nitrogen.cue@hotmail.com sale, rental and repair of dive gear.

Ocean Passion, St. Francois, 0590-88-72-73

Plongee Note Bleue, Deshaies, 0590-28-53-74/28-56-89

Tropical Sub, Deshaies, 0590-28-52-67, F: 0590-28-53-489, tropical.sub@outremeronline.com

MARIE GALANTE

Marie Galante is on the Guadeloupe exchange. Numbers are ten digits, starting with 0590 (fixed phones) and 0690 (mobile units). From French territories dial this ten-digit number. If you are calling from outside French territory, dial the international exit code (usually 011for NANP countries), then 590, then the full number we give but leave off the first 0.Thus, from overseas if we give 0590-97-82-64, you dial 011-590-590-97-82-64.This dou-bling of 590 is a little confusing, but absolutely necessary.

Directory

EMERGENCY/OFFICIAL

Hospital Ste-Marie,
0590-97-89-70/97-82-64
Ambulance, 0590-97-78-44/46

AIRLINES
(SEE ALSO GUADELOUPE)
Air Guadeloupe, 0590-97-94-11
Airport, 0590-97-90-25

COMMUNICATIONS
M.J.C. de Saint Louis,
0590-97-10-86,
mjc.saint.louis@wanadoo.fr, internet
Pegases, (G. Bourg),
0590-97-38-95,

MISCELLANEOUS
Tourist Office, 0590-97-56-51,
info@ot-mariegalante.com

TRANSPORT
E. Castanet, 0590-97-80-65, taxi
Magauto, (G. Bourg),
0590-97-98-75/97-34-49,
car and scooter rental
Auto Moto Location,
(St. Louis), 0590-97-19-42,
0690-53-20-39,
automoto-location@wanadoo.fr,
bike, scooter and car rental
Loca Sol, (G. Bourg),
0590-97-76-58, car rental

PROVISIONING
Bagg Cash, 0590-97-8192,
mgcash@wanadoo.fr
Caraibe Food, 0590-97-78-26

RESTAURANTS
Auberge Abre et Pain, (G.
Bourg), 0590-97-73-69, $B-C
Chez Henry, (St. Louis),
0590-97-04-57, $C
Kawann Beach Hotel, (St.
Louis),
0590-97-50-50, F: 0590-97-97-96,
cohoba@leaderhotels.com, $B-C
La Brise des Mers (G. Bourg),
$D, 0590-97-46-22,
sabine.ypreeuw@wanadoo.fr
Le Royale Cafe, (St. Louis), $C-D

**Le Skipper/ L'Assiette des
Iles,** (St. Louis),
0590-97-16-28, $C-D
Maria Galanda, (G. Bourg),
0590-97-50-56, $C

Man Balaou, (G. Bourg),
0590-97-75-24/17-94,
manbalaou@wanadoo.fr, dive shop

MONTSERRAT

Montserrat phone numbers work
like the USA with an area code of
664, dial 1 plus the number, within
Montserrat just dial the last 7-digits.

EMERGENCY/OFFICIAL
Customs, 664-491-2456
Port Authority, 664-491-2791/2
**Montserrat Volcano
Observatory,** 664-491-5647
Hospital, 664-491-2836, emergency: 664-491-2802
Police, 664-491-2555

AIRLINES
Winair, 664-491-6988/6030,
asl2006@yahoo.com

MISCELLANEOUS
Tourist Office,
664-491-2230/8370,
F: 664-491-7430,
info@montserrattourism.ms
Montserrat National Trust,
664-491-3086, mnatrustandw.ms

TRANSPORT
Avalon's Taxi and Tours,
664-491-3432, Cell: 664-492-
1565, VHF: 16 "Avalon",
citrusseeker@gmail.com
Be-Peeps, 664-491-3787, car
rentals
Neville Bradshaw Agencies,
664-491-5270/5235, car rentals
Sam Sword Taxi, 664-493-
1973/496-1973
(Many other taxis and car rental
firms can be accessed through the
tourist office)

BANKING
Bank of Montserrat,
664-491-3843
Royal Bank or Canada,
664-491-2426

FUN SHOPPING
Carol's Corner, 664-491-5210
Luv's Cotton Store,
664-491-3906

PROVISIONING
Ram's Emdee,
664-491-2289/5847,
F: 664-491-2568

RESTAURANTS
JJ's Cuisine, 664-491-9024, $B-D,
Oriole Restaurant,
664-491-7144, $C-D
La Collage, 664-491-4236, $C-D
The Lyme, 664-491-5559, $D
Tina's Restaurant,
664-491-3538, $D
Tropical Mansions,
664-491-8767, F: 664-491-8275,
hotel@candw.ms, $B
Vue Point Hotel, 664-491-5210,
vuepointe@candw.ms, $D
Ziggy's, 664-491-8282,
F: 664-491-8282, $A-B
Ziggys@candw.ms

Green Monkey Dive Shop,
664-496-2960/491-2960/2628,
troy@divemontserrat.com

NEVIS

St. Kitts/Nevis phone numbers
work like the USA with an area
code of 869, dial 1 plus the number, within St. Kitts/Nevis just dial
the last 7-digits

EMERGENCY/OFFICIAL
General Emergency, 911
Nevis Customs, 869-469-
5521/5419 (for Charlestown ext
2183)
Nevis Port Authority,
869-496-0788/0651, VHF: 16,
nevports@sisterisles.kn
Alexandra Hospital,
869-469-5473
Evelyn's Drug Store,
869-469-5278

AIRLINES
Evelyn's Travel, 869-469-7447,
travel agent
Nevis Express, 869-469-9756,

F: 869-469-9751

COMMUNICATIONS

Double Deuce, 869-469-2222, marknevis@hotmail.com, wifi
Federal Express, Main Street, 869-469-5351, courier
Nevis

GENERAL YACHT SERVICES

A&M Enterprises, 869-469-5966, F: 869-469-5966, caribsurfqueen@hotmail.com, ship and yacht agent
CCCL Nevis, 1-869-469-1166, mark@cccl.kn or info@cccl.kn, sail and canvas work,
Kustom Airbrush, 1-869-663-8358, kustomairbrushhandsigns@yahoo.com

MISCELLANEOUS

Botanical Gardens of Nevis, 869-469-3509, F: 869-469-1354, worldart2@yahoo.com botanical gardens, shop and restaurant
Carino Hamilton Development, 869-469-1315/0353, F: 869-469-3105, Real estate sales rentals and management.
Equestrian Center, 869-469-8118/3106, guilbert@Caribsurf.com, horse riding
Hermitage Plantation, 869-469-3477, horse riding
Nevis Water Sports, Oualie Beach Club, Nevis, 869-469-9060, F: 869-469-9690, VHF: 16, seabrat@sisterisles.kn, deep sea fishing
Nevis Historical Society, 869-469-5786, F:869-469-0274, nhcs@sisterisles.kn
Nevis Gases, 869-469-5409, fill cooking gas
Nevis Tourism Authority, 869-469-7550, F: 869-469-7551, dliburd@nevisisland.com
Oualie Realty, 869-469-9829/9403
Sugar Mill Real Estate, 869-469-1093, limehill@sisterisles.kn
Top to Bottom, 869-469-9080, walknevis@sisterisles.kn, hiking tours with Jim Johnson

Under the Sea, 869-469-1291, touch and go snorkeling trip with Barbara Whitman

TRANSPORT

3 KB's Scooter Rental, 869-765-7701/667-6702
Abba's Tours, 869-663-7155, VHF Ch 16 or 88
City Stand, Nevis, 869-469-5621, taxis
Nevis Windsurfing and Mountain Bike Center, 869-469-9682/469-9178 F: 869-469-9176, windsurf@sisterisles.kn
Noel's Car Rental, T&F: 869-469-5199/1972, VHF: 16
TDC, 869-469-5690/1005, F: 869-469-1239, VHF: 18, car rentals
Strikers Car rental, 869-469-2654, strikers@sisterisles.kn
St. Kitts Sea Bridge, 869-662-7002, car ferry
Teach Tours and Taxi Service, 869-662-9022/469-1140, teachtours@sisterisles.kn, VHF: 16, good taxi driver also car rentals

NEVIS SHOPPING

BANKING

Barclays Bank, 869-469-5467/5309, F: 869-469-5106.

FUN SHOPS

Bocane Ceramics, 869-469-5437, F: 869-469-4437, bocaneceramics@sisterisles.kn
Caribco Gifts, 869-469-1432, F: 869-469-0072
Crafthouse Boutique, 869-469-5505
Knick Knacks, 869-469-5784,
Island Fever Boutique, 869-469-0620, home: 869-469-9613, F: 869-469-8089, gigi@islandfever.biz
Nevis Handicrafts Cooperative, 869-469-1746
TDC Plaza, 869-469-5430/5364, tdcnevis@sisterisles.kn, VHF: 18

PROVISIONING

Deli by Wendy, 869-469-1191, info@delibywendy.com
Nevis Bakery, 869-469-5219,

F: 869-469-0165, nevisbakery@sisterisles.kn
Rams, 869-469-7777
Superfoods, 869-469-1267, F: 869-469-0297
Nevis Center, (Hardware) 869-469-5600

RESTAURANTS/ ACCOMODATION

Bananas 869-469-1891, $A-C
Cafe Des Arts, 869-667-8768, $D
Chevy's Calypso Bar, 869-664-5164, chevy@yahoo.com , $B-C
Chrichi Beach Club, 869-662-3958, Christian@zenithnevis.com, $B-C
Coconut Grove, 869-469-1020, cocnutgrove@caribcable.com, $A
Croney's Old Manor, 869-469-3445, $A
Double Deuce, 869-469-2222, marknevis@hotmail.com, $B-D
Golden Rock Plantation Inn, 869-469-3346, F: 869-469-2113, goldenrockhotel@sisterisles.kn, $A
Eddy's 869-469-5958, F: 869-469-0129, adesbay@sisterisles.kn, VHF: 16, $B-D
Gallipot, 869-469-8230, F: 869-469-9690, VHF: 16, seabrat@sisterisles.kn, $B-C
Hermitage Inn, 869-469-3477, F: 869-469-2481, contactus@hermitagenevis.com, $A
Montpelier, 869-469-3462, F: 869-469-2932, info@montpeliernevis.com, $A
Mt. Nevis Hotel, 869-469-9373, $A-B
Nisbet Plantation, 869-469-9325, F: 869-469-9864, $A
Old Manor, 869-469-3445, $B
Oualie Beach Club, 869-469-9735, F: 869-469-9176, VHF: 16, $C
Sunshine's Bar and Grill, T&F: 869-469-5817, sunshines@sisterisles.kn, $B-D
Unella's By the Sea, 869-469-5574, $B-D
Yachtman Grill, 869-665-

Directory

6045/6245/762-1610,
gslagon@aol.com, $B-C

NEVIS SCUBA DIVING

Scuba Safaris, Oualie Beach Club, Nevis, 869-469-9518, info@scubanevis.com, VHF: 16, Ellis Chaderton

SABA

Saba numbers begin with 599. If calling within Saba, leave off the 599. If calling from abroad, dial the exit code plus the number. Thus, from the USA dial 011 and the full number given here. If calling from another Dutch island, leave off the 599 and just dial 0 plus the last 7-digits. If that does not work, start by dialing 0 then 599.

SABA SERVICES

EMERGENCY/OFFICIAL

Edwards Medical Center, 599-416-3288/9, medical emergencies
Port Authority, 599-416-3294, VHF: 16, 11, fortbayharbor@hotmail.com, or travisjohnson83@hotmail.com

AIRLINES

Windward Island Airways, 599-416-2255

COMMUNICATIONS

Island Communications, 599-416-2881. F: 416-2781, info@ICSsaba.com

GENERAL YACHT SERVICES

Laundry, 599-416-3461/2

MISCELLANEOUS

Saba Marine Park and Conservation Society, Box 18, The Bottom, Saba, N.A., 599-416-3295, F: 599-416-3435, VHF: 16, info@sabapark.org
Tourist Office, 599-416-2231/2/2322, F: 599-416-2350, iluvsaba@unspoiledqueen.com

TRANSPORT

Taxis: Call Marine Park or Port Office on VHF 16 when you are still south of the island and ask them to call for you, or
Garvis Hasell (taxi), 599-552-3418/416-6114

The Edge Ferry, 599-544-2640, info@stmaarten-activities.com

SABA SHOPPING

FUN SHOPS

Peanut Gallery, 599-416-2509, local art
El Mono Folk Art, 599-416-2518, handicrafts
Hellsgate Community Cottage, 599-416-2300, lacework
Jobean Designs, T&F: 599-416-2490/9, 599-416-2638, jobean@unspoiledqueen.com, hand-blown glass and other fine gifts, glass workshops
Saba Artisans, 599-416-3260, handicrafts
Saba Trail Shop, 599-416-2360, nature type gifts

PROVISIONING

Big Rock Market, 599-416-2280
My Store, 599-416-3263
Saba Self-Service Supermarket, 599-416-3218

SABA HOTELS AND RESTAURANTS

ACCOMMOCATION ONLY

Cottage Club, 599-416-2386, F: 599-416-2434
Cranston's Antique Inn, 599-416-3203, F: 599-416-3469
Juliana's, 599-416-2269, F: 599-416-2389
Saba Real Estate (apartments), 599-416-2299, F: 599-416-2415

RESTAURANTS / ACCOMODATION

Brigadoon, 599-416-2380, $B-C
Chinese Place, 599-416-2353, $C
Copa Sabana, 580-2398, $C-D
Ecolodge, 599-416-3888/3348, info@ecolodge-saba.com, $C-D
In Two Deep, 599-416-3438, $C-D
Lime Time, 599-416-3351
Lollipop's, 599-416-3330, $C
Restaurant Eden, 599-416-2539, restaurant.eden@gmail.com, $A-B
Queen's Garden, 599-416-3694, info@quyeensaba.com, $A-B
Saba's Treasures, 599-416-2819
Scout's Place,

599-416-2740, F: 599-416-2471, VHF: 16, info@scoutsplace.com, $B-D
Swinging Door, 599-416-2506, $D
Tropics Cafe, 599-416-2469, $B
Willard's of Saba, 99-416-2498, F: 599-416-2482, info@willardsofsaba.com, $A-B

SABA SCUBA DIVING

Saba Deep, 599-416-3347, F: 599-416-3397, VHF: 16, Tony and Cheri Waterfield, diving@sabadeep.com, diving, dive shop, sale of dive equipment
Saba Divers, 599-416-2740, Port dive shop: 599-416-3840, F: 599-416-2741, VHF: 16, Barbara and Wolfgang, info@scoutsplace.com,
Sea Saba, 599-416-2246/ F: 599-416-2362, VHF: 16, Lynne Costenaro and John Magor, diving@seasaba.com, dive shop, sale of dive equipment

ST. EUSTATIUS (STATIA)

Statia numbers begin with 599-3. If dialing from overseas, dial the exit code plus this number. Thus, from the USA dial 011 plus the 10-digit number. If calling within Statia, leave off the 599. If calling from another Dutch island, leave off the 599 and dial the last seven digits. If that does not work, start by dialing 0 then 599.

STATIA SERVICES

EMERGENCY/OFFICIAL

Emergency (all), 911
Marine Park, 599-318-2884, F: 599-318-2913, VHF: 17, fpsxe2@sintmaarten.net
Queen Beatrix Hospital, 599-318-2371/2211
Port Authority, 599-318-2205, VHF: 16, 14

AIRLINES

WinAir, 599-318-2381

CHANDLERY - FISHING GEAR

Dive Statia, 599-318-2435, F: 599-318-2539,

info@divestatia.com, VHF: 16

COMMUNICATIONS

Computers and More,
599-318-2596,
MBVI@goldenrock.net (email,
faxes)
Federal Express, 599-318-2451,
courier

GENERAL
YACHT SERVICES

Golden Rock Dive Center,
T&F: 599-318-2964, VHF: 16,
grdivers@gmail.com,
water available in emergency

MISCELLANEOUS

Tourist Office,
599-318-2371/2211, F: 599-318-
2324,
info@statiatourism.com

TRANSPORT

Taxi Stand: 599-318-2620
ARC car rental, 599-318-2595
Rivers Rental, 599-318-2566
Brown's Rental, 599-318-2266
LPN Scooter Rental, 599-318-
4152/581-8395

TECHNICAL
YACHT SERVICES

Carti, 599-524-1050, mechanic
Reynaldo Redan,
599-523-6323/580-0503,
mechanic, underwater work

FUN SHOPS

Mazinga, 599-318-2245,
F: 599-318-2230, gifts, postcards,
essentials and more

PROVISIONING

Duggins Supermarket,
599-318-2241, F: 599-318-2737.
Sandbox Tree Bakery,
599-318-2469, F: 599-318-2202.

RESTAURANTS /
ACCOMODATION

Blue Bead Restaurant,
599-318-2873, $C-D
Cool Corner, 599-554-7989, $D
Franky's, 599-318-3575, $D
Golden Era Hotel,
599-318-2345, $B-C
King's Well Resort,
T&F: 599-318-2538, VHF:16,
kingswellresort2000@yahoo.com,

$B-C
Ocean View, 599-318-2934
Old Gin House, 599-318-2319,
info@oldginhouse.com, $A-B
Smoke Alley, 599-318-2002,
statiagal@hotmail.com, $B-D
San Yen, 599-318-2915, $C-D

Dive Statia, 599-318-2435,
F: 599-318-2539, VHF: 16,
(In USA, 1-405-843-7846),
info@divestatia.com,
Rudy and Rinda Hees.
Golden Rock Dive Center,
T&F: 599-318-2964, VHF: 16,
(In USA 1-800- 311-6658),
grdivers@goldenrocknet.com,
Glen, Michele Faires
Scubaqua,
T&F: 599-318-5450/2873,
dive@scubaqua.com,
Ingred and Menno

ST. BARTS

St. Barts numbers are ten digits,
starting with 0590 (fixed phones)
and 0690 (mobile units). Within
French territories dial this ten-
digit number. If you are calling
from outside French territory, dial
the international exit code then
590, then the full number we give
but leave off the first 0. Thus, from
the USA if we give 0590-27-85-
78, you dial 011-590-590-27-85-
78. This doubling of 590 is a little
confusing, but absolutely
necessary.

EMERGENCY/OFFICIAL

Hospital de Bruyn,
0590-27-60-35, F: 27-60-35
Police, 0590-27-11-70
Fire Department,
0590-27-62-31 or just 18
Dr. Husson, 0590-27-66-84
Doctor on call: 0590-27-76-03
(holidays/weekends)
Port Captain, 0590-27-66-97,
Fax: 590-27-81-54,
port.de.gustavia@wanadoo.fr
Pharmacie St. Barts,
0590-27-61-82

AIRLINES

Air Antilles, 0590-87-35-03
Air Caraibes, 0590-27-71-90
Winair, 0590-27-61-01

CHANDLERY -
FISHING GEAR

Le Shipchandler,
0590-27-86-29, F: 0590-27-85-73,
VHF: 16, leship@wanadoo.fr

COMMUNICATIONS

Centre@lizes,
0590-29-89-89, F: 0590-29-81-10,
centralizes971@yahoo.fr,
Phone, fax, email, internet access
Nautica FWI,
0590-27-56-50/51, F: 590-27-56-
52. nfyachts@wanadoo.fr,
phone and fax
Port of Gustavia,
0590-27-66-97,
Fax: 590 27-81-54, VHF: 16,
port.de.gustavia@wanadoo.fr
mail drop, fax service, wifi

GENERAL
YACHT SERVICES

Port of Gustavia,
0590-27-66-97, VHF: 16,
marina about 100 berths all size
yachts including super-yachts. See
also communications

MISCELLANEOUS

**St. Barthelemy
Marine Reserve**,
0590-27-88-18, emergency: 0690-
31-70-73,
resnatbarth@wanadoo.fr
St. Barts Tourist Office,
0590-27-87-27

SAILMAKERS , CANVAS,
CUSHIONS

Alcatraz Sewing,
0590-52-05-98, F: 0590-27-94-41
Le Voilerie de Port Franc,
0590-27-56-58, F: 0590-27-85-73,
alexaber@wanadoo.fr
West Indies Sails,
0590-27-63-89,
westindies.sails@wanadoo.fr

TRANSPORT

Chez Berenger, 0590-27-89-00,
F: 0590-27-80-28,
chezberenger@wanadoo.fr
car and scooter rentals
Taxi Stand, 0590-27-66-31

TECHNICAL
YACHT SERVICES

Boatinox, 0590-27-99-14,
stainless steel work
Chez Beranger, 0590-27-89-00,
F: 0590-27-71-97,

Directory

chezberanger@wanadoo.fr, outboard sales and repair, mechanical help
JCC, 0590-27-63-06, Cell: 0690-55-32-40, jcgreparateir@wandoo,fr, chris to check OK electrical and tool repair
Hughes Marine, 0590-27-50-70, hughesmarine@orange.fr
Kuka, 0690-58-77-59, 0590-29-74-49, VHF:12, underwater anchor work
Le Shipchandler, 0590-27-86-29, F: 0590-27-85-73, VHF: 16, leship@wanadoo.fr rigging shop, sailmaker, stainless and aluminum welding and fabrication
2-Swedes, 0690-41-88 -14/34-37-51, F: 0590-29-04-03, info@2swedes.com, fiberglass work, woodwork, most yacht repairs and refits

ST. BARTS SHOPPING

FUN SHOPS

Happy Bazaar, 0590-52-85-66
Gallery Spindler, 0596-52-93-66, lequaidesartistes@yahoo.com
Quicksilver Boardriders Club, 0590-29-69-40, F: 0590-29-60-81, quiksbh@orange.com

PROVISIONING

American Gourmet, 0590-52-38-80, 0690-81-15-96, gourmet store, yacht provisioning
Libre Service AMC, 0590-27-60-09, F: 0590-27-85-71, AMC.LS@wanadoo.fr Good supermarket and liquor store, orders can be faxed in advance
La Cave de Port Franc, 0590-27-65-27, lacaveduportfranc@hotmail.com
Segeco, 0590-27-60-10, F: 0590-27-81-34, liquors, some foods
Tom Food, 0590-27-60-43, F: 0590-27-72-77

ST. BARTS HOTELS AND RESTAURANTS

RESTAURANTS

Eddie's, 0590-27-54-17, $B-C
La Cantina, 0590-27-55-66, $D
L'Entracte, 0590-27-70-11, $C-D
Le Repaire, 0590-27-72-48, $B

Le Sapotillier, 0590-27-60-28, $A
Le Select, 0590-27-86-87, $D
Maya's, 0590-27-75-73, $A
News Born, 0590-27-67-07
Pipiri Palace, 0590-27-53-20, $B-C
Santa Fe, 0590-27-61-04, $A-B

ST. BARTS SCUBA DIVING

La Bulle, Ocean Must Marina, 0590-27-62-25, 0690-73-77-85 charley.ce.line@wanadoo.fr, dive shop, tank refills

ST. KITTS

St. Kitts/Nevis phone numbers work like the USA with an area code of 869, dial 1 plus the number. Within St. Kitts/Nevis just dial the last 7-digits.

ST. KITTS SERVICES

EMERGENCY/OFFICIAL

General emergency, 911
Customs Boarding officer, 869-465-8121 ext 100, VHF: 16
City Drug, 869-465-2156, pharmacy
Medical Associates Dr. Kathleen Allen and partners, 869-465-5349. (Offices on Victoria Road)

AIRLINES

American Airlines, 869-465-2273
BWIA, 869-465-2286
Caribbean Sun, 869-466-2690
Kantours, 869-465-2098, F: 869-465-3168, VHF: 16, travel agent
LIAT, 869-465-8613
Nevis Express, 869-469-9755
TDC Airline Service, 869-465-2286, travel agent
WinAir, 869-465-8010, 869-469-9583

CHANDLERY - FISHING GEAR

Builders Paradise (hardware) 869-466-5488
Horsfords, (hardware) 869-465-2262
TDC, (hardware) 869-465-2988
Leeward Island Charters, 869-465-7474, F: 869-465-7070, saillic@thecable.net, chart agent

COMMUNICATIONS

Federal Express, 869-465-4155
The Tour Store, 466-0712/6624400
UPS, 869-465-5978

GENERAL YACHT SERVICES

Delisle Walywn, 869-662-4872/465-2631, VHF: 16 ship's agent
Warner's One Stop, 869-465-8630, F: 869-465-6661, laundry
Port Zante, 869-466-5021, F: 869-466-5020, VHF: 68, udcorp@sisterisles.kn, fuel dock, marina, water
Serviciz, 869-466-8814/762-8130/663-8130, F: 869-465-4188, rick-ie@serviciz.com, yacht agent
St. Kitts Marine Works, 869-662-8930/465-4004/4005, bentels@sisterisles.kn Haul out yard, 150-ton travel lift

MISCELLANEOUS

Clay Villa Plantation House, 869-465-2353, philliphurdskb@hotmail.com, tour
Brimstone Hill Fort National Park, 869-465-2609, F: 869-466-7784, brimstonehill@sisterisles.kn
Christopher Harbour, 869-466-4557, marina development
Royal St. Kitts Golf Course, 869-465-8339, F: 869-465-4463, golfing
Royal Stables, 869-465-2222, horse riding
Scenic Railways, 869-465-7263, F: 869-466-4815
St. Christopher Heritage Society, 869-465-5584, schs@ sisterisles.kn
St. Kitts Tourist Office, 869-465-4040, (1-800-582-6208 USA), info@stkitts-nevis.com
Trinity Stables, 869-465-3226, horse riding

SAILMAKERS, CANVAS, CUSHIONS

Caribbean Canvas Company, 869-466-9636, F: 869-466-9635, canvasup@ sisterisles.kn, sail repair, canvas work

TRANSPORT

Avis, 869-465-5607
City Taxi Stand, 869-466-5621, Taxis
Delisle Walwyn, 869-465-8449/2631, F: 869-465-1125, VHF: 16, car rental
Free Wheelers, 869-466-3912, /466-4257, bike rentals & tours
Gibraltar Tours and Taxi Service, 869-664-8110/465-4223, gibraltar-tours@msn.com
Junie Taxi Service, 869-664-2458/663-2686, VHF:16/68, junietaxi@gmail.com
Island Spice Taxi Service, 869-664-1497, VHF:16/68
Leeward Island Charters, 869-465-7474, F: 869-465-7070, day charters
Quality Time Taxi, 869-466-5185/663-0503, Pager: 467-7027
Set Up Taxi, 869-465-4933, set-up79@hotmail.com
Sunny Blue Scooter Rentals, 869-664-8755/667-2880
Tangerine Tours, 869-664-5058, rummustdrink@yahoo.com
TDC Rentals, 869-465-2991, F: 869-465-4330, tdcrent@ sisterisles.kn, VHF: 18, car rental
Unique Tours and Taxi, 869-466-5948/664-1820, VHF: 16, taxi, tours

TECHNICAL YACHT SERVICES

Fortress Marine, 869-663-4307, dougbrookes2000@yahoo.com, boatbuilders
Indigo Yachts, 869-466-1753, F: 869-466-1754, info@indigoyachts.com, boatyard
Ossie, 869-466-6736, machine shop
Original Boatbuilders, 869-465-1152, boatyard
Yamaha, 869-465-2511, Yamaha agents

BANKING

Kantours (American Express), 869-465-2098, F: 869-465-3168,
VHF: 16, delwal@ sisterisles.kn, American Express agency
Barclays Bank, 869-465-2449, Visa Group

FUN SHOPS

Ashburry's, 869-465-8175
Caribbean Treasures, 869-466-5541/466-2341 caribbeantreasures@yahoo.com
Caribelle Batik, 869-465-6253, F: 869-465-3629, batiks
Faaces, 869-466-1002
Glass Island, 869-466-6771/660-7847 glassisl@ sisterisles.kn, handmade glass ornaments, windows, ash-trays and jewelry
Island Fever Boutique, 869-469-0620, home: 869-469-9613, F:869-469-8089, gigi@ sisterisles.kn, clothing, handicrafts
Island Hopper, 869-465-2905, F: 869-465-1887, Caribelle batik and souvenirs
Spencer Cameron Art Gallery, 869-465-1617, art, prints
The Potter's House, 869-465-5947

PROVISIONING

Horsford's Value Mart, 869-465-1600, 869-465-1037 info@horsfords.com
Ram's Supermarket, 869-466-6065, town: 869-465-2145

RESTAURANTS / ACCOMODATION

Ballahoo, 869-465-4197, F: 869-465-7627, pete@ballahoo.com, $C
Bird Rock Beach Hotel, 869-465-8914, F: 869-465-1675, brbh@ sisterisles.kn
Circus Grill, 869-465-0143, $B-C
Fisherman's Wharf, 869-465-2754, VHF: 18, $B-D
King's Palace, 869-466-3685, $D
Ottley Plantation Inn, 869-465-7234, $A
Ocean Terrace Inn (OTI), 869-465-2754, F: 869-465-1057, otistkitts@ sisterisles.kn

PJ's Bar and Restaurant, 869-465-8373, F: 869-465-8236, leigh@sisterisles.kn, $B-D
Rawlins Plantation, 869-465-6221, F: 869-465-4954, rawplant@ sisterisles.kn, $B
Serendipity, 869-465-9999/8999, $A, serendipity@ sisterisles.kn
Stone Walls, 869-465-5248, simonemestier@hotmail.com, $B-C
The Beach House, 869-469-5299/762-1521, guish@christopheharbour.com
The Golden Lemon, 869-465-7260, F:869-465-4019, $B-D
Reggae Beach Bar and Grill, 869-662-2661, gary@ reggaebeachbar.com, $B-D

Kenneth's Dive Center, 869-465-2670, F: 869-465-1950, kdcsk@yahoo.com, VHF: 16, Kenneth Samuel. Best to call early in the morning, or between 1300 and 1400 or after 1600. After 2100, call 869-465-7043\1601 or better still use the cell any time: 869-664-6809
Pro Divers, 869-465-3483, prodiver@sisterisles.kn
Dive St. Kitts, 869-465-1189, F: 869-465-3696, brbh@sisterisles.kn

ST. MARTIN

French St. Martin numbers are part of the Guadeloupe exchange. They are ten digits, starting with 0590 (fixed phones) and 0690 (mobile units). Within French territories dial this ten-digit number. If you are calling from outside French territory, dial the international exit code then 590, then the full number we give but leave off the first 0. Thus, from the USA if we give 0590-27-85-78, you dial 011-590-590-27-85-78. This doubling of 590 is a little confusing, but absolutely necessary. The exit code for both sides is 00. Dutch Sint Maarten numbers start with 599 5. From overseas dial the exit code plus the

Directory

number. Thus, to call the Dutch side from the French, dial 00-590 and the 10-digit number. To call from the USA, dial 011 then the10-digit number. If calling from the Dutch islands, just dial the last seven digits. (If that does not work, dial 0 and then the last seven digits, seems to work for some mobiles)

ST MARTIN SERVICES
EMERGENCY/MEDICAL
Ambulance, Dutch
912 or 599-520-6262
Ambulance, French
0590-87-74-14
Central Drugstore,
599-542-2321, F: 599-542-5576
Dr. Johan Datema, or Ubbo Tjaden, Simpson Bay Yacht Club, 599-544-5312, F: 599-544-5650
Emergency, 911
Simpson Bay Dental Clinic, Simpson Bay Yacht Club, 599-544-3208
Dutch side Hospital, 599-3-1111
Dutch side Ambulance, 599-542-2111
Dutch side Dentist, 599-542-3584
French side Hospital, 0590-52-25-25
Friendly Island/Simpson Bay Drugstores, 599-544-4290/3653, FIPnicole@caribserve.net includes a pharmacy by Simpson Bay Yacht Club
Vet, Dr. Gary Swanston, 599-542-0111, sxmvetclinic@megatroc.com
Police, Dutch 911
Police, French marine, 0590-87 73 84
Simpson Bay Lagoon Authority, 599-545-3183
SNSM (French lifeboat), VHF: 16, 0690-76-75-00, MRCC (coordinators)
0596-70-92-92
St. Martin Sea Rescue 199, VHF: 16

AIRLINES
Air France, 599-54-67-47
American Airlines, 599-545-2040
Continental, 599-546-7670
Delta, 599-546-7616

KLM, 599-546-7747
Let's Travel, 599-542-2381/3303, F: 599-542-5042, letstravelsxm.net
LIAT, 599-545-4203/546-7675
Maduro & Sons, 599-542-3407/8, travel agent
Winair, 599-545-2568

CHANDLERY - FISHING GEAR
Boat Paint and Stuff, 0690-55-65-41,
F: 0590-51-99-80,
bbvl@domaccess.com
Budget Marine, (Simpson Bay) 599-544-5577/3134, F: 599-544-4409,
sales@budmar.an
Island Water World, 599-544-5310/4-5278, F:599-544-3299, VHF: 74, sales@islandwaterworld.com
L'Ile Marine, (Marigot), 0590-29-08-60, F: 0590-29-08-96, l.ile.marine@wanadoo.fr
Marine Trading, (I. de Sol & at Skip Jacks), 599-522-5651/522-9894/ 544-5020/ 5445019, VHF: 68, smileymt@caribserve.net
Madco, (Marigot), 0590-51-05-40, F: 0590-29-43-70, madco@sadwifi.com
Team Number One, 0590-87-58-27, F: 0590-87-95-75, fishing gear

COMMUNICATIONS
(Some businesses charge for holding mail.)
Business Point, 599-544-3315, F: 599-544-3319, hiyosxm@thebusinesspoint.com, email, internet access, mail, communications and travel
Captain Oliver's, (Oyster Pond, 97150, St. Martin, FWI) 0590-87-33-47/690-56-21-40, F: 0590-87-33-47, captainoliver@wanadoo.fr, mail drop, phone, fax, email
DVPRO, 0590-29-22-32 Grand Case
Mailbox, The Palapa Center #30, Airport Blvd., St. Maarten, NA., 599-545-3890/70, F: 599-545-3893, themailbox@caribserve.net, Phones, fax, email, internet, mail out, secretarial, couriers
Radisson Marina,

0590-87-31-94, F: 0590-87-33-96, VHF: 16/1, marinas martin@radisson.com,
BP 521, Anse Marcel, 97056, Saint-Martin, mail drop, phone & fax; Free wifi on your own computer at: Ric's and Jimbo's

GENERAL YACHT SERVICES
Anyway Marine, 0690-37-62-69/75-65-88, 0590-87-91-41, anyway@wanadoo.fr, yacht brokers
Bay Island Yachts, 599-544-2798, 690-47-71-45, heather@bayislandyachts.com, yacht brokers Boat Cleaning and Services, 0690-47-65-93, info@www.bc-serv.com
Bobby's Marina Group, 599-542-2366, F: 599-542-5442, VHF: 16,
Simpson Bay Bobby's, 599-545-2890, VHF:14 switch 69, info@bobbysmarina.com, marina, water, fuel, haul out, dry storage (2 yards), machining, mechanics, glass and paintwork, all kinds of repairs
Captain Oliver's, (Oyster Pond), 0590-87-33-47/87-31-94/87-40-26,
F: 0590-87-33-96/87-40-84, VHF: 16/67, captoli@wanadoo.fr, marina, water, fuel, absentee yacht management
Harel Yacht Broker, (Oyster Pond), 0590-29-43-85, Cell: 0690-76-22-22
F: 0590-87-01-79, yachtbroker@wanadoo.fr
Dock Martin, 599-542-5705, Cell: 599-557-5434, F: 599-542-4940, brian@dockmaarten.com, marina
Geminga, (Marigot), 0590-29-35-52, F:0590-29 65 36, geminga@domaccess,com, VHF:71, haul out, dry storage
Great House Marina, cell: 599-571416, F: 599-543-6427, marina
Island Water World, 599-542-2675/4-5310/4-5278, F: 599-544-3299, VHF: 74, boatssxm@saintmartin.net, haul out, all kinds of repairs

JMC Boatyard, 0590-77-10-05, F: 0590 77 10 06, haul-out

Lagoon Marina, (Simpson B.), 599-544-2611, info@lagoon-marina.com, Marina, laundromat,

Marina Fort St. Louis, 0590-51-11-11, F: 0590-51-11-12, VHF: 16, marinafort-louis@wanadoo.fr, marina

Marina Port La Royale, 0590-87-20-43, 0690-62-90-93, F: 0590-87-55-95, VHF: 16, semreginel@wanadoo.fr, marina

MP Yachting, 0690-53-37-98, mpyachting@gmail.com, (Marigot), agents for Jeanneau

Must, 0590-29-17-18, 0690 40 99 95, F: 0590-29-16-65, m.u.s.t@wanadoo.fr, yacht brokers

Palapa Marina, 599-545-2735, F: 599-545-2510, VHF: 68, office@palapamarina.com, marina

Radisson Marina, 0590-87-31-94, F: 0590-87-33-96/ 87-30-45. VHF: 16/11, marina, water, fuel

Portofino Marina, 599-544-5174, cell: 599-520-1588, yachtclub@caribserve.net, marina

Polypat, (Marigot), 0590-87-12-01, Cell: 0690-58-58-20, F: 0590-87-22-13, polypat.caraibes@gmail.com, haul out, dry storage

Radio Shack, 599-542-3310, F: 599-542-2497, sale of electronics, electrics and components

Simpson Bay Marina, 599-544-2309, F: 599-544-3378, VHF: 16/79A, sbm@IGYmarinas.com, water, fuel, marina

Sun Maintenance, 0690-74-97-14

Total Cleaning, 599-544-2122, Cell: 599-554-2122/2165, F:599-544-2435, cleaning@sintmaarten.net

Time Out Boatyard (TOBY), (Marigot), 0590-52-02-88, F: 0590-52-02-89, timeoutboat@hotmail.com, haul out, dry storage

Weather Eye Yacht Sales, 599-552-6286, moreinfo@weathereyeyachts.com

Yacht Club Isle de Sol, (Simpson B.), 599-544-2408, Fax: 599-544-5175,

IDS@IGYmarinas.com

Yacht Club Port de Plaisance, 599-544-4565, F: 599-544-4566, info@yachtclubportdeplaisance.com, marina

Yacht Services, 0590-52-92-38, 0690-88-88-47, 599-553-7526

MISCELLANEOUS

Inter Coiffure, 599-454-2985

Nature Foundation 599-542-0267, F: 599-542-0268,

St. Martin Yacht Club, 599-544-2079, commodore@smyc.com

Sunset Theaters, 599-544-3630

Tourist Office - Dutch side, 599-542-2337

Tourist Office - French side, 0590-87-57-23/21, F: 0590-87-56-43

Tricia Massage, 0690-50-08-60

Tri Sport, 599-545-4384, trisport@caribsurf.net, bike rentals, sales, repair

SAILMAKERS , CANVAS, CUSHIONS

Grenadine Sails, (Sandy Ground), 0590-87-41-35, Cell: 0690-27-11-94, F: 0590-87-00-99, allaire@deltavoiles.com

St. Maarten Sails, (Simpson Bay), 599-544-5231/520-8765, F: 599-544-5044, info@stmaartensails.com, sail, canvas and cushion work. Agent for Quantum

SXM Sellerie, 0690-36-23-36

Tailor by the Sea, 599-526-1324

Tropical Sail Loft, (Simpson Bay), 599-544-5472/553-2759 ernst@tropicalsailloft.com, sailmaker and canvas work, North Sails agent, sells fabrics and needles

Voile Caraibes (Incidences), (Sandy Ground), 0590-87-06-04, F:0590-29-41-68, incidences.caraibes@wanadoo.fr, sailmaker

TRANSPORT

Avis, 599-545-2847

Deep Blue, lagoon water taxi, 599-580-3314

Dollar Car Rental, 599-545-3281

Excellent Rentals,

599-545-2448

Europcar, 599-544-2168,

Johan Romney (good taxi driver), 599-552-2213/557-2333

Tri-Sport, 599-545-4384, F: 599-545-4385, bike rentals

Taxis, (Marigot), 0590-87-56-54, Airport, 599-546-7758/9 (Philipsburg), 147

TECHNICAL YACHT SERVICES

Advanced Marine Systems, 599-544-3482, cell: 599-552-9760, info@advancedmarinesystems.com satellite communications, commercial electronics

Aquatic Solutions, 599-557-2979, deonosaurus@yahoo.com

Atlantis Marine, 599-544-3788/553-7061, gsbguima@hotmail.com. Electronics

Atlantic Spirit, 599-580-6677, yacht/project manangement

Bobby's Marina, (Philipsburg), 599-542-2366, VHF: 16, mechanics, machinists, paint and glass work

Brokaar Marine Services, cell: 599-571416, F: 599-543-6427, brokaar@sintmaarten.net, towing, salvage, commercial diving

Caamano Marine, 599-524-0075, F: 590-87-29-09, info@caamano-marine.com

Caraibes Diesel Services, 0590-87-03-73, 0690-38-39-75, mechanic

Dinghy Spot, 0690-32-82-11 (inflatable repair)

Diesel Outfitters, (Simpson bay),T&F: 599-544-2320, repair of all diesel engines, Perkins agent E&MSC, 599-527-3812, 544-2912, e-msc07@yahoo.com, metal-work

Electec, 599-544-4512/2051, F: 599-544-3641, sales@electec.info, electrical installation and repair and instrumentation, also water makers

Enertech, 599-544-2460, F: 559-544-4608, service@enertechnv.com, refrigeration & air conditioning specialists

Erik Marine, 599-580-1998, eric-marine@hotmail.com

FKG Rigging (Cole Bay Marine Center),

599-544-4733/5691,
F: 599-544-2171,
cell: 599 557-8502,VHF: 71,
kevin@fkg-marine-rigging.com,
dry storage, all kinds of repairs,
work berths, rigging, welding &
machining, rigging a specialty, large
stock wire and fitting, swaging,
profurl and furlex, woodworking
Frostline, 599-544-3263/526-
2763, glyn@frostline.biz, refrigeration
Greg S Mechanique, 0690-54-
83-24
Havin's, 599-552-0530, F:599-
544-2293
havin_ramnauth@yahoo.com
metalwork - t-top and fuel tank
specialists
Island Water World,
599-544-5310/45278,
F: 599-544-3299, haul-out, hull
repairs and painting, Evinrude
sales, and OMC repairs
JMC Hydraulic Marine,
0690 62 15 21, F: 0590 29 09 79,
jmcstmartin@wanadoo.fr
Kenny Awlgrip,
599-587-6942,
Kenny@caribserve.com, yacht
refinishing.
Lagoon Diving, 599-552-5511,
lagoondivers@caribsurf.net
VHF: 14, hull scrubbing, all underwater work.
Maintech, 599-544-3146, F: 599-
544-3146,
maintech@sintmaarten.net,
woodworking, glasswork, electrics.
Mendall,
0590-29-69-40/87-05-94/51-01-46,
F: 0590-87-07-78,VHF: 16,
mendol@wanadoo.fr, machining,
fabrication, mechanics, hydraulics,
refrigeration
MGS, 0590-87-07-95, 0690-56-
06-37, Christian-pinho-teixi-
ra@orange.com, fabrication
MJC Fabrication,
0690-53-74-89/65-75-23,
Fax: 0590-87-33-91,
markcarlatempleton@yaho.com
Necol, 599-545-2363/4,
F: 599-545-2349, info@necol.com,
VHF: 4int, Electrics, electronics,
watermakers
Minville Marine,
0590-87-19-13, F: 0590-87-19-73,
Suzuki sales and service

Ocean Xperts, 0590-52-24-72,
0690-62-16-02 F: 0590-52-24-73,
info@oceanxperts.com,Yamaha
agent
Palapa Shipwrights,
599-554-1584
Pascal Register, 0690-35-84-45,
glasswork
Permafrost,
T&F: 599-557-5780,
F: 599-545-5599,VHF: 68, serv-
ice@permafrostrefrigeration.com,
refrigeration & air-conditioning
specialists
Rob Marine, 599-554-6333,
robmarine@megatropic.com
Simpson Bay Diesel,
599-544-5397, F: 599-544-5747,
VHF: 74, info@sbdiesel.com
repair of diesels,Yamaha and
Perkins agent
Star Marine, 0690-73-05-88
glass and paintwork
Teamwork Marine, 599-555-
4555, 522-0393, VHF: 62, team-
work-marine@yahoo.com
The Wired Sailor, 599-580-
7733/ 527-2896, electronics, IT
The Yacht Shop, 599-524-9903,
mike@theyacht-shop.com, all
repairs, storage lockers.
TMTT, 0590-52-97-86, 599-557-
1479
Yacht Rigging, 0590-29-52-82,
F: 0590-29-45-15, mustyachtrig-
ging@domaccess.com

ST. MARTIN SHOPPING
BANKING
American Express agents:
Maduro & Sons, 599-542-2678
The Windward Bank,
599-542-2313, Cash from VISA

FUN SHOPPING
Guavaberry, 599-542-2965,
F: 599-542-4598,
manager@Guavaberry.com

PROVISIONING
(Yacht agents)
Dockside Management,
599-544-4096/, F: 599-544-4097
VHF: 16,
office@docksidemanagement.net
super-yacht agent
**Food Express & Lido
Provisioning,** 599-544-3824,
cell: 599-581-2779, fax: 599-544-
3823, mitch@lidofoodgroup.com,

full provisioning
IDSYacht Provisioning,
599-544-2408/599-523-7616, fax:
599-544-2725,
admin@stmaartenyachtpro.com
provisioning
**International Yacht
Collection,** (Simpson B.),
599-544-3780/2515,
F: 599-544-3779, mel-
liot@yachtcollection.net
MegaYacht Services,
599-544-4440,
Cell: 599-557-5835, F: 599-57-
3835,
harrison@megayachtservice.com
**Simpson Bay Yacht
Provisioning,** 599-520-3336,
danny@caribserve.net
**Super Yacht Services (Crew
Network),**
599-544-2436/522-9746,
simon@superyachtservices.net
Yacht Services, 0590-52-92-38,
0690-88=88-47, 599-553-7526

PROVISIONING
Cost-U-Less, 5995-429860,
Fax: 5995-429861
Daily Extra, 599-544-2577,
afoo@sintmaarten.net
Georgie's Gourmet Galley,
599-544-3852, F: 599-544-4031,
georgie@caribsurf.com
Gourmet Marche, 599-545-
3055, legrandmarche.net
La Sucriere, 599-544-3530
Le Grande Marche,
(Philipsburg) 599-542-4400,
F: 599-542-4401,
email@legrandmarche.net
Match, 0590-87-92-36,
Simpson Bay Pharmacy,
599-544-3653, F: 599-544-3654
sbpharmacy@hotmail.com, phar-
macy at Simpson Bay Yacht Club
Sang's Supermarket, 599-542-
3447,
F: 599-542-3189, sangstrad-
ing@sintmaarten.net.
Seascape Lobster Wholesale,
0690-35-09-36
US Import Export, 0590-87-
03-80, F: 0590-87-03-69

ST. MARTIN HOTELS & RESTAURANTS

RESTAURANTS / ACCOMODATION

Bistrot du Port, 0590-29-25-16, Marigot, $C-D

Buccaneer Bar, 599-522-9700, bernyachtmaster@yahoo.com

Calmos Cafe, 0590-29-01-85, $D, Grand Case

Captain Oliver's, 0590-87-30-00, $A-B, Oyster Pond

Chesterfields, 599-542-3484, $B-C, Philipsburg

Dinghy Dock, VHF: 16, $D, Oyster Pond

El Rancho, 599-545-2495, $B, Simpson Bay

Fish Pot, 0590-87-50-88, $A, Grand Case

Green House, 599-542-2941, $B-C

Jimbo's, $C-D

La Baguette, 599-542-1601, Philipsburg

Kangaroo Court, $D, Philispburg

L'Escapade, 0590-87-75-04, $AB, Grand Case

L'Escargot, T&F: 599-542-2483, $A-B, Philispburg

LaGuinguette, 599-544-4507, $B-C

Lagoonies, $B-D, 524-1143, bradsxm@yahoo.co.uk

La Vie en Rose, 0590-87-54-42, F: 0590-87-82-63 $A, Marigot

Le Bar de la Mer, 0590-87-81-79 $C-D, Marigot

Le Planteur, 0590-29 53 21, $AB, Oyster Pond

Le Pressoir, 0590-87-76-62, $B, Grand Case

Mario's Bistro, 0590-87-06-36

Mr. Busby, 599-543-6083, $D, Oyster Pond

Peg Leg Pub, 599-544-5859, peglegpubsxm@aol.com, $B-C, Simpson Bay

Pineapple Pete, 599-544-6030, $B-C, Simpson Bay

Ric's Place, 599-545-3630, F: 599-545-3630, ricsplace@caribsurf.com, $C-D, Simpson Bay

Top Carrot, 599-544-3381,

Simpson Bay

The Boathouse, 599-544-5409, $B-D

Tropicana, 0590-87-79-07, $C-D

Zee Best, 0590 690 39 79 59, $D, Simpson Bay

ST MARTIN SCUBA DIVING

2-Limits Dive Center, (Marigot) 0696-34-14-00/50-04-00, contact@2limits.com

Dive Safaris (Philipsburg) 599-542-9001 F: 599-542-8983, divesafaris@caribserve.net, dive trips, dive school, shark awareness dive

Dive Safaris (Simpson Bay) 599-545-2401 Cell: 599-557-3436 divesafari@caribserve.net, dive trips, dive school, hydrostatic testing and tank annual service

Ocean Explorers, Simpson Bay Lagoon, T: 599-544-5252, divesm@caribserve.net, Leroy French, dive shop plus sales of snorkeling and diving gear stmaartendiving.com

Octoplus, Grande Case, 0590-87-20-62, F: 0590-87-20-63

Scuba Fun Caraibes, Anse Marcel, 0590-87-36-13, F: 0590-87-36-52, Philipsburg, 599-557-0505/542-3966, dive shop plus sales of snorkeling and diving gear

Scuba Shop, Oyster Pond, 0590-87-48-01, F: 0590-87-48-01, info@thescubashop.net, Peter Frye, excellent prices on equipment, gear rentals to charter yachts, free diving site booklet.

Scuba Shop, Simpson Bay, 599-545-3213, T: 599-545-3209, info@thescubashop.net, authorized dealer, retail, rental, equipment service

THE SAINTES

The Saintes phones work off the Guadeloupe exchange. They are ten digits, starting with 0590 (fixed phones) and 0690 (mobile units). Within French territories dial this ten-digit number. If you are calling from outside French territory, dial the international exit code (usually 011), then 590, then the full number we give but

leave off the first 0. Thus, from overseas if we give 0590-99-59-45, you dial 011-590-590-99-59-45. This doubling of 590 is a little confusing, but absolutely necessary.

SAINTES SERVICES

EMERGENCY/MEDICAL

Pharmacy des Saintes, 0590-99-52-48, 0690-49-41-11, pharmacie.dessaintes@hotmail.fr

Doctor, 0590-99-50-66/99-51-33

CHANDLERY - FISHING GEAR

Saintes Brico, 0590-99-56-38, F: 590-99-56-37, fishing gear, general hardware, some yacht chandlery, wood, resins and glass

COMMUNICATIONS

Maogany, 0590-99-50-12, F: 590-99-55-69, maogony@outremer.com, help in emergencies

Terre de Haut.net, 0590-81-53-37, terredehaut.net@wanadoo.fr, internet

GENERAL YACHT SERVICES

Roches a Move Baie de Marigot, 0590-99-53-15, fuel by dinghy

Yacht Club de Saintes, 0590-99-57-82, F: 0590-99-57-82, VHF: 68, water buoy, block ice, laundry, water taxi, showers, mechanics and technical assistance

MISCELLANEOUS

Ludo Coiff, 0590-99-53-69, F: 0590-99-50-51, dabriou.ludovic@wanadoo.fr, unisex hairstylist

Office de Tourism, 0590-99-58-60, F: 0590-99-58-58, omt.lessaintes@wanadoo.fr

SAILMAKERS, CANVAS, CUSHIONS

Phil a Voile, 0590-99-58-69, 0690-81-43-28, philavoile@wanadoo.fr, sailmaker, canvas and cushion work

TRANSPORT

Club de Kayak des Saintes, 0690-65-79-81, lexan kayaks.

Tropico Velo, 0590-99-56-62, bikes, electric bikes

Directory

Les Saintes Travel Services, 0690-37-55-42/81-61-00, F: 0590-99-56-77, lessaintestravel@orange.fr travel agent and taxi

TECHNICAL YACHT SERVICES

Chantier Naval a Foy, 0590-99-50-75, fiberglass and wood boat construction

Chantier Judes, 0590-99-51-63

SAINTES SHOPPING

FUN SHOPS

Cafe de la Marine, samson.herve@wanadoo.fr, 0590-99-53-78, boutique

CB, 0590-99-88-01, F: 0590-99-51-99, samsonherve@wanadoo.fr, costume and fine jewelry

Galerie d'Art Les Saintes, 0590-92-70-98, lequaidesartistes@yahoo.com

Galerie Martine Cotten, 0590-99-55-22, martine.cotten@wanadoo.fr

L'Atelier su Savon des Saintes, 0590-99-56-24/99-56-26, caraibes.plaisirs@wanadoo.fr soaps, lotions and more

Kazannou, (Pascal Foy), 0590-99-52-29, artistic models of Saintes house facades

Maogany, 0590-99-50-12, F: 0590-99-55-69, maogany@outremer.com, elegant hand painted and silk screened clothing

PROVISIONING

8 a Huit, 0590-95-19-16, F: 0590-99-61-98, 8ahuit.lessaintes@wanadoo.fr, supermarket

Delco Distribution, 0690-59-88-01/0590-92-63-86, delcodistribution@wandoo.fr, wholesale beer, wine and more

Le Jardin des Iles, 0590-99-55-91, greengrocer, frozen goods

Superette Sampson, 0590-99-53-68, supermarket

Vival, 0590-99-88-03, supermarket

RESTAURANTS / ACCOMODATION

3-Boats,, 0590-81-72-94, 0690-83-85-68, $C

Auberge Les Petits Saints, 0590-99-50-99, F: 0590-99-54-51, info@petitssaints.com, $A-B

Cafe de la Marine, 0590-99-53-78, F: 0590-99-52-41, $B

Couleurs du Monde, couleurs.dumonde971@orange.fr

Hotel Bois Joli, 0590-99-52-53, F: 0590-99-05, Bois.joli@wanadoo.fr $A-B

Kaz a Man Albe, 0590-99-52-53, $B-C

La Case aux Epices, 0590-98-07-88, lacaseauxepices@wanadoo.fr, $B

Le Kanaoa, 0590-99-51-36, $B-C

La Fringale, 0590-98-14-65, manobadie@wanadoo.fr, $B-C

La Saladerie, T&F: 0590-99-53-43, $B-C, Edouardclaude885@orange.fr

La Teranga, 0690-49-64-13/0590-41-90-35, $B

Le Genois, 0590-98-25-99, guillaume.molza@wanadoo.fr, $C-D

Le Mambo, 0590-99-56-18, guillaume.molza@wanadoo.fr, $ D

Restaurant la Toumbana, 0590-99-57-56, $C-D

Le Triangle Restaurant, 0590-99-50-50, $C, pedro.fox@wanadoo.fr

Sole Mio, T&F: 0590-99-56-46, $B-D

Tropic Gelato, 0590-99-88-12

Ti Kaz La, 0590-99-57-63, $B-D

SAINTES SCUBA DIVING

La Dive Bouteille, 0590-99-54-25, F: 0590-99-50-96, mail@dive-bouteille.com

Pisquettes, 0590-99-88-80, F: 0590-99-88-20, plongee@pisquettes.com

INTERNATIONAL COMPANIES OF INTEREST

AB inflatables, 239-231-4905, F: 239-231- 3389, info@ABinflatables.com

Doyle Offshore Sails, Barbados, 246-423-4600, F: 246-423-4499, doyle@sunbeach.net

French For Cruisers, 361-798-4159, F: 928-832-2066, kathy@forcruisers.com

Sea Hawk Paints, FL, 727-523-8053, F: 727-523-7325 emorrie@seahawkpaints.com

OceanWorld Marina, 809-970-3373, concierge@ocianworld.com

SVG Air, 84-457-5124,, F: 784-456-9238, paulgravel@svgair.com

Winch Buddy, 617-680-7747, winchbuddy@safe-mail.net

Advertisers Index

Cruising Guide Publications

CRUISING GUIDE TO THE VIRGIN ISLANDS

By Nancy &
Simon Scott
14th Edition,
2009-2011
ISBN 0-944428-86-X
6 X 9, 350pp. **$31.95**

Completely revised and up-dated with full color sketch charts, these guides have been indispensable companions for sailors and visitors to these islands since 1982. Includes a free 17" x 27" color planning chart covering the Virgin Islands from St. Thomas to Anegada.

- Anchoring and mooring information and fees.
- Customs, immigration and National Parks regulations.
- Particulars on marina facilities and the amenities they offer.
- Water sports - where to go and where to rent equipment.
- Shore-side facilities, restaurants, beach bars, shops, provisions, Internet connections.
- Alphabetical - by island - Directory of goods and services.

Everything you will need to help make your vacation an enjoyable and memorable experience in a concise easy-to-use format.

CRUISING GUIDE TO THE LEEWARD ISLANDS

Chris Doyle
11th Edition, 2010-2011
ISBN 0-944428-87-8
6 x 9, 529pp
$34.95

This Eleventh edition covers the islands from Anguilla to Dominica, and is an essential tool for all cruisers sailing this region. Chris Doyle, the author spends months sailing these islands to update each edition. This book includes over a hundred up-to-date color sketch charts, full-color aerial photos of most anchorages, island pictures, and detailed shore-side information covering services, restaurants, provisioning, travel basics and island history. Information is linked to the author's website where you can download the GPS waypoints given in the sketch charts, learn of essential updates, print town maps, and obtain links to local weather, news and businesses.

VIRGIN ANCHORAGES

By Nancy & Simon Scott
2009 Edition
ISBN 0-944428-50-9
8.5 x 11, 96pp.
$29.95

Contact for availabilit Virgin Anchorages features stunning color aeria photography of 46 of the most popular anchorages i the Virgin Islands. Graphic overlays aid in navigat ing to safe anchorages. This is an excellent compan ion to Cruising Guide to the Virgin Islands.

LAMINATED PLANNING CHART O THE VIRGIN ISLAND

Color, 17" x 27"   **$9.95**

Printed on two sides th chart includes the US & BVI from St. Thomas to Anegada, includin anchorage and moorings locations. Pre-folded an plastic laminated for protection from sea spray, th chart is a convenient size for cockpit navigation.

LEEWARD ANCHORAGES

By Chris Doyle
2009 Edition
ISBN 0-944428-82-7
8.5 x 11, 91pp
$29.95

Contact for availability. Leeward Anchorages show aerial photographs of all the favorite anchorage from Anguilla through Dominica with graphic over lays to illustrate dangerous and safe passages from a bird's eye view. Carefully researched and recorded by Chris Doyle, safe passages, markers, buoys and hazards are all marked to guide you to safe, enjoyable anchorages. This is a companion book to use with The Cruising Guide to the Leeward Islands.

CRUISING GUIDE TO CARIBBEAN MARINAS & SERVICES

By Ashley & Nancy Scott
ISBN 0-944428-60-6
8.5 x 11, 96pp **$10.00**

An indispensable book for vessels needing routine or emergency maintenance throughout the Caribbean, this directory contains depths, slip sizes, amenities, fees, websites, telephone numbers and is organized for easy reference.

www.cruisingguides.com
For more titles, charts, cookbooks and more.

SAILORS GUIDE TO THE WINDWARD ISLANDS
By Chris Doyle
14th Edition,
2009-2010
ISBN 978-0-944428-85-1
6 x 9, 430pp. **$29.95**

Revised and updated for 2009-2010, this guide features detailed sketch charts based on the author's own surveys, and aerial photos of most anchorages. It also includes clear and concise navigational information. By far the most popular guide to the area, it covers the islands from Martinique to Grenada, with dazzling scenic photography, unsurpassed onshore information, sections on exploring, provisioning, water sports, services, restaurants and photography. Information is linked to the author's website where you can download town maps, GPS waypoints from the sketch charts, and obtain links to local weather, news and more.

CRUISING GUIDE TO VENEZUELA & BONAIRE
By Chris Doyle
3rd Edition, 2007 -2008
ISBN 0-944428-78-9
6 x 9, 290pp. **$27.95**

This is the latest updated version of the only seriously researched guide to this area. The book includes color aerial photos of many anchorages, clear and concise navigational charts, with information on things to do and places to go while on shore. The guide is linked to the author's website where you can download updates, town maps and much more.

CRUISING GUIDE TO TRINIDAD, TOBAGO PLUS BARBADOS AND GUYANA
By Chris Doyle
Third Edition 2007-2008
ISBN 0-9444282-77-0
6 x 9, 256pp. **$25.95**

This new, completely updated edition has been expanded to include Guyana. Including 53 sketch charts, aerial photographs, dazzling scenic photography throughout, unsurpassed onshore information with sections on exploring, provisioning, services and restaurants. The guide is linked to the author's website where you can download town maps, GPS waypoints given in the sketch charts and much more.

WINDWARD ANCHORAGES
By Chris Doyle
2009 Edition
ISBN 0-944428-83-5
8.5 x 11, 96pp
$29.95

Contact for availability. Windward Anchorages is the third in the Anchorages series and a companion book to the Sailors Guide to the Windward Islands by Chris Doyle. Stunning aerial images depict anchorages from Martinique south through Dominica. These aerial images are overprinted to show the hazards to avoid, as well as, markers and buoys to guide you to the safe passages and anchorages of the Windward Islands.

GENTLEMAN'S GUIDE TO PASSAGES SOUTH
By Bruce Van Sant
ISBN 0-944428-79-7
6 x 9, 330 pp. **$29.95**

Updated for 2007 the guide includes many sketch charts and GPS coordinates, plus a wealth of information for the sailor who would rather take it slow and easy en-route to paradise. Many cruising yachtsmen traveling between Florida and Venezuela consider this guide the "Bible".

From the preface, "PASSAGES SOUTH TODAY, if followed, can give you thornless island hopping. Its windward strategies, backed by many years of continuous observation and testing, beat any instant expertise based on just a few voyages. Tune out the two-trip Globetrotter who says, "Aw, that's malarkey! Why, I did that last year and ...." He'll get his on the third trip."

TRICKS OF THE TRADES
By Bruce Van Sant
2001 ISBN 0-944428-62-2
6 x 9, 182pp. **$14.95**

The author of Gentleman's Guide to Passages South widens the scope of his book to include stratagems and tips for sailors cruising aboard for the first time. Not how to sail, but how to live safely and comfortably while aboard - in short "tricks" he has learned during his many years of cruising.

Cruising Guides

Cruising Guide Publications
P.O. Box 1017, Dunedin, FL 34697-1017 • phone 800-330-9542
International Orders 727-733-5322, Fax 727-734-8179